Microsoft®
PowerShell, VBScript, and JScript® Bible

Microsoft® PowerShell, VBScript, and JScript® Bible

William R. Stanek

James O'Neill

Jeffrey Rosen

Wiley Publishing, Inc.

Microsoft® PowerShell, VBScript, and JScript® Bible

Published by
Wiley Publishing, Inc.
10475 Crosspoint Boulevard
Indianapolis, IN 46256
www.wiley.com

Copyright © 2009 by Wiley Publishing, Inc., Indianapolis, Indiana

Published simultaneously in Canada

ISBN: 978-0-470-38680-4

Manufactured in the United States of America

10 9 8 7 6 5 4 3 2 1

Library of Congress Cataloging-in-Publication Data is available from the publisher.

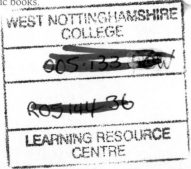

About the Authors

William R. Stanek (http://www.williamstanek.com/) has over 20 years of hands-on experience with advanced programming and development. He is a leading technology expert, an award-winning author, and a pretty-darn-good instructional trainer. Over the years, his practical advice has helped millions of technical professionals all over the world. He has written more than 75 books, including *Microsoft Exchange Server 2007 Administrator's Pocket Consultant*, *Microsoft Windows Vista Administrator's Pocket Consultant*, *Microsoft Windows Server 2008 Administrator's Pocket Consultant,* and *Windows Server 2008 Inside Out.*

Mr. Stanek has been involved in the commercial Internet community since 1991. His core business and technology experience comes from over 11 years of military service. He has substantial experience in developing server technology, encryption, and Internet solutions. He has written many technical white papers and training courses on a wide variety of topics. He frequently serves as a subject matter expert and consultant.

Mr. Stanek has an MS with distinction in information systems and a BS magna cum laude in computer science. He is proud to have served in the Persian Gulf War as a combat crewmember on an electronic warfare aircraft. He flew on numerous combat missions into Iraq and was awarded nine medals for his wartime service, including one of the United States of America's highest flying honors, the Air Force Distinguished Flying Cross. Currently, he resides in the Pacific Northwest with his wife and children.

James O'Neill was born in 1965, used his first Microsoft product at the age of 13, and has scarcely stopped since. He describes himself as a compulsive explainer, which led him to work as a technical trainer and run a small training company in the 1990s. He joined Microsoft Consulting Services in 2000, and after six years there working with a wide variety of clients he moved back to a role where he can explain more, becoming an evangelist, talking to IT professionals primarily about Windows platform technologies. He is a veteran of every Microsoft operating system and network technology since DOS 3.1 MS-Net and Windows 1.03, and has used a dozen or so programming and scripting languages. Over the last two years, he has become increasingly evangelical about PowerShell, using it to write libraries that support Windows 2008 virtualization and Office Communications Server. He lives near Oxford, England with his wife and two children, and occasionally manages to find time for photography and scuba diving. He has a worrying tendency to write about himself in the third person.

Jeffrey Rosen has a Masters of Business Administration from Case Western Reserve, Weatherhead School of Management, specializing in Information Systems. He is a Microsoft Certified Architect, an MCSE specializing in messaging and security, and a CISSP. He began his career working with Microsoft Mail and Novell Netware. Since then, Jeffrey has worked for Microsoft Consulting Services for nine years on large and complex Exchange deployments. He is a co-author of *Professional PowerShell for Exchange 2007 SP1.*

About the Technical Editor

Andrew Edney has been an IT professional for more than 12 years and has, over the course of his career, worked for a range of high-tech companies, such as Microsoft, Hewlett-Packard, and Fujitsu Services. He has a wide range of experience in virtually all aspects of Microsoft's computing solutions, having designed and architected large enterprise solutions for government and private-sector customers. Over the years, Andrew has made a number of guest appearances at major industry events, presenting on a wide range of information systems subjects, such as an appearance at the annual Microsoft Exchange Conference in Nice where he addressed the Microsoft technical community on mobility computing. Andrew is currently involved in numerous Microsoft beta programs, including next-generation Windows operating systems and next-generation Microsoft Office products. He actively participates in all Windows Media Center beta programs and was heavily involved in the Windows Home Server beta program. In addition, Andrew has written a number of books including: *Windows Home Server User's Guide* (2007), *Pro LCS: Live Communications Server Administration* (2007), *Getting More from Your Microsoft Xbox 360* (2006), *How to Set Up Your Home or Small Business Network* (2006), *Using Microsoft Windows XP Media Center 2005* (2006), *Windows Vista: An Ultimate Guide* (2007), *PowerPoint 2007 in Easy Steps* (2007), *Windows Vista Media Center in Easy Steps* (2007), and *Using Ubuntu Linux* (2007).

Credits

Acquisitions Editor
Katie Mohr

Development Editor
Ed Connor

Technical Editor
Andrew Edney

Production Editor
Melissa Lopez

Copy Editor
Nancy Rapoport

Editorial Manager
Mary Beth Wakefield

Production Manager
Tim Tate

**Vice President and
Executive Group Publisher**
Richard Swadley

Vice President and Executive Publisher
Barry Pruett

Associate Publisher
Jim Minatel

Compositor
James D. Kramer, Happenstance Type-O-Rama

Proofreaders
Corina Copp and Sheilah Ledwidge

Indexer
Jack Lewis

Cover Image
Joyce Haughey

Cover Designer
Michael E. Trent

Acknowledgments

Writing *PowerShell, VBScript, and JScript Bible* took a lot of work and research. Much of the time was spent searching for undocumented features, resolving problems with poorly documented interfaces, and exploring uncharted areas of Windows. Then, I had to write about the hidden features and the many interfaces I had discovered. I hope you'll agree that the result was worth all of the effort. The book contains over 300 code examples and dozens of working scripts, all designed to provide a top-notch tutorial and reference.

PowerShell, VBScript, and JScript Bible wouldn't have been possible without a lot of help from others and, especially, the team at Wiley: Katie Mohr, the Acquisitions Editor, and Ed Connor, the Development Editor.

A big thank you goes out to my close contacts and friends at Microsoft. Thanks also to Studio B literary agency and my agents, David Rogelberg and Neil Salkind. Neil has a terrific knack for helping me find projects that are both fun and challenging.

I hope I haven't forgotten anyone, but if I have, it was an oversight. *Honest.* ;-)

William R. Stanek

There are a few people without whom I wouldn't have been able to contribute to this book. Neil Salkind at Studio B who asked is perhaps first in the queue to be thanked. Richard Siddaway, who started the first PowerShell user group, is probably the person most responsible for the depth of my interest in the subject. At Microsoft, I should mention Jeffrey Snover for his encouragement and Eileen Brown, my manager but also my friend, mentor, and when I least deserve it, my advocate. She deserves far greater thanks than a mention here. And finally, my family: my wife, Jackie, and my children, Lisa and Paul. Kids: the book in your hands is one of the reasons why Daddy kept asking you to be quiet.

James O'Neill

To my wife, Christine, and our daughters, Madison and Isabel, I love you, and thanks for always being there for me. Also, thanks to the authors, editors, and other invaluable staff that I've had the pleasure of working with.

Jeffrey Rosen

If you've purchased *PowerShell, VBScript, and JScript Bible* or are thumbing through the book in a bookstore somewhere, you probably want to know how this book can help you. Our goal in writing *PowerShell, VBScript, and JScript Bible* is to create the best resource available on scripting the Windows operating system.

As you'll learn in this book, Windows scripting involves many different technologies. These technologies include:

- Windows operating systems
- Windows Script Host (WSH)
- Scripting languages, such as VBScript and JScript
- Windows PowerShell
- ActiveX and COM (Component Object Model) components
- Microsoft Active Directory
- ADSI (Active Directory Services Interfaces)
- WMI (Windows Management Instrumentation)

We've tried to pack in as much information about these topics as possible, and to present the information in a way that is both clear and concise. We've also tried to present Windows scripting in a unique way, offering both VBScript and JScript solutions throughout the text and then discussing how to accomplish similar tasks using PowerShell. In this way, you can learn exactly how VBScript, JScript, and PowerShell can be used with Windows. With this approach, you gain insight into unique scripting techniques necessary to implement solutions in VBScript, JScript, and PowerShell, and, if you prefer one technique over the other, there's no more guesswork.

Contents at a Glance

Part V: Windows Scripting Libraries

Part VI: Appendixes

Contents

Part II: Windows VBScript and JScript

Contents

Contents

Part III: Network and Directory Service Scripting

Contents

Part IV: Windows PowerShell

Contents

Part VI: Appendixes

Contents

Contents

Introduction

PowerShell, VBScript, and JScript Bible is a work in progress, just like the Windows operating system itself and the body of work that's grown up around it. It is quite likely that errors will make themselves apparent after this book has gone to press and found its way onto your desktop. I very much appreciate the efforts of readers who go to the trouble of pointing out mistakes in the text so I can fix them in future editions. Even more, I am grateful for readers who offer their own hints, tricks, code, and ideas to me for inclusion in future editions of this book.

I truly hope you find that *PowerShell, VBScript and JScript Bible* provides everything you need to perform essential scripting tasks. You can contact me through e-mail at `williamstanek@aol .com`. You're always welcome to write me with ideas, suggestions, improvements, or questions. If you provide an example that's used in a future edition of this book, I'll be especially grateful for your help and will credit you in that edition. I also have a Web site, which contains support material for this book, among other things. Point your browser to `www.williamstanek.com/ scripting/` for corrections, enhancements, news, and additional thoughts. I'll post the source code from this book as well.

Thank you!

William R. Stanek

The best introduction to a book I ever saw was from Machiavelli's *The Discourses*, where he says something like, "I'm sending you something, and if it doesn't meet the obligations I owe you, is at any rate the best I can send. For in it I have set down all I know from long experience and constant reading...you may perhaps lament my lack of skill should my narratives be thin and also errors of judgment if I have made mistakes."

The longer the piece that I write, the more likely I am to think of that. The experience I have in PowerShell builds on decades of seeing different scenarios and using different tools: and that experience has been gained working with people who don't think of themselves as Programmers. Graphical management tools make it easy to find how to do a one-off task, but some repetitive tasks aren't efficient with the GUI. Some information can't be extracted easily from a graphical tool: some tasks just weren't anticipated by the Programmer who wrote it. UNIX system administrators have known for a long time that there is an area, which isn't Programming in the customary sense, of creating a large beast, with considerations such as user interface design to be taken into account. It produces something that a dictionary would define as a program—a sequence of instructions to be followed by the computer. A script is a program but not a Program (the capitalization is deliberate). Scripts are written mostly by people who are not Programmers, but just know the job they need to get done. And, usually a script will involve less time to create than a "proper" Program and will pay back the time that went into it very quickly. Want to know which of the servers you manage don't have a key patch on them—without logging onto each one? It's a few lines of script; a system administrator can put it together in a couple of minutes. A Programmer (capital P) won't have fired up Visual Studio and roughed out the user interface in that time.

Better still for the Windows system administrator, most of the work has been done by someone else. Want a list of your servers? A couple of lines of script will get it from Active Directory. Want the installed patches on each of those servers? One line of PowerShell will get that. Most of the knowledge needed isn't of a programming or scripting language—whether you use PowerShell, VBScript, or any other environment, it is a question of understanding the task and the objects that you can call on *from* that environment. PowerShell has all of .NET, WMI, AD, and ActiveX/COM at its disposal. It needs a whole bookshelf to explain all of those things, so what we do in this book is to try to equip you, the reader, with the skills you need to use them—which is why I worry that my narratives may be thin.

Who Should Read This Book

If you are someone who is interested in any of the previously mentioned technologies, *PowerShell, VBScript and JScript Bible* is definitely a book you should read. This comes with several caveats. This book is designed for:

- Administrators who support Windows systems
- Developers who create scripts or programs for Windows systems
- Advanced users working with Windows systems

To pack in as much information as possible, We had to assume that you have basic networking skills, a basic understanding of Windows, and that Windows is already installed on your systems. With this in mind, we don't devote entire chapters to understanding, installing, or using Windows. Beyond the introductory information in Chapters 1, 2, and 3, we don't cover scripting basics either. We do, however, cover every facet of Windows scripting, so if you want to learn Windows scripting inside and out—including techniques not published elsewhere—you've come to the right source.

Although the book highlights the latest and greatest features of Windows Vista and Windows Server 2008, just about everything you learn in this book can also be applied to script Windows XP. Keep in mind that if you are using a pre–Windows Vista system, however, you may need to check your scripts to ensure they are fully compatible.

How This Book Is Organized

Learn the basics of what goes into Windows and you will be able to use all sorts of devices and computers in the future. The book is organized in a way that enables you to start off at the very beginning with Windows, but still grow to the point where you can get going with some powerful server and programming features, if you care to.

Part I assumes that someone has set up a Windows system in front of you. After being introduced to Windows script in Chapter 1, you learn the basics of how to:

- VBScript Essentials (Chapter 2)
- JScript Essentials (Chapter 3)
- PowerShell Essentials (Chapter 4)

In Part II, you learn how to:

- Creating Scripts and Scripting Files (Chapter 5)
- VBScript and JScript Scripting Basics (Chapter 6)
- Input, Output, and Error Handling with VBScript and JScript (Chapter 7)
- Working with Files and Folders in VBscript and JScript (Chapter 8)
- Reading and Writing Files (Chapter 9)
- Managing Drives and Printers with VBScript and JScript (Chapter 10)
- Configuring Menus, Shortcusts, and Startup Applications (Chapter 11)
- Working with the Windows Registry and Event Logs (Chapter 12)

In Part III, you learn network and directory service scripting:

- Scheduling One-time and Recurring Tasks (Chapter 13)
- Managing Computer and User Scripts (Chapter 14)
- Introducing Active Directory Service Interfaces (Chapter 15)
- Using Schema to Master ADSI (Chapter 16)
- Managing Local and Domain Resources with ADSI (Chapter 17)
- Service and Resource Administration with ADSI (Chapter 18)
- Maintaining Shared Directories, Printer Queues, and Print Jobs (Chapter 19)
- Managing Active Directory Domain Extensions (Chapter 20)

In Part IV, you learn Windows PowerShell:

- Input, Output and Error Handling in PowerShell (Chapter 21)
- Working with Files and Registry in Powershell (Chapter 22)
- Event Logging, Services, and Process Monitoring with PowerShell (Chapter 23)
- Working with Active Directory Using ADSI and PowerShell (Chapter 24)
- Working with WMI and PowerShell (Chapter 25)

In Part V, you develop a set of programming libraries:

- Library: File-System Utilities (Chapter 26)
- Library: I/O Utilities (Chapter 27)
- Library: Network Resource Utilities (Chapter 28)
- Library: Account Management Utilities (Chapter 29)
- Library: Building a PowerShell Library (Chapter 30)

In Part VI, you'll learn more about:

- Windows Scripting API (Appendix A)
- Core ADSI Reference (Appendix B)
- Essential Command-Line Utilities for Use with WSH (Appendix C)

Conventions and Features

As with most computer books, you'll see that some text is highlighted by special formatting or with special icons. Here's a field guide to the things you'll see.

NOTE Notes provide additional details and often contain information that you should read before trying to implement a referenced technique.

CROSS-REF Cross-references tell you where you can find more information on a particular topic.

TIP Tips inform you of little factoids that may be useful to you as you work with Windows scripting. Tips provide helpful information that isn't always essential to getting things to work correctly. Rather, Tip material can be used to make things run better.

CAUTION Cautions provide a specific warning about things you should watch out for, or things you shouldn't do. You should pay particular attention to Cautions when reading the text.

Source-Code Formatting

The text contains source-code listings as well as in-text references to objects, methods, properties, and other source-code elements. In order to minimize line wrapping and formatting issues, we generally use in-line code lists for code examples. For example:

VBScript

```
Set fs = CreateObject ("Scripting.FileSystemObject")
Set f = fs.OpenTextFile (aFile, ForAppending)
f.WriteLine theLine
f.Close
```

JScript

```
var fs = new ActiveXObject("Scripting.FileSystemObject");
var f = fs.OpenTextFile (aFile, ForAppending)
f.WriteLine(theLine)
f.Close()
```

In-text references to source-code elements are highlighted with a monospace font, as in the following sentence. The `OpenTextFile` method is used to open text files. Don't confuse monospace type with in-text elements printed in bold. When you see bold text in the middle of a paragraph, it means that this is something you should type in at the keyboard, such as, "Type **cls** at the command prompt to clear the screen."

What's on the Companion Web site

On the companion Web site, you will find the following:

- **Sample code:** Each chapter has its own subfolder on the Web site, and you will find all the code output that was discussed in each chapter organized accordingly.

What You'll Learn from This Book

Every how-to book is supposed to teach its readers how to do something, and in the process convey some body of knowledge to the reader. *PowerShell, VBScript and JScript Bible* is no exception. This book teaches you about Windows scripting and includes in-depth coverage of related technologies.

PowerShell, VBScript and JScript Bible isn't meant to be a do-everything guide to scripting. Rather, the book focuses on techniques you'll use to script the Windows operating system. Chapter by chapter, you learn how to create scripts. The detailed explanations provided are backed by hundreds of hands-on examples and over 300 complete source-code listings. This book also develops extensive utility libraries that you can use to quickly and efficiently perform complex tasks.

Part I

Getting Started with Windows Scripting

P art I of the *PowerShell, VBScript, and JScript Bible* introduces you to the powerful administrative tool that is Windows scripting. You'll get an overview of Windows scripting and its potential, and an introduction to three technologies you can use for Windows scripting: VBScript, JScript, and PowerShell.

Chapter 1

Introducing Windows Scripting

Windows scripting gives everyday users and administrators the ability to automate repetitive tasks, complete activities while away from the computer, and perform many other time-saving activities. Windows scripting accomplishes all of this by enabling you to create tools to automate tasks that would otherwise be handled manually, such as creating user accounts, generating log files, managing print queues, or examining system information. By eliminating manual processes, you can double, triple, or even quadruple your productivity and become more effective and efficient at your job. Best of all, scripts are easy to create and you can rapidly develop prototypes of applications, procedures, and utilities; and then enhance these prototypes to get exactly what you need, or just throw them away and begin again. This ease of use gives you the flexibility to create the kinds of tools you need without a lot of fuss.

Introducing Windows Scripting

You've heard the claims about scripting and now you're thinking, so what? What's in it for me? You may be an administrator rather than a developer. Or maybe you're a power user who helps other users from time to time. Either way, scripting will prove useful to your situation and needs. So in answer to the question, "What's in it for me?" consider the following:

- **Would you like to have more free time?** Windows scripting frees you from mundane and repetitive tasks, enabling you to focus on more interesting and challenging tasks.

- **Would you like to be able to analyze trends and be proactive rather than reactive?** You can use Windows scripting to extract and manipulate huge quantities of information and turn out easy-to-use reports.

- **Would you like to be able to seize opportunities before they disappear?** Windows scripting enables you to take advantage of opportunities and be more effective. You can solve problems quickly and efficiently.

- **Would you like to be a top performer and receive the praise you deserve?** Windows scripting enables you to accomplish in hours or days what would otherwise take weeks or months with traditional techniques. You'll be more successful and more productive at work.

- **Would you like to be able to integrate activities and applications?** Windows scripting enables you to integrate information from existing systems and applications, allowing you to kick off a series of tasks simply by starting a script.

- **Would you like to have fun at work?** Windows scripting can be fun, challenging, and rewarding. Give it a try and you'll see!

If Windows scripting can do so much, it must be terribly complex, right? On the contrary—it is its simplicity that enables you to do so much, not complexity. Many Windows scripts are only a few lines long and you can create them in a few minutes!

Taking a look at Windows Scripting

Two different architectures are used for scripting in Windows. The older one uses the Windows Script Host and the newer one uses PowerShell. A lot of the tasks that can be carried out using the VBScript in the Windows Scripting Host can be transferred to PowerShell. However not all the tasks that can be run in PowerShell can be transferred to Windows Script Host scripts so easily. For a lot of organizations using various derivatives of Visual Basic—in Web pages, Office applications, Windows forms applications—makes a de-facto standard.

Windows Script Host Architecture

Windows Script Host (WSH) has been part of Windows since Windows NT4. Windows Script Host provides architecture for building dynamic scripts that consist of a core object model, scripting hosts, and scripting engines—each of which is discussed in the sections that follow.

Getting Started with Windows Script Host

Windows Script Host is a core component of the Windows operating system and, as such, is installed by default when you install Windows. Like other components, Windows Script Host can be uninstalled. It can also be upgraded through downloads or by installing service packs. To ensure that Windows Script Host is installed on your system, type **cscript** at a command prompt. You should see version information for Windows Script Host as well as usage details. If you don't see this information, Windows Script Host may not be installed and you'll need to install it as you would any other Windows component.

The key components of Windows Script Host are as follows:

- **WScript:** A Windows executable for the scripting host that is used when you execute scripts from the desktop. This executable has GUI controls for displaying output in pop-up dialog boxes.

- **CScript:** A command-line executable for the scripting host that is used when you execute scripts from the command line. This executable displays standard output at the command line.

- **WSH ActiveX Control:** An ActiveX control that provides the core object model for the scripting host.

- **Scripting Engines:** Scripting engines provide the core functions, objects, and methods for a particular scripting language. VBScript and JScript scripting engines are installed by default on Windows.

A Windows script is a text file containing a series of commands. Unlike shell scripts, Windows script commands don't resemble commands that you'd type in at the keyboard. Instead, they follow the syntax for the scripting language you are using, such as VBScript or JScript.

Windows scripts can be created in Notepad. When you finish creating the script, save it with an extension appropriate for the scripting language (.vbs for VBScript, .js for JScript, or .wsf for batch scripts that combine scripts with markup). Once you create a Windows script, you run it with WScript or CScript.

Using and running scripts

Windows scripts can be run with either WScript or CScript, and most of the time the application you use depends on your personal preference. However, you'll find that WScript works best for scripts that interact with users, especially if the script displays results as standard text output. For tasks that you want to automate or run behind the scenes, you'll probably prefer CScript, with which you can suppress output and prompts for batch processing.

You can use WScript and CScript with scripts in several different ways. The easiest way is to set WScript as the default application for scripts and then run scripts by clicking their file name in Windows Explorer. Don't worry—you don't have to do anything fancy to set WScript as the default. The first time you click a Windows script, you'll be asked if you'd like to associate the file extension with WScript. Click Yes. Alternatively, you may see an Open With dialog box that asks which program you would like to use to open the file. Choose WScript, and then check the "Always use this program to open this file" checkbox.

You can also set CScript as the default interface. When you do this, clicking a Windows script runs CScript instead of WScript. Or, you could run scripts from the Run prompt just as you could when WScript was the default. To run scripts with CScript from the command line, enter **cscript** followed by the pathname of the script you want to execute. For now, don't worry about the details; you'll find detailed instructions in Chapter 4.

Core object model

The core object model and scripting hosts are packaged with WSH for Windows. The core object model is implemented in the WSH.ocx ActiveX control. WSH.ocx provides the key functionality necessary for scripts to interact with the operating system. In WSH, objects are simply named containers that you'll use to interact with operating system components. For example, you'll use the WshNetwork object to access and configure network resources, such as printers and drives.

Each object has properties and methods that are used to perform certain types of tasks. Properties are attributes of an object that you can access. Methods are procedures that you'll use to perform operations. As with other object-based programming languages, you can work with objects in a variety of ways. You can use built-in objects, create new objects based on the built-in objects, or define your own objects using unique methods and properties.

Table 1-1 provides a summary of the WSH object model. The WSH object hierarchy can be broken down into two broad categories: exposed objects and non-exposed objects. Exposed objects, such as WScript, are the ones you'll work with in your scripts. Non-exposed objects, such as WshCollection, are accessed through the methods or properties of other objects. These objects do the behind-the-scenes work.

TABLE 1-1

Core WSH Objects

Object Type	Object	Description
Exposed Object	Script.Signer	An object that allows you to sign scripts with a digital signature and to verify signed scripts
	WScript	Top-level object that provides access to core objects and other functionality such as object creation
	WScript.WshNetwork	Automation object used to access and configure network resources, such as printers and drives, also provides user, domain, and computer information
	WScript.WshShell	Automation object that provides access to the environment and file folders

Object Type	Object	Description
	WshController	Automation object that provides the control functions necessary for creating a remote script process
Non-exposed Object	WshArguments	Accessed through the WScript.Arguments property, obtains command-line arguments
	WshCollection	Accessed through WshNetwork.EnumNetwork Drives or WshNetwork.EnumPrinter Collection, used for iteration through a group of items, such as printers or drives
	WshEnvironment	Accessed through the WshShell.Environment property, allows you to work with environment variables
	WshNamed	Accessed through the WScript.Arguments .Named property, allows you to work with named arguments passed to a script
	WshRemote	Accessed through the WshController .WshRemote method, allows you to start, stop, and track the status of remote scripts
	WshRemote.Error	Accessed through the WshRemote.Error property, used to track runtime errors related to remote scripts
	WshScriptExec	Accessed through the WshShell.Exec method, allows you to track the status of program or scripts started with the WshShell.Exec method, also provides access to the related input, output, and error streams
	WshShortcut	Accessed through the WshShell.CreateShortcut method, used to create and manage file shortcuts
	WshSpecialFolders	Accessed through the WshShell.SpecialFolders property, used to work with file folders
	WshUnnamed	Accessed through the WScript.Arguments .Unnamed property, allows you to work with unnamed arguments passed to a script
	WshUrlShortcut	Accessed through the WshShell.CreateShortcut method, used to create and manage URL shortcuts

NOTE With the JScript scripting engine, the letter case for object, method, and property names is important. The JScript engine doesn't recognize an object unless you reference it properly. For example, with `WScript`, the JScript engine does not recognize `Wscript`. Because VBScript really doesn't care about letter case, either `Wscript` or `WScript` works just fine.

More on scripting hosts

To execute Windows scripts, you'll use one of the two scripting hosts available, either WScript or CScript. WScript has GUI controls for displaying output in pop-up dialog boxes and is used primarily when you execute scripts from the desktop. CScript is the command-line executable for the scripting host that is used when you execute scripts from the command line. Although you can work with both of these hosts in much the same way, there are some features specific to each, which we discuss later in Chapter 4. For now, let's focus on how the scripting hosts work.

Several file extensions are mapped for use with the scripting hosts. These file extensions are:

- .js: Designates scripts written in JScript
- .vbs: Designates scripts written in VBScript
- .wsf: Designates a Windows script file
- .wsh: Designates a WSH properties file

A limitation of .js and .vbs files is that they can contain only JScript or VBScript statements, respectively, and you cannot mix and match. This is where .wsf files come into the picture. You can use .wsf files to create WSH jobs, or what I call *batch* scripts. These batch scripts can combine multiple types of scripts and can also include type libraries containing constants.

Batch scripts contain markup tags that identify elements within the batch, such as individual jobs and the scripting language being used. These markup tags are defined as XML (Extensible Markup Language) elements. XML is structured much like HTML and uses plain-text characters. You can use any text editor to create batch scripts and, because batch scripts contain XML, you can also use an XML editor.

Windows scripts can also use .wsh files. These files contain default settings for scripts, such as timeout values and script paths. Because of the introduction of .wsf files and direct in-script support for most script properties, .wsh files are rarely needed.

More on scripting engines

Scripting engines provide the core language functionality for Windows scripts and are packaged separately from the Windows Script Host itself. You can obtain scripting engines for JScript, VBScript, Perl, TCL, Python, and more. The official Microsoft scripting engines for VBScript and JScript are standard components on Windows and are the focus of this book.

With Windows scripting, many of the features available for scripting with Internet Explorer and the Web aren't available. Functions needed for Web scripting simply aren't needed for Windows scripting and vice versa. For example, in JScript, none of the window-related objects are available in WSH because, in Windows, you normally don't need to access documents, forms, frames, applets, plug-ins, or any of those other browser-related features. The exception to this is if you create a script that starts a browser session; within the browser session, you can use the browser-related objects as much as you want.

Right now, you may be wondering what exactly is and isn't supported by Windows scripts. In a nutshell, the scripting engines support core language and language runtime environments. The core language includes operators, statements, built-in objects, and built-in functions. Operators are used to perform arithmetic, comparisons, and more. Statements are used to make assignments, to conditionally execute code, and to control the flow within a script. For example, you can use `for` looping to execute a section of code for a specific count. These types of statements are all defined in the core language. Beyond this, the core language also defines the core functions and objects that perform common operations such as evaluating expressions, manipulating strings, and managing data.

The runtime environment adds objects to the core object model. These objects are used to work with the operating system and are available only with Windows Scripting. Table 1-2 provides a complete list of the available VBScript objects. The list is organized according to where the objects originate, either in the runtime environment or the core object model.

TABLE 1-2

VBScript Objects for Windows Scripting

Runtime Objects	Core Objects
Dictionary object	Class object
Drive object	Debug object
Drives collection	Dictionary object
File object	Err object
Files collection	FileSystemObject object
FileSystemObject object	Match object
Folder object	Matches collection
Folders collection	RegExp object
TextStream object	SubMatches collection

Table 1-3 provides a complete list of available JScript objects. Again, the list is organized according to where the objects originate.

TABLE 1-3

JScript Objects for Windows Scripting

Runtime Objects	Core Objects
Arguments Object	ActiveXObject Object
Dictionary object	Array object
Drive object	Boolean object
Drives collection	Date object
File object	Debug object
Files collection	Dictionary object
FileSystemObject object	Enumerator object
Folder object	Error object
Folders collection	FileSystemObject object
TextStream object	Function object
	Global object
	Math object
	Number object
	Object object
	RegExp object
	Regular Expression object
	String object
	VBArray object

Windows PowerShell Architecture

The name "PowerShell" explains the key architectural difference from the Windows Scripting Host. PowerShell began life as a command-line shell—like Windows CMD.EXE, and you can interact with it—so where VBScript or JScript programs are written in Notepad and run using the appropriate language inside the scripting host, the lines of a PowerShell script might be tested at a command prompt one by one and then gathered into a script.

As a shell, PowerShell can chain commands together using piping—that is, sending the output of one command into another using the | symbol. Often, development consists of running a command, checking its output, piping that output into something, checking that, and building up a long and complex line.

One of the important things that sets PowerShell apart from CMD.EXE is that where a command returns text to CMD, PowerShell's commands return objects. The properties and methods of those objects can be used by commands further along a pipeline.

Compared with the WSH languages, PowerShell's use of objects is both broader and deeper. Its use is deeper because .NET defines types such as text strings, and provides methods for working with them. PowerShell does not need to write a function for getting a substring from a bigger string—that's inherited from .NET, as is PowerShell's file handling, arithmetic, and so on (so PowerShell doesn't need to implement the core functions found in the WSH languages). PowerShell's use of objects is broader, because PowerShell has access to .NET objects, as well as COM ones and ready-made commands for getting to WMI and Active Directory objects.

WMI objects provide management, configuration, and performance information for many server applications and Windows components—indeed you could do a lot with just piping the output of PowerShell's Get-WMIObject command into its Format-Table command.

PowerShell was designed to be highly extensible. Not only can your own scripts become part of the working environment, but also developers can write *snap-ins* that extend the environment with compiled code. These add to the set of commands available inside PowerShell—the term "command" in PowerShell covers all the different things that can be invoked from the prompt: external programs, scripts, functions loaded from scripts, and what PowerShell terms "CMDlets" from the snap-ins. PowerShell provides five snap-ins by default.

TABLE 1-4

PowerShell Snap-ins

Snap-in	Functions
Core	Loads other snap-ins, provides access to command history, implements for loop, and where functionality
Host	Handles the console, manages transcripts
Management	Provides the commands to manage Windows components
Security	Handles credentials and secure strings
Utility	Provides the commands to format and output data

Other products that run on Windows can provide their own snap-ins—for example, Exchange2007, SQL Server 2008, and various members of the system center family provide their own snap-ins to allow PowerShell to be used as the scripting environment to manage them. At the time of this writing, Windows Server 2008 R2 has only just been announced: It will include an updated version of PowerShell, and more Windows components will have snap-ins to manage them.

The CMDLets snap-ins can also implement *providers*. The Security snap-in loads a provider for the Certificate store, so you can browse through it as if it were a file system. The Core snap-in has one for the registry, so you can treat branches of the registry like folders on your hard disk. Again, additional snap-ins can add to the list of providers.

Although PowerShell is a shell, it is possible to use the engine from another program without loading the "host"—the command Window that is wrapped around the engine. Increasingly it is expected that management tools for Microsoft products will be written as PowerShell snap-ins and then the GUI management tools will invoke CMDlets in these. This allows you to carry out a task in the GUI, discover the script that would carry it out, and use that as the basis for your own scripts.

PowerShell scripts have a .ps1 file extension, but to avoid the dangers of PowerShell automatically running a malicious script, the file type is not tied to the PowerShell executable. You can run PowerShell.exe with a command line that is the name of a script. Or you can invoke the script inside the shell. There is no equivalent to the choice between CScript and WScript.

Is there any need to learn anything other than PowerShell? That's less of a point of argument between the contributors of this book than you might imagine. It's going to become harder to be a properly rounded IT professional in a Microsoft environment without PowerShell, but the other languages will be with us for many years. Few organizations will see sense in re-writing a perfectly good VB or JScript script as a PowerShell one, and there are libraries and code samples that exist only in those languages. Sometimes it will make sense to translate them into PowerShell (which requires the ability to understand the script) and sometimes it will make sense to adapt an existing script in its existing language.

Summary

Now that you have a taste of what Windows scripting is all about, it's time to go to the next level. Chapters 2, 3, and 4 provide essential scripting techniques for VBScript, JScript, and PowerShell, respectively. Carefully study these chapters before proceeding as they describe the core mechanics of scripting, covering variables, arrays, operators, conditional statements, control loops, procedures, and more. Once we have covered these core mechanics, we won't waste your time rehashing how these features work with every future scripting example. Instead, we will trust that you've reviewed and understand the core mechanics and want to focus on the new materials we are discussing in a particular chapter. Even if you know some scripting basics, we recommend that you use these chapters to brush up on your VBScript, JScript, and PowerShell knowledge.

Chapter 2

VBScript Essentials

Microsoft Visual Basic scripting edition (VBScript) has long been the favorite scripting language of Microsoft developers and soon it will be your favorite as well. VBScript is easy to learn and use, making the language a great choice, especially if you don't have a programming background.

Working with Variables

Variables are a part of most scripting languages, and VBScript is no exception. A variable is simply a placeholder for a value you want to work with.

Variable naming

You can create a variable by assigning the variable a name, which you can refer to in your code later. Variable names, like other VBScript structures, follow standard naming conventions. These naming rules are as follows:

- Names must begin with an alphabetic character.
- Names cannot contain periods.
- Names must be less than 256 characters in length.

Variable names also have an additional property, which isn't the case of other structures in VBScript. They are case-sensitive, meaning `value1`, `Value1`, and `VALUE1` are all different variables. However, method, function, and object references in VBScript are not case-sensitive. For example, you can echo to the screen using any of the following commands:

```
wscript.echo "This is a test!"
Wscript.echo "This is a test!"
WScript.Echo "This is a test!"
```

But in reality, the correct capitalization for this reference is WScript.Echo.

Declaring variables

In VBScript, variables are declared either explicitly or implicitly. To declare a variable explicitly, use the keyword Dim to tell VBScript that you are creating a variable and then specify the variable name, such as:

```
Dim newString
```

You can then assign a value to the variable, such as:

```
newString = "I really love VBScript!"
```

You can also declare multiple variables at the same time. You do this by separating the variable names with commas:

```
Dim firstName, lastName, middleInitial
```

To declare a variable implicitly, use the variable name without first declaring it; you don't need to use the Dim keyword. In this instance, VBScript creates the variable for you.

The problem with implicit variables is that any name is assumed to be valid, so you can mistakenly assign values to the wrong variable and you won't know it. Consider the following example, in which you assign a value to theTotal and later assign a value to a variable called theTotals:

```
theTotal = sumA + sumB + sumC

'working with the variable

'now you need to increase the total
theTotals = theTotals + 1
```

 Everything following a single quotation mark is interpreted as a comment. You can use comments anywhere in a line of code.

In this example, we meant to increase theTotal, but increased theTotals instead. To avoid situations like this, set Option Explicit, which requires that all variables be declared explicitly with the Dim keyword and also ensures the validity of your variables. This option should be placed at the beginning of your script, as shown in Listing 2-1.

LISTING 2-1

Using Variables

vars.vbs

```
Option Explicit
'Setting variables
Dim sumA, sumB, sumC
Dim theTotal

sumA = 100
sumB = 10*10
sumC = 1000/10

'Get the total
theTotal = sumA + sumB + sumC

'write total to command-line using WScript.Echo
wScript.Echo "Total = ", theTotal
```

Output

```
300
```

Variable types

VBScript assigns all variables to the `variant` data type. Variants can hold numeric or string data and each is handled differently. The primary way in which VBScript determines if something is a number or a string is through the use of double quotation marks. In the previous code sample, `sumA`, `sumB`, and `sumC` are all handled as numbers. If you add double quotation marks to the values, they are treated as strings, as in the following example:

```
sumA = "100"
sumB = "10*10"
sumC = "1000/10"
```

The use of strings yields very different results when you add the values together, and as a result, the value of `theTotal` is:

```
10010*101000/10
```

The reason for this is that while numbers are summed, strings are concatenated so you get the literal sum of all characters in the string. To complicate things a bit more, VBScript also uses *variable subtypes*. Variable subtypes are summarized in Table 2-1. Subtypes enable you to put certain types of information into categories, which allows for better handling of dates, floating-point numbers, integers, and other types of variables. For example, if you are working with dates and you need to add two dates together, you wouldn't want the result to be an integer. Instead, you'd want the dates to be handled as dates and the result of any operations to be dates, which is exactly what subtypes offer.

TABLE 2-1

Variable Subtypes in VBScript

Subtype	Description
Boolean	A Boolean value that contains either True or False.
Byte	An integer byte value in the range 0 to 255.
Currency	A floating-point number in the range –922,337,203,685,477.5808 to 922,337,203,685,477.5807. Note the use of up to four decimal places.
Date (Time)	A number that represents a date between January 1, 100 to December 31, 9999.
Double	A double-precision, floating-point number in the range –1.79769313486232E308 to –4.94065645841247E–324 for negative values; 4.94065645841247E–324 to 1.79769313486232E308 for positive values.
Empty	An uninitialized variant. Value is 0 for numeric variables or an empty string ("") for string variables.
Error	An error number used with runtime errors.
Integer	An integer in the range –32,768 to 32,767.
Long	An integer in the range –2,147,483,648 to 2,147,483,647.
Null	A variant set to NULL that contains no valid data.
Object	An object reference.
Single	A single-precision, floating-point number in the range –3.402823E38 to –1.401298E–45 for negative values; 1.401298E–45 to 3.402823E38 for positive values.
String	A variable-length string.

Generally, if you use whole numbers, such as 3 or 5, with a variable, VBScript creates the variable as an Integer. Variables with values that use decimal points, such as 3.125 or 5.7, are generally assigned as Doubles, double-precision floating-point values. Variables with values entered with a mixture of alphabetical and numeric characters, such as Yeah! and Q3, are created as Strings.

Converting variable types

VBScript can automatically convert between some variable types, and this eliminates most variable conflict. However, if you try to add a string variable to a numeric variable type, you will get an error. Because of this, do not try to perform numeric calculations with alphanumeric data.

That said, VBScript includes many different functions for converting data from one subtype to another. These functions are summarized in Table 2-2.

TABLE 2-2

Functions for Converting Variable Subtypes

Function	Description
CBool(expression)	Converts any valid expression to a Boolean value. Returns either True or False.
CByte(expression)	Converts any valid expression to a Byte value.
CCur(expression)	Converts any valid expression to a Currency value.
CDate(date)	Converts any valid date string to a Date value. Returns a date value that can be used when adding dates and times.
CDbl(expression)	Converts any valid expression to a Double value.
CInt(expression)	Converts any valid expression to an Integer value.
CLng(expression)	Converts any valid expression to a Long value.
CSng(expression)	Converts any valid expression to a Single value.
CStr(expression)	Converts any valid expression to a String value.

Working with conversion functions is a lot easier than you may think. To convert a value, just pass the value to the conversion function, as follows:

```
stringA = "42"
stringB = "37"

intA = CInt(stringA) 'Set to integer value 42
intB = CInt(stringB) 'Set to integer value 37
```

The CBool(), CDate(), and CString() functions deserve a special note because they return output that is a bit different from what you might be used to. To learn more about these functions, take a look at Listing 2-2.

LISTING 2-2

Using Conversion Functions

changetype.vbs

```
sumA = 30: sumB = 15        'Initialize variables
wscript.echo "sumA: " & TypeName(sumA)
wscript.echo "sumB: " & TypeName(sumB)

Test = CBool(sumA = sumB) 'Test contains false

sumB= sumB * 2              'Double value of sumB
Test = CBool(sumA = sumB) 'Test contains true
wscript.echo "Test: " & TypeName(Test)

dateStr = "December 10, 2005" 'Define a date as a string
wscript.echo "dateStr: " & TypeName(dateStr)

theDate = CDate(dateStr)      'Convert to Date data type
wscript.echo "theDate: " & TypeName(theDate)

timeStr = "8:25:10 AM"        'Define a time as a string
theTime = CDate(timeStr)      'Convert to Date data type
wscript.echo "timeStr: " & TypeName(timeStr)
wscript.echo "theTime: " & TypeName(theTime)

aDouble = 715.255            'Define a numeric value
aString = CStr(aDouble)      'Convert to a string
wscript.echo "aDouble: " & TypeName(aDouble)
wscript.echo "aString: " & TypeName(aString)
```

This code produces the following output:

```
sumA: Integer
sumB: Integer
Test: Boolean
dateStr: String
theDate: Date
timeStr: String
theTime: Date
aDouble: Double
aString: String
```

Working with Constants

Constants provide an easy way to use specific values without actually having to remember related value codes or strings. By using constants, you make it easier to maintain your code should the value of a constant ever change. You'll also see constants referred to as literals. To help differentiate constants from variables, you should use a unique prefix or formatting.

Using built-in constants

In VBScript, constants are either intrinsic (built-in) or declared explicitly. VBScript has many built-in constants. Because built-in constants are already defined, you don't need to explicitly declare them in your scripts. All VBScript constants begin with the prefix vb.

Table 2-3 shows the available color constants. Table 2-4 shows the available date and time constants. Many other constants are defined as well, and are referenced in the appropriate sections of this book.

TABLE 2-3

Color Constants

Constant	Value	Description
vbBlack	&h00	Black
vbRed	&hFF	Red
vbGreen	&hFF00	Green
vbYellow	&hFFFF	Yellow
vbBlue	&hFF0000	Blue
vbMagenta	&hFF00FF	Magenta
vbCyan	&hFFFF00	Cyan
vbWhite	&hFFFFFF	White

TABLE 2-4

Date and Time Constants

Constant	Value	Description
vbSunday	1	Sunday
vbMonday	2	Monday

continued

TABLE 2-4	(continued)	
Constant	Value	Description
vbTuesday	3	Tuesday
vbWednesday	4	Wednesday
vbThursday	5	Thursday
vbFriday	6	Friday
vbSaturday	7	Saturday
vbUseSystemDayOfWeek	0	First day of the week specified in system settings
vbFirstJan1	1	Week in which January 1 occurs (default)
vbFirstFourDays	2	First week that has at least four days in the new year
vbFirstFullWeek	3	First full week of the year

Declaring constants

You declare a constant explicitly using the keyword `Const` to tell VBScript that you are creating a constant, specify the constant name, and then assign a value to the constant, such as:

```
Const COMPANYID = "4876-54-32-87A"
```

 Constant names don't need to be in all caps. However, to give constants a unique format-ting that differentiates them from variables, we decided to use all caps in the examples in this section.

Here, you are declaring the COMPANYID constant and setting a string value of 4876-54-32-87A. With string constants, the quotation marks are necessary to differentiate a string value from other types of values.

When you declare a numeric constant, you don't need to use quotation marks. The following exam-ple declares a numeric constant:

```
Const PROJECTNUMBER = 789
```

Here, you are declaring the PROJECTNUMBER constant and setting a numeric value of 789.

You declare date and time constants by enclosing them in number signs (#), such as:

```
Const PROJECTSTARTDATE = #12-15-07#
```

Working with Arrays

Using arrays, you can group related sets of data together. The most common type of array you'll use is one-dimensional, but you can create arrays with up to 60 dimensions if you want to. While a one-dimensional array is like a column of tabular data, a two-dimensional array is like a spreadsheet with rows and columns, and a three-dimensional array is like a 3D grid.

Initializing arrays

Arrays are declared much like regular variables except you follow the variable name with information describing the size and dimensions of the array. You can initialize an array with ten data elements as follows:

```
Dim bookArray(9)
```

Values in an array always begin at 0 and end at the number of data points in the array minus 1. This is the reason an array with 10 data points is initialized as `bookArray(9)`. To access elements in an array, reference the element's index position within the array. For example, `bookArray(0)` references the first element, `bookArray(1)` references the second element, and so on. Use the index position to set values for the array as well, as in the following:

```
bookArray(0) = "A Tale Of Two Cities"
bookArray(1) = "Grapes Of Wrath"
```

Using arrays with multiple dimensions

Multiple dimensions are created by separating the size of each dimension with commas, such as `currentArray(3,3,3)` or `testArray(2,5,5,4)`. You can create a two-dimensional array with five columns each with four rows of data points as follows:

```
Dim myArray(4,3)
```

Then, if you want to obtain the value of a specific cell in the spreadsheet, you can use the following:

```
theValue = arrayName(columns -1, rows -1)
```

in which `columns` is the column position of the cell and `rows` is the row position of the cell. Following this, you can get the value of the cell in column 3, row 2 with this statement:

```
myValue = myArray(2,1)
```

Sizing arrays

Sizing arrays on-the-fly allows you to use input from users to drive the size of an array. You declare a dynamic array without specifying its dimensions, as follows:

```
Dim userArray()
```

Then size the array later using the ReDim function:

```
ReDim userArray(currValues - 1)
```

or

```
ReDim userArray(numColumns - 1, numRows - 1)
```

You can also use ReDim to change the size of an existing array. For example, you can increase the size of an array from 10 elements to 20 elements. However, when you change the size of an existing array, the array's data contents are destroyed. To prevent this, use the Preserve keyword, as follows:

```
ReDim Preserve userArray(numColumns - 1, numRows - 1)
```

VBScript Operators

Operators are used to perform mathematical operations, to make assignments, and to compare values. The two key types of operators you'll use in VBScript are arithmetic operators and comparison operators. As you'll see, VBScript supports fewer operators than the command line. While this may seem limiting, VBScript makes up for this by allowing you to use floating-point values and integers with high precision.

 VBScript also has logical operators such as AND, NOT, OR, **and** XOR. **With the exception of** NOT, **these operators are rarely used.**

Arithmetic operators

VBScript supports a standard set of arithmetic operators. These operators are summarized in Table 2-5.

TABLE 2-5

Arithmetic Operators in VBScript

Operator	Operation
+	Addition
=	Assignment
/	Division
^	Exponent
Mod	Modulus
*	Multiplication
−	Subtraction/Negation

As you can see in Table 2-5, there are few surprises when it comes to VBScript operators. Still, a few standouts are worth mentioning. In VBScript, you determine remainders using the Mod function versus the % for the command line. But the syntax is essentially the same. With the expression:

```
Answer = 9 Mod 3
```

Answer is set to 0. With the expression:

```
Answer = 9 Mod 2
```

Answer is set to 1.

You can multiply by an exponent with the ^ operator. To achieve the same result as 8 *8 * 8 * 8, you would use:

```
Answer = 8^4
```

You can negate a value using the – operator, such as:

```
Answer = -6 * 2
```

If you mix operators, VBScript performs calculations using the same precedence order you learned in school. For example, multiplication and division in equations are carried out before subtraction and addition, which means:

7 + 2 * 2 = 11

and

5 / 5 + 6 = 7

Table 2-6 shows the complete precedence order for operators. As the table shows, exponents have the highest precedence order and are always calculated first.

TABLE 2-6

Operator Precedence in VBScript

Order	Operation
1	Exponents (^)
2	Negation (-)
3	Multiplication (*) and Division (/)
4	Remainders (Mod)
5	Addition (+) and Subtraction (-)

Comparison operators

When you perform comparisons, you check for certain conditions, such as whether A is greater than B, or if A is equal to C. You primarily use comparison operators with conditional statements, such as `If Then` and `If Then Else`. The available operators are summarized in Table 2-7.

TABLE 2-7

Comparison Operators in VBScript

Operator	Description
=	Equality; evaluates to `True` if the values are equal.
<>	Inequality; evaluates to `True` if the values are not equal.
<	Less than; evaluates to `True` if `value1` is less than `value2`.
<=	Less than or equal to; evaluates to `True` if `value1` is less than or equal to `value2`.
>	Greater than; evaluates to `True` if `value1` is greater than `value2`.
>=	Greater than or equal to; evaluates to `True` if `value1` is greater than or equal to `value2`.

Listing 2-3 shows how you can use comparison operators in a script. Note that you can use these operators to compare numbers as well as strings and that there is no set precedence order for comparisons. Comparisons are always performed from left to right.

LISTING 2-3

Scripting with Comparison Operators

checktotal.vbs

```
currTotal = 519
prevTotal = 321
if currTotal = 0 Then
  WScript.Echo "The total is zero."
End If
if currTotal = prevTotal Then
  WScript.Echo "The totals are
    equal."
End If
if currTotal <> 0 Then
  WScript.Echo "The total does NOT
    equal zero."
End If
if currTotal <> prevTotal Then
```

```
   WScript.Echo "The totals are NOT
      equal."
End If
if currTotal < 0 Then
  WScript.Echo "The total is less
      than zero."
End If
if currTotal > 0 Then
  WScript.Echo "The total is
      greater than zero."
End If
if currTotal <= prevTotal Then
  WScript.Echo "currTotal is less
      than or equal to prevTotal."
End If
if currTotal >= 0 Then
  WScript.Echo "The total is
      greater than or equal to zero."
End If
```

Output

```
The total does NOT equal zero.
The totals are NOT equal.
The total is greater than zero.
The total is greater than or equal
```

One other comparison operator you should learn about is the special operator Is. You use Is to compare objects, such as buttons. If the objects are of the same type, the result of the comparison is True. If the objects are not of the same type, the result of the comparison is False. You can test to see if the object theButton references the VBScript object Button as follows:

```
Answer = theButton Is Button
If Answer = True Then
   WScript.Echo "theButton is equivalent to Button."
Else
   WScript.Echo "theButton is NOT equivalent to Button."
End If
```

You can also perform the comparison directly in an if statement:

```
If theButton Is Button Then
   WScript.Echo "theButton is equivalent to Button."
Else
   WScript.Echo "theButton is NOT equivalent to Button."
End If
```

Performing operations on strings

The most common string operations you'll want to perform are assignment and concatenation. You assign values to strings using the equals sign, ensuring that the value is enclosed in double quotation marks, such as:

```
aString = "This is a String."
```

Concatenation is the technical term for adding strings together. Although you can use the + operator to concatenate strings, the normal operator for string concatenation is the & operator. Using the & operator, you can add strings together as follows:

```
custAddress = streetAdd & " " & cityState & " " & zipCode
```

Sometimes you may also want to display the value of a string in a message box. In such an instance, you will use the & operator as well. For example:

```
aString = "I get it!"
WScript.Echo "The string value is: " & aString
```

would display a dialog box with the message:

```
The string value is: I get it!
```

Conditional Statements

Traffic lights control the flow of traffic on the street. Conditional instructions control the flow of instructions in your code.

Using If...Then

You use If statements to execute a set of instructions only when certain conditions are met. In VBScript, If...Then structures follow this syntax:

```
If condition = True Then
  'Handle the condition
End If
```

or

```
If condition Then
    'Handle the condition
End If
```

Note the use of the `End If` statement. This is what makes it possible to execute multiple commands when a condition exists, such as:

```
If sum > 25 Then
    WScript.Echo "The sum exceeds the expected Result"
    'Reset sum to zero
    sum = 0
End If
```

You can control the execution of instructions based on a false condition as follows:

```
If condition = False Then
    'The condition is false
End If
```

or

```
If Not condition Then
    'The condition is false
End If
```

Using Else and ElseIf

You can extend the `If...Then` condition with `Else` statements. The `Else` statement provides an alternative when a condition that you specified is not met. The structure of an `If...Then Else` statement is as follows:

```
If checkValue = "Yes" Then
    WScript.Echo "The condition has been met."
Else
    WScript.Echo "The condition has not been met."
End If
```

To add more conditions, you can use `ElseIf` statements. Each additional condition you add to the code is then checked for validity. An example using `ElseIf` is shown in Listing 2-4.

LISTING 2-4

Working with ElseIf

testvalue.vbs

```
currValue = 5
If currValue < 0 Then
  WScript.Echo "The value is less than zero."
ElseIf currValue = 0 Then
  WScript.Echo "The value is equal to zero."
```

continued

LISTING 2-4   *(continued)*

```
ElseIf currValue = 1 Then
  WScript.Echo "The value is equal to one."
ElseIf currValue = 2 Then
  WScript.Echo "The value is equal to two."
ElseIf currValue = 3 Then
  WScript.Echo "The value is equal to three."
ElseIf currValue = 4 Then
  WScript.Echo "The value is equal to four."
ElseIf currValue = 5 Then
  WScript.Echo "The value is equal to five."
Else
  WScript.Echo "Value doesn't match expected parameters."
End If
```

Select Case

Checking for multiple conditions using `ElseIf` is a lot of work for you and for the VB interpreter. To make things easier, use `Select Case` anytime you want to check more than three conditions. Using `Select Case`, you can rewrite Listing 2-4 in a way that is clearer and easier to understand, which you can see in Listing 2-5.

LISTING 2-5

Working with Select Case

multicond.vbs

```
currValue = 9
Select Case currValue
  Case currValue < 0
    WScript.Echo "The value is less than zero."
  Case 0
    WScript.Echo "The value is equal to zero."
  Case 1
    WScript.Echo "The value is equal to one."
  Case 2
    WScript.Echo "The value is equal to two."
  Case 3
    WScript.Echo "The value is equal to three."
  Case 4
    WScript.Echo "The value is equal to four."
  Case 5
    WScript.Echo "The value is equal to five."
  Case Else
```

```
    WScript.Echo "Value doesn't match expected parameters."
End Select
```

Output

```
Value doesn't match expected parameters.
```

If you compare the ElseIf example and the Select Case example, you will see that the Select Case example requires less code and has a simpler structure. You can apply this same structure anytime you want to check for multiple conditions. Start the structure with the name of the variable whose value you want to check. Here, you compare the value of userInput:

```
Select Case userInput
```

Afterward, you can check for specific conditions, such as:

```
Case < 0
  'less than zero
Case > 0
  'greater than zero
Case = 0
  'equal zero
```

or

```
Case "Yes"
  'value is yes
Case "No"
  'value is no
```

Use Case Else to specify statements that should be executed if no match is found in the specified Case statements, such as:

```
Case Else
    WScript.Echo "Value doesn't match expected parameters."
    WScript.Echo "Please check your input again."
```

Conditional controls and strings

When you perform string comparisons with conditional controls, pay particular attention to the letter case. VBScript automatically performs case-sensitive comparisons. Because of this, a comparison of "No" and "NO" returns False.

To avoid potential problems you should convert the string to upper- or lowercase for the comparison. Use lcase() to convert strings to lowercase. Use ucase() to convert strings to uppercase. Listing 2-6 shows how these functions can be used with If...Then. You can also use these functions with Select Case.

LISTING 2-6

Changing the Case of a String

changecase.vbs

```
'Setting variables
m = "No"
n = "NO"
If m = n Then
  WScript.Echo "Anything? Nope, I didn't think so."
End If
If lcase(m) = lcase(n) Then
  WScript.Echo "Values are equal when converted to lowercase."
End If
if ucase(m) = ucase(n) Then
  WScript.Echo "Values are equal when converted to uppercase."
End If
```

Output

```
Values are equal when converted to lowercase.
Values are equal when converted to uppercase.
```

Control Loops

Sometimes you want to repeatedly execute a section of code. In VBScript, you can do this in several ways, including:

- `For Next` looping
- `For Each` looping
- `Do While` looping
- `Do Until` looping
- `While` looping

For Next looping

VBScript `For` loops are very basic. You use VBScript `For` loops to execute a code segment for a specific count. The structure of `For` loops is as follows:

```
For Counter = startNum to endNum
    'add the code to repeat
Next
```

The following example uses a For loop to initialize an array of 10 elements:

```
For i = 0 to 9
    myArray(i) = "Placeholder"
Next
```

After the For loop is executed, all 10 elements in the array are initialized to the value Placeholder. Using the Step keyword, you can step through the counter at specific intervals. You can step by 2s as follows:

```
For i = 0 to 20 Step 2
    myArray(i) = "Even"
Next
```

When you use a negative step value, you reverse the normal order of the counter. So instead of going in ascending order, go in descending order, as in the following:

```
For i = 20 to 0 Step -1
    myArray(i) = "Unknown"
Next
```

For Each looping

With For Each loops, you iterate through each element in an object or array. For Each loops are very similar to standard For loops. The key difference is that the number of elements in an object or array determines the number of times you go through the loop. In Listing 2-7, you initialize an array using a regular For loop and then display its values using a For Each loop.

LISTING 2-7

Using For Each Loops

foreach.vbs

```
'initialize array
Dim myArray(9)

'set array values
For i = 0 to 9
   myArray(i) = "Placeholder" & i
Next

'display array values
For Each i IN myArray
  WScript.Echo i
Next
```

continued

LISTING 2-7   *(continued)*

Output

```
Placeholder0
Placeholder1
Placeholder2
Placeholder3
Placeholder4
Placeholder5
Placeholder6
Placeholder7
Placeholder8
Placeholder9
```

As you can see, the basic syntax of a `For Each` loop is:

```
For Each element IN objArray
'add code to repeat
Next
```

where `element` is the counter for the loop and `objArray` is the object or array you want to examine.

Using Exit For

With `For` and `For Each` loops, you'll sometimes want to exit the loop before iterating through all of the possible values. To exit a `For` loop ahead of schedule, you can use the `Exit For` statement. The best place for this statement is within an `If Then` or `If Then Else` condition test, such as:

```
For Each i IN myArray
  WScript.Echo i

  If i = "Unknown" Then
    Exit For
  EndIf

Next
```

Using Do While loops

Sometimes you'll want to execute a code segment while a condition is met. To do this, you will use `Do While` looping. The structure of this loop is as follows:

```
Do While condition
    'add the code to repeat
Loop
```

With Do While, the loop is executed as long as the condition is met. This means to break out of the loop, you must change the condition at some point within the loop. Here is an example of a Do While loop that changes the status of the condition:

```
Do While continue = True
    y = y + 1
    If y < 10 Then
        WScript.Echo "Y is less than 10."
    ElseIf Y = 10 Then
        WScript.Echo "Y equals 10."
    Else
        WScript.Echo "Exiting the loop."
        continue = False
    EndIf
Loop
```

By placing the condition at the top of the loop, you ensure that the loop is only executed if the condition is met. In the previous example, the loop won't be executed at all if continue is set to False beforehand. However, sometimes you want to execute the loop at least once before you check the condition. To do this, you can place the condition test at the bottom of the loop, as in the following:

```
Do
    y = y + 1
    If y < 10 Then
        WScript.Echo "Y is less than 10."
    ElseIf Y = 10 Then
        WScript.Echo "Y equals 10."
    Else
        WScript.Echo "Exiting the loop."
        continue = False
    EndIf

Loop While continue = True
```

Using Do Until loops

Another form of control loop is a Do Until loop. With Do Until, you execute a loop *until* a condition is met instead of *while* a condition is met. As with Do While, you can place the condition test at the beginning or end of the loop. The following loop is executed zero or more times until the condition is met:

```
Do Until Answer = "No"
    'Add code to execute
    'Be sure to allow the condition to be changed
Loop
```

To ensure that the loop is executed at least once, use the following structure:

```
Do
    'Add code to execute
    'Be sure to allow the condition to be changed
Loop Until Answer = "No"
```

Using Exit Do

Using Exit Do, you can exit a Do While and Do Until before a condition occurs. As with Exit For, the best place for an Exit Do statement is within an If Then or If Then Else condition test, such as:

```
Do Until Answer = "No"
    'Add code to get answer
    'check to see if user wants to quit
    If Answer = "Quit" Then
      Exit Do
    End If
Loop
```

While…WEnd loops

The final type of control loop available in VBScript is a While…WEnd loop. With this type of loop, you can execute a loop while a condition is met, as in the following:

```
While x < 10
    'Execute this code
    x = x+1
    WScript.Echo x
WEnd
```

With a While…WEnd loop, the condition can only be placed at the beginning of the loop.

Using Procedures

Procedures are used to handle routine operations. You can pass in arguments and return values. You can even use Call to call a procedure if you want to. VBScript supports two types of procedures:

- **Functions:** Procedures that return a value to the caller
- **Subroutines:** Procedures that do not return a value to the caller

 VBScript also supports a special type of subroutine called an event. Events occur when a certain condition exists, such as when a key is pressed, and can also be simulated in the code with method calls. We don't discuss events in this book. You just don't use them much with Windows scripting.

VBScript Essentials 2

Working with functions

Many different built-in functions are available in VBScript. In earlier examples, you've seen lcase(), ucase(), and more. You can also create your own functions, which can perform many different types of tasks. Yet all functions have one thing in common: They are designed to return a value.

The basic structure of a function declaration is:

```
Function functionName(arg1, arg2, ..., argN)
    'Add your function code here.
End Function
```

As you can see, you declare the function, specify a name, and then set arguments that you want to pass to the function. Afterward, you add statements the function should execute and then end the function. When the function finishes executing, control returns to the caller and execution of the script continues from there.

You can call a function using several different techniques. You can use the Call statement, such as:

```
Call getTotal()
```

You can call a function directly in an assignment, such as:

```
value = getTotal()
```

You can also call a function within a statement:

```
WScript.Echo "The name you entered is: " & getUserName()
```

When there are no parameters to pass to the function, the parentheses are optional. This means you can use the following:

```
userName = getUserName
```

To return a value from a function, assign a value to a variable with the same name as the function. For example, if you create a function called getSum, you can return a value from the function as follows:

```
Call getSum(3,4,2)
Function getSum(varA, varB, varC)
    total = varA + varB + varC
    getSum = total / 2
End Function
```

Typically, all variables initialized within functions are temporary and exist only within the scope of the function. Thus, you can think of these variables as having a local scope. However, if you use a variable that is initialized outside the function, that variable has global scope. In the following example, you use a global variable in the function:

```
sample = "Placeholder"
WScript.Echo test
Function test()
    test = sample
End Function
```

The output is:

```
Placeholder
```

Listing 2-8 creates a function called getName(). The function accepts no parameters and so none are defined. A temporary variable called tempName is used to store input, and the function InputBox is used to display an input prompt to users. Once the user enters a name, the Do While loop is exited and the value the user entered is assigned to the function, allowing the value to be returned to the calling statement. The result is that the user input is echoed after the text "You entered:".

LISTING 2-8

Using Functions in a Script

testfunction.vbs

```
WScript.Echo "You entered: " & getName()

Function getName()
    Dim tempName
    tempName = ""
    Do While tempName = ""
       tempName = InputBox("Enter your name:")
    Loop
    getName = tempName
End Function
```

When the script runs, the user is prompted with an input dialog box. If "William Stanek" is entered, the output is:

```
You entered: William Stanek
```

 InputBox is a built-in function for getting user input. VBScript also supports message boxes with graphical buttons that can be selected. You learn about both of these features in Chapter 7.

You can break out of a function and return to the caller using the Exit Function statement. This statement is useful when a condition has been met and you want to return to the calling statement without finishing the execution of the function.

Working with subroutines

A *subroutine* is a procedure that does not return a value to the caller. Other than this, subroutines behave almost exactly like functions. Variables initialized within subroutines have local scope. You can call subroutines and pass in arguments. You can even exit the subroutine when a condition has been met, and you do this with Exit Sub.

Following this procedure, the basic structure of a subroutine is:

```
Sub subroutineName(argument1, argument2, ..., argumentN)
    'Add subroutine code here.
End Sub
```

You can use a subroutine in your code as follows:

```
Sub showError(errorMessage,title)
    MsgBox "Input Error: " & errorMessage,, title
End Sub
```

 MsgBox is listed as a function in most documentation, but it is actually a built-in subroutine for displaying messages. Also, the double comma used in the example isn't a mistake. This is how you enter a null value for a parameter that you don't want to use. You learn about message boxes in Chapter 6.

In the example, showError is the name of the subroutine. The subroutine expects one parameter to be passed in, and this parameter holds an error message to display to the user. You can call this subroutine in several different ways. You can use a Call statement, such as the following:

```
Call showError "Input is invalid.","Error"
```

or you can call the subroutine directly:

```
showError "Input is invalid.","Error"
```

 When you call subroutines, you shouldn't use parentheses to enclose parameters. Parentheses are only used with functions.

When there are no parameters to pass to the subroutine, the parentheses are optional as well, such as:

```
Call mySub
```

However, subroutines cannot be used in expressions. For example, the following call causes an error:

```
test = showError()
Sub showError(errorMessage)
    MsgBox "Input Error: " & errorMessage
End Sub
```

Summary

As you've seen in this chapter, VBScript has much to offer programmers, administrators, and power users. VBScript provides extensive functions, procedures, control flow statements, and expressions. VBScript also provides top-notch array-handling capabilities and multidimensional arrays. Beyond the basics, you'll find good error-handling capabilities, routines for manipulating strings, and solid support for standard mathematical functions. All of these features make VBScript a good choice as your preferred scripting language.

Chapter 3

JScript Essentials

JScript is Microsoft's version of JavaScript. If you are familiar with Java or JavaScript, you'll be able to jump right into the swing of things with JScript. Many advanced programmers prefer JScript to VBScript. JScript offers more features and more control over many elements of your scripts. More features and controls also mean that, in some ways, JScript is more complex than VBScript.

Variables and Data Types

Like VBScript, JScript allows you to work with constants and variables. Constants are distinguished from variables in that their values do not change within the program.

Variables and naming conventions

JScript variable names are case-sensitive, which means `valueA`, `ValueA`, and `VALUEA` all refer to different variables. Variable names can include alphabetic and numeric characters as well as the underscore (_) character, but must begin with an alphabetic character or the underscore character. Further, variable names cannot include spaces or punctuation characters. Using these variable-naming rules, the following are all valid names for variables:

```
myvar
user_name
_varA
theAnswer
```

Unlike VBScript, the case-sensitivity rule applies to all objects in JScript. This means you can't call WScript using anything but `WScript` and that all of the following statements result in errors:

```
wscript.echo("This is a test!")
Wscript.echo("This is a test!")
WSCRIPT.echo("This is a test!")
```

As with VBScript, variables can have a global or local scope. By default, all variables have a global scope, meaning they can be accessed anywhere in the script. Variables declared within a function, however, cannot be accessed outside the function. This means the variables have a local scope.

In JScript, variables are generally initialized with the `var` keyword, such as:

```
var theAnswer = "Invalid"
```

But you don't have to use the `var` keyword all the time. The `var` keyword is optional for global variables but mandatory for local variables. We talk more about functions in the section "Using Functions" later in this chapter.

Working with data types

Much like VBScript, JScript assigns a data type to variables based on their contents. This means you don't have to worry about assigning a specific data type. That said, you should learn how to use the basic data types shown in Table 3-1.

TABLE 3-1

Data Types in JScript

Data Type	Description	Example
Undefined	No value assigned; a variable that has been initialized but doesn't have a value has this data type.	`Var resultA`
Boolean	A logical value; either `true` or `false`.	`aBool = true`
Number	An integer or floating-point value.	`theSum = 202.5`
String	Characters within single or double quotation marks.	`theString = "Yes!"`
Null	The value of an undefined variable.	`myVar = null`

JScript automatically converts between data types whenever possible, which eliminates most variable conflicts. However, if you try to add a string variable to a numeric variable type, you will usually have problems. You will also have problems if JScript expects a string and you reference a numeric value. You'll find solutions for these problems in the next section "Using Strings".

With numerical data, JScript supports base 8, base 10, and base 16. Numbers with a leading zero are considered to be octal — base 8. Numbers with the 0x prefix are considered to be hexadecimal — base 16. All other number formats are considered to be standard decimal numbers — base 10. Examples of numbers in these formats include:

- **Decimal:** 12, 126, 8
- **Octal:** 032, 016, 061
- **Hexadecimal:** 0x3D, 0xEE, 0xA2

 NOTE JScript does not support base 2 (binary) but does support bitwise operators and functions that can perform binary operations.

Using Strings

Because JScript automatically types variables, you do not need to declare a variable as a string. Yet in order for JScript to recognize a variable as a string, you must use single or double quotation marks to enclose the value associated with the variable, such as:

```
myString = "This is a String."
```

When you work with strings, the two most common operations you'll perform are concatenation and conversion. These topics are covered in the sections that follow.

Concatenating strings

In your scripts, you will often need to add strings together. For example, if a user enters his or her full name as three separate variables representing the first, middle, and last names, you may want to add these strings together. To do this, you will use the + operator to concatenate the strings, such as:

```
userName = firstName + " " + middle + " " + lastName
```

Keep in mind that if you enclose numeric values within quotation marks, JScript still interprets the value as a string. This can lead to strange results when you try to add values together. As shown in the following example, if you add variables that contain strings, you will not get the desired results:

```
varA = "25"
varB = "32"
varC = 8
total1 = varA + varB //the result is "2532" not 57.
total2 = varB + varC //the result is "328" not 40.
```

Now that you know not to enclose numeric values in quotation marks, you probably will not have problems with strings and variables in your code. However, this problem can also occur when you accept user input and try to perform calculations based on user input, because user input is interpreted as a string unless you tell JScript otherwise by converting the string to a number.

Converting to and from strings

As with VBScript, JScript supports built-in functionality for converting data types but this functionality isn't implemented in the same way. In JScript, you use method calls more often than function calls. Think of a method as a predefined function that is related to an object. Normally, to call a method, you reference the object by name followed by a period, and then the name of the method you are invoking. For example, to convert a number to a string, use the `toString()` method of a variable or object, such as:

```
varA = 900
varB = varA.toString() // varB is set to a string value of "900"
```

However, some built-in methods don't require an object reference. For example, to convert string values to numbers, you will use one of two built-in methods: `parseInt()` or `parseFloat()`. The `parseInt()` method converts a string to an integer. The `parseFloat()` method converts a string to a floating-point number. These methods can be used without referencing an object, as in the following:

```
varA = "27.5"
varB = "15"
theFloat = parseFloat(varA) //theFloat is set to 27.5
theInt = parseInt(varB) //theInt is set to 15
```

Using Comments

JScript supports two types of comments:

- Single-line comments that begin with a double slash (//):

  ```
  //This is a comment
  ```

- Multiple-line comments that begin with the /* delimiter and end with the */ delimiter:

  ```
  /* This is a comment */
  ```

If you have a begin-comment delimiter, you must have a matching end-comment delimiter. JScript interprets everything between the begin- and end- comment tags as a comment.

Using Arrays

Compared to VBScript, JScript arrays are very simple. JScript arrays can be only a single dimension and are initialized with the `new Array()` statement. As with VBScript, arrays always begin at 0 and end at the number of data points in the array minus 1. Following this, an array with six data points can be initialized as follows:

```
favBooks = new Array(5)
```

If the size of your array is determined by user input or otherwise subject to change, you can initialize the array without specifying its size, such as:

```
theArray = new Array()
```

Unlike VBScript, however, you don't have to set the size of the array before using it. You simply assign values to the array.

After you initialize an array, you can insert values for elements in the array. The most basic way to do this is with individual statements that reference the array element by its index. Listing 3-1 shows an example of setting values for the cities array.

LISTING 3-1

Creating an Array and Assigning Values

testarray.js

```
favBooks = new Array(5)
favBooks[0] = "Grapes Of Wrath"
favBooks[1] = "All Over But The Shouting"
favBooks[2] = "On Walden's Pond"
favBooks[3] = "Childhood's End"
favBooks[4] = "Life On the Mississippi"
favBooks[5] = "Dune"
```

After you set values for array elements, you access those values by referencing the element's index, such as:

```
theValue = favBooks[2]
```

Here, theValue is set to On Walden's Pond.

Another way to populate an array with values is to set the values directly in the array declaration. Following is how you would do this for the favBooks array:

```
favBooks = new Array("Grapes of Wrath",
"All over But the Shouting",
"On Walden's Pond",
"Childhood's End",
"Life on the Mississippi",
"Dune")
```

JScript Operators

JScript supports many different types of operators. You'll find arithmetic operators, comparison operators, assignment operators, and bitwise operators. You'll also find logical operators, such as && and ||.

Arithmetic operators

JScript's arithmetic operators are summarized in Table 3-2. The syntax is nearly identical in every case to VBScript, so there are few surprises.

TABLE 3-2

Arithmetic Operators

Operator	Operation
*	Multiplication
/	Division
+	Addition
-	Subtraction
%	Modulus
=	Assignment
++	Increment
- -	Decrement

You must pay special attention to the ++ and - - operators, which are called unary operators. Typically, if you want to increment a value by one, you can write out the statement as follows:

```
A = A + 1
```

Alternately, you can use the increment operator (++), as follows:

```
++A
```

The result of the previous statement is that A is incremented by one. Similarly, you can decrease the value of A using the decrement operator (- -), such as:

```
- -A
```

When using the increment or decrement operator in a statement, the placement of the operator is extremely important. The result of this statement is that A and B are set to 6:

```
B = 5
A = ++B
```

The JScript interpreter reads the statement as "add 1 to B and store the result in A." If you change the position of the increment operator as follows:

```
A = B++
```

the JScript interpreter reads the statement as "set A equal to B, and then add 1 to B." The result is that A is set to 5 and B is incremented to 6.

Table 3-3 lists the precedence order for operators in JScript. As the table shows, negation operators have the highest precedence order and are always calculated first.

TABLE 3-3

Precedence of Arithmetic Operators

Order	Operation
1	Negation (-)
2	Multiplication (*) and Division (/)
3	Modulus (%)
4	Addition (+) and Subtraction (-)

Comparison operators

Comparison operators are used to check for certain conditions, such as whether A is equal to B. Generally, you will use a control flow, such as conditional looping, in conjunction with your comparison. For example, if A is equal to B, then you will perform a specific task. If A is not equal to B, then you will perform a different task.

When performing comparisons, you are often comparing objects as well as numeric and textual data. To see if a variable is equal to another variable, you will use the comparison operator (==). This operator returns a result that is true if the objects are equivalent, false if they are not equivalent. Here is an example of code that checks for equality:

```
if (aValue == varA) {
    //The variables are equal
}
```

To see if variables are not equal, use the inequality operator. Here is an example of code that checks for inequality:

```
if (aValue != varA) {
    //The variables are not equal
}
```

To see if one variable is less than or greater than another variable, use the less than and greater than operators. You can check for values greater than or less than a variable as follows:

```
if (aValue < varA) {
    //aValue is less than varA
}
if (aValue > varA) {
    //aValue is greater than varA
}
```

Another type of comparison you can perform will tell you whether a variable is less than or equal to a value. Likewise, you can see whether a variable is greater than or equal to a value. Here is an example of this type of comparison:

```
if (theValue <= varA) {
    //theValue is less than or equal to varA
}
if (theValue >= 0) {
    //theValue is greater than or equal to varA
}
```

Table 3-4 summarizes the comparison operators available in JScript. As you've seen from the examples in this section, JScript and VBScript support a slightly different set of comparison operators. JScript uses a separate equality operator (==) and also has a different inequality operator (!=).

TABLE 3-4

Comparison Operators in JScript

Operator	Description
==	Equality; evaluates to true if the values or objects are equal.
!=	Inequality; evaluates to true if the values or objects are not equal.
<	Less than; evaluates to true if value1 is less than value2.
<=	Less than or equal to; evaluates to true if value1 is less than or equal to value2.
>	Greater than; evaluates to true if value1 is greater than value2.
>=	Greater than or equal to; evaluates to true if value1 is greater than or equal to value2.

Assignment operators

Assignment operators are useful for assigning a value to a named variable. Some assignment operators, such as the equals sign (=), are used in just about every statement you will write. Other assignment operators, such as divide by value, are used rarely — if at all.

Like the increment and decrement operators, you can use assignment operators to save some typing. Instead of typing

```
a = a +3
```

you can type

```
a += 3
```

Although both statements perform the same operation, the second statement does so with less typing. Saving a few keystrokes becomes increasingly important in long scripts and in a series of repetitive statements. Assignment operators are summarized in Table 3-5.

TABLE 3-5

Assignment Operators

Operator	Descriptions
+=	Increments (adds and assigns value)
-=	Decrements (subtracts and assigns value)
*=	Multiplies and assigns value
/=	Divides and assigns value
%=	Performs modulus arithmetic and assigns value

Logical operators

Logical operators are great for performing several comparisons within a control flow. For example, if you want to check whether A is greater than B, and C is less than B before you perform a calculation, you can use a logical operator.

Like comparison operators, logical operators return either true or false. Generally, if the operation returns true, you can perform a set of statements. Otherwise, you can skip the statements or perform other statements.

The most commonly used logical operators are logical And (&&) and logical Or (||). These operators compare two Boolean expressions, the results of comparison operators, or other logical expressions to produce a Boolean value, which can be true or false. The logical And returns a true value only when both expressions being compared return a true value. The logical Or returns a true value when either or both expressions return a true value.

Another logical operator available in JScript is Not (!). You will use the Not operator just as you do the keyword `Not` in VBScript. Listing 3-2 shows how logical operators can be used in your scripts.

LISTING 3-2

Using Logical Operators

compare.js

```
varA = 12
varB = 5
varC = 6
varD = 2

if (varA > varC && varB < varD) {
   //evaluates when the results of both tests are true
   WScript.Echo("Both tests are true.")
}
if (varA > varB || varC < varB) {
   //evaluates when at least one side is true
   WScript.Echo("At least one side is true.")
}
if (!(varA <= varB)) {
   //evaluates when varB is less than varA
   WScript.Echo("Less than.")
}
```

OutPut

```
At least one side is true.
Less than.
```

Table 3-6 summarizes the available logical operators.

TABLE 3-6

Logical Operators

Operator	Operation
&&	Logical And
||	Logical Or
!	Logical Not

Bitwise operators

Bitwise operators are used to perform binary math. There is little use for binary math in JScript and you will probably never need to use JScript's bitwise operators. Just in case, however, the bitwise operators are summarized in Table 3-7.

TABLE 3-7

Bitwise Operators

Operator	Description
&	Bitwise And; returns 1 if both bits compared are 1.
|	Bitwise Or; returns 1 if either bit compared is 1.
^	Bitwise Or; returns 1 only if one bit is 1.
~	Bitwise Not; turns zeros to ones and ones to zeros.
<<	Shift Left; shifts the values left the number of positions specified by the operand on the right.
>>	Shift Right; shifts the values right the number of positions specified by the operand on the right.
>>>	Zero Fill Shift Right; shifts the values right; fills the bits with zeros from the left.

Conditional Statements

When you want to execute a set of instructions only if a certain condition is met, you can use `if` or `if...else` structures. Unlike VBScript, JScript does not support `elseif` statements.

Using if

You can use `if` statements to control execution based on a true or false condition. The syntax for JScript `if` statements is a bit different than you are used to. Note the use of parentheses and curly brackets in the following example that tests for a true condition:

```
if (choice = "Y") {
    //then condition is true and choice equals Y
    //execute these statements
}
```

You can also control the execution of instructions based on a false condition. To do this, use the `!` operator and add an extra set of parentheses, such as:

```
if (!(choice = "Y")) {
    //then condition is false and choice doesn't equal Y
    //execute these statements
}
```

Using if...else

You can extend if statements with the else statement. The else statement provides an alternative when a condition you specified is not met. The structure of an if...else condition is as follows:

```
if (choice="Y") {
   //condition is true and choice equals Y
  //execute these statements
}
else {
   //condition is false and choice doesn't equal Y
   //execute these statements
}
```

Control Flow with Looping

Sometimes you want to repeatedly execute a section of code. You can do this several ways in JScript. You can use:

- for and for in
- while and do while
- switch case

Using for loops

Using for loops in your code is easy. The following example uses this structure to initialize an array of ten elements:

```
for (x = 0; x < 10; x++) {
   myArray(x) = "Test"
}
```

This for loop initializes a counter to zero, and then sets the condition that the loop should continue as long as x is less than 10. During each iteration of the loop, the counter is incremented by 1. When the loop finishes, all ten elements in the array are initialized to the value Placeholder. The structure of a for loop in JScript is as follows:

```
for (initialize counter; condition; update counter) {
  code to repeat
}
```

Using for in loops

JScript's for in loops work much like VBScript's For Each loops. Both looping techniques are designed to iterate through each element in an object or array. They differ only in the syntax used.

Listing 3-3 shows how you can examine the elements in an array using a `for in` loop. Note that with JScript, you have to index into the array even when you are in the `for in` loop.

LISTING 3-3

Checking Values in an Array

arrayvalues.js

```
currArray = new Array()

for (x = 0; x < 10; x++) {
   currArray[x] = "Initial"
}

counter = 0
for (i in currArray) {
  WScript.Echo("Value " + counter + "
    equals: " + currArray[i])
  counter++

}
```

Output

```
Value 0 equals: Initial
Value 1 equals: Initial
Value 2 equals: Initial
Value 3 equals: Initial
Value 4 equals: Initial
Value 5 equals: Initial
Value 6 equals: Initial
Value 7 equals: Initial
Value 8 equals: Initial
Value 9 equals: Initial
```

Using while and do while loops

JScript's `while` loops are used much like the `While` loops in VBScript. To execute a code segment while a condition is met, you will use `while` looping. The structure of a loop that checks for a true condition is as follows:

```
while (condition) {
   //add code to repeat
}
```

The structure of a loop that checks for a false condition is as follows:

```
while (!condition) {
   /add code to repeat
}
```

As long as the condition is met, the loop is executed. This means to break out of the loop, you must change the condition at some point within the loop.

You can put the condition check at the bottom of the loop using a `do while` construct, such as the following:

```
do {
   //add code to repeat
} while (condition)
```

Using continue and break statements

When you are working with conditional looping, you will often want to break out of a loop or continue with the next iteration of the loop. In JScript, the break statement enables you to end the execution of a loop, and the continue statement enables you to begin the next iteration of a loop without executing subsequent statements. Whenever your script begins the next iteration of the loop, the condition is checked and the counter is updated as necessary in for loops.

Using switch case

JScript's switch case is the functional equivalent of VBScript's Select Case. To see how similar the structures are, compare Listing 3-4 with Listing 2-5. As you'll see, these listings check for similar information. However, JScript doesn't support the less-than operation used with VBScript, so we omitted this from the example. JScript doesn't support any other case either, such as VBScript's Case Else. Instead, JScript supports a default case.

LISTING 3-4

Working with Switch Case

case1.js

```
currValue = 5
switch (currValue) {
   case 0 :
     WScript.Echo("The value is equal to zero.")
   case 1 :
     WScript.Echo("The value is equal to one.")
   case 2 :
     WScript.Echo("The value is equal to two.")
   case 3 :
     WScript.Echo("The value is equal to three.")
   case 4 :
     WScript.Echo("The value is equal to four.")
   case 5 :
     WScript.Echo("The value is equal to five.")
   default :
     WScript.Echo("Value doesn't match expected parameters.")
}
```

Output

```
The value is equal to five.
Value doesn't match expected parameters.
```

If you run Listing 3-4, you learn another interesting fact concerning switch case — JScript can execute multiple case statements. In this case, the script executes case 5 and the default. To prevent JScript from executing multiple case statements, you need to exit the switch case using the break keyword, as shown in Listing 3-5.

LISTING 3-5

Revised Switch Case Example

case2.js

```
currValue = 5
switch (currValue) {
   case 0 :
     WScript.Echo("The value is equal to zero.")
     break
   case 1 :
     WScript.Echo("The value is equal to one.")
     break
   case 2 :
     WScript.Echo("The value is equal to two.")
     break
   case 3 :
     WScript.Echo("The value is equal to three.")
     break
   case 4 :
     WScript.Echo("The value is equal to four.")
     break
   case 5 :
     WScript.Echo("The value is equal to five.")
     break
   default :
     WScript.Echo("Value doesn't match expected
        parameters.")
}
```

Output

```
The value is equal to five.
```

Using Functions

In JScript, functions are the key structure you use to create customizable procedures. JScript doesn't support subroutines or goto. As you will quickly discover, JScript functions work much like VBScript functions and, again, the main difference is syntax.

Function structure

In JScript, the basic structure of a function is:

```
function functionName(parameter1, parameter2, ..., parameterN) {
    //Insert function code here.
}
```

You can use functions in your code as follows:

```
function getInput() {
    var userInput
    var timeOut = 10;    // set wait time
    var title = "Getting Input"; // set title
    var button = 4;       // Yes/No
    // create object
    var wshell = WScript.CreateObject("WScript.Shell");
    userInput = wshell.Popup ("Do you want to continue?",
                 timeOut,title,button)

    return userInput
}
```

 **Note the use of** Popup() **in the example. Unlike VBScript, none of the standard JScript dialog or input boxes are available in Windows Script Host and as a result,** Popup() **is the only way to display messages and get user input. For more information on** Popup()**s, see Chapter 6.**

In the example, getInput is the name of the function. Because the function accepts no parameters, none are defined after the function name. A temporary local variable called userInput is created to store the user's input. Once the user enters a value, the while loop is exited. This value is then returned to the calling statement. Generally, all functions return one or more values using the return statement.

Calling functions

Calling a function in JScript is just like calling a function in VBScript. You can call a function as follows:

```
getInput()
```

or

```
Input = getInput()
```

When you call a function, you can pass in parameters as well. To better understand how parameters are used, we'll create a function that converts a time entry to seconds. This function, called numSeconds(), accepts four parameters: xYears, xDays, xHours, and xMinutes. Because these parameters are passed directly to the function, you do not need to create temporary variables to hold their values within the function. The code for the function `numSeconds ()` is as follows:

```
function numSeconds(xYears, xDays, xHours, xMinutes) {
    var count
    tempSeconds = ((365 * xYears + xDays) * 24 + xHours) * 3600 + 60@@1b
        * xMinutes
    return count
}
```

When you call this function, the parameters are expected and must be entered in the order defined. Here is a statement that calls the `numSeconds()` function:

```
theSeconds = numSeconds(5,25,10,30)
```

Summary

JScript provides an alternative to VBScript that is often preferred by people with a background in programming. In JScript, you'll find numerous functions, procedures, and control flow statements. You'll also find good support for arrays with access to multidimensional arrays through VBScript; extensive sets of ready-to-use objects with methods, properties, and events; strong support for mathematical functions (with many more functions supported than in VBScript); and a very dynamic framework for handling errors.

Chapter 4

PowerShell Fundamentals

Let's start by getting the obvious thing about PowerShell out of the way. It is a shell. The UNIX world has had a number of shells (the C shell, Korn shell, BASH, and so on), but the Microsoft world has a single shell, COMMAND.COM in the DOS-based operating systems, and its successor CMD.EXE in the NT-based ones. The term "shell" refers to a piece of software that wraps around the operating system kernel. The shell is an environment where commands can be entered to run other programs and text output from those programs can be displayed. Some basic tasks might be built into the shell itself—such as getting a listing of files in the current directory, copying and deleting files, and so on. With the Microsoft shells, it is sometimes difficult to know which commands are built into the shell (such as `copy`) and which are separate utility programs (such as `Xcopy`).

Shell Fundamentals

Most shells include some kind of scripting language; at their simplest, these are simply lists of commands that could have been typed in the interactive shell, but are executed as a batch task. The Microsoft shells have had batch files from the early days of DOS and although each new release has added some features, the language has remained largely unchanged for more than 20 years. PowerShell aims to give Windows a modern shell.

The final feature of most shells is the capability to link commands together—the mechanism is normally called a "pipe". Unix uses the | sign to link the output of one to the input of the next. It might be more accurate to say that DOS copied the idea of "standard output"—the Console screen by default, and the > symbol redirected standard output to a file. Both DOS and UNIX also had the idea of *standard input*—the Console keyboard by default, and the < symbol redirected input from a file. When DOS first implemented the pipe it was simply in the form:

```
Command1 > ~number.tmp
Command2 < ~number.tmp
```

The most commonly used *pipe command* in COMMAND.COM, and probably in CMD.EXE was ¦ more.

This was commonly used in the form:

```
Type filename ¦ more
```

although the form:

```
More < filename
```

would have been more efficient and needed less typing.

You will see later in this chapter how PowerShell exploits the pipe to a much greater degree than other shells, and in later chapters you will see the things you can do with scripts. The first experience most people will have with PowerShell is entering simple commands. As you would expect, you can start a shell and enter:

```
Notepad myFile.Txt
```

You can use familiar commands to start editing a text file, or to manipulate files and folders, for example: MD, Copy, Del, Dir, Type. If you come from a UNIX background you'll find commands such as ls, cat, and cp also work, and you shall see how it is that PowerShell supports multiple names for the same task.

PowerShell Aliases

PowerShell understands several different kinds of commands:

- External programs, such as Format, Xcopy, Notepad, and so on
- Scripts, analogous to batch files, VBScript files, or UNIX shell scripts
- Cmdlets
- Functions and filters
- Aliases

Let's deal with aliases first.

In PowerShell, if you enter the command `Get-Alias` it will list about 100 predefined aliases, most of which are alternative names for Cmdlets. This shows that some familiar commands from CMD or from UNIX are aliased into PowerShell `Cmdlets`.

Aliases	Definitions
Copy, CP	Copy-Item
Dir, ls	Get-ChildItem
Cat, type	Get-Content
Move	Move-Item
Rm, rmdir, erase, del ,rd	Remove-Item
Chdir, Cd	Set-Location

There are several things to note here. First, PowerShell Cmdlets are usually in the form:

    Verb-Noun

Another PowerShell command, `Get-Command`, takes –Verb or -noun switches, so the command:

    Get-Command -verb get

will give a list of all the commands that start with `get-`.

This is important because it enforces consistency. If you think about different ways in Windows that you might get information or stop something you'll understand that there is a lot of vocabulary to memorize. Stopping a service might use the `Net` command with a `stop` parameter, stopping a process uses the `TaskKill` command, and stopping a computer uses the `shutdown` command. PowerShell tries to use standard verbs throughout.

Another thing to note is that you can define your own aliases. For example, if you use `notepad.exe` to edit your files, you could define an alias N for `notepad` like this:

    Set-Alias -Name N -value notepad

There is nothing to stop you from redefining aliases; for example, you could delete the alias for `CD` and re-create it as an alias for `Push-Location`. So each `CD` operation stacks the previous directory. Another alias, say `CD-`, could be defined for `Pop-Location`, taking you back to the previous directory.

Finally, aliases are very useful at the command line to save typing. For example the percent (%) sign is an alias for the Cmdlet `ForEach-Object`, and the `Set-Alias` Cmdlet has its own alias SAL. But when you write scripts, using aliases does make them harder to maintain, so try to use the full command names where possible. Similarly the parameters passed at the command line do not need to be specified in full; Cmdlets (and user written functions and filters) can accept parameters by position as well as by name, and when names are specified they only need to be long enough to be unambiguous. The Set-Alias command can be re-written as:

```
SAL n notepad
```

The second way of writing the command needs a better understanding of PowerShell than the first. As a best practice when writing code that you will have to go back to or others will need to read, use the full name and name the parameters.

It's also worth noting at this early stage that while older command-line tools use a mixture of the / and - signs to indicate parameters and switches, PowerShell uses the - sign throughout.

Cmdlets, Snap-ins, and Providers

At the beginning of the last section, you saw that PowerShell commands divide up into external programs, aliases, user-written commands, and Cmdlets.

Cmdlets are analogous to the built-in commands in CMD.EXE or COMMAND.COM. There, the functionality of DIR, for example, is provided by code in the command processor itself. By contrast, PowerShell can be broken down into multiple parts. Commands do not need to be run in the PowerShell command window—the PowerShell engine can be invoked separately from the *host* window so that, for example, the management console for Microsoft Exchange or a tool such as Quest's Power Gui (see www.powerGUI.org) can invoke the engine without ever showing the command-line host. PowerShell takes this modularity a stage further because the Cmdlets are not built into the engine, but are provided in a series of snap-ins. PowerShell V1 provides five snap-ins:

- Microsoft.PowerShell.Core
- Microsoft.PowerShell.Host
- Microsoft.PowerShell.Management
- Microsoft.PowerShell.Security
- Microsoft.PowerShell.Utility

The previews of PowerShell V2 have included additional snap-ins.

Snap-ins are .NET DLL files that have been registered with the system. You can check which snap-ins are registered but not loaded with the following command:

```
Get-PSSnapin -Registered
```

It is worth noting that some install routines register their snap-in only for the 32 bit or for the 64 bit version of PowerShell; if you need to register the DLL manually, it is a one-off task that you can do with the commands:

```
C:\Windows\Microsoft.NET\Framework\v2.0.50727\InstallUtil.exe "<PathToDll>"
C:\Windows\Microsoft.NET\Framework64\v2.0.50727\InstallUtil.exe "<PathToDll>"
```

The snap-ins' design means that the set of Cmdlets in PowerShell is completely extensible. For example, PowerShell V1 does not have a Cmdlet to send mail. However, when a group of PowerShell users put together the PowerShell Community Extensions (`www.codePlex.com/PSCX`) one of the Cmdlets in their DLL was `Send-SMTPmail`. Similarly PowerShell doesn't have any built-in understanding of Exchange 2007—the Exchange group in Microsoft provided the snap-in support for their product, and other teams have followed. Snap-ins follow a simple template, which developers can download from MSDN, and so it is easy to take existing code for a task and re-package it as one or more Cmdlets that can be loaded from a snap-in.

PowerShell encourages developers to be consistent. Not only are parameters always prefixed with the - sign but the format `Verb-Noun` is standardized, with developers encouraged to stick to the existing verbs (for example, using `NEW` rather adding `Create`). In addition, it defines a standard way for all snap-ins to provide help, so that help maintains the same format as the range of Cmdlets is extended. `New-PsDrive -?` or `Del -?` will return help, as will `Get-Help newPsDrive` or `Get-Help Del`.

`Get-Help *` will provide a list of help topics.

PowerShell's startup files determine which snap-ins are loaded, and these are covered in detail later.

Snap-ins do more than add Cmdlets. They can also add *providers*. Providers allow PowerShell to see drives so, for example, there is a file system provider that enables PowerShell to see the first hard disk partition as C: and so on. This idea is extended with additional providers that give access to aliases, environment variables, PowerShell variables, functions, the registry, and the Certificate store as though they were drives. All of these providers are implemented in the `Microsoft.PowerShell` `.Core` snap-in, except for the Certificate one, which is implanted in the `Microsoft.PowerShell` `.Security` snap-in. Each of the providers enables one or more drives so you can set the current location to the `HKEY_CURRENT_USER` branch of the registry with the command:

```
CD HKCU:
```

(Remember that `CD` is an alias for `Set-Location`.) Then you can manipulate registry items in the same way that you would manipulate other files.

Similarly, to see the functions that are currently defined in PowerShell you can use:

```
Dir Function:
```

Or, to delete the CD alias before re-defining it you can use the following:

```
Del Alias:CD
```

The PowerShell command `Get-PsDrive` shows a list of the drives that have been defined and the provider used. And `New-PsDrive` allows new ones to be defined, like this:

```
New-PSDrive -Name HOME -PSProvider filesystem -Root "C:\users\administrator"
```

After this, a `HOME:` drive will exist, and it can be treated in the same way as `C:` or `Function`.

Functions and Filters

Providers and Cmdlets in snap-ins are not the only way that PowerShell can be expanded.

The simplest way to add a command to PowerShell is to write a function or filter. For all practical purposes, the two are the same except in the way they handle input from the pipe.

When you looked at aliases, you saw that commands such as CD were simply substituted for the PowerShell Cmdlet Set-Location. PowerShell doesn't have a "make directory" command (MD or MKDIR). It has New-Item, which takes switches -Type and -Path. Simply aliasing MD to New-Item won't work because you need to include the command-line switch to set the type to Directory. An alias can't specify the switch.

Earlier, you saw that one of PowerShell's providers gives you a FUNCTION: drive so you can see the available functions using the command:

```
Dir Function:
```

If you try this, you will see there are functions MD and MKDIR; you can see the content of the function by using any of the three following commands:

```
Type Function:md
Cat Function:Md
Get-Content Function:md
```

The first two work because Type and cat are aliases for Get-Content.

The function is:

```
param($paths); New-Item -type directory -path $paths
```

This is pretty easy to follow. First, the function takes a parameter named "$Paths"—PowerShell Variable names are usually written with a $ sign—which you can read as *the value of*. The semicolon (;) separates commands on the same line, and then the New-Item Cmdlet creates a directory item, using $paths to specify the Path. Here you can see another thing about PowerShell's consistency: the nouns used in commands and their switches are written in the singular New-Item, not New-Items, and -Path not -Paths, but in many cases they will accept <u>multiple</u> values, separated by commas. So, to create three directories one can use the following command:

```
MD sub1,sub2,sub3
```

This is why the variable name is $Paths (in the plural). You will see later in this chapter that PowerShell does not require you to declare formally that $Paths is a text string, or an array of strings, and it copes well with converting between types. You'll also have a look at writing your own functions and filters.

Objects and Types and the PowerShell Pipe

At the start of this chapter, you saw several core aspects of a shell. The last of these to look at is the facility to pipe commands together. And this is the area where PowerShell differs radically from what has gone before.

Do you ever wonder about the stupidity of faxing word-processed documents—faxing is great for handwritten stuff or pre-existing documents, but why send a picture of the document instead of sending the document itself by e-mail? The way we handle information from a lot of sources in older shells is like fax to PowerShell's e-mail: these shells have to output a *view* of the information, not the information itself. Consider getting a list of files: ls in the UNIX world or DIR in the Microsoft world. In each case, the command returns a block of text with one line for each file or subdirectory. That text can be re-directed to a file with the > operator or sent into another command with ¦ but it is always *text*. Just as you can use optical character recognition to turn a fax back into a document, you can write code to parse the text and try to extract the file size or date stamp but the process is long winded and may fail. Similarly, trying to isolate an individual item from a list is hard. So let's try a couple of lines of PowerShell and see how it's different. If you start PowerShell and enter the command DIR, it will list the contents of the current directory.

```
PS C:\Users\Administrator> dir

    Directory: Microsoft.PowerShell.Core\FileSystem::C:\Users\Administrator


Mode                LastWriteTime     Length Name
----                -------------     ------ ----
d-r--        14/07/2008     21:25            Contacts
d-r--        16/07/2008     19:26            Desktop
d-r--        17/07/2008     18:18            Documents
d-r--        15/07/2008     07:50            Downloads
d-r--        15/07/2008     08:28            Favorites
d-r--        14/07/2008     21:25            Links
d-r--        16/07/2008     19:20            Pictures
d-r--        14/07/2008     21:25            Saved Games
d-r--        14/07/2008     21:25            Searches
d----        17/07/2008     09:54            sub1
d----        17/07/2008     09:54            sub2
d----        17/07/2008     09:54            sub3
d-r--        14/07/2008     21:25            Videos
-a---        18/08/2006     00:39    9564507 bar.wmv
-a---        10/04/2007     14:48    2983995 Prev_ver.wmv
-a---        10/04/2007     15:00    1627967 Prev_ver2.wmv
```

One thing to point out is that the Directory line at the top shows the full path in the form SNAPIN\ Provider::Path so doing a directory of a certificate store will tell you than it is a directory-based on a different snap-in and provider; for example:

```
PS C:\Users\Administrator> dir cert:\LocalMachine\CA


    Directory: Microsoft.PowerShell.Security\Certificate::LocalMachine\CA


Thumbprint                                Subject
----------                                -------
FEE449EE0E3965A5246F000E87FDE2A065FD89D4  CN=Root Agency
8B24CD8D8B58C6DA72ACE097C7B1E3CEA4DC3DC6  OU=www.verisign.com/CPS Incorp.by...
7B02312BACC59EC388FEAE12FD277F6A9FB4FAC1  CN=VeriSign Class 2 CA - Individua...
12519AE9CD777A560184F1FBD54215222E95E71F  CN=VeriSign Class 1 CA Individual...
109F1CAED645BB78B3EA2B94C0697C740733031C  CN=Microsoft Windows Hardware Comp...
```

Although PowerShell doesn't enforce the use of data types on you, it still understands them so you can test to see if dir returns an array, and if it does, you can have a look at items in the array and their types, as follows:

```
PS C:\Users\Administrator> (dir) -is [array]
True
PS C:\Users\Administrator> (dir).count
16
PS C:\Users\Administrator> (dir)[0]


    Directory: Microsoft.PowerShell.Core\FileSystem::C:\Users\Administrator


Mode            LastWriteTime     Length Name
----            -------------     ------ ----
d-r--      14/07/2008     21:25          Contacts

PS C:\Users\Administrator> (dir)[-1]


    Directory: Microsoft.PowerShell.Core\FileSystem::C:\Users\Administrator


Mode            LastWriteTime     Length Name
----            -------------     ------ ----
-a---      10/04/2007     15:00   1627967 Prev_ver2.wmv

PS C:\Users\Administrator> (dir)[-1].gettype()

IsPublic IsSerial Name                                     BaseType
-------- -------- ----                                     --------
True     True     FileInfo                                 System.IO.FileSys...

PS C:\Users\Administrator> (dir cert:\LocalMachine\CA)[0].GetType()

IsPublic IsSerial Name                                     BaseType
-------- -------- ----                                     --------
True     False    X509Certificate2                         System.Security.C...
```

So Dir returns an array—it is, after all, an alias for a function that Gets a set of Child Items. You can see a count property for the array and you can access its items with [index]. PowerShell arrays start from 0, and negative indices work back from the last item toward the beginning.

Everything in PowerShell has a data type and you can discover this with Get-Type(). Directories accessed via the FileSystem provider contain FileInfo and DirectoryInfo objects and those accessed through the Certificate provider contain X509Certificate2 objects.

This is the beginning of understanding the power of PowerShell. Everything it returns as a result, stores as a variable, or passes as a parameter is an object. For example, you can try the following:

```
PS C:\Users\Administrator> [system.math]::pi
3.14159265358979
PS C:\Users\Administrator> [system.math]::pi.gettype()

IsPublic IsSerial Name                                     BaseType
-------- -------- ----                                     --------
True     True     Double                                   System.ValueType

PS C:\Users\Administrator> "hello world"
hello world
PS C:\Users\Administrator> "Hello World".getType()

IsPublic IsSerial Name                                     BaseType
-------- -------- ----                                     --------
True     True     String                                   System.Object
```

The first two commands show that you can get the value of PI from the System.Math .NET library (you'll see more on using .NET later), and it is a Double Precision Floating Point number.

These examples reinforce something that has been implied in what you have seen so far. Given an object and not told to redirect it or pipe it, or save it in variable PowerShell, outputs it to the Host console. So the "Hello World" program for PowerShell is simply "Hello World". Incidentally, if you work with editors that like to use smart quotes, "hello world" written using straight quotes and "Hello World" written using smart quotes are treated identically by PowerShell. Calling its GetType()method shows "Hello World" is a text-string.

Exploring PowerShell Variables

In the older command shells, it is possible to hold text information in *environment* variables—in every Microsoft operating system from the early DOS through to the present you have been able to use SET to create an environment variable and refer back to it with %name%, so %comspec% holds the name of the command processor, %userProfile% holds the users home directory, and so on. But environment variables are always text and PowerShell—as you have just seen—understands a richer set of variable types. PowerShell also has variables—a value can be assigned to a variable like this:

```
$username = "James"
```

It is easiest to think of the $ sign in this as *the value of* so the first line reads "the value of username becomes James." Note that we say *becomes* for the *equals* sign. PowerShell uses operators -lt, -eq, and -gt for "is less than," "is equal to," and "is greater than." The symbols < and > are reserved for redirecting input and output, and the = sign is only used for "becomes equal to."

You also saw earlier that PowerShell has providers for its own variables and for Environment variables. You can refer to the contents of the variable you have just declared, as $username (again read the $ as *the value of*). As it happens, there is a username environment variable and you can refer to that as $Env:username. You never need to explicitly specify $variable:, but if a *PowerShell* variable name is the same as an *Environment* variable name, you can refer to it explicitly as $variable:username in order to avoid misunderstanding when someone else reads your script.

PowerShell also has *scopes*, and these have a similar notation. You can also refer to this variable as $Global:Username, because it is available in all scripts and functions, and at the prompt. If you try to set $UserName in a script or a function, that change applies only in the script unless you specify the global: scope. This is easier to see with an example:

```
> function scope-test
 { " Local:var is initially $local:var "
   "        var is initially $var"
   "Global:var is intitally $global:var"
   "now we will set VAR "
   $var = 1
   " Local:var is now $local:var "
   "        var is now $var"
   "Global:var is now $Global:var"
 }
>$var = 99
> Scope-test
 Local:var is initially
        var is initially 99
Global:var is intitally 99
now we will set VAR
 Local:var is now 1
        var is now 1
Global:var is now 99
> $var
 99
```

So you can see that:

- $local:var is empty until $var is set in the function.
- $var will return $local:var if it exists, or $global:var otherwise.
- Setting $var creates a $local:var, and the global $var is unaffected.

So you can see what type of information that username variable contains, as follows:

```
> $username.getType().name
String
```

In some programming languages, variables are given a type when they are first used. PowerShell variables are much looser—when the value "James" was assigned to the variable, PowerShell figured out that it was a string so $username contains a string. If you now change $username to something else, its type might change; for example:

```
> $username=[system.math]::pi
> $username.getType()name
Double
>$username * 4
12.5663706143592
```

As you can see, assigning PI to the $username changed the variable from holding a text string to holding a double precision floating point number, and you can do calculations with that number.

You can force the variable to be a text string if you declare it like this:

```
> [string]$username="james"
> $username.getType().name
string
> $username=[system.math]::pi
> $username.getType().name
String
```

So $username still contains a string—it's the text "3.14159265358979," which looks like a number but when you try to process it, PowerShell knows it is a string. If you try to multiply it—which worked in the previous example—you get this:

```
> $username * 4
3.141592653589793.141592653589793.141592653589793.14159265358979
```

Generally, it is better to let PowerShell make the decisions about types, rather than to force a variable to a particular type, but sometimes you want an error to be generated if you assign the wrong kind of thing to a variable. Let's reverse the case discussed previously and explicitly say that a variable p holds the value of pi and is a double-precision floating-point number.

```
> [double]$p=[system.math]::pi
> $P*4
12.5663706143592
```

Notice that PowerShell variable names are case-insensitive. You can use $p and $P interchangeably. Now what happens if you try to store text in p?

```
> $p="james"
Cannot convert value "james" to type "System.Double".
    Error: "Input string was not in a correct format."
At line:1 char:3
```

PowerShell tried to convert the text to a number but it couldn't do it, and generated an error.

Left to its own devices, PowerShell will examine numbers and, if they have a fraction part, it will use the Double (double precision floating point number) type; if they don't have a fraction it will use the INT32 (32 bit, signed integer) type. There are two ways of presenting PowerShell with a text string. Some languages use single quotes and some use double quotes. PowerShell will expand variables in a double quoted string and not in a single quoted one so in the example earlier:

```
"Global:var is now $Global:var"
```

returned:

```
Global:var is now 99
```

If you had used single quotes, it would have returned the literal text $Global:var instead of substituting 99 in its place. You can "escape" characters in a string with the ` (back quote) character. Used on its own, the backquote acts as a continuation character, allowing one line of PowerShell to be typed as two—the ` at the end of the line telling the parser that there is more to come.

Inside a string, ` is used to indicate special characters, so writing:

```
"Global:var is now `$Global:var"
```

would also cause the literal text to be output. There are a few escape characters listed in the PowerShell documentation, the most useful of which is probably `n for newline.

One other useful trick PowerShell has is that it can take a sequence of numbers written in the form 1..10 or 456..789 and convert them into an array of integers; for example:

```
>1..5
1
2
3
4
5
```

PowerShell uses the [TypeName] syntax in other places as well as setting the type for a variable. For example, in addition to the string type, PowerShell understands the Char (single character) type, so you can convert an ASCII value into a character, as follows:

```
>[Char]65
A
```

If you try to convert a string to a single character you will get an error:

```
> [char]"hello"
Cannot convert value "hello" to type "System.Char".
    Error: "String must be exactly one character long."
```

You need to convert to an *array* of characters, which you can write as [Char[]], which breaks the string down into its characters like this:

```
> [char[]]"Hello"
H
e
l
l
o
```

You can convert the array of characters into an array of bytes (8 bit unsigned integers) to give the ASCII values of the characters.

```
> [byte[]][char[]]"Hello"
72
101
108
108
111
```

You can't convert from a string directly to an array of bytes, even if it contains only a single character. Converting a string to bytes is beyond its limitations.

Richer Types and .NET Objects

So far, the only variable things you have touched in the examples have been files and text and numeric variables—and that was about as far as other shells went. These shells understood the world as strings of text and files, and perhaps some arithmetical types. PowerShell understands the much richer world of *objects*.

It is often difficult to explain the concept of objects to people who are new to the subject. An object defines something in terms of its properties and methods. Properties tell us something *about* the object and methods are things you can *do* with it or do to it. Even the numbers, characters, and text strings you've looked at so far are implemented in PowerShell as .NET objects. If you've worked in older versions of basic, you might be used to using functions such as Len(S) to return the length of a string S. In an object-based world, length is a *property* of a string, so in PowerShell we refer to $S.length. In a non-object world, if you wanted to convert a string to all uppercase, it was the job of the programming language to provide an UpCase function so you could say U=Upcase(s); in the object world, converting to uppercase is something you can do with or to a string, so strings have a toUpper method and you would write $U=$S.toUpper().

Superficially, this looks like just a change of syntax. If you have a variable of an arbitrary type—let's call it a *widget*—and you can carry out an arbitrary action on a widget, say *fettling* then instead of writing `Fettle(widget,parameter)`, you write `widget.fettle (parameter)`. And it would be just a change of syntax if it weren't for the fact that object-oriented environments such as PowerShell can use objects that their designers had never even imagined.

If someone asks you to create a Virtual Machine on Server 2008 using a batch file, you can't do it because batch files understand the world of files and text strings. In PowerShell, you can ask for a virtual system management object, which includes a method of `defineVirtualSystem()`. Some other executable implements the object: neither you nor PowerShell need to know *what* happens when a new VM is defined. Under the surface, PowerShell (or any object-oriented environment) knows how to access the executables that implement the objects you want and get them to do your bidding. And there are thousands of such objects out there at your beck and call.

This is good news for system administrators because they know the things they want to work with—user accounts, virtual machines, processes, and so on (these are *objects*). They know the things they do with them—resetting passwords, starting VMs, stopping processes (these are *methods*), and they know that there are things they can see or change about them. User accounts have a full name, virtual machines have connected hard disks, and processes have a CPU time used, (these are *properties*). Instead of having to learn a lot of PowerShell, administrators only need to know enough to manipulate the objects, and they've already got an understanding of what the objects do.

Taken together, properties and methods are known as *members* of an object; one of the most used Cmdlets when developing in PowerShell is `Get-Member`, which lists the available properties and methods for an object.

Remember that all the PowerShell commands that you have seen return objects, so let's look at members of the objects you have seen before by redirecting them into `Get-member`.

```
PS C:\Users\Administrator> [system.math]::pi | get-member


   TypeName: System.Double
Name        MemberType Definition
----        ---------- ----------
CompareTo   Method     System.Int32 CompareTo(Object value
Equals      Method     System.Boolean Equals(Object obj)
GetHashCode Method     System.Int32 GetHashCode()
GetType     Method     System.Type GetType()
GetTypeCode Method     System.TypeCode GetTypeCode()
ToString    Method     System.String ToString()
```

```
PS C:\Users\Administrator> "Hello, world" | get-member


    TypeName: System.String
Name                MemberType           Definition
----                ----------           ----------
Clone               Method               System.Object Clone()
CompareTo           Method               System.Int32 CompareTo(Object value),...
Contains            Method               System.Boolean Contains(String value)
CopyTo              Method               System.Void CopyTo(Int32 sourceIndex,...
EndsWith            Method               System.Boolean EndsWith(String value)...
Equals              Method               System.Boolean Equals(Object obj), Sy...
GetEnumerator       Method               System.CharEnumerator GetEnumerator()
GetHashCode         Method               System.Int32 GetHashCode()
GetType             Method               System.Type GetType()
GetTypeCode         Method               System.TypeCode GetTypeCode()
IndexOf             Method               System.Int32 IndexOf(Char value, Int3...
IndexOfAny          Method               System.Int32 IndexOfAny(Char[] anyOf,...
Insert              Method               System.String Insert(Int32 startIndex...
IsNormalized        Method               System.Boolean IsNormalized(), System...
LastIndexOf         Method               System.Int32 LastIndexOf(Char value, ...
LastIndexOfAny      Method               System.Int32 LastIndexOfAny(Char[] an...
Normalize           Method               System.String Normalize(), System.Str...
PadLeft             Method               System.String PadLeft(Int32 totalWidt...
PadRight            Method               System.String PadRight(Int32 totalWid...
Remove              Method               System.String Remove(Int32 startIndex...
Replace             Method               System.String Replace(Char oldChar, C...
Split               Method               System.String[] Split(Params Char[] s...
StartsWith          Method               System.Boolean StartsWith(String valu...
Substring           Method               System.String Substring(Int32 startIn...
ToCharArray         Method               System.Char[] ToCharArray(), System.C...
ToLower             Method               System.String ToLower(), System.Strin...
ToLowerInvariant    Method               System.String ToLowerInvariant()
ToString            Method               System.String ToString(), System.Stri...
ToUpper             Method               System.String ToUpper(), System.Strin...
ToUpperInvariant    Method               System.String ToUpperInvariant()
Trim                Method               System.String Trim(Params Char[] trim...
TrimEnd             Method               System.String TrimEnd(Params Char[] t...
TrimStart           Method               System.String TrimStart(Params Char[]...
Chars               ParameterizedProperty System.Char Chars(Int32 index) {get;}
Length              Property             System.Int32 Length {get;}
```

As you can see, numbers have only a core set of methods so that they can be turned into text strings for output, compared, and have their type checked. Every type in PowerShell supports the GetType() method, which was shown before. Notice that when you invoke a method of an object, its parameters are enclosed in brackets—even if there are none! If you omit the brackets, PowerShell assumes you are asking for information about the GetType member—so it tells you it is a method of the object.

Text strings have many more methods than numbers; they allow them to be cut and sliced, or the contents to be checked or parts of them to be changed. Strings also have a `length` property (12 for "Hello, World") and a `chars` property, which takes a parameter `"Hello, world".chars(0)` is returns H.

Not surprisingly, `FileInfo` objects have even more properties and methods, as you can see in the code that follows:

```
PS C:\Users\Administrator> dir *.wmv | Get-Member


    TypeName: System.IO.FileInfo

Name                        MemberType      Definition
----                        ----------      ----------
Mode                        CodeProperty    System.String Mode{get=Mode;}
AppendText                  Method          System.IO.StreamWriter AppendText()
CopyTo                      Method          System.IO.FileInfo CopyTo(String de...
Create                      Method          System.IO.FileStream Create()
CreateObjRef                Method          System.Runtime.Remoting.ObjRef Crea...
CreateText                  Method          System.IO.StreamWriter CreateText()
Decrypt                     Method          System.Void Decrypt()
Delete                      Method          System.Void Delete()
Encrypt                     Method          System.Void Encrypt()
Equals                      Method          System.Boolean Equals(Object obj)
GetAccessControl            Method          System.Security.AccessControl.FileS...
GetHashCode                 Method          System.Int32 GetHashCode()
GetLifetimeService          Method          System.Object GetLifetimeService()
GetObjectData               Method          System.Void GetObjectData(Serializa...
GetType                     Method          System.Type GetType()
InitializeLifetimeService   Method          System.Object InitializeLifetimeSer...
MoveTo                      Method          System.Void MoveTo(String destFileN...
Open                        Method          System.IO.FileStream Open(FileMode ...
OpenRead                    Method          System.IO.FileStream OpenRead()
OpenText                    Method          System.IO.StreamReader OpenText()
OpenWrite                   Method          System.IO.FileStream OpenWrite()
Refresh                     Method          System.Void Refresh()
Replace                     Method          System.IO.FileInfo Replace(String d...
SetAccessControl            Method          System.Void SetAccessControl(FileSe...
ToString                    Method          System.String ToString()
PSChildName                 NoteProperty    System.String PSChildName=bar.wmv
PSDrive                     NoteProperty    System.Management.Automation.PSDriv...
PSIsContainer               NoteProperty    System.Boolean PSIsContainer=False
PSParentPath                NoteProperty    System.String PSParentPath=Microsof...
PSPath                      NoteProperty    System.String PSPath=Microsoft.Powe...
PSProvider                  NoteProperty    System.Management.Automation.Provid...
Attributes                  Property        System.IO.FileAttributes Attributes...
CreationTime                Property        System.DateTime CreationTime {get;s...
CreationTimeUtc             Property        System.DateTime CreationTimeUtc {ge...
Directory                   Property        System.IO.DirectoryInfo Directory {...
```

```
DirectoryName            Property         System.String DirectoryName {get;}
Exists                   Property         System.Boolean Exists {get;}
Extension                Property         System.String Extension {get;}
FullName                 Property         System.String FullName {get;}
IsReadOnly               Property         System.Boolean IsReadOnly {get;set;}
LastAccessTime           Property         System.DateTime LastAccessTime {get...
LastAccessTimeUtc        Property         System.DateTime LastAccessTimeUtc {...
LastWriteTime            Property         System.DateTime LastWriteTime {get;...
LastWriteTimeUtc         Property         System.DateTime LastWriteTimeUtc {g...
Length                   Property         System.Int64 Length {get;}
Name                     Property         System.String Name {get;}
BaseName                 ScriptProperty   System.Object BaseName {get=if ($th...
VersionInfo              ScriptProperty   System.Object VersionInfo {get=[Sys...
```

Because all of these properties are available to anything that uses the object, it is easy to write a command where two Cmdlets are piped together and the second uses properties of the objects found in the first.

Arrays

We have already referred to arrays. PowerShell handles arrays slightly differently from other environments. Usually an array is a collection of identical objects, but PowerShell arrays can be collections of dissimilar objects. But in some senses an array is just another variable. An array can be declared with the following syntax:

```
$a=@("a" , 3.14, (dir *.jpg) )
```

In fact, the third item of the array is itself an array.

As you will see shortly, it is possible to process each of the items in an array with the ForEach-object Cmdlet, and you index into arrays by using a number. Array indexes start at zero, and PowerShell allows negative numbers to be used in indexes: –1 represents the last item, –2 the second to last, and so on. For example, strings have a *Last index of* function and a *Substring* function, but there is no *Substring after the last index of*. So if you want to check if a string contains a file name ending in .jpg you could write:

```
if ($f.substring($f.lastindexof("."))  -eq ".jpg") { some action
```

or you could write:

```
if ($f.split(".")[-1] -eq "jpg" ) {some action}
```

One of the guiding principles in PowerShell is that commands should not force parameters to be single items, if it is possible to take multiple ones. Typically, if a command is called once with an array as a parameter, it will carry out the same actions as being called multiple times—once for each member of the array.

For example, the following code:

```
Get-WmiObject -class Win32_QuickfixEngineering -Server Srv1,Srv2,Srv3
```

is the same as calling:

```
Get-WmiObject -class Win32_QuickfixEngineering -Server Srv1
Get-WmiObject -class Win32_QuickfixEngineering -Server Srv2
Get-WmiObject -class Win32_QuickfixEngineering -Server Srv3
```

You may be used to separating unnamed parameters on a command line with commas, but this can cause unexpected results because the parser in PowerShell will treat a list separated by commas as a single array, not multiple items.

There is a second kind of array, which is different from the first; PowerShell documentation usually calls it an *associative array* but if you test for its type with GetType(), a variable of this type reports it is a HashTable, which is how most people know it.

In an associative array, there are two columns: *keys* and *values*. A normal array has keys—they are 0, 1, 2, and so on up to whatever the upper bound of the array is. In an associative array, the key can be anything, so here is a declaration of an associative array:

```
$BootMedia= @{"Floppy"=0 ; "CD"=1 ; "IDE"=2 ; "NET"=3 }
```

You can refer to the elements of the associative array in the same way as you would refer to elements in a conventional array as follows:

```
$bootMedia["floppy"]
```

Or you can use the following syntax to handle them as if they were properties:

```
$bootMedia.floppy
```

This is useful in this case because instead of a script making references to setting a boot device to 0 and needing to then discover what 0 actually means, you have something that contains all the values in one line rather than having to declare four separate constants. This also works well for decoding error response codes, which might appear more than once in a script. For example, you might define an associative array like this one:

```
$ReturnCode=  @{0="OK" ; 4096="Job Started" ; 32768="Failed";
               32769="Access Denied"; 32770="Not Supported"; 32771="Unknown" }
```

Then, elsewhere in the script, you can report what happened by using the following:

```
Write-host "Result was " + $returncode[$result]
```

The PowerShell Pipe

You saw in the last section that the Get-ChildItem Cmdlet—called using its alias DIR—can output an array of FileInfo objects. Depending on which directory it is looking at, it may return a mixture of FileInfo and DirectoryInfo objects, or Sertificate objects, Registry key objects, and so on. These objects, which have numerous methods and properties, including DirectoryName, Name, and Extension, as well as FullName, which is the three combined. You also saw that the output of DIR can be sent into another command, using the ¦ symbol—a process known as *piping*.

When DIR in CMD.EXE (or the old COMMAND.COM) is piped into another command, that command has only text to work with. In PowerShell, the next command in the pipe will have access to all the object's properties and methods. So, PowerShell's Sort-object Cmdlet can be told which of the properties of the FileInfo objects handed to it is the sorting key. For example, the following:

```
Dir | sort-object -property Name
```

will sort objects according to their name (without the file extension).

One of the PowerShell Cmdlets that saves a lot of scripting work is Format-Table. It, too, has a property parameter and this tells it which properties of the object that was passed to it should be displayed in tabular format. To display your own style of directory you could use the following:

```
Dir | Format-table -property name, length, mode -autosize
```

And frequently you need to filter objects so you might use:

```
Dir -Recurse | where-object {$_.length -gt 8mb}
```

Here, the -recurse switch causes dir to get child items from subdirectories; but the syntax of where-object takes a moment to understand.

Where-object looks at each item passed to it and evaluates the *Scriptblock* in the braces. If the Scriptblock evaluates to true the object is passed on to the next step, and if it evaluates to false, the object is discarded. PowerShell uses script blocks in lots of places, and they are just blocks of script—one or more commands that are executed, and in almost every situation they are surrounded by braces. User-defined functions and filters are just stored script blocks, and many Cmdlets take a script block as a parameter.

Inside the braces, $_ means *The current object*, so $_.length is the file size. The -gt operator is "is greater than," and PowerShell understands KB, MB, GB, and TB suffixes, so you don't need to write 8*1024*1024 when you can't remember exactly how many bytes there are in 1MB. So the clause selects items greater than 8MB in size.

Of course there is nothing to stop all three commands from being linked together:

```
Dir -Recurse | where-object {$_.length -gt 8mb} | sort-object -property Name |
    Format-table -property name, length, mode autosize
```

As you've seen already, this command can be reduced in size using aliases and by not being so explicit with the switches—giving this:

```
Dir -R | ? {$_.length -gt 8mb} | sort Name | Ft name, length, mode -a
```

It is worth noting that PowerShell has *Tab Expansion*. In the newer versions of CMD the [tab] key allows you to type part of a path or file name and then expand it to the full version. If there is more than one match, pressing Tab repeatedly cycles through the possible choices. PowerShell has a customizable tab-expansion function, which will do more sophisticated things: get-ch[tab] will expand to get-childItem (get-C [tab] will cycle through Get-Command, Get-Credential, and so on). If you aren't sure what you can do with an item, you can type *Item [tab] and PowerShell will cycle through Clear-Item, Clear-ItemProperty, Copy-Item, and so on.

Tab expansion by default won't expand aliases and expands Cmdlets only once the - sign has been typed. However it does recognize aliases as well as the canonical names when expanding parameters, so once DIR is entered, -R [Tab] will expand to -Recurse, and once FormatTable or FT is entered, -a [Tab] will expand to Autosize. If you are unsure what options are available, you can just type -[Tab] to cycle through all of them.

The Where-object Cmdlet has two aliases—the question mark (?) and where, and it looks at each object in turn. Sometimes it is necessary to explicitly tell PowerShell to process a scriptblock for each object that is passed along the pipe. For example, the following command will take a collection of image files from a digital camera and return only their names:

```
dir _igp* | foreach-object {$_.name}
```

You cannot write dir _igp* | $_.name because the $_.name isn't a command that can receive input from the pipe, so you need to be explicit and pass that information to ForEach-Object, which can. PowerShell will pass the output of any command into the next command and it is the responsibility of each command to see if there is piped input for it. You can write your own functions and filters that can be executed at any point in the pipeline even if they ignore what the previous command is trying to pass.

As with the preceding example, which uses where-object, the code block in the braces after ForEach-Object is evaluated for each object that is passed down the pipe. In this example, PowerShell gets the item's name property, and having nothing else to do with it, prints it out in the host console. Let's make it do something a little more sophisticated:

```
dir _igp* | foreach-object {$_.name.replace ("_IGP","Party") }
```

The Name Property is a text string, and as you saw previously, strings have a Replace() method. Calling that method means this command replaces the "_IGP", which the camera used at the start of all the image-file names with something more descriptive of the picture—while preserving the serial number the camera gave each image.

You can probably guess that the next step is to change the name of the files. PowerShell has a Rename-Item Cmdlet (with an alias Ren so it works like its CMD equivalent), so to rename the files, that line evolves into:

```
dir _igp* | foreach-object { rename-item -path $_.Fullname -newname
    $_.name.replace("_IGP","Party")  }
```

In fact, rename-item is a Cmdlet that accepts a set of files from the pipe and processes each one, so it doesn't need to be called using foreachobject or by specifying the path to the object. The command can be simplified to:

```
dir _igp* | rename-item -newname {$_.name.replace("_IGP","Party") }
```

Notice that one little quirk of PowerShell syntax is that you need to enclose the section where the passed object's name is evaluated in braces.

As before, this could be shortened for typing at the command line. Rennane-item can become ren and the -newname switch can become, simply, -n. However, more important than how to enter the command with the smallest number of keystrokes, you may be more concerned with renaming files to something nonsensical. Fortunately, PowerShell has a standard switch on many Cmdlets: WhatIf tells the Cmdlet to show what it would do without actually doing it, like this:

```
> dir _igp* | rename-item -newname {$_.name.replace("_IGP","Party") } -whatif

What if: Performing operation "Rename File" on Target
    "Item: C:\Pictures\Image dump\_IGP5499.JPG
      Destination: C:\Pictures\Image dump\Party5499.JPG".
What if: Performing operation "Rename File" on Target
    "Item: C:\Pictures\Image dump\_IGP5510.JPG
      Destination: C:\Pictures\Image dump\Party5510.JPG".
What if: Performing operation "Rename File" on Target
    "Item: C:\Pictures\Image dump\_IGP5511.JPG
      Destination: C:\Pictures\Image dump\Party5511.JPG".
What if: Performing operation "Rename File" on Target
    "Item: C:\Pictures\Image dump\_IGP5512.JPG
      Destination: C:\Pictures\Image dump\Party5512.JPG".
What if: Performing operation "Rename File" on Target
    "Item: C:\Pictures\Image dump\_IGP5513.JPG
      Destination: C:\Pictures\Image dump\Party5513.JPG".
```

Having proved that the command does what you want it to do, you can remove the -WhatIf switch and run it for real.

Looping in PowerShell

You have already seen how PowerShell can loop through all the items in an array. PowerShell provides three kinds of looping construction: For, ForEach-Object, and while.

The `while` statement is the simplest of the three. The syntax is `While (condition) {script block}`. It tests to see if a condition evaluates to true; if it does, it executes the script block. Then it tests the condition again; if it is still true, it executes the script block again, and it keeps repeating the process until the condition is no longer true. The script block won't execute at all if the condition initially returns false. For example, this code is used to suspend a script as long as a job is running: 4 indicates *running*.

```
while ($job.jobstate -eq 4)
{Start-Sleep -seconds 1
 $Job.PSBase.Get() }
```

It may sound obvious, but it is important that something happen in the script block that causes the condition to change. Sooner or later, you will write something that loops forever. Fortunately, when you do that, PowerShell traps the [Ctrl]+[c] key to break out.

This version of `while` will not run the script block at if the condition is false. Sometimes it is useful to put the test at the end, which runs the script block at least once. The syntax for this is `Do {scriptblock} while (condition)`.

The `For` statement is a C-style loop, and may seem a little unfriendly to the people who have come from other languages. Typically in those languages you might write:

```
For x = 0 to 100 step 10
Do something with x
Next X
```

A PowerShell `for` is written like this:

```
For ($x=0; x -lt 100 , $x += 10 ) {do something with x}
```

Inside the brackets are an *initialization* statement, a *condition*, and a *repeated* statement. The first thing to be executed is the *initialization statement*, which sets $x to 0. Next, if the *condition*—$x is less than 100—is true, the script block in the braces will be executed. Each time the script block completes, the *repeated statement*—adding 10 to $x—is run. If the *condition* is still true the script block is run again followed by the repeated statement and so on, until eventually the *condition* ceases to be true.

Each of the three blocks is optional and there is no reason why they have to deal with incrementing a counter. For example, the *initialization statement* could fetch records from a database, the *condition* could be that the current record doesn't contain a particular value in a particular field, and the *repeated statement* could move to the next record—this would return a the desired record in the set without needing a script block at all.

You might also have noticed that the `for` loop could be rewritten as a `while` loop.

```
$x=0
While ($x -lt 100) {
Do something with x
$x += 10
}
```

Because the initialize, condition, and repeat parts of the `for` are all optional, any `while` can also be written as a `for`.

```
for(; $job.jobstate -eq 4 ; )
{Start-Sleep -seconds 1
 $Job.PSBase.Get() }
```

Or better:

```
for(; $job.jobstate -eq 4 ; $Job.PSBase.Get())
{Start-Sleep -seconds 1 }
```

The command to get the job object could be inserted as the initialize part:

```
for($job=[wmi]$jobID; $job.jobstate -eq 4 ; $Job.PSBase.Get())
    {Start-Sleep -seconds 1 }
```

`ForEach-object` is a Cmdlet you have seen already.

Without `ForEach-object`, you would have to write a `for` loop to work through each item in an array. In the renaming example, you would need to do something like this:

```
$Files = (dir *.jpg)
For (I = 0; I -lt files.count ; i++) {
    rename-item $files[i] -newName $files[i].name.replace("img_", "party") }
```

Most people think of for each as a construction which was introduced by Microsoft Visual Basic, but in fact the language in COMMAND.COM and later had `for...do`, which achieved the same effect. In CMD.EXE you can write:

```
for %f in (*.JPG) do if exist ..\%f del %f
```

This looks at all the files with a .JPG extension in the current folder, and if a file with the same name exists in the parent folder, the copy in the current folder is removed.

`ForEach-Object` has two aliases—`foreach` and `%`—and can be used with more than one syntax; you have already seen it used receiving objects via the pipe. In that form, you could enter the following at the command prompt to replicate the preceding duplicate removal line:

```
dir *.jpg | % {if (test-path "..\$($_.name)") {del $_ } }
```

As well as the Cmdlet, PowerShell has a ForEach Statement, which specifies what is being looped through, like this:

```
Foreach ($f in (dir *.jpg)) {if (test-path "..\$($f.name)")
    {del $f -verbose} }
```

This could also be written as:

```
$files=(dir *.jpg)
Foreach ($f in $files) {if (test-path "..\$($f.name)") {del $f -verbose} }
```

Earlier, you saw that PowerShell understands 1..10 to mean an array of integers and this can be used to make forEach behave like a simple for loop. For example, the following will return the squares of numbers from 1 to 10:

```
1..10 | ForEach-object {$_ * $_ }
```

Foreach-object has one more trick worth noting: It can run three code blocks, not just one. These are named process, begin, and –end. If only one block is supplied, it is assumed to be process. It is the only one that is required. begin and end blocks are optional: they allow you to do in one command something that would otherwise need to be divided into two or three. For example, you could count the number of duplicate files deleted by initializing a counter, incrementing it with each deletion, and then outputting it at the end.

```
dir *.jpg | % -begin {$c=0} `
            -process {if (test-path "..\$($_.name)") {del $_ ; $C ++}} `
            -end {"Removed $c duplicates"}
```

Conditions

You have already seen that PowerShell makes decisions on what to do next based on certain conditions. In the previous section, you saw conditions used in if statements, for statements, and while statements, and before that you saw them used in where statements.

Although you've seen conditions in use, they haven't been formally described. A PowerShell if statement is written in the form:

```
If (condition) {script block to execute if the condition evaluates to true}
Else {script block to execute if the condition evaluates to false}
```

Conditions can be built up from subconditions using the Boolean operators -and, -or, and -not. Consider the following:

(-not (subCondition))	Returns true if the subcondition is false and false if it is true
((subCondition a) -and (subConditionb))	Returns true only if the subConditions are both true and false if either or both are false
((subcondition a) -or (subcondition b))	Returns true if either or both of the conditions are true and false only if both are false

A condition (or a subcondition) can be a variable or an expression that returns something. PowerShell has two special variables—$true and $false—and these can be assigned to a variable. Otherwise, any non-empty, non-zero result is treated as True. Some languages have special ways to handle empty, or null, objects. PowerShell treats them as false, and the condition of being empty can be tested for by comparing with a special variable, $null:

```
> $notDefined1 -eq $null
True
```

```
> $notDefined2 -eq $null
True
$notDefined1 -eq $notDefined2
True
```

The last one of these causes some issues in environments that say an empty argument can't be equal to anything because it has no content. (This is a bit like the old zero divided by zero paradox. Any number divided by itself is 1. Any number divided by zero is infinity, and zero divided by anything is zero. So what *is* zero divided by zero?) PowerShell is quite happy to treat null as just another value.

Most commonly, a *condition* will be two terms linked by one of the comparison operators. PowerShell has quite a full set of comparison operators, of which the most commonly used are shown in Table 4-01 that follows:

TABLE 4-01

PowerShell Comparison Operators	
-eq	Is equal to
-ne	Is not equal to
-ge	Is greater than or equal to
-gt	Is greater than
-lt	Is less than
-le	Is less than or equal to
-like	Wildcard comparison
-notlike	Wildcard comparison
-match	Regular expression comparison
-notmatch	Regular expression comparison
-contains	Containment operator
-notcontains	Containment operator

The first few of these are obvious: greater than and less than, equal to, and combinations of them. The question of string comparison does arise: Will PowerShell return True or False if you ask it to evaluate:

```
"THIS" -eq "this"
```

The answer is that PowerShell returns True. By default, all the comparison operators are case insensitive, but they all have case-sensitive versions, which are prefixed with a C. Although redundant, PowerShell provides additional versions that are case insensitive, prefixed with an i, so if you want to be emphatic that a comparison is case insensitive, you could write the previous comparison as:

```
"THIS" -ieq "this"
```

The -like, -match, and -contains operators cause some confusion. Contains checks to see if an array has a member, so the following is an incorrect use of the operator:

```
"this" -contains "t"
```

In the preceding line of code, "this" is a string, not an array, so it can't have an array member "t". Strings do have a method to convert them to an array of characters so this would be a valid test:

```
$s.ToCharArray() -contains "t"
```

Any kind of array can appear on the left of the -contains operator so you can test to see if $x is a value between 1 and 10 with the following:

```
1..10 -contains $x
```

You should be careful about using this, however—it might save a little typing but it takes more computation to evaluate than test for ($x -gte 1) -and ($x -lte 10).

like is a wildcard operator so that a simple test for a string containing t could be written as follows:

```
"this" -like "*t*"
```

The * sign in a -like comparison stands for "any number of characters including none." A question mark (?) stands for "any single character" so if you evaluate each of the following:

```
"this" -like "*t*"
"this" -like "th*"
"that" -like "th*"
"these" -like "th*"
"this" -like "th??"
"these" -like "th??"
"this" -like "th?"
```

all but the last two will return true.

like has one other test you can apply and that is to test for one of a set of characters: -like "*[aeiou]*" will test for any of the vowels, and -like "*[a-e]*" will test for any of the letters a–e.

This begins to overlap with the more complex regular expression operator -match. We will look at regular expressions in detail in Chapter 30. However it is important not to confuse -match and like. "A*" in a -like means "beginning with A" and in a -match means "containing any number of As" including 0. This will match *everything*.

Scripts, Script Blocks, and Functions

At the beginning of this chapter, we explained that PowerShell commands included built-in Cmdlets, Aliases, Functions, Filters, Scripts, and external programs.

Script blocks have been referred to in several places already. A *script block* is nothing more than a collection of commands (of any of the types listed above) enclosed in a set of braces. Script blocks can be nested—for example, you saw the following script in the section about loops:

```
dir *.jpg | % -begin {$c=0} `
            -process {if (test-path "..\$($_.name)") {del $_ ; $C ++}} `
            -end {"Removed $c duplicates"}
```

This contains four script blocks, one for each of the begin, process, and end stages, and one inside the process block to run if the `test-path` Cmdlet returns `true`.

Script blocks can be stored—either in an active instance of PowerShell or in a script—and called up later. Inside PowerShell are two very similar constructions—Functions and Filters—that are commonly used. In fact, a Function is very little more than a named code block accessible under the Function: drive, as you saw earlier for MKDIR.

Functions can take arguments and although it is possible to reference everything on the command line passed to the function, it is usual to use a set of named parameters, declared using a `param` statement.

For example, in the preceding section on loops there was a script , which removed duplicates. This could be made into a function to remove duplicates of any given extension, which you could write as follows:

```
Function Remove-Duplicates
{Param ($fileExt)
dir "*.$fileExt" | % -begin {$c=0} `
                   -process {if (test-path "..\$($_.name)")
                            {del $_ ; $C ++}}`
                   -end {"Removed $c duplicates"}
}
```

Parameters can be given a type like any other variable and also assigned a default value. For example:

```
Param ([string]$fileExt=".jpg")
```

The default value can also be used to produce an error if no value is provided:

```
Param ([string]$fileExt= $(throw "error"))
```

As before $ sign is used for the "the value of". `Throw` is a core *Statement*. not a Cmdlet and statements must be *explicitly* evaluated before they can be stored. Syntactically this tells PowerShell the default is the value of throwing an error.

When the function is called, parameters can be passed to it by position—i.e., by the sequence in which they appear in the Param statement—or they can be passed by name, and the name used need only be long enough to be unambiguous; so this function could be invoked using any of the following:

```
Remove-Duplicates -fileExt "JPG"
Remove-Duplicates -f  "JPG"
Remove-Duplicates "JPG"
```

This function can be stored in a script file—simply by removing the function definition from the top and the opening and closing braces, and saving with a .ps1 extension. If the script was on the path and named Remove-Duplicates.ps1, the same command lines would be used to invoke it.

Functions and filters differ in only one regard and that is how they are treated when they are included in the pipeline. Filters work better here because each item passed in via the pipe is available in the default variable $_. Under the surface, both functions and filters can have the same -Begin, -Process, and End-Blocks that you saw in ForEach-Object. If they have only one block, a filter treats it as the Process-Block and a function treats it as an End-Block; explicitly declaring the blocks allows you to cancel out this difference. With functions, all the input is passed in an automatically created variable, $input. With filters, it is in $_.

If you use the remove-duplicates function as an example, you might want to use some more options to select the files so rather than finding the files in the function, you might want to have a remove-duplicates filter into which you can pipe files:

```
Filter Remove-Duplicates
{if (test-path "..\$($_.name)") {del $_ }}
```

So now you can issue a command like this:

```
Dir *.jpg -recurse | remove-duplicates
```

Obviously, when you have created functions, filters, and useful variable declarations you will want to use them again. It's a good idea to add comments to scripts so other people can understand what you did—in fact, when you come back to your scripts months after writing them, *you* are effectively someone else so you can do it for your own benefit.

Anything following a # sign is taken to be a comment.

Also critical when using functions and filters again are saving and loading them from a *script*. A script can do anything you can do at the prompt including defining functions, but, by default, any functions and variables created are only in scope while the script is running. To keep anything that is set by the script, it needs to be *dot sourced*, as PowerShell terms it. This is a fancy name for putting a dot (.) in the command line before the name of the script.

This will load a library of functions to manage Windows server Hyper-V.

```
. .\hyper-v.ps1
```

In contrast, the following is little more than a syntax check:

```
.\hyper-v.ps1
```

Scripts and Security

So, knowing that PowerShell allows commands to be stored in script files, you might choose to test it out with a very simple script. If you create a file in Notepad containing a single command—Dir, for example—and save it using the name test.ps1 you might expect to be able to run it just by entering the command TEST at the PowerShell prompt, but doing so will generate an error:

```
PS C:\Users\Administrator> notepad test.ps1
PS C:\Users\Administrator> test
The term 'test' is not recognized as a cmdlet, function,
    operable program, or script file. Verify the term and try again.
At line:1 char:5
+ test <<<<
```

Unlike CMD.EXE and COMMAND.COM, PowerShell doesn't treat the current folder as part of the path. So you need to specify .\test.ps1. On a newly installed copy of PowerShell, this will still generate an error:

```
PS C:\Users\Administrator> .\test
File C:\Users\Administrator\test.ps1 cannot be loaded because
    the execution of scripts is disabled on this system. Please
    see "get-help about_signing" for more details.
At line:1 char:7
+ .\test <<<<
```

You can see from the error that PowerShell initially deploys in a secure state. PowerShell's online help tells you that you need to set an execution policy and, by default, this is set to Restricted—no scripts run. You can tell PowerShell to run only signed scripts, or to run all scripts, or to require a signature on downloaded scripts but not locally authored ones.

Figure 4-1 shows the file properties dialog for a downloaded file—the blocking attribute can be manually removed if the script is trusted.

FIGURE 4-1

The file properties dialog for a downloaded file

If you are running PowerShell as a user other than the built-in Administrator account on Windows Vista or Server 2008, you will need to explicitly run PowerShell as Administrator in order to make the change:

```
PS C:\Users\Administrator> Get-ExecutionPolicy
Restricted
PS C:\Users\Administrator> Set-ExecutionPolicy remoteSigned
PS C:\Users\Administrator> .\test


    Directory: Microsoft.PowerShell.Core\FileSystem::C:\Users\Administrator


Mode                LastWriteTime     Length Name
----                -------------     ------ ----
d-r--         14/07/2008     21:25           Contacts
d-r--         16/07/2008     19:26           Desktop
d-r--         18/07/2008     18:10           Documents
```

If signing is not required, then PowerShell doesn't even look at the signature block in the script. If the policy is set to *all signed* or the script was downloaded and the policy is set to *remote signed* then trying to run a script with no signature generates an error:

```
File C:\Users\Administrator\test.ps1 cannot be loaded. The file C:\Users\
Administrator\test.ps1 is not digitally signed. The script will not execute
on the system. Please see "get-help about_signing" for more details.
```

There are three main ways to get a certificate to sign your scripts. The first is to create a local certificate—the PowerShell online help refers to the MAKECERT utility, which is part of the Windows Software Development Kits. Microsoft Office includes a rather more user friendly tool for signing macros. If you run this, it creates a certificate and installs it into the personal certificates folder.

Here you can use PowerShell's certificate provider to find the certificate, the following will show *codeSigning* certificates:

```
dir cert:\CurrentUser\my -codesigning
```

If there is only one certificate, you can store it in a variable with:

```
$myCodeCert= dir cert:\CurrentUser\my -codesigning
```

If you have more than one you can index to the one you want—using 0 for the first one. For example:

```
$myCodeCert= (dir cert:\CurrentUser\my -codesigning)[0]
```

Then the certificate can be used to sign a file. For example:

```
> Set-AuthenticodeSignature .\test.ps1  $MyCodeCert

    Directory: C:\Users\Administrator
SignerCertificate                         Status                  Path
-----------------                         ------                  ----
3EB59EF3815C43071149710E48F7127D5EF45BC9  Valid                   test.ps1
```

And the certificate on a file can be checked with `Get-AuthenticodeSignature`. In this case it returns the following:

```
    Directory: C:\Users\Administrator
SignerCertificate                         Status                  Path
-----------------                         ------                  ----
3EB59EF3815C43071149710E48F7127D5EF45BC9  UnknownError            test.ps1
```

That doesn't look right—now the status column has changed from "Valid" to "Unknown error," which doesn't bode well for running the script.

```
>  .\test
File C:\Users\Administrator\test.ps1 cannot be loaded. A certificate chain
processed, but terminated in a root certificate which is not trusted by the
trust provider.
```

Oh dear. This is actually expected behavior because the certificate is not listed as a trusted certificate provider so you have to copy the certificate into the trusted certificate provider's folder. This is done via the GUI. (PowerShell's certificate provider doesn't support copying certificates from one store to another.) To do this is to start the Microsoft Management console (run MMC.EXE) and load the certificates MMC snap-in. Then you can copy the certificate from the user's personal certificates to the trusted Root Certification authorities' folder. Figure 4-2 shows the process of copying the certificate. You can copy the certificate from one store and paste into another using the MMC.

Now running `Get-AuthenticodeSignature` again will show the file has a valid signature.

However, PowerShell *still* wants reassurance that you mean to trust this publisher:

```
>  .\test.ps1
Do you want to run software from this untrusted publisher?
File: C:\Users\Administrator\test.ps1 is published by CN=James Test-Cert and
is not trusted on your system. Only run scripts from trusted publishers.
[V] Never run  [D] Do not run  [R] Run once  [A] Always run  [?] Help
(default is "D"):
```

This is not the clearest of PowerShell's messages because you would think it is asking you about this script. It is actually asking about all scripts from this publisher.

FIGURE 4-2

Copying the certificate

These certificates to help developers sign their code are helpful, but anything that involves adding a random publisher to your list of trusted Root CAs is to be regarded with suspicion. It is far better to use a corporate PKI to issue signing certificates. All the managed computers within an organization can have the corporate CA's certificate pushed to them and those charged with managing the servers can ensure that they trust only appropriate certificates, which are then used to sign scripts that run on those servers. The person who signs the scripts does not need to be the author of the scripts but becomes the change control authority for putting those scripts into a production environment.

Summary

In this chapter, you have seen that PowerShell is a modern shell for Windows—it understands rich objects and data types. PowerShell commands are aliased to their equivalents in other shells. New Cmdlets and providers can be added to PowerShell using snap-ins, making it a general-purpose tool. PowerShell users can extend the set of commands available by writing their own functions and defining aliases. PowerShell helps discoverability with consistent help, tab expansion, the widespread use of the `-WhatIf` switch, and the `Get-Member` function. `-WhatIf` and script restrictions help PowerShell to be safer than other shells. A lot of the power of PowerShell comes from being able to return objects from functions' Cmdlets, and pipe those objects into other functions and Cmdlets. PowerShell doesn't need to explicitly echo things to the console—anything not piped somewhere else goes to the console.

Although we have not looked at the details of what you can do in PowerShell, you have seen that it has functions such as `Format-table`, which shorten the amount of script needed for common tasks. You will see more examples of this in the coming chapters.

Part II

Windows VBScript and JScript

P art II gets you into the nuts and bolts of scripting: the Windows Script Host and the basic commands you can use in scripts. Part II also shows you how to run scripts, perform input and output, and handle errors. You'll learn how to work with the most common objects you can control with scripts: files and folders, drives and printers, and the applications themselves. Finally, you'll learn how to use scripts to work with the Windows Registry and event logs.

Chapter 5

Creating Scripts and Scripting Files

W indows Script Host (WSH) provides several different ways to work with Windows scripts. The easiest technique is to create scripts using only a single scripting language and then save the script using the appropriate extension for the scripting engine. If you use VBScript, you save the script with the .vbs extension. If you use JScript, you save the script with the .js extension. Unlike script files used with Web pages, WSH script files don't need to contain any special markup or any kind of instructions.

You can also combine multiple types of scripts in a batch script. With batch scripts, you can use a single file and save it with the .wsf file extension. Because batch scripts can use scripts written in multiple scripting languages, you must somehow identify the type of scripts you are using and other important aspects of these scripts. You do this using markup tags written in XML (Extensible Markup Language). Don't worry — you don't need to become an XML or HTML expert to work with batch scripts. However, you do need to learn a bit about the markup tags available for use with WSH.

IN THIS CHAPTER

Running scripts

XML and Windows Script files

Working with batch scripts

Creating jobs and packages

Debugging and error handling

Running Scripts

You run scripts using the scripting hosts provided by WSH. These scripting hosts are:

- **WScript:** WScript is a scripting host with GUI controls for displaying output in pop-up dialog boxes and is used primarily when you execute scripts from the desktop. The related executable is WScript.exe and it isn't related to the WScript object that is a part of the core object model.

- **CScript:** CScript is the command-line version of the scripting host. All output from CScript is displayed at the Windows command prompt unless you specify otherwise by using a pop-up box or dialog box. The related executable for CScript is CScript.exe.

The techniques you use to work with WScript and CScript are the same regardless of whether you are working with standard script files or batch script files.

Starting a Script

When you install WSH and the scripting engines on a system, several file types are mapped for use with the scripting hosts. These mappings allow you to run scripts like any other executable program. You can run scripts using any of the following techniques:

- Start Windows Explorer, and then browse until you find a script. Double-click on the script.
- Double-click on a desktop shortcut to a script.
- Enter a script name at the Run command on the Start menu. Be sure to enter the full file extension, and path if necessary, such as C:\scripts\myscript.vbs.
- At the command-line prompt, type **wscript** followed by a script name, such as:

  ```
  wscript myscript.vbs
  ```

- At the command-line prompt, type **cscript** followed by a script name, such as:

  ```
  cscript myscript.js
  ```

Setting script properties

You can set script properties for Wscript in Windows Explorer, or when you run scripts at the command line. If you want to set properties for scripts in Windows Explorer, follow these steps:

1. Right-click a script file in Windows Explorer.
2. Select Properties on the shortcut menu.
3. Choose the Script tab, as shown in Figure 5-1.
4. You can now set the default timeout value and determine whether a scripting logo is displayed when you execute WScript from the command line. Use the timeout value to stop execution of a script that has been running too long and to possibly prevent a runaway process from using up precious processor time.
5. Choose OK or Apply.

As we stated, you can also set script properties at the command line. You can do this only when you execute a script using CScript. We show you how to do this in the next section.

FIGURE 5-1

You can set script properties through the Script tab in Windows Explorer.

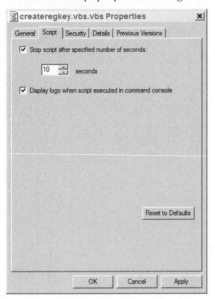

Command-line options for scripts

When you run scripts from the desktop or Windows Explorer, property settings can be applied as outlined in the previous section. These settings are for WScript. CScript, on the other hand, is a command-line executable, and like most command-line programs, can be configured using switches and modifiers.

The command-line syntax for Cscript is:

```
cscript [host_options] [script_name] [script_args]
```

in which host_options are options to set for CScript, script_name is the name of the script, and script_args are arguments to pass in to the script. The script name must include the file extension and any necessary path information, as in the following:

```
cscript copyfiles.js
cscript c:\scripts\copyfiles.js
cscript c:\"my scripts"\copyfiles.js
```

Table 5-1 shows the available options for CScript. As you can see, options and arguments are differentiated using slashes. Host options are preceded with two slashes (//) and script arguments don't use slashes. For example, you can set a timeout for a script and pass in the script parameter "basic" as follows:

```
cscript //t:45 logon.vbs basic
```

TABLE 5-1

Options for CScript

Option	Description
//?	Shows command usage.
//b	Sets batch mode, which suppresses command-line display of user prompts and script errors. (Opposite of //i.)
//d	Turns on the debugger.
//e:engine	Runs the script with the specified scripting engine.
//h:Cscript	Registers Cscript.exe as the default application for running scripts.
//h:Wscript	Registers Wscript.exe as the default application for running scripts. If not specified, Wscript.exe is assumed to be the default.
//i	Sets interactive mode for scripts, which allows display of user prompts and script errors. Interactive mode is the default.
//Job:"Job Name"	Runs the specified job from a WSC file.
//logo	Displays CScript logo at runtime. This is the default setting.
//nologo	Turns off display of the CScript logo at runtime.
//s	Saves the current command-line options for the user logged on to the system.
//t:nn	Sets a timeout for the script, which is the maximum number of seconds (nn) the script can run. By default, scripts have no limit.
//x	Executes the program in the debugger.

As you can see from the table, scripts can be run in interactive mode or batch mode. In batch mode, scripts don't display prompts or errors, and this behavior is very useful when you want to schedule scripts to run with the Task Scheduler service. For example, if you want to run a Windows script every weekday at midnight, you would probably want to run in batch mode. For example:

```
AT 00:00 /every:M,T,W,Th,F "cscript //b backupdata.js"
```

Whether you run scripts from the command line or via the Task Scheduler, you'll often want to set more than one option. Having to retype scripting options each time you use a script isn't fun, which is why the //s option is provided. With this option, you can set default options to use each time you run CScript. For example, if you enter the following command:

```
cscript //b //nologo //t:30 //d //s
```

CScript is set to use batch mode, no logo, a timeout of 30 seconds, and debugging whenever you run scripts. The only way to override the default setup is to save a different set of options, like this:

```
cscript //i //s
```

As you work with WScript and CScript, you may find that you prefer one over the other. Don't worry, you can switch the default scripting host at any time. To use CScript as the default, enter the following command:

```
cscript //h:CScript
```

To use WScript as the default, enter:

```
cscript //h:WScript
```

Using drag and drop with scripts

Windows Script Host supports drag and drop. Drag and drop allows you to drag one or more files onto a script file. The script is then automatically executed with the files as arguments.

When you drag files onto a WSH script, the filenames are translated into arguments on the command line. These filenames can be managed just like any other script arguments. The number of files you can drag onto a script is limited by the maximum command-line length your computer allows. If the total number of characters in all filenames (including the spaces added between filenames) exceeds this limit, the drag-and-drop operation will fail.

To give drag and drop a test run, create the script shown as Listing 5-1; then save the file to the Windows desktop. Afterward, start Windows Explorer. In Windows Explorer, select several files and then, while holding down the right mouse button, drag the files onto the script. The script displays the filenames in separate pop-up dialog boxes.

LISTING 5-1

Using Drag and Drop

echoargs.vbs

```
Set objArgs = WScript.Arguments
For I = 0 to objArgs.Count - 1
  WScript.Echo "File " + CStr(I) + ": " + objArgs(I)
Next
```

Creating Batch Scripts

Batch scripts allow you to combine multiple scripts in a single file. These scripts can use the same scripting language or different scripting languages — it doesn't matter. The advantage of batch scripts is that they make it possible for scripts to interact. You can pass values back and forth between scripts. You can even call functions of scripts that aren't included in the file directly, which is the technique you'll use if you create utility libraries like those discussed in Part V of this book.

Batch scripts are saved in files with the .wsf file extension and make use of XML markup tags to tell the scripting host how to handle the batch scripts. As with HTML (Hypertext Markup Language), most XML markup tags have a begin tag and an end tag that, together, specify an element. An element that you may already be familiar with is script. The script element is used to specify the start and end of scripts in Web pages, as well as to specify information needed to locate and interpret scripts.

The scripting hosts support a special set of XML tags. These tags include:

- `<?job ?>`: Sets special instructions for all scripts in the batch
- `<?XML ?>`: Sets special instructions for parsing file as XML
- `<description>`: Marks the descriptive text shown when the user runs ShowUsage() or runs the script with the /? command line switch
- `<example>`: Provides an example of usage when the ShowUsage method is called
- `<named>`: Describes a named argument for the script
- `<package>`: Encloses multiple job definitions
- `<job>`: Identifies the job (or script name)
- `<object>`: Exposes objects for use in scripts
- `<reference>`: References an external-type library
- `<resource>`: Sets text or numeric data that should not be hard coded into a script
- `<runtime>`: Creates a set of runtime arguments for a script
- `<unnamed>`: Describes an unnamed argument for the script
- `<usage>`: Allows the user to override the default usage display
- `<script>`: Identifies the scripting language and source

The sections that follow examine each of these tags in turn. If you've never worked with markup tags before, don't worry — you don't need to know anything about XML or HTML, I promise.

Identifying the job name

Batch scripts are really designed to help administrators create scripting libraries with functions that can be easily accessed. Because you can potentially have dozens of scripts in a single library, you may need a container to be able to reference the script you want to run. You do this with the job element. As with most elements, the job element has a pair of markup tags associated with it. The <job> tag marks the beginning of the job element, and the </job> tag marks the end of the job element, like this:

```
<job>
  Insert body of job here
</job>
```

To identify the name of the job, you use the id *attribute*. An attribute is simply a property of an element that can be used to set values. Using the id attribute, you set the job name as follows:

```
<job id="WriteLogs">
</job>
```

The job element is a top-level element that can contain zero or more occurrences of these other elements: object, reference, and script. The job element itself can also be used more than once in a .wsf file, provided that you enclose the jobs within a package element. Enclosing multiple jobs is the only purpose of the package element and its use is mandatory when you have two or more jobs in a .wsf file.

When you use multiple jobs, you shouldn't nest job elements within job elements. Instead, you should start one job, end it, and then start another, as shown in Listing 5-2.

LISTING 5-2

Using multiple jobs

multijobs.wsf

```
<package>
<job id="WriteLogs">
 Insert body of job here
</job>
<job id="DeleteOldLogs">
 Insert body of job here
</job>
<job id="PublishLogs">
 Insert body of job here
</job>
</package>
```

Adding scripts and setting the scripting language

When you add scripts to the batch, you need to tell the scripting hosts about the script you are using. You do this with the script element. The `<script>` tag marks the beginning of a script and the `</script>` tag marks the end of a script. You always use the script element within a job element, like this:

```
<job id="WriteLogs">
<script>
 Insert script here
</script>
</job>
```

The scripting host also needs to know which language you are using. You specify the scripting language with the language attribute. Valid values for the language attribute include VBScript, JScript, JavaScript, and PerlScript. You can set the scripting language to VBScript as follows:

```
<script language="VBScript">
 'Insert VBScript here
</script>
```

WSH jobs can contain multiple scripts. When they do contain multiple scripts, you need to insert additional script elements. In Listing 5-3, the job uses scripts written in VBScript and JScript.

LISTING 5-3

Using Multiple Scripts within a Single Job

multiscripts.wsf

```
<job id="WriteLogs">
<script language="VBScript">
 'Insert VBScript here
</script>
<script language="JScript">
 'Insert JScript here
</script>
</job>
```

Setting the script source

The source code for scripts doesn't have to be in the batch file. You can store the source code in separate .js, .vbs, and .pl files, and then reference the source file from within the batch. Source files that aren't located in the batch are referred to as external scripts, and their location is set with the src attribute.

The src attribute expects you to reference source locations using URLs (Universal Resource Locators). URLs are what you use when you browse the Web. However, while a typical Web URL looks like this: `http://www.centraldrive.com/index.html`, a typical file URL looks like this: `file://c:\working\myscript.vbs`. where `http:` identifies the Hypertext Transfer Protocol used on the Web, and `file:` identifies the file protocol used with file systems.

Source files can be referenced with *relative* file paths or *absolute* file paths. You access local files — files on your local system — using a relative file path. URLs with relative file paths generally do not name a protocol. When you use a relative path to locate a file, you locate the file in relation to the current batch script. You can use relative file paths in the following three key ways:

- To access a file in the current directory, such as:
  ```
  <script language="JScript" src="test.js" />
  ```

- To access a file in a parent directory of the current directory, such as:
  ```
  <script language="JScript" src="../test.js" />
  ```

- To access a file in a subdirectory of the current directory, such as:
  ```
  <script language="JScript" src="scripts/test.js" />
  ```

Another way to access files is directly. You do this by specifying the complete path to the file you want to access, such as:

```
<script language="JScript" src="file://c:\scripts/test.js" />
```

As shown in the previous examples, you don't use an end script tag when you specify a script source. Instead, you tell the scripting host to end the element with the `/>` designator. A more complete example of using external scripts is shown in Listing 5-4.

LISTING 5-4

Working with Multiple Jobs and External Source Files

multijobs2.wsf

```
<package>
<job id="WriteLogs">
  <script language="VBScript" src="fget.vbs" />
  <script language="JScript" src="fcreate.js" />
</job>
<job id="DeleteOldLogs">
  <script LANGUAGE="VBScript" src="testfolder.vbs" />
  <script LANGUAGE="VBScript" src="delcreate.vbs" />
</job>
<job id="PublishLogs">
<script LANGUAGE="VBScript">
 'Insert VBScript here
</script>
```

```
<script language="JScript">
 'Insert JScript here
</script>
</job>
</package>
```

One of the primary reasons for placing multiple scripts in the same file is the ability to take advantage of the strengths of a particular scripting language. For example, VBScript features extensive support for arrays, while JScript doesn't. You can create a script that makes use of VBScript's arrays and then pass this information back to JScript where you can then take advantage of JScript's extensive mathematical functions to manipulate the data in the arrays.

 You'll find specific examples of combining scripting languages throughout this book. For specific pointers and helpful tips, see "Combining JScript and VBScript" in Chapter 6.

Referencing external objects and type libraries

External objects and type libraries enable you to extend the functionality of Windows scripts. With external objects, you can gain additional features. With type libraries, you can define sets of constants to use with scripts.

Windows scripts can use external objects and type libraries as long as those objects and libraries are defined appropriately for use with WSH. External objects must be defined as ActiveX objects and installed on the system that is running the script. Type libraries must be accessible for external calls and saved as .tlb, .olb, or .dll files.

When you use external objects in scripts, you need a way to tell your system about an object. You do this with the `classid` attribute of the `object` element. The `classid` attribute is a reference to the globally unique identifier (GUID) for the ActiveX object you want to use. Each ActiveX object has a GUID, and when the object is installed on a system, this value is stored in the Windows Registry. An ActiveX object has the same GUID on your system as it does on any other system.

The value {0002DF01-0000-0000-C000-000000000046} is the GUID for Internet Explorer. This value is also referred to as the CLSID or class ID for Internet Explorer. Your system accesses the appropriate object by looking up the class ID in the Windows Registry. Using the `classid` attribute, you reference controls by their CLSID value, such as:

```
<object classid="clsid:0002DF01-0000-0000-C000-000000000046" />
```

 In the previous example, the curly braces are removed from the CLSID. You must remove the curly braces from all CLSIDs before referencing them.

You are probably wondering how to obtain such a monstrous CLSID value. The easiest way to obtain the CLSID value is through the Registry Editor. You can run the Registry Editor by starting regedit.exe (or regedt32.exe).

As shown in Figure 5-2, the Registry Editor files entries by category into directories. For OLE and ActiveX objects, the directory you want to use is the HKEY_CLASSES_ROOT directory. Although the Registry Editor features a Find function under the Edit menu, this feature is useful only if you know the exact name of the object for which you are searching. Therefore, you will probably want to browse for the object you are looking for. To do this, select HKEY_CLASSES_ROOT on the local machine from the Window menu. With the HKEY_CLASSES_ROOT folder open, you will see folders for each registered item. Entries are listed by file extension, name, and GUID. The named entries are what you are looking for. Many ActiveX objects are filed beginning with the keyword "Internet."

FIGURE 5-2

Working with the Windows Registry

When you find the entry you are looking for, click in its folder to view subfolders associated with the entry. The CLSID subfolder contains the CLSID you need, so click on the CLSID subfolder associated with the entry. Now, in the right pane of the Registry Editor, you should see the CLSID associated with the entry.

Double-click on the CLSID entry in the right pane to display the Edit String dialog box. With the CLSID highlighted, you can press Ctrl+C to copy the CLSID to the clipboard. When you are ready to use the CLSID, paste the value from the clipboard using Ctrl+V.

Before you can use the object, you need to create a reference to it. You do this by giving the object an identifier, such as IE for Internet Explorer. This identifier is assigned with the id attribute, such as:

```
<job id="WorkwithIE">
  <object ID="IE"
   classid="clsid:0002DF01-0000-0000-C000-000000000046" />
  <script language="VBScript" src="useie.vbs" />
</job>
```

Once you create an object reference, you can work with the object's methods and properties as you would any other object. The object is also available to multiple scripts associated with the current job.

The Reference element can also use CLSIDs to reference type libraries containing constants that you want to use in your scripts. With the Reference element, you set the CLSID with the guid attribute and should also specify the library version with the version attribute. If you do not specify a version, version 1.0 is assumed. Because you are referencing a GUID directly, you do not need the CLSID: prefix and you can use these attributes as follows:

```
<job id="WorkwithTypeLib">
  <reference guid="0002DF01-0000-0000-C000-000000000046"
            version=1.2/>
  <script language="VBScript" src="uselib.vbs" />
</job>
```

Rather than specifying the guid and version, you can specify a file location for the type library using the url attribute. When you do this, you set the relative or absolute location of the library file. In the source code, you must then create instances of the object class or classes that the library contains.

 If using CLSIDs and the Registry seems like a lot of work, that's because it is. In practice, you'll probably want to create instances of objects within scripts rather than reference external objects. To do this, you'll use the CreateObject() method of the WScript object. You learn more about CreateObject() in Chapter 6.

Setting job properties

Another element you may want to work with in a batch script is <?job ?>. This element sets error-handling instructions for the scripting host on a per-job basis. Each job in a .wsf file can have a separate <?job ?> element. The basic syntax for <?job ?> is:

```
<?job error="flag"
      debug="flag" ?>
```

where *flag* is a Boolean value, such as True or False. You can use the error and debug attributes as follows:

- error: Set to true to allow error messages for syntax or runtime errors. Default is false.

- debug: Set to true to enable debugging. When enabled, you can start the script debugger. Default is false. (This assumes a debugger is configured.)

Listing 5-5 shows an example of using error-handling in a script. Note that each job has a separate instruction.

LISTING 5-5

Setting Special Instructions in a Batch Script

errorhandling.wsf

```
<package>
<job id="Backup">
<?job error="true" ?>
  <reference URL="file:c:\components\comp.lib">
  <script language="VBScript" src="backupset1.vbs" />
  <script language="VBScript" src="backupset2.vbs" />
  <script language="VBScript" src="backupset3.vbs" />
</job>
<job id="Restore">
<?job error="true" ?>
  <reference url="file:c:\components\comp.lib">
  <script language="VBScript" src="restore.vbs" />
</job>
</package>
```

Setting parsing instructions

The <?XML ?> element enables you to set parsing instructions for the .wsf file. If you use this element, the batch script is parsed as XML. The element has two attributes: version and standalone.

You use the version attribute to set the version of the XML specification to which the file conforms, such as 1.0. You use the standalone attribute to specify whether the file includes a reference to an external Document Type Definition (DTD). Normally, you want to set the value of standalone to Yes, which indicates that the batch script is a standalone document that does not use an external DTD.

If used, parsing instructions are set on the first line of the .wsf file; for example:

```
<?XML version="1.0" standalone="yes" ?>
<package>
<job id="job1">
</job>
<job id="job2">
</job>
</package>
```

Each file should have only one parsing instruction.

Documentation and Usage

Several elements are used for providing instructions to a user on how to execute the script. The tags <description>, <example>, <named>, <unnamed>, and <usage> are all grouped together within a <runtime> element.

For example, Listing 5-6 shows the use of the <runtime> along with other elements to provide usage instructions for the script.

LISTING 5-6

Runtime Documentation

runtimedemo.wsf

```
<job>
    <runtime>
<description>This script demonstrates the documentation elements</description>
        <named
            name="globalcatalog"
            helpstring="A global catalog server to run the script against"
            type="string"
            required="true"
        />
<unnamed
    name="object"
    helpstring="the objects in the global catalog"
    many="true"
    required="2"
/>

<example>Example: RuntimeDemo /globalcatalog:GCServer1 userAccount1 group1
    </example>
    </runtime>
    <script language="JScript">
      if (!WScript.Arguments.Named.Exists("globalcatalog"))
     {
        WScript.Arguments.ShowUsage();
     }
    // ...do an interesting script here...
    </script>
</job>
```

Output

```
This script demonstrates the documentation elements
Usage: runtimedemo.wsf /globalcatalog:value object1 object2 [object3...]
```

```
Options:

globalcatalog : A global catalog server to run the script against
object        : the objects in the global catalog
Example: RuntimeDemo /globalcatalog:GCServer1 userAccount1 group1
```

The <usage> element overrides all other elements in the <runtime> XML block. It is called in the same way as the other elements. For example, adding the <usage> element to the runtimedemo.wsf in Listing 5-6:

```
 <runtime>
<usage>
This overrides the other elements.
</usage>
<description>This script demonstrates the documentation elements
    </description>
        <named
            name="globalcatalog"
            helpstring="A global catalog server to run the script
                        against"
            type="string"
            required="true"
        />
<unnamed
    name="object"
    helpstring="the objects in the global catalog"
    many="true"
    required="2"
/>
```

produces the following output:

```
This overrides the other elements.
```

Finally, the <resource> element allows the developer a way to make strings or textual data more flexible to reference in the script. This is an easy way to provide strings that can be used for localization, as in the following example:

```
<job>
<resource id="localizedWelcome">
    Bonjour World!
</resource>
<script language="VBScript">
```

```
localString=getResource("localizedWelcome")
wscript.echo localString

</script>
</job>
```

This code produces the following output:

```
Bonjour World!
```

Summary

As you've seen in this chapter, the Windows Script Host provides a versatile environment for working with scripts. You can execute scripts from the command line, from the Windows desktop, and from Windows Explorer. WSH also supports drag and drop. Both CScript and WScript support batch script files as well. With batch script files, you can combine multiple types of scripts in a single file.

Chapter 6

VBScript and JScript Scripting Basics

N ow that you know a bit about creating script files and running scripts, you are ready to start working with the features Windows Script Host has to offer. You'll find that WSH structures are surprisingly powerful. You can perform many advanced tasks with only a few basic commands.

Key WSH Objects

As you learned in Chapter 1, the WSH object model contains exposed and unexposed objects. Exposed objects are the ones you can access directly in your scripts and include `WScript`, `WScript.WshNetwork`, and `WScript.WshShell`. In this chapter, you work with basic methods and properties of each of these objects.

Table 6-1 lists the methods and properties of `WScript`.

IN THIS CHAPTER

Displaying text strings

Examining script information

Accessing environment variables

Running programs from within scripts

Combining JScript and VBScript

TABLE 6-1

WScript Methods and Properties

Methods	Properties
CreateObject	Application
DisconnectObject	Arguments
Echo	FullName
GetObject	Name
Quit	Path

continued

TABLE 6-1	*(continued)*
Methods	**Properties**
Sleep	ScriptFullName
	ScriptName
	Version

WScript.WshNetwork is the object you'll use to manage network resources such as printers and network drives. The methods and properties of this object are listed in Table 6-2.

TABLE 6-2

WScript.WshNetwork Methods and Properties

Methods	**Properties**
AddPrinterConnection	ComputerName
EnumNetworkDrives	UserDomain
EnumPrinterConnection	UserName
MapNetworkDrive	
RemoveNetworkDrive	
RemovePrinterConnection	
SetDefaultPrinter	

Another important object is WScript.WshShell. You'll use this object to work with the environment and the operating system. Table 6-3 lists the methods and properties of this object.

TABLE 6-3

WScript.WshShell Methods and Properties

Methods	**Properties**
CreateShortcut	Environment
ExpandEnvironmentStrings	SpecialFolders
LogEvent	
Popup	

Methods	Properties
RegDelete	
RegRead	
RegWrite	
Run	

Displaying Text Strings

The first command you are going to learn about is Echo. You call Echo as a method of the WScript object. If you are using CScript and are in interactive mode, output from Echo is written to the command line. If you are using WScript and are in interactive mode, output from Echo is displayed in a pop-up dialog box.

Using Echo

You can use Echo in VBScript and JScript as shown in Listing 6-1. Note the difference in syntax between the two. With VBScript, you pass Echo strings and can use the standard concatenation rules to add strings together. You can also pass values in a comma-separated list. In JScript, you must use parentheses and can only pass values in a comma-separated list, which is then concatenated for you.

LISTING 6-1

Using Echo in VBScript and JScript

VBScript
echo.vbs

```
theAnswer = "Yes"
WScript.Echo 1, 2, 3
WScript.Echo "Run, run, run!"
WScript.Echo "1: " + theAnswer
```

JScript
echo.js

```
theAnswer = "Yes"
WScript.Echo(1, 2, 3)
WScript.Echo("Run, run, run!")
WScript.Echo("1: ", theAnswer)
```

Running the Echo script

You can run these scripts from the command line or from Windows Explorer. At the command line, change to the directory containing the scripts and then type:

```
cscript echo.vbs
```

or

```
cscript echo.js
```

The following output is then written to the command line:

```
1 2 3
Run, run, run!
1: Yes
```

With Windows Explorer, you access the directory containing the scripts and then double-click the script you want to run. Each call to `Echo` produces a separate pop-up dialog box. The first dialog box displays 1 2 3. When you click OK to close the first dialog box, a second dialog box displays `Run, run, run!`. When you click OK to close the second pop-up, a third dialog box displays `1: Yes`. Click OK again and then the script completes execution.

Examining Script Information

To accommodate a variety of user environments, your scripts will often need to test for version information before running. For example, if the user system is running the version 4 script engines, you don't want to try to run a version 5 script on the system because doing so could have unpredictable results. To prevent problems, you should at least check the script host version and the script engine version. Other scripting information you may want to check includes the location of the script hosts on the user's system, arguments passed in to the script at startup, and environment variables set on the system.

Last, with user scripts, you also may want to run other applications from within a script. For example, you may want to create a logon script that provides a menu for selecting the type of applications the user may want to start, such as Development Tools or Productivity Tools. Then, based on the response, you would start the related set of applications.

Getting script host information

When you want to examine information related to the script hosts (WScript or CScript), you use these properties of the `WScript` object:

- `WScript.Fullname`: Returns the full path to the current script host, such as:
  `C:\WIN2000\System32\cscript.exe`

- WScript.Path: Returns the path to the script host, such as:
  C:\WIN2000\System32

- WScript.Version: Returns the script host version, such as:
  5.1

You can use these properties in VBScript and JScript as shown in Listing 6-2. Note the If Else condition used to call main() and error() functions. If the version is greater than or equal to 5, the main() function is executed. Otherwise, the error() function is executed.

LISTING 6-2

Validating Script Host Information

VBScript
wshinfo.vbs

```
vs = WScript.Version

If vs >= 5 Then
  main()
Else
  error()
End If


Function main
 WScript.Echo "Starting execution..."
End Function

Function error
 WScript.Echo "WSH version error!"
End Function
```

JScript
wsinfo.js

```
vs = WScript.Version

if (vs >= 5) {
main()
}
else {
error()
}
```

continued

LISTING 6-2   *(continued)*

```
function main() {
  WScript.Echo("Starting execution...")
}

function error() {
  WScript.Echo("WSH version error!")
}
```

If you use script host information to determine whether to run a script, you may want to use the Quit method. The Quit method quits execution of a script and returns an error code. For example, if you wanted to return an error code of 1 you would use:

VBScript

```
WScript.Quit 1
```

JScript

```
WScript.Quit(1)
```

Listing 6-3 shows how to rewrite the previous example using the Quit method. Here, you eliminate the error() method and replace the check for a version greater than or equal to 5 with a check for a version less than 5. If the version is less than 5, the script quits executing and returns an error code of 1. So, Listing 6-3 should execute the main() function because the version of WSH is greater than 5.

LISTING 6-3

Ending Script Execution with an Error Code

VBScript
wshquit.vbs

```
vs = WScript.Version

If vs < 5 Then
 WScript.Quit 1
End If

main()

Function main
WScript.Echo "Starting execution..."
End Function
```

JScript
wshquit.js

```
vs = WScript.Version

if (vs < 5) {
 WScript.Quit(1)
}

main()
function main() {
WScript.Echo("Starting execution...")
}
```

Getting scripting information

Just as you can examine information related to the script host, you can also examine information related to the script engine and the current script. To examine properties of the script engine, you use built-in functions available in VBScript and JScript. To examine script properties, you use properties of the WScript object. Following is a list of these functions and properties:

- ScriptEngine(): A built-in function that returns the script engine language, such as VBScript or JScript.

- ScriptEngineMajorVersion(): A built-in function that returns the script engine version, such as 5 or 6.

- ScriptEngineMinorVersion(): A built-in function that returns the revision number of the script engine, such as 1 or 2.

- ScriptEngineBuildVersion(): A built-in function that returns the build version of the script engine, such as 3715.

- ScriptFullName: A property of WScript that returns the full path to the current script, such as c:\scripts\createspreadsheet.vbs.

- ScriptName A property of WScript that returns the file name of the current script, such as createspreadsheet.vbs.

Listing 6-4 shows an example of how you can use these functions and properties in a script. The listing builds the script information using two functions: GetSEInfo and GetScript. The GetSEInfo function returns script engine information. The GetScript function returns script path and name information.

LISTING 6-4

Getting Script Information

VBScript
scriptinfo.vbs

```
WScript.Echo GetSEInfo()

WScript.Echo GetScript()

Function GetSEInfo
  Dim info
  info = ""
  info = ScriptEngine & " Version "
  info = info & ScriptEngineMajorVersion & "."
  info = info & ScriptEngineMinorVersion & "."
  info = info & ScriptEngineBuildVersion
  GetSEInfo = info
End Function

Function GetScript
  Dim info
  scr = "Name: "
  scr = WScript.ScriptName & " Full path: "
  scr = scr & WScript.ScriptFullName
  GetScript =  scr
End Function
```

JScript
scriptinfo.js

```
se = GetSEInfo()
WScript.Echo(se)

sc = GetScript()
WScript.Echo(sc)

function GetSEInfo()
{
   var info;
   info = "";
   info += ScriptEngine() + " Version";
   info += ScriptEngineMajorVersion() + ".";
   info += ScriptEngineMinorVersion() + ".";
   info += ScriptEngineBuildVersion();
   return(info);
```

```
}
function GetScript()
{
    var scr;
    scr = "Name: ";
    scr += WScript.ScriptName + " Full path: ";
    scr += WScript.ScriptFullName;
    return(scr);
}
```

Getting script arguments

Arguments set information needed by the script at runtime and are often needed with Windows scripts. WSH interprets any text following the script name as arguments. For example, in the following code:

```
cscript testarg.vbs Test Code 52
```

the first argument is Test, the second is Code, and the third is 52. As you can see, spaces are used to determine where one argument ends and another begins. This can cause some problems if you want to enter multiple words as a single argument. The workaround is to enclose the argument in double quotation marks, as follows:

```
cscript testarg.vbs "Test Code 52"
```

Now the first argument is interpreted as Test Code 52.

Script arguments are placed in a container object called WshArguments. You can think of container objects as arrays with properties that are used to work with elements in the array. You need to create an instance of WshArguments before you can work with it. You do this with the WScript. Arguments property. For example:

VBScript

```
Set theArgs = WScript.Arguments
```

JScript

```
var theArgs = WScript.Arguments
```

 Note the use of Set and var in the example. In VBScript, you assign an object reference to a variable with the Set statement. In JScript, you do so with the var statement.

After you create the object instance, you can use the Item property of the WshArguments object to access arguments passed to a script according to their index position in the WshArguments object.

The first script argument is at index position 0, the second at 1, and so on. You can assign argument 1 to a variable as follows:

VBScript

```
arg1 = theArgs.Item(0)
```

JScript

```
arg1 = theArgs.Item(0)
```

Both VBScript and JScript support a property for determining how many arguments were passed in as well. In VBScript, you use the Count property. In JScript, you use the corresponding Count() method or the Length property. If two arguments were passed to a script, these statements would return 2:

VBScript

```
numArgs = theArgs.Count
```

JScript

```
numArgs = theArgs.Length
numArgs = theArgs.Count()
```

You can also use For loops to examine each argument in turn. When you do this, use the argument count to determine how many times to loop while examining the WshArguments object. Then use the Item() method to examine or display the value of each argument. An example of this technique is shown in Listing 6-5.

LISTING 6-5

Examining Script Arguments Using a Loop

VBScript
getargs.vbs

```
Set theArgs = WScript.Arguments
For I = 0 to theArgs.Count - 1
  WScript.Echo theArgs(I)
Next
For Each i IN theArgs
  WScript.Echo i
Next
```

JScript
getargs.js

```
var theArgs = WScript.Arguments
for (x = 0; x < theArgs.Length; x++)
```

```
{
   WScript.Echo(theArgs.Item(x))
}
```

Working with Environment Variables

Environment variables play an important role in Windows scripting. In Windows scripts, you can access environment variables is several ways. In this section, we focus on two techniques. The first technique is one that you can rely on time and again, rather than the other technique, which may cause problems in your scripts.

Understanding environment variables

Environment variables come from many different sources. Just as you can look around and describe your personal surroundings, Windows looks around and describes what it sees in terms of processors, users, paths, and so on. Some variables are built into the operating system or derived from the system hardware during startup. These variables are called *built-in system variables* and are available to all Windows processes regardless of whether anyone is logged in interactively. System variables can also come from the Windows Registry. These variables are stored in the Registry's HKEY_LOCAL_MACHINE hive and are set when the system boots.

Other variables are set during logon and are called *built-in user variables*. The built-in user variables available are the same no matter who is logged on at the computer and, as you might expect, are only valid during an actual logon session. Because of this, shell scripts executed with the AT command cannot rely on user variables to be available. User variables can also come from the Windows NT Registry where they are stored in the Registry's HKEY_CURRENT_USER hive and are set during user login. These user variables are valid only for the current user and are not available for other users.

Table 6-4 lists the key built-in system and user variables you may want to work with in shell scripts. Additional variables can be created by users and the operating system.

TABLE 6-4

Built-in System and User Variables

Variable Name	Description	Sample Value
`ALLUSERS PROFILE`	Default profile for users	`F:\Documents and Settings\ All Users`
`APPDATA`	Location of the current user's application data	`F:\Documents and Settings\ wrstanek\Application Data`

continued

TABLE 6-4	(continued)	
Variable Name	**Description**	**Sample Value**
COMMON PROGRAMFILES	Location of common program files on the computer	`F:\Program Files\Common Files`
COMPUTERNAME	Computer account name	`Pluto`
COMSPEC	Complete path to the current instance of CMD.EXE	`C:\WIN2000\system32\cmd.exe`
HOMEDRIVE	Drive name on which the current user's profile resides	`C:`
HOMEPATH	Location of the root directory on the home drive	`\`
LOGONSERVER	UNC name of the logon domain controller	`\\Sun`
NUMBER_OF _PROCESSORS	Number of CPUs on the system	`3`
OS	Operating system name	`Windows_NT`
PATH	Executable path used by Windows	Path=C:\;C:\WIN2000system32;C:\WIN2000
PATHEXT	File name extensions for executable files	.COM;.EXE;.BAT;.CMD;.VBS;.VBE;.JS;.VBE;.WSF;.WSH
PROCESSOR _ARCHITECTURE	Architecture of the processors	`X86`
PROMPT	Command prompt settings on the current machine	`$P$G`
SYSTEMDRIVE	Drive name on which the operating system resides	`C:`
SYSTEMROOT	Path to the operating system	`C:\WIN2000`
USERDOMAIN	Name of the logon domain	`WEBONE`
USERNAME	Username of the current user	`WRSTANEK`
USERPROFILE	Path to the current user's user profile	`F:\Documents and Settings\WRSTANEK`

Accessing environment variables

Environment variables are accessed via the `WScript.WshShell` object, so you need to create an instance of `WScript.WshShell` before you can work with environment variables. Unfortunately, there isn't a property of the `WScript` object that you can use to return the `WScript.WshShell` object. Because of this, you must create the object instance yourself. You can do this with the `CreateObject` method of the `WScript` object. For example:

VBScript

```
Set ws = WScript.CreateObject("WScript.Shell")
```

JScript

```
var ws = WScript.CreateObject("WScript.Shell");
```

Next, as shown in Listing 6-6, use the `ExpandEnvironmentStrings()` method of `WScript.Shell` to specify the environment variable you want to work with. All of the environment variables described previously in Table 6-4 are available. You can use the paths returned by `ExpandEnvironment Strings()` to set file and directory locations.

LISTING 6-6

Using Environment Variables

VBScript
envar.vbs

```
Set WshShell = WScript.CreateObject("WScript.Shell")
WScript.Echo WshShell.ExpandEnvironmentStrings("%PATH%")
WScript.Echo WshShell.ExpandEnvironmentStrings("%COMPUTERNAME%")
```

JScript
envar.js

```
var WshShell = WScript.CreateObject("WScript.Shell")
WScript.Echo(WshShell.ExpandEnvironmentStrings("%PATH%"))
WScript.Echo(WshShell.ExpandEnvironmentStrings("%COMPUTERNAME%"))
```

Working with environment variables: An alternative

In Windows scripts, you can access environment variables in several ways. In the previous section, we examined a technique that you can rely on time and again to get the job done. In this section, we examine an alternative technique that may or may not work in your particular circumstance.

With this technique, you access environment variables through `WshEnvironment`; then you use the `WshShell.Environment` method to specify which type of environment variables to work with. Environment variables, broken down into four possible classes, are as follows:

- `System`: Refers to system environment variables
- `User`: Refers to user environment variables

- Volatile: Refers to temporary environment variables
- Process: Refers to process variables

You specify the type of environment variable you want to work with as follows:

VBScript

```
Set ws = WScript.CreateObject("WScript.Shell")
Set sysEnv = ws.Environment("SYSTEM")
```

JScript

```
var ws = WScript.CreateObject("WScript.Shell");
var sysEnv = ws.Environment("SYSTEM")
```

Afterward, you can work with individual environment variables, as shown in Listing 6-7. As you work with the environment variable classes, you'll often find that a variable you want to use isn't available in a particular class. If this happens, you'll have to use a different class. Rather than learning which variables are used with which classes, we recommend using the technique outlined in the previous section.

LISTING 6-7

Working with Environment Variable Classes

VBScript
sysenv.vbs

```
Set WshShell = WScript.CreateObject("WScript.Shell")

Set sysEnv = WshShell.Environment("SYSTEM")
os = sysEnv("OS")
thePath = sysEnv("PATH")
Set usrEnv = WshShell.Environment("USER")
inc = usrEnv("INCLUDE")
theLib = usrEnv("LIB")

Set usrEnv = WshShell.Environment("VOLATILE")
lsvr = usrEnv("LOGONSERVER")
```

JScript
sysenv.js

```
var WshShell = WScript.CreateObject("WScript.Shell");

var sysEnv = WshShell.Environment("SYSTEM")
os = sysEnv("OS")
thePath = sysEnv("PATH")
var usrEnv = WshShell.Environment("USER")
inc = usrEnv("INCLUDE")
```

```
theLib = usrEnv("LIB")

var usrEnv = WshShell.Environment("VOLATILE")
lsvr = usrEnv ("LOGONSERVER")
```

Running Programs from Within Scripts

The Run() method of the WScript.Shell object lets you run programs. You can:

- Start Windows applications, such as Microsoft Word, Excel, or PowerPoint
- Run command-line programs, such as shutdown.exe or regedt32.exe
- Run command shell scripts

 **TIP** Not only can you run programs, you can also pass in arguments and keystrokes. You can activate program windows and pause programs temporarily as well.

Starting an application

To use the Run() method, create an instance of WScript.Shell and then access Run(). The following example starts the Windows Notepad in VBScript and JScript:

VBScript

```
Set ws =  WScript.CreateObject("WScript.Shell")
ws.Run("notepad")
```

JScript

```
var ws = WScript.CreateObject("WScript.Shell");
ws.Run("notepad")
```

The file path you pass to Run() is parsed by WSH. This allows you to use any available environment variable in the file path. However, you must tell WSH that you are using an environment variable that has a path that needs to be expanded. Do so by enclosing the variable name in percent signs (%). You can use %SystemRoot% for the SystemRoot environment variable, shown as follows:

VBScript

```
Set ws = WScript.CreateObject("WScript.Shell")
ws.Run("%SystemRoot%\system32\notepad")
```

JScript

```
var ws =  WScript.CreateObject("WScript.Shell");
ws.Run("%SystemRoot%\\system32\\notepad")
```

 As you can see in the example, JScript file paths are referenced in a slightly different way than they are in VBScript. The reason is that JScript treats the slash character as a special character and, as a result, you must escape it with another slash character.

Passing arguments to an application

You can also pass in arguments to command-shell programs and to Windows applications that support command-line parameters. Simply follow the application name with the parameters you want to use. Be sure to add a space between the application name and the parameters. The following example starts Notepad with the active script accessed for editing:

VBScript

```
Set ws = WScript.CreateObject("WScript.Shell")
ws.Run("notepad " & WScript.ScriptFullName)
```

JScript

```
var ws = WScript.CreateObject("WScript.Shell");
ws.Run("notepad " + WScript.ScriptFullName)
WScript.ScriptFullName)
```

Additional features for Run

The Run() method has more features than you'll probably ever use; but just in case, you can set additional features using the following syntax:

```
object.Run ("command", [winStyle], ["waitOnReturn"])
```

in which command is the program or shell script you want to run, winStyle is the window style, and waitOnReturn specifies whether the script should wait or continue execution. If waitOnReturn is not specified or set to False, the script continues execution without waiting on process termination. If waitOnReturn is set to True, script execution pauses until the application stops running or is exited — at which time, the Run() method returns any error code returned by the application, and script execution resumes.

If you want to track error codes, assign Run() to a variable and then check the error code returned by the application. Generally, a non-zero error code indicates an error of some kind. Listing 6-8 shows how you can run a shell script and check the error code the script returned. In this example, note that VBScript allows you to evaluate the error code as a number, but JScript treats the error code as a string.

 Note if you try to run the scripts in Listing 6-8, you will get a "file not found error" because the example illustrates how to call a file, in this case log.bat, and we have not actually created this file.

LISTING 6-8

Checking for Run Errors

VBScript
runerrors.vbs

```
Set ws = WScript.CreateObject("WScript.Shell")
ret = ws.Run("log.bat",0,"TRUE")
If ret = 0 Then
    WScript.Echo "No error"
Else
    WScript.Echo "Error"
End If
```

JScript
runerrors.js

```
var ws =
  WScript.CreateObject
  ("WScript.Shell");
ret = ws.Run("log.bat",0,"TRUE")
if (ret="0") {
    WScript.Echo("No error")
} else {
    WScript.Echo("Error")
}
```

 If you specify an invalid program or script name, WSH won't report an error and an error code won't be set. In this case, `ret` would be a null string.

Table 6-5 shows the options you can use for window style. The most useful styles are 0 for running programs and scripts in the background, and 1 for displaying the window normally. You can use the other options to minimize or maximize the application.

TABLE 6-5

Window Style Options

Option	Description
0	Runs a program or script in the background
1	Runs a program or script normally and displays a window if necessary; generally, use this option before options 2–10.
2	Activates a program and displays it as a minimized window

continued

TABLE 6-5	*(continued)*
Option	**Description**
3	Activates a program and displays it as a maximized window
4	Activates a program and displays it in its most recent size and position
5	Activates a program and displays it in its current size and position
6	Minimizes the specified window and activates the next top-level window in the Z order
7	Minimizes the program window without activating it
8	Displays the program window in its current state but doesn't activate it
9	Activates and restores the window; if the window is minimized or maximized, the system restores it to its original size and position.
10	Sets the display state based on the state of the Windows script

Running Scripts Remotely

Windows Script Host version 5.6 introduced the ability to remotely execute scripts. This is achieved with the new WshController object. The remote script can be any one of the valid script file types, such as .vbs, .js, .wsh, and so on. It's even possible to load scripts onto multiple remote computers and start them all simultaneously.

The WshController object has one method called CreateScript. The method takes the path to the script to be executed, and specifies the remote machine to run the script on. The file path can even be located on a file share.

Before the scripts can be executed on the remote computer, security must be configured to allow remote script execution. You can do this by by editing the registry. Add a new REG_SZ subkey to HKEY_LOCAL_MACHINE\SOFTWARE\Microsoft\Windows Script Host\Settings.

Setting the key to a value of 1 enables remote execution, and a value of 0 or removing the key disables remote execution. You will also need to add your account to the remote machine's Local Administrators group. It is not possible to use alternate credentials when executing remote scripts. Let's now take a look at an example shown in Listing 6-9: a controller script, remotecaller, which executes the script callme. If successful, the callme script will create a text file called helloworld.txt.

LISTING 6-9

Remote Execution

VBScript
remotecaller.vbs

```vbscript
dim oController, oRemoteScript
set oController = createobject("WSHController")
set oRemoteScript = oController.CreateScript("C:\temp\callme.vbs","client")
wscript.connectObject oRemoteScript, "remote_"
oRemoteScript.Execute
do while oRemoteScript.Status <> 2
 wscript.sleep 100
loop
Sub remote_Error
 dim theError
 set theError = oRemoteScript.Error
 wscript.echo "Error " & theError.Number & " - Line: " & theError.Line & ",
    Char: " & theError.Character & vbCrLf\
end sub
```

Callme.vbs

```vbscript
set fso = CreateObject("Scripting.FileSystemObject")
set fout = fso.CreateTextFile("C:\temp\helloworld.txt",true)
fout.WriteLine Now
fout.Close
```

JScript
remotecaller.js

```javascript
var oController = WScript.CreateObject("WSHController");
var oRemoteScript = oController.CreateScript("C:\\temp\\callme.js","client");
WScript.ConnectObject(oRemoteScript, "remote_")
oRemoteScript.Execute();

while (oRemoteScript.Status != 2) {
 WScript.Sleep(100);
}

function remote_Error()
{
 var theError = oRemoteScript.Error;
 WScript.Echo("Error " + theError.Number + " - Line: " + theError.Line + ",
    Char: " + theError.Character)
}
```

continued

LISTING 6-9   *(continued)*

Callme.js

```
var fso = new ActiveXObject("Scripting.FileSystemObject");
var fout = fso.CreateTextFile("C:\\temp\\helloworld.txt",true);
fout.WriteLine(new Date);
fout.Close();
```

There are some interesting things to note from these scripts. First, the loop in remotecaller monitors the status of the remote script. The possible status values are:

- **0:** The remote script has not yet started to run.
- **1:** The remote script is running.
- **2:** The remote script has finished running.

Also, the remotecaller script implements error checking with the WshRemoteError object. The error handler function is called on an error event from the connection established in the `connectObject` method. There are two other events that can also be hooked `Start` and `_End`. To use these events, simply add the corresponding functions similar to the Error function in Listing 6-9.

Combining JScript and VBScript

You'll often encounter situations in which you implement a script in one scripting language and then wish you could use features of another scripting language in the same script. Well, when you use batch scripts (.WSF files), you can combine scripts written in JScript and scripts written in VBScript in the same file. You can then call functions in one script from another script and return values to the caller.

In VBScript, you can:

- Call JScript functions and return values

In JScript, you can:

- Call VBScript subroutines to execute a section of code
- Call VBScript functions and return values

When the function or subroutine you've called finishes executing, control returns to the caller and execution of the original script continues from there. Listing 6-10 provides a detailed example of calling VBScript and JScript functions. You can use this technique in your own scripts as well.

LISTING 6-10

Combining Functions of Multiple Scripting Languages

cfunctions.wsf

```
<!-- Author: William R. Stanek -->
<!-- Descr: Combined example for JScript and VBScript -->

<Job ID="MyJob">
<Script LANGUAGE="JScript">
function GetInfoJS()
{
    var info;
    info = "";
    info += ScriptEngine() + " Version ";
    info += ScriptEngineMajorVersion() + ".";
    info += ScriptEngineMinorVersion() + ".";
    info += ScriptEngineBuildVersion();
    return(info);
}

</Script>
<Script LANGUAGE="VBSCript">
Function GetInfoVB
  Dim info
  info = ""
  info = ScriptEngine & " Version "
  info = info & ScriptEngineMajorVersion & "."
  info = info & ScriptEngineMinorVersion & "."
  info = info & ScriptEngineBuildVersion
  GetInfoVB =  info
End Function
</Script>

<Script LANGUAGE="VBSCript">
WScript.Echo "VB2VB: " + GetInfoVB()
WScript.Echo "VB2JS: " + GetInfoJS()
</Script>

<Script LANGUAGE="JSCript">
versionVB = GetInfoVB()
WScript.Echo("JS2VB: ", versionVB)

versionJS = GetInfoJS()
WScript.Echo("JS2JS: ", versionJS)
</Script>
</Job>
```

continued

LISTING 6-10   *(continued)*

Output

```
VB2VB: VBScript Version 5.7.18068
VB2JS: JScript Version 5.7.18068
JS2VB:  VBScript Version 5.7.18068
JS2JS:  JScript Version 5.7.18068
```

You'll find additional examples of combining VBScript and JScript throughout this book. In particular, examine Part V, "Windows Scripting Libraries" where you'll find many advanced examples of working with multiple scripting languages.

Summary

In this chapter, you learned scripting basics such as displaying text strings and examining script information. You also learned how to access environment variables and run programs from within scripts. As you've seen, both VBScript and JScript can be used to perform these actions — although each scripting language has a different syntax. As we explore more of the features of Windows Script Host, we'll point out many additional areas where VBScript and JScript differ. If you are interested in using both scripting languages, be sure to keep track of these differences.

Chapter 7

Input, Output, and Error Handling with VBScript and JScript

IN THIS CHAPTER

Understanding input and output

Using input boxes, message boxes, and pop-up dialog boxes

Standard input and output

Detecting and handling errors

Displaying output to readers using `WScript.Echo` is useful but you often need to implement more powerful techniques in your scripts. For example, you may want to display a dialog box that allows users to make a selection, or you may want users to input a file path or directory name. In either case, you need to display a prompt that enables users to pass information to a script. This prompt can be an input box that allows users to type in text, a message box with clickable buttons, or a pop-up dialog box with clickable buttons.

As you work with input and output, you'll also need to learn error-handling techniques. If a user enters the wrong information, the script should handle the error appropriately. Some error-handling techniques are very basic, such as using control loops to ensure that users enter information. Other error-handling techniques are more advanced and usually involve the built-in error-detection capabilities of VBScript and JScript.

Input and Output Essentials

Chapter 6 discusses how you can use `WScript.Arguments` to access arguments passed to a script, and how you can display output with `WScript.Echo`. What that chapter doesn't discuss, however, is how Windows Script Host handles these standard input and output mechanisms. Basic I/O is handled through the standard input and standard output streams — much like I/O is handled in most programming languages. Errors are written to the standard error stream.

The WScript object has three special properties for working with the input, output, and error streams. These special properties are:

- StdIn: A read-only input stream
- StdOut: A write-only output stream
- StdErr: A write-only error stream

These properties return text stream objects. These objects are similar to the FileSystemObject .TextStream object, discussed in Chapter 9. The properties and methods for these streams are listed in Table 7-1.

TABLE 7-1

Methods and Properties of Input, Output, and Error Streams

Methods	Properties
StdIn Stream	
WScript.StdIn.Close()	WScript.StdIn.AtEndOfLine
WScript.StdIn.Read()	WScript.StdIn.AtEndOfStream
WScript.StdIn.ReadAll()	WScript.StdIn.Column
WScript.StdIn.ReadLine()	WScript.StdIn.Line
WScript.StdIn.Skip()	
WScript.StdIn.SkipLine()	
StdErr Stream	
WScript.StdErr.Close()	
WScript.StdErr.Write()	
WScript.StdErr.WriteBlankLines()	
WScript.StdErr.WriteLine()	
StdOut Stream	
WScript.StdOut.Close()	
WScript.StdOut.Write()	
WScript.StdOut.WriteBlankLines()	
WScript.StdOut.WriteLine()	

Windows Script Host exposes these streams whenever you run scripts using the command-line script host, CScript. Because of this, you can use the StdIn, StdOut, and StdErr streams in scripts that you intend to run from the command line. You cannot, however, use these streams in scripts that you run with the graphical script host, WScript.

CROSS-REF You'll find examples that use streams in Chapters 17, 18, and 19.

Using Input Boxes

Input boxes are available in VBScript only. You can think of input boxes as customizable dialog boxes that you can use to get input from users. This input can be any kind of text, such as a file path, the user's login name, or a response to a question.

Input box basics

To create input boxes, use the InputBox() function and add a prompt and title as necessary. In the example shown in Figure 7-1, InputBox() sets a display prompt and a title for the input box using the following statement:

```
Input = InputBox("Please enter the logon ID:","Setup Script")
```

Here, the Input variable holds the value of the user's response and can be used later in the script to test the validity of the input. As shown, the prompt and title you want to use are strings enclosed in double quotation marks and separated with a comma.

FIGURE 7-1

Input boxes are used to get user input. They can have titles and display prompts.

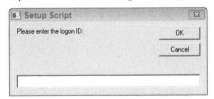

The order of elements in an input box must be exact. You cannot enter a title without entering a prompt — even if the prompt used is just an empty string, such as:

```
Input = InputBox("","Setup Script")
```

Input boxes have an OK button and a Cancel button. If the user types a value and then clicks OK, or types a value and then presses Enter on the keyboard, the value is returned by the input function. The user can click OK or Cancel without entering a value, which will cause the function to return an empty string. To ensure the user enters text, you can use a control loop to examine the value entered.

In the following example, the script continues to loop until the user enters a value:

```
Do
    theInput = InputBox("Enter your name:","Test Script")
Loop While theInput = ""
```

Setting default values for input boxes

If necessary, you can follow the prompt and the title with a default value for the input. This value is then used when the user clicks OK without entering a value. For example, with the logon example, you might want to set the default user to anonymous, like this:

```
Input = InputBox("Please enter the logon ID:","Setup
Script","anonymous")
```

As stated before, the quotes around the default value aren't necessary when you use numeric values, though the order of input parameters is important. If you don't use a prompt or title, you must insert placeholder values; for example:

```
Input = InputBox("Please enter the logon ID:", "","anonymous")
```

Positioning input boxes

By default, input boxes are centered on the screen, but if you want, you can specify where you want it displayed as well. You do this by specifying the *x/y coordinate* for the upper-left corner of the input box. The *x* coordinate sets the horizontal distance in pixels from the left edge of the screen. The *y* coordinate sets the vertical distance in pixels from the top of the screen. The *x* and *y* coordinates follow the prompt and title in sequence. For example:

```
Input = InputBox("Please enter your login name:","Setup
Script",,300,300)
```

If you position an input box, you must always set both coordinates. In the examples for this section, the basic syntax for input boxes is:

```
varA = InputBox("prompt","title",defaultValue,X,Y)
```

where *prompt* is the text to display in the input box, *title* is the title for the input box, and *defaultValue* is the value to use when no input is entered.

Converting input values

Values entered into an input box are interpreted as strings provided they contain alphanumeric characters. If the value entered is a number, the value can be handled as a numeric value. This means you can perform arithmetic operations on the input; for example:

```
Dim theTotal: theTotal=0
For i = 1 to 3
  theTotal = theTotal + InputBox("Enter value " & i, "Compute Average")
```

```
Next
theAvg = theTotal/3
WScript.Echo theAvg
```

If you are looking for a particular type of numeric value such as an integer versus a real number, you can convert the value as necessary. In this example, the user could enter a value such as 1.8 or 2.2, which you handle by converting the input to an integer:

```
Do
    theValue = InputBox("Enter a value 1 to 100:","Setup Script",,300,300)
Loop While (theValue < 1 OR theValue > 100)
theValue = CInt(theValue)
```

Other conversion functions could also be used, such as CDbl() or CCur(). Conversion functions are listed in Chapter 2.

Using Message Boxes

Message boxes are available in VBScript only. You use message boxes to display information and to allow users to make selections. Because message boxes can have customized buttons and icons, they are a bit more complex than input boxes.

Constant	Value	Description
vbCr	Chr(13)	Carriage return
vbCrLf	Chr(13) & Chr(10)	Carriage return–linefeed combination
vbFormFeed	Chr(12)	Form feed; not useful in Microsoft Windows
vbLf	Chr(10)	Line feed
vbNewLine	Chr(13) & Chr(10) or Chr(10)	Platform-specific newline character; whatever is appropriate for the platform
vbNullChar	Chr(0)	Character having the value 0
vbNullString	String having value 0	Not the same as a zero-length string (""); used for calling external procedures
vbTab	Chr(9)	Horizontal tab
vbVerticalTab	Chr(11)	Vertical tab; not useful in Microsoft Windows

Message box basics

The most basic type of message box is one that calls the Msgbox function and displays a message, such as this:

```
Msgbox "Time to run the scripts…"
```

133

When you use a basic message box, you get a plain dialog box with an OK button. To add pizzazz to message boxes, you can customize the dialog box with titles, icons, and multiple button styles. To add these elements to message boxes, use the following syntax:

```
Msgbox "Message to display", buttonType + iconType,"Message box title"
```

As with input boxes, message box parameters must be used in the order specified and you can't skip parameters. For example, if you want to add a title to a message box without specifying a button or icon type, you can use the following command:

```
Msgbox "Time to run the scripts…",,"User Alert!"
```

Adding buttons

As stated previously, the OK button is the default button for all message boxes. However, you can use many different buttons including Yes, No, Cancel, Retry, Ignore, and Abort. Use the following code to add Yes, No, and Cancel buttons to a message box:

```
dim vbYesNoCancel
vbYesNoCancel = 3
Msgbox "Do you want to continue?", vbYesNoCancel
```

In the preceding code, vbYesNoCancel represents the button types you want to add and 3 is the parameter value for this type of button. A message box with the Yes, No, and Cancel buttons is shown in Figure 7-2.

FIGURE 7-2

Message boxes can use Yes, No, and Cancel buttons. They can also use OK, Retry, Ignore, and Abort buttons.

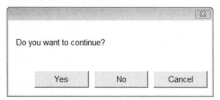

If you want to, you can specify other types of buttons to use as well, such as vbOkCancel or vbAbortRetryIgnore. These button types are constants, which are variables whose values don't change. Because the script engine knows these values, you don't actually have to use the constant and you can refer to the value directly in the call to Msgbox. However, if you do this, you lose the advantage of being able to tell, at a glance, what types of buttons are used with a particular message box.

Table 7-2 provides a complete list of constants you can use to set button types and their corresponding values. These constants represent all of the available button combinations.

TABLE 7-2

Buttons for Message Boxes

Constant	Description	Value
VbOkOnly	Displays the OK button	0
VbOkCancel	Displays OK and Cancel buttons	1
VbAbortRetryIgnore	Displays Abort, Retry, and Ignore buttons	2
VbYesNoCancel	Displays Yes, No, and Cancel buttons	3
VbYesNo	Displays Yes and No buttons	4
VbRetryCancel	Displays Retry and Cancel buttons	5

Adding icons

By default, message boxes use an information icon, but you can change this icon if you want to. Adding a unique icon to a message box is easy. Just keep in mind that buttons and icons are part of the same parameter, which is why you use the plus sign to separate the button types from the icon type. Following is an example message box with an icon:

```
Dim vbYesNo: vbYesNo=4
Dim vbQuestion: vbQuestion=32
Msgbox "Would you like to continue?", vbYesNo + vbQuestion
```

In this example, we've combined the initialization of the value with the actual declaration that sets the value. You can rewrite these statements on separate lines as follows:

```
Dim vbYesNo
vbYesNo=4
Dim vbQuestion
vbQuestion=32
Msgbox "Would you like to continue?", vbYesNo + vbQuestion
```

If you don't want to use constants to represent the numerical values you want to use, you can rewrite these statements as follows:

```
Msgbox "Error writing to disk", 36
```

where 36 is the sum of 4 + 32.

Table 7-3 shows a complete list of icons you can add to message boxes. As with buttons, the use of a constant is optional but a constant makes it easier to work with the script.

TABLE 7-3

Icons for Messages Boxes

Constant	Description	Value
VbCritical	Displays an icon with an X, used for critical errors	16
VbQuestion	Displays an icon with a question mark, used for questions	32
VbExclamation	Displays an icon with an exclamation point, used for minor errors, cautions, and warnings	48
VbInformation	Displays an icon with an I, used for informational messages (this is the default)	64

Evaluating button clicks

When you present users with multiple options, such as Yes/No or Retry/Cancel, you need a way to determine which button the user selected. You do this by storing the return value from MsgBox in a variable, like this:

```
returnValue = Msgbox ("Message to display", buttonType + iconType,
"Message box title.")
```

Note that the syntax has changed. You must now use parentheses after the function name.

Table 7-4 provides a summary of the status codes returned when message box buttons are pressed. Once you assign a variable to store the returned status code, you can use an If Then or Select Case structure to perform actions in response to the button click.

TABLE 7-4

Button Status Codes

Button	Constant	Return Value
OK	VbOk	1
Cancel	VbCancel	2
Abort	VbAbort	3
Retry	VbRetry	4
Ignore	VbIgnore	5
Yes	VbYes	6
No	VbNo	7

A script that evaluates button clicks in message boxes and then handles the result is shown in Listing 7-1. While the example uses an `If Then` loop to evaluate the button click, you can easily use a `Select Case` structure as well.

LISTING 7-1

Determining Button Selection in a Script

checkbuttons.vbs

```
Dim vbYesNoCancel: vbYesNoCancel=3
Dim vbQuestion: vbQuestion=32
Dim vbYes: vbYes=6
Dim vbNo: vbNo=7
Dim vbCancel: vbCancel=2

retry = Msgbox ("Write to log failed. Try again?",vbYesNoCancel + VBQuestion)

If retry = vbYes Then
    WScript.Echo "Yes"
ElseIf retry = vbNo Then
    WScript.Echo "No"
Else
    WScript.Echo "Cancel"
End If
```

Help files for message boxes

Windows help files can be used with message boxes. To do this, you need to specify the name of the help file to use as an additional parameter. Following the help file name, you can add a context identifier, which is a numerical value that points to a specific location in the help file. To specify a help file and context identifier, use the following syntax:

```
Msgbox "Message to display", buttonType + iconType,
        "Message box title", "helpFile", helpContextID
```

Here's an example:

```
Msgbox "Continue?", 4, "", "windows.hlp", 0
```

This message box will be displayed with Yes, No, and Help buttons. The Help button is added to allow users to access the Windows help files.

Using pop-up dialog boxes

JScript doesn't support `InputBox()` or `Msgbox()`. In the browser implementation of JScript, dialog and input boxes are associated with the `window` object. Unfortunately, the `window` object is not available in WSH (unless you start a browser instance). To work around this problem, the developers of WSH created the Popup() function. Popup() is essentially an implementation of the VBScript Msgbox() function that is available in both JScript and VBScript.

Everything you've learned about VBScript message boxes applies to pop-up dialog boxes. The only real difference is that these dialog boxes are accessed through the Popup() method of the Shell object and they have a timeout mechanism. The basic syntax for Popup() is:

VBScript

```
answ = object.Popup("msg",
                    ["title"],
                    [wait],
                    [type])
```

JScript

```
answ = object.Popup(msg,
                    [wait],
                    ["title"],
                    [type])
```

These options are used in the following ways:

- msg: The message you want to display
- wait: The number of seconds to wait before closing the pop-up
- title: The title for the pop-up
- type: The value representing the button and icon types to use; these values are the same as those listed previously in Tables 7-1 and 7-2.

Because the Popup() method is accessed through the Shell object, you must create an instance of Shell and then reference the Popup() method of this object. You create instances of objects using the CreateObject method of the WScript object. Creating an object instance is a bit different in VBScript and JScript. In VBScript, you create an object reference using the Set keyword. In JScript, you create an object reference using the var keyword. The object reference is then used in the code to access methods and properties of the object you instantiated.

The following code creates an object instance in both VBScript and JScript:

VBScript

```
Set w = WScript.CreateObject("WScript.Shell")
```

JScript

```
var w = WScript.CreateObject("WScript.Shell");
```

Listing 7-2 shows how you can use `CreateObject()` and `Popup()` in a script. As discussed, you create an instance of `Shell` and then reference its `Popup()` method. Note that the value for the buttons (4) comes from Table 7-1. You can also set icons for the pop-up using values in Table 7-2. When you use both icons and buttons, you add the values together and then assign this value in the type property.

LISTING 7-2

Displaying a Pop-up Dialog Box

VBScript
popup.vbs

```
answer = getResponse()

function getResponse()
Dim answ
timeOut = 10
title = "Error!"
button = 2
'create object
Set w = WScript.CreateObject("WScript.Shell")
getResponse = w.Popup ("Write failure. Try again?",timeOut,title,button)

End Function
```

JScript
popup.js

```
answer = getResponse()

function getResponse() {
    var answ
    var timeOut = 10;
    var title = "Error!"
    var button = 2
    //create object
    var w = WScript.CreateObject("WScript.Shell");
    answ = w.Popup ("Write failure. Try again?", timeOut, title, button)
    return answ
}
```

The return value from `Popup` tells you which button the user selected. Return values are the same as those listed previously in Table 7-3, but with one important addition. If the user doesn't press a button and the timeout interval elapses, the method returns −1.

Listing 7-3 shows how you can handle user selections and errors in both VBScript and JScript. Note that the primary difference between the two is syntax.

LISTING 7-3

Checking the User Selection and Handling a Timeout Error

VBScript
usersel.vbs

```
function getInput()
Dim answ
timeOut = 30
title = "Write Failure!"
btype = 2
'create object
Set w = WScript.CreateObject("WScript.Shell")

getInput = w.Popup ("Error writing to the drive. Try again?",timeOut,title,btype)

End Function

answer = getInput()
Select Case answer
  Case 3
    WScript.Echo "You selected Abort."

  Case 4
    WScript.Echo "You selected Retry."

  Case 5
    WScript.Echo "You selected Ignore."

  Case Else
    WScript.Echo "No selection in the time allowed. "

End Select
```

JScript
usersel.js

```
function getInput() {
   var answ;
   var timeOut = 30;
   var title = "Write Failure!";
   var type = 2;
   //create object
   var w =
WScript.CreateObject("WScript.Shell");
```

```
    answ = w.Popup ("Error writing to the drive. Try again?",timeOut,title,type);
    return answ;
}

answer = getInput()
switch (answer) {
  case 3 :
    WScript.Echo("You selected Abort.")
    break
  case 4 :
    WScript.Echo("You selected Retry.")
    break
  case 5 :
    WScript.Echo("You selected Ignore.")

    break
  default :
WScript.Echo("No selection in the time allowed.")
    break
}
```

Error Detection and Handling

Errors can occur for a variety of reasons. The user may have entered the wrong type of value, or the script may not be able to find a necessary file, directory, or drive. In previous examples, we've handled errors using basic techniques, such as control loops. Now let's look at the error detection and handling functionality that's built into VBScript and JScript.

Handling runtime errors in VBScript

The most common type of error you'll encounter is a runtime error. Runtime errors occur while a script is running and is the result of the script trying to perform an invalid operation, such as dividing by zero. The sections that follow examine techniques you can use to handle runtime errors in VBScript.

Preventing runtime errors from halting script execution

In VBScript, any runtime error that occurs is fatal. This means that an error message is displayed and execution of the script stops. To prevent runtime errors from halting script execution, you need to add an On Error Resume Next statement to the script. This statement tells VBScript that execution should continue with the statement that immediately follows the statement that causes an error.

To see how On Error Resume Next works, consider the example shown in Listing 7-4. The user is asked to enter the number of values to total. If the user doesn't enter a value or enters zero, a "Type Mismatch Error" occurs on line 5 but script execution isn't halted. Instead, an error number, its description, and source are pushed onto the current error stack and script execution continues on line 6. Line 7 will again generate a "Type Mismatch Error." The related error number, its description, and source are pushed onto the error stack. This error replaces the previous error and script execution continues. Line 8 generates a "For Loop Not Initialized Error" and then line 9 generates a "Type Mismatch Error."

LISTING 7-4

Computing the Average Value

resume.vbs

```
On Error Resume Next
Dim theTotal: theTotal=0
Dim vals: vals=0
vals = InputBox("Number of values to total:"," Average")
vals = CInt(vals)
For i = 1 to vals
  theTotal = theTotal + InputBox("Enter value " & i," Average")
Next
theAvg = theTotal/vals
WScript.Echo theAvg
```

Table 7-5 shows other common runtime errors that you may see. These errors are listed by error number and description. Both error values are set by the runtime environment.

TABLE 7-5

Common Runtime Errors in VBScript

Error Number	Error Description
5	Invalid procedure call or argument
6	Overflow
7	Out of memory
9	Subscript out of range
10	Array fixed or temporarily locked
11	Division by zero
13	Type mismatch
14	Out of string space
28	Out of stack space

Error Number	Error Description
35	Sub or Function not defined
48	Error in loading DLL
51	Internal error
53	File not found
57	Device I/O error
58	File already exists
61	Disk full
67	Too many files
70	Permission denied
75	Path/File access error
76	Path not found
91	Object variable or With block variable not set
92	For loop not initialized
94	Invalid use of Null
322	Can't create necessary temporary file
424	Object required
429	ActiveX component can't create object
438	Object doesn't support this property or method
440	Automation error
445	Object doesn't support this action
446	Object doesn't support named arguments
447	Object doesn't support current locale setting
448	Named argument not found
449	Argument not optional
450	Wrong number of arguments or invalid property assignment
451	Object not a collection
500	Variable is undefined
501	Illegal assignment

Checking for and catching errors in VBScript

While the `On Error Resume Next` statement prevents VBScript from halting execution on an error, it doesn't actually handle the error. To handle the error, you need to add statements to the script that check for an error condition and then handle an error if it occurs. Generally, you'll want to check for errors at key places within your code. For example, in Listing 7-5 you would check for errors after line 4 and line 8. These are places where the user enters values that can affect the execution of the code.

You may also be thinking that you could have prevented an error by checking to see if the user entered a value or by checking for a range of values, as you see in Listing 7-5.

LISTING 7-5

Computing the Average Value

alternative1.vbs

```
On Error Resume Next
Dim theTotal: theTotal=0
Dim vals: vals=0
Do
 vals = InputBox("Number of values to total:"," Average")
Loop While vals = ""
vals = CInt(vals)
For i = 1 to vals
 Do
  theTotal = theTotal + InputBox("Enter value " & i," Average")
 Loop While theTotal = 0
Next
theAvg = theTotal/vals
WScript.Echo theAvg
```

Unfortunately, you can't always predict the values users may enter or the results of operations that are based on user input. The previous example assumes that the user enters numerical values and this may not be the case. The example also has a logic flaw in that it allows the user to enter no value on the second and subsequent iterations of the `For` loop.

Obviously, you need basic controls such as those provided in Listing 7-6. You also need to look at other ways to manage errors; this is where the `Err` object comes into the picture. The `Err` object has methods and properties for displaying and setting information about the current error. These methods and properties are listed in Table 7-6.

TABLE 7-6

Methods and Properties of the Err Object

Methods	Properties
Clear	Description
Raise	HelpContext
	HelpFile
	Number
	Source

The error number is your most valuable tool in determining if an error has occurred. When a script is executing normally, the error number is set to zero. This means that no error has occurred. When a runtime error occurs, the runtime environment sets a nonzero error number, description, and source. The source of a runtime error is set as "Microsoft VBScript runtime error" instead of "Microsoft VBScript compilation error."

One way to detect an error is to use an If Then conditional that checks for an error number other than zero, such as this:

```
If Err.Number <> 0 Then
  'An error has occurred.
   WScript.Echo Err.Number & " " & Err.Description & " " & Err.Source
End If
```

As you've seen, the error number, description, and source are set automatically. Values that you can configure when an error occurs are the name of a Windows help file and the context identifier within the help file, that can be used to provide detailed help for the user. You set the file name of a help file with the HelpFile property and the context identifier with the HelpContext property, like this:

```
Err.Helpfile = "myHelpFile.hlp"
Err.HelpContext = 0
```

After handling an error, you should clear the error from the error stack using the Clear method. The Clear method resets the error code, description, and source to allow normal execution to continue. If you want to catch each individual error, you'll need to add error detection and handling code wherever errors may occur in the code.

Listing 7-6 shows how you can use the Clear method and some other techniques discussed in this section to handle an error. If a runtime error occurs, a message box similar to the one shown in Figure 7-3 is displayed. Note that a Help button is displayed to enable users to access online help files, as well as the additional parameters specified for the message box in the script.

LISTING 7-6

Detecting and Handling Errors

alternative2.vbs

```
On Error Resume Next
Dim Msg
Err.HelpFile = "myHelpFile.hlp"
Err.HelpContext = 0

Dim theTotal: theTotal=0
Dim vals: vals=0
Do
 vals = InputBox("Number of values to total:"," Average")
Loop While vals = ""

vals = CInt(vals)
For i = 1 to vals
 Do
  theTotal = theTotal + InputBox("Enter value " & i," Average")
 Loop While theTotal = 0
Next
theAvg = theTotal/vals
WScript.Echo theAvg
If Err.Number <> 0 Then
 Msg = "Press F1 or click Help to view a help file."
 MsgBox Msg,1, Err.Description, Err.Helpfile, Err.HelpContext
 Err.Clear
End If
```

FIGURE 7-3

Message boxes have a special format and syntax for Windows help.

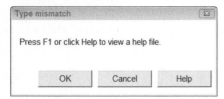

Manually generating runtime errors

In advanced scripts, there are times when you may want to generate a runtime error. For example, a user enters a file path and your script checks the file path before using it. If the file path isn't valid, the script generates a runtime error and displays a message box that enables the user to access help on setting file paths.

You can use the `Raise` method of the `Err` object to generate runtime errors. The complete syntax for the method is:

```
Err.Raise(number, "source", "description", "helpfile", helpcontext)
```

The arguments for the `Raise` method are used much like the related property values for the `Err` object. If you wanted to generate a "Path Not Found error," you could use the following code:

```
On Error Resume Next
Err.Raise 76
MsgBox "Error " & Err.Number & ": " & Err.Description
Err.Clear
```

You can also set custom errors. When you do this, you should use an error code above 50,000, which is the range set aside for user-defined errors. This example sets a custom error designated as error number 50001:

```
On Error Resume Next
Err.Raise 50001,,"Not a valid choice"
MsgBox "Error " & Err.Number & ": " & Err.Description
Err.Clear
```

You can also generate an error with an associated help file, like this:

```
On Error Resume Next
Dim Msg
Err.Raise 50001,,"Not a valid choice","usage.hlp",0
Msg = "Error " & Err.Number & ": " & Err.Description
MsgBox Msg,1, Err.Description, Err.Helpfile, Err.HelpContext
Err.Clear
```

Handling runtime errors in JScript

JScript takes a different approach to error handling. In many ways, this approach is more intuitive and more powerful than the VBScript approach, so let's take a look.

Checking for and catching errors in JScript

The core mechanisms for error handling are `try...catch` statements. Use a `try` statement to identify a section of code where an error may occur and a `catch` statement to handle any resulting errors. The basic syntax for `try catch` is:

```
try {
  //code where an error might occur
}
catch(exception) {
  //catch errors that may occur
}
```

If an error occurs within the `try` statement, control is passed to the `catch` statement and the value of `exception` is set to the value of the error that occurred. You may be wondering why the developers of JScript decided to use the keywords `try catch` rather than `detect handle` or something else. Primarily this is because errors that occur in scripts are said to be thrown by the runtime environment and thus, the `catch` statement catches them so they don't cause problems in the script.

As with VBScript, errors can be generated both automatically and manually. For example, if you call a function that doesn't exist, an object error occurs which you can handle in the following way:

```
try {
  nosuchfunction()
}
catch(e) {
  if (e == "[object Error]")
    WScript.Echo(e)
}
```

If you want to manually set error values, you can throw errors as well, which we will discuss next.

Throwing errors

You manually generate errors using the `throw` statement. The `throw` statement expects a single argument, which is an expression that yields a string, number, or object. This argument sets the error value. If you pass `throw` the following string:

```
throw "division by zero"
```

the error value is set to:

```
division by zero
```

You can use `throw` with `try` and `catch` as follows:

```
try {
  if (x < 0)
    throw "value less than zero";
  else if (x == 0)
    throw "value equals zero";
  }
  catch(e) {
    WScript.Echo("Error: " + e)
}
```

This example sets error values based on the value of x. If x is less than zero, the error value is set to "value less than zero." If x equals zero, the error value is set to "value equals zero." The `catch` statement is used to detect and handle an error if it occurs. If an error occurs, the script displays an error statement.

So far, we've been looking at how you can handle localized errors directly. Unfortunately, you may not want to handle errors directly. Instead, you may want to detect one or more errors locally and then pass unresolved errors to a higher context to handle them globally, like this:

```
try {
  if (x < 0)
    throw "value less than zero";
  else if (x == 0)
    throw "value equals zero";
  }
  catch(e) {
    if (e == "value less than zero")
      return("Error handled locally.");
    else
      throw e; //error not handled locally, pass exception on.
  }
```

Listing 7-7 shows a more complete example of handling errors locally and globally. The first call to the tryTest function passes in a value of –1, causing the script to throw an exception and set the error value to "value less than zero." The catch statement uses If Else to determine whether to handle the error. Here, the error value matches the value expected by the If statement, and the error is handled locally. The subsequent call to tryTest, however, sets x to 0, and this error isn't handled locally. Instead, the error is thrown to a higher context and then handled globally.

LISTING 7-7

Throwing an Error

throwerror.js

```
function tryTest(x)
{
 try {
  if (x < 0)
    throw "value less than zero";
  else if (x == 0)
    throw "value equals zero";
  }
  catch(e) {
    if (e == "value less than zero")
      return("Error handled locally.");
    else
      throw e;
  }
}
```

```
try {
 WScript.Echo("Result A: " + tryTest(-1))
}
catch(e) {
 WScript.Echo("Error passed to higher context. Handled globally.");
}
try {
 WScript.Echo("Result B: " + tryTest(0))
}
catch(e) {
 WScript.Echo("Error passed to higher context. Handled globally.");
}
```

Output

```
Result A: Error handled locally.
Error passed to higher context. Handled globally.
```

Other error-handling techniques

As with VBScript, you can examine error codes and descriptions in JScript. Table 7-7 shows the common errors by error code and description.

TABLE 7-7

Common Runtime Errors in JScript

Error Code	Error Description
5	Invalid procedure call or argument
6	Overflow
7	Out of memory
9	Subscript out of range
10	This array is fixed or temporarily locked
11	Division by zero
13	Type mismatch
14	Out of string space
17	Can't perform requested operation
28	Out of stack space

Error Code	Error Description
35	Sub or Function not defined
48	Error in loading DLL
51	Internal error
52	Bad file name or number
53	File not found
54	Bad file mode
55	File already open
57	Device I/O error
58	File already exists
61	Disk full
62	Input past end of file
67	Too many files
68	Device unavailable
70	Permission denied
71	Disk not ready
74	Can't rename with different drive
75	Path/File access error
76	Path not found
91	Object variable or With block variable not set
92	For loop not initialized
93	Invalid pattern string
94	Invalid use of Null
322	Can't create necessary temporary file
424	Object required

To access the error code and description, use the Error object. The Error object is created automatically by the catch statement and has two properties: Description and Number. The Description property returns or sets the error message. The Number property returns or sets the error number associated with the error.

You access the `Description` property directly through the `Error` object, like this:

```
try {
 nosuchfunction()
}
catch(e) {
 WScript.Echo(e.description)
}
```

On the other hand, the `Number` property is accessed through a 32-bit value. The upper 16-bit word from this value is a facility code, which you won't use in most cases. The lower 16-bit word is the actual error code. You can examine both codes as follows:

```
try {
 nosuchfunction()
}
catch(e) {
 WScript.Echo("Facility Code: " + e.number>>16 & 0x1FFF)
 WScript.Echo("Error Code: " + e.number & 0xFFFF)
}
```

Again, the error code is the value you'll want to use in your scripts.

Summary

Input, output, and error handling are important parts of any script. The most common techniques for displaying output and gathering input are dialog boxes. In the runtime environment, three types of dialog boxes are available: input boxes, message boxes, and pop-up dialog boxes. While VBScript supports all three types of dialog boxes, JScript only supports pop-ups. This support for VBScript and JScript is different from what you may be used to if you've worked with browser-based scripting, and it is something you should keep in mind whenever you work with Windows scripts.

Chapter 8

Working with Files and Folders in VBScript and JScript

The file system is one of the most important parts of any operating system and Windows is no exception. Your scripts will often need to manage files and folders. For example, before you can extract information from a log file you must learn how to find files, how to check for a file's existence, and how to read files. This chapter examines high-level techniques for working with files and folders. You'll learn how to create files and folders, how to examine file and folder properties, and how to move and delete files and folders. Reading and writing files is the subject of Chapter 9.

Whenever you work with files or folders in protected locations, such as those used by the operating system, you'll want to ensure you use an elevated command prompt with administrator privileges, in order to have the appropriate permissions to work with files and folders. When you are working with files and folders on remote computers, keep in mind that the remote script is copied to the temporary directory of the account that accesses the remote computer and runs with the security settings for the remote computer and the temporary directory.

> **NOTE** Some of the scripts in this chapter are not fully working examples. The scripts may highlight only the syntax of how the commands could be used in a complete script. Also, you may need to replace files and file paths with your own if you are trying the examples on your own computer.

Understanding the FileSystemObject

The top-level object for working with the Windows desktop and file systems is the `FileSystemObject` (FSO). It is through FSO that you access most of the other file system-related objects. Because this object is so

153

complex, let's take a step-by-step look at its components including related objects, methods, and properties.

FSO objects and collections

The FileSystemObject is implemented in the scripting runtime library (Scrrun.dll) and as such, it is an extension of the JScript and VBScript scripting engines rather than a part of the Windows Script Host object model. This distinction is important if you plan to use Windows Script Host with other scripting engines. For example, if you plan to use the PerlScript scripting engine, you will use PerlScript's file system objects, or you can define file system functions in VBScript and JScript and access them from PerlScript as part of a batch script job.

Many different objects and collections are accessed through the FileSystemObject. These elements are summarized in Table 8-1. As you already know, objects are containers for related sets of methods and properties. Collections, on the other hand, may be new to you. *Collections* are containers for groups of related items, such as the Drives collection that contains references for all the drives on a particular system. Normally, collections are accessed through the properties and methods of other objects. For example, to examine drives on a system, you'll use the Drives property of the FileSystemObject.

TABLE 8-1

Objects and Collections Accessed Through FileSystemObject

Object/Collection	Description
Drive Object	Used to examine information on storage devices, including disk drives, CD-ROM drives, RAM disks, and network drives
Drives Collection	Provides a list of physical and logical drives on the system
File Object	Used to examine and manipulate files
Files Collection	Provides a list of files in a folder
Folder Object	Used to examine and manipulate folders
Folders Collection	Provides a list of subfolders in a folder
TextStream Object	Used to read and write text files

FSO methods and properties

As shown in Table 8-2, the FileSystemObject provides many different methods for working with file systems. These methods sometimes provide the same functionality as the methods of lower-level objects. For example, the FileSystemObject's CopyFile method is identical to the File object's Copy method. They both expect the same arguments and have the same syntax.

TABLE 8-2

Methods of FileSystemObject

Method	Description
BuildPath	Appends file path information to an existing file path
CopyFile	Copies files from one location to another
CopyFolder	Copies folders and their contents from one location to another
CreateFolder	Creates a folder
CreateTextFile	Creates a text file and returns a TextStream object
DeleteFile	Deletes a file
DeleteFolder	Deletes a folder and all of its contents
DriveExists	Determines if a drive exists
FileExists	Determines if a file exists
FolderExists	Determines if a folder exists
GetAbsolutePathName	Returns the full path to a file or folder
GetBaseName	Returns the base name of a file or folder
GetDrive	Returns a Drive object
GetDriveName	Returns a drive name
GetExtensionName	Returns a file extension from a path
GetFile	Returns a File object
GetFileName	Returns a file name from a path
GetFolder	Returns a Folder object
GetParentFolderName	Returns the parent folder name from a path
GetSpecialFolder	Returns an object pointer to a special folder
GetTempName	Returns a randomly generated file or folder name that can be used with CreateTextFile
MoveFile	Moves files from one location to another
MoveFolder	Moves folders and their contents from one location to another
OpenTextFile	Opens an existing text file and returns a TextStream object

The only property of the `FileSystemObject` is `Drives`. This property returns a `Drives` collection that contains a list of all physical and logical drives on the system.

Using the FileSystemObject

As stated earlier, the `FileSystemObject` isn't a part of the Windows Script Host object model and is instead a part of the scripting type library. Because of this, you access the `FileSystemObject` via the `Scripting` object, like this:

VBScript

```
Set fs = WScript.CreateObject("Scripting.FileSystemObject")
```

JScript

```
fs = new ActiveXObject("Scripting.FileSystemObject");
```

In these examples, note that you create the `FileSystemObject` in JScript using the `ActiveXObject` method rather than the `CreateObject` method. `ActiveXObject` is a JScript method designed to return references to ActiveX Automation objects.

Once you create an instance of the `FileSystemObject` you can use its objects, methods, and properties. You need only one instance of the `FileSystemObject` in a script, and when you are finished using it, you may want to destroy the object instance and free up the memory it uses. To do this, you can set the reference variable to null, like this:

VBScript

```
Set fs = Nothing
```

JScript

```
fs = ""
```

 `Nothing` **is a reserved keyword in VBScript. You use** `Nothing` **in an assignment to null the object (free the memory associated with the object).**

Working with Folders

Folders are an important part of the file system, and whether you want to access existing folders or create new folders, you can use Windows scripts to get the job done. Often, the way you work with folders depends on the tasks you want to perform. For example, if you want to examine folder properties, you first need to create a `Folder` object and then you can work with the `Folder` object. The sections that follow examine key folder administration tasks, including:

- Viewing folder contents
- Examining and working with folder properties

- Checking for and creating folders
- Deleting, copying, and moving folders
- Working with special folders

Checking folder contents

Before you can view the contents of a folder, you must create a reference to the folder. This is done with the GetFolder method of the FileSystemObject. Pass the GetFolder method the path of the folder, and the method returns a Folder object. Once you have this Folder object, you can use it in your scripts. The following example shows how you can call GetFolder:

VBScript

```
Set fs = CreateObject("Scripting.FileSystemObject")
Set f = fs.GetFolder("C:\Windows")
```

JScript

```
fs = new ActiveXObject("Scripting.FileSystemObject");
var f = fs.GetFolder("C:\\WINDOWS")
```

 **Don't forget that you must use escaped directory paths in JScript. If you forget to use double slashes, your scripts may not work.**

After calling GetFolder, you can use the Subfolders and Files properties of the File object to examine the elements contained in the specified folder. These properties return Folder and File collections respectively, which you can iterate through with a For loop.

Listing 8-1 shows an example using GetFolder. The example displays a pop-up dialog box that contains a list of all subfolders under the C:WINDOWS directory.

LISTING 8-1

Examining Collections of Subfolders and Files

VBScript
viewfolder.vbs

```
Set w = WScript.CreateObject("WScript.Shell")
w.Popup ShowFolders("C:\WINDOWS")
Function ShowFolders(folderName)

Dim fs, f, f1, fc, s
s = ""
Set fs = CreateObject("Scripting.FileSystemObject")

Set f = fs.GetFolder(folderName)
```

continued

LISTING 8-1   *(continued)*

```
Set fc = f.SubFolders
For Each f1 in fc
   s = s & f1.name
   s = s &  (Chr(13) & Chr(10))
Next
  ShowFolders = s
End Function
```

JScript
viewfolder.js

```
var w = WScript.CreateObject("WScript.Shell");
w.Popup (ShowFolders("C:\\WINDOWS"))

function ShowFolders(folderName)
{
  var fs, f, fc, s;
  s = ""
  fs = new ActiveXObject("Scripting.FileSystemObject");
  f = fs.GetFolder(folderName);
  fc = new Enumerator(f.SubFolders);
  for (; !fc.atEnd();fc.moveNext())
  {
    s += fc.item();
    s += "\r\n";
  }
  return(s);
}
```

As Listing 8-1 shows, the techniques you use to examine collections in VBScript and JScript differ. In VBScript, you can use a simple For Each structure to examine the contents of the collection. The structure of the For Each loop isn't really any different from structures we've used in past examples. You start out by obtaining a Folder object:

```
Set fs = CreateObject("Scripting.FileSystemObject")
Set f = fs.GetFolder(folderName)
```

Next, you obtain the SubFolders collection within the folder:

```
Set fc = f.SubFolders
```

Then, you examine each item in the collection using a For Each loop:

```
For Each f1 in fc
s = s & f1.name
```

```
s = s & (Chr(13) & Chr(10))
Next
```

You use the s variable to hold the list of folder names, placing the names on separate lines by combining Chr(13) and Chr(10). Chr(13) is a carriage return and Chr(10) is a line feed.

With JScript, on the other hand, accessing collections requires some new techniques. You start out by obtaining a pointer to a Folder object:

```
fs = new ActiveXObject("Scripting.FileSystemObject");
f = fs.GetFolder(folderName);
```

Next, because the items in a collection aren't directly accessible in JScript, you use the Enumerator() method to obtain the SubFolders collection within the specified folder:

```
fc = new Enumerator(f.SubFolders);
```

Enumerator() provides access to special methods for working with collections. These methods are:

- atEnd: Returns True if the current item is the last in the collection. Otherwise, returns False.

- item: Returns an item in a collection.

- moveFirst: Resets the collection pointer to the beginning of the collection. Returns undefined if there aren't any items.

- moveNext: Advances to the next item in the collection. Returns undefined if the pointer is at the end of the collection.

In the example below, these methods are used to move through the collection. The following For loop iterates through the available items:

```
for (; !fc.atEnd(); fc.moveNext())
  {
    s += fc.item();
    s += "\r\n"
  }
```

You use the s variable to hold the list of folder names, placing the names on separate lines by combining \r and \n. The special character \r is a carriage return and \n is a line feed.

Examining folder properties

When you work with folders, you often want to examine their properties, such as the creation date or the date last modified. You can use these properties to view folder attributes, to display folder information to users, and more. Before you can examine folder properties, you must reference the folder through its `Folder` object. You can then work with any of the folder properties available. The following example shows how you can examine the creation date of a specified folder:

VBScript

```
Set fs = CreateObject("Scripting.FileSystemObject")
Set f = fs.GetFolder("C:\WINDOWS")
creDate = f.DateCreated
wscript.echo creDate
```

JScript

```
fs = new ActiveXObject("Scripting.FileSystemObject");
var f = fs.GetFolder("C:\\WINDOWS")
creDate = f.DateCreated
WScript.echo(creDate);
```

A complete list of folder properties is shown in Table 8-3. All folder properties are read-only, except for the `Attributes` property. This means you can read the properties but you can't change their values.

TABLE 8-3

Properties of the Folder Object

Property	Description	Sample Return Value
Attributes	Sets or returns folder properties; see the section, "Examining and Working with File Properties" for complete details.	16
DateCreated	Returns the folder creation date and time	10/15/10 6:11:21 PM
DateLastAccessed	Returns the date the folder was last accessed	10/21/10
DateLastModified	Returns the date and time the folder was last modified	10/21/10 6:52:12 PM
Drive	Returns the drive letter on which the folder resides	C:
Files	Returns a Files collection	-
IsRootFolder	Returns 1 (True) if the folder is the root folder, such as C:\ or D:\; otherwise, returns zero.	0
Name	Returns the folder name	Windows
ParentFolder	Returns the Folder object of the parent folder	C:\
Path	Returns the path to the folder	C:\WINDOWS
ShortName	Returns the MS DOS–compliant name of the folder	Windows
ShortPath	Returns the MS DOS–compliant path to the folder	C:\WINDOWS

Property	Description	Sample Return Value
Size	Returns the byte size of all files and subfolders in the folder	1576524
SubFolders	Returns a SubFolders collection	-
Type	Returns the folder type	File Folder

Most of the folder properties have fairly obvious uses. For example, you use the CreationDate property when you want to display the folder's creation date to a user, or perform a calculation based on the creation date.

Some properties are more useful than you might imagine. For example, you can use IsRootFolder and ParentFolder to move through directory structures. You create an instance of a folder and set it to a path, like this: C:\WINDOWS\System32\LogFiles. Then use the ParentFolder property to move through each of the parent folders, stopping when you reach the root folder C:\. An example that uses this technique is shown in Listing 8-2.

LISTING 8-2

Using IsRootFolder and ParentFolder

VBScript
checkfolder.vbs

```
folderP = CheckFolders("C:\WINDOWS\System32\LogFiles")
Set w = WScript.CreateObject("WScript.Shell")
w.Popup folderP

Function CheckFolders(folderPath)
  Dim fs, f, n, s
  s = ""
  n = 0
  Set fs = CreateObject("Scripting.FileSystemObject")
  Set f = fs.GetFolder(folderPath)
  If f.IsRootFolder Then
    s = "This is the root folder."
  Else
    Do Until f.IsRootFolder
      Set f = f.ParentFolder
      n = n + 1
  Loop
  End If
 'Work with folder
  s = "Folder is nested " & n & " levels deep."
  CheckFolders = s
End Function
```

continued

LISTING 8-2   (continued)

JScript
checkfolder.js

```
folderP = CheckFolders("C:\\WINDOWS\\System32\\LogFiles")
var w = WScript.CreateObject("WScript.Shell");
w.Popup (folderP)

function CheckFolders(folderPath)
{
   var fs, f, n, s;
   s = "";
   n = 0;
   fs = new ActiveXObject("Scripting.FileSystemObject");
   f = fs.GetFolder(folderPath);
   if (f.IsRootFolder)
     s = "Root folder."
   else {
     do
      {
         f = f.ParentFolder;
         n++;
      }
      while (!f.IsRootFolder)
     //Work with folder
     s = "Folder is nested " + n + " levels deep."
     return(s);
     }
}
```

Output

```
Folder is nested three levels deep.
```

As shown, the ParentFolder property returns a Folder object that you can manipulate. If you just want the name of the parent folder, use the GetParentFolderName method instead. This method returns a string containing the name of the parent folder and can be used as follows:

VBScript

```
Set fs = CreateObject("Scripting.FileSystemObject")
par = fs.GetParentFolderName folderpath
```

JScript

```
fs = new ActiveXObject("Scripting.FileSystemObject");
var par = fs.GetParentFolderName(folderpath)
```

Here, if the folder path is C:\WINDOWS\System32, the par variable is set to C:\WINDOWS. Note that if the folder path is a root folder, such as C:\, the GetParentFolderName method returns an empty string. The reason for this is that root folders don't have parent folders.

Creating folders

In the previous examples, we've assumed that the folder exists on the user's system. As this may not always be the case, you may want to test for a folder's existence before you try to work with it. To do this, you can use the FolderExists method of FileSystemObject. This method returns True if the folder exists and can be used as shown in Listing 8-3.

LISTING 8-3

Using FolderExists

VBScript
checkfolder2.vbs

```
WScript.Echo(CheckFolder("C:\WINDOWS"))
Function CheckFolder(foldr)
Dim fs, s
  Set fs = CreateObject("Scripting.FileSystemObject")
  If (fs.FolderExists(foldr)) Then
    s = foldr & " is available."
  Else
    s = foldr & " doesn't exist."
  End If
  CheckFolder = s
End Function
```

JScript
checkfolder2.js

```
WScript.Echo(CheckFolder("C:\\WINDOWS"))
function CheckFolder(foldr)
{
  var fs, s = foldr;
  fs = new ActiveXObject("Scripting.FileSystemObject");
  if (fs.FolderExists(foldr))
    s += " is available.";
  else
    s += " doesn't exist.";
  return(s);
}
```

Output

```
C:\WINDOWS is available.
```

After checking for a folder's existence, one of the most common tasks you'll want to perform is the creation of a necessary folder. You can create folders with the `CreateFolder` method of the `FileSystemObject`. The main argument for this method is a string containing the path to the folder you want to create, such as:

VBScript

```
Set fs = CreateObject("Scripting.FileSystemObject")
Set foldr = fs.CreateFolder("d:\data")
```

JScript

```
var fs = new ActiveXObject("Scripting.FileSystemObject");
var foldr = fs.CreateFolder("d:\\data");
```

Copying, moving, and deleting folders

With Windows scripts, there are two different ways to copy, move, and delete files. You can use methods of `FileSystemObject` to work with multiple folders or you can use methods of the `Folder` object to work with individual folders.

Issues for multiple folders

Using `FileSystemObject`, the methods for copying, moving, and deleting folders are:

- `DeleteFolder`
- `CopyFolder`
- `MoveFolder`

Using DeleteFolder

The `DeleteFolder` method is used to delete a folder and all of its contents, which can include subfolders and files. When you use the method, specify the path to the folder you want to delete and optionally force the method to delete read-only files. For example, you can delete a working directory in `C:\working\data` as follows:

VBScript

```
Set fs = CreateObject("Scripting.FileSystemObject")
fs.DeleteFolder("C:\working\data")
```

JScript

```
var fs = new ActiveXObject("Scripting.FileSystemObject");
fs.DeleteFolder("C:\\working\\data");
```

 The `DeleteFolder` method can be very dangerous. It allows you to specify the root folder for deletion, which will delete all contents on an entire drive.

If the directory contains read-only files that you want to delete, an error occurs and the delete operation is cancelled. To prevent this from happening, you must set the force flag to True. For example:

VBScript

```
fs.DeleteFolder "C:\working\data",True
```

JScript

```
fs.DeleteFolder("C:\\working\\data", "True");
```

You can also use wildcards when deleting folders. To do this, specify the wildcard as the last element of the path. For example, you can delete the folders C:\working\test and C:\working\test2 as follows:

VBScript

```
fs.DeleteFolder "C:\working\tes*"
```

JScript

```
fs.DeleteFolder("C:\\working\\tes*");
```

Using CopyFolder

The CopyFolder method copies a folder and all of its contents—which can include subfolders and files — to a new location. Using CopyFolder, you specify the source path of the folder you want to copy and the destination path for the folder. For example, you can copy C:\working to D:\data as follows:

VBScript

```
Set fs = CreateObject("Scripting.FileSystemObject")
fs.CopyFolder "C:\working", "D:\data"
```

JScript

```
var fs = new ActiveXObject("Scripting.FileSystemObject");
fs.CopyFolder("C:\\working", "D:\\data");
```

You can also use CopyFolder to copy between existing folders. For example if both C:\working and D:\data exist, you can copy files and subfolders from C:\working to D:\data. However, when you do this, there are several rules you must follow. If the destination directory already exists and any files are overwritten during the copy, an error occurs and the copy operation stops. To force the method to overwrite existing files, you must set the overwrite flag to True, like this:

VBScript

```
fs.CopyFolder "C:\working","D:\data", True
```

JScript

```
fs.CopyFolder ("C:\\working","D:\\data", "True");
```

If the destination directory already exists and you want to copy specific files and folders, use a wildcard as the final element of the source folder name. The following example copies the C:\Working\test and C:\Working\test2 folders to D:\data\test and D:\data\test2:

VBScript

```
fs.CopyFolder "C:\working\tes*","D:\data"
```

JScript

```
fs.CopyFolder("C:\\working\tes*","D:\\data");
```

> **TIP** Normally, you don't want to specify the last element of the destination path as a folder separator (\). If you do, the CopyFolder method assumes the destination folder exists and will not create it if it is necessary to do so.

Using MoveFolder

If you want to move a folder and all of its contents to a new location, use MoveFolder. When you use the MoveFolder method, you specify the source path of the folder you want to move and the destination path. For example, you can move C:\data to D:\work\data as follows:

VBScript

```
Set fs = CreateObject("Scripting.FileSystemObject")

fs.MoveFolder "C:\data","D:\work\data"
```

JScript

```
var fs = new ActiveXObject("Scripting.FileSystemObject");
fs.CopyFolder("C:\\data","D:\\work\\data");
```

You can also use MoveFolder to move files and subfolders between existing folders. For example if both C:\working and D:\data exist, you can move files and subfolders from C:\working to D:\data. To do this, use wildcards to match subfolders and file contents, like this:

VBScript

```
fs.MoveFolder "C:\working\tes*","D:\data"
```

JScript

```
fs.MoveFolder("C:\\working\\tes*","D:\\data");.
```

> **NOTE** If you specify the last element of the destination path as a folder separator (\), the MoveFolder method assumes that the destination folder exists and will not create it if it is necessary to do so. Also, the move operation will not overwrite existing files or folders. In such a case, the move fails the first time it tries to overwrite.

Issues for individual folders

With the Folder object, the methods for copying, moving, and deleting folders are:

- Delete
- Copy
- Move

 You cannot use wildcards when copying, moving, or deleting individual folders.

Using Delete

The Delete method of the Folder object works almost the same as the DeleteFolder method discussed previously. The method deletes a folder and all of its contents, which can include subfolders and files, and can also force the deletion of read-only contents. The Delete method works with a specific Folder object reference and, as a result, can delete a folder just by calling the method, like this:

VBScript

```
Set fs = CreateObject("Scripting.FileSystemObject")
Set f = fs.GetFolder("C:\working")
f.Delete
```

JScript

```
var fs = new ActiveXObject("Scripting.FileSystemObject");
var f = fs.GetFolder("C:\\working");
f.Delete()
```

If the folder contains read-only subfolders and files that you want to delete, you must set the force flag to True, like this:

VBScript

```
f.Delete True
```

JScript

```
f.Delete("True")
```

Using Copy

The Copy method copies a folder and all of its contents to a new location. With Copy, you obtain a Folder object and then set the destination path for the folder in the Copy method. For example, you can copy C:\working to D:\data as follows:

VBScript

```
Set fs = CreateObject("Scripting.FileSystemObject")
Set f = fs.GetFolder("C:\working")
f.Copy "D:\data"
```

JScript

```
var fs = new ActiveXObject("Scripting.FileSystemObject");
var f = fs.GetFolder("C:\\working");
f.Copy("D:\\data");
```

As with CopyFolder, you can also use the Copy method to copy between existing folders. For example if both C:\working and D:\data exist, you can copy files and subfolders from C:\working to D:\data. In this case, you may want to force the method to overwrite existing files, which you do by setting the overwrite flag to True, like this:

VBScript

```
f.Copy "D:\data", True
```

JScript

```
f.Copy("D:\\data", "True");
```

 If you try to overwrite existing files and don't set the overwrite flag, an error occurs and the Copy operation stops.

Using Move

The Move method moves a folder and all of its contents to a new location. Before you use Move, you must first obtain a Folder object and then you can set the destination path for the folder in the Move method. For example, you can move C:\data to D:\work\data like this:

VBScript

```
Set fs = CreateObject("Scripting.FileSystemObject")
Set f = fs.GetFolder("C:\data")
f.Move "D:\work\data"
```

JScript

```
var fs = new ActiveXObject("Scripting.FileSystemObject");
var f = fs.GetFolder("C:\\data");
f.Move("D:\\work\\data");
```

You can also use Move to move files and subfolders between existing folders. For example if both C:\data and D:\backups\data exist, you can move files and subfolders from C:\data to D:\backups\data. However, the Move method will not overwrite existing files. If you try to do this, an error occurs and the operation stops.

Using Special Folders

Entering a specific value for folder paths works in many cases, but there are times when you'll need to work with certain folders in a way that isn't specific to a particular system. For example, if you create a login script, users may log in from Windows XP, Windows Vista, Windows Server 2003, or

Windows Server 2008. With these operating systems, system files are installed in same locations by default but can be set to just about any directory name during installation.

So, if you want to create a script that works with operating system files, you shouldn't enter a precise path. Instead, you should work with environment variables that act as pointers to the location of the operating system files, `SystemRoot` for example. As you will learn in Chapter 10, you can use the `ExpandEnvironmentStrings` method of the `Shell` object to obtain a string representation of the `SystemRoot` environment variable. You can then assign this value to a method that uses the path information. An example is shown in Listing 8-4.

LISTING 8-4

Working with Paths and Environment Variables

VBScript
envpaths.vbs

```
Set fs = CreateObject("Scripting.FileSystemObject")
Set WshShell = WScript.CreateObject("WScript.Shell")
osdir = WshShell.ExpandEnvironmentStrings("%SystemRoot%")
Set f = fs.GetFolder(osdir)
WScript.Echo f
```

JScript
envpaths.js

```
var fs = new ActiveXObject("Scripting.FileSystemObject");
var WshShell = WScript.CreateObject("WScript.Shell")
osdir = WshShell.ExpandEnvironmentStrings("%SystemRoot%")
var f = fs.GetFolder(osdir);
WScript.Echo(f)
```

Output

```
C:\WINDOWS
```

Accessing environment variables before working with folders requires a few extra steps that can be avoided by using the `GetSpecialFolder` method of `FileSystemObject`. With this method, you can directly obtain one of three folders: the `Windows folder`, the `System folder`, or the `Temp folder`. The method accepts a value that represents the folder you want to work with. The three values are listed here:

- **0:** For the `Windows folder`, such as `C:\WINDOWS`. Associated constant is `WindowsFolder`.

- **1:** For the `System folder`, such as `C:\WINDOWS\System32`. Associated constant is `SystemFolder`.

- **2:** For the `Temp folder`, such as `C:\TEMP`. Associated constant is `TemporaryFolder`.

An example using `GetSpecialFolder` is shown in Listing 8-5.

LISTING 8-5

Working with Special Folders

VBScript
specialfolder.vbs

```vbscript
Set fs = CreateObject("Scripting.FileSystemObject")
'Get the Windows folder
Set wfolder = fs.GetSpecialFolder(0)
'Get the System folder
Set sfolder = fs.GetSpecialFolder(1)
'Get the Temp folder
Set tfolder = fs.GetSpecialFolder(2)
```

JScript
specialfolder.js

```javascript
var fs = CreateObject("Scripting.FileSystemObject")
//Get the Windows folder
var wfolder = fs.GetSpecialFolder(0)
//Get the System folder
var sfolder = fs.GetSpecialFolder(1)
//Get the Temp folder
var tfolder = fs.GetSpecialFolder(2)
```

Working with Files

Many of the tasks you perform in Windows scripts will relate to files. You can use scripts to copy, move, and delete files. You can also use scripts to create, read, and write text files. The types of text files you can work with include HTML, XML, scripts, and other types of files containing standard ASCII or Unicode text. The sections that follow examine key file administration tasks, including:

- Examining and working with file properties
- Copying, moving, and deleting files
- Checking for and creating files
- Reading and writing files

Examining file properties

Files have many different properties. Some of these properties can only be read. Others are read/write, which means you can change their values. A complete list of folder properties is shown as Table 8-4.

TABLE 8-4

Properties of the File Object

Property	Description	Sample Return Value
Attributes	Sets or returns file properties	32
DateCreated	Returns the file creation date and time	7/15/10 12:05:11 AM
DateLastAccessed	Returns the date the file was last accessed	9/10/10
DateLastModified	Returns the date and time the file was last modified	9/10/10 8:26:35 PM
Drive	Returns the drive letter on which the file resides	D:
Name	Returns the file name	index.html
ParentFolder	Returns the Folder object of the parent folder	C:\working
Path	Returns the path to the file	C:\working\index.html
ShortName	Returns the MS DOS-compliant name of the file	index.htm
ShortPath	Returns the MS DOS–compliant path to the file	C:\working\index.htm
Size	Returns the byte size of the file	45225
Type	Returns the file type	Netscape Hypertext Document

Before you can examine file properties, you must reference the file through its related File object. You can then work with any of the file properties available. The following example shows how you can examine the size of a file:

VBScript

```
Set fs = CreateObject("Scripting.FileSystemObject")
Set f = fs.GetFile("D:\index.htm")
fileSize = f.size
```

JScript

```
fs = new ActiveXObject("Scripting.FileSystemObject");
var f = fs.GetFile("D:\\index.htm")
fileSize = f.size
```

One of the key properties you'll work with is Attributes. The value that is returned by the Attributes property is the combination of the related values for all the flags set for the file or folder. You can change file properties by setting Attributes to a new value or by adding and subtracting from its current value. With folders, however, you can only display attribute values.

Table 8-5 provides a complete list of `Attribute` values that can be used with files and folders. While read-only values cannot be changed, read/write values can be combined to set multiple attributes.

TABLE 8-5

Attribute Values for Files and Folders

Constant	Value	Description
Normal	0	A normal file with no attributes set
ReadOnly	1	A read-only file; attribute is read/write.
Hidden	2	A hidden file; attribute is read/write.
System	4	A system file; attribute is read/write.
Volume	8	A disk drive volume label; attribute is read-only.
Directory	16	A folder or directory; attribute is read-only.
Archive	32	A file with the archive bit set (meaning it has changed since last backup); attribute is read/write.
Alias	64	A link or shortcut; attribute is read-only.
Compressed	128	A compressed file; attribute is read-only.

Changing read/write file attributes is easy. The following example sets the read-only flag for a file named `log.txt`:

VBScript

```
Set fs = CreateObject("Scripting.FileSystemObject")
Set f = fs.GetFile("D:\log.txt")
f.Attributes = f.Attributes + 1
```

JScript

```
fs = new ActiveXObject("Scripting.FileSystemObject");
var f = fs.GetFile("D:\\log.txt")
f.Attributes += 1
```

Now you may be wondering what would happen if the file was read-only already and you added one to its value. The result is unpredictable, but a hidden, read-only file (value 3) would become a system file (value 4). To ensure that you only set a particular flag—that is, if it's not set already—you can use an AND test. In Listing 8-6, the file is changed to read-only, but only if this flag isn't already set.

LISTING 8-6

Checking for Attributes Before Making Changes

VBScript
attribs.vbs

```
Set fs = CreateObject("Scripting.FileSystemObject")
Set f = fs.GetFile("c:\log.txt")
If f.Attributes And 1 Then
 f.Attributes = f.Attributes + 1
End If
```

JScript
attribs.js

```
fs = new ActiveXObject("Scripting.FileSystemObject");
var f = fs.GetFile("D:\\log.txt")
if (f.Attributes & 1)
{
 f.Attributes += 1
}
```

Creating files

So far, we've assumed that the file we want to work with exists on the user's system. However, this may not always be the case, so you may want to test for a file's existence before you try to work with it. To do this, use the `FileExists` method of `FileSystemObject`. This method returns `True` if the folder exists and `False` if not.

Listing 8-7 shows how you can test for a file's existence.

LISTING 8-7

Using FileExists

VBScript
testfile.vbs

```
WScript.Echo(CheckFile("C:\data.txt"))

Function CheckFile(aFile)
Dim fs, s
  Set fs = CreateObject("Scripting.FileSystemObject")

  If (fs.FileExists(aFile)) Then
    s = aFile & " is available."
```

continued

LISTING 8-7   (continued)

```
  Else
    s = aFile & " doesn't exist."
  End If
CheckFile = s
End Function
```

JScript
testfile.js

```
WScript.Echo(CheckFile("C:\\data.txt"))
function CheckFile(aFile)
{
  var fs, s = aFile;
  fs = new ActiveXObject("Scripting.FileSystemObject");
  if (fs.FileExists(aFile))
    s += " is available.";
else
    s += " doesn't exist.";
    return(s);
}
```

Output

```
C:\data.txt is available.
```

If a file you want to write to doesn't exist, you may want to create it. To do this, you can use the CreateTextFile method of the FileSystemObject. The main argument for this method is a string containing the path to the file you want to create:

VBScript

```
Set fs = CreateObject("Scripting.FileSystemObject")
Set aFile = fs.CreateTextFile("d:\data\data.txt")
```

JScript

```
var fs = new ActiveXObject("Scripting.FileSystemObject");
var aFile = fs.CreateTextFile("d:\\data\\data.txt");
```

The Folder object also has a CreateTextFile method. With the Folder object, you specify only the file name rather than a complete path, like this:

VBScript

```
Set fs = CreateObject("Scripting.FileSystemObject")
Set f = fs.GetFolder("D:\data")
Set aFile = f.CreateTextFile("data.txt")
```

JScript

```
var fs = new ActiveXObject("Scripting.FileSystemObject");
var f = fs.GetFolder("D:\\data")
var aFile = f.CreateTextFile("data.txt");;
```

The CreateTextFile method returns a TextStream object that you can use to work with the newly created file. If you try to create a file with the same name and path as an existing file, an error occurs. By default, CreateTextFile won't overwrite an existing file. You can change this behavior by setting the overwrite flag, like this:

VBScript

```
Set aFile = f.CreateTextFile("data.txt", True)
```

JScript

```
var aFile = f.CreateTextFile("data.txt", "True");
```

Another default behavior of the CreateTextFile method is to create files in ASCII text mode. You can also set Unicode mode. To do this, you need to set the Unicode flag to True, as follows:

VBScript

```
Set aFile = f.CreateTextFile("data.txt", False, True)
```

JScript

```
var aFile = f.CreateTextFile("data.txt", "False", "True");
```

 You cannot skip the overwrite flag when you set the Unicode flag. Instead, set the overwrite flag to True or False explicitly and then set the Unicode flag.

Copying, moving, and deleting files

You can manage files using methods of FileSystemObject or methods of the File object. Use FileSystemObject methods when you want to work with multiple files. Use the File object when you want to work with individual files.

Issues for multiple files

FileSystemObject methods for copying, moving, and deleting files are:

- DeleteFile
- CopyFile
- MoveFile

Using DeleteFile

You can use the DeleteFile method to delete one or more files. When you use this method, specify the path to the file you want to delete and optionally force the method to delete read-only files. Delete one file by specifying an absolute path, such as C:\working\data.txt. Delete multiple files by using wildcards in the file name. For example, you can delete all .txt files in C:\working as follows:

VBScript

```
Set fs = CreateObject("Scripting.FileSystemObject")
fs.DeleteFile("C:\working\*.txt")
```

JScript

```
var fs = new ActiveXObject("Scripting.FileSystemObject");
fs.DeleteFile("C:\\working\\*.txt");
```

The DeleteFile method deletes only read-only files when you set the force flag to True, like this:

VBScript

```
fs.DeleteFile
"C:\working\data.txt",True
```

JScript

```
fs.DeleteFile
("C:\\working\\data.txt", "True");
```

 If DeleteFile **encounters a read-only file and you haven't set the force flag, the operation stops and no other files are deleted.**

Using CopyFile

The CopyFile method copies one or more files to a new location. To copy a single file, specify the absolute path to the file you want to copy and then the destination path. For example, you can copy C:\working\data.txt to D:\backup\data.txt as follows:

VBScript

```
Set fs = CreateObject("Scripting.FileSystemObject")
fs.CopyFile "C:\working\data.txt","D:\backup\data.txt"
```

JScript

```
var fs = new ActiveXObject("Scripting.FileSystemObject");
fs.CopyFile("C:\\working\\data.txt","D:\\backup\\data.txt");
```

You can copy multiple files by using wildcards in the file name as well. For example, to copy all .html files from C:\working to D:\webdata you can use the following code:

VBScript

```
Set fs = CreateObject("Scripting.FileSystemObject")
fs.CopyFile "C:\working\*.html","D:\webdata"
```

JScript

```
var fs = new ActiveXObject("Scripting.FileSystemObject");
fs.CopyFile("C:\\working\\*.html","D:\\webdata");
```

You can also use CopyFile to copy files between directories that already exist. For example, if both C:\working and D:\data exist, you can copy files from C:\working to D:\data. However, when you do this, there are several rules you must follow. If the files you are copying exist at the destination, an error occurs and the copy operation stops. To force the method to overwrite existing files, set the overwrite flag to True, like this:

VBScript

```
fs.CopyFile
"C:\working\*.txt","D:\data", True
```

JScript

```
fs.CopyFile("C:\\working\*.txt",
"D:\\data", "True");
```

CopyFile will not write into a read-only directory and it will not write over read-only files either. You cannot change this behavior with the overwrite flag.

Using MoveFile

If you want to move one or more files to a new location, use MoveFile. To move a single file, specify the absolute path to the file as the source and then set the destination path. For example, you can move C:\data.txt to D:\work\data.txt as follows:

VBScript

```
Set fs = CreateObject("Scripting.FileSystemObject")
fs.MoveFile "C:\data.txt","D:\work\data.txt"
```

JScript

```
var fs = new ActiveXObject("Scripting.FileSystemObject");
fs.CopyFile("C:\\data.txt","D:\\work\\data.txt");
```

To move multiple files, you can use wildcards. For example, if you want to move all .txt files from C:\working to D:\backup, you can use the following code:

VBScript

```
Set fs = CreateObject("Scripting.FileSystemObject")
fs.MoveFile "C:\working\*.txt","D:\backup"
```

JScript

```
var fs = new ActiveXObject("Scripting.FileSystemObject");
fs.CopyFile("C:\\working\\*.txt","D:\\backup");
```

You can also use MoveFile to move files to an existing directory. For example, if both C:\working and D:\data exist, you can move all .html files from C:\working to D:\data, as follows:

VBScript

```
fs.MoveFile "C:\working\*.HTML","D:\data"
```

JScript

```
fs.MoveFile ("C:\\working\\*.HTML","D:\\data");
```

 **If you specify the last element of the destination path as a folder separator (\), the** MoveFile **method assumes the destination folder exists and will not create it if it is necessary to do so. Also, the move operation will not overwrite existing files. In such a case, the move fails the first time it tries to overwrite.**

Issues for individual files

With the File object, the methods for copying, moving, and deleting files are:

- Delete
- Copy
- Move

 **You cannot use wildcards when copying, moving, or deleting individual files.**

Using Delete

The Delete method of the File object deletes a file and can also force the deletion of a read-only file. This method works with a specific File object reference and, as a result, you can delete a file just by calling the method, like this:

VBScript

```
Set fs = CreateObject("Scripting.FileSystemObject")
Set f = fs.GetFile ("C:\working\data.txt")
f.Delete
```

JScript

```
var fs = new ActiveXObject("Scripting.FileSystemObject");
var f = fs.GetFile ("C:\\working\\data.txt");
f.Delete()
```

If the file is read-only, you must set the force flag to True, like this:

VBScript

```
f.Delete True
```

JScript

```
f.Delete("True")
```

Using Copy

The Copy method copies a file to a new location. With Copy, you must obtain a File object and then set the destination path for the file in the Copy method. For example, you can copy C:\data.txt to D:\data\data.txt as follows:

VBScript

```
Set fs = CreateObject("Scripting.FileSystemObject")
Set f = fs.GetFile("C:\data.txt")
f.Copy "D:\data\data.txt"
```

JScript

```
var fs = new ActiveXObject("Scripting.FileSystemObject");
var f = fs.GetFile("C:\\data.txt");
f.Copy("D:\\data\\data.txt");
```

As with CopyFile, you can also use the Copy method to copy over an existing file. To do this, you must set the overwrite flag to True, like this:

VBScript

```
f.Copy "D:\data\data.txt", True
```

JScript

```
f.Copy("D:\\data\\data.txt", "True");
```

 **If you try to overwrite a file and don't set the overwrite flag to** True, **an error occurs and the copy operation fails.**

Using Move

Use the Move method to move a file to a new location. Before you use Move, you must first obtain a File object and then you can set the destination path for the file in the Move method. You can move C:\data.txt to D:\work\data.txt as follows:

VBScript

```
Set fs = CreateObject("Scripting.FileSystemObject")
Set f = fs.GetFile("C:\data.txt")
f.Move "D:\work\data.txt "
```

JScript

```
var fs = new ActiveXObject("Scripting.FileSystemObject");
var f = fs.GetFile("C:\\data.txt");
f.Move("D:\\work\\data.txt");
```

 **You cannot use** Move **to overwrite an existing file.**

Summary

As you've seen in this chapter, the FileSystemObject is used to manipulate files and folders. File and folder operations you can perform include create, copy, move, and delete. You can examine folder and file information as well. In the next chapter, you learn how to read and write files.

Chapter 9

Reading and Writing Files

Now that you know how to manage files and folders, you're ready to take a closer look at manipulating the contents of files. Many different methods and properties are available for working with files. But before you can work with a file, you need to open it for reading, writing, or appending.

> **NOTE** Some of the scripts in this chapter are not fully working examples. The scripts may only highlight the syntax of how the commands could be used in a complete script. Also, you may need to replace files and file paths with your own if you are trying the examples on your own computer.

Opening Files

Two methods are provided for opening files. You can use the `OpenTextFile` method of `FileSystemObject` or the `OpenAsTextStream` method of the `File` object. While both methods return a `TextStream` object, they are used in slightly different ways.

Using OpenTextFile

The OpenTextFile method expects to be passed the full path to the file you want to open, such as:

VBScript

```
Set fs = CreateObject("Scripting.FileSystemObject")
Set ts = fs.OpenTextFile("D:\data\log.txt")
```

JScript

```
var fs = new ActiveXObject("Scripting.FileSystemObject");
var ts = fs.OpenTextFile("D:\\data\\log.txt")
```

If you plan to work with the file, you should set the access mode as well. Three access modes are provided:

- 1: Opens a file for reading. Associated constant is ForReading.
- 2: Opens a file for writing to the beginning of the file. Associated constant is ForWriting.
- 8: Opens a file for appending (writing to the end of the file). Associated constant is ForAppending.

As you can see, the access modes are designed for specific tasks, such as reading, writing, or appending. You must use the appropriate mode for the task you want to perform and then close the file before performing a different task. For example, if you want to write to a file, you must open it in ForWriting mode. Later, if you want to read from the file, you must close it and then open it in ForReading mode.

Beyond access modes, you can also specify that you want to create the referenced file if it doesn't already exist and set the file's format mode. To create a file if it doesn't exist, set the create flag to True. Otherwise, the file isn't created and an error may occur. To set a file's format mode, use one of these values:

- -2: Opens the file using the system default. Associated constant is TristateUseDefault.
- -1: Opens the file as Unicode. Associated constant is TristateTrue.
- 0: Opens the file as ASCII. Associated constant is TristateFalse.

Listing 9-1 opens a file in ForWriting mode. If the file doesn't exist, it is created automatically, which is handy, as you don't have to test for the file with FileExists. The file is also set to ASCII text mode, which is the default mode on most systems. The listing also creates an extensive set of constants for working with files. Use constants when you want your scripts to be easy to read. If the directory does not exist, you will get a "path not found" error.

LISTING 9-1

Using OpenTextFile

VBScript
usefile.vbs

```
Const ForReading = 1
Const ForWriting = 2
Const ForAppending = 8
Const TristateUseDefault = -2
Const TristateTrue = -1
Const TristateFalse = 0

Set fs = CreateObject("Scripting.FileSystemObject")
Set ts = fs.OpenTextFile("D:\data\log.txt", ForWriting, True, TristateFalse)
```

JScript
usefile.js

```
ForReading = 1
ForWriting = 2
ForAppending = 8
TristateUseDefault = -2
TristateTrue = -1
TristateFalse = 0
var fs = new ActiveXObject("Scripting.FileSystemObject");
var ts = fs.OpenTextFile("D:\\data\\log.txt",ForWriting, "True", TristateFalse)
```

Using OpenAsTextStream

The OpenAsTextStream method is used much like OpenTextFile. The key differences are that you already have a file reference, so you don't have to set a file path, and you cannot set a create flag. Other than that, the methods are identical. Listing 9-2 shows how you can open an ASCII text file in ForReading mode.

LISTING 9-2

Using OpenAsTextStream

VBScript
usestream.vbs

```
Const ForReading = 1
Const TristateFalse = 0
```

continued

LISTING 9-2   *(continued)*

```
Set fs = CreateObject("Scripting.FileSystemObject")
Set f = fs.GetFile("D:\data\log.txt")
Set ts = f.OpenAsTextStream(ForReading, TristateFalse)
```

JScript
usestream.js

```
ForReading = 1
TristateFalse = 0
var fs = new ActiveXObject("Scripting.FileSystemObject");
var f = fs.GetFile("D:\\data\\log.txt");
var ts = f.OpenAsTextStream(ForReading, TristateFalse)
```

Reading Text Files

You can read from a text file only when you open it in the ForReading access mode. Once you open the file for reading, you can read information for the file in several different ways. You can read the entire contents of the file, or just character strings or lines of information from the file.

Preparing to read

Just because you can open a file doesn't mean it contains any information. Therefore, before you try to read the file, you should verify that it contains information. To do this, you can use the AtEndOfStream property of the TextStream object. The AtEndOfStream property returns True when you are at the end of a file and False otherwise. If the file exists but is empty, the AtEndOfStream property returns True immediately after you open the file.

You should also use the AtEndOfStream property to test for the end-of-file marker prior to reading additional information from a file. One way to test for an empty file and to check for the end-of-file marker prior to reading it is to use a Do While loop as shown in Listing 9-3. If you run this example on an empty file, it will complete execution. If you run it against a file containing text, the script will never stop running because it is not actually reading the file at this point.

LISTING 9-3

Using AtEndOfStream

VBScript
checkeos.vbs

```
Const ForReading = 1
Const TristateFalse = 0
```

```
Set fs = CreateObject("Scripting.FileSystemObject")
Set f = fs.GetFile("D:\data\log.txt")
Set thefile = f.OpenAsTextStream(ForReading, TristateFalse)

Do While theFile.AtEndOfStream <> True
  'Read from the file
Loop
```

JScript
checkeos.js

```
ForReading = 1
TristateFalse = 0
var fs = new ActiveXObject("Scripting.FileSystemObject");
var f = fs.GetFile("D:\\data\\log.txt");
var ts = f.OpenAsTextStream(ForReading, TristateFalse)
while (!ts.AtEndOfStream) {
//Read from the file
}
```

Another helpful property is AtEndOfLine, which returns True if you've reached an end-of-line marker. This property is useful if you are reading characters from files where fields or data records are stored on individual lines. Here, you read from the file until the end of line is reached, at which point you know you've reached the end of a field or record. An example using AtEndOfLine is shown here:

VBScript

```
Do While theFile.AtEndOfLine <> True
  'Read characters from the file
Loop
```

JScript

```
while (!f.AtEndOfLine) {
  //Read characters from the file
}
```

Your window into text files is gained through column and line pointers. The column pointer indicates the current column position within a file. The line pointer indicates the current line position within a file. To check the value of these pointers, use the Column and Line properties of the TextStream object, respectively.

After opening a file, the column and line pointers are both set to 1. This means you are at column 1, line 1. If you then read in a line from the file, you are at column 1, line 2. If you read 10 characters from a file without advancing to the next line, you are at column 11, line 1. Being able to check the column and line position is very useful when you work with fixed-length records or you want to examine specific lines of data.

Listing 9-4 shows how you could check the column and line position at various stages of reading a file. You'll find more pointers for using these properties later in this chapter.

LISTING 9-4

Using the Column and Line Properties

VBScript
fpointers.vbs

```
Const ForReading = 1
Const TristateFalse = 0

Set fs = CreateObject("Scripting.FileSystemObject")
Set f = fs.GetFile("D:\data\log.txt")
Set ts = f.OpenAsTextStream(ForReading, TristateFalse)

currColumn = ts.Column
currLine = ts.Line

WScript.Echo "Position is: Column " & currColumn & " Line " & currLine
```

JScript
fpointers.js

```
ForReading = 1
TristateFalse = 0

var fs = new ActiveXObject("Scripting.FileSystemObject");
var f = fs.GetFile("D:\\data\\log.txt");
var ts = f.OpenAsTextStream(ForReading, TristateFalse)

currColumn = ts.Column
currLine = ts.Line

WScript.Echo("Position is: Column " + currColumn + " Line " + currLine)
```

You can read from a file using any of these three methods:

- Read(x): Reads *x* number of characters from a file.
- ReadLine: Reads a line of text from a file.
- ReadAll: Reads the entire contents of a file.

Whether you read in a file all at once, a few characters at a time, or line by line depends on the type of information the file contains. If the file contains fixed-length records or is written as a single line of data, you'll usually want to use Read or ReadAll. If the file contains lines of data and each line ends with an end-of-line marker, you'll usually want to use ReadLine or ReadAll.

Reading characters

You use the Read method to read a specific number of characters from a file. The read begins at the current column position and continues until the number of characters specified is reached. Because you want to maintain the information returned from Read, assign the return value to a variable. Listing 9-5 shows how you can open a file and read 20 characters.

LISTING 9-5

Reading Characters from a File

VBScript
readchars.vbs

```
Const ForReading = 1
Const TristateFalse = 0

Set fs = CreateObject("Scripting.FileSystemObject")
Set f = fs.OpenTextFile("D:\data\log.txt", ForReading, True)
returnValue = f.Read(20)
```

JScript
readchars.js

```
ForReading = 1
TristateFalse = 0
var fs = new ActiveXObject("Scripting.FileSystemObject");
var f = fs.OpenTextFile("D:\\data\\log.txt", ForReading, "True")
returnValue = f.Read(20)
```

The Read method doesn't stop at end-of-line markers. Instead, the method reads the individual characters that make up this marker as one or two characters (either carriage return, or carriage return and line feed). To have the Read method stop when the end of the line is reached, you should read one character at a time and test for the end-of-line before each successive read, like this:

VBScript

```
Do While theFile.AtEndOfLine <> True
   val = val + theFile.Read(1)
Loop
```

JScript

```
while (!theFile.AtEndOfLine)
{
    val += theFile.Read(1);
}
```

Reading lines

For files written using lines, you can use the ReadLine method to read a line from the file. As with the Read method, you store the value returned by the ReadLine method in a variable so you can use the results. An example is shown as Listing 9-6.

LISTING 9-6

Using ReadLine

VBScript
readlines.vbs

```
Const ForReading = 1
Const TristateFalse = 0

Set fs = CreateObject("Scripting.FileSystemObject")
Set f = fs.OpenTextFile("D:\data\log.txt", ForReading, True)
theLine = f.ReadLine
```

JScript
readlines.js

```
ForReading = 1
TristateFalse = 0

var fs = new ActiveXObject("Scripting.FileSystemObject");
var f = fs.OpenTextFile("D:\\data\\log.txt", ForReading, "True")
theLine = f.ReadLine()
```

NOTE   When you read files that include end-of-line designators, you normally use ReadLine rather than Read. If, however, you read the first 20 characters in a line without reaching the end-of-line designator and then issued a ReadLine command, the ReadLine method would read from the current pointer position to the end of the current line.

Unless you know that each line of a file has a fixed length, you probably won't use the Column pointer in conjunction with the ReadLine method. Instead, you'll use the individual lines of data to move around within the file. Let's say you want to extract data from a file five lines at a time. To do this, you can open the file for reading and then use a loop to advance through the file as is shown in Listing 9-7.

LISTING 9-7

Reading Data Sets with ReadLine

VBScript
readdatasets.vbs

```
Const ForReading = 1
count = 5
dataSet = 0

Set fs = CreateObject("Scripting.FileSystemObject")
Set f = fs.OpenTextFile("D:\data.txt", ForReading, True)

Do While f.AtEndOfStream <> True
  data = ""
  For a = 1 to count
   If f.AtEndOfStream <> True Then
    data = data + f.ReadLine
   End If
  Next
  dataSet = dataSet + 1
  WScript.Echo "Data Set " & dataset & ": " & data
Loop
```

JScript
readdatasets.js

```
ForReading = 1
count = 5
dataSet = 0
var fs = new ActiveXObject("Scripting.FileSystemObject");
var f = fs.OpenTextFile("D:\\data.txt", ForReading, "True")
while (!f.AtEndOfStream){
  var data = ""
  for (a = 0; a < count; a++) {
    if (!f.AtEndOfStream) {
      data += f.ReadLine()
    }
  }
  dataSet++
  WScript.Echo("Data Set " + dataSet +": " + data)
}
```

Reading an entire file

The ReadAll method enables you to read in the entire contents of a file and is useful if you want to manipulate the file contents all at once, or display the contents to a user. Listing 9-8 shows how you can read in the contents of a file and display the results in a pop-up dialog box.

LISTING 9-8

Using ReadAll

VBScript
readfile.vbs

```
Const ForReading = 1

Set fs = CreateObject("Scripting.FileSystemObject")
Set f = fs.OpenTextFile("D:\data.txt", ForReading, True)

fContents = f.ReadAll
f.Close

Set w = WScript.CreateObject("WScript.Shell")
a = w.Popup(fContents,60,"Display File",1)
```

JScript
readfile.js

```
ForReading = 1

var fs = new ActiveXObject("Scripting.FileSystemObject");
var f = fs.OpenTextFile("D:\\data.txt", ForReading, "True")

fContents = f.ReadAll()
f.Close()

var w = WScript.CreateObject("WScript.Shell");
a = w.Popup(fContents,60,"Display File",1)
```

Skipping Lines in a File

Skipping characters and lines are common tasks you'll want to perform when you read from a file. To do this, you can use these methods:

- Skip(x): Skips x number of characters.
- SkipLine: Skips one line of text.

You cannot skip characters in a file you open to write in or append. In the ForWriting mode, the file is initialized and any existing contents are deleted. In the ForAppending mode, the file pointer is set to the end of the file, so there are no characters to skip.

Skipping characters

In a file you are reading, you can set the number of characters to skip when you call the Skip method. In Listing 9-9, you skip the first 30 characters and then read the next 30 characters.

LISTING 9-9

Working with Skip

VBScript
skipchars.vbs

```
Const ForReading = 1

Set fs = CreateObject("Scripting.FileSystemObject")
Set f = fs.OpenTextFile("D:\data.txt", ForReading, True)
f.Skip(30)
record = f.Read(30)
```

JScript
skipchars.js

```
ForReading = 1
var fs = new ActiveXObject("Scripting.FileSystemObject");
var f = fs.OpenTextFile("D:\\data.txt", ForReading, "True")
f.Skip(30)
record = f.Read(30)
```

Skipping lines

The SkipLine method is also pretty straightforward. Each time you call the method, it skips one line in a file. It does this by looking for the next occurrence of the end-of-line designator. If you know the first three lines of a file have comments that you don't want to use in a data set, you can skip them as follows:

VBScript

```
For a = 1 to 3
  If f.AtEndOfStream <> True Then
    f.SkipLine
  End If
Next
```

JScript

```
for (a = 0; a < 3; a++) {
    if (!f.AtEndOfStream) {
        f.SkipLine()
    }
}
```

NOTE The `SkipLine` method looks for the end-of-line designator to determine when it has reached the end of a line. So if you called the method after reading part of a line with the `Read` method, but before reaching the end of the line, `SkipLine` would find the end-of-line designator for the current line and then set the pointer to the beginning of the next line.

Writing to a File

You can write to text files using the `ForWriting` and the `ForAppending` modes. The access mode determines the initial position of the pointer within the file. With the `ForWriting` mode, the file is initialized, erasing any existing data. The pointer is then set at the beginning of the file. With the `ForAppending` mode, the pointer is set to the end of the file and any data you write is added to the existing data in the file.

Preparing to write

While you may want to overwrite temporary data files, you probably don't want to inadvertently overwrite other types of files. If you have any doubts about whether a file exists, you should use the `FileExists` method to check for the file before trying to access it in `ForWriting` mode. The `FileExists` method returns `True` if the file exists and `False` if it does not exist. As shown in Listing 9-10, you can use the results of the `FileExists` test to determine whether you open a file in the `ForWriting` mode or the `ForAppending` mode.

LISTING 9-10

Setting Mode Based on FileExists

VBScript
setmode.vbs

```
Const ForWriting = 2
Const ForAppending = 8

aFile = "C:\temp\data.txt"
Set fs = CreateObject("Scripting.FileSystemObject")
If (fs.FileExists(aFile)) Then
  Set f = fs.OpenTextFile(aFile, ForAppending)
```

```
Else
  Set f = fs.OpenTextFile(aFile, ForWriting, True)
End If
```

JScript
setmode.js

```
ForWriting = 2
ForAppending = 8
aFile = "C:\\temp\\data.txt"
var fs = new ActiveXObject
("Scripting.FileSystemObject");
if (fs.FileExists(aFile))
  var f = fs.OpenTextFile(aFile, ForAppending)
else
  var f = fs.OpenTextFile(aFile, ForWriting, "True")
```

When you are finished writing to a file, you should close the file by calling the `Close` method. `Close` writes the end-of-file marker to the file and releases the file. You are then free to open the file in a different mode, such as `ForReading`. You close a file as follows:

VBScript

```
f.Close
```

JScript

```
f.Close()
```

 **NOTE**   Closing a file after a write is essential. If you forget to do this, the end-of-file marker may not be written to the file and this may cause problems when trying to read the file later.

Writing to a new file or appending data to the end of an existing file is fairly easy. You start by creating a `TextStream` object. Afterward, you open the file for writing or appending, and then write to the file. Regardless of which write-related method you use, the write begins at the pointer position set when the file was opened (which is either the beginning or end of the file). You can write to a file using any of these methods:

- `Write(x)`: Writes *x* number of characters to a file.
- `WriteLine`: Writes a line of text to a file.
- `WriteBlankLines(n)`: Writes *n* blank lines to a file.

Writing characters

The `Write` method writes strings to a file. You set the string to write when you call the `Write` method, like this:

VBScript

```
Set fs = CreateObject("Scripting.FileSystemObject")
Set f = fs.OpenTextFile(aFile, ForAppending)
f.Write theData
f.Close
```

JScript

```
var fs = new ActiveXObject("Scripting.FileSystemObject");
var f = fs.OpenTextFile(aFile, ForAppending)
f.Write(theData)
f.Close()
```

Writing lines

The `WriteLine` method is used to write lines of data to a file. The runtime engine terminates lines with an end-of-line marker (the carriage return and line-feed characters). You can use the `WriteLine` method as follows:

VBScript

```
Set fs = CreateObject("Scripting.FileSystemObject")
Set f = fs.OpenTextFile(aFile, ForAppending)
f.WriteLine theLine
f.Close
```

JScript

```
var fs = new ActiveXObject("Scripting.FileSystemObject");
var f = fs.OpenTextFile(aFile, ForAppending)
f.WriteLine(theLine)
f.Close()
```

Writing blank lines

The `WriteBlankLines` method is used to write blank lines to a file. The only contents on a blank line are end-of-line markers (the carriage return and line-feed characters). When you call the `WriteBlankLines` method, you set the number of blank lines to add to the file, such as 3 or 5.

Normally, you'll use this method in conjunction with `WriteLine`, like this:

VBScript

```
Set fs = CreateObject("Scripting.FileSystemObject")
Set f = fs.OpenTextFile(aFile, ForAppending)

f.WriteLine theHeaderLine
f.WriteBlankLines
f.WriteLine theDataLine
f.WriteBlankLines 1
f.WriteLine theFooterLine
```

JScript

```
var fs = new ActiveXObject("Scripting.FileSystemObject");
var f = fs.OpenTextFile(aFile, ForAppending)
f.WriteLine(theHeaderLine)
f.WriteBlankLines(1)
f.WriteLine(theDataLine)
f.WriteBlankLines(1)
f.WriteLine(theFooterLine)
```

Writing a blank line to a file is useful when you are managing text files, such as logs or flat-file data-bases in which multiple blank lines serve as record separators. But keep in mind that blank lines usually aren't shown in HTML documents. To create a blank line in an HTML document, you'll need to insert an empty paragraph element. You learn more about using scripts to create HTML documents in other chapters.

Summary

Reading and writing files is one of the fundamental tasks that you'll need to master. As you set out to create your own scripts to read and write files, don't forget the essential lessons learned from this chapter. You open files for reading, writing, and appending using `ForReading`, `ForWriting`, and `ForAppending`. Then, once you have the file open in the appropriate mode, you can read, write, or skip within the file.

Chapter 10

Managing Drives and Printers with VBScript and JScript

This chapter completes our look at managing the file system and then moves on to examine managing network resources. You learn how to work with drives and how to examine drive properties. You also learn how to map network drives and configure network printer connections.

Managing Drives

Two different ways of working with drives are available. You can work with a specific drive, such as the C: drive, or you can work with drive collections. *Drive collections* are containers for all of the local and network drives on a particular system.

Obtaining Drive Information

Most functions that work with drives allow you to reference drive paths in any of these ways:

- By drive letter, such as C or D
- By drive path, such as C:\ or D:\
- By network share path, such as \\PLUTO\MYSHARE or \\SATURN\DATA

Most network drives have a drive designator associated with them as well as a path. For example, the network drive \\PLUTO\MYSHARE may be mapped on the system as the H: drive. You can obtain a drive designator for a network drive using the GetDriveName method of FileSystemObject. This method requires a drive path. The following are a few examples of how it is used:

VBScript

```
Set fs = CreateObject("Scripting.FileSystemObject")
drv = fs.GetDriveName ("\\PLUTO\DATA")
WScript.Echo drv
```

JScript

```
fs = new ActiveXObject("Scripting.FileSystemObject");
drv = fs.GetDriveName("\\PLUTO\\DATA")
WScript.Echo (drv)
```

Checking for a drive

You'll usually want to test for a drive's existence before you try to work with it. To do this, you can use the DriveExists method of FileSystemObject. This method returns True if a drive exists and can be used (shown in Listing 10-1).

LISTING 10-1

Checking for a Drive

VBScript
testdrive.vbs

```
WScript.Echo (CheckDrive("C"))

Function CheckDrive(drv)
 Dim fs, s
  Set fs = CreateObject("Scripting.FileSystemObject")
  If (fs.DriveExists(drv)) Then
    s = drv & " is available."
  Else
    s = drv & " doesn't exist."
  End If
 CheckDrive = s
End Function
```

JScript
testdrive.js

```
WScript.Echo (CheckDrive("C"))
function CheckDrive(drv) {
var fs, s = drv;
fs = new ActiveXObject("Scripting.FileSystemObject");
if (fs.DriveExists(drv))
```

```
    s += " is available.";
else
    s += " doesn't exist.";
 return(s);
}
```

Output

```
C is available.
```

Using the Drive object

After checking for a drive's existence, one of the most common tasks you'll want to perform is to obtain a Drive object. You can then use this object to check drive properties.

To obtain a Drive object, use the GetDrive method of FileSystemObject. The main argument for this method is a string containing the path to the drive you want to work with, such as:

VBScript

```
Set fs = CreateObject("Scripting.FileSystemObject")
Set drv = fs.GetDrive("D")
```

JScript

```
var fs = new ActiveXObject("Scripting.FileSystemObject");
var drv = fs.GetDrive("D")
```

Once you have a Drive object, you can examine its properties. To do this, use the Drive object properties summarized in Table 10-1.

TABLE 10-1

Properties of the Drive Object

Property Value	Description	Sample
AvailableSpace	Returns the amount of available space on the drive in bytes, this is a per-user value that can be affected by quotas.	1632116580
DriveLetter	Returns the drive letter without a colon	C
DriveType	Returns the drive type as an integer value: 0 for Unknown, 1 for Removable, 2 for Fixed, 3 for Network, 4 for CD/DVD-ROM, and 5 for RAM Disk	2
FileSystem	Returns the file system type such as FAT, FAT32, NFTS, or CDFS	NTFS

continued

TABLE 10-1	(continued)	
Property Value	**Description**	**Sample**
FreeSpace	Returns the total amount of free space on the drive	192975478
IsReady	For removable-media drives and CD/DVD drives, returns True if the drive is ready	True
Path	Returns the drive path	C:\
RootFolder	Returns a Folder object containing the root folder on the specified drive	-
SerialNumber	With removable media, returns the serial number of the media	329941809
ShareName	With network drives, returns the network share name	work
TotalSize	Returns the total size of the drive in bytes	928282853399
VolumeName	Returns the volume name of the drive	Primary

One of the most useful drive properties is FreeSpace. You can use this property to help you keep track of system resources throughout the network. For example, you can create a script that runs as a periodically scheduled job on your key servers, such as your email and file servers. When the script runs, it logs the free space on system drives. If any of the drives has less free space than is desirable, you can log a warning that the drive is getting low on space as well.

 Because the DriveInfo.js script may run through the Task scheduler, you'll need to map the drives you want to use to the network. Mapping network drives is covered later in this chapter.

Listing 10-2 shows an example script for displaying drive information. You can use this script to obtain summary information for a specific drive. Using the Drive collection, you could extend the script to obtain a report for all drives on a system.

LISTING 10-2

Obtaining Drive Information

driveinfo.js

```
drvpath = "C"
WScript.Echo(GetDriveInfo(drvpath))

function GetDriveInfo(drvpath)
{
  var fs, d, s, t, wnet, cname;
```

```
wNet = WScript.CreateObject ("WScript.Network");
cname = wNet.ComputerName;

fs = new ActiveXObject("Scripting.FileSystemObject");
d = fs.GetDrive(drvpath);
switch (d.DriveType)
{
  case 0: t = "Unknown"; break;
  case 1: t = "Removable"; break;
  case 2: t = "Fixed"; break;
  case 3: t = "Network"; break;
  case 4: t = "CD/DVD-ROM"; break;
  case 5: t = "RAM Disk"; break;
}
s = "=========================" + "\r\n";
s += cname + "\r\n";
s += "=========================" + "\r\n";
s += "Drive " + d.DriveLetter + ": - " + t;
s += " - " + d.FileSystem + "\r\n";
if (d.VolumeName)
 s += "Volume: " + d.VolumeName + "\r\n"
if (d.ShareName)
 s += " Share: " + d.ShareName + "\r\n"
s += "Total space " + Math.round(d.TotalSize/1048576)
s += " Mbytes" + "\r\n";
s += "Free Space: " + Math.round(d.FreeSpace/1048576)
s += " Mbytes" + "\r\n";
s += "=========================" + "\r\n";
return(s);
}
```

Output

```
=========================
PLUTO
=========================
Drive C: - Fixed - FAT
Volume: Primary
Total space 20047 Mbytes
Free Space: 5057 Mbytes
=========================
```

The drive information script uses a few new techniques. First, a Switch Case structure is used to convert the integer value returned by DriveType to a string:

```
switch (d.DriveType)
  {
```

```
    case 0: t = "Unknown"; break;
    case 1: t = "Removable"; break;
    case 2: t = "Fixed"; break;
    case 3: t = "Network"; break;
    case 4: t = "CD/DVD-ROM"; break;
    case 5: t = "RAM Disk"; break;
}
```

Next, the script builds the output by concatenating a series of strings. Tucked away in these strings is a function that converts the byte values returned by TotalSize and FreeSpace to a value in megabytes. The bytes to megabytes conversion is handled by dividing the return value by 1,048,576, which is the number of bytes in a megabyte. The result is then rounded to the nearest integer value using the Math.round() method. In the script, this results in:

```
s += "Total space " + Math.round(d.TotalSize/1048576)
s += " Mbytes" + "\r\n";
s += "Free Space: " + Math.round(d.FreeSpace/1048576)
```

Examining all drives on a system

The easiest way to examine all drives on a system is to use the Drives collection. You work with the Drives collection much like any other collection discussed in this book. In VBScript, you obtain the collection, and then use a For Each loop to examine its contents. In JScript, you obtain the collection through an Enumerator object and then use the methods of the Enumerator object to examine each drive in turn.

Listing 10-3 shows a sample script that works with the Drives collection. The output provided is a partial listing of drives from our system. Note that the A: drive is a floppy drive. Because the drive didn't contain a disk when checked, the drive wasn't ready for certain tasks, such as reading the volume name or obtaining the amount of free space. Running this example on your system will result in different output than shown below.

LISTING 10-3

Working with the Drives Collection

VBScript
checkdrives.vbs

```
WScript.Echo GetDriveList()

Function GetDriveList
'Initialize variables
Dim fs, d, dc, s, n, CRLF
'Specify EOL designator
  CRLF = Chr(13) & Chr(10)
```

```
  Set fs = CreateObject("Scripting.FileSystemObject")
  Set dc = fs.Drives

  For Each d in dc
    n = ""
    s = s & d.DriveLetter & " - "
    If d.DriveType = Remote Then
      n = d.ShareName
    ElseIf d.IsReady Then
      n = d.VolumeName
    End If
    s = s & n & CRLF
  Next
  GetDriveList = s
End Function
```

JScript
checkdrives.js

```
WScript.Echo(GetDriveList())
function GetDriveList()
{
  //Initialize variables
  var fs, s, n, e, d;
  fs = new ActiveXObject("Scripting.FileSystemObject");
  e = new Enumerator(fs.Drives);
  s = "";
  for (; !e.atEnd(); e.moveNext())
  {
    d = e.item();
    s = s + d.DriveLetter + " - " ;
    if (d.DriveType == 3)
      n = d.ShareName;
    else if (d.IsReady)
      n = d.VolumeName;
    else
      n = "(Drive not ready)";
    s +=  n + "\r\n";
  }
  return(s);
}
```

Output

```
C - PRIMARY
D - SECONDARY
E - HISTORY
```

Mapping Network Drives

Network drives enable users and scripts to access remote resources on the network. If you are using a script to configure network drives for a particular user, you should log in as this user and then run the script, or have the user log in and then run the script. This ensures that the network drives are configured as necessary in the user's profile. On the other hand, if you are using a network drive in a script, such as a script that runs as a scheduled job, you should connect to the drive, use the drive, and then disconnect from the drive.

Connecting to a network share

Network shares aren't automatically available to users or to scripts. You must specifically map a network share to a network drive before it is available. In Windows scripts, you map network drives using the MapNetworkDrive method of the Network object. The basic structure for this method requires the drive letter to map the name of the network share to the local system, like this:

VBScript

```
Set wn = WScript.CreateObject("WScript.Network")
wn.MapNetworkDrive "H:","\\Saturn\data"
```

JScript

```
var wn = WScript.CreateObject("WScript.Network")
wn.MapNetworkDrive("H:", "\\\\Saturn\\data")
```

 The four backslashes used with JScript aren't typos. Remember, in JScript you must escape each slash in a directory path with a slash.

By default, the network drive mapping isn't permanent, and the next time the user logs on, the drive isn't mapped. To change this behavior, you can specify that the drive is persistent by setting the optional persistent flag to True. This updates the user profile to ensure the drive is automatically mapped in subsequent user sessions. You can set the persistent flag like this:

VBScript

```
Set wn = WScript.CreateObject("WScript.Network")
wn.MapNetworkDrive "H:","\\Saturn\data", True
```

JScript

```
var wn = WScript.CreateObject("WScript.Network")
wn.MapNetworkDrive("H:", "\\\\Saturn\\data", "True")
```

When mapping a network drive for use by scripts that run as scheduled jobs, you may need to set a username and password in order to establish the connection. You do this by supplying the username and password as the final parameters. In this example, scriptAdmin is the username and gorilla is the password:

VBScript

```
Set wn = WScript.CreateObject("WScript.Network")
wn.MapNetworkDrive "H:","\\Saturn\data", True,"scriptAdmin", "gorilla"
```

JScript

```
var wn = WScript.CreateObject("WScript.Network")
wn.MapNetworkDrive("H:", "\\\\Saturn\\data", "True","scriptAdmin", "gorilla")
```

CAUTION   Placing passwords in a script isn't a sound security practice. If you are going to set passwords in scripts, you should A) place the scripts in a directory with very limited access,
and B) create a special account that is used only for scripts and has limited permissions.

Disconnecting from a network share

When you are finished working with a network drive, you may want to disconnect the associated
drive. To do this, you can use the RemoveNetworkDrive method of the Network object. Specify
the designator of the network drive you want to disconnect, like this:

VBScript

```
Set wn = WScript.CreateObject("WScript.Network")
wn.RemoveNetworkDrive "H:"
```

JScript

```
var wn = WScript.CreateObject("WScript.Network")
wn.RemoveNetworkDrive("H:")
```

If a drive is still in use, it won't be disconnected. You can force the drive to disconnect by setting the
optional force flag to True, like this:

VBScript

```
Set wn = WScript.CreateObject("WScript.Network")
wn.RemoveNetworkDrive "H:", True
```

JScript

```
var wn = WScript.CreateObject("WScript.Network")
wn.RemoveNetworkDrive("H:", "True")
```

The third and final parameter for RemoveNetworkDrive removes the persistent mapping for the
drive. If you want to remove the persistent mapping for the drive in the user's profile, set this flag to
True, like this:

VBScript

```
Set wn = WScript.CreateObject("WScript.Network")
wn.RemoveNetworkDrive "H:", True, True
```

JScript

```
var wn = WScript.CreateObject("WScript.Network")
wn.RemoveNetworkDrive("H:", "True", "True")
```

Managing Network Printers

Windows scripts can configure default printers, as well as add and remove network printers. A net-work printer is a shared printer that is accessible to other systems on the network. If you are using a script to configure printers for a particular user, you should log in as the user and run the script, or have the user log in and then run the script. This ensures that the printers are configured as neces-sary in the user's profile. If you are using a printer in a script, such as one that runs in a scheduled job, you should connect to the printer, use the printer, and then disconnect from the printer.

Setting a default printer

The default printer is the primary printer for a user. This printer is used whenever a user prints a document and doesn't select a specific destination printer. You can set a default printer using the SetDefaultPrinter method of the Network object. This method automatically updates the user's profile to use the default printer in the current session as well as subsequent sessions.

When you use SetDefaultPrinter, you must specify the network share for the printer to use as the default, such as \\NPSERVER\SW12. The network share path is the only parameter for SetDefaultPrinter. You can use the method in a script as follows:

VBScript

```
Set wn = WScript.CreateObject("WScript.Network")
wn.SetDefaultPrinter "\\NPSERVER\SW12"
```

JScript

```
var wn = WScript.CreateObject("WScript.Network")
wn.SetDefaultPrinter("\\\\NPSERVER\\SW12")
```

Adding printer connections

Windows scripts manage connections to network printers much like they manage connections to network drives. You map printer connections using AddPrinterConnection or AddWindows PrinterConnection. You remove printer connections using RemovePrinterConnection.

AddPrinterConnection adds a remote MS-DOS based computer connection to a computer. As you cannot use AddPrinterConnection to add a Windows-based printer connection, you'll need to use AddWindowsPrinterConnection with Windows-based printers.

The basic structure for `AddPrinterConnection` requires a local resource name for the printer, and the path to the network printer name. For example, if you work in an office building, you may want to map to the printer in the southwest corner of the 12th floor. If the printer is shared as \\NPSERVER\SW12, you can map the printer to the local LPT1 port as follows:

VBScript

```
Set wn = WScript.CreateObject("WScript.Network")
wn.AddPrinterConnection "LPT1", "\\NPSERVER\SW12"
```

JScript

```
var wn = WScript.CreateObject("WScript.Network")
wn.AddPrinterConnection("LPT1", "\\\\NPSERVER\\SW12")
```

You can also enter `""` for the port parameter, for example:

VBScript

```
Set wn = WScript.CreateObject("WScript.Network")
wn.AddPrinterConnection "", "\\NPSERVER\SW12"
```

JScript

```
var wn = WScript.CreateObject("WScript.Network")
wn.AddPrinterConnection("", "\\\\NPSERVER\\SW12")
```

If you just need to use the printer temporarily, you probably don't want to update the user's profile to maintain the printer connection in subsequent user sessions. On the other hand, if you are configuring printers that will be used regularly, you can set the optional persistent flag to `True`. This updates the user profile to ensure that the printer is automatically connected to in subsequent user sessions. You can set the persistent flag as follows:

VBScript

```
Set wn = WScript.CreateObject("WScript.Network")
wn.AddPrinterConnection "LPT1", "\\NPSERVER\SW12",True
```

JScript

```
var wn = WScript.CreateObject("WScript.Network")
wn.AddPrinterConnection("LPT1", "\\\\NPSERVER\\SW12","True")
```

When mapping a network printer for use by scripts that run as scheduled jobs, you may need to set a username and password in order to establish the connection. You do this by supplying the username and password as the final parameters. In this example, `prUser` is the user name and `gorilla` is the password:

VBScript

```
Set wn = WScript.CreateObject("WScript.Network")
wn.AddPrinterConnection "LPT1","\\NPSERVER\SW12", False, "prUser", "gorilla"
```

JScript

```
var wn = WScript.CreateObject("WScript.Network")
wn.AddPrinterConnection("LPT1","\\\\NPSERVER\\SW12", "False","prUser", "gorilla")
```

An alternative to AddPrinterConnection is AddWindowsPrinterConnection. The AddWindows PrinterConnection method expects to be passed the path to the network printer, such as:

VBScript

```
Set wn = WScript.CreateObject("WScript.Network")
wn.AddWindowsPrinterConnection "\\NPSERVER\SW12"
```

JScript

```
var wn = WScript.CreateObject("WScript.Network")
wn.AddWindowsPrinterConnection("\\\\NPSERVER\\SW12")
```

Removing printer connections

When you are finished working with a network printer, you may want to remove the connection. To do this, you can use the RemovePrinterConnection method of the Network object. Specify the local designator of the printer you want to disconnect, like this:

VBScript

```
Set wn = WScript.CreateObject("WScript.Network")
wn.RemovePrinterConnection "PrinterSW12"
```

JScript

```
var wn = WScript.CreateObject("WScript.Network")
wn.RemovePrinterConnection("PrinterSW12")
```

You can force the printer to disconnect by setting the optional force flag to True, like this:

VBScript

```
Set wn = WScript.CreateObject("WScript.Network")
wn.RemovePrinterConnection "PrinterSW12", True
```

JScript

```
var wn = WScript.CreateObject("WScript.Network")
wn.RemovePrinterConnection("PrinterSW12", "True")
```

You can also remove the persistent mapping for a printer in the user's profile. To do this, set the third and final parameter to True, like this:

VBScript

```
Set wn = WScript.CreateObject("WScript.Network")
wn.RemovePrinterConnection "PrinterSW12", True, True
```

JScript

```
var wn = WScript.CreateObject("WScript.Network")
wn.RemovePrinterConnection("PrinterSW12", "True", "True")
```

If you create a printer connection for a script, you'll usually want to remove the connection before the script exits. On other hand, if you create a connection in a user logon script, you usually won't remove the printer connection.

Summary

As you've seen, you can create scripts to manage drives and to create reports detailing drive information. Drive reports can be extremely useful when you want to track drive usage and free space on enterprise servers. Windows scripts can also be used to map network drives and network printers—essential tasks that you may need to implement in logon scripts.

Chapter 11

Configuring Menus, Shortcuts, and Startup Applications

S hortcuts, menu options, and startup applications are items that most people don't give much thought. After all, menu options are configured when you add and remove programs. Startup applications are configured based on desktop configuration, and you can create shortcuts without a whole lot of thought. In Windows, you can move items around the menu simply by clicking on them and dragging them to a new location. So you may be wondering, why in the world would you need to do this with a script?

Well, have you ever tried to track down a startup application that you didn't want to start anymore? If you have, you know that you have to browse several different folders to determine where the startup application is defined. You then have to delete the reference to the startup application and hope that you didn't miss another reference somewhere else. To make this process easier, you can use a script to examine all startup application definitions and then delete the unnecessary ones. The script takes care of the dirty work for you and can be used on one system or a thousand quite easily. Starting to see how scripts can be useful in this area?

NOTE Some of the scripts in this chapter are not fully working examples. The scripts may only highlight the syntax of how the commands could be used in a complete script. Also, you may need to replace files and file paths with your own if you are trying the examples on your own computer. You may receive errors if you do not have permissions. For example, if using Windows Vista, run the command shell as an administrator.

Working with Menus, Desktops, and Startup Applications

In the Windows operating system, menus, desktops, and startup applications are all configured with shortcuts and it is the location of the shortcut that determines how the shortcut is used. For example, if you want to add a menu option for a user, you add a shortcut to the user's Programs or Start folder. These shortcuts then appear on the user's menu. If you want to configure startup applications for all users, you add shortcuts to the AllUsersStartup folder. These applications then automatically start when a user logs in to the system locally.

In Chapter 8, we talked about special folders that you may want to use when managing files and folders. There's also a set of special folders that you may want to use when configuring menus, desktops, and startup applications — for example, Programs, Start, and AllUsersStartup.

Table 11-1 provides a summary of special folders you can use with shortcuts. Keep in mind that these folders aren't available on all Windows systems. For example, Windows 95 systems can't use any of the global user folders. (These folders are AllUsersDesktop, AllUsersPrograms, AllUsersStartMenu, and AllUsersStartup.)

TABLE 11-1

Special Folders for Use with Shortcuts

Special Folder	Usage
AllUsersDesktop	Desktop shortcuts for all users
AllUsersPrograms	Programs menu options for all users
AllUsersStartMenu	Start menu options for all users
AllUsersStartup	Startup applications for all users
Desktop	Desktop shortcuts for the current user
Favorites	Favorites menu shortcuts for the current user
Fonts	Fonts folder shortcuts for the current user
MyDocuments	My Documents menu shortcuts for the current user
NetHood	Network Neighborhood shortcuts for the current user
Printers	Printers folder shortcuts for the current user
Programs	Programs menu options for the current user
Recent	Recently used document shortcuts for the current user

Special Folder	Usage
SendTo	SendTo menu shortcuts for the current user
StartMenu	Start menu shortcuts for the current user
Startup	Startup applications for the current user
Templates	Templates folder shortcuts for the current user

Before you can work with a special folder, you need to obtain a `Folder` object that references the special folder. The easiest way to do this is to use the `SpecialFolders` method of the `WScript.WshShell` object. This method expects a single parameter, which is a string containing the name of the special folder you want to work with. For example, if you want to add or remove desktop shortcuts, you can obtain the Desktop folder as follows:

VBScript

```
Set ws = WScript.CreateObject("WScript.Shell")
dsktop = ws.SpecialFolders("Desktop")
```

JScript

```
var ws = WScript.CreateObject("WScript.Shell")
dsktop = ws.SpecialFolders("Desktop")
```

Creating Shortcuts and Menu Options

Creating a shortcut is a very different process from most other administrative tasks we've looked at so far. In fact, you don't really *create* a shortcut — rather, you *build* shortcuts. The process goes like this:

1. Obtain a target folder for the shortcut.
2. Obtain a shortcut object.
3. Set properties for the shortcut.
4. Save the shortcut, which writes it to the target folder or menu.

Each of these steps is examined in the sections that follow.

Obtaining a target folder for the shortcut

Previously, we covered how to obtain a special folder for a shortcut. You aren't limited to creating shortcuts for special folders, however. You can create shortcuts in any type of folder.

With a standard folder, you can obtain a pointer to the folder you want to use with the `GetFolder` method or any other method that returns a `Folder` object. If you want to create a shortcut in the `C:\Data` folder, you can do so like this:

VBScript

```
Set fs = CreateObject("Scripting.FileSystemObject")
Set f = fs.GetFolder("C:\Data")
```

JScript

```
fs = new ActiveXObject("Scripting.FileSystemObject");
var f = fs.GetFolder("C:\\Data");
```

Obtaining a shortcut object

Shortcuts can point to local and network files as well as remote Internet resources. With local or network files, the shortcut name must end with .lnk, which stands for link. With remote Internet resources, the shortcut must end with .url, which indicates a Universal Resource Locator. For brevity, we refer to these shortcuts as *link shortcuts* and *URL shortcuts*.

Regardless of type, you can obtain the necessary object for working with a shortcut via the `Create Shortcut` method of the `Shell` object. For link shortcuts, the method returns a `WshShortcut` object. For URL shortcuts, the method returns a `WshUrlShortcut` object. These objects have different sets of properties, which we examine later in this chapter.

The name of the shortcut is the text that immediately precedes the file extension. For example, if you want to create a shortcut to Microsoft Word, you can name the shortcut MS Word using the following designator:

```
MS Word.lnk
```

Listing 11-1 shows how you can create a link shortcut named Notes. The shortcut is set to execute the Notepad text editor along the path `%WINDIR%\notepad.exe`. Then the shortcut is saved to the Windows desktop with the `Save` method. `Save` is the only method for shortcut-related objects.

LISTING 11-1

Creating a Link Shortcut

VBScript
links.vbs

```
Set ws = WScript.CreateObject("WScript.Shell")
dsktop = ws.SpecialFolders("Desktop")
Set scut = ws.CreateShortcut(dsktop & "\Notes.lnk")
scut.TargetPath = "%windir%\notepad.exe"
scut.Save
```

JScript
links.js

```
var ws = WScript.CreateObject("WScript.Shell")
dsktop = ws.SpecialFolders("Desktop")
var scut = ws.CreateShortcut(dsktop + "\\Notes.lnk")
scut.TargetPath = "%windir%\\notepad.exe"
scut.Save()
```

As you examine the previous listing, note how the folder path and the link path are concatenated. In VBScript, you add the paths together using:

```
dsktop & "\Notes.lnk"
```

In JScript, you use:

```
dsktop + "\\Notes.lnk"
```

Listing 11-2 shows how you can create a URL shortcut named IDG BOOKS. This shortcut is set to access the URL www.idgbooks.com. Then the shortcut is saved with the Save method. The shortcut is created without a folder path and, as a result, is created in the current working directory.

LISTING 11-2

Creating a URL Shortcut

VBScript
urls.vbs

```
Set ws = WScript.CreateObject("WScript.Shell")
Set scut = ws.CreateShortcut("IDG BOOKS.URL")
scut.TargetPath = "http://www.idgbooks.com/"
scut.Save
```

JScript
urls.js

```
var ws = WScript.CreateObject("WScript.Shell")
var scut = ws.CreateShortcut("IDG BOOKS.URL")
scut.TargetPath ="http://www.idgbooks.com/"
scut.Save()
```

 The forward slash is not a special character in JScript. Thus, the forward slash doesn't need to be escaped.

Setting properties for link shortcuts

Link shortcuts are usually used to start applications or open documents rather than access a URL in a browser. Because of this, link shortcuts have different properties than URL shortcuts. The properties are summarized in Table 11-2. At first glance, it seems like a truckload of options, but you can work through the properties one step at a time.

TABLE 11-2

Properties of WshShortcut

Property	Description	Sample VBScript Value
Arguments	Arguments to pass to an application started through the shortcut.	"C:\data\log.txt"
Description	Sets a description for the shortcut.	"Starts Notepad"
Hotkey	Sets a hotkey sequence that activates the shortcut. Can only be used with desktop shortcuts and Start menu options.	"ALT+SHIFT+Z"
IconLocation	Sets the location of an icon for the shortcut. If not set, a default icon is used. The zero indicates the index position of the icon. Few applications have multiple icons indexed, so the index is almost always zero.	"netscape.exe, 0"
TargetPath	Sets the path of the file to execute.	"%windir%\notepad.exe"
WindowStyle	Sets the window style of the application started by the shortcut. The default style is 1. The available styles are the same as options 0-6 discussed in Chapter 10, Table 10-4.	1
WorkingDirectory	Sets the working directory of the application started by the shortcut.	"C:\Working"

CAUTION   If you set any property incorrectly or set a property that isn't supported by a linked application, the shortcut may not be created. In this case, you'll need to correct the problem and try to create the shortcut again.

Setting shortcut arguments

One of the most valuable options is the Arguments property. You can use this property to set arguments to pass in to an application you are starting. Using this property, you can create a shortcut that starts Microsoft Word and loads in a document at C:\Data\Todo.doc as shown in Listing 11-3. Note the location of Microsoft Word may differ when trying these scripts on your own machine.

LISTING 11-3

Setting Arguments for Link Shortcuts

VBScript
largs.vbs

```
Set ws = WScript.CreateObject("WScript.Shell")
Set scut = ws.CreateShortcut("To-do List.lnk")
scut.TargetPath = "C:\Program Files\Microsoft Office\OFFICE\WINWORD.EXE"
scut.Arguments = "C:\temp\Todo.doc"
scut.Save
```

JScript
largs.js

```
var ws = WScript.CreateObject("WScript.Shell")
var scut = ws.CreateShortcut("To-do List.lnk")
scut.TargetPath = "C:\\Program Files\\Microsoft Office\\OFFICE\\WINWORD.EXE"
scut.Arguments = "C:\\Data\\Todo.doc"
scut.Save()
```

Setting shortcut hotkeys

When you add shortcuts to the Windows desktop or the Start menu, you can set a hotkey sequence that activates the shortcut. The hotkey sequence must be specified with at least one modifier key and a key designator. The following modifier keys are available:

- ALT: The Alt key
- CTRL: The Ctrl key
- SHIFT: The Shift key
- EXT: The Windows key

Modifier keys can be joimed in any combination, such as ALT+CTRL or ALT+SHIFT+CTRL, but shouldn't duplicate existing key combinations used by other shortcuts. Key designators include alphabetic characters (A–Z) and numeric characters (0–9) as well as Back, Clear, Delete, Escape, End, Home, Return, Space, and Tab.

Listing 11-4 creates a shortcut for the Start menu. The shortcut uses the hotkey ALT+SHIFT+E.

LISTING 11-4

Setting Hotkeys for Link Shortcuts

VBScript
lkeys.vbs

```
Set ws = WScript.CreateObject("WScript.Shell")
smenu = ws.SpecialFolders("StartMenu")
Set scut = ws.CreateShortcut(smenu & "\Internet Explorer.LNK")
scut.TargetPath = "C:\Program Files\Plus!\Microsoft Internet\IEXPLORE.EXE"
scut.Hotkey = "ALT+SHIFT+E"
scut.Save
```

JScript
lkeys.js

```
var ws = WScript.CreateObject("WScript.Shell")
smenu = ws.SpecialFolders("StartMenu")
var scut = ws.CreateShortcut(smenu + "\\Internet Explorer.LNK")
scut.TargetPath = "C:\\Program Files\\Plus!\\Microsoft Internet\\IEXPLORE.EXE"
scut.Hotkey = "ALT+SHIFT+E"
scut.Save()
```

Setting icon locations

When you create shortcuts for applications, the applications normally have a default icon that is displayed with the shortcut. For example, if you create a shortcut for Internet Explorer, the default icon is a large E. When you create shortcuts to document files, the Windows default icon is used in most cases.

If you want to use an icon other than the default, you can use the IconLocation property. This property expects to be passed an icon location and an icon index. Normally, the icon location equates to an application name, such as iexplore.exe or notepad.exe, and the icon index is set to 0. Listing 11-5 adds an option to the Programs menu for all users. The icon for this option is the Internet Explorer icon.

LISTING 11-5

Setting Icons for Link Shortcuts

VBScript
licons.vbs

```
Set ws = WScript.CreateObject("WScript.Shell")
pmenu = ws.SpecialFolders("AllUsersPrograms")
Set scut = ws.CreateShortcut(pmenu & "\Current Script.LNK")
scut.TargetPath = "%windir%\notepad.exe"
scut.Arguments = "C:\data\curr.vbs"
```

```
scut.IconLocation = "iexplore.exe, 0"
scut.Save
```

JScript
licons.js

```
var ws = WScript.CreateObject("WScript.Shell")
pmenu = ws.SpecialFolders("All(pmenu + "\\Current Script.LNK")UsersPrograms")
var scut = ws.CreateShortcut
scut.TargetPath = "%windir%\\notepad.exe"
scut.Arguments = "C:\\data\\curr.vbs"
scut.IconLocation = "iexplore.exe, 0"
scut.Save()
```

 **Windows has to be able to find the executable. If the executable can't be found in the path, the icon can't be set. In this case, enter the full path to the executable, like this:**

```
scut.IconLocation = "C:\\Program Files\\Plus!\\Microsoft Internet\\
IEXPLORE.EXE, 0"
```

Setting working directories

The working directory sets the default directory for an application. This directory is used the first time you open or save files. Listing 11-6 creates a Start menu shortcut for Windows Notepad. The default directory is set to D:\working.

LISTING 11-6

Setting a Working Directory for Link Shortcuts

VBScript
workingdir.vbs

```
Set ws = WScript.CreateObject("WScript.Shell")
smenu = ws.SpecialFolders("StartMenu")
Set scut = ws.CreateShortcut(smenu & "\Notepad for Working.LNK")
scut.TargetPath = "%windir%\notepad.exe"
scut.WorkingDirectory = "C:\working"
scut.Save
```

JScript
workingdir.js

```
var ws = WScript.CreateObject("WScript.Shell")
smenu = ws.SpecialFolders("StartMenu")
var scut = ws.CreateShortcut(smenu + "\\Notepad for Working.LNK")
scut.TargetPath ="%windir%\\notepad.exe"
scut.WorkingDirectory = "C:\\working"
scut.Save()
```

Setting properties for URL shortcuts

URL shortcuts open Internet documents in the appropriate application. For example, Web pages are opened in the default browser, such as Internet Explorer. With URL shortcuts, the only property you can use is `TargetPath`, which sets the URL you want to use. Listing 11-7 creates a URL shortcut on the Start menu.

LISTING 11-7

Setting the Target Path for URL Shortcuts

VBScript
urlshortcut.vbs

```
Set ws = WScript.CreateObject("WScript.Shell")
smenu = ws.SpecialFolders("StartMenu")
Set scut = ws.CreateShortcut(smenu & "\Cool Web Site.URL")
scut.TargetPath = "http://www.centraldrive.com/"
scut.Save
```

JScript
urlshortcut.js

```
var ws = WScript.CreateObject("WScript.Shell")
smenu = ws.SpecialFolders("StartMenu")
var scut = ws.CreateShortcut(smenu + "\\Cool Web Site.URL")
scut.TargetPath ="http://www.centraldrive.com/"
scut.Save()
```

Managing Shortcuts and Menus

As you've seen, creating shortcuts isn't that difficult. Now let's extend what you've learned to new areas, such as creating, updating, and deleting menus.

Creating menus

Windows scripts can also create new menus. When you create menus, you add folders to existing special folders, such as Start or Programs. Start by obtaining a reference to the menu you want to add onto, like this:

VBScript

```
Set ws = WScript.CreateObject("WScript.Shell")
pmenu = ws.SpecialFolders ("Programs")
```

JScript

```
var ws = WScript.CreateObject("WScript.Shell")
pmenu = ws.SpecialFolders ("Programs")
```

Then create a new menu by adding a folder to the special menu. The following example creates a submenu called Work Files under the Programs menu:

VBScript

```
Set fs = CreateObject("Scripting.FileSystemObject")
Set foldr = fs.CreateFolder(pmenu & "\Work Files")
```

JScript

```
fs = new ActiveXObject("Scripting.FileSystemObject");
var foldr = fs.CreateFolder(pmenu + "\\Work Files")
```

After you create the menu, you can add options to it. You do this by creating shortcuts that point to a location in the new menu. The following example creates a URL shortcut in the Work Files menu:

VBScript

```
Set ws = WScript.CreateObject("WScript.Shell")
Set scut = ws.CreateShortcut(pmenu & "\Work Files\CentralDrive.URL")
scut.TargetPath = "http://www.centraldrive.com/"
scut.Save
```

JScript

```
var ws = WScript.CreateObject("WScript.Shell")
var scut = ws.CreateShortcut(pmenu + "\\Work Files\\CentralDrive.URL")
scut.TargetPath ="http://www.centraldrive.com/"
scut.Save()
```

Accessing and listing menu options

When you manage menus, you'll often find that you need to display or manipulate all of the available options on a particular menu. Unfortunately, accessing a complete list of menu options is a bit more complex than one would imagine. For starters, you need to obtain a WshShell object and then use this object to access the special folder you want to work with, like this:

VBScript

```
Set ws = WScript.CreateObject("WScript.Shell")
 smenu = ws.SpecialFolders(mname)
```

JScript

```
var ws = WScript.CreateObject("WScript.Shell")
smenu = ws.SpecialFolders(mname)
```

Afterward, you need to access the file collection associated with the special folder. You do this through the `FileSystemObject`, like this:

VBScript

```
Set fs = WScript.CreateObject("Scripting.FileSystemObject")
Set f = fs.GetFolder(smenu)
Set fc = f.Files
```

JScript

```
fs = new ActiveXObject("Scripting.FileSystemObject");
f = fs.GetFolder(smenu);
fc = new Enumerator(f.Files);
```

Once you have the file collection, you can use `For` looping to examine the contents of the collection. This example places the full name and path for menu options on separate lines:

VBScript

```
For Each fl in fc
   s = s & fl
   s = s & Chr(10) & Chr(13)
Next
CheckMenu = s
End Function
```

JScript

```
for (; !fc.atEnd(); fc.moveNext())
{
  fl = fs.GetFile(fc.item());
  s += fl + "\r\n"
}
return (s)
}
```

If you want to display only the option name, you can use the `name` property of the `File` object, like this:

VBScript

```
For Each fl in fc

   s = s & fl.name
   s = s & Chr(10) & Chr(13)
Next
CheckMenu = s
End Function
```

JScript

```
for (; !fc.atEnd(); fc.moveNext())
{
  f1 = fs.GetFile(fc.item());
  s += f1.name + "\r\n"
}
return (s)
}
```

Listing 11-8 shows how these procedures could come together in an actual script. This example displays all of the options on the current user's Programs menu.

LISTING 11-8

Viewing Menu Options

VBScript
viewoptions.vbs

```
Function CheckMenu(mname)
 Dim fs, f, f1, fc, s, smenu, ws
 Set ws = WScript.CreateObject("WScript.Shell")
 smenu = ws.SpecialFolders(mname)
 Set fs = WScript.CreateObject("Scripting.FileSystemObject")
 Set f = fs.GetFolder(smenu)
 Set fc = f.Files
 For Each f1 in fc
    s = s & f1.name
    s = s & Chr(10) & Chr(13)
 Next
 CheckMenu = s
End Function

WScript.Echo CheckMenu("Programs")
```

JScript
viewoptions.js

```
function CheckMenu(mname)
{
    var fs, f, fc, s;
    var ws = WScript.CreateObject("WScript.Shell")
    smenu = ws.SpecialFolders(mname)
    fs = new ActiveXObject("Scripting.FileSystemObject");
    f = fs.GetFolder(smenu);
    fc = new Enumerator(f.Files);
```

continued

LISTING 11-8   *(continued)*

```
    s = "";
    for (; !fc.atEnd(); fc.moveNext())
    {
        fl = fs.GetFile(fc.item());
        s += fl.name + "\r\n"
    }
    return (s)
}
WScript.Echo(CheckMenu("Programs"))
```

Updating current shortcuts and menu options

Through Windows scripts, you can update the properties of any shortcut or menu option. You do this by creating a new shortcut with the exact same name as the old shortcut. For example, if you created a Start menu shortcut named Notes.lnk, you can update its settings by creating a new shortcut named Notes.lnk.

In most cases, only the options you specifically set for the shortcut are overwritten. If necessary, you can clear an existing option by setting its value to an empty string. For example, Listing 11-5 creates a shortcut for Notepad. This shortcut sets an argument that opens a document called curr.vbs. If you delete curr.vbs and don't want to use it anymore, you can update the shortcut as shown in Listing 11-9.

LISTING 11-9

Updating a Shortcut

VBScript
update.vbs

```
Set ws = WScript.CreateObject("WScript.Shell")
pmenu = ws.SpecialFolders("AllUsersPrograms")
Set scut = ws.CreateShortcut(pmenu & "\Web Script.LNK")
scut.TargetPath = "%windir%\notepad.exe"
scut.Arguments = ""
scut.IconLocation = "iexplore.exe, 0"
scut.Save
```

JScript
update.js

```
var ws = WScript.CreateObject("WScript.Shell")
pmenu = ws.SpecialFolders("AllUsersPrograms")
```

```
var scut = ws.CreateShortcut(pmenu + "\\Web Script.LNK")
scut.TargetPath ="%windir%\\notepad.exe "
scut.Arguments = ""
scut.IconLocation = "iexplore.exe, 0"
scut.Save()
```

Deleting shortcuts and menu options

Shortcuts and menu options are specified in files. You can delete them as you would any system file. If a shortcut called Notes.lnk is in the current working directory, you can delete it as follows:

VBScript

```
Dim fs
Set fs = CreateObject("Scripting.FileSystemObject")
fs.DeleteFile "Notes.LNK"
```

JScript

```
var fs
fs = new ActiveXObject("Scripting.FileSystemObject");
fs.DeleteFile("Notes.LNK")
```

If a shortcut is in a special folder, such as the Start menu folder, you need to obtain the related folder object before trying to delete the shortcut. Use the path to the folder to retrieve the shortcut using the GetFile method of FileSystemObject. Afterward, call the Delete method of the File object. This removes the shortcut. Listing 11-10 shows an example of deleting a shortcut from the Start menu.

LISTING 11-10

Deleting Start Menu Options

VBScript
deleteoption.vbs

```
Dim ws, fs, f, smenu
Set ws = WScript.CreateObject("WScript.Shell")
Set smenu = ws.SpecialFolders("StartMenu")

Set fs = CreateObject("Scripting.FileSystemObject")
Set f = fs.GetFile(smenu & "\Notes.LNK")
f.Delete
```

continued

LISTING 11-10   *(continued)*

JScript
deleteoption.js

```
var ws = WScript.CreateObject("WScript.Shell")
smenu = ws.SpecialFolders("StartMenu")
fs = new ActiveXObject("Scripting.FileSystemObject");
f = fs.GetFile(smenu +"\\Notes.LNK")
f.Delete();
```

Deleting menus

You can delete menus in much the same way as you delete menu options. However, you normally delete submenus of special folders rather than the special folders themselves. Also, when you create a menu for all users, you must delete the menu via the related special folder. For example, if you create a submenu of AllUsersStartMenu, you must delete the submenu via the AllUsersStartMenu special folder.

The first step in deleting a menu is to obtain a reference to the appropriate special folder, for example:

VBScript

```
Set ws = WScript.CreateObject("WScript.Shell")
pmenu = ws.SpecialFolders ("Programs")
```

JScript

```
var ws = WScript.CreateObject("WScript.Shell")
pmenu = ws.SpecialFolders ("Programs")
```

Afterward, use the `DeleteFolder` method to delete the submenu. Listing 11-11 shows how you can delete a submenu called Work Files under the Programs menu.

LISTING 11-11

Deleting a Menu

VBScript
deletemenu.vbs

```
Set ws = WScript.CreateObject("WScript.Shell")
pmenu = ws.SpecialFolders ("Programs")
Set fs = CreateObject("Scripting.FileSystemObject")
fs.DeleteFolder(pmenu & "\Work Files")
```

JScript
deletemenu.js

```
var ws = WScript.CreateObject("WScript.Shell")
pmenu = ws.SpecialFolders ("Programs")
fs = new ActiveXObject("Scripting.FileSystemObject");
var foldr = fs.DeleteFolder(pmenu + "\\Work Files")
```

Adding and Removing Startup Applications

You specify applications that should be started after a user logs on by creating shortcuts in the AllUsersStartup and Startup folders. The AllUsersStartup folder sets startup applications for all users that log onto a system. The Startup folder sets startup applications for the current user.

Adding startup options

Because these shortcuts are used for automatic startup, the only option you need to set in most cases is the target path. Occasionally, you may also want to set a working directory for the application. The following example shows how you can set Internet Explorer as a startup application for all users:

VBScript

```
Set ws = WScript.CreateObject("WScript.Shell")
smenu = ws.SpecialFolders("AllUsersStartup")
Set scut = ws.CreateShortcut(smenu & "\Internet Explorer.LNK")
scut.TargetPath = "C:\Program Files\Plus!\Microsoft Internet\IEXPLORE.EXE"
scut.Save
```

JScript

```
var ws = WScript.CreateObject("WScript.Shell")
smenu = ws.SpecialFolders("AllUsersStartup")
var scut = ws.CreateShortcut(smenu + "\\Internet Explorer.LNK")
scut.TargetPath = "C:\\Program Files\\Plus!\\Microsoft Internet\\IEXPLORE.
EXE"
scut.Save()
```

Removing startup options

If you later want to remove Internet Explorer as a startup application, you delete its related shortcut, like this:

VBScript

```
Dim ws, fs, f, smenu
Set ws = WScript.CreateObject("WScript.Shell")
```

```
Set smenu = ws.SpecialFolders("AllUsersStartup")
Set fs = CreateObject("Scripting.FileSystemObject")
Set f = fs.GetFile(smenu & "\Internet Explorer.LNK")
f.Delete
```

JScript

```
var ws = WScript.CreateObject("WScript.Shell")
smenu = ws.SpecialFolders("AllUsersStartup")
fs = new ActiveXObject("Scripting.FileSystemObject");
f = fs.GetFile(smenu +"\\Internet Explorer.LNK")
f.Delete();
```

Moving startup options

You may want to move it to the Startup folder so that only the current user (rather than all users) runs the application on startup. To do this, you need to obtain a reference to the original folder and the destination folder, and then move the shortcut with the MoveFile method. Listing 11-12 shows how this can be handled.

LISTING 11-12

Moving a Shortcut to a New Location

VBScript
moveoption.vbs

```
Set ws = WScript.CreateObject("WScript.Shell")
m1 = ws.SpecialFolders("AllUsersStartup")
m2 = ws.SpecialFolders("Startup")
orig = m1 & "\Internet Explorer.LNK"
dest = m2 & "\Internet Explorer.LNK"
Set fs = WScript.CreateObject("Scripting.FileSystemObject")
fs.MoveFile orig, dest
```

JScript
moveoption.js

```
var ws = WScript.CreateObject("WScript.Shell")
m1 = ws.SpecialFolders("AllUsersStartup")
m2 = ws.SpecialFolders("Startup")
orig = m1 + \\Internet Explorer.LNK
dest = m2 + "\\Internet Explorer.LNK"
var fs = WScript.CreateObject("Scripting.FileSystemObject")
fs.MoveFile(orig, dest)
```

Summary

Use the techniques examined in this chapter any time you want to work with shortcuts, menus, and startup applications. Windows Script Host makes it possible to create and manage shortcuts in many different ways. Through shortcuts, you can manage menu options and startup applications as well.

Chapter 12

Working with the Windows Registry and Event Logs

Through Windows Script Host, you can manage the Windows Registry and the Windows event logs. The registry stores configuration information for the operating system, applications, services, and more. By examining and changing registry information in scripts, you can reconfigure a system so that it runs exactly the way you want it to. The event logs track essential processes on a system and can also be used in auditing system activity. By examining event logs through scripts, you can analyze system activity and monitor a system for problems.

IN THIS CHAPTER

Understanding the Windows Registry

Reading and writing Registry values

Working with Windows event logs

Reading and writing event logs

NOTE Some of the scripts in this chapter are not fully working examples. The scripts may only highlight the syntax of how the commands could be used in a complete script. Also, you may need to replace registry paths with your own if you are trying the examples on your own computer.

Working with the Windows Registry

The Windows Registry stores configuration settings. Through Windows scripts, you can read, write, and delete registry entries. Because the registry is essential to the proper operation of the operating system, you should only make changes to the registry when you know how these changes will affect the system. Improperly modifying the Windows Registry can cause serious problems. If the registry gets corrupted, you may have to reinstall the operating system. Always double-check registry scripts before running them, and make sure that they do exactly what you intend.

> **NOTE** Before you edit the registry in any way, you should create or update the system's existing emergency repair disk. This way, if you make a mistake, you can recover the registry and the system. Details on how to back up and restore the registry for Windows XP and Windows Vista can be found in Microsoft knowledgebase article 322756 (http://support.microsoft.com/kb/322756).

Understanding the registry structure

The registry stores configuration values for the operating system, applications, user settings, and more. Registry settings are stored as keys and values. These keys and values are placed under a specific root key, which controls when and how the keys and values are used.

The root keys are summarized in Table 12-1. This table also shows the short name by which you can reference the root key in a script. The three keys with short names are the ones you'll work with most often.

TABLE 12-1

Working with the Windows Registry and Event Logs

Short Name	Long Name	Description
HKCU	HKEY_CURRENT_USER	Controls configuration settings for the current user.
HKLM	HKEY_LOCAL_MACHINE	Controls system-level configuration settings.
HKCR	HKEY_CLASSES_ROOT	Configuration settings for applications and files. Ensures the correct application is opened when a file is started through Windows Explorer or OLE.
-	HKEY_USERS	Stores default-user and other-user settings by profile.
-	HKEY_CURRENT_CONFIG	Contains information about the hardware profile being used.

Under the root keys, you'll find the main keys that control system, user, and application settings. These keys are organized into a tree structure where folders represent keys. For example, under HKEY_CURRENT_USER\Software\Microsoft, you'll find folders for all Microsoft applications installed by the current user. Under HKEY_LOCAL_MACHINE\SYSTEM\CurrentControlSet\Services, you'll find folders for all services installed on the computer. These folders are officially referenced as keys.

Through Windows scripts, you change the values of existing keys or you can assign values to new keys. Keys are designated by a folder path; for example:

```
HKEY_LOCAL_MACHINE
    \SYSTEM
        \CurrentControlSet
            \Services
                \WINS
                    \Parameters
```

Here, the key is `Parameters`. This key has values associated with it. Key values have three components: a value name, a value type, and the actual value. In the following example, the value name is `DbFileNm`, the type is `REG_EXPAND_SZ`, and the actual value is `%windir%\system32\wins\wins.mdb`:

> `DbFileNm : REG_EXPAND_SZ : %windir%\system32\wins\wins.mdb`

NOTE   The `DbFileNm` **value controls the location of the WINS database on a Windows server. Another useful value for controlling WINS is** `LogFilePath`, **which controls the location of WINS log files on a Windows server. This value is written as:**

> `LogFilePath : REG_EXPAND_SZ : %windir%\system32\wins`

For more information, see the section, "Managing WINS through Windows scripts."

Key values are written by default as normal string values (type `REG_SZ`), but you can assign any of these data types:

- `REG_BINARY`: Identifies a binary value. Binary values must be entered using base-2 (0 or 1 only).

- `REG_SZ`: Identifies a string value containing a sequence of characters.

- `REG_DWORD`: Identifies a `DWORD` value, which is composed of hexadecimal data with a maximum length of four bytes.

- `REG_MULTI_SZ`: Identifies a multiple string value.

- `REG_EXPAND_SZ`: Identifies an expandable string value, which is usually used with directory paths.

Reading registry keys and values

You can read registry values by passing the full path and name of a key to the `RegRead` method of the `WshShell` object. `RegRead` then returns the value associated with the key. Listing 12-1 shows how you can read the `DbFileNm` value.

LISTING 12-1

Reading the Windows Registry

VBScript
readkey.vbs

```
Set ws = WScript.CreateObject("WScript.Shell")
v=ws.RegRead("HKLM\SYSTEM\CurrentControlSet\Services\WINS\Parameters\DbFileNm")
WScript.Echo v
```

continued

LISTING 12-1   *(continued)*

JScript
readkey.js

```
var ws = WScript.CreateObject ("WScript.Shell")
v=ws.RegRead("HKLM\\SYSTEM\\CurrentControlSet\\Services\\WINS\\Parameters\\
DbFileNm")
WScript.Echo(v)
```

The RegRead method only supports the standard data types: REG_SZ, REG_EXPAND_SZ, REG_MULTI_SZ, REG_DWORD, and REG_BINARY. If the value contains another data type, the method returns DISP_E_TYPEMISMATCH.

Writing registry keys and values

Creating keys and writing registry values is a bit different than reading key values. To write keys and value entries to the registry, use the RegWrite method of the WshShell object. This method expects to be passed the key name as well as the value you want to set. You can also set an optional parameter that specifies the value type. If you don't set the type parameter, the value is set as a string of type REG_SZ. If you set the value type, the type must be one of the following: REG_SZ, REG_EXPAND_SZ, REG_DWORD, or REG_BINARY.

Some value types are converted automatically to the appropriate format. With REG_SZ and REG_EXPAND_SZ, RegWrite automatically converts values to strings. With REG_DWORD, values are converted to integers in hexadecimal format. However, REG_BINARY must be set as integers. If you set an incorrect data type or an incorrect value, RegWrite returns E_INVALIDARG.

You can use RegWrite to update existing registry keys and values as well as to create new keys and values. If the path ends with a slash (or double slash for JScript), the entry is written as a key. Otherwise, the entry is written as a value entry. Listing 12-2 changes the value entry for the DbFileNm key and then confirms the change by reading the new value.

LISTING 12-2

Modifying an Existing Key

VBScript
modkey.vbs

```
Dim Path
Path = "HKLM\SYSTEM\CurrentControlSet\Services\WINS\Parameters\"
Set ws = WScript.CreateObject("WScript.Shell")
o=ws.RegWrite(Path & "DbFileNm", "%windir%\system32\wins.mdb", "REG_EXPAND_SZ")
v=ws.RegRead(Path & "DbFileNm")
WScript.Echo v
```

JScript
modkey.js

```
var Path
Path = "HKLM\\SYSTEM\\CurrentControlSet\\Services\\WINS\\Parameters\\"
var ws = WScript.CreateObject("WScript.Shell")
o=ws.RegWrite(Path + "DbFileNm","%windir%\\system32\\wins.mdb",
  "REG_EXPAND_SZ")
v=ws.RegRead(Path + "DbFileNm")
WScript.Echo(v)
```

> **TIP** If you change the settings of a Windows service, you will need to restart the service before the changes take effect. If the service won't start after you've made changes, you should change the key values back to their original settings.

Creating new keys

When you create new keys, you don't have to worry about creating the tree structure that may be associated with the key. The registry automatically creates additional folders as necessary.

Usually, you'll want to add new keys to the HKEY_CURRENT_USER root key. For example, you can create a new key for Windows scripts called HKEY_CURRENT_USER\WSHBible and then add values to it. Because these values are stored in the current user's profile, they are persistent and aren't destroyed when the user logs out. This makes it possible to retain values across multiple user sessions.

Listing 12-3 shows an example of creating registry keys and assigning values to the keys. The key created is HKEY_CURRENT_USER\WSHBible. The values associated with the key are named Author and Comments.

LISTING 12-3

Creating Registry Keys and Values

VBScript
Createregkey.vbs

```
Set ws = WScript.CreateObject("WScript.Shell")
val = ws.RegWrite("HKCU\WSHBible\Author","William Stanek")
val = ws.RegWrite("HKCU\WSHBible\Comments","Covers Windows Script Host")
```

JScript
createregkey.js

```
var ws = WScript.CreateObject("WScript.Shell")
val = ws.RegWrite("HKCU\\WSHBible\\Author","William Stanek")
val = ws.RegWrite("HKCU\\WSHBible\\Comments","Covers Windows Script Host")
```

Deleting registry keys and values

You delete registry keys using the RegDelete method of the WshShell object. The only argument for the method is the full path for the key or the value you want to delete. When you delete a key, the path should end with a slash, like this: HKCU\WSHBible\. When you delete a key value, the slash isn't necessary. For example, you can delete the Author value using HKCU\WSHBible\Author as the argument to RegDelete.

Listing 12-4 shows an example of how you can delete the Author and Comment values created in the previous section. The example doesn't delete the HKEY_CURRENT_USER\WSHBible key.

LISTING 12-4

Deleting Registry Values

VBScript
deleteregkey.vbs

```
Set ws = WScript.CreateObject("WScript.Shell")
val = ws.RegDelete("HKCU\WSHBible\Author")
val = ws.RegDelete("HKCU\WSHBible\Comments")
```

JScript
deleteregkey.js

```
var ws = WScript.CreateObject("WScript.Shell")
val = ws.RegDelete("HKCU\\WSHBible\\Author")
val = ws.RegDelete("HKCU\\WSHBible\\Comments")
```

If you want to delete the HKEY_CURRENT_USER\WSHBible key, you change the listing as follows:

VBScript

```
Set ws = WScript.CreateObject("WScript.Shell")
val = ws.RegDel("HKCU\WSHBible\")
```

JScript

```
var ws = WScript.CreateObject("WScript.Shell")
val = ws.RegDel("HKCU\\WSHBible\\")
```

 When you delete a key, you permanently delete all of the values associated with the key as well.

Reconfiguring network services through the registry

To better understand how the registry controls system and network settings, let's take a detailed look at how you can manage WINS and DHCP through the Windows Registry.

Managing WINS through Windows scripts

WINS is the Windows Internet Name Service and it is used to resolve computer names to IP addresses. If you log on to a domain, your computer may use WINS to access resources on the network.

The `Parameters` key is the primary key that controls WINS configuration. This key is located in the folder:

```
HKEY_LOCAL_MACHINE
    \SYSTEM
        \CurrentControlSet
            \Services
                \WINS
                    \Parameters
```

Table 12-2 summarizes the main values that you'll use to configure WINS.

TABLE 12-2

Key Values for Configuring WINS

Key Value	Value Type	Value Description
BackUpDirPath	REG_EXPAND_SZ	Sets the location for WINS backup files. You can change this location to any valid folder path on the local system.
BurstHandling	REG_DWORD	Determines whether WINS uses burst handling mode. Set to 1 to turn the mode on. Set to 0 to turn the mode off.
BurstQueSize	REG_DWORD	Sets the size of the burst queue threshold. The default value is 500, but you can use any value from 50 to 5,000. When the threshold you've set is reached, WINS switches to burst handling mode.
DbFileNm	REG_EXPAND_SZ	Sets the full file path to the WINS database; for example, %windir%\system32\wins.mdb.
DoBackupOnTerm	REG_DWORD	Determines whether the WINS database is backed up when the WINS server is stopped. Set to 1 to turn backups on. Set to 0 to turn backups off.
LogDetailedEvents	REG_DWORD	Determines whether detailed logging of WINS activity is used. All WINS events are logged in the System event log automatically and usually you will want to turn on detailed logging only for troubleshooting. Set to 1 to turn on detailed logging. Set to 0 to turn off detailed logging.
LogFilePath	REG_EXPAND_SZ	Sets an alternative log file path.

continued

TABLE 12-2	*(continued)*	
Key Value	**Value Type**	**Value Description**
LoggingOn	REG_DWORD	Determines whether logging is enabled. Set to 1 to turn on logging. Set to 0 to turn off logging. If you turn off logging, WINS events are not logged in the System event log.
RefreshInterval	REG_DWORD	Sets the interval during which a WINS client must renew its computer name. The minimum value is 2,400 seconds and the default value is 518,400 seconds (six days).
TombstoneInterval	REG_DWORD	Sets the interval during which a computer name can be marked for removal. The value must be equal to or greater than the renewal interval or 345,600 seconds (four days), whichever is smaller.
TombstoneTimeout	REG_DWORD	Sets the interval during which a computer name can be removed from the WINS database. The value must be greater than or equal to the refresh interval.
VerifyInterval	REG_DWORD	Sets the interval after which a WINS server must verify computer names originating from other WINS servers. This allows inactive names to be removed. The minimum value is 2,073,600 seconds (24 days).

Now that you know the key values and how they are used, you can create a script that manages the WINS configuration. You can then use this script on other WINS servers to ensure that the configurations are exactly the same, which is usually what you want. An example script is shown as Listing 12-5.

LISTING 12-5

Configuring WINS

VBScript
updatewins.vbs

```
Dim Path
Path = "HKLM\SYSTEM\CurrentControlSet\Services\WINS\Parameters\"
Set ws = WScript.CreateObject("WScript.Shell")
ws.RegWrite Path & "BackUpDirPath","%windir%\system32", "REG_EXPAND_SZ"
ws.RegWrite Path & "BurstHandling",1, "REG_DWORD"
ws.RegWrite Path & "BurstQueSize",500, "REG_DWORD"
ws.RegWrite Path & "DbFileNm","%windir%\system32\wins.mdb", "REG_EXPAND_SZ"
ws.RegWrite Path & "DoBackupOnTerm",1, "REG_DWORD"
```

```
ws.RegWrite Path & "LogDetailedEvents",0, "REG_DWORD"
ws.RegWrite Path & "LogFilePath","%windir%\system32", "REG_EXPAND_SZ"
ws.RegWrite Path & "LoggingOn",1, "REG_DWORD"
ws.RegWrite Path & "RefreshInterval",518400, "REG_DWORD"
ws.RegWrite Path & "TombstoneInterval",518400, "REG_DWORD"
ws.RegWrite Path & "TombstoneTimeout",518400, "REG_DWORD"
ws.RegWrite Path & "VerifyInterval",2073600, "REG_DWORD"
```

JScript
updatewins.js

```
var Path
Path = "HKLM\\SYSTEM\\CurrentControlSet\\Services\\WINS\\Parameters\\"
var ws = WScript.CreateObject("WScript.Shell")
ws.RegWrite(Path + "BackUpDirPath","%windir%\\system32", "REG_EXPAND_SZ")
ws.RegWrite(Path + "BurstHandling",1, "REG_DWORD")
ws.RegWrite(Path + "BurstQueSize",500, "REG_DWORD")
ws.RegWrite(Path + "DbFileNm","%windir%\\system32\\wins.mdb", "REG_EXPAND_SZ")
ws.RegWrite(Path + "DoBackupOnTerm",1, "REG_DWORD")
ws.RegWrite(Path + "LogDetailedEvents",0, "REG_DWORD")
ws.RegWrite(Path + "LogFilePath","%windir%\\system32", "REG_EXPAND_SZ")
ws.RegWrite(Path + "LoggingOn",1, "REG_DWORD")
ws.RegWrite(Path + "RefreshInterval",518400, "REG_DWORD")
ws.RegWrite(Path + "TombstoneInterval",518400, "REG_DWORD")
ws.RegWrite(Path + "TombstoneTimeout",518400, "REG_DWORD")
ws.RegWrite(Path + "VerifyInterval",2073600, "REG_DWORD")
```

Managing DHCP through Windows scripts

DHCP is the Dynamic Host Configuration Protocol and it is used to dynamically assign network configuration settings to computers. If you log on to a workstation in an Active Directory domain, your computer probably uses DHCP to obtain the settings it needs to access the network.

DHCP configuration is located in the folder:

```
HKEY_LOCAL_MACHINE
    \SYSTEM
        \CurrentControlSet
            \Services
                \DHCPServer
                    \Parameters
```

The main values that you'll want to work with to configure DHCP are summarized in Table 12-3.

TABLE 12-3

Key Values for Configuring DHCP

Key Value	Value Type	Value Description
BackupDatabasePath	REG_EXPAND_SZ	Sets the location for DHCP backup files. You can change this location to any valid folder path on the local system.
BackupInterval	REG_DWORD	Sets the interval for automatic backups. The default value is 60 minutes.
DatabaseCleanupInterval	REG_DWORD	Sets the interval for cleaning up old records in the DHCP database. The default value is 1,440 minutes (24 hours).
DatabaseLoggingFlag	REG_DWORD	Determines whether audit logging is enabled. Audit logs track DHCP processes and requests. Set to 1 to turn on. Set to 0 to turn off.
DatabaseName	REG_SZ	Sets the file name for the DHCP database, for example, dhcp.mdb.
DatabasePath	REG_EXPAND_SZ	Sets the directory path for the DHCP database, for example, %SystemRoot%\System32\dhcp.
DebugFlag	REG_DWORD	Determines whether debugging is enabled. If debugging is enabled, detailed events are created in the event logs. Set to 1 to turn on. Set to 0 to turn off.
DetectConflictRetries	REG_DWORD	Sets the number of times DHCP checks to *continued* see if an IP address is in use before assigning. Generally, you'll want to check IP addresses at least once before assigning them, which helps to prevent IP address conflicts.
DhcpLogDiskSpaceCheckInterval	REG_DWORD	Determines how often DHCP checks the amount of disk space used by DHCP. The default interval is 50 minutes.
DhcpLogFilePath	REG_SZ	Sets the file path for audit log, for example, %windir%\system32\dhcp.
DhcpLogFilesMaxSize	REG_DWORD	Sets the maximum file size for all audit logs. The default is 7MB.
DhcpLogMinSpaceOnDisk	REG_DWORD	Sets the free-space threshold for writing to the audit logs. If the disk drive has less free space than the value specified, logging is temporarily disabled. The default value is 20MB.

Key Value	Value Type	Value Description
RestoreFlag	REG_DWORD	Determines whether the DHCP is restored from backup when the DHCP server is started. Set this option to 1 only if you want to restore a previously saved DHCP database.

Using the key values shown in Table 12-3, you can create scripts that help you manage DHCP. Listing 12-6 shows an example script that reconfigures DHCP settings.

LISTING 12-6

Configuring DHCP

VBScript
updatedhcp.vbs

```
Dim Path
Path = "HKLM\SYSTEM\CurrentControlSet\Services\DHCPServer\Parameters\"
Set ws = WScript.CreateObject("WScript.Shell")
ws.RegWrite Path & "BackupDatabasePath","%windir%\dhcp\backup", "REG_EXPAND_SZ"
ws.RegWrite Path & "BackupInterval",60, "REG_DWORD"
ws.RegWrite Path & "DatabaseCleanupInterval",1440, "REG_DWORD"
ws.RegWrite Path & "DatabaseLoggingFlag",1, "REG_DWORD"
ws.RegWrite Path & "DatabaseName","dhcp.mdb", "REG_SZ"
ws.RegWrite Path & "DatabasePath","%windir%\system32\dhcp", "REG_EXPAND_SZ"
ws.RegWrite Path & "DebugFlag",0, "REG_DWORD"
ws.RegWrite Path & "DetectConflictRetries",2, "REG_DWORD"
ws.RegWrite Path & "DhcpLogDiskSpaceCheckInterval",50, "REG_DWORD"
ws.RegWrite Path & "DhcpLogFilePath","d:\logs\dhcp", "REG_SZ"
ws.RegWrite Path & "DhcpLogFilesMaxSize",7, "REG_DWORD"
ws.RegWrite Path & "DhcpLogMinSpaceOnDisk",20, "REG_DWORD"
ws.RegWrite Path & "RestoreFlag",0, "REG_DWORD"
```

JScript
updatedhcp.js

```
var Path
Path = "HKLM\\SYSTEM\\CurrentControlSet\\Services\\DHCPServer\\Parameters\\"
var ws = WScript.CreateObject("WScript.Shell")
ws.RegWrite(Path+"BackupDatabasePath","%windir%\\dhcp\\backup","REG_EXPAND_SZ")
ws.RegWrite(Path + "BackupInterval",60, "REG_DWORD")
ws.RegWrite(Path + "DatabaseCleanupInterval",1440, "REG_DWORD")
ws.RegWrite(Path + "DatabaseLoggingFlag",1, "REG_DWORD")
ws.RegWrite(Path + "DatabaseName","dhcp.mdb", "REG_SZ")
ws.RegWrite(Path + "DatabasePath","%windir%\\system32\\dhcp","REG_EXPAND_SZ")
ws.RegWrite(Path + "DebugFlag",0, "REG_DWORD")
```

continued

LISTING 12-6   *(continued)*

```
ws.RegWrite(Path + "DetectConflictRetries",2, "REG_DWORD")
ws.RegWrite(Path + "DhcpLogDiskSpaceCheckInterval",50, "REG_DWORD")
ws.RegWrite(Path + "DhcpLogFilePath","d:\\logs\\dhcp", "REG_SZ")
ws.RegWrite(Path + "DhcpLogFilesMaxSize",7, "REG_DWORD")
ws.RegWrite(Path + "DhcpLogMinSpaceOnDisk",20, "REG_DWORD")
ws.RegWrite(Path + "RestoreFlag",0, "REG_DWORD")
```

Using Event Logs

Windows event logs track activity on a particular system. You can use the logs to track system processes, to troubleshoot system problems, and to monitor system security. On Windows servers and workstations, you'll find the following logs:

- **Application Log:** Tracks events logged by applications, such as by SQL Server.
- **Security Log:** Tracks events you've set for auditing with local or global group policies. Only authorized users can access security logs.
- **System Log:** Tracks events logged by the operating system or its components, such as WINS or DHCP.
- **Directory Service:** Tracks events logged by Active Directory.
- **DNS Server:** Tracks DNS queries, responses, and other DNS activities.
- **File Replication Service:** Tracks file replication activities on the system.

Viewing event logs

You can view event logs through Event Viewer. This utility is in the Administrative Tools folder and can also be accessed through the System Tools node in the Computer Management console. Windows Vista has a slightly updated look and feel from Windows XP. As shown in Figure 12-1, Event Viewer's main window is divided into three panels. The left panel is called the console tree. The middle panel is the view pane, and the right panel is the actions menu. To view a log, click its entry in the console tree and then the selected log is displayed in the middle panel.

When you start Event Viewer, the utility automatically accesses event logs on the local system. You can access event logs on remote computers as well. Right-click Event Viewer in the console tree and then select Connect to Another Computer. You can then use the Select Computer dialog box shown in Figure 12-2 to connect to a remote computer. Choose the Another Computer radio button and then enter the name or IP address of the computer to which you want to connect in the input field provided. Afterward, click OK.

FIGURE 12-1

Event Viewer displays events on local and remote computers.

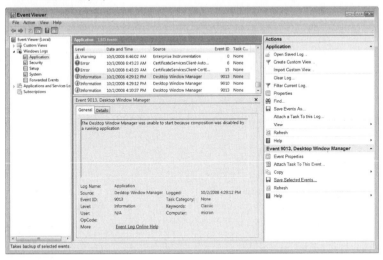

FIGURE 12-2

To display events on a remote computer, select Another Computer and then enter the computer name or IP address.

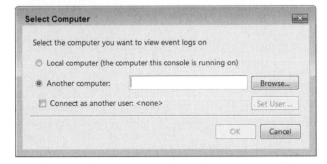

Understanding event entries

When you select a log in the console tree, current entries for the log are displayed in the view pane. Each entry provides an overview of why, when, where, and how an event occurred. This information is organized under column headings that provide the following information:

- **Type:** The type of event that occurred, such as an error event
- **Date:** The date the event occurred

- **Time:** The time the event occurred
- **Source:** The component that generated the event
- **Category:** The class of the event, such as Online Defragmentation or Logging/Recovery
- **Event:** An identifier for the specific event that occurred
- **User:** The user account that triggered the event
- **Computer:** The computer name where the event occurred

You can obtain detailed information on an event by double-clicking its entry in the view pane. The additional information provided is:

- **Description:** Provides a text description of the event
- **Record Data:** Provides any data or error code output by the event

Of all the various kinds of information that you can gather from event logs, the most valuable for determining the relevance of an event is the event type. Event types include:

- **Error:** An event for an application, component, or service error. You should examine all error events.
- **Failure Audit:** An event related to the failed execution of an action. If you are auditing user activities to help you monitor network security, you should keep track of all failed audit events.
- **Information:** An information event, which is generally related to a successful action. You don't need to watch information events closely, but may want to track totals on various categories of information events.
- **Success Audit:** An event related to the successful execution of an action. You don't need to watch these events closely, but may want to track totals on various categories of these events.
- **Warning:** An event that may cause problems on the system, but isn't necessarily the result of an error. You should examine all warning events.

Archiving event logs

On most servers, administrators will archive event logs periodically. When you archive event logs, you store logs for later use. Logs can be archived in three formats:

- **Event log format:** This archive type is designed for viewing logs in Event Viewer. You can also access these logs from *Dumpel*, an event log analysis utility. To access an old log in Event Viewer, right-click Event Viewer in the console tree, point to New, and then select Log View. You can now load a previously saved log.
- **Text (Tab Delimited):** This archive type works best for viewing in a text editor or word processor. Individual entries are placed on separate lines with each data column representing a field. Tabs are used to separate the fields.

■ **Text (Comma Delimited):** This archive type works best for importing logs into spreadsheets and databases. You can also work with the logs in Dumpel.

When you save log files to a comma-delimited file, each field in the event entry is separated by a comma. Example event entries look like this:

```
Error,08/15/2008,5:35:07 PM,LicenseService,None,202,N/A,ZETA
Information,08/15/2008,11:25:19 AM,SceCli,None,1704,N/A,ZETA
Information,08/15/2008,11:24:36 AM,ESENT,Logging/Recovery ,302,N/A,ZETA
Information,08/15/2008,11:24:31 AM,Remote Storage,Agent ,1000,N/A,ZETA
Information,08/15/2008,11:24:19 AM,ESENT,Logging/Recovery ,302,N/A,ZETA
Information,08/15/2008,11:22:49 AM,Oakley,None,542,N/A,ZETA
Information,08/15/2008,11:20:38 AM,ESENT,Logging/Recovery ,301,N/A,ZETA
Information,08/15/2008,11:20:35 AM,EvntAgnt,None,2018,N/A,ZETA
```

The format for the entries is as follows:

```
Type, Date, Time, Source, Category, Event, User, Computer
```

As you can see, the event description and record data is not saved with text-based archives. This saves space and you won't really need the detailed descriptions in most instances. If you do, you can use the event code to find the description. The Windows Resource Kit has an Event log database that provides detailed information on events and their meaning.

Writing to Event Logs

In Chapter 13, you learn how to create scripts that can run automatically, such as scripts that are scheduled to run periodically at a scheduled time, or scripts that run when a user logs on. To help you keep track of the success or failure of these scripts, you can write information related to the scripts directly to the application event log. In this way, when you are browsing or analyzing the logs, you'll know immediately if scripts are running properly or failing.

Event logging basics

When you write events to the application event log, you specify the event ID and the event description. Windows Script Host then directs the event to the event logging service. The event logging service then:

■ Sets the event type based on the event identifier

■ Records the event with the current date and time

■ Sets the source as WSH and the category as None

■ Sets the event ID based on the event type

■ Sets the user to N/A and then sets the computer name

The results look like this:

```
Type       Date         Time         Source    Category   Event   User   Computer
Warning    08/15/2008   7:24:36 PM   WSH       None       2       N/A    ZETA
Error      08/15/2008   7:13:08 PM   WSH       None       1       N/A    ZETA
```

The event description is available, but only if you double-click on the event in the Event Viewer. Keep in mind that if you save the event log to a text file, the description is not saved, which will probably mean that you won't be able to determine the meaning of the event.

Working with the LogEvent method

To write events to the application event log, use the LogEvent method of the WshShell object. The syntax for this method is:

```
LogEvent(eventType, eventDescription [,remoteSystem])
```

in which *eventType* is a numeric identifier for the event type, *eventDescription* is a text description of the event, and *remoteSystem* is an optional value that specifies the system on which you want to log the event.

Event types you can specify are summarized in Table 12-4. You set the event type as the first argument for LogEvent. If the logging succeeds, LogEvent returns True. If the logging fails, LogEvent returns False.

TABLE 12-4

Specifying Event Types for the LogEvent Method

Event	Value	Event Type
Successful execution	0	Information
Execution error	1	Error
Warning; possible problem	2	Warning
Information	4	Information
Audit of successful action	8	Success Audit
Audit of failed action	16	Failure Audit

Typically, you'll want to use the event log to record the successful or failed execution of the script. For example, if the script is performing nightly backups, you'd want to track the success or failure of the backup process. If you build a main function into the script, you can record the outcome of the execution as shown in Listing 12-7. Of course, there are many other ways that you can handle event logging.

LISTING 12-7

Writing to an Event Log

VBScript
writelog.vbs

```vbscript
Set ws = WScript.CreateObject("WScript.Shell")
ex = main()
If ex Then
 ws.LogEvent 0, "WriteLog.VBS Script Completed Successfully"
Else
 ws.LogEvent 1, "Error executing WriteLog.VBS"
End If

Function main()
 'add main routine
 WScript.Echo "Write log test..."
If err.Number <> 0 Then
 main = 1
Else
 main = 0
End If
End Function
```

JScript
writelog.js

```jscript
var ws = WScript.CreateObject("WScript.Shell")
ex = main()
if (ex == 0) {
 //successful execution
 ws.LogEvent(0, "WriteLog.JS Script Completed Successfully")
 }
else {
 //failed execution
 ws.LogEvent(1, "Error executing WriteLog.JS")
}

function main() {
 //add main routine
 try {
 //add code to try
 WScript.Echo("Write log test...")
 }
 catch(e) {
  return 1
 }
 return 0
}
```

Reading Event Logs

The EventLog method makes writing to event logs fairly easy. Unfortunately, there isn't a simple method that you can use to read event logs. Primarily, this is because event logs have a complex structure and you really need a tool that can search the event logs for relevant information, rather than a tool that simply reads the events. While you can use the built-in capabilities of VBScript and JScript to create log-searching and extraction routines, you don't need to do this. Instead, you can use Dumpel to handle all of the dirty work for you. Dumpel is a resource kit utility designed to help you analyze event logs.

> **NOTE** To use the examples in this section, Dumpel must be in a directory that is accessible to the command path. The default installation location for resource kit utilities is Program Files\Resource Kit. This directory is not in the standard command path. You can add this directory to the path or you can move the Dumpel utility to the %SystemRoot% directory. To view the current command path, start a command prompt and then type path. To add the resource kit directory to the command path, start a command prompt and then type the following command:
>
> ```
> set PATH=%PATH%;F:\Program Files\Resource Kit
> ```
>
> in which F:\Program Files\Resource Kit is the location of the resource kit.

Introducing Dumpel

Dumpel provides many different ways to examine information in event logs. You can dump entire event logs on specific systems and write the logs to files, search the event logs for specific events by ID, or even search event logs for events logged by a specific user. The syntax for Dumpel follows:

```
dumpel [/f <filename>] [/s <servername>] [/l <logname> [/m <source>
[/r]]]
        [/e <eventlist>] [/c] [/ns] [/t] [/d <days>]
```

Each of the arguments for Dumpel is summarized in Table 12-5.

TABLE 12-5

Arguments for Dumpel

Argument	Description
/b	Filters an existing dump log.
/c	Uses commas to separate fields. If not specified, a space is used.
/d <days>	Filters events for the past *n* days. Value must be greater than 0.
/e <eventlist>	Filters by event ID. You can specify up to 10 event IDs in a space-separated list. You must use /m to specify a source as well.

Argument	Description
/f <filename>	Sets the output file name. If none is specified, the output is sent to the standard output stream.
/format <fmt>	Sets the output format for event fields. Formatting is discussed later in this chapter.
/l <logname>	Examines the specified log, such as system, application, or security.
/m <source>	Filters for events logged by source.
/ns	Specifies that the description should not be dumped.
/r	Reverses the source filtering for /m. All events except those logged by the source are dumped.
/s <servername>	Sets the name of the remote server to use.
/t	Uses a tab to separate fields. If not specified, a space is used.

Using Dumpel

Working with Dumpel is a lot easier than you might imagine, especially after seeing that long list of arguments. With Dumpel, the event log you want to examine is specified with the /l switch. Follow the /l switch with the log type, such as system, application, or security. If you use the /l switch without specifying any other switches, the utility dumps the specified log on the current system to the command line. To dump logs to a file, use the /f switch and specify a file name. The following example dumps the system log to a file on a shared network drive:

```
dumpel /l system /f \\ZETA\DATA\LOG\%computername%.log
```

If the local system is named Gandolf, the result would be a text file named Gandolf.log. The file would contain the entire contents of the system log and each field would be separated with a space. Although Dumpel works with the local system by default, you can access event logs on remote systems as well. Use the /s switch to specify the system name. For example:

```
dumpel /l system /f omega-sys.log /s omega
```

Fields in the event entry are normally separated by spaces, but you can use /t to specify tabs or /c to specify commas as delimiters. You can also use the /format switch to determine which fields to store in the event entries, and their exact order. To do this, follow the /format switch with any combination of the modifiers shown in Table 12-6. The following example dumps the security log on the local system and restricts output to the date, time, event ID, and event type fields:

```
dumpel /l security /format dtIT
```

TABLE 12-6

Formatting Modifiers for Dumpel

Modifier	Description
C	Event category
c	Computer name
d	Date
I	Event ID
s	Event comment string
S	Event source
t	Time of day
T	Event type
U	Username

To search the event logs for specified events by identifier, use the /e switch and then enter one to 10 event identifiers. Each event must be separated with a space. You must also specify an event source, such as LicenseService or WINS. The following example shows how you can track multiple events in the system log:

```
dumpel /l system /f loc-sys.log /e 401 402 403 404 405 /m netlogon
```

 The Windows Resource Kit contains a comprehensive database of events and their mean-ing. If you've installed the resource kit, look for the Windows Event Log Database in the Tools A to Z listing.

When you use the /m switch, you can search for events logged by specified sources, such as Netlogon or WINS. Unfortunately, you cannot specify multiple sources, but you can use the /r switch with the /m switch to specify that you want to see all events except those for the specified source. In the following example, you search for events logged by the Netlogon service:

```
dumpel /l system /f loc-sys.log /m netlogon
```

In this example, you search for all events *except* those logged by Netlogon:

```
dumpel /l system /f loc-sys.log /m netlogon /r
```

CAUTION Watch out; if you combine /r, /m, and /e, you'll get a list of all events except the desig-nated events for the specified source.

You'll often have existing log files and may not need to create new ones. In this case, use the /b switch to search the existing log file specified with /l. In the following example, you search the loc-sec.log:

```
dumpel /b /l loc-sec.log /e 401
```

In this example, you search the loc-sec.log and write the results to a file:

```
dumpel /b /l loc-sec.log /e 401 /f sec-e401.log
```

So far we've focused on how Dumpel works and how you can use Dumpel from the command line. Now let's look at how you can work with Dumpel in scripts.

Working with Dumpel in scripts

Dumpel is a command-line utility and as with other command-line utilities, you can run it within a Windows script using the Run method of the WshShell object. As discussed in Chapter 6, the basic syntax for Run is:

```
object.Run ("command", [winStyle], ["waitOnReturn"])
```

When you use the Run method, you can pass Dumpel any necessary arguments in the command parameter. An example of this is shown as Listing 12-8.

LISTING 12-8

Reading an Event Log with Dumpel

VBScript
readlog.vbs

```
Set ws = WScript.CreateObject("WScript.Shell")
ret = ws.Run("dumpel /l system /f loc-sys.log /m netlogon",0,"TRUE")

If ret = 0 Then
 ws.LogEvent 0, "ReadLog.VBS Script Completed Successfully"
Else
 ws.LogEvent 1, "Error executing ReadLog.VBS"
End If
```

JScript
readlog.js

```
var ws = WScript.CreateObject("WScript.Shell");
ret = ws.Run("dumpel /l system /f loc-sys.log /m netlogon",0,"TRUE")

if (ret == 0) {
 //successful execution
```

continued

LISTING 12-8   *(continued)*

```
ws.LogEvent(0, "ReadLog.JS Script Completed Successfully")
 }
else {
 //failed execution
 ws.LogEvent(1, "Error executing ReadLog.JS")
}
```

If you are dumping multiple event logs or event logs on multiple systems, you can enter additional Run statements in the script. Listing 12-9 shows how you can examine the system, security, and application logs on a remote server, and then store the logs on a network drive. Keep in mind that if you run this script as a scheduled task, you'll need to map the drive before you can use it as discussed in Chapter 10.

LISTING 12-9

Working with Multiple Logs

VBScript
createlogs.vbs

```
Set ws = WScript.CreateObject("WScript.Shell")
c = ws.ExpandEnvironmentStrings("%computername%")
ret = ws.Run("dumpel /l system /f \\ash\log\" & c & "-sys.log",0,"TRUE")
ret = ret + ws.Run("dumpel /l security /f \\ash\log\" & c & "-sec.log",0,"TRUE")
ret = ret + ws.Run("dumpel /l application /f \\ash\log\" & c & "-app.
log",0,"TRUE")

If ret = 0 Then
 ws.LogEvent 0, "CreateLogs.VBS Script Completed Successfully"
Else
 ws.LogEvent 1, "Error executing CreateLogs.VBS"
End If
```

JScript
createlogs.js

```
var ws = WScript.CreateObject("WScript.Shell")
c = ws.ExpandEnvironmentStrings("%computername%")
ret = ws.Run("dumpel /l system /f \\\\ash\\log\\" + c + "-sys.log",0,"TRUE")
ret += ws.Run("dumpel /l security /f \\\\ash\\log\\" + c + "-sec.log",0,"TRUE")
ret += ws.Run("dumpel /l application /f \\\\ash\\log\\" + c + "-app.
log",0,"TRUE")

if (ret == 0) {
```

```
//successful execution
ws.LogEvent(0, "CreateLogs.JS Script Completed Successfully")
 }
else {
 //failed execution
 ws.LogEvent(1, "Error executing CreateLogs.JS")
}
```

Generating Event Log Reports

Event logs are only useful if you can analyze the information they contain. One way to do this is to create a daily event log report for key systems on the network and then publish the results on the corporate intranet. Let's break this process down into a series of steps and then analyze how each step can be implemented.

Step 1: Creating the logs

Step one is to create a script that dumps logs on critical systems and stores the logs on a network drive. If these systems are named Gandolf, Bilbo, and Dragon, the first part of the script would look like Listing 12-10. Each time you run the script, the original logs are overwritten.

LISTING 12-10

Creating Logs for the Report

JScript
logstep1.js

```
var ret; ret=0
var ws = WScript.CreateObject("WScript.Shell")

//create array of computers to check from string; no spaces
computers = "gandolf,bilbo,dragon"
sysArray = computers.split(",")

//create array of logs to check from string; no spaces
logs = "system,application,security"
logArray = logs.split(",")

evArray = parseInt(logs.split(","))

//examine each item in the systems array and then the log array
for (s in sysArray) {
```

continued

LISTING 12-10   *(continued)*

```
for (1 in logArray) {

    ws.Run("dumpel /l " + logArray[l] + " /f \\\\zeta\\corpdatashare\\" +
sysArray[s] + "-" +  logArray[l] + ".log /d 1 /ns /s " + sysArray[s],0,"TRUE")

    WScript.Echo("Executing dumpel /l " + logArray[l] + " /f \\\\zeta\\
corpdatashare\\" + sysArray[s] + "-" + logArray[l] + ".log /d 1 /ns /s " +
sysArray[s],0,"TRUE")

 }
}
```

The output from the script tells you what the script is doing and can really help in understanding the script's logic. The output looks like this:

```
Executing dumpel /l system /f \\zeta\corpdatashare\gandolf-system.log
/d 1 /ns /s gandolf 0 TRUE

Executing dumpel /l application /f \\zeta\corpdatashare\gandolf-application.log
 /d 1 /ns /s gandolf 0 TRUE

Executing dumpel /l security /f \\zeta\corpdatashare\gandolf-security.log
/d 1 /ns /s gandolf 0 TRUE

Executing dumpel /l system /f \\zeta\corpdatashare\biblo-system.log
/d 1 /ns /s biblo 0 TRUE

Executing dumpel /l application /f \\zeta\corpdatashare\biblo-application.log
/d 1 /ns /s biblo 0 TRUE

Executing dumpel /l security /f \\zeta\corpdatashare\biblo-security.log
/d 1 /ns /s biblo 0 TRUE

Executing dumpel /l system /f \\zeta\corpdatashare\dragon-system.log
/d 1 /ns /s dragon 0 TRUE

Executing dumpel /l application /f \\zeta\corpdatashare\dragon-application.log
 /d 1 /ns /s dragon 0 TRUE

Executing dumpel /l security /f \\zeta\corpdatashare\dragon-security.log
/d 1 /ns /s dragon 0 TRUE
```

As you can see from the output, the script dumps the logs for the first system specified in the computer's variable, and then dumps the logs for the seconds system, and so on. The order of the logs is specified in the logs variable. The output contains events for the current day only (/d 1) and does not contain descriptions (/ns).

To dump the log files daily, you can schedule the script to run with the Task Scheduler. Scheduling scripts to run periodically is covered in Chapter 13. Rather than dumping the log to a file and then browsing the file in a text editor, it would be a lot easier if you could browse the file on the corporate intranet. Before you do this, you may want to clean up the files, search for specific events, or format the files in HTML.

Step 2: Formatting the logs for viewing

You can format the logs for viewing in many different ways. If you are running the script manually, the easiest way to do this is to display the contents of each log file in a pop-up dialog box. The code that does this is shown in Listing 12-11. Figure 12-3 shows sample output for a log file.

LISTING 12-11

Displaying the Log Reports in a Pop-up Dialog Box

JScript
logstep2a.js

```jscript
var ret; ret=0
var ws = WScript.CreateObject("WScript.Shell")

//create array of computers to check from string; no spaces
computers = "gandolf,bilbo,dragon"
sysArray = computers.split(",")

//create array of logs to check from string; no spaces
logs = "system,application,security"
logArray = logs.split(",")

//examine each item in the systems array and then the log array
for (s in sysArray) {
 for (l in logArray) {

    ws.Run("dumpel /l " + logArray[l] + " /f \\\\zeta\\corpdatashare\\" +
sysArray[s] + "-" + logArray[l] + ".log /d 1 /ns /s " + sysArray[s],0,"TRUE")

    WScript.Echo("Executing dumpel /l " + logArray[l] + " /f \\\zeta\\
corpdatashare\\" +

sysArray[s] + "-" + logArray[l] + ".log /d 1 /ns /s " + sysArray[s],0,"TRUE")

 }
}

ForReading = 1
```

continued

LISTING 12-11   *(continued)*

```
for (s in sysArray) {
 for (l in logArray) {

  fname = "\\\\zeta\\corpdatashare\\" + sysArray[s] + "-" + logArray[l] + ".log"

  var fs = new ActiveXObject ("Scripting.FileSystemObject");
  var f = fs.OpenTextFile (fname, ForReading, "True")
  fContents = f.ReadAll()
  f.Close()

  var w = WScript.CreateObject("WScript.Shell");
  a = w.Popup (fContents,60,"Display File",1)

 }
}
```

FIGURE 12-3

Viewing partial logs in a pop-up dialog box

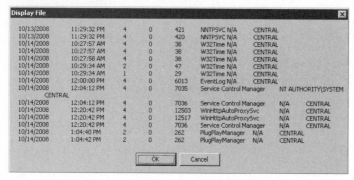

As you can see from the listing, For loops are used to display the contents of each log in turn. These For loops are implemented in the same way as the For loops that dump the logs in the first place. The key difference is that instead of dumping logs, you are reading the contents of the logs and displaying them in a pop-up dialog box. You can extend this technique to format the logs as HTML, which then makes the daily log report easier to work with.

Listing 12-12 shows how you can add an HTML header and footer to the log files. Don't worry — we'll analyze the script one step at a time following the listing.

LISTING 12-12

Creating HTML Documents for the Log Reports

JScript
logreports.js

```
// ************************
// Script: The Log Reporter
// Version: 1.1.5
// Creation Date: 02/15/2007
// Last Modified: 02/15/2007
// Author: William R. Stanek
// Email: williamstanek@aol.com
// Copyright (c) 2007 William R. Stanek
// ************************
// Description: Uses the Dumpel utility to dump specified
//              logs on local and remote systems. The script
//              then generates reports formatted as HTML.
//
// Maintenance: When installing this script, you should update
//              computers, logs, netDrive and fname.
//              Computers sets the name of the systems to check.
//              Logs sets the type of event logs to dump.
//              netDrive sets the log creation directory.
//              fname sets the full file path to the publishing directory for
//              the HTML reports.
// ************************
theMonth = new Array(12)
theMonth[1] = "January"
theMonth[2] = "February"
theMonth[3] = "March"
theMonth[4] = "April"
theMonth[5] = "May"
theMonth[6] = "June"
theMonth[7] = "July"
theMonth[8] = "August"
theMonth[9] = "September"
theMonth[10] = "October"
theMonth[11] = "November"
theMonth[12] = "December"
theDays = new Array(7)
theDays[1] = "Sunday"
theDays[2] = "Monday"
theDays[3] = "Tuesday"
theDays[4] = "Wednesday"
theDays[5] = "Thursday"
theDays[6] = "Friday"
theDays[7] = "Saturday"
```

continued

LISTING 12-12 *(continued)*

```
function theDate(aDate) {
   var currentDay = theDays[aDate.getDay() + 1]
   var currentMonth = theMonth[aDate.getMonth() + 1]
   return currentDay + ", " + currentMonth + " " + aDate.getDate()
}

var ret; ret=0
var ws = WScript.CreateObject("WScript.Shell")

//create array of computers to check from string; no spaces
computers = "gandolf,bilbo,dragon"
sysArray = computers.split(",")

//sets the network drive where logs are created
netDrive = "\\\\zeta\\corpdatashare\\"

//create array of logs to check from string; no spaces
logs = "system,application,security"
logArray = logs.split(",")

//examine each item in the systems array and then the log array
for (s in sysArray) {
 for (l in logArray) {

    ws.Run("dumpel /l " + logArray[l] + " /f " + netDrive + sysArray[s] + "-"
+ logArray[l] + ".log /d 1 /ns /s " + sysArray[s],0,"TRUE")
    WScript.Echo("Executing dumpel /l " + logArray[l] + " /f " + netDrive +
sysArray[s] + "-" + logArray[l] + ".log /d 1 /ns /s " + sysArray[s],0,"TRUE")

 }
}

ForReading = 1
ForAppending = 8

for (s in sysArray) {
 for (l in logArray) {

  fname = "\\\\zeta\\corpdatashare\\" + sysArray[s] + "-" + logArray[l]

  var fs = new ActiveXObject ("Scripting.FileSystemObject");
  var f = fs.OpenTextFile (fname + ".log", ForReading, "True")
  fContents = f.ReadAll()
  f.Close()

  var f = fs.OpenTextFile (fname + ".html", ForAppending, "True")

  fHeader = "<html><head><title>Daily "
```

```
fHeader += logArray[l]
fHeader += " Log Report for "
fHeader += sysArray[s]
fHeader += "</title></head>"
fHeader += "<body bgcolor='#FFFFFF' text='#000000'>"
fHeader += "<h1>Daily "
fHeader += logArray[l]
fHeader += " Log Report for "
fHeader += sysArray[s]
fHeader += "</h1>"
fHeader += "<h3>"

today = new Date()
fHeader += theDate(today)

fHeader += "</h3>"
fHeader += "<pre>"

f.Write(fHeader)
f.Write(fContents)

fFooter = "</pre></body></html>"

f.Write(fFooter)

f.Close()
    }
}
```

FIGURE 12-4

Viewing the customized log report in Internet Explorer

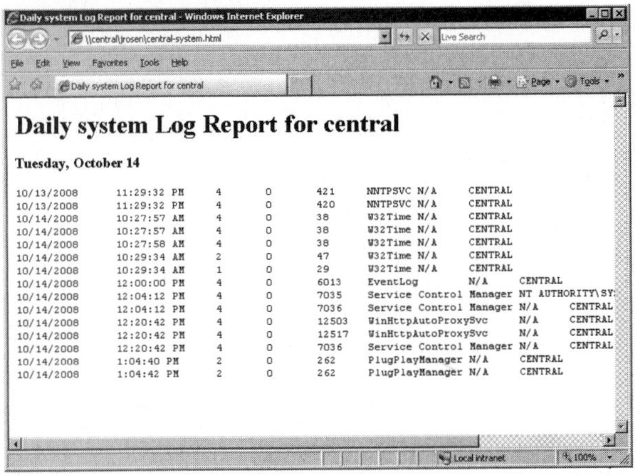

The first section of the script sets up a custom `Date` function. The function looks like this:

```
function theDate(aDate) {
    var currentDay = theDays[aDate.getDay() + 1]
    var currentMonth = theMonth[aDate.getMonth() + 1]
    return currentDay + ", " + currentMonth + " " + aDate.getDate()
}
```

The purpose of the `Date` function is to output the date in a custom format. Thus, rather than the standard date format:

```
Sun Sep 5 15:48:52 PDT 2008
```

you get a date that looks like this:

```
Sunday, September 5
```

Another new section of code creates a header for the HTML document you are creating. This code sets a title for the document and sets a level-1 header that will make it easier to work with the log files:

```
fHeader = "<html><head><title>Daily "
fHeader += logArray[1]
fHeader += " Log Report for "
fHeader += sysArray[s]
fHeader += "</title></head>"
fHeader += "<body bgcolor='#FFFFFF' text='#000000'>"
fHeader += "<h1>Daily "
fHeader += logArray[1]
fHeader += " Log Report for "
fHeader += sysArray[s]
fHeader += "</h1>"
fHeader += "<h3>"

today = new Date()
fHeader += theDate(today)

fHeader += "</h3>"
```

After creating the header, the code starts a preformatted text element in which the contents of the log file are placed. The code then writes the document header and contents:

```
fHeader += "<pre>"

f.Write(fHeader)
f.Write(fContents)
```

The final steps are to write the document footer and then close the file:

```
fFooter = "</pre></body></html>"

f.Write(fFooter)

f.Close()
```

As shown in Figure 12-4, the result is a customized report that can be viewed on the corporate intranet using any standard Web browser, such as Internet Explorer or Netscape Navigator. The script is designed to append each day's report to the same HTML document. If you don't want historical data, you can open the HTML document's ForWriting rather than ForAppending. Simply replace the lines that read:

```
ForAppending = 8
var f = fs.OpenTextFile (fname + ".html", ForAppending, "True")
```

with these lines:

```
ForWriting = 2
var f = fs.OpenTextFile (fname + ".html", ForWriting, "True")
```

Now, a new HTML document is created each time the script runs. If you plan to publish the reports on the corporate intranet, the network drive you use for the HTML documents should point to an appropriate directory on the intranet server. In the example, the files are written to the network share \\zeta\corpdatashare. This is the same directory where the log files are written. To change this, set the fname variable to the directory you want to use for publishing to the intranet, for example:

```
fname = "\\\\iServer\\webdatashare\\" + sysArray[s] + "-" + logArray[l]
```

Summary

The registry and the event logs are important resources on Windows computers. As you've learned in this chapter, you can manipulate these resources in many different ways. You can read, write, and modify registry keys. You can use the registry to reconfigure network services, such as DHCP and WINS. You can use the event logs to monitor critical systems, and you can create customized reports based on event log entries as well.

Part III

Network and Dictionary Service Scripting

Part III takes you into the heart of scripting Windows: working with network and directory service objects. In Part III, you'll learn to plumb the depths of Active Directory Services Interfaces (ADSI) and master the art of scheduling one-time and recurring network tasks using Startup/Shutdown and login scripts; controlling local and domain resources, services, shared directories, printer queues, and print jobs. By the end of this Part, you'll be an expert Windows scripter.

Chapter 13

Scheduling One-time and Recurring Tasks

O ne of the most powerful aspects of Windows scripting is the ability
to schedule scripts to run automatically. You can schedule scripts
to run one time only at 5 p.m. on Wednesday, every day at 11
p.m., every other Monday at 2 a.m., and at other times that are convenient.
Just as important, you can schedule scripts to run on any network computer and you can manage those scripts through an easy-to-use graphical
interface or an equally powerful command-line utility.

IN THIS CHAPTER

Scheduling scripts to run automatically

Working with the Task Scheduler Wizard

Scheduling jobs with the AT Scheduler

Scheduling Local and Remote Jobs

Windows Scripts that run automatically on a periodic or one-time basis are
referred to as scheduled jobs or scheduled tasks. While these scheduled
jobs can perform any regular scripting duty, there are some important differences in how scheduled jobs are used. So before we dive into job scheduling, let's look at these differences.

> **NOTE** Only authorized users can manage services and network time.
> You may need administrative privileges to perform the tasks in
> this section.

Scheduling basics

Scheduled jobs are started by a Windows service called Task Scheduler.
This service must be running on the local or remote system in order for
task scheduling to operate. You can check the status of the Task Scheduler
in the Services node of the Computer Management console or through the
Services console itself.

Figure 13-1 shows the Services console. You start the Services console by clicking Start ⇨ Programs ⇨ Administrative Tools ⇨ Services. As shown in the figure, the Task Scheduler Status should be Started. The Startup Type should be Automatic. If the service isn't started, right-click its entry, and then select Start on the pop-up menu. If the startup type isn't set to automatic, double-click Task Scheduler, choose Automatic on the Startup Type selection list, and then click OK.

FIGURE 13-1

The Task Scheduler must be configured properly for scheduled jobs to run.

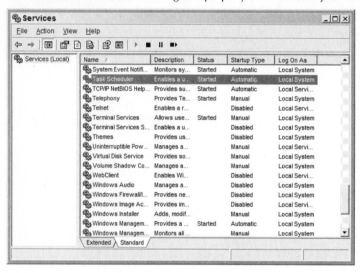

If you plan to use the command-line scheduler rather than the graphical scheduler, you should configure the logon account for the Task Scheduler. Task Scheduler logs on as the LocalSystem account by default. This account usually doesn't have adequate permissions to perform administrative tasks. Because of this, you should configure Task Scheduler to use a specific user account that has adequate user privileges and access rights to run the tasks you want to schedule. You can change the logon account for Task Scheduler as follows:

1. Double-click Task Scheduler in the Services console.
2. On the Log On tab, choose the This Account radio button as shown in Figure 13-2.
3. Type the name of the authorized account in the field provided, then enter and confirm the password for the account.
4. Click OK.

FIGURE 13-2

Configuring the startup account for Task Scheduler

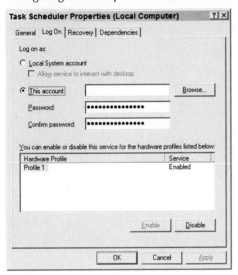

Synchronizing the system time

Task Scheduler uses the local system time to determine when scripts should run. If the local system time isn't in sync with the rest of the network, scripts may not run when expected. You can specify a timeserver that the computer should synchronize with using the `net time` command.

The syntax for `net time` is:

```
net time [\\computername | /domain[:domainname] |
         /rtsdomain[:domainname]] [/set]
net time [\\computername] /querysntp
net time [\\computername] /setsntp[:ntp server list]
```

The options for the `net time` command are summarized in Table 13-1.

TABLE 13-1	

Arguments for the net time Command

Arguments	Description
\\computername	Sets the name of the computer you want to check or synchronize with
/domain[:domainname]	Specifies that you want to synchronize with a Primary Domain Controller for domainname
/rtsdomain[:domainname]	Specifies that you want to synchronize with a Reliable Timeserver from domainname
/set	Sets the computer time on the computer
/querysntp	Displays the DNS name of the currently configured network timeserver for this computer
/setsntp[:ntp_server_list]	Sets the DNS name or IP address of the network timeservers to be used by this computer; if you list multiple timeservers, you must use quotation marks.

In an Active Directory domain, the primary domain controller at the root of the domain tree is designated as the master timeserver. All other computers in the domain can synchronize with this computer or with other designated timeservers. You designate the timeserver that a computer should use with the /setsntp command. If you want the Gandolf.tvpress.com server to be the timeserver for a computer, enter the following command:

```
net time /setsntp:gandolf.tvpress.com
```

You can also set the timeserver using its IP address, like this:

```
net time /setsntp:204.67.12.18
```

When you designate a timeserver for a computer, the time is automatically synchronized, provided the timeserver is available. If the timeserver goes off line, the computer won't be able to sync time. You can, however, specify alternative timeservers to use in case of outage. Simply enter the servers in a space-separated list, like this:

```
net time /setsntp:"gandolf.tvpress.com omega.tvpress.com"
```

Here, the server Gandolf.tvpress.com is the primary timeserver and omega.tvpress.com is an alternative timeserver.

Once you designate a timeserver, system time will be synchronized automatically. If you want to determine the current timeserver for a computer, enter the net time command with the /querysntp option, like this:

```
net time /querysntp
```

The results will look similar to this:

```
The current SNTP value is: gandolf.tvpress.com omega.tvpress.com
```

Scheduling utilities

As mentioned previously, there are two scheduling utilities: Task Scheduler Wizard and the AT Scheduler. Both utilities are useful.

The Task Scheduler Wizard provides a graphical interface for task assignment. Using this wizard, you can quickly configure tasks without having to worry about syntax issues. The disadvantage is that you don't have a central location for managing scheduled tasks in the enterprise. You access the wizard separately on each individual system that you want to configure and you view the scheduled tasks on each system individually through the related Scheduled Tasks folder.

The AT Scheduler is a command-line utility. Because the AT Scheduler doesn't have a point-and-click interface, you'll have to learn its command syntax, which isn't all that friendly. Still, AT has a definite advantage when it comes to script management. Using AT, you can schedule jobs to run on remote systems without having to access those systems, and you can check the status of jobs in the same way.

Regardless of which scheduling utility you decide to use, you'll need to ensure that the script can access resources with which it needs to work. Scripts don't automatically have access to the environment settings and may not have mapped drives, environment variables, and other necessary resources available. Because of this, you may need to map drives, set environment variables, or perform other preliminary tasks that aren't necessary when you run the script yourself. In fact, if you can run a script from the command line and it operates normally but fails when run as a scheduled task, something in the user environment isn't set properly.

Using the Graphical Task Scheduler

The graphical Task Scheduler makes scheduling and viewing tasks fairly easy. You create new tasks using the Task Scheduler Wizard. You view current tasks and manage their options through the Scheduled Tasks folder.

NOTE Group policy and user permissions can affect your ability to schedule tasks with the Task Scheduler Wizard. If you can't run the wizard or you can't access the Scheduled Tasks folder, you don't have the right privileges.

Running the wizard

You can use the Task Scheduler Wizard to create recurring or one-time tasks as follows:

1. Start Windows Explorer, and then double-click My Network Places.
2. In My Network Places, access the computer you want to work with and then double-click the Scheduled Tasks folder.

3. Start the Task Scheduler Wizard by double-clicking Add Scheduled Task. A Welcome dialog box is displayed. Click Next.

4. Click Browse to display the Select Program to Schedule dialog box shown in Figure 13-3. This dialog box is basically a File Open dialog box that you can use to find the script you want to schedule. When you find the script you want to use, click it and then click Open.

FIGURE 13-3

Use the Select Program to Schedule dialog box to find the script you want to run as a scheduled task.

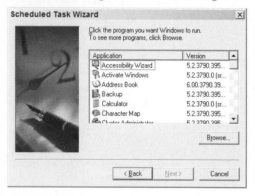

5. Type a name for the task, as shown in Figure 13-4. The task name should help you determine what the task does. For example, if you are scheduling a script that generates event log reports, type the name **Generate Nightly Log Reports.**

6. Choose a run schedule, and then click Next. Tasks can be scheduled to run one time only, daily, weekly, or monthly. They can also be set to run when a specific event occurs, such as when the computer starts or when the current user logs in.

FIGURE 13-4

Enter a descriptive name for the task and then select a run schedule.

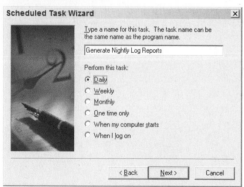

7. The next dialog box you see depends on your previous selection. If you want to run the task daily, the date and time dialog box appears as shown in Figure 13-5. Set a start time and date. Daily scheduled tasks can be configured to run:

   ■ **Every Day:** Sunday to Saturday.

   ■ **Weekdays:** Monday to Friday only.

   ■ **Every...Day:** Every 2nd, 3rd,...nth day.

FIGURE 13-5

Schedule daily tasks using this dialog box.

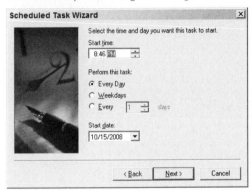

8. If you want the task to run weekly, the date and time dialog box appears as shown in Figure 13-6. Weekly scheduled tasks can be configured to run using the following fields:

   ■ **Start Time:** Sets the start time of the task.

   ■ **Every...Week:** Runs the task every week, every other week, or every nth week.

   ■ **Day of Week:** Sets the day of the week the task runs, such as on Monday, or on Monday and Friday.

FIGURE 13-6

Schedule weekly tasks using this dialog box.

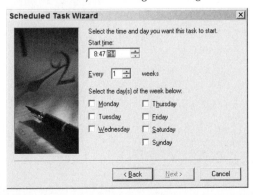

9. If you want the task to run monthly, the date and time dialog box appears as shown in Figure 13-7. Monthly scheduled tasks can be configured to run using the following fields:

   - **Start Time:** Sets the start time of the task.

   - **Day:** Sets the day of the month the task runs. If you select 2, the task runs on the second day of the month.

   - **The...Day:** Sets task to run on the *n*th occurrence of a day in a month, such as the third Monday or the fourth Wednesday of every month.

   - **Of the Months:** Sets the months the task runs in.

FIGURE 13-7

Schedule monthly tasks using this dialog box.

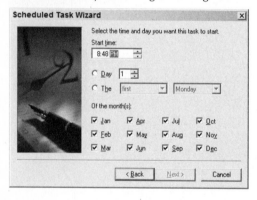

10. If you want the task to run one time only, the date and time dialog box appears as shown in Figure 13-8. Set the start time and start date.

FIGURE 13-8

Schedule one-time tasks using this dialog box.

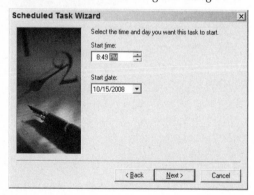

11. If the task runs when the computer starts or when the current user logs on, you don't have to set a start date and time. The task runs automatically when the startup or logon event occurs.

12. Once you configure a start date and time, click the Next button to continue. As shown in Figure 13-9, enter a username that can be used when running the scheduled task. This username must have appropriate permissions and privileges to run the scheduled task.

13. Enter and confirm the user's password, and then click Next.

CAUTION Be careful when running scripts using an account with administrative privileges in the domain. If users have access to the scripts, they may be able to enter malicious code into the script and, in this way, cause problems on the network. If you must use an administrator account to start a script, give the script the same strict security consideration you'd give to the administrator password. Ideally, you place the script in a protected folder on an NTFS volume and then set appropriate NTFS security restrictions on the script.

FIGURE 13-9

When you use the Scheduled Task Wizard, tasks can be run by any designated user. Enter an appropriate username and password.

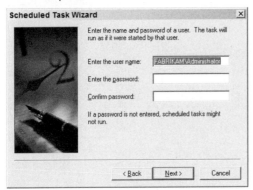

14. Click Finish to complete the scheduling process. Errors that occur while creating a task don't normally cause failure. Instead, you'll see a prompt telling you something went wrong and you can click OK to continue. After the task is created, double-click the task in Windows Explorer and then correct the problem in the Properties dialog box.

Viewing wizard tasks

All tasks that you create with the Task Scheduler Wizard are accessible through the Scheduled Tasks folder. In Windows Explorer, you can access this folder in the following ways:

- On a local system, double-click Control Panel and then click Scheduled Tasks.

- On a remote system, double-click My Network Places and then access the computer you want to work with. Afterward, double-click the Scheduled Tasks folder.

Once you access the Scheduled Tasks folder, you can manage tasks in the following ways:

■ To examine properties for scheduled tasks, double-click the task with which you want to work. Set advanced options through the Settings tab.

■ To delete a task, click it and then press Delete.

■ Instead of deleting a task, you may want to temporarily disable it. If you do this, you can start the task at a later date without having to re-create it. You disable a task by double-clicking it and then clearing the Enabled checkbox on the Task tab.

Changing task properties

You can change the properties of a task at any time. Double-click the task's entry in the Scheduled Tasks folder. This displays the properties dialog box shown in Figure 13-10. As shown in the figure, the Properties dialog box has the following tabs:

■ **Task:** Used to set general task settings. These settings are the same as those set through the Task Scheduler Wizard.

■ **Scheduled:** Used to set the task's run schedule. These settings are the same as those set through the Task Scheduler Wizard.

■ **Settings:** Used to set advanced options for the task.

■ **Security:** Used to restrict access to the task's property settings.

FIGURE 13-10

You can change the configuration of a scheduled task at any time.

Scheduling Jobs with AT

You can schedule jobs at the command line or within your scripts using the AT utility. With AT, you can schedule tasks anywhere on the network and you don't have to log on to remote systems.

 NOTE   You may need special permissions to schedule tasks on remote systems. If you aren't a member of the local Administrators group, you may not be able to use AT.

Using the AT Scheduler

When you schedule tasks with AT, you use a 24-hour clock on which 00:00 is midnight and 12:00 is 12 p.m. When you schedule tasks using AT, you must ensure that:

- The Task Scheduler service is running on the local or remote system.
- The Task Scheduler service uses an appropriate startup account.
- The scripts you want to use are located in directories that can be found along the command path set for the service logon account.

The syntax for the AT utility is:

```
AT [\\computername] [ [id] [/delete] | /delete [/yes]]
AT [\\computername] time [/interactive]
    [ /every:date[,…] | /next:date[,…]] "command"
```

The arguments for the AT utility are summarized in Table 13-2.

TABLE 13-2

Arguments for the AT Utility

Argument	Description
\\computername	Sets the name of a remote computer on which to schedule the task
Id	Sets the ID number of a task to delete
/delete	Deletes a scheduled task; if a specific ID isn't set, all scheduled tasks are deleted.
/yes	Cancels scheduled tasks without prompting to confirm the action
Time	Sets the time when task is to run
/interactive	Turns on interactive mode, which allows the task to interact with the desktop
/every:date[,…]	Runs the task on each specified day of the week or month; if date is omitted, the current day of the month is assumed.
/next:date[,…]	Runs the task on the next occurrence of the day; if date is omitted, the current day of the month is assumed.
"command"	Sets the command, program, or script to run

When you use numeric dates, you can use any value in the range 1–31. Here's how you can schedule a backup script to run every other day at 5 a.m.:

```
AT 05:00 /every:2,4,6,8,10,12,14,16,18,20,22,24,26,28,30 checkstatus.js
```

Another way to schedule tasks by date is to specify the day of the week. The values are:

- **M:** Monday
- **T:** Tuesday
- **W:** Wednesday
- **Th:** Thursday
- **F:** Friday
- **S:** Saturday
- **Su:** Sunday

You can schedule tasks to run relative to the current date as well. To do this, specify only a start time, and not a run date. You can start a backup script at 7 p.m., today as follows:

```
AT 19:00 backup.js
```

You can also schedule tasks to run on the next occurrence of a date. For example, if today is Monday and you want the task to run Wednesday, you can use the following command:

```
AT 07:30 /next:W starttest.js
```

Scheduled tasks usually run as background processes. However, you can specify that tasks run interactively, like this:

```
AT 05:00 /interactive /every:M,W,F copylogs.js
```

So far, all of the examples have assumed that you want to schedule tasks to run on the local system. The local system is the default for the AT Scheduler. If you want to schedule tasks on a remote system, type the UNC name or IP address of the remote system before you specify other parameters, like this:

```
AT \\Bilbo 09:45 /next:Su update.js
```

or, like this:

```
AT \\207.17.12.8 09:45 /every:T,Th backupmainservers.js
```

Viewing scheduled AT jobs

If a task is scheduled with the AT utility, you can view its status and configuration from anywhere on the network. To view scheduled jobs on a local system, type **at** on a line by itself and press Enter.

On a remote system, type **at** followed by the UNC name or IP address of the system you want to check, for example:

```
at \\Bilbo
```

When you view tasks, the output you get is similar to the following:

```
Status ID  Day                          Time       Command Line
--------------------------------------------------------------------
         1   Each T Th                  7:00 AM    checkstatus.js
         2   Each M F                   9:00 AM    copylogs.js
         3   Each S Su                  8:00 AM    backup.js
```

From the output you can determine the following:

- **Status:** Shows the status of a task. A blank entry indicates a normal status. Otherwise, you'll see an error message, such as ERROR.
- **ID:** Shows the unique identifier for the task.
- **Day:** Shows when the task is scheduled to run. Recurring tasks begin with the keyword Each. One-time tasks begin with the keyword Next.
- **Time:** Shows the time the command is scheduled to run.
- **Command Line:** Shows the command, program, or script scheduled to run.

If you enter the status ID, you can get information on an individual task, for example:

```
AT 3
```

or

```
AT \\Gandolf 3
```

Deleting scheduled AT jobs

You delete tasks by ID or you can cancel all scheduled tasks. You can delete a specific task like this:

```
AT 3 /delete
```

or

```
AT \\Gandolf 3 /delete
```

You cancel all tasks by typing the /delete switch without a task ID, like this:

```
AT /delete
```

or

```
AT \\Gandolf /delete
```

When deleting all tasks, you'll be prompted to confirm the action:

```
This operation will delete all scheduled jobs.
Do you want to continue this operation? (Y/N) [N]:
```

Type **y** to confirm that you want to delete all tasks. If you want to delete all tasks without having to confirm the action, use the /yes option:

```
AT /delete /yes
```

or

```
AT \\Gandolf /delete /yes
```

Scheduling with Scripts

The sections that follow show how you can schedule jobs on local and remote systems using scripts. As you'll see, there are many different ways you can schedule jobs in the enterprise.

Using AT in a script

Because the AT Scheduler is a command-line utility, you can access it within scripts using the Run method of the WshShell object. When you use the Run method, you can pass AT arguments as command parameters. An example of this is shown as Listing 13-1.

LISTING 13-1

Scheduling Tasks Within a Script

VBScript
schedtask.vbs

```
Set ws = WScript.CreateObject("WScript.Shell")
ret = ws.Run("at 5:00 /every:M,W,F copylogs.vbs",0,"TRUE")

If ret = 0 Then
 ws.LogEvent 0, "SchedTask.VBS Script Completed Successfully"
Else
 ws.LogEvent 1, "Error executing SchedTask.VBS"
End If
```

JScript
schedtask.js

```
var ws = WScript.CreateObject("WScript.Shell");
ret = ws.Run("at 5:00 /every:M,W,F copylogs.js",0,"TRUE")
```

```
if (ret == 0) {
 //successful execution
 ws.LogEvent(0, "SchedTask.JS Script Completed Successfully")
 }
else {
 //failed execution
 ws.LogEvent(1, "Error executing SchedTask.JS")
 }
```

If you are scheduling multiple tasks, you can enter additional Run statements in the script. Listing 13-2 shows how you could schedule tasks on three different systems.

LISTING 13-2

Scheduling Multiple Tasks Through a Script

VBScript
multitasks.vbs

```
Set ws = WScript.CreateObject("WScript.Shell")
ret = ws.Run("at 5:00 \\Gandolf /every:T,TH log.vbs",0,"TRUE")
ret = ret + ws.Run("at 5:00 \\Bilbo /every:T,TH log.vbs",0,"TRUE")
ret = ret + ws.Run("at 5:00 \\Dragon /every:T,TH log.vbs",0,"TRUE")
If ret = 0 Then
 ws.LogEvent 0, "SchedTask.VBS Script Completed Successfully"
Else
 ws.LogEvent 1, "Error executing SchedTask.VBS"
End If
```

JScript
multitasks.js

```
var ws = WScript.CreateObject("WScript.Shell");
ret = ws.Run("at 5:00 \\\\Gandolf /every:T,TH log.js",0,"TRUE")
ret += ws.Run("at 5:00 \\\\Bilbo /every:T,TH log.js",0,"TRUE")
ret += ws.Run("at 5:00 \\\\Dragon /every:T,TH log.js",0,"TRUE")

if (ret == 0) {
 //successful execution
 ws.LogEvent(0, "SchedTask.JS Script Completed Successfully")
 }
else {
 //failed execution
 ws.LogEvent(1, "Error executing SchedTask.JS")
 }
```

Automated job creation

In a network environment, you'll often want scheduled tasks to run on multiple computers. Rather than scheduling each script to run manually, you can automate the chore with a script. You'd probably want to use a separate file that the script can read to determine where and how to set up the jobs.

If the text file contains the system names and the jobs to execute, the format can look like this:

```
\\gandolf 00:00 /every:1,5,10,15,20,25,30 cleanup.js
```

You can then create a script that reads the file and executes the necessary commands, such as the one shown in Listing 13-3.

LISTING 13-3

Creating Jobs Automatically

schedule.txt

```
\\gandolf 00:00 /every:1,5,10,15,20,25,30 cleanup.js
\\bilbo 00:00 /every:1,5,10,15,20,25,30 cleanup.js
\\dragon 00:00 /every:1,5,10,15,20,25,30 cleanup.js
```

autosched.js

```
var ws = WScript.CreateObject("WScript.Shell")

ForReading = 1
 data = new Array()
 count = 0

 var fs = new ActiveXObject ("Scripting.FileSystemObject");
 var f = fs.OpenTextFile("schedule.txt", ForReading, "True")
 while (!f.AtEndOfStream) {
  data[count] = f.ReadLine()
  count++
 }

for (s in data) {
  ws.Run("at " + data[s],0,"True")
  WScript.Echo("Creating job " + data[s])
 }
```

If you are scheduling the same jobs on multiple computers, you may want to have a file that specifies the computers to use and a script that specifies the jobs to run. If you do this, you don't have to create separate entries when you want to run the same jobs on multiple computers. You can then modify the job creation script as shown in Listing 13-4.

LISTING 13-4

Scheduling the Same Jobs on Multiple Systems

sched-sys.txt

```
gandolf
bilbo
dragon
```

sched-jobs.txt

```
00:00 /every:1,5,10,15,20,25,30 cleanup.js
02:00 /every:M,W,F backup.js
05:00 /every:T,Th copylogs.js
```

autosched2.js

```
var ws = WScript.CreateObject("WScript.Shell")

ForReading = 1
data = new Array()
count = 0

var fs = new ActiveXObject ("Scripting.FileSystemObject");
var f = fs.OpenTextFile("sched-sys.txt", ForReading, "True")
while (!f.AtEndOfStream) {
 data[count] = "\\\\" + f.ReadLine()
 count++
}

ForReading = 1
jobs = new Array()
count = 0

var fs = new ActiveXObject ("Scripting.FileSystemObject");
var f = fs.OpenTextFile("sched-jobs.txt", ForReading, "True")
while (!f.AtEndOfStream) {
 jobs[count] = f.ReadLine()
 count++
}
```

continued

LISTING 13-4 *(continued)*

```
for (s in data) {
  for (j in jobs) {
    ws.Run("at " + data[s] + " " + jobs [j],0,"True")
    WScript.Echo("Creating job " + jobs [j] + " on " + data[s])
  }
}
```

Deleting jobs using scripts

You can delete jobs using scripts as well. This is useful if you make a mistake during automated scheduling or simply want to delete jobs that are no longer needed. You can delete jobs using the same techniques that you used to create jobs. The key difference is that instead of specifying jobs to create, you set the job identifiers to delete. You can also delete all scheduled jobs and then re-create them.

Listing 13-5 shows how you can delete all jobs on multiple computers. A text file is again used to specify the names of the systems you want to work with.

LISTING 13-5

Deleting Scheduled Jobs

sched-del.txt

```
\\gandolf
\\bilbo
\\dragon
```

deletejobs.js

```
var ws = WScript.CreateObject("WScript.Shell")

ForReading = 1
data = new Array()
count = 0

var fs = new ActiveXObject ("Scripting.FileSystemObject");
var f = fs.OpenTextFile("sched-del.txt", ForReading, "True")
while (!f.AtEndOfStream) {
 data[count] = f.ReadLine()
 count++
}
```

```
for (s in data) {
 ws.Run("at " + data[s] + " /delete /yes",0,"True")
 WScript.Echo("Deleting jobs on " + data[s])
}
```

Creating a scheduling manager script

Previous sections outlined several different techniques for creating and deleting scripts. Now let's take this concept a few steps further by developing a script that handles both job creation and job deletion. You'll again use text files to designate where and how jobs should be handled.

A file named sched-svr.txt lists the servers on which you want to create or delete jobs. The file should contain the UNC name of the server, for example:

```
\\Gandolf
\\Bilbo
\\Dragon
\\Goblin
```

A file named sched-repl.txt lists the jobs you want to schedule on the designated servers. The file should only contain the job text:

```
00:00 /every:1,5,10,15,20,25,30 cleanup.js
00:20 /every:M,W,F backup.js
01:00 /every:Su copylogs.js
```

To make the script more dynamic, you'll configure the script to handle arguments. If the user doesn't enter an argument, the script should provide basic instruction on how to use the script. If the user enters an argument, the script should check the value of the argument and determine if the proper value has been entered. These features are implemented as follows:

```
var theArgs = WScript.Arguments

if (theArgs.Count() == 0) {
  WScript.Echo("Configure the text files:")
  WScript.Echo("sched-svr.txt and sched-repl.txt")
  WScript.Echo("Then enter c to copy or d to delete jobs.")
  WScript.Quit(1)
}
else {
  arg1 = theArgs.Item(0)
  WScript.Echo(arg1)
}

if (arg1 == "c") {
  WScript.Echo("Preparing to create Jobs…")
```

```
      createJobs()
      WScript.Quit(0)
}

if (arg1 == "d") {
   WScript.Echo("Preparing to delete Jobs…")
   deleteJobs()
   WScript.Quit(0)
}
```

Next, the `createJobs()` and `deleteJobs()` functions should perform the appropriate tasks. Because these functions both read the sched-svr.txt file, there is no reason to code the file-reading functionality twice. Instead, you can call another function that reads the files and returns the data neatly packed away in an array. The functions can then use the array values to configure or delete jobs, for example:

```
function deleteJobs() {

sysArray = getData("sched-svr.txt")

  for (s in sysArray) {
   ws.Run("at " + sysArray[s] + " /delete /yes",0,"True")
   WScript.Echo("Deleting jobs on " + sysArray[s])
  }
}

function createJobs() {

 sysArray = getData("sched-svr.txt")
 jobsArray = getData("sched-repl.txt")

 for (s in sysArray) {
  for (j in jobsArray) {
   ws.Run("at " + sysArray[s] + " " + jobsArray[j],0,"True")
   WScript.Echo("Creating job " + jobsArray[j] + " on " + sysArray[s])
  }
 }
}
```

The `getData()` function is very similar to the other functions for reading files we've examined. The key difference is that the function expects to be passed the file name to use as the first parameter. In this way, you can call the function to read both sched-svr.txt and sched-repl.txt. This function is implemented using the following code:

```
function getData(fname) {

ForReading = 1
data = new Array()
count = 0
```

```
var fs = new ActiveXObject ("Scripting.FileSystemObject");
var f = fs.OpenTextFile(fname, ForReading, "True")
while (!f.AtEndOfStream) {
 data[count] = f.ReadLine()
 count++
 }
 return data
}
```

The complete text for the scheduling manager script is shown in Listing 13-6.

LISTING 13-6

Managing Job Scheduling

sched-svr.txt

```
\\Gandolf
\\Bilbo
\\Dragon
\\Goblin
```

sched-repl.txt

```
00:00 /every:1,5,10,15,20,25,30 cleanup.js
00:20 /every:M,W,F backup.js
01:00 /every:Su copylogs.js
```

schedmgr.js

```
// ***********************
// Script: Enterprise Scheduling Manager
// Version: 1.1.5
// Creation Date: 05/23/2008
// Last Modified: 07/14/2008
// Author: William R. Stanek
// Email: williamstanek@aol.com
//
// Copyright (c) 2008 William R. Stanek
// ***********************
// Description: Manages scheduled tasks on local and
//              remote systems.
// ***********************
// Copy jobs to multiple systems
// Enter c at first parameter
// *
// Delete jobs on a group of servers
// Enter d at first parameter
// *
```

continued

LISTING 13-6 *(continued)*

```
// Server list comes from sched-svr.txt in current directory
// Enter server names on separate lines, such as:
// \\Gandolf
// \\Bilbo
// *
// Scheduled jobs are entered in sched-jobs.txt in the
// current directory. Enter the job information without
// the at or system name, such as:
// 01:00 /every:M,T,W,Th,F,S,Su cleanup.js
// 05:00 /next:1,15 checkstatus.js
// ************************

var ws = WScript.CreateObject("WScript.Shell")

var theArgs = WScript.Arguments

if (theArgs.Count() == 0) {
  WScript.Echo("Configure the text files:")
  WScript.Echo("sched-svr.txt and sched-repl.txt")
  WScript.Echo("Then enter c to copy or d to delete jobs.")
  WScript.Quit(1)
}
else {
  arg1 = theArgs.Item(0)
  WScript.Echo(arg1)
}

if (arg1 == "c") {
  WScript.Echo("Preparing to create Jobs…")
  createJobs()
  WScript.Quit(0)
}

if (arg1 == "d") {
  WScript.Echo("Preparing to delete Jobs…")
  deleteJobs()
  WScript.Quit(0)
}

function deleteJobs() {

sysArray = getData("sched-svr.txt")

 for (s in sysArray) {
  ws.Run("at " + sysArray[s] + " /delete /yes",0,"True")
  WScript.Echo("Deleting jobs on " + sysArray[s])
 }
```

```
}

function createJobs() {

 sysArray = getData("sched-svr.txt")
 jobsArray = getData("sched-repl.txt")

 for (s in sysArray) {
  for (j in jobsArray) {
   ws.Run("at " + sysArray[s] + " " + jobsArray[j],0,"True")
   WScript.Echo("Creating job " + jobsArray[j] + " on " + sysArray[s])
  }
 }
}

function getData(fname) {

 ForReading = 1
 data = new Array()
 count = 0

 var fs = new ActiveXObject ("Scripting.FileSystemObject");
 var f = fs.OpenTextFile(fname, ForReading, "True")
 while (!f.AtEndOfStream) {
  data[count] = f.ReadLine()
  count++
 }
 return data
}
```

Summary

Task scheduling is one of the primary administrative tasks you'll need to perform in a network environment. As an administrator or a power user with extended permissions, you can use the techniques discussed in this chapter to create and manage scheduled tasks anywhere on the network. When you set out to manage tasks on multiple computers, don't forget that you can use scripts to handle the grunt work. In fact, you can use the scheduling manager script to handle most of your scheduling needs.

Chapter 14

Managing Computer and User Scripts

Automation is the key to Windows scripting. The previous chapter showed how you can create scripts to run automatically based on the time, day of the week, or date. This chapter focuses on creating scripts that execute based on user logon and logoff, as well as computer startup and shutdown.

Why Use Computer and User Scripts?

Every once in a while, an administrator or user asks "Why would I want to use computer and user scripts?" I always think back to my days in the military when I often needed to logon to a system and be able to immediately begin troubleshooting critical network problems in a real-time environment. I simply didn't have time to start all the tools I needed, run background checks, or perform any other setup tasks, so I automated these processes. When I logged in, the tools I needed to work with started automatically, the background checks initialized and began running, and other configuration tasks were executed as well. The result was that instead of it taking five or six minutes to get ready to troubleshoot, I could start immediately, which helped me earn a reputation as someone who could resolve problems quickly.

While seconds may not count in the environment you work in, you can certainly benefit from auto-mation. Any routine tasks that you or others in your office need to perform on a daily basis can be automated. You can automate these tasks:

- After system startup
- After logging on to the network
- Before logging off
- Before shutting down a system

The limits for computer and user scripts are the limits of your imagination. Scripts can run any Windows shell command, work with Windows Script Host, access Windows applications through COM (Component Object Model), and more. You just have to know how to write the script you need. For example, with logon scripts you may want to:

- Display a message of the day
- Display a network usage policy or disclaimer
- Start applications or run commands
- Configure default printers and set up other printers
- Map network drives and set default drive paths
- Track the users logon and logout times
- Build a daily report from log files and display it in a browser

So the answer to the question, "Why use computer and user scripts?" is clear. You use computer and user scripts because you want to become more efficient and you want to help others become more efficient.

NOTE   You'll need special privileges and permissions to manage computer and user scripts. If you aren't an administrator and don't have power user permissions on the local com-puter, you won't be able to manage startup, shutdown, logon, and logoff scripts.

Introducing Group Policies

In Windows, you normally assign computer and user scripts through group policies. Think of a group policy as a set of rules that helps you manage users and computers.

How are policies used?

Group policies can be applied at various levels in the organization. Policies that apply to individual computers are referred to as *local group policies* and are stored on an individual computer. Other group policies affect multiple computers and are stored in the Active Directory directory service.

We'll refer to policies that affect multiple computers as *global group policies*. This will help differentiate between policies that affect individual computers (local group policies) and policies that affect multiple computers (global group policies).

The way policies are applied depends on the structure of the organization. To help you understand the available structures, you need to know a bit about Active Directory. Active Directory is the primary directory service for Windows. Active Directory provides the logical and physical structure of the company's network.

Logical structures defined by Active Directory are:

- **Domains:** A domain is a group of computers that share a common directory structure. For example, the computers named Gandolf, Bilbo, and Dragon are all a part of the tvpress.com domain. This means that their full computer names are Gandolf.tvpress.com, Bilbo.tvpress.com, and Dragon.tvpress.com.

- **Organizational units:** An organizational unit is a subgroup of domains. Organizational units often mirror the company's functional or business structure. For example, you may have organizational units named Marketing, Engineering, and IS.

- **Domain trees:** A domain tree is one or more domains that share a contiguous namespace. For example, the domains hr.tvpress.com and eng.tvpress.com are all a part of the tvpress.com master domain and are thus a part of the same domain tree.

- **Domain forests:** A domain forest is one or more domain trees that share common directory information. If your company has multiple domains, such as tvpress.com and centraldrive.com, these domains form separate domain trees. However, because they are all defined through your organization's directory, they are a part of the same forest, and can thus share directory information.

The physical structures defined by Active Directory are:

- **Subnets:** A subnet is a network group with a specific IP address range and network mask. For example, the IP addresses for Gandolf, Bilbo, and Dragon are all a part of the 207.19.67 network group. Their IP addresses are 207.19.67.12, 207.19.67.14, and 207.19.67.16, respectively. This means they are all a part of the same subnet.

- **Sites:** A site is a group of one or more subnets. For example, if the company used the network groups 207.19.67 and 204.12.5, they could all be part of the same site.

Group policies apply to domains, organizational units, and sites. This means you can set group policies based on the physical and logical structure of the network. When multiple policies are in place, they are applied in the following order:

1. Windows NT 4.0 policies (NTConfig.pol)
2. Local group policies
3. Site group policies

4. Domain group policies

5. Organizational unit group policies

6. Child organizational unit group policies

When there are conflicts in policy settings, settings applied later have precedence and overwrite previously set policy settings. For example, site policies have precedence over local group policies.

NOTE Windows does define ways to override and block policy settings. These changes can affect the way policies are inherited and applied. A good resource to learn more about group policy is the *Microsoft Windows Administrator's Pocket Consultant*.

When are policies applied?

The way policies are applied depends on whether the policies affect computers or users. Computer-related policies are normally applied during system startup. User-related policies are normally applied during logon. The events that take place during startup and logon are as follows:

- After the network starts, Windows applies computer policies. The computer policies are applied one at a time as outlined previously. No user interface is displayed while computer policies are being processed.

- Windows runs any startup scripts. These scripts are executed one at a time by default. Here, each script must complete or time out before the next starts. Script execution is not displayed to the user unless otherwise specified.

- When a user logs on, Windows loads the user profile.

- Windows applies user policies. The policies are applied one at a time as outlined previously. The user interface is displayed while user policies are being processed.

- Windows runs logon scripts. These scripts are executed simultaneously by default. Normally script execution is not displayed to the user. Scripts in the Netlogon share are run last.

- Windows displays the startup interface configured in Group Policy.

How are local group policies managed?

All Windows computers have a local group policy. You manage local policies on a computer through an extension for the Microsoft Management Console (MMC) called Local Computer Policy. You can access Local Computer Policy as follows:

1. Click the Start menu, and then click Run. This displays the Run dialog box.

2. Type mmc in the Open field and then click OK. This displays the Microsoft Management Console (MMC).

3. Click File, and then click Add/Remove Snap-in. This displays the Add/Remove Snap-in dialog box shown in Figure 14-1.

FIGURE 14-1

Use the Add/Remove Snap-in dialog box to select snap-ins that you want to add to the console.

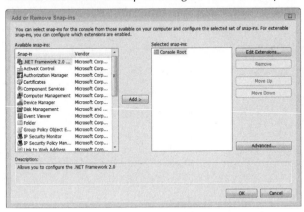

4. On the Standalone tab, click Add.

5. Next, in the Add Snap-in dialog box, click Group Policy, then click Add. This displays the Select Group Policy Object dialog box.

6. Click Local Computer to edit the local policy on your computer or Browse to find the local policy on another computer.

7. Click Finish in the Group Policy Object dialog box, and then click Close in the Add Snap-in dialog box.

8. Click OK. As Figure 14-2 shows, the Local Computer Policy snap-in is then added to the console.

Once you've added the Local Computer Policy snap-in to the console, you can manage the local policy on the selected computer.

FIGURE 14-2

Use the Local Computer Policy snap-in to manage local group policies.

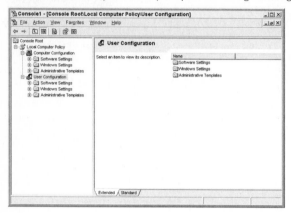

How are global group policies managed?

You work with global group policies through the Group Policy snap-in. The way you access this snap-in depends on the type of policy you are working with. For sites, you start the Group Policy snap-in from the Active Directory Sites and Services console. For domains and organizational units, you start the Group Policy snap-in from the Active Directory Users and Computers console.

Once you start the appropriate console, you access the Group Policy snap-in as follows:

1. Right-click on the site, domain, or organizational unit you want to work within the console root. Then select Properties. This displays a Properties dialog box.

2. In the Properties dialog box, select the Group Policy tab, as shown in Figure 14-3. You can now:

   ▓ Create a new policy or edit an existing policy by clicking New.

   ▓ Edit an existing policy by selecting a policy, then clicking Edit.

   ▓ Change the priority of a policy by selecting it and then using the Up/Down buttons to change its position in the Group Policy Object Links list.

   ▓ Delete an existing policy by selecting it and then clicking Delete.

FIGURE 14-3

Use the Group Policy tab to view, edit, and delete policies.

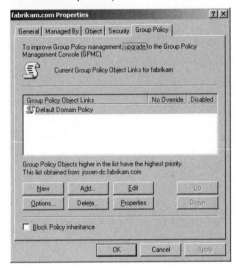

Using the policy consoles

Figure 14-4 shows the Group Policy snap-in in an MMC console. If you compare this figure to Figure 14-2, you'll see that the Local Computer Policy and the Group Policy snap-ins are configured similarly. These snap-ins have two main nodes:

- **Computer Configuration:** Used to set computer policies
- **User Configuration:** Used to set user policies

You'll usually find that both Computer Configuration and User Configuration have subnodes for:

- Software Settings
- Windows Settings
- Administrative Templates

You configure user and computer scripts through Windows Settings.

FIGURE 14-4

Use the Group Policy snap-in to manage global group policies.

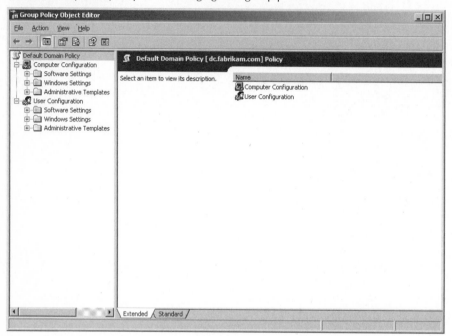

Working with Computer and User Scripts

As you've seen, group policies play an important role in the way startup, shutdown, logon, and logoff scripts are assigned. Now let's look at how you can assign these scripts as part of group policies.

Managing startup and shutdown scripts

You assign startup and shutdown scripts to individual computers through local group policy, or to groups of computers through global group policies. By doing this, computers can execute scripts automatically when they are booted-up or shut down. You assign a startup or shutdown script to a computer by completing the following steps:

1.   Access the policy console you want to work with as described previously in the chapter.

2.   In the Computer Configuration node, double-click the Windows Settings folder.

3. In the console root, select Scripts. You can now:

   ▪ Specify startup scripts by right-clicking Startup and then selecting Properties.

   ▪ Specify shutdown scripts by right-clicking Shutdown and then selecting Properties.

4. Either technique opens a dialog box similar to the one shown in Figure 14-5. You can now add, delete, or reconfigure script properties.

FIGURE 14-5

Use the Startup Properties dialog box to manage computer scripts.

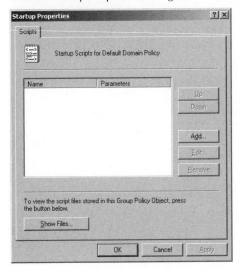

5. To assign a script, click Add. This displays the Add a Script dialog box. In the Script Name field, type the full file path to the script you want to use, or click Browse to find a script. In the script parameter field, enter any parameters to pass to the scripting host for a Windows script. Repeat this step to add other scripts.

6. During startup or shutdown, scripts are executed in the order that they are listed in the Properties dialog box. Use the Up/Down buttons to change the order of the scripts if necessary.

7. Click OK when you are finished. If you later want to edit the script name or parameters, select the script in the Script For list, and then click Edit. You can delete a script by selecting it in the Script For list and then clicking Remove.

Managing logon and logoff scripts

Logon and logoff scripts are also managed through local and global group policies. Scripts you assign through local group policies affect all users that log in to that particular computer. Scripts you assign through global group policies affect all computers in the organizational unit, domain, or site. You assign a logon or logoff script by completing the following steps:

1. Access the policy console you want to work with as described previously in the chapter.

2. In the User Configuration node, double-click the Windows Settings folder.

3. In the console root, select Scripts. You can now:

   ▣ Specify logon scripts by right-clicking Logon and then selecting Properties.

   ▣ Specify logoff scripts by right-clicking Logoff and then selecting Properties.

4. Either technique opens a dialog box similar to the one shown in Figure 14-6. You can now add, delete, or reconfigure script properties.

FIGURE 14-6

Use the Logoff Properties dialog box to manage user scripts.

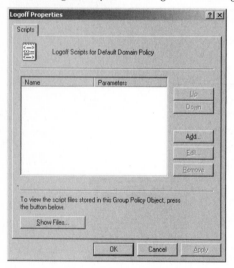

5. To assign a script, click Add. This displays the Add a Script dialog box. In the Script Name field, type the full file path to the script you want to use, or click Browse to find a script. In the script parameter field, enter any parameters to pass to the scripting host for a Windows script. Repeat this step to add other scripts.

6. During logon or logoff, scripts are executed in the order that they are listed in the Properties dialog box. Use the Up/Down buttons to change the order of the scripts if necessary.

7. Click OK when you are finished. If you later want to edit the script name or parameters, select the script in the Script For list, and then click Edit. You can delete a script by selecting it in the Script For list and then clicking Remove.

Alternatives to group policy

The sections that follow look at alternatives to assigning scripts through group policy. Group policies only apply to Windows 2000 and later. In a Windows domain, the main scripts that you'll work with are logon scripts. These scripts are handled by a domain controller, which is a Windows server acting as a domain controller for the Windows NT domain.

You can use command-shell scripts as logon scripts. These scripts must end with the .bat or .cmd extension. You can also use Windows scripts or call Windows scripts from command-shell scripts.

Listing 14-1 shows basic logon scripts that are executed through a shell script. The scripting hosts use the user's default working directory and all paths must be set relative to this directory; or you should use a full file path. This example accesses the Netlogon share on the primary domain controller. For logon scripts to be available, you need to configure directory replication or have an administrator do this for you.

LISTING 14-1

Executing Windows Logon Scripts through a Shell Script

startup.bat

```
cscript \\Gandolf\NETLOGON\start.vbs
cscript \\Gandolf\NETLOGON\start.js
```

start.vbs

```
Set ws = WScript.CreateObject("WScript.Shell")
ws.Run "notepad " & WScript.ScriptFullName
```

start.js

```
var ws = WScript.CreateObject("WScript.Shell");
ws.Run("notepad " + WScript.ScriptFullName)
```

Another thing to note is that when you work with Windows systems, you don't have to assign computer and user scripts through Group Policy. The following options can be used in addition to, or instead of, Group Policy:

- Assign startup and logon scripts as scheduled tasks. You schedule tasks using the Task Scheduler Wizard.

- Assign logon scripts to individual user accounts through the Active Directory Users and Computers console. To do this, access the Profile tab of the User Properties dialog box.

Summary

In this chapter, you learned about the benefits of computer and user scripts. Computer scripts help you automate tasks when a computer is started or shut down. User scripts help you automate tasks when a user logs on or logs off. Both types of scripts can be powerful automation tools if used properly.

Chapter 15

Introducing Active Directory Services Interfaces

With Active Directory Service Interfaces, you can manage local accounts, domain accounts, Windows services, and other resources through Windows scripts. ADSI is very complex and is designed primarily for programmers that use Visual Basic or C++. Because of this complexity, you'll need to learn a few important concepts before you can start working with ADSI, which are exactly what this chapter covers. Don't worry; we won't try to teach you Visual Basic or C++ programming. We won't try to cover every facet of ADSI either. Instead, we'll focus on the core tasks that you can use time and again to manage network and system resources.

NOTE Rather than provide a ton of background material that you may not need, the focus of this chapter is on using ADSI and not on directory service basics. If you aren't familiar with directory services, you may want to brush up on the basics. A good resource for Active Directory is *Windows Server 2008 Administrator's Pocket Consultant*. Chapters 7 through 11 cover Active Directory in detail.

ADSI Essentials

Directory services are an important part of many network operating systems, including Novell NetWare and Microsoft Windows. In Novell NetWare, the directory service is called Novell NetWare Directory Services (NDS). In Microsoft Windows, the directory service is called Active Directory. Some directory services implement a common communication protocol called *the Lightweight Directory Access Protocol (LDAP)*. LDAP is an Internet standard protocol and you use it to access any compliant directory service.

Directory services often use objects to describe and provide access to various network components, such as users and groups. You can access these objects through the Active Directory Service Interfaces. While it's possible to fill several chapters with background material on how ADSI works, you really don't need to know ADSI internals to be able to create Windows scripts that use ADSI. The key concepts you should know are as follows:

- ADSI provides access to directory services by exposing their objects as COM objects.
- The interfaces of these COM objects provide methods and properties that can be used in Windows Scripts.
- You don't manipulate the COM interfaces directly and instead access the interfaces through an ADSI provider.
- ADSI uses a multi-tier architecture with clients, routers, and providers.

The sections that follow examine ADSI providers and the ADSI architecture.

Understanding ADSI providers

For Windows scripts, the ADSI provider is the most important aspect of the ADSI model. Each ADSI provider is specific to a particular directory service. You can get ADSI providers from Microsoft and from third-party vendors. ADSI providers from Microsoft include:

- **ADSI LDAP Provider:** A standard provider for LDAP-compliant services and applications. You can use this provider to manage Windows Active Directory, Microsoft Exchange 5.5/6.0, and more.
- **ADSI WinNT Provider:** A standard provider for accessing Windows NT 4.0 domains, workstations, and servers. You also use this provider to access local resources on Windows systems, such as local users and local groups.
- **ADSI NDS Provider:** A standard provider for accessing Novell NetWare Directory Services (NDS).
- **ADSI NWCOMPAT Provider:** A standard provider for accessing Novell NetWare 3.

 The provider name is case-sensitive and must be used exactly as shown in your scripts.

Providers can be extended at any time by installing new versions, service packs, or other add-ons. As you might expect, many different provider extensions are available. Two extensions that you may want to use are GC and IIS. Both are extensions to the ADSI LDAP Providers.

GC provides access to global catalogs. Global catalogs contain partial replicas of all the domains in a domain forest and are a part of Windows Active Directory. You can use the GC extension to search for objects in the enterprise regardless of which domain they are in. For example, if your domain forest contains the domains tvpress.com, centraldrive.com, and weblearningcenter.com, you can search the global catalog for an object without having to know which domain it is in. Once you find the object, you could discover its relative domain and then obtain the object.

IIS provides access to Internet Information Services (IIS). Through IIS, you can create and configure FTP, Web, and SMTP sites. You can also manage logs and the IIS metabase. The *IIS metabase* contains definitions for various aspects of IIS and essentially allows you to read and change the configurations of related sites and services.

Understanding the ADSI architecture

ADSI uses a multi-tier architecture. Without going into all of the unnecessary details, the basic structure of this architecture looks like this:

Client ⇨ ADSI Router ⇨ ADSI Provider

Following this simple structure, you can see that clients are used to access ADSI and that a middle-man called a router is used to access providers. The router implements a core set of objects. These objects present a common set of features and services to providers. Because of this, any feature supported by the ADSI router is also supported by an ADSI provider (unless the provider chooses otherwise).

Any computer that wants to make use of ADSI must have the ADSI client installed. The client is installed automatically with Windows Professional and Windows Server. Computers running other operating systems must install the ADSI client. For example, if you run Windows scripts on a Windows 95 or Windows NT 4.0 computer and these scripts use ADSI, you'll need to install the ADSI client prior to running the scripts.

The standard providers distributed with the ADSI Software Developers Kit and in ADSI client distributions are referred to as ADSI system providers. Because ADSI is fully extensible, newer versions of providers are being created all the time. You can take advantage of these extensions by installing the latest version. Most of the features for ADSI providers and the ADSI router are implemented as *Dynamically Linked Libraries (DLLs)*. The key DLLs for system providers include:

- Activeds.dll, which implements the ADSI router module
- Adsldp.dll, adsldpc.dll, and adsmsext.dll, which implement the ADSI LDAP provider
- Adsnt.dll, which implements the ADSI WinNT provider
- Adsnds.dll, which implements the ADSI NDS provider
- Adsnw.dll, which implements the ADSI NWCompat provider

 **If a DLL that's needed by a provider isn't installed on a computer, you can't use the provider. You'll need to install the provider.**

Binding ADSI objects

You use the ADSI provider interfaces by binding to objects in the related directory service. In WSH, you can bind objects using the `WScript.GetObject` method. With ADSI, the syntax for the `GetObject` method is:

VBScript

```
Set obj = GetObject("AdsPathString")
```

JScript

```
var obj = GetObject("AdsPathString")
```

The AdsPath string identifies the ADSI provider and the object to which you want to bind. The following example obtains an object reference to the organizational unit called IT in the seattle.tvpress. com domain:

VBScript

```
Set ou = GetObject("LDAP://OU=IT,DC=seattle,DC=tvpress,DC=com")
```

JScript

```
var ou = GetObject("LDAP://OU=IT,DC=seattle,DC=tvpress,DC=com")
```

Although the AdsPath string is different for each provider, the basic syntax of the string is summarized in Table 15-1. As you can see from the table, the AdsPath string has two basic elements: special characters and components. Special characters serve primarily as separators but also join class designators and escape special characters. Components identify ADSI providers and designate component classes, such as domain components and organizational units.

TABLE 15-1

Syntax for AdsPath Strings

String Element Special Characters	
Character	**Description**
Backward slash (\)	Escapes special characters to signify that they should be used as literals.
Forward slash (/)	Separates elements in the AdsPath string
Semicolon (;)	Separates elements in the AdsPath string
Comma (,)	Separates elements in the AdsPath string
Equal sign (=)	Joins a class specifier with a component
Components	
Designator	**Description**
Provider://	Designates an ADSI provider, such as LDAP://; the provider name is case-sensitive and must be exact.
OU=	Designates an organizational unit class, such as OU=IT
DC=	Designates a domain component class, such as DC=tvpress

Components Designator	Description
O=	Designates an organization, such as `O=Internet`
CN=	Designates a common name, such as `CN=user`

All directory objects have a unique identifier. The identifier is a representation of each element, from the root of the directory hierarchy to the object you want to work with. When you use commas to separate elements in the hierarchy, you use a reverse order, starting from the object you want to work with and moving to the top-most object. In the previous example, the `AdsPath` string starts in the organizational unit and works up to the top-level of the domain hierarchy. The example could have started with a common name as well, for example:

```
CN=Administrator,OU=IT,DC=seattle,DC=tvpress,DC=com
```

When you use forward slashes to separate objects in the domain hierarchy, you move from the highest-level object to the lowest-level object, like this:

```
DC=com/DC=tvpress/DC=seattle/OU=IT/CN=Administrator
```

When you first start working with the `AdsPath` string, one of the most difficult concepts to understand is how domain names are represented through domain component classes. A technique that is helpful is to remember that domain names, such as `tvpress.com`, represent elements in the domain hierarchy. Here, `tvpress` represents the organizational domain and `com` is the top-level domain. Top-level domains form the root of the domain hierarchy and are also called root domains. *Root domains* are organized by function, organization type, and geographic location.

Normal domains, such as `tvpress.com`, are also referred to as parent domains. Parent domains can be divided into subdomains. These subdomains can be used for divisions or office locations. For example, the fully qualified domains `seattle.tvpress.com`, `portland.tvpress.com`, and `la.tvpress.com` could be used for your company's Seattle, Portland, and Los Angeles offices respectively.

Each level of the domain hierarchy is represented by a domain component class. In the `portland.tvpress.com` domain:

- `DC=PORTLAND` represents the subdomain level
- `DC=TVPRESS` represents the parent level
- `DC=COM` represents the root level

By specifying these component classes in an `AdsPath`, you gain access to objects within the subdomain container, such as organizational units. If you wanted to work with objects in the parent domain (`tvpress.com`), you reference only the parent level and the root level, for example:

VBScript

```
Set ou = GetObject("LDAP://OU=Marketing,DC=tvpress,DC=com")
```

JScript

```
var ou = GetObject("LDAP://OU=Marketing,DC=tvpress,DC=com")
```

Once you have the object that you want to work with, you can use the available methods and properties to manipulate the object. Through these directory objects you can then:

- Manage domain accounts for users and groups
- Manage local accounts for users and groups
- Administer printers and print jobs
- Control file services and sharing
- Manage user sessions and connections
- Control other system and network resources

Taking Advantage of ADSI

Now that you know ADSI essentials, let's look at how you can take advantage of ADSI. ADSI implements dozens of interfaces that can be used in scripts. You access these interfaces through a named provider, such as the ADSI LDAP provider. Each provider implements interfaces for objects that are available through its related directory service. If an object isn't available, the interface isn't implemented. If an object property or method isn't available, the related interface method or property method isn't implemented.

 The sections that follow offer overviews of using the various providers. Later in the chapter and in other chapters in this part of the book, you'll find more detailed examples.

Working with the ADSI·LDAP provider

The *ADSI LDAP provider* is used to manage Windows Active Directory, Microsoft Exchange, and other LDAP-compliant applications. With Active Directory, you use the provider as outlined previously in the section titled, "Binding ADSI objects." As you'll recall, the basic syntax for the `AdsPath` string is:

```
LDAP://OU=IT,DC=seattle,DC=tvpress,DC=com
```

You can also reference a specific server or domain in the `AdsPath`. In the following example, you bind to the ADSI object through a server named Zeta:

VBScript

```
Set ou = GetObject("LDAP://Zeta/OU=Marketing,DC=tvpress,DC=com")
```

JScript

```
var ou = GetObject("LDAP://Zeta/OU=Marketing,DC=tvpress,DC=com")
```

In this example, you bind to an ADSI object through a domain on the Internet:

VBScript

```
Set ou = GetObject("LDAP://tvpress.com/OU=Marketing,
DC=tvpress,DC=com,O=Internet")
```

JScript

```
var ou = GetObject("LDAP://tvpress.com/OU=Marketing,
DC=tvpress,DC=com,O=Internet")
```

TIP   When you access objects outside your local domain, you may need to authenticate your-self. To do this, use the `OpenDSObject` method. See the section in this chapter titled, "Handling authentication and security" for details.

When you access Microsoft Exchange, you must reference the server name in the `AdsPath`. Then, instead of referencing domain components, you reference the organization, site, container, and mail-box names, for example:

```
LDAP://ServerName/cn=Mailbox,cn=Container,ou=SiteName,o=OrgName
```

In this example, you bind to the `Recipients` container in the mailbox for `wrstanek`:

VBScript

```
Set cont = GetObject("LDAP://qmail/cn=wrstanek,cn=Recipients,
ou=Seattle,o=tvpress")
```

JScript

```
var cont = GetObject("LDAP://qmail/cn=wrstanek,cn=Recipients,
ou=Seattle,o=tvpress")
```

You can also use forward slashes as shown here:

VBScript

```
Set cont = GetObject("LDAP://qmail/o=tvpress/ou=Seattle/ cn=Recipients/
cn=wrstanek")
```

JScript

```
var cont = GetObject("LDAP://qmail/o=tvpress/ou=Seattle/ cn=Recipients/
cn=wrstanek")
```

With Microsoft Exchange, common names are mapped to actual display names rather than directory names. This means you access mailboxes and their components using the name displayed in Exchange Administrator, Outlook, or another mail client.

When you use the LDAP provider, you'll use a different set of objects than you'll use with other providers. Table 15-2 lists the objects you'll use most often with the LDAP provider. The table also lists the ADSI interfaces for those objects that are supported by the LDAP provider.

CAUTION   Some LDAP provider objects inherit from GenObject, which allows them to access interfaces supported by this object. For example, although the User object doesn't support IADs directly, the object can use the interface. The reason is that the interface is inherited from GenObject.

TABLE 15-2

Common Objects and Interfaces for the LDAP Provider

ADSI Object	Supported Interfaces	Description
Class	IADs IADsClass	Represents class definitions in the schema
GenObject	IADs IADsContainer IADsDeleteOps IADsObjectOptions IADsPropertyList IDirectoryObject IDirectorySearch	Provides common services to most other ADSI objects for the provider
Group	IADsGroup IADsExtension	Represents a group account
GroupCollection	IADsMembers	Represents a collection of group accounts
Locality	IADsLocality IADsExtension	Represents geographical locales of users, organizations, and so forth
Namespace	IADs IADsContainer IADsOpenDSObject	Represents the LDAP namespace
Organization	IADsO IADsExtension	Represents an organization
OrganizationalUnit	IADsOU IADsExtension	Represents an organizational unit

ADSI Object	Supported Interfaces	Description
Pathname	IADsPathname	Represents AdsPath
PrintQueue	IADsPrintQueue IADsPrintQueueOperations IADsExtension	Represents a print queue
Property	IADs IADsProperty	Represents attribute definitions in the schema
RootDSE	IADs IADsPropertyList	Represents the root of the directory tree
Schema	IADs IADsContainer	Represents the schema container
Syntax	IADs IADsSyntax	Represents the attribute syntax
User	IADsUser IADsExtension	Represents a user account
UserCollection	IADsMembers	Represents a collection of user accounts

Working with the ADSI WinNT provider

The ADSI WinNT provider is used to access resources in Windows NT 4.0 domains, as well as local resources on Windows systems. With the WinNT provider, the basic syntax for the Ads/Path string is:

```
WinNT://DomainName/ServerName/ObjectName
```

In many ways this syntax makes the WinNT provider easier to work with, but it also limits the reach of the provider. You can access objects in the current NT domain or other accessible NT domains, but you can't access Internet domains. The following example shows how you can access the user account for wrstane in the tvpress domain:

VBScript

```
Set user = GetObject("WinNT://TVPRESS/wrstane")
```

JScript

```
var user = GetObject("WinNT://TVPRESS/wrstane")
```

You can also access a specific server in the domain. In the following example, you access the Primary Domain Controller named Zeta:

VBScript

```
Set user = GetObject("WinNT://TVPRESS/Zeta/wrstane")
```

JScript

```
var user = GetObject("WinNT://TVPRESS/Zeta/wrstane")
```

If a computer named Omega had a local printer named EngPrinter, you could access it as follows:

VBScript

```
Set ptr = GetObject("WinNT://TVPRESS/Omega/EngPrinter")
```

JScript

```
var ptr = GetObject("WinNT://TVPRESS/Omega/EngPrinter")
```

For the WinNT provider, the AdsPath can also include the class name of the object to which you want to bind. The main reason to do this is to improve the response time for binding the object. In this example, you specify the user class:

VBScript

```
Set user = GetObject("WinNT://TVPRESS/Zeta/wrstane,user")
```

JScript

```
var user = GetObject("WinNT://TVPRESS/Zeta/wrstane,user")
```

Table 15-3 shows the objects you'll use most often with the WinNT provider. The table also shows the ADSI interfaces for those objects that are supported by the WinNT provider.

TABLE 15-3

Common Objects and Interfaces for the WinNT Provider

ADSI Object	Supported Interfaces	Description
Class	IADs IADsClass	Represents a class definition
Computer	IADs IADsComputer IADsComputerOperations IADsContainer IADsPropertyList	Represents a computer account

ADSI Object	Supported Interfaces	Description
Domain	IADs IADsContainer IADsDomain IADsPropertyList	Represents a domain
FileService	IADs IADsContainer IADsFileService IADsFileServiceOperations IADsPropertyList	Represents a file service
FileShare	IADs IADsFileShare IADsPropertyList	Represents a file share
Group	IADs IADsGroup IADsPropertyList	Represents a group account
GroupCollection	IADs IADsMembers	Represents a collection of group accounts
LocalGroup	IADs IADsGroup IADsPropertyList	Represents a local group account
LocalgroupCollection	IADs IADsMembers	Represents a collection of local group accounts
Namespace	IADs IADsContainer IADsOpenDSObject	Represents the WinNT namespace
PrintJob	IADs IADsPrintJob IADsPrintJobOperations IADsPropertyList	Represents a print job
PrintJobsCollection	IADsCollection	Represents a collection of print jobs
PrintQueue	IADs IADsPrintQueue IADsPrintQueueOperations IADsPropertyList	Represents a print queue
Property	IADs IADsProperty	Represents an attribute definition

continued

TABLE 15-3	*(continued)*	
ADSI Object	**Supported Interfaces**	**Description**
Resource	IADs IADsPropertyList IADsResource	Represents a resource
ResourcesCollection	IADsCollection	Represents a collection of resources
Schema	IADs IADsContainer	Represents the schema container
Service	IADs IADsPropertyList IADsService IADsServiceOperations	Represents a service
Session	IADs IADsSession IADsPropertyList	Represents a user session
SessionsCollection	IADsCollection	Represents a collection of user sessions
Syntax	IADs IADsSyntax	Represents the syntax of an attribute
User	IADs IADsPropertyList IADsUser	Represents a user account
UserGroupCollection	IADsMembers	Represents a collection of user groups

Working with the ADSI NDS provider

When you need to work with Novell NetWare Directory Services, you'll use the ADSI NDS provider. With NDS, you use an AdsPath string that is very similar to the string for the LDAP provider. The key differences are that you use the NDS:// designator and you normally specify the server or domain you want work with, for example:

```
NDS://Goober/CN=Trailer,DC=seattle,DC=tvpress,DC=com,O=Internet
```

or

```
NDS://Goober/O=Internet/DC=com/DC=tvpress/DC=seattle/CN=Trailer
```

In the following example, you bind to the ADSI object through an Internet domain:

VBScript

```
Set cont = GetObject("NDS://seattle.tvpress.com/O=Internet/ DC=com/
DC=tvpress/DC=seattle/CN=Trailer ")
```

JScript

```
var cont = GetObject("NDS://seattle.tvpress.com/O=Internet/ DC=com/
DC=tvpress/DC=seattle/CN=Trailer ")
```

The objects you'll use most often with the NDS provider are shown in Table 15-4. The table also lists the ADSI interfaces for those objects that are supported by the NDS provider.

TABLE 15-4

Common Objects and Interfaces for the NDS Provider

ADSI Object	Supported Interfaces	Description
Acl	IADsAcl	Represents an access control list
BackLink	IADsBackLink	Represents the Back Link attribute
CaseIgnoreList	IADsCaseIgnoreList	Represents a list of strings that aren't case-sensitive
Class	IADs IADsClass	Represents a class definition
Email	IADsEmail	Represents an e-mail account
FaxNumber	IADsFaxNumber	Represents a fax number
GenObject	IADs IADsContainer IADsPropertyList IDirectoryObject IDirectorySearch	Provides common services to most of the ADSI objects in the NDS provider
Group	IADs IADsGroup IADsPropertyList IDirectoryObject IDirectorySearch	Represents a group account
GroupCollection	IADs IADsMembers	Represents a collection of group accounts
Hold	IADsHold	Represents the Hold attribute in NDS

continued

TABLE 15-4	(continued)	
ADSI Object	**Supported Interfaces**	**Description**
Locality	IADsContainer IADsLocality IADsPropertyList IDirectoryObject IDirectorySearch	Represents the geographical locale of users, organizations, and so forth
Namespace	IADs IADsContainer IADsOpenDSObject	Represents the namespace
NetAddress	IADsNetAddress	Represents the NetAddress attribute in NDS
OctetList	IADsOctetList	Represents a list of octet strings
Organization	IADsContainer IADsO IADsPropertyList IDirectoryObject IDirectorySearch	Represents an organization
OrganizationalUnit	IADsContainer IADsOU IADsPropertyList IDirectoryObject IDirectorySearch	Represents an organizational unit
Path	IADsPath	Represents the Path attribute in NDS
PostalAddress	IADsPostalAddress	Represents a postal address
PrintQueue	IADsPrintQueue IADsPrintQueueOperations IADsPropertyList	Represents a print queue
Property	IADs IADsProperty	Represents an attribute definition
ReplicaPointer	IADsReplicaPointer	Represents the ReplicaPointer attribute in NDS
Schema	IADs IADsContainer	Represents the schema container
Syntax	IADs IADsSyntax	Represents the syntax of an attribute
Timestamp	IADsTimestamp	Represents the Timestamp attribute in NDS

ADSI Object	Supported Interfaces	Description
Tree	IADs IADsContainer	Represents a NDS directory tree
TypedName	IADsTypedName	Represents the TypedName attribute in NDS
User	IADs IADsPropertyList IADsUser IDirectoryObject IDirectorySearch	Represents a user account
UserCollection	IADs IADsMembers	Represents a collection of user accounts

Working with the ADSI NWCOMPAT provider

When you need to work with Novell NetWare Directory Services, you use the ADSI NDS provider. With NDS, you use an AdsPath string that is very similar to the string for the LDAP provider. The key differences are that you use the NDS:// designator and you normally specify the server or domain you want work with the ADSI NWCOMPAT provider is used to access Novell NetWare 3. The provider designator is NWCOMPAT://. When you use this provider, you should reference the server or domain you want to work with—for example:

    NWCOMPAT://Goober/CN=Trailer,DC=seattle,DC=tvpress,DC=com,O=Internet

or

    NWCOMPAT://Goober/O=Internet/DC=com/DC=tvpress/DC=seattle/CN=Trailer

As you can see, the syntax is nearly identical to the syntax for the NDS provider. Table 15-5 shows the objects you'll use most often with the NWCOMPAT provider. The table also shows the ADSI interfaces for those objects that are supported by the NWCOMPAT provider.

TABLE 15-5

Common Objects and Interfaces for the NWCOMPAT Provider

ADSI Object	Supported Interfaces	Description
Class	IADs IADsClass	Represents a class definition of the schema

continued

TABLE 15-5 *(continued)*

ADSI Object	Supported Interfaces	Description
Computer	IADs IADsComputer IADsComputerOperations IADsContainer IADsPropertyList	Represents a computer on the network
FileService	IADs IADsContainer IADsFileService IADsFileServiceOperations IADsPropertyList	Represents a file service
FileShare	IADs IADsFileShare IADsPropertyList	Represents a file share on the network
Group	IADs IADsGroup IADsPropertyList	Represents a group account
GroupCollection	IADs IADsMembers	Represents a collection of group accounts
JobCollection	IADs IADsCollection	Represents a collection of print jobs
Namespace	IADs IADsContainer	Represents the namespace of the directory
PrintJob	IADs IADsPrintJob IADsPrintJobOperations IADsPropertyList	Represents a print job
PrintQueue	IADs IADsPrintQueue IADsPrintQueueOperations IADsPropertyList	Represents a print queue
Property	IADs IADsProperty	Represents an attribute definition of the schema
Schema	IADs IADsContainer	Represents the schema container of the provider
Syntax	IADs IADsSyntax	Represents the syntax of an attribute

ADSI Object	Supported Interfaces	Description
User	IADs IADsPropertyList IADsUser	Represents a user account
UserCollection	IADs IADsMembers	Represents a collection of users

ADSI Provider Basics

As you've seen, the ADSI providers make a dizzying array of objects and interfaces available to your Windows scripts. Before going into the specifics of key objects and interfaces, let's look at basic tasks you may need to perform regardless of which provider you use. These basic tasks are:

■ Generic object binding

■ Handling authentication and security

■ Accessing properties and updating objects

Generic object binding

To create effective Windows scripts that use ADSI, you shouldn't make direct assignments in bindings. In most of the previous examples, we created bindings to specific servers, domains, and objects. We did so through a direct assignment, such as:

```
Set user = GetObject("WinNT://TVPRESS/wrstane")
```

Because domain resources can (and frequently do) change, you should be very careful when you bind directly to specific objects. Instead, you should make variable assignments that designate which objects you plan to use and then reference the variables. Ideally, you should make these assignments in the top section of the script so that they are easy to identify and change. You could re-write the previous example and have the outcome look like Listing 15-1.

LISTING 15-1

Setting Up the Object Binding

VBScript
bind.vbs

```
'Set up NT domain information
NTDomain = "TVPRESS"
NTUser = "wrstane"
```

continued

LISTING 15-1   *(continued)*

```
'Get user object
Set user = GetObject("WinNT://" & NTDomain & "/" & NTUser)
```

JScript
bind.js

```
//Set up NT domain information
NTDomain = "TVPRESS"
NTUser = "wrstane"

//Get user object
var user = GetObject("WinNT://" + NTDomain + "/" + NTUser)
```

You should also use server-less binding whenever possible. So instead of referencing a specific server, such as Zeta or Goober, you reference the domain only. This allows the provider to locate and use the best server. For example, with LDAP and Active Directory, the LDAP provider would locate the best domain controller to work with and then use this domain controller.

TIP   With LDAP you can bind to the root of the directory tree through the `rootDSE` object. You can then use the `rootDSE` object to access objects in the domain. In this way, you can create scripts that can be used in any domain. For details, see the section of Chapter 20 titled, "Working with Naming Contexts and the rootDSE Object."

Handling authentication and security

When you work with local domains you usually don't have to authenticate yourself to gain access to ADSI objects. If you want to work with objects outside the local domain, or you need to use a controlled account to access objects, you'll need to authenticate yourself through the `OpenDSObject` method of the `IADsOpenDSObject` interface. If you check Tables 15-2 through 15-6, you'll see this interface is supported by the LDAP, NDS, and WinNT providers only.

The `IADsOpenDSObject` interface is accessible when you obtain an object reference to the ADSI provider you want to work with—for example:

VBScript

```
Set prov = GetObject("WinNT:")
```

JScript

```
var prov = GetObject("WinNT:")
```

You can then call the `OpenDSObject` method to obtain the object you want to work with. The basic syntax for this method is:

```
ProvObj.OpenDSObject(ADSPath, UserID, Password, Flags)
```

> **NOTE** The script returns the local and domain administrators accounts. These accounts are different and the *Globally Unique Identifier (GUID)* associated with the accounts shows this. As you set out to work with the providers, don't forget that local objects are different than domain objects.

Accessing properties and updating objects

Providers access objects through various interfaces. The core interface is IADs. This interface defines a set of properties and methods for working with objects. These properties and methods are examined in the sections that follow.

Working with IADs Properties

The properties you'll want to use in Windows scripts are summarized in Table 15-7. These properties allow you to examine (but not set) object properties.

IADs Properties for Windows Scripts

Description	Sample Return Value
Retrieves the object's AdsPath	LDAP://CN=Administrator, CN=Users,DC=SEATTLE, DC=DOMAIN,DC=COM
Retrieves the name of the object's class	User
Retrieves the GUID of the object	21fa96966f2b5341ba91257c73996825
Retrieves the object's relative name	CN=Administrator
Retrieves the AdsPath string for the parent object	LDAP://CN=Users,DC=SEATTLE,DC=DOMAIN,DC=COM
Retrieves the AdsPath string for the schema class object	LDAP://schema/user

The properties for the parent and schema are very useful in your Windows scripts. You can use these to retrieve the related parent and schema objects. Another useful property is GUID. The globally unique identifier that was assigned when the object instance was created. The identifiers are 128-bit numbers that are guaranteed to be unique in the namespace. Once assigned, the GUID never changes—even if the object is moved or renamed. Thus, while the path to the object may change, the GUID won't. Because of this, you may want to reference and manage objects in scripts.

The following detailed example of how you read property values and display them. You'll be accessing the parent and schema properties to retrieve the related objects.

Here's an example:

```
ProvObj.OpenDSObject("WinNT://TVPRESS/Administrator", "wrstane",
"jiggyPop", ADS_SECURE_CREDENTIALS)
```

When you use this method with other providers, be sure to use the correct syntax. For example, with the LDAP provider and Active Directory, you must specify the user ID in the format:

```
Username@domain
```

Here is an example:

```
wrstanek@seattle.tvpress.com
```

You should also be sure to use the correct flags. Most of the time you'll want to use the ADS_SECURE_CREDENTIALS flag, which tells the provider to request secure authentication. Still, there are times when you may want to use a different flag. You may also want to use multiple flags, and you can do this as well.

Table 15-6 provides a summary of the available flags. Because the flags represent constant values, you use multiple flags by adding together the flag values or by adding the constants themselves. While the constants are available in VBScript, they aren't available in JScript. Thus in JScript, you'll have to assign the constant a value, or simply use the expected value. The constant values are specified in octal format and use the 0x prefix.

TABLE 15-6

Flags for Use with OpenDSObject

Flag	Constant Value	Description
ADS_SECURE_ AUTHENTICATION	0x1	Requests secure authentication
ADS_USE_ ENCRYPTION	0x2	Tells ADSI to use SSL (Secure Socket Layer) encryption whenever exchanging data over the network; you must have a Certificate Server installed to use this option.
ADS_USE_SSL	0x2	Tells ADSI to use SSL (Secure Socket Layer) encryption. You must have a Certificate Server installed to use this option.
ADS_READONLY_ SERVER	0x4	Allows the provider to use a read-only connection
ADS_PROMPT_ CREDENTIALS	0x8	Tells ADSI to prompt for user credentials when the authentication is initiated. An interface must be available to display the prompt.

continued

Part I

TABLE 15-6	*(continued)*	
Flag	**Constant Value**	**Description**
ADS_NO_AUTHENTICATION	0x10	Requests no authentication; the WinNT provider does not support this flag. With Active Directory, the security context is set as "Everyone."
ADS_FAST_BIND	0x20	Requests quick bind with minimum interfaces only (rather than full-interface support)
ADS_USE_SIGNING	0x40	Checks data integrity to ensure the data received is the same as the data sent; to use this flag, you must also set the ADS_SECURE_AUTHENTICATION flag.
ADS_USE_SEALING	0x80	Tells ADSI to use Kerberos encryption. To use this flag, you must also set the ADS_SECURE_AUTHENTICATION flag.

Listing 15-2 shows a more complete example of working with OpenDSObject. Technically, when you obtain a reference to the provider object, you are obtaining a reference to the root of the provider's namespace. You can then work your way through this namespace in a variety of ways. As you examine the listing, compare the VBScript and the JScript code carefully and note the differences. You should also note the output, which demonstrates that the local Administrator account accessed by the WinNT provider is different from the domain Administrator account accessed by the LDAP provider. The accounts have different GUIDs and thus, they are different.

LISTING 15-2

Authenticating Your Access to the Directory

VBScript
auth.vbs

```
NTDomain = "seattle"
NTUser = "Administrator"

Set prov = GetObject("WinNT:")
Set user = prov.OpenDSObject("WinNT://" & NTDomain & "/" & NTUser,
"wrstane","jiggyPop", ADS_SECURE_AUTHENTICATION)

'Work with the object
WScript.Echo user.Name
WScript.Echo user.Class
WScript.Echo user.GUID
WScript.Echo ""

Container = "CN=Administrator,CN=Users,DC=SEATTLE,DC=DOMAIN,DC=COM"
```

```
Set prov2 = GetObject("LDAP:")
Set user2 = prov2.OpenDSObject("LDAP://" & Container, "wrstane
.com","snoreLoud", ADS_SECURE_AUTHENTICATION)

'Work with the object
WScript.Echo user2.Name
WScript.Echo user2.Class
WScript.Echo user2.GUID
WScript.Echo ""
```

JScript
auth.js

```
ADS_SECURE_AUTHENTICATION  = 0x1

NTDomain = "seattle"
NTUser = "Administrator"

var prov = GetObject("WinNT:")
var user = prov.OpenDSObject("WinNT://" + NTDomain +
   NTUser,"wrstane","jiggyPop", ADS_SECURE_AUTHENTICA

//Work with the object
WScript.Echo(user.Name)
WScript.Echo(user.Class)
WScript.Echo(user.GUID)
WScript.Echo("")

Container = "CN=Administrator,CN=Users,DC=SEA

var prov2 = GetObject("LDAP:")
var user2 = prov2.OpenDSObject("LDAP://" +
   "wrstanek@seattle.domain.com","snoreLou

//Work with the object
WScript.Echo(user2.Name)
WScript.Echo(user2.Class)
WScript.Echo(user2.GUID)
WScript.Echo("")
```

Output

```
Administrator
User
(D83F1060-1E71-11CF-B1F3-02608

CN=Administrator
user
21fa96966f2b5341ba91257c739
```

LISTING 15-3

Using IADs Properties

VBScript
iads.vbs

```
Container = "CN=Administrator,CN=Users,DC=SEATTLE,DC=DOMAIN,DC=COM"

Set prov = GetObject("LDAP:")
Set user = prov.OpenDSObject("LDAP://" & Container,
  "wrstanek@seattle.domain.com","lolly", ADS_SECURE_AUTHENTICATION)

'Work with the object
WScript.Echo "Object AdsPath: " & user.AdsPath
WScript.Echo "Object Class: " & user.Class
WScript.Echo "Object GUID: " & user.GUID
WScript.Echo "Object Name: " & user.Name
WScript.Echo "Object Parent: " & user.Parent
WScript.Echo "Object Schema: " & user.Schema

Set cls = GetObject(user.Schema)
WScript.Echo "Class Name: " & cls.Name

Set parcls = GetObject(user.Parent)
WScript.Echo "Parent Class Name: " & parcls.Name
```

JScript
iads.js

```
ADS_SECURE_AUTHENTICATION  = 0x1
Container = "CN=Administrator,CN=Users,DC=SEATTLE,DC=DOMAIN,DC=COM"

var prov = GetObject("LDAP:")
var user = prov.OpenDSObject("LDAP://" + Container, "wrstanek@seattle.domain.
com","lolly",
  ADS_SECURE_AUTHENTICATION)

//Work with the object
WScript.Echo("Object AdsPath: " + user.AdsPath)
WScript.Echo("Object Class: " + user.Class)
WScript.Echo("Object GUID: " + user.GUID)
WScript.Echo("Object Name: " + user.Name)
WScript.Echo("Object Parent: " + user.Parent)
WScript.Echo("Object Schema: " + user.Schema)

var cls = GetObject(user.Schema)
WScript.Echo("Class Name: " + cls.Name)
```

continued

LISTING 15-3 *(continued)*

```
var parcls = GetObject(user.Parent)
WScript.Echo("Parent Class Name: " + parcls.Name)
```

Output

```
Object AdsPath: LDAP://CN=Administrator,CN=Users,DC=SEATTLE,DC=DOMAIN,DC=COM
Object Class: user
Object GUID: 21fa96966f2b5341ba91257c73996825
Object Name: CN=Administrator
Object Parent: LDAP://CN=Users,DC=SEATTLE,DC=DOMAIN,DC=COM
Object Schema: LDAP://schema/user
Class Name: user
Parent Class Name: CN=Users
```

You can modify the script to run on your system by changing the following lines to reflect proper settings for your network:

```
Container = "CN=Administrator,CN=Users,DC=SEATTLE,DC=DOMAIN,DC=COM"
Set user = prov.OpenDSObject("LDAP://" & Container,
    "wrstanek@seattle.domain.com","lolly", ADS_SECURE_AUTHENTICATION)
```

or

```
Container = "CN=Administrator,CN=Users,DC=SEATTLE,DC=DOMAIN,DC=COM"
var user = prov.OpenDSObject("LDAP://" + Container,
    "wrstanek@seattle.domain.com","lolly", ADS_SECURE_AUTHENTICATION)
```

Once you do this, you should get a GUID for the Administrator object. Now replace the Container line with the following code:

```
Container = "<GUID=guid>"
```

where *guid* is the actual GUID for the Administrator account. When you run the script again, you should see output similar to the following:

```
Object AdsPath: LDAP://<GUID=21fa96966f2b5341ba91257c73996825>
Object Class: user
Object GUID: 21fa96966f2b5341ba91257c73996825
Object Name: <GUID=21fa96966f2b5341ba91257c73996825>
Object Parent: LDAP:
Object Schema: LDAP://schema/user
Class Name: user
Parent Class Name: LDAP:
```

The output shows the important differences between using a GUID and using a precise object reference. When you access an object by its GUID, you access it directly from the root of the namespace. This is why the parent object and parent class name are LDAP:. In your scripts, this difference may cause poorly written scripts to behave differently when you use GUIDs. To prevent problems, ensure that the parent and schema objects you obtain reflect the objects with which you want to work.

Working with IADs methods

As you've seen, the IADs properties are used to obtain standard properties for objects, such as the object name and class. When you want to go beyond standard properties or want to set properties of an object, you'll need to use the methods of the IADs interface. The key methods are:

- Get(): Gets a property value from the property cache.
- Put(): Sets a new value in the property cache.
- GetEx(): Gets an array of cached values.
- PutEx(): Sets an array of cached values.
- GetInfo(): Gets property values for an object from the directory cache.
- GetInfoEx(): Gets property values for an object from the directory cache.
- SetInfo(): Saves the object's cached values to the data store.

TIP During the testing of VBScript and JScript compatibility with ADSI, we found it difficult to obtain reliable results with GetEx(), GetInfoEx(), and PutEx() in JScript. The reason for this is that ADSI interfaces use safe arrays, which are designed for VBScript. Before you can use safe arrays in JScript, you must convert them to a standard JScript array with the toArray() method. Similarly, you can only update a safe array by creating a safe array with the VBArray() method.

When you use any of these methods, you obtain the property value by referencing the property name, for example:

```
phone = user.Get("homePhone")
```

or

```
pager = user.Get("pager")
```

You can retrieve any available property with the Get() method. Although the Get() method is designed to work with single values, it does return two types of values: strings or arrays. This can lead to problems in your scripts. If you are unsure whether a property returns one value or many, you may want to use GetEx(). With GetEx() you get an array regardless of whether there is one value or multiple values. You can then examine the contents of the array to work with the property values.

You can examine multi-value properties in Listing 15-4. We've used a side-by-side code example so you can make a direct comparison of safe array-handling techniques in VBScript and JScript.

LISTING 15-4

Viewing Multi-Value Properties

VBScript

```
Set user = GetObject("LDAP://CN=William R. Stanek,CN=Users,DC=SEATTLE,DC=DOMAIN,
DC=COM")
Nums = user.GetEx("otherTelephone")
For Each a In nums
  WScript.Echo a
Next
```

JScript

```
var user = GetObject("LDAP://CN=William R. Stanek, CN=Users, DC=SEATTLE,
DC=DOMAIN, DC=COM")
nums = user.GetEx("otherTelephone")
e = nums.toArray()
for (opt in e)
{
  WScript.Echo(e[opt])
}
```

When you use the Put() or PutEx() methods, you modify property values in the property cache. To set the changes, you call SetInfo(). With Put(), you can set the home telephone number for a user as shown in Listing 15-5.

LISTING 15-5

Setting Property Values

VBScript

```
Set user = GetObject("LDAP://CN=William R. Stanek,CN=Users,
  DC=SEATTLE,DC=DOMAIN,DC=COM")
user.Put "homePhone", "808-555-1212"
user.SetInfo
```

JScript

```
var user = GetObject("LDAP://CN=William R. Stanek,CN=Users,
  DC=SEATTLE,DC=DOMAIN,DC=COM")
user.Put("homePhone", "808-555-1212")
user.SetInfo()
```

The GetInfo() and SetInfo() methods are strongly related. GetInfo() retrieves a snapshot of an object from the directory store and puts it in the cache. When you obtain an object property using Get() or GetEx(), the GetInfo() method is called for you and this is how you are able to obtain a property value. When you check property values later for the same object, these values are retrieved directly from cache and GetInfo() is not called (unless you explicitly call it).

Once you change property values in the cache, you should commit those changes by calling SetInfo(). Keep in mind, however, that you shouldn't call SetInfo() each time you change property values. Rather, you should call SetInfo() when you are finished working with the object and want to update the directory store.

The PutEx() method has an interesting syntax that you should know about. When you call PutEx(), you pass in three parameters:

- A flag that determines how a property value should be updated
- A string containing the property name
- An array containing the new value(s) for the property

These parameters give PutEx() the following syntax:

```
Obj.PutEx(Flag, "Property", Array("str1", "str2", … "strN")
```

Table 15-8 provides an overview of the flags for PutEx().

TABLE 15-8

Flags for Use with PutEx()

Flag	Constant Value	Description
ADS_PROPERTY_CLEAR	1	Sets the property value to an empty string
ADS_PROPERTY_UPDATE	2	Replaces the current property value with the array value(s)
ADS_PROPERTY_APPEND	3	Adds the array value(s) to the current property value
ADS_PROPERTY_DELETE	4	Deletes the specified value(s) in the array from the property

An example of modifying multi-value properties is shown in Listing 15-6. Note that you normally wouldn't make all of these changes on the same object.

LISTING 15-6

Working with Multiple Property Values

VBScript
multiprops.vbs

```
Set user = GetObject("LDAP://CN=William R. Stanek,CN=Users,DC=SEATTLE,DC=DOMAIN,
DC=COM")

'Replace current value
Dim r
r = Array("808-555-1212","808-678-1000")
user.PutEx ADS_PROPERTY_UPDATE, "otherTelephone", r
user.SetInfo

'Add another phone number
Dim a
a = Array("206-905-55555")
user.PutEx ADS_PROPERTY_APPEND, "otherTelephone", a
user.SetInfo

'Delete a value while leaving other values
Dim d
d = Array("808-555-1212")
user.PutEx ADS_PROPERTY_DELETE, "otherTelephone", d
user.SetInfo

'Clear all values
user.PutEx ADS_PROPERTY_CLEAR, "otherTelephone",  vbNullString
user.SetInfo
```

JScript
multiprops.js

```
var user = GetObject("LDAP://CN=William R. Stanek,CN=Users,DC=SEATTLE,DC=DOMAIN,
DC=COM")

//Replace current value
r = new VBArray("808-555-1212","808-678-1000")
user.PutEx(ADS_PROPERTY_UPDATE, "otherTelephone", r)
user.SetInfo()
```

```
//Add another phone number
a = new VBArray("206-905-55555")
user.PutEx(ADS_PROPERTY_APPEND, "otherTelephone", a)
user.SetInfo()

//Delete a value while leaving other values
d = new VBArray("808-555-1212")
user.PutEx(ADS_PROPERTY_DELETE, "otherTelephone", d)
user.SetInfo()

//Clear all values
user.PutEx(ADS_PROPERTY_CLEAR, "otherTelephone",  "")
user.SetInfo()
```

Summary

ADSI provides a powerful set of interfaces that you can use to manage system and network resources. To work with these interfaces, you use an ADSI provider, such as WinNT or LDAP. Each provider supports an extensible set of objects and these objects implement specific interfaces. The supported interfaces determine the functions you can script. Most objects implement the IADs interface. This interface provides basic functions for reading and writing object properties.

Chapter 16

Using Schema to Master ADSI

One of the most important features of ADSI is its extensibility. ADSI will change and evolve over time, and to adapt to these changes, you'll need to know how to navigate the schema. Schemas provide the basic structures that you can script. By examining the schema, you can determine the exact feature set a particular computer supports. You can also determine the acceptable parameters for properties. These elements together provide everything you need to master the provider features and to get detailed information on objects and their properties. As you study this chapter, keep in mind that Appendix B has detailed information on all of the interfaces that this chapter examines.

Exploring ADSI Schema

In ADSI, you manage groups of objects through collections. You'll encounter collections in a wide variety of circumstances. For example, user sessions are represented through a collection and you use this collection to examine individual Session objects. You also manage services, print jobs, and open resources through collections.

Collections are implemented through the IADsCollection interface. This interface has methods for obtaining, adding, and removing elements. ADSI defines two special types of collections:

- **Containers:** Containers contain other objects and are implemented with the IADsContainer interface. The IADsContainer interface has properties and methods for examining and managing objects.

- **Membership groups:** Membership groups represent collections of objects belonging to groups and are implemented with the IADsMembers interface. The IADsMembers interface has methods for determining and summarizing group membership. Only users and groups have membership groups.

The Schema object is a top-level container for other objects, and these objects in turn contain other objects. All system providers support a Schema object. Schema is implemented through three interfaces:

- IADsClass: Used to manage schema class objects
- IADsProperty: Used to view object properties
- IADsSyntax: Used to view data types supported by object properties

An object that is not a container is referred to as a leaf element. Only users and groups have membership groups. You can determine this because they implement the IADsMembers interface.

Knowing the object model structure is essential to working with Active Directory schema. So before we cover the schema in depth, we'll map out the object model for WinNT and LDAP. These providers are the ones you'll use the most.

The core WinNT object model

The WinNT provider has the most complex object model, primarily because WinNT serves a multipurpose role for domains, Windows NT 4.0 computers, and Windows computers.

With the WinNT provider, the core container objects are Domain, User, and Group. The Domain object represents the top of the domain hierarchy. The User object represents domain user accounts. The Group object represents domain group accounts. While the Domain object holds other containers, the User and Group objects contain individual user and group accounts at the leaf level.

The core hierarchy comes together like this:

```
WinNT:
    - Domain
        - User
        - LocalGroup
            LocalGroupCollection
        - Computer
            - Service
            - FileService
                - FileShare
                - ResourcesCollection
                - SessionsCollection
            - PrintQueue
                - PrintJobsCollection
        - User
        - Group
            UserGroupCollection
            GroupCollection
```

You can use the object model to determine how you can access a specific object. For example, to access the alert service you must go through the `Domain` and `Computer` objects:

VBScript

```
Set service = GetObject("WinNT://tvpress/zeta/alerter,service")
```

JScript

```
var service = GetObject("WinNT://tvpress/zeta/alerter,service")
```

where `tvpress` is the domain name, `zeta` is the computer name, and `alerter` is the name of the service you want to work with.

The core LDAP object model

Compared to the WinNT object model, the LDAP object model is fairly basic, primarily because the LDAP model seeks to be generic so that it can be used with multiple applications, such as Windows and Exchange Server. Because of this, the only meaningful way to examine the object models related to the LDAP provider is in the context of a specific implementation. The implementation you'll use the most is the Windows object model.

The Windows object model is tied to Active Directory. The root of the Active Directory directory tree is represented with the `RootDSE` object. The `RootDSE` provides information about individual directory servers and is not a part of the standard namespace. In addition to the directory root, you'll find the standard naming contexts for Windows. A naming context is a top-level container for the directory tree. The available naming contexts are:

- **Domain container:** A top-level container for the domain. It contains users, groups, computers, organizational units, and other domain objects.
- **Schema container:** A top-level container that allows you to access schema objects.
- **Configuration container:** A top-level container for the entire domain forest. It contains sites, which in turn contain individual sites, subnets, inter-site transports, and other configuration objects.

As you'd expect, these naming contexts hold other containers. You can view other domain containers through Active Directory Users and Computers. As Figure 16-1 shows, the default domain containers are:

- **Builtin:** Stores built-in local groups.
- **Computers:** Stores computer accounts.
- **ForeignSecurityPrincipals:** Stores security identifiers for external objects associated with external, trusted domains.
- **Users:** Stores user and group accounts.

The default containers are designed to hold specific types of objects. However, you can add just about any type of object to these containers, including:

- Computers
- Contacts
- Users
- Groups
- Printers
- Shared Folders

FIGURE 16-1

You can use Active Directory Users and Computers to view high-level domain containers and their contents.

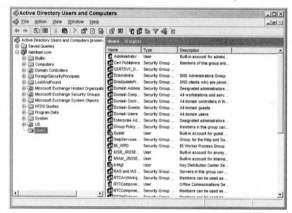

We refer to these types of objects as common-name objects. You access objects in default containers through the *common-name identifier*, CN. For example, if you want to access the built-in Administrators group, you can use the following:

VBScript

```
Set acc = GetObject("LDAP://CN=Administrators,CN=Builtin,DC=tvpress,DC=com")
```

JScript

```
var acc = GetObject("LDAP://CN=Administrators,CN=Builtin,DC=tvpress,DC=com")
```

New domain containers can be created as well. To do this, you create organizational units. Organizational units can contain the same objects as the default domain containers. The only default organizational unit is Domain Controllers, which is designed to store computer accounts for domain controllers. To access Domain Controllers, you must use the *organizational unit identifier*, OU.

If you create or move objects into the organizational unit container, you access the objects through the organizational unit—for example:

VBScript

```
Set acc = GetObject("LDAP://CN=William R. Stanek,OU=IT,DC=tvpress,DC=com")
```

JScript

```
var acc = GetObject("LDAP://CN=William R. Stanek,OU=IT,DC=tvpress,DC=com")
```

You can view other configuration containers through Active Directory Sites and Services. As Figure 16-2 shows, the default configuration containers are:

- **Sites:** A high-level container for subnets, transports, and individual sites.
- **Default-First-Site:** The default site for the domain tree.
- **Subnets:** A high-level container for subnets in the domain tree.
- **Inter-Site Transports:** A high-level container for transports. Transports like IP and SMTP transfer information throughout the domain tree.

FIGURE 16-2

You can use Active Directory Sites and Services to view high-level configuration containers and their contents.

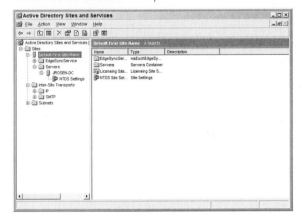

Putting all this together, you see that the Windows object model looks similar to the following:

```
RootDSE
     - Domain Container
          - Default Containers
          - Common Name Objects
          - Organizational Units
          - Common Name Objects
```

```
- Schema Container
    - Schema Objects
- Configuration Container
    - Sites Container
        - Site Container
        - Subnets Container
        - Inter-site Transports Container
```

Working with Schema Class Objects

Schema class objects provide a window into the world of the ADSI provider. If you know nothing else about a provider except its name and the core objects it supports, you can—with a bit of trial and error—explore every key feature of the provider. To do this, you access the IADsClass interface of the object you want to work with and then you use the properties of this interface to explore the object.

Accessing an object's schema class

You access an object's schema class through its Schema property. For example, if you want to access the schema for a computer, you can use the following:

VBScript

```
'WinNT Provider
Set obj = GetObject("WinNT://zeta,computer")
Set cls = GetObject(obj.Schema)

'LDAP Provider
Set obj = GetObject("LDAP://CN=Zeta,CN=Computers, DC=tvpress, DC=com")
Set cls = GetObject(obj.Schema)
```

JScript

```
//WinNT Provider
var obj = GetObject("WinNT://zeta,computer")
var cls = GetObject(obj.Schema)

//LDAP Provider
var obj = GetObject("LDAP://CN=Zeta,CN=Computers, DC=tvpress, DC=com")
var cls = GetObject(obj.Schema)
```

Once you've accessed the schema for an object, you can use any of the available properties of IADsClass to work with the schema. These properties are summarized in Table 16-1.

TABLE 16-1

Properties of IADsClass

Property	Status	Description
Abstract	Read/Write	Boolean value that indicates whether the schema class is abstract
AuxDerivedFrom	Read/Write	Array of AdsPath strings that specify the super Auxiliary classes of this schema class
Auxiliary	Read/Write	Boolean value that determines whether this schema class is an Auxiliary class
CLSID	Read/Write	A provider-specific string that identifies the COM object that implements this schema class
Container	Read/Write	Boolean value that indicates whether this is a Container object
Containment	Read/Write	Array of strings that identify object types that can be contained within this container
DerivedFrom	Read/Write	Array of AdsPath strings that indicate which classes this class is derived from
HelpFileContext	Read/Write	The context identifier for an optional help file
HelpFileName	Read/Write	The name of an optional help file
MandatoryProperties	Read/Write	An array of strings that lists the mandatory properties for an ADSI object
NamingProperties	Read/Write	An array of strings that lists the properties that are used for naming attributes
OID	Read/Write	A directory-specific object identifier string
OptionalProperties	Read/Write	An array of strings that lists the optional properties for an ADSI object
PossibleSuperiors	Read/Write	An array of AdsPath strings that lists classes that can contain instances of this class
PrimaryInterface	Read Only	A globally unique identifier string for the interface defining this schema class

Checking to see if an object is a container

Often when you work with objects, you'll want to determine if an object is a container and, if so, what objects it contains. You can do this with the Container and Containment properties. An example is shown as Listing 16-1.

As you examine the listing, note the different VBScript and JScript techniques used to access the `Containment` array. ADSI returns arrays as safe arrays, which are designed to be used with VBScript. To use these arrays in JScript, you can convert the safe array to a normal JScript array.

LISTING 16-1

Checking Containers and Containment

VBScript
Container.vbs

```
Set dom = GetObject("WinNT://tvpress")
Set cls = GetObject(dom.Schema)
If cls.Container = True Then
  WScript.Echo "The domain object contains the following objects: "
  e = cls.Containment
  For each op in e
    WScript.Echo op
  Next
End If
```

JScript
Container.js

```
var dom = GetObject("WinNT://tvpress")
var cls = GetObject(dom.Schema)
if (cls.Container == 1) {
  WScript.Echo("The domain object contains the following objects: ")
  e = cls.Containment.toArray()
  for (op in e)
  {
    WScript.Echo(e[op])
  }
}
```

Output

```
The domain object contains the
 following children:
Computer
User
Group
```

Examining mandatory and optional properties

Whether you are creating users, modifying groups, or working with other objects, you often need to be able to determine if a property must be set, or if the property is optional. You can determine mandatory and optional properties using `MandatoryProperties` and `OptionalProperties`, respectively.

Listing 16-2 examines properties of the `Computer` object using both WinNT and LDAP. With WinNT, you can bind directly to the object. With LDAP, you must bind to the object via its container, which in this case is the `Computers` container.

LISTING 16-2

Examining Mandatory and Optional Properties

VBScript
Checkproperties.vbs

```
Set obj = GetObject("WinNT://zeta,computer")
Set cls = GetObject(obj.Schema)
WScript.Echo obj.AdsPath
displayProps(cls)

Set obj =GetObject("LDAP://CN=Omega,CN=Computers,DC=tvpress,DC=com")
Set cls = GetObject(obj.Schema)
WScript.Echo obj.AdsPath
displayProps(cls)

Sub displayProps(obj)
  For Each p in obj.MandatoryProperties
    WScript.Echo "Mandatory: " & p
  Next
  For Each p in obj.OptionalProperties
    WScript.Echo "Optional: " & p
  Next
End Sub
```

JScript
Checkproperties.js

```
var obj = GetObject("WinNT://zeta,computer")
var cls = GetObject(obj.Schema)
WScript.Echo(obj.AdsPath)
displayProps(cls)

var obj =GetObject("LDAP://CN=Omega,CN=Computers,DC=tvpress,DC=com")
var cls = GetObject(obj.Schema)
WScript.Echo(obj.AdsPath)
displayProps(cls)

function displayProps(obj) {

  mprop = obj.MandatoryProperties.toArray()
  for ( p in mprop) {
    WScript.Echo("Mandatory: " + mprop[p])
  }
```

continued

LISTING 16-2 *(continued)*

```
  oprop = obj.OptionalProperties.toArray()
  for ( p in oprop) {
    WScript.Echo("Optional: " + oprop[p])
  }
}
```

Output

```
WinNT://SEATTLE/ZETA
Optional: Owner
Optional: Division
Optional: OperatingSystem
Optional: OperatingSystemVersion
Optional: Processor
Optional: ProcessorCount
LDAP://CN=Omega,CN=Computers,DC=SEATTLE,DC=DOMAIN,DC=com
Mandatory: cn
Mandatory: instanceType
Mandatory: nTSecurityDescriptor
Mandatory: objectCategory
Mandatory: objectClass
Mandatory: objectSid
Mandatory: sAMAccountName
Optional: accountExpires
Optional: accountNameHistory
Optional: aCSPolicyName
Optional: adminCount
...
Optional: x121Address
```

As the output shows, LDAP and Active Directory report many mandatory properties for most objects. Fortunately, some of these properties are set automatically when you create an object instance. The pre-set properties are as follows:

- ■ `instanceType`
- ■ `nTSecurityDescriptor`
- ■ `objectCategory`
- ■ `objectClass`
- ■ `objectSid`

Because of this, you can create a computer object by setting only the cn and samAccountName properties—for example:

VBScript

```
Set cont = GetObject("LDAP://CN=Computers,DC=tvpress,DC=com")
Set comp = cont.Create("computer", "CN=theta")
comp.Put "samAccountName", "theta"
comp.SetInfo
```

JScript

```
var cont = GetObject("LDAP://CN=Computers,DC=tvpress,DC=com")
var comp = cont.Create("computer", "CN=theta")
comp.Put("samAccountName", "theta")
comp.SetInfo()
```

Viewing Property Syntax, Ranges, and Values

Once you know which properties are available for an object, you may want to take a more detailed look at a particular property. For example, you may want to know the minimum and maximum values the property accepts. You may also want to know which type of values you can pass to the property. You can examine the individual properties of an object using the IADsProperty interface.

Accessing the IADsProperty interface

The IADsProperty interface is designed for managing attributes of schema objects. You gain access to an object's properties by binding to the parent schema object. In this example, you bind to the schema for the Computer object:

VBScript

```
Set cls = GetObject(obj.Schema)
Set par = GetObject(obj.Parent)
```

JScript

```
var cls = GetObject(obj.Schema)
var par = GetObject(obj.Parent)
```

Once you bind to the parent schema object, you can retrieve a specific property using the GetObject() method and the following syntax:

```
SchemaObject.GetObject("Property","PropertyName")
```

where *SchemaObject* is the schema object you obtained and *PropertyName* is the name of the property you want to examine—for example:

VBScript

```
Set prop = cls.GetObject("Property","Owner")
```

JScript

```
var prop = cls.GetObject("Property","Owner")
```

Once you've accessed a property, you can use any of the properties of IADsProperty to work with the schema. These properties are summarized in Table 16-2.

TABLE 16-2

Properties of IADsProperty

Property	Status	Description
MaxRange	Read/Write	Numeric value that sets the upper limit of values for the property
MinRange	Read/Write	Numeric value that sets the lower limit of values for the property
MultiValued	Read/Write	Boolean value that indicates whether this property supports multiple values
OID	Read/Write	The directory-specific object identifier string
Syntax	Read/Write	A string that specifies the acceptable data type(s) for the property

Examining object properties

Now that you know the features of IADsProperty that are available to you, you can put these features to use to help you determine syntax, range, and value types for properties. One way to examine this information is to identify a specific property you want to learn about and then display its schema. Listing 16-3 examines the OperatingSystem property of the Computer Object.

LISTING 16-3

Examining Schema for Object Properties

VBScript
viewpropertyschema.vbs

```
Set obj = GetObject("WinNT://zeta,computer")
Set cls = GetObject(obj.Schema)
```

```
Set sch = GetObject(cls.Parent)
Set pr = sch.GetObject("Property","OperatingSystem")

WScript.Echo "Property:    " & pr.Name
WScript.Echo "Syntax:      " & pr.Syntax
WScript.Echo "MaxRange:    " & pr.MaxRange
WScript.Echo "MinRange:    " & pr.MinRange
WScript.Echo "Multivalued: " & pr.Multivalued
```

JScript
viewpropertyschema.js

```
var obj = GetObject("WinNT://zeta,computer")
var cls = GetObject(obj.Schema)
var sch = GetObject(cls.Parent)
var pr = sch.GetObject("Property","OperatingSystem")

WScript.Echo("Property:    " + pr.Name)
WScript.Echo("Syntax:      " + pr.Syntax)
WScript.Echo("MaxRange:    " + pr.MaxRange)
WScript.Echo("MinRange:    " + pr.MinRange)
WScript.Echo("Multivalued: " + pr.Multivalued)
```

Output

```
Property:    OperatingSystem
Syntax:      String
MaxRange:    256
MinRange:    0
Multivalued: False
```

If you want to examine all the properties of an object, you can set up a control loop through optional and mandatory object properties (much as you did in Listing 16-2). You'll run into a problem, however. While all properties of WinNT objects have maximum and minimum ranges, this isn't necessarily true with objects in other providers. The only properties that are supported for all objects across all providers are Syntax and Multivalued.

To work around the property-support problem, you'll need to set up error-handling for the script as described in Chapter 7. In Listing 16-4, we've implemented error-handling in a VBScript routine that examines all properties of a given object for WinNT and LDAP. The objects the script examines are Domain, Computer, User, and Group. The key to accessing these objects is to obtain a reference to a representative object and then to access the parent schema object.

LISTING 16-4

Examining Schema for All Object Properties

VBScript
viewall.vbs

```
'Get domain properties for WinNT
Set obj = GetObject("WinNT://seattle")
Set cls = GetObject(obj.Schema)
Set sch = GetObject(cls.Parent)
WScript.Echo obj.AdsPath
displayProps(cls)

'Get computer properties for WinNT
Set obj = GetObject("WinNT://zeta,computer")
Set cls = GetObject(obj.Schema)
Set sch = GetObject(cls.Parent)
WScript.Echo obj.AdsPath
displayProps(cls)

'Get user properties for WinNT
Set obj = GetObject("WinNT://zeta/Administrator,user")
Set cls = GetObject(obj.Schema)
Set sch = GetObject(cls.Parent)
WScript.Echo obj.AdsPath
displayProps(cls)

'Get group properties for WinNT
Set obj = GetObject("WinNT://zeta/administrators,group")
Set cls = GetObject(obj.Schema)
Set sch = GetObject(cls.Parent)
WScript.Echo obj.AdsPath
displayProps(cls)

'Get domain properties for LDAP
Set obj = GetObject("LDAP://DC=tvpress,DC=com")
Set cls = GetObject(obj.Schema)
Set sch = GetObject(cls.Parent)
WScript.Echo obj.AdsPath
displayProps(cls)

'Get computer properties for LDAP
Set obj = GetObject("LDAP://CN=Omega,CN=Computers, DC=tvpress,DC=com")
Set cls = GetObject(obj.Schema)
Set sch = GetObject(cls.Parent)
WScript.Echo obj.AdsPath
displayProps(cls)
```

```
'Get user properties for LDAP
Set obj = GetObject("LDAP://CN=William R. Stanek,CN=Users,DC=tvpress,DC=com")
Set cls = GetObject(obj.Schema)
Set sch = GetObject(cls.Parent)
WScript.Echo obj.AdsPath
displayProps(cls)

'Get group properties for LDAP
Set obj = GetObject("LDAP://CN=Administrators,CN=Builtin,DC=tvpress,DC=com")
Set cls = GetObject(obj.Schema)
Set sch = GetObject(cls.Parent)
WScript.Echo obj.AdsPath
displayProps(cls)

'Subroutine to display object properties
Sub displayProps(obj)
  On Error Resume Next

  For Each p in obj.MandatoryProperties
    Set prop = sch.GetObject("Property",p)
    WScript.Echo "Property: " & prop.Name
    WScript.Echo "Syntax: " & prop.Syntax
    WScript.Echo "MinRange: " & prop.MinRange
    WScript.Echo "MaxRange: " & prop.MaxRange
    WScript.Echo "Multivalued:" & prop.Multivalued
    WScript.Echo
  Next

  For Each p in obj.OptionalProperties
    Set prop = sch.GetObject("Property",p)
    WScript.Echo "Property: " & prop.Name
    WScript.Echo "Syntax: " & prop.Syntax
    WScript.Echo "MinRange: " & prop.MinRange
    WScript.Echo "MaxRange: " & prop.MaxRange
    WScript.Echo "Multivalued:" & prop.Multivalued
    WScript.Echo
  Next
End Sub
```

One of the properties that deserves additional discussion is Multivalued. If you are unsure whether a property returns a single value or multiple values, use the Multivalued property. If you create general-purpose functions for handling properties, you can use this to determine whether you use Get(), GetEx(), Put(), or PutEx()—for example:

VBScript

```
If prop.Multivalued = True Then
  'use GetEx() or PutEx()
```

```
Else
  'use Get() or Put()
End If
```

JScript

```
if (prop.Multivalued == 1) {
  //use GetEx() or PutEx()
else {
  //use Get() or Put()
}
```

Summary

As you've seen in this chapter, schemas are an important aspect of ADSI scripting. If you know how to access schema, you can examine objects and the properties they support. Some properties are optional when you create a new instance of an object. Other properties are mandatory. You must set mandatory properties when you create an object, such as a user, group, or computer account.

Chapter 17

Managing Local and Domain Resources with ADSI

Windows scripts and ADSI can help you build powerful tools for managing computers and domain resources. The ADSI provider you'll use to manage local resources on Windows computers is WinNT. You will also use the WinNT provider to manage domain resources. The focus of this chapter is on using WinNT to manage the following:

- Domain account policies for both Windows Vista and Windows Server 2008

- Domain user accounts for both Windows Vista and Windows Server 2008

- Domain group accounts for both Windows Vista and Windows Server 2008

- Local computer properties for both Windows Vista and Windows Server 2008

- Local user and group accounts for both Windows Vista and Windows Server 2008

IN THIS CHAPTER

Managing domain settings

Viewing and modifying local computer settings

Local and global user account administration

Local and global group account administration

Managing Domain Account Policies

Using the WinNT provider, you can view and set domain account policies for Windows Vista and Windows Server 2008. In Windows NT, you normally access these properties through the User Manager's Account Policy dialog box. In Windows, you normally access these properties through Group Policy.

Working with domain objects

Before you can manage domain account policies, you must first obtain a reference to a domain object. In this example, you obtain the domain object for a domain named `tvpress`:

VBScript

```
Set dom = GetObject("WinNT://tvpress")
```

JScript

```
var dom = GetObject("WinNT://tvpress")
```

The domain name you use with WinNT is always the NT domain name whether you are working with Windows NT or Windows. With the domain `seattle.tvpress.com`, the NT equivalent would normally be `seattle`, but with the domain `tvpress.com`, the NT equivalent would normally be `tvpress`.

Once you obtain the `Domain` object, you can get and set the properties of the object, for example:

VBScript

```
dom.Put "MinPasswordLength", 8
dom.SetInfo
```

JScript

```
dom.Put("MinPasswordLength", 8)
dom.SetInfo()
```

Table 17-1 summarizes the available `Domain` object properties. A status of RW means that you can set and get the property (i.e., it is readable and writable).

TABLE 17-1

WinNT Domain Object Summary

Property	Status	Value Type	Min Range	Max Range	Multiple Values
MinPasswordLength	RW	Integer	0	14	False
MinPasswordAge	RW	Integer	0	86227200	False
MaxPasswordAge	RW	Integer	86400	86313600	False
MaxBadPasswordsAllowed	RW	Integer	0	2147483647	False
PasswordHistoryLength	RW	Integer	0	8	False
AutoUnlockInterval	RW	Integer	0	2147483647	False
LockoutObservationInterval	RW	Integer	0	2147483647	False

> **NOTE** Note that if you used the techniques described in Chapter 16 to obtain a summary for the Domain object, you'd get slightly different results. The primary reason for this is that the syntax often reports –1 as the highest value when a property restriction can be turned off with a setting of 0. Another interpretation for this is that there isn't an upper range when the property is turned off.

Preparing to view and set account policies

Before you can manage account policies, you must ensure that the related policies are enabled through group policies. If a policy is disabled or inactive, you won't be able to manipulate the related property. Group policy is discussed in Chapter 14. As discussed in that chapter, you access the domain group policy container through Active Directory Users and Computers. Once you start Active Directory Users and Computers, you can view the group policy for accounts as follows:

1. Right-click on the domain you want to work with in the console root. Then select Properties. This displays a Properties dialog box.

2. In the Properties dialog box, select the Group Policy tab, and then click Edit. You can now view and set group policies.

3. Expand Computer Configuration, Windows Settings, and Security Settings. Then click the Account Policies node.

4. Select the Password Policy node and note which policies are enabled or disabled.

5. Select the Account Lockout Policy node and note which policies are enabled or not defined.

6. If you need to enable a policy, double-click it and then select the Define This Policy checkbox or the Enabled radio button as appropriate.

Domain object properties map to password and account lockout policies as follows:

Password Policy:

- PasswordHistoryLength sets Enforce Password History.
- MaxPasswordAge sets Maximum Password Age.
- MinPasswordAge sets Minimum Password Age.
- MinPasswordLength sets Minimum Password Length.

Account Lockout Policy:

- MaxBadPasswordsAllowed sets Account Lockout Threshold.
- AutoUnlockInterval sets Account Lockout Duration.
- LockoutObservationInterval sets Reset Account Lockout Counter After.

Viewing and setting account policies

Properties of the domain object can be tricky to use because you must set them in a specific way. To help you get around the pitfalls, we'll examine each property briefly.

Using MinPasswordLength

The MinPasswordLength property sets the minimum number of characters for passwords. The value must be between 0 and 14. You can view and set the minimum password length, as shown in Listing 17-1.

LISTING 17-1

Setting and Viewing the Minimum Password Length

VBScript
minpass.vbs

```
'Set minimum password length
Set dom = GetObject("WinNT://seattle")
Dom.Put "MinPasswordLength", 8
Dom.SetInfo
'Confirm the change
WScript.Echo("MinPasswordLength")
```

JScript
minpass.js

```
//Set minimum password length
var dom = GetObject("WinNT://seattle")
dom.Put("MinPasswordLength", 8)
dom.SetInfo()
//Confirm the change
dom.Get
WScript.Echo(dom.Get("MinPasswordLength"))
```

Using MinPasswordAge and MaxPasswordAge

The MinPasswordAge and MaxPasswordAge properties are closely related. MinPasswordAge determines what length of time users must keep a password before they can change it and MaxPasswordAge determines how long users can keep a password before they must change it. The maximum password age must be set to a duration that is longer than the minimum password age. Otherwise, an error occurs when you try to set the property value.

Both MinPasswordAge and MaxPasswordAge have maximum ranges of 998 and 999 days, respectively. You have to set the values in seconds, however, because this is how the Windows Registry handles the values. The easiest way to convert seconds to days is to use 86,400 as a multiplier. This value is the number of seconds in a day. Following this, you can set a minimum password age of 3 days and a maximum password age of 90 days like this:

VBScript

```
Set d = GetObject("WinNT://seattle")
d.Put "MinPasswordAge", 86400*3
d.Put "MaxPasswordAge", 86400*90
d.SetInfo
```

JScript

```
var d = GetObject("WinNT://seattle")
d.Put("MinPasswordAge", 86400*3)
d.Put("MaxPasswordAge", 86400*90)
d.SetInfo()
```

You can then confirm the changes by examining the current property values:

VBScript

```
WScript.Echo d.Get("MinPasswordAge")
WScript.Echo d.Get("MaxPasswordAge")
```

JScript

```
WScript.Echo(d.Get("MinPasswordAge"))
WScript.Echo(d.Get("MaxPasswordAge"))
```

Using PasswordHistoryLength

The password history determines how often a user can reuse an old password. For example, if you set the password history length to 3, the history remembers up to three passwords for each user. If Sally has the passwords coolDays, rainBows, and rubberDuck in the history, she won't be able to reuse those passwords.

You can set and then confirm the password history length, as shown in Listing 17-2.

LISTING 17-2

Setting and Viewing the Password History Length

VBScript
passhist.vbs

```
'Set password history length
Set dom = GetObject("WinNT://seattle")
dom.Put "PasswordHistoryLength", 4
dom.SetInfo
```

continued

LISTING 17-2 *(continued)*

```
'Confirm the change
WScript.Echo("PasswordHistoryLength: " & dom.PasswordHistoryLength)
```

JScript
passhist.js

```
//Set password history length
var dom = GetObject("WinNT://seattle")
dom.Put("PasswordHistoryLength", 4)
dom.SetInfo()

//Confirm the change
WScript.Echo("PasswordHistoryLength: " + dom.Get("PasswordHistoryLength "))
```

Using MaxBadPasswordsAllowed, AutoUnlockInterval, and LockoutObservationInterval

The `MaxBadPasswordsAllowed`, `AutoUnlockInterval`, and `LockoutObservationInterval` properties all relate to whether accounts get locked out when users enter bad passwords repeatedly. The `MaxBadPasswordsAllowed` property determines the number of bad passwords a user can enter before he or she is locked out. The `AutoUnlockInterval` property determines how long the user is locked out. The `LockoutObservationInterval` property determines when previously entered bad passwords no longer count toward locking out the account. If the interval is set to 30 minutes, bad passwords entered more than 30 minutes ago don't count.

Both `AutoUnlockInterval` and `LockoutObservationInterval` properties have maximum ranges of 99,999 minutes. Again, the value is set in seconds because this is how the Windows Registry handles the values. To convert seconds to minutes, use 60 as a multiplier. Listing 17-3 shows how you can set unlock and lockout intervals of 50 and 5 minutes, respectively.

LISTING 17-3

Setting and Viewing the Lockout

VBScript
passlock.vbs

```
'Set lockout
Set dom = GetObject("WinNT://seattle")
dom.Put "MaxBadPasswordsAllowed", 4
dom.Put "AutoUnlockInterval", 60*50
dom.Put "LockoutObservationInterval",60*5
dom.SetInfo

'Confirm lockout
```

```
WScript.Echo dom.Get("MaxBadPasswordsAllowed")
WScript.Echo(dom.Get("AutoUnlockInterval")
WScript.Echo(dom.Get("LockoutObservationInterval")
```

JScript
passlock.js

```
//Set lockout
var dom = GetObject("WinNT://seattle")
dom.Put("MaxBadPasswordsAllowed", 4)
dom.Put("AutoUnlockInterval", 60*50)
dom.Put( "LockoutObservationInterval",60*5)
dom.SetInfo()

//Confirm lockout
WScript.Echo(dom.Get("MaxBadPasswordsAllowed"))
WScript.Echo dom.Get("AutoUnlockInterval"))
WScript.Echo dom.Get("LockoutObservationInterval"))
```

Working with Local Computer Properties

The WinNT Computer object is used to work with properties of a computer in a Windows NT or Windows domain. You can't use this object to create computer accounts or to authorize computers in the domain. You can perform these functions with the LDAP provider, however, and this is discussed in Chapter 19.

To work with local computers, you need to obtain an object reference to the computer. In the following example, you obtain the Computer object for a local computer named Omega:

VBScript

```
Set dom = GetObject("WinNT://omega,computer")
```

JScript

```
var dom = GetObject("WinNT://omega,computer")
```

Once you obtain the necessary Computer object, you can get and set the properties of the object:

VBScript

```
dom.Put "Owner", "William R. Stanek"
dom.SetInfo
```

JScript

```
dom.Put("Owner", "William R. Stanek")
dom.SetInfo()
```

Table 17-2 summarizes the properties of the WinNT Computer object. These properties are fairly straightforward so we don't go into each property individually.

TABLE 17-2

WinNT Computer Object Summary

Property	Status	Value Type	Min Range	Max Range	Multiple Values
Owner	RW	String	0	256	False
Division	RW	String	0	256	False
OperatingSystem	RW	String	0	256	False
OperatingSystemVersion	RW	String	0	256	False
Processor	RW	String	0	256	False
ProcessorCount	RW	String	0	256	False

When you work with the Computer object, you may need to examine or update all of the computers on the network. One way you can do this is shown as Listing 17-4.

NOTE Note that with JScript, you must create Enumerator objects to examine the Domain and Computer objects. Enumerators are discussed in Chapter 8 in the section entitled "Working with folders." As you examine the sample output, note also that on Windows, the operating system is set to Windows NT, but the OS version is set to 6.0.

LISTING 17-4

Examining All Computer Objects in the Domain

VBScript
checkcomp.vbs

```
'Handle Errors
On Error Resume Next
'Get the provider object
Set prov = GetObject("WinNT:")

'Examine the available domains the provider can reach
For each dom in prov

 'Examine the objects in the domain and check for Computer objects
  For each o in dom
```

```
  If o.Class = "Computer" Then

    'Display properties of the Computer
    WScript.Echo o.Class & " " & o.Name
    WScript.Echo " Owner: " & o.Owner
    WScript.Echo " Division: " & o.Division
    WScript.Echo " OperatingSystem: "  & o.OperatingSystem
    WScript.Echo " OS Version: " & o.OperatingSystemVersion
    WScript.Echo " Processor: " & o.Processor
    WScript.Echo " ProcessorCount: " & o.ProcessorCount

  End If

 Next
Next
```

JScript
checkcomp.js

```
//Get the provider object
var prov = GetObject("WinNT:")

tlist = new Enumerator(prov)

//Examine the available domains the provider can reach
for (; !tlist.atEnd(); tlist.moveNext())
 {

 s = new Enumerator(tlist.item())

 //Examine the objects in the domain and check for Computer objects
 for (; !s.atEnd(); s.moveNext())
  {

  o = s.item();
  if (o.Class == "Computer") {

    try {
    //Display properties of the Computer
    WScript.Echo(o.Class + " " + o.Name)
    WScript.Echo(" Owner: " + o.Owner)
    WScript.Echo(" Division: " + o.Division)
    WScript.Echo(" OperatingSystem: "  + o.OperatingSystem)
    WScript.Echo(" OS Version: " + o.OperatingSystemVersion)
    WScript.Echo(" Processor: " + o.Processor)
    WScript.Echo(" ProcessorCount: " + o.ProcessorCount)
    }
    catch(e) {
```

continued

LISTING 17-4 (continued)

```
      WScript.Echo(" Not online at this time")
    }
  }


  }
}
```

Output

```
Computer OMEGA
 Owner: William Stanek
 Division: Stanek & Associates
 OperatingSystem: Windows NT
 OperatingSystemVersion: 6.0
 Processor: x86 Family 6 Model 6 Stepping 0
 ProcessorCount: Uniprocessor Free
Computer ZETA
 Owner: William R. Stanek
 Division: Stanek & Associates
 OperatingSystem: Windows NT
 OperatingSystemVersion: 6.0
 Processor: x86 Family 6 Model 3 Stepping 3
 ProcessorCount: Uniprocessor Free
```

Creating and Modifying User Accounts

User accounts are represented with the User object. Of all the objects available for WinNT, the User object is the most complex. You can use this object to create, delete, update, and move local user accounts as well as domain accounts. You will also find that WinNT is easier to work with than LDAP in most respects. However, you cannot use WinNT to perform tasks that are specific to Active Directory, such as moving accounts to different containers or organizational units. Beyond this, you also can't manage extended properties for user accounts that are specific to Active Directory. For details on Active Directory and LDAP, see Chapter 20.

User properties for WinNT

Before getting into the specifics of working with user accounts, you should examine Table 17-3. This table provides a brief summary of User object properties. A status of RO means the property is read-only and cannot be updated. A status of RW means the property is read-write and can be updated.

TABLE 17-3

WinNT User Object Summary

Property	Status	Value Type	Min Range	Max Range	Multiple Values
AccountDisabled	RW	Boolean	0	1	False
AccountExpirationDate	RW	Date String	n/a	n/a	False
BadPasswordAttempts	RO	Integer	0	2147483647	False
Description	RW	String	0	257	False
FullName	RW	String	0	257	False
HomeDirDrive	RW	String	0	340	False
HomeDirectory	RW	Path String	0	340	False
IsAccountLocked	RO	Boolean	0	1	False
LastLogin	RO	Date String	n/a	n/a	False
LastLogoff	RO	Date String	n/a	n/a	False
LoginHours	RW	OctetString	0	0	False
LoginScript	RW	Path String	0	340	False
LoginWorkstations	RW	Safe Array	0	256	True
MaxLogins	RW	Integer	0	2147483647	False
MaxPasswordAge	RW	Integer	86400	86313600	False
MaxStorage	RW	Integer	0	2147483647	False
MinPasswordAge	RW	Integer	0	86227200	False
MinPasswordLength	RW	Integer	0	15	False
ObjectSid	RO	OctetString	0	0	False
Parameters	RO	String	0	340	False
PasswordAge	RO	Date String	n/a	n/a	False
PasswordExpired	RO	Integer	0	1	False
PasswordHistoryLength	RO	Integer	0	8	False
PrimaryGroupID	RW	Integer	0	2147483647	False

continued

TABLE 17-3			Min		Multiple
Property	**Status**	**Value Type**	**Range**	**Max Range**	**Values**
Profile	RW	Path String	0	340	False
RasPermissions	RW	Integer	0	0	False
UserFlags	RW	Integer	0	0	False

TABLE 17-3 (continued) label appears above the table.

When you work with object properties, you can get them by name or through the Get() method. Listing 17-5 shows an example of working with User object properties by name. As you take a look at the example, note the sample output for each property.

LISTING 17-5

Viewing User Properties

VBScript
viewuser.vbs

```
On Error Resume Next
Set usr = GetObject("WinNT://seattle/omega/tgreen,user")

WScript.Echo "AccountDisabled        " & usr.AccountDisabled
WScript.Echo "AccountExpirationDate  " & usr.AccountExpirationDate
WScript.Echo "BadPasswordAttempts    " & usr.BadPasswordAttempts
WScript.Echo "Description             " & usr.Description
WScript.Echo "FullName                " & usr.FullName
WScript.Echo "HomeDirDrive            " & usr.HomeDirDrive
WScript.Echo "HomeDirectory           " & usr.HomeDirectory
WScript.Echo "IsAccountLocked         " & usr.IsAccountLocked
WScript.Echo "LastLogin               " & usr.LastLogin
WScript.Echo "LastLogoff              " & usr.LastLogoff
WScript.Echo "LoginHours              " & usr.LoginHours
WScript.Echo "LoginScript             " & usr.LoginScript
WScript.Echo "LoginWorkstations       " & usr.LoginWorkstations
WScript.Echo "MaxLogins               " & usr.MaxLogins
WScript.Echo "MaxPasswordAge          " & usr.MaxPasswordAge
WScript.Echo "MaxStorage              " & usr.MaxStorage
WScript.Echo "MinPasswordAge          " & usr.MinPasswordAge
WScript.Echo "MinPasswordLength       " & usr.MinPasswordLength
WScript.Echo "Parameters              " & usr.Parameters
WScript.Echo "PasswordAge             " & usr.PasswordAge
WScript.Echo "PasswordExpired         " & usr.PasswordExpired
WScript.Echo "PasswordHistoryLength   " & usr.PasswordHistoryLength
WScript.Echo "PrimaryGroupID          " & usr.PrimaryGroupID
```

```
WScript.Echo "Profile              " & usr.Profile
WScript.Echo "RasPermissions       " & usr.RasPermissions
WScript.Echo "UserFlags            " & usr.UserFlags
```

Output

```
AccountDisabled       False
AccountExpirationDate 12/31/2009
BadPasswordAttempts   0
Description           Systems Engineer
FullName              Tom Green
HomeDirDrive
HomeDirectory         d:\home
IsAccountLocked       False
LastLogin             10/3/2008 3:05:55 PM
LoginScript           log.vbs
MaxPasswordAge        432000
MaxStorage            -1
MinPasswordAge        172800
MinPasswordLength     8
Parameters
PasswordAge           1401
PasswordExpired       0
PasswordHistoryLength 3
PrimaryGroupID        513
Profile               d:\data
RasPermissions        1
UserFlags             66115
```

Working with user account properties

The User object properties are very useful in managing user accounts. Some more so than others, and because of this, several properties deserve special attention. These properties include AccountDisabled, IsAccountLocked, and UserFlags.

You can use AccountDisabled and IsAccountLocked to troubleshoot basic problems with accounts and to track down possible security problems. For example, you may want to schedule a script to run nightly that checks the status of all user accounts to see if they are disabled or locked. You can use this information to help users that are having problems accessing the network and may not want to tell you that they forgot their password for the third time in a row, or to track patterns that may tell you someone is trying to hack into accounts.

Listing 17-6 provides a basic script you can use to check all of the user accounts in a Windows NT or Windows domain. If an account is disabled or locked, the script writes the account name and status.

LISTING 17-6

Checking for Account Problems

VBScript
secuser.vbs

```
'Get the provider object
Set prov = GetObject("WinNT:")

'Examine the available domains the provider can reach
For each dom in prov
 'Examine the objects in the domain and check for User objects
  For each o in dom
    If o.Class = "User" Then
       If o.AccountDisabled = "True" Then
         WScript.Echo o.Name & " is disabled"
       End If
       If o.IsAccountLocked = "True" Then
         WScript.Echo o.Name & " is locked"
       End If
    End If
  Next
Next
```

JScript
secuser.js

```
//Get the provider object
var prov = GetObject("WinNT:")

tlist = new Enumerator(prov)

//Examine the available domains the provider can reach
for (; !tlist.atEnd(); tlist.moveNext())
 {
 s = new Enumerator(tlist.item())
 //Examine the objects in the domain and check for User objects
 for (; !s.atEnd(); s.moveNext())
  {
  o = s.item();
   if (o.Class == "User") {
      if (o.AccountDisabled == 1) {
        WScript.Echo(o.Name + " is disabled")
      }
      if (o.IsAccountLocked == 1) {
        WScript.Echo(o.Name + " is locked")
      }
    }
  }
 }
```

Output

```
Guest is disabled
testAcc is disabled
Theta is disabled
```

Knowing that an account is disabled or locked isn't very useful if you can't resolve the problem as necessary, and this is where the UserFlags property comes into the picture. This property provides an integer value that is the sum of all the flags associated with an account.

Table 17-4 provides a summary of the user flags. Each individual flag represents an account state, such as the password cannot be changed, or the account is disabled, and so forth. By adding the flag value to the total, you can apply the flag. By removing the flag value from the total, you can remove the flag.

TABLE 17-4

User Flags

Flag	Value	Description
ADS_UF_SCRIPT	0X0001	A logon script will be executed.
ADS_UF_ACCOUNTDISABLE	0X0002	The account is disabled.
ADS_UF_HOMEDIR_REQUIRED	0X0004	A home directory is required.
ADS_UF_LOCKOUT	0X0010	The account is locked out.
ADS_UF_PASSWD_NOTREQD	0X0020	No password is required.
ADS_UF_PASSWD_CANT_CHANGE	0X0040	User cannot change the password.
ADS_UF_ENCRYPTED_TEXT_ PASSWORD_ALLOWED	0X0080	User can send an encrypted password.
ADS_UF_TEMP_DUPLICATE_ACCOUNT	0X0100	This is an account for users whose primary account is in another domain.
ADS_UF_NORMAL_ACCOUNT	0X0200	This is a normal account.
ADS_UF_INTERDOMAIN_TRUST_ ACCOUNT	0X0800	Trusted account
ADS_UF_WORKSTATION_TRUST_ ACCOUNT	0X1000	This is a computer account that is a member of this domain.
ADS_UF_SERVER_TRUST_ACCOUNT	0X2000	This is a computer account for a backup domain controller that is a member of this domain.

continued

TABLE 17-4	(continued)	
Flag	**Value**	**Description**
ADS_UF_DONTEXPIREPASSWD	0X10000	The account password doesn't expire.
ADS_UF_MNS_LOGON_ACCOUNT	0X20000	This is an MNS logon account.
ADS_UF_SMARTCARD_REQUIRED	0X40000	Forces the user to log on with a smart card.
ADS_UF_TRUSTED_FOR_DELEGATION	0X80000	The user or computer account under which a service runs is trusted for Kerberos delegation.
ADS_UF_NOT_DELEGATED	0X100000	The security context of the user will not be delegated to a service even if it is trusted.

If you go back to the output of Listing 17-5, you'll see that the sample value for `UserFlags` is 66115. If you convert that value to hexadecimal format, you get 0ts10243. Now if you review the values in Table 17-4, you'll see that the hexadecimal value is the result of the following flags being set on the account:

```
ADS_UF_DONTEXPIREPASSWD 0X10000
ADS_UF_NORMAL_ACCOUNT    0X0200
ADS_UF_PASSWD_CANT_CHANGE         0X0040
ADS_UF_ACCOUNTDISABLE    0X0002
ADS_UF_SCRIPT    0X0001
```

What these flags tell you about the account is:

- You are looking at a normal user account that has been assigned a logon script.
- The account password doesn't expire.
- The user can't change the password.
- The account is disabled.

If you want to enable the account, you need to remove the related flag. You do this by removing the related value from the `UserFlags` property. Because you normally wouldn't want to compute flags by hand and then remove flags individually, you need a safe way to remove the flag if it is set, and to leave the `UserFlags` property alone otherwise. This way you can automate the process and not worry about the details.

The best way to handle this procedure is to use the `AccountDisabled` and `IsLockedOut` properties to tell you when an account is disabled or locked, and then to take appropriate corrective action. An example of this is shown as Listing 17-7. In this example, you examine the tgreen account on a computer named omega. If the account is disabled or locked, the code in this listing enables or unlocks the account as appropriate.

LISTING 17-7

Enabling and Unlocking a User Account

VBScript
restoreuser.vbs

```
Set usr = GetObject("WinNT://seattle/omega/tgreen,user")

If usr.AccountDisabled = "True" Then
  'ADS_UF_ACCOUNTDISABLE 0X0002
  flag = usr.Get("UserFlags") - 2
  usr.Put "UserFlags", flag
  usr.SetInfo

  WScript.Echo usr.Name & " is now enabled"

End If

If usr.IsAccountLocked = "True" Then
  'ADS_UF_LOCKOUT 0X0010
  flag = usr.Get("UserFlags") - 16
  usr.Put "UserFlags", flag
  usr.SetInfo

  WScript.Echo usr.Name & " is now unlocked"

End If
```

JScript
restoreuser.js

```
var usr = GetObject("WinNT://seattle/omega/tgreen,user")

if (usr.AccountDisabled == 1) {
  //ADS_UF_ACCOUNTDISABLE 0X0002
  flag = usr.Get("UserFlags") - 2
  usr.Put("UserFlags", flag)
  usr.SetInfo()

  WScript.Echo(usr.Name + " is now enabled")

}

if (usr.IsAccountLocked == 1) {
  //ADS_UF_LOCKOUT 0X0010
  flag = usr.Get("UserFlags") - 16
  usr.Put("UserFlags", flag)
  usr.SetInfo()
```

continued

LISTING 17-7 *(continued)*

```
    WScript.Echo(usr.Name + " is now unlocked")

}
```

NOTE Actually, the best way to handle this operation is to use a logical XOr. When you perform an XOr comparison of `UserFlags` and the flag you want to remove, you get the desired result. The flag is always removed if set. Otherwise, the `UserFlags` property is not changed. To set a flag, you can do a logical Or. Unfortunately, this technique works great in Visual Basic, but not in scripts.

With a few simple modifications, you can create a script to enable/unlock or disable/lock any account on the network. An example script is shown as Listing 17-8. In this example, Seattle is the NT-equivalent domain name. Replace this with your domain name for the script to work on your network.

LISTING 17-8

Enabling and Unlocking a User Account

VBScript
maccounts.vbs

```
lf = Chr(13) + Chr(10)
WScript.Echo "======================================" & lf
WScript.Echo "==      Account Management Script     ==" & lf
WScript.Echo "======================================" & lf

WScript.Echo "Enter account to work with: " & lf

r = WScript.StdIn.ReadLine()


WScript.Echo "Enter R to restore or D to disable: " & lf

n = WScript.StdIn.ReadLine()

WScript.Echo "======================================" & lf
WScript.Echo "==               Working             ==" & lf
WScript.Echo "======================================" & lf

Set usr = GetObject("WinNT://seattle/" & r & ",user")

select case LCase(n)

case "r"

  If usr.AccountDisabled = "True" Then
```

```
 'ADS_UF_ACCOUNTDISABLE 0X0002

 flag = usr.Get("UserFlags") - 2
 usr.Put "UserFlags", flag
 usr.SetInfo

 WScript.Echo usr.Name & " is enabled"

End If

If usr.IsAccountLocked = "True" Then

 'ADS_UF_LOCKOUT  0X0010

 flag = usr.Get("UserFlags") - 16
 usr.Put "UserFlags", flag
 usr.SetInfo

 WScript.Echo usr.Name & " is unlocked"

 End If

case "d"

 If usr.AccountDisabled = "False" Then

 'ADS_UF_ACCOUNTDISABLE 0X0002

 flag = usr.Get("UserFlags") + 2
 usr.Put "UserFlags", flag
 usr.SetInfo

 WScript.Echo usr.Name & " is disabled"

 End If

 If usr.IsAccountLocked = "False" Then

 'ADS_UF_LOCKOUT  0X0010

 flag = usr.Get("UserFlags") + 16
 usr.Put "UserFlags", flag
 usr.SetInfo

 WScript.Echo usr.Name & " is locked"

 End If

End Select
```

continued

LISTING 17-8   *(continued)*

JScript
maccounts.js

```jscript
lf = "\r\n"
WScript.Echo("========================================" + lf)
WScript.Echo("==         Account Management Script      ==" + lf)
WScript.Echo("========================================" + lf)

WScript.Echo("Enter account to work with: " + lf)

r = WScript.StdIn.ReadLine()

WScript.Echo("Enter R to restore or D to disable: " + lf)

n = WScript.StdIn.ReadLine()

WScript.Echo("========================================" + lf)
WScript.Echo("==                  Working               ==" + lf)
WScript.Echo("========================================" + lf)

var usr = GetObject("WinNT://seattle/" + r + ",user")

switch (n) {

case "r" :

 if (usr.AccountDisabled == 1) {

  //ADS_UF_ACCOUNTDISABLE 0X0002

  flag = usr.Get("UserFlags") - 2
  usr.Put("UserFlags", flag)
  usr.SetInfo()

  WScript.Echo(usr.Name + " is enabled")

 }

 if (usr.IsAccountLocked == 1) {

  //ADS_UF_LOCKOUT 0X0010

  flag = usr.Get("UserFlags") - 16
  usr.Put("UserFlags", flag)
  usr.SetInfo()

  WScript.Echo(usr.Name + " is unlocked")
```

```
    }

    break

  case "d" :

    if (usr.AccountDisabled == 0) {

      //ADS_UF_ACCOUNTDISABLE 0X0002

      flag = usr.Get("UserFlags") + 2
      usr.Put("UserFlags", flag)
      usr.SetInfo()

      WScript.Echo(usr.Name + " is disabled")

    }

    if (usr.IsAccountLocked == 0) {

      //ADS_UF_LOCKOUT 0X0010

      flag = usr.Get("UserFlags") + 16
      usr.Put("UserFlags", flag)
      usr.SetInfo()

      WScript.Echo(usr.Name + " is locked")

    }

    break
}
```

Output

```
========================================

==       Account Management Script     ==

========================================

Enter account to work with:

tgreen
Enter R to restore or D to disable:

r
```

continued

LISTING 17-8   *(continued)*

```
=======================================

==              Working              ==

=======================================

tgreen is enabled
```

NOTE   As with many examples in the text, this script is designed to run from the command line with CScript.exe. If you run the script with WScript.exe, you won't get the results you expect and you'll have a lot of pop-up dialog boxes to deal with.

As you examine the script, you should note the techniques used to display output and handle input. So the output is easy to follow, we added blank lines with Chr(13) and Chr(10) or \r\n. To read from the command line, the script reads a line from the standard input stream. The code for this is:

```
r = WScript.StdIn.ReadLine()
```

The StdIn.ReadLine() method allows you to type in characters and pass the result to a variable when you press Enter. To get the sample output, we typed **tgreen** and then pressed Enter. Afterward, we typed **r** and then pressed Enter.

Managing user accounts with WinNT

With WinNT, you can perform many common user account tasks. You can create and delete accounts. You can also set and change account passwords. Another interesting user-management task is to examine the group membership for users.

Creating user accounts with WinNT

To create user accounts, you use the Create() method of the IADsContainer interface. This method expects to be passed the two parameters: the class and the relative name of the object to create.

Before you can use the Create() method, you must bind to the container in which you will create the account. To create a local account, you bind to the local computer object. To create a domain account, you bind to the domain object. When you create an account with WinNT, you must also set the account password. You do this with the SetPassword() method which expects a single string that contains the new password.

The following example binds to the seattle domain and creates a user account for jfranklin:

VBScript

```
Set obj = GetObject("WinNT://seattle")
Set usr = obj.Create("user", "jfranklin")
```

```
usr.SetPassword("gres$#42g")
usr.SetInfo
```

JScript

```
var obj = GetObject("WinNT://seattle")
var usr = obj.Create("user","jfranklin")
usr.SetPassword("gres$#42g")
usr.SetInfo()
```

As stated previously, you can also create local computer accounts. In the next example, you create the same account on a computer named omega:

VBScript

```
Set obj = GetObject("WinNT://seattle/omega")
Set usr = obj.Create("user", "jfranklin")
usr.SetPassword("gres$#42g")
usr.SetInfo
```

JScript

```
var obj = GetObject
("WinNT://seattle/omega")
var usr = obj.Create("user", "jfranklin")
usr.SetPassword("gres$#42g")
usr.SetInfo()
```

You can, of course, set other properties for the new account before you create it. You can also set these properties at a later time.

Deleting user accounts with WinNT

You delete accounts with the Delete() method of the IADsContainer interface. As with Create(), this method expects to be passed the two parameters: the class and the relative name of the object to create.

Before you can use the Delete() method, you must bind to the container from which you will delete the account. The following example deletes the user account for jfranklin from the seattle domain:

VBScript

```
Set obj = GetObject("WinNT://seattle")
obj.Delete "user", "jfranklin"
```

JScript

```
var obj = GetObject("WinNT://seattle")
obj.Delete("user", "jfranklin")
```

Setting and changing passwords

You set passwords for new or existing user accounts with the SetPassword() method. This method was discussed previously in the chapter. The User object also provides a ChangePassword() method. To change a password, you can use ChangePassword(); however, you must know the old password, which is why this method isn't very practical for day-to-day administration. Instead, you'll usually want to use SetPassword().

Examples of using SetPassword() and ChangePassword() follow.

VBScript

```
Set usr = GetObject("WinNT://seattle/jsmith,user")
usr.SetPassword "NewPassword"

Set usr = GetObject("WinNT://seattle/omega/hwilder,user")
usr.ChangePassword "OldPassword","NewPassword"
```

JScript

```
var usr = GetObject("WinNT://seattle/jsmith,user")
usr.SetPassword("NewPassword")

var usr = GetObject("WinNT://seattle/omega/hwilder,user")
usr.ChangePassword("OldPassword","NewPassword")
```

Checking group membership

Often you'll need to check group membership for users on the network. One way to do this quickly and efficiently is to use a script that examines group membership on a user-by-user basis with the Groups() method of the User object. The Groups() method returns a collection of group objects to which a user belongs.

You can use Groups() to examine all of the groups sjohnson belongs to, as follows:

VBScript

```
Set usr = GetObject("WinNT://seattle/sjohnson,user")
For Each grp In usr.Groups
    WScript.Echo grp.Name
Next
```

JScript

```
var usr = GetObject("WinNT://seattle/sjohnson,user")
mList = new Enumerator(usr.Groups());
for (; !mList.atEnd();mList.moveNext())
{
    s = mList.item()
    WScript.Echo(s.Name)
}
```

Output

```
Domain Users
Enterprise Admins
Schema Admins
Domain Admins
Administrators
Backup Operators
```

To make it easier to monitor group membership, you can create a function to check all user accounts in the domain and then create a report. A sample function is shown in Listing 17-9.

LISTING 17-9

Tracking Group Membership

VBScript
groupmembership.vbs

```vbscript
Set prov = GetObject("WinNT:")
For each dom in prov

 For each o in dom

  If o.Class = "User" Then
    WScript.Echo "======================="
    WScript.Echo "Account: " & o.FullName
    For Each grp In o.Groups
      WScript.Echo "  " & grp.Name
    Next
  End If

 Next
Next
```

JScript
groupmembership.js

```jscript
//Get the provider object
var prov = GetObject("WinNT:")
tlist = new Enumerator(prov)

for (; !tlist.atEnd(); tlist.moveNext())
 {

 s = new Enumerator(tlist.item())

 for (; !s.atEnd(); s.moveNext())
  {
```

continued

LISTING 17-9   *(continued)*

```
o = s.item();
if (o.Class == "User") {
 WScript.Echo("=======================")
 WScript.Echo("Account: " + o.FullName)

 mList = new Enumerator(o.Groups());


     for (; !mList.atEnd(); mList.moveNext())
  {
   usr = mList.item()
   WScript.Echo(usr.Name)
  }


 }
 }
}
```

Output

```
=======================
Account: Thomas Franklin
 Domain Users
=======================
Account: George Johnson
 Domain Users
=======================
Account: William R. Stanek
 Domain Users
 Enterprise Admins
 Schema Admins
 Domain Admins
 Administrators
 Backup Operators
```

Creating and Modifying Group Accounts

WinNT supports basic functions for managing group accounts. You can create local group accounts on member servers and workstations. You can create domain local and global security groups in domains. You can manipulate any type of group.

Understanding Windows group types

In Windows, there are several different types of groups and each type of group can have a different scope. The group type affects how the group is used. The three group types are as follows:

- **Local:** Groups are used only on a local workstation or server.

- **Security:** Groups have security controls associated with them and are available in domains.

- **Distribution:** Groups are used as e-mail distribution lists and do not have security controls. You define distribution groups in domains.

Group scope further defines the area in which groups are valid. The group scopes are:

- **Domain local:** These special groups exist only on Domain Controllers and have domain local permissions. Members of domain local groups can only include user accounts, computer accounts, and groups from the domain in which they are defined.

- **Built-in local:** These special groups exist only on Domain Controllers and have domain local permissions. Built-in local groups differ from other groups in that they cannot be created or deleted, but you can modify their membership.

- **Global:** These groups are used to grant permissions to any domain in the domain tree or forest. However, members of global groups can only include user accounts, computer accounts, and groups from the domain in which they are defined.

- **Universal:** These groups are used to grant wide access throughout a domain tree or forest. Members of global groups include user accounts, computer accounts, and groups from any domain in the domain tree or forest.

Creating groups with WinNT

Creating groups with WinNT is much like creating user accounts. You start by obtaining the domain or local computer container in which you want to create the group. If you obtain a domain container, you create a global domain group by default. If you obtain a local computer container, you create a local group on that computer.

In the following example, you create a local group on a computer named omega and set the group name to myGroup:

VBScript

```
Set obj = GetObject("WinNT://seattle/omega,computer")
Set grp = obj.Create("group", "myGroup")
grp.SetInfo
```

JScript

```
var obj = GetObject("WinNT://seattle/omega,computer")
var grp = obj.Create("group", "myGroup")
grp.SetInfo()
```

Using a similar technique you could create a global domain group as well. If you want to create a domain local group, you must set the groupType property. This property is set with an integer value. The default value of 2 sets the group type to domain local. A value of 4 sets the group type to domain local. Following this, you could create a domain local group called Marketing like this:

VBScript

```
Set obj = GetObject("WinNT://seattle")
Set grp = obj.Create("group", "Marketing")
grp.groupType = 4
grp.SetInfo
```

JScript

```
var obj = GetObject("WinNT://seattle")
var grp = obj.Create("group", "Marketing")
grp.groupType = 4
grp.SetInfo()
```

The only other property that you may want to set for a group is Description, which is used to describe the group. You can set a description for the group when you create it. You can also view or change the value if necessary. In the following example, you add a description to the Marketing group we created previously:

VBScript

```
Set grp = GetObject("WinNT://seattle/Marketing,group")
grp.Description = "Sales and Marketing Group"
grp.SetInfo
```

JScript

```
var grp = GetObject("WinNT://seattle,Marketing,group")
grp.Description = "Sales and Marketing Group"
grp.SetInfo()
```

Checking group membership

Often when you work with groups, you'll want to determine if a particular account or other group is a member. You can do this with the IsMember() method of the Group object. Start by obtaining the group object you want to work with and then passing IsMember the AdsPath string of the member you want to check, for example:

VBScript

```
Set grp = GetObject("WinNT://seattle/Marketing,group")
mem = grp.IsMember("WinNT://seattle/jsmith,user")
WScript.Echo mem
```

JScript

```
var grp = GetObject("WinNT://seattle,Marketing,group")
mem = grp.IsMember("WinNT://seattle/jsmith,user")
WScript.Echo(mem)
```

The IsMember method returns True (or 1) if the member is found and False (or 0) otherwise.

Another way you can work with groups is to obtain a list of current members. You can do this by calling the Members() method, for example:

VBScript

```
Set grp = GetObject("WinNT://seattle/Marketing,group")
mem = grp.Members
```

JScript

```
var grp = GetObject("WinNT://seattle,Marketing,group")
mem = grp.Members()
```

The Members() method returns a collection of members using the IADsMembers interface. You can examine each member using a For loop; for example:

VBScript

```
Set grp = GetObject("WinNT://seattle/Domain Users")
Set mList = grp.members
For Each member In mList
   WScript.Echo member.Name & " " & member.Class
Next
```

JScript

```
var grp = GetObject("WinNT://seattle/Domain Users")
mList = new Enumerator(grp.members());

for (; !mList.atEnd(); mList.moveNext())
{
 s = mList.item()
 WScript.Echo(s.Name)
}
```

Adding and removing group members

You can use the WinNT provider to add and remove members from any type of group. To do this, first obtain the group object you want to work with and then add or remove members using their AdsPath string.

After you add or remove a member, you can use `IsMember()` to confirm the action; for example:

VBScript

```
Set grp = GetObject("WinNT://seattle/Marketing,group")
mem = grp.Add("WinNT://seattle/jsmith,user")
WScript.Echo grp.IsMember("WinNT://seattle/jsmith,user")
```

JScript

```
var grp = GetObject("WinNT://seattle/Marketing,group")
mem = grp.Add("WinNT://seattle/jsmith,user")
WScript.Echo(grp.IsMember("WinNT://seattle/jsmith,user"))
```

Summary

The WinNT provider is very useful when you want to manage basic settings for domains, users, and groups. As you've seen, you can also use WinNT to create, delete, and modify both user and group accounts. When using WinNT with Windows, it is useful to keep in mind the limitations discussed in this chapter. To perform extended functions, such as moving user accounts to different containers or creating organizational units, you'll need to use the LDAP provider.

Chapter 18

Service and Resource Administration with ADSI

You can use ADSI to control many different aspects of workstations and servers. In this chapter, we look at managing services, opening files, and handling user sessions. When services and resources aren't configured or managed properly, your organization's productivity can grind to a halt. E-mail messages may not get delivered. Users may get locked out of files and databases. Critical systems may even crash. To help avoid problems with services and resources, you can use scripts to monitor their status, update configuration settings, and more.

Managing Windows Services

Windows services provide essential functions for workstations and servers. Without these services, computers could not perform many important tasks. If you've worked with Windows for awhile, you know that the operating system has many different features that help you automatically manage services. For example, you can configure the automatic restart of a service and the automatic restart of a computer if a service fails to restart.

With Windows scripts, you gain more control over how and when services are started, stopped, and restarted. You can use scripts to view service status and manage configuration settings as well.

Using and understanding Windows services

The standard utility for managing Windows services is the Services node of the Computer Management console. You can use the entries in the Services node to control and monitor services. When you examine services in the

Computer Management console, you find that each service is displayed with summary information. As shown in Figure 18-1, this includes the following fields:

- **Name:** Shows the name of the service installed on the system.

- **Description:** Shows a brief description of the service.

- **Status:** Shows the service status. For example, a stopped service is indicated by a blank entry.

- **Startup Type:** Shows the startup setting for the service. Manual services can be started by users or other services. Automatic services are started when the computer boots. Disabled services are configured so that they cannot be started.

- **Log On As:** Shows the account the service logs on as. Usually, this is the local system account.

FIGURE 18-1

You can view and manage services with the Services node in the Computer Management console.

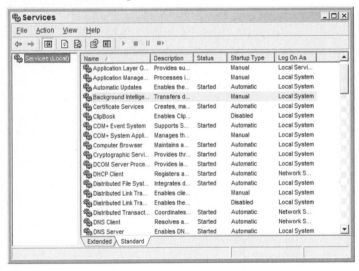

The services that are available on a system depend on the system's configuration. Table 18-1 lists some of the most commonly used services and their default configuration settings.

TABLE 18-1

Common Windows Services and Their Default Configuration

Display Name	Description	Startup Type	Log On As
Alerter	Notifies users and computers of administrative alerts	Automatic	LocalSystem
Application Management	Provides software installation services	Manual	LocalSystem

Display Name	Description	Startup Type	Log On As
ClipBook	Supports the ClipBook Viewer for remote viewing of ClipBooks	Manual	LocalSystem
COM+ Event System	Provides automatic distribution of COM events	Manual	LocalSystem
Computer Browser	Maintains an up-to-date list of computers on the network	Automatic	LocalSystem
DHCP Client	Provides dynamic host configuration information	Automatic	LocalSystem
DHCP Server	Provides dynamic configuration for DHCP clients	Automatic	LocalSystem
Distributed File System	Manages distributed file systems	Automatic	LocalSystem
Distributed Transaction Coordinator	Coordinates distributed transactions	Automatic	LocalSystem
DNS Client	Resolves and caches Domain Naming System (DNS) names	Automatic	LocalSystem
DNS Server	Answers DNS requests	Automatic	LocalSystem
Event Log	Logs event messages	Automatic	LocalSystem
File Replication Service	Replicates directory data	Automatic	LocalSystem
File Server for Macintosh	Enables Macintosh users to work with files on a Windows server	Automatic	LocalSystem
FTP Publishing Service	Provides FTP connectivity and administration through the Internet Information Services snap-in	Automatic	LocalSystem
IIS Admin Service	Permits administration of Web and FTP services through the Internet Information Services snap-in	Automatic	LocalSystem
Indexing Service	Indexes files and provides quick access	Manual	LocalSystem
Internet Authentication Service	Enables authentication of dial-up and VPN users	Automatic	LocalSystem
Internet Connection Sharing	Allows computers to share Internet connections	Manual	LocalSystem
License Logging Service	Logs license-related events	Automatic	LocalSystem
Logical Disk Manager	Monitors the Logical Disk Manager	Automatic	LocalSystem
Logical Disk Manager Administrative Service	Used to manage logical disks	Manual	LocalSystem
Messenger	Sends and receives administrative messages	Automatic	LocalSystem
Net Logon	Supports authentication of account logon events	Automatic	LocalSystem

continued

TABLE 18-1	*(continued)*		
Display Name	**Description**	**Startup Type**	**Log On As**
Network DDE	Provides network transport and security for dynamic data exchange (DDE)	Manual	LocalSystem
Network DDE DSDM	Used by Network DDE to manage shared data exchanges	Manual	LocalSystem
NT LM Security Support Provider	Provides security for remote procedure calls (RPC)	Manual	LocalSystem
Performance Logs and Alerts	Configures performance logs and alerts	Manual	LocalSystem
Plug and Play	Manages device installation and configuration	Automatic	LocalSystem
Print Server for Macintosh	Enables Macintosh users to send print jobs to a spooler on a Windows server	Automatic	LocalSystem
Print Spooler	Loads files to memory for later printing	Automatic	LocalSystem
Protected Storage	Provides protected storage for sensitive data	Automatic	LocalSystem
Remote Registry Service	Allows remote registry manipulation	Automatic	LocalSystem
Removable Storage	Manages removable media	Automatic	LocalSystem
Routing and Remote Access	Used to manage routing and remote access	Disabled	LocalSystem
RunAs Service	Allows users to start process using alternate credentials	Automatic	LocalSystem
Security Accounts Manager	Stores security information for local user accounts	Automatic	LocalSystem
Server	Provides essential server services	Automatic	LocalSystem
Simple Mail Transport Protocol (SMTP)	Transports e-mail across the network	Automatic	LocalSystem
Smart Card	Manages and controls access to smart cards	Manual	LocalSystem
Smart Card Helper	Provides support for legacy smart card readers	Manual	LocalSystem
System Event Notification	Tracks system events	Automatic	LocalSystem
Task Scheduler	Enables task scheduling	Automatic	LocalSystem
TCP/IP NetBIOS Helper Service	Supports NetBIOS over TCP/IP (NetBT) service and NetBIOS name resolution	Automatic	LocalSystem

Display Name	Description	Startup Type	Log On As
TCP/IP Print Server	Provides a TCP/IP-based printing	Automatic	LocalSystem
Telephony	Provides Telephony support	Manual	LocalSystem
Telnet	Allows a remote user to log on to the system and run console programs	Manual	LocalSystem
Windows Installer	Installs, repairs, and removes software using .MSI files	Manual	LocalSystem
Windows Internet Name Service (WINS)	Provides a NetBIOS name service	Automatic	LocalSystem
Windows Time	Used to synchronize system time	Automatic	LocalSystem
Workstation	Provides network connections and communications	Automatic	LocalSystem
World Wide Web Publishing Service	Provides Web connectivity and administration through the Internet Information Services snap-in	Automatic	LocalSystem

Windows has built-in controls for monitoring and restarting services. You configure these recovery features on a per-service basis. To check or manage the recovery settings for a service, follow these steps:

1. Start the Computer Management console. Choose Start ➪ Programs ➪ Administrative Tools ➪ Computer Management.

2. In the Computer Management console, right-click the Computer Management entry in the console tree. Then, select Connect to Another Computer on the shortcut menu. You can now choose the system whose services you want to manage.

3. Click the plus sign (+) next to System Tools and then choose Services.

4. Right-click the service you want to configure and then choose Properties.

5. Choose the Recovery tab as shown in Figure 18-2. Now check or reconfigure recovery options for the first, second, and subsequent recovery attempts.

6. If you choose the Run A File option, you can specify a script that you want to run if the service fails. Enter the full directory path to the script in the File field, or click Browse to find the file. If you want to pass parameters to the script, enter these parameters in the Command Line Parameters field.

7. Click OK.

FIGURE 18-2

You set recovery options on a per-service basis and you can designate scripts to run if the service fails.

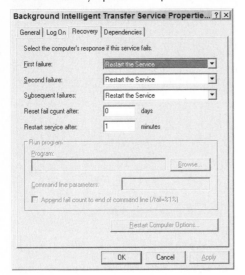

Working with service objects

Services are specific to a particular computer. So if you want to manage services, you must do so via the related `Computer` object. You don't access services by their display name. Instead, you access them using the object name for the service. For example, if you want to access the Windows Internet Name Service on a computer called HodgePodge, you would do so as follows:

```
Set service = GetObject("WinNT://seattle/hodgepodge/wins,service")
```

In this example, `seattle` is the domain name (part of `seattle.tvpress.com`) and `wins` is the actual name of the `Service` object. Table 18-2 provides a detailed mapping of service display names to service object names. When you want to examine a particular service, use the table to help you determine the necessary object name.

TABLE 18-2

Service Name Map

Display Name	Object Name
Alerter	`Alerter`
Application Management	`AppMgmt`
ClipBook	`ClipSrv`

Display Name	Object Name
COM+ Event System	EventSystem
Computer Browser	Browser
DHCP Client	Dhcp
DHCP Server	DHCPServer
Distributed File System	Dfs
Distributed Link Tracking Client	TrkWks
Distributed Link Tracking Server	TrkSvr
Distributed Transaction Coordinator	MSDTC
DNS Client	Dnscache
DNS Server	DNS
Event Log	Eventlog
Fax Service	Fax
File Replication Service	NtFrs
File Server for Macintosh	MacFile
FTP Publishing Service	MSFTPSVC
IIS Admin Service	IISADMIN
IMDB Server	ImdbServer
Indexing Service	cisvc
Internet Authentication Service	IAS
Internet Connection Sharing	SharedAccess
Intersite Messaging	IsmServ
IPSEC Policy Agent	PolicyAgent
Kerberos Key Distribution Center	kdc
License Logging Service	LicenseService
Logical Disk Manager	dmserver
Logical Disk Manager Administrative Service	dmadmin
Messenger	Messenger
Net Logon	Netlogon

continued

TABLE 18-2   *(continued)*

Display Name	Object Name
NetMeeting Remote Desktop Sharing	mnmsrvc
Network Connections	Netman
Network DDE	NetDDE
Network DDE DSDM	NetDDEdsdm
NT LM Security Support Provider	NtLmSsp
Performance Logs and Alerts	SysmonLog
Plug and Play	PlugPlay
Print Server for Macintosh	MacPrint
Print Spooler	Spooler
Protected Storage	ProtectedStorage
QoS Admission Control (RSVP)	RSVP
Remote Access Auto Connection Manager	RasAuto
Remote Access Connection Manager	RasMan
Remote Procedure Call (RPC)	RpcSs
Remote Procedure Call (RPC) Locator	RpcLocator
Remote Registry Service	RemoteRegistry
Removable Storage	NtmsSvc
Routing and Remote Access	RemoteAccess
RunAs Service	seclogon
Security Accounts Manager	SamSs
Server	lanmanserver
Simple Mail Transport Protocol (SMTP)	SMTPSVC
Simple TCP/IP Services	SimpTcp
Smart Card	SCardSvr
Smart Card Helper	SCardDrv
SNMP Service	SNMP
SNMP Trap Service	SNMPTRAP

Display Name	Object Name
System Event Notification	SENS
Task Scheduler	Schedule
TCP/IP NetBIOS Helper Service	LmHosts
TCP/IP Print Server	LPDSVC
Telephony	TapiSrv
Telnet	TlntSvr
Terminal Services	TermService
Uninterruptible Power Supply	UPS
Utility Manager	UtilMan
Windows Installer	MSIServer
Windows Internet Name Service (WINS)	WINS
Windows Management Instrumentation	WinMgmt
Windows Management Instrumentation Driver Extensions	Wmi
Windows Time	W32Time
Workstation	lanmanworkstation
World Wide Web Publishing Service	W3SVC

If a service you need to work with isn't listed in Table 18-2, you may need to create a list of all services on the computer and then filter this list by the display name. Listing 18-1 shows how you can search for the Windows Internet Name Service (WINS).

<hr>

LISTING 18-1

Searching for a Service Object Name

VBScript
servicename.vbs

```
Set comp = GetObject("WinNT://seattle/zeta")

 'Check for Service objects
  For each s in comp
   If s.Class = "Service" Then
     If s.DisplayName = "Windows Internet Name Service (WINS)" Then
```

continued

LISTING 18-1   *(continued)*

```
        WScript.Echo s.DisplayName & ": " & s.Name
      End If
    End If
  Next
```

JScript
servicename.js

```
var comp = GetObject("WinNT://seattle/zeta")

tlist = new Enumerator(comp)
for (; !tlist.atEnd(); tlist.moveNext())
  {
    s = tlist.item()
    if (s.Class == "Service") {
      if (s.DisplayName == "Windows Internet Name Service (WINS)") {
        WScript.Echo(s.DisplayName + " " + s.Name)
      }
    }
  }
```

Output

```
Windows Internet Name Service (WINS): WINS
```

Using service object properties

All service objects have a set of properties that you can work with. These properties are summarized in Table 18-3. (A status of RO means the property is read-only and cannot be updated. A status of RW means the property is read-write and can be updated.)

TABLE 18-3

Service Object Properties

Property	Status	Value Type	Min Range	Max Range	Multiple Values
Dependencies	RW	Array or String	0	256	True
DisplayName	RW	String	0	256	False
ErrorControl	RW	Integer	–2147483648	2147483647	False

Property	Status	Value Type	Min Range	Max Range	Multiple Values
HostComputer	RW	AdsPath String	0	256	False
LoadOrderGroup	RW	String	0	256	False
Path	RW	Path String	0	340	False
ServiceAccountName	RW	String	0	273	False
ServiceType	RW	Integer	-2147483648	2147483647	False
StartType	RW	Integer	-2147483648	2147483647	False
Status	RO	Integer	1	8	False

As with most object properties, you can access property values by name or through the get() method. Listing 18-2 shows how you could examine all of the services running on a particular computer. Services can have multiple dependencies. If they do, these dependencies can be accessed through the Dependencies array. Note the sample values listed in the output, which we discuss later in the chapter.

LISTING 18-2

Viewing Service Settings

VBScript
viewservices.vbs

```
'Handle Errors
On Error Resume Next

lf = Chr(13) + Chr(10)
'Get the provider object
Set comp = GetObject("WinNT://seattle/zeta")

 'Check for Service objects
  For each s in comp

   If s.Class = "Service" Then

    'Display service properties
     WScript.Echo s.Class & " " & s.Name
     WScript.Echo "==============================="
```

continued

LISTING 18-2   *(continued)*

```
    WScript.Echo "StartType: " & s.StartType
    WScript.Echo "ServiceType: " & s.ServiceType
    WScript.Echo "DisplayName: " & s.DisplayName
    WScript.Echo "Path: " & s.Path
    WScript.Echo "ErrorControl: " & s.ErrorControl
    WScript.Echo "HostComputer: " & s.HostComputer
    WScript.Echo "LoadOrderGroup: " & s.LoadOrderGroup
    WScript.Echo "ServiceAccountName: " & s.ServiceAccountName

      WScript.Echo "Dependency: " & a
      Set ds = c.GetObject("Service", a)
    Next
  End If
  WScript.Echo(lf)
End If

Next
```

JScript
viewservices.js

```
lf = "\r\n"

var comp = GetObject("WinNT://seattle/zeta")

tlist = new Enumerator(comp)

for (; !tlist.atEnd(); tlist.moveNext())
 {

 s = tlist.item()

 if (s.Class == "Service") {

      //Display service properties
      WScript.Echo(s.Class + " " + s.Name)
      WScript.Echo("==============================")
      WScript.Echo("StartType: " + s.StartType)
      WScript.Echo("ServiceType: " + s.ServiceType)
      WScript.Echo("DisplayName: " + s.DisplayName)
      WScript.Echo("Path: " + s.Path)
      WScript.Echo("ErrorControl: " + s.ErrorControl)
      WScript.Echo("HostComputer: " + s.HostComputer)
      WScript.Echo("LoadOrderGroup: " + s.LoadOrderGroup)
      WScript.Echo("ServiceAccountName: " + s.ServiceAccountName)
```

```
try {
 WScript.Echo("Dependencies: " + s.Dependencies)
 }
 catch (e) {
 //property setting not available or is array
 }
 try {
 //services can have multiple dependencies
 e = s.Dependencies.toArray()
  for (opt in e)
  {
    WScript.Echo("Dependencies: " + e[opt])
  }
 }
 catch (e) {
  //property setting not available
 }
 try {
   WScript.Echo("Status: " + s.Get("Status"))
 }
 catch (e) {
   //property setting not available
 }

 WScript.Echo(lf)
 }

 }
```

Output

```
Service WINS
================================
StartType: 2
ServiceType: 16
DisplayName: Windows Internet Name Service (WINS)
Path: F:\WIN2000\System32\wins.exe
ErrorControl: 1
HostComputer: WinNT://seattle/zeta
LoadOrderGroup:
ServiceAccountName: LocalSystem
Dependencies: RPCSS
Dependencies: NTLMSSP
Dependencies: SAMSS
Status: 4
```

continued

LISTING 18-2   *(continued)*

```
Service Wmi
===============================
StartType: 3
ServiceType: 32
DisplayName: Windows Management Instrumentation Driver Extensions
Path: F:\WIN2000\system32\Services.exe
ErrorControl: 1
HostComputer: WinNT://seattle/zeta
LoadOrderGroup:
ServiceAccountName: LocalSystem
Dependencies: RPCSS
Dependencies: NTLMSSP
Dependencies: SAMSS
Status: 4
```

NOTE   We had a problem accessing the `Status` property in JScript on our system. This property wasn't directly accessible by name for some service types. To resolve this problem, we had to use `s.Get("Status")` instead of `s.Status`, in which `s` is the name of the current `Service` object.

Checking Service Status and Dependencies

One of the key properties that you'll use while troubleshooting service problems is `Status`. This property returns a code that indicates the state of the service. The status codes are:

Service Stopped	1	Attempting to Continue Service	5
Attempting to Start Service	2	Attempting to Pause Service	6
Attempting to Stop Service	3	Service Paused	7
Service Running	4	Service Error	8

Another important property that's used in troubleshooting service problems is `Dependencies`. The `Dependencies` property returns an array of services that must be running before the parent service can run. For example, the WINS service can only run if the RPCSS, NTLMSSP, and SAMSS services are running. So if you determine that WINS is a critical service that you want to track or manage through a Windows script, you also want to track and manage these additional services.

Using the `Status` and `Dependencies` properties together, you can determine if a service isn't running because of problems with dependent services. In Listing 18-3, the user is prompted to enter a computer name and service name. The script then checks to see if the service is running normally. If the service isn't running normally, the script checks the status of dependent services.

LISTING 18-3

Resolving Service-Related Problems

VBScript
trservices.vbs

```vbscript
' ***********************
' Script: Service Troubleshooter
' Version: 1.1.5
' Creation Date: 6/16/2008
' Last Modified: 7/23/2008
' Author: William R. Stanek
' Email: williamstanek@aol.com
' Copyright (c) 2008 William R. Stanek
' ***********************

On Error Resume Next
lf = Chr(13) & Chr(10)

WScript.Echo "======================================" & lf
WScript.Echo "==    Service Troubleshooting Script    ==" & lf
WScript.Echo "======================================" & lf

WScript.Echo "Enter local or remote host name: " & lf

host = WScript.StdIn.ReadLine()

WScript.Echo lf & "Enter service to troubleshoot: " & lf

servName = WScript.StdIn.ReadLine()

Set c = GetObject("WinNT://" & host & ",computer")
Set s = c.GetObject("Service", servName)

WScript.Echo lf & "======================================" & lf
WScript.Echo "Checking Status for " & s.Name
WScript.Echo "======================================" & lf

checkStatus(s)

sub checkStatus(obj)

 Select Case obj.Status
  Case 1

    WScript.Echo "======================================"
    WScript.Echo "Service not running."
    WScript.Echo "Checking dependent services."
```

continued

LISTING 18-3 *(continued)*

```
   WScript.Echo "=========================================" & lf

   deps = obj.Dependencies

   If VarType(deps) = vbString Then
      WScript.Echo "Dependency: " & deps & lf

      Set ds = c.GetObject("Service", deps)
      checkStatus(ds)
   Else

     For Each a In deps
       WScript.Echo "Dependency: " & a & lf

       Set ds = c.GetObject("Service", a)
       checkStatus(ds)

     Next
   End If

 Case 4

   WScript.Echo obj.Class & " " & obj.Name & " is running normally"
   WScript.Echo lf

 Case 7

   WScript.Echo obj.Class & " " & obj.Name & " is paused." & lf

 Case 8

   WScript.Echo "====================================="
   WScript.Echo "Service error!"
   WScript.Echo "Checking dependent services."
   WScript.Echo "=====================================" & lf
    deps = obj.Dependencies

   If VarType(deps) = vbString Then
      WScript.Echo "Dependency: " & deps & lf

      Set ds = c.GetObject("Service", deps)
      checkStatus(ds)
   Else

     For Each a In deps
       WScript.Echo "Dependency: " & a & lf
```

```
        Set ds = c.GetObject("Service", a)
        checkStatus(ds)

    Next
    End If


  Case Else

    WScript.Echo obj.Class & " " & obj.Name & " is changing states."
    WScript.Echo lf

 End Select
End Sub
```

Output

```
=========================================

==   Service Troubleshooting Script   ==

=========================================

Enter local or remote host name:

zeta

Enter service to troubleshoot:

w3svc


=========================================

Checking Status for w3svc
=========================================


=========================================
Service not running or error.
Checking dependent services.
=========================================

Dependency: IISADMIN

Service IISADMIN is running normally
```

We've configured the script to use recursive calls to the checkStatus subroutine. This enables the script to check the next level of service dependencies in case of service failure. In the previous example, the W3SVC depends on the IISADMIN service. In turn, IISADMIN depends on other services. If both W3SVC and IISADMIN aren't running properly, the script checks the dependent services of IISADMIN. To see how this works, consider the following output from this service troubleshooting script:

```
========================================

==   Service Troubleshooting Script   ==

========================================


Enter local or remote host name:

zeta

Enter service to troubleshoot:

w3svc


========================================

Checking Status for w3svc
========================================


========================================
Service not running or error.
Checking dependent services.
========================================


Dependency: IISADMIN

========================================
Service not running or error.
Checking dependent services.
========================================


Dependency: RPCSS

Service RPCSS is running normally

Dependency: ProtectedStorage

Service ProtectedStorage is running normally
```

In this example, niether W3SVC nor IISADMIN are running normally. Because of this, the script checks the dependencies of both services. The section of code driving most of the script is:

```
deps = obj.Dependencies

    If VarType(deps) = vbString Then
```

```
        WScript.Echo "Dependency: " & deps & lf

        Set ds = c.GetObject("Service", deps)
        checkStatus(ds)
    Else

      For Each a In deps
        WScript.Echo "Dependency: " & a & lf

        Set ds = c.GetObject("Service", a)
        checkStatus(ds)

      Next
    End If
```

This snippet of code is responsible for checking service dependencies. A single dependency is repre-sented with a string. Multiple dependencies are represented with an array. Because of this, you need a section of code that checks for a string value if one is present, and otherwise handles the depen-dencies as an array.

Viewing and Setting Service Information

These other service object properties let you view and configure service settings:

- DisplayName: Specifies the service display name.

- ErrorControl: Specifies the actions taken in case of service failure. A value of 0 indicates no recovery settings. A value greater than zero indicates recovery options have been set.

- HostComputer: Displays the AdsPath string of the host computer running the service.

- LoadOrderGroup: Identifies the load order group of which the service is a member.

- Path: Specifies the path and file name of the executable for the service.

- ServiceAccountName: Designates the account used by the service at startup.

- ServiceType: Specifies the process type in which the service runs.

- StartType: Identifies the start type for the service.

 For detailed information on these properties, see Appendix B. Service properties and methods are defined in the IADsService and IADsServiceOperations interfaces.

In scripts, you'll often need to view values for the service object properties, and you can do this as shown in Listing 18-2. However, unless you are creating a script to install a service, you won't need to set most of these properties. Because of this, we'll focus on the two properties that you may want to configure: DisplayName and ServiceAccountName.

As you've seen in previous examples, the `Service` object name isn't tied to the display name. This means you can change the display name without affecting the service. For example, if you want to rename the Windows Management Instrumentation Driver Extensions service as Wmi, you can do so as follows:

VBScript

```
Set s = GetObject("WinNT://seattle/zeta/wmi,service")
s.Put "DisplayName", "Wmi"
s.SetInfo
```

JScript

```
var s = GetObject("WinNT://seattle/zeta/wmi,service")
s.Put("DisplayName", "Wmi")
s.SetInfo()
```

Changing the `ServiceAccoutName` property, on the other hand, does affect the service. This property controls which domain or system account is used to start the service. If you use a domain account, you must enter the domain name as well as the account name. For example, if the domain is Seattle and the account is Administrator, you enter Seattle/Administration as the account name.

When you set the account name, you must also enter the password for the account. To do this, use the `SetPassword()` method of the service object. The only parameter for this method is a string containing the account password. You can configure a new service startup account as follows:

VBScript

```
Set s = GetObject("WinNT://seattle/zeta/snmp,service")
s.Put "ServiceAccountName", "Seattle/Administrator"
s.SetPassword "MamboKings"
s.SetInfo
```

JScript

```
var s = GetObject("WinNT://seattle/zeta/snmp,service")
s.Put("ServiceAccountName", "Seattle/Administrator")
s.SetPassword("MamboKings")
s.SetInfo()
```

Starting, Stopping, and Pausing Services

The service object has methods for controlling services in scripts as well. These methods are:

- `Start()`: Starts a service.
- `Stop()`: Stops a service.
- `Pause()`: Pauses a service.
- `Continue()`: Resumes a paused service.

Using these methods is rather straightforward. If you want to start the W3SVC, you obtain the related service object and then call Start( ), for example:

VBScript

```
Set s = GetObject("WinNT://seattle/zeta/w3svc,service")
s.Start
```

JScript

```
var s = GetObject("WinNT://seattle/zeta/w3svc,service")
s.Start()
```

You can use the other methods in a similar manner. Keep in mind that if you stop a service, you must use Start( ) to start it, but if you pause a service, you must use Continue( ) to resume it.

A problem arises when you want to stop a service that other services depend on. For example, if you want to stop the IISADMIN service and haven't stopped dependent services, you'll get the following error message:

```
A stop control has been sent to a service that other running services
are dependent on.
```

You'll need to stop the dependent services before you can stop this service. Fortunately, if you try to start a service that is dependent on another service that is stopped, Windows is smart enough to start the dependent service as well. To see how this works, stop the IISADMIN and W3SVC services and then try to start W3SVC. You'll discover that both IISADMIN and W3SVC start.

Listing 18-4 shows a script that you can use to manage services. This script combines some of the techniques we've discussed previously and is not meant to be complete. You'll need to add to the script to suit your needs.

LISTING 18-4

Managing Services

VBScript
servicemgr.vbs

```
' ************************
' Script: Service Manager
' Version: 1.1.5
' Creation Date: 06/15/2008
' Last Modified: 07/20/2008
' Author: William R. Stanek
' Email: williamstanek@aol.com
' Copyright (c) 2008 William R. Stanek
' ************************
```

continued

LISTING 18-4   *(continued)*

```
On Error Resume Next
lf = Chr(13) & Chr(10)

WScript.Echo "========================================" & lf
WScript.Echo "==    Service Manager Script    ==" & lf
WScript.Echo "========================================" & lf

WScript.Echo "Enter local or remote host name: " & lf

host = WScript.StdIn.ReadLine()

WScript.Echo lf & "Enter service to manage: " & lf

servName = WScript.StdIn.ReadLine()

WScript.Echo lf & "G) Start Service" & lf
WScript.Echo "S) Stop Service" & lf

action = WScript.StdIn.ReadLine()

action = LCase(action)

Set c = GetObject("WinNT://" & host & ",computer")
Set s = c.GetObject("Service", servName)

manageService s, action

sub manageService(obj, a)

 On Error Resume Next

 Select Case a
  Case "g"

    If obj.Status = 1 Then

     obj.Start

     WScript.Echo "========================================"
     WScript.Echo "Starting Service..."
     WScript.Echo "========================================" & lf

    Else

     WScript.Echo "========================================"
     WScript.Echo "Service is running already."
     WScript.Echo "========================================"
```

```
   WScript.Echo "Checking dependent services."
   WScript.Echo "========================================" & lf
   deps = obj.Dependencies

   If VarType(deps) = vbString Then
     WScript.Echo "Dependency: " & deps & lf

     Set ds = c.GetObject("Service", deps)
     checkStatus(ds)
   Else

   For Each a In deps
     WScript.Echo "Dependency: " & a & lf

     Set ds = c.GetObject("Service", a)
     checkStatus(ds)

   Next
  End If
 End If

Case "s"

  If obj.Status = 4 Then

   obj.Stop
   WScript.Echo "========================================"
   WScript.Echo "Stopping Service..."
   WScript.Echo "========================================" & lf

  Else

   WScript.Echo "========================================"
   WScript.Echo "Service is already stopped."
   WScript.Echo "========================================"
   WScript.Echo "Checking dependent services."
   WScript.Echo "========================================" & lf
   deps = obj.Dependencies

   If VarType(deps) = vbString Then
     WScript.Echo "Dependency: " & deps & lf

     Set ds = c.GetObject("Service", deps)
     checkStatus(ds)
   Else

   For Each a In deps
     WScript.Echo "Dependency: " & a & lf
```

continued

LISTING 18-4   *(continued)*

```
         Set ds = c.GetObject("Service", a)
         checkStatus(ds)

      Next
     End If

    End If

  Case Else

     WScript.Echo "Please re-run script and enter a valid option"

 End Select
End Sub

sub checkStatus(obj)

 On Error Resume Next

 Select Case obj.Status
  Case 1

     WScript.Echo "========================================"
     WScript.Echo "Service not running."
     WScript.Echo "Checking dependent services."
     WScript.Echo "========================================" & lf
      deps = obj.Dependencies

     If VarType(deps) = vbString Then
        WScript.Echo "Dependency: " & deps & lf

        Set ds = c.GetObject("Service", deps)
        checkStatus(ds)
     Else

      For Each a In deps
        WScript.Echo "Dependency: " & a & lf

        Set ds = c.GetObject("Service", a)
        checkStatus(ds)

      Next
     End If

   Case 4

     WScript.Echo obj.Class & " " & obj.Name & " is running normally"
```

```
      WScript.Echo lf

   Case 7

      WScript.Echo obj.Class & " " & obj.Name & " is paused." & lf

   Case 8

      WScript.Echo "========================================"
      WScript.Echo "Service error!"
      WScript.Echo "Checking dependent services."
      WScript.Echo "========================================" & lf
       deps = obj.Dependencies

      If VarType(deps) = vbString Then
         WScript.Echo "Dependency: " & deps & lf

         Set ds = c.GetObject("Service", deps)
         checkStatus(ds)
      Else

       For Each a In deps
         WScript.Echo "Dependency: " & a & lf

         Set ds = c.GetObject("Service", a)
         checkStatus(ds)

       Next
      End If

   Case Else

      WScript.Echo obj.Class & " " & obj.Name & " is changing states."
      WScript.Echo lf

  End Select
End Sub
```

Output

```
========================================

==    Service Manager Script    ==

========================================

Enter local or remote host name:

zeta
```

continued

LISTING 18-4 *(continued)*

```
Enter service to manage:

w3svc

G) Start Service

S) Stop Service

g
========================================
Starting Service...
========================================
```

The script relies on the manageService and checkStatus subroutines to perform most of the work. The manageService subroutine expects to be passed a service object and an action to be performed. For example:

```
sub manageService(obj, a)
  ...
end sub
```

The subroutine then uses these arguments to start or stop services. If the referenced service is already started (or stopped), the script calls checkStatus to display the status of dependent services. You'll find this useful when you want to control services and the services they depend on.

Managing Open Resources and User Sessions

User sessions are created each time users connect to shared resources on a server. If a user opens a file for editing, the file is also listed as an open resource on the server. Problems with open files and user sessions can often affect network operations. If a file is listed as open but no user is actually using it, another user may not be able to access the file. To resolve this problem you need to end the user session causing the problem or close the open file. For this and other reasons, you'll find that you often need to manage user sessions and open resources, especially in a busy network environment.

Viewing open files and user sessions

In Windows, you normally manage open files and user sessions through the Computer Management console. You view connections to shared resources as follows:

1. In the Computer Management console, right-click the Computer Management entry in the console tree. Then select Connect to Another Computer on the shortcut menu. You can now choose the system whose services you want to manage.

2. Click the plus sign (+) next to System Tools, and then click the plus sign next to Shared Folders.

3. Select Sessions to view or manage user sessions. The information provided in the Sessions node tells you the following information:

   ▪ **User:** Names of users or computers connected to shared resources. Computer names are shown with a $ suffix to differentiate them from users.

   ▪ **Computer:** IP address of the computer being used.

   ▪ **Type:** Type of computer being used.

   ▪ **Open Files:** Number of files the user has open.

   ▪ **Connected Time:** Elapsed time since the connection was established.

   ▪ **Idle Time:** Elapsed time since the connection was last used.

   ▪ **Guest:** Identifies users accessing the computer through a guest account or default guest access.

4. Select Open Files to view or manage open files. The Open Files node provides the following information about resource usage:

   ▪ **Open File:** File or folder path to the open file on the local system.

   ▪ **File Locks:** Total number of file locks.

   ▪ **Accessed By:** Name of the user accessing the file.

   ▪ **Type:** Type of computer being used.

   ▪ **# Locks:** Number of locks on the resource.

   ▪ **Open Mode:** Access mode used when the resource was opened, such as Read or Read+Write mode.

Figure 18-3 shows Computer Management with the Open Files node selected. As you would expect, you can obtain similar information through Windows scripts. We'll show you how in the next section.

You can use Computer Management to get summary information on open files and user sessions.

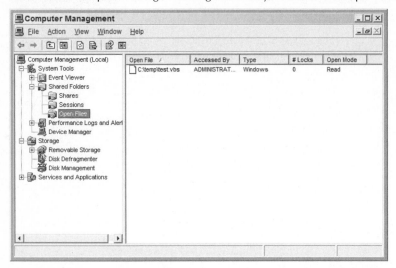

Viewing resources and sessions in scripts

In scripts, you view open files and user sessions through the `Resource` and `Session` objects. These objects can only be accessed through a `FileService` object. You obtain a `FileService` object through the LanManServer service. The `AdsPath` string should either not state the object type:

    WinNT://seattle/zeta/lanmanserver

or it should state the object type as `FileService`:

    WinNT://seattle/zeta/lanmanserver,fileservice

`FileService` is a special type of object that extends the standard `Service` object, adding several new properties and methods that you can use to work with resources and sessions. If you state the object type as `Service`, as was done in previous examples, you won't get the extended `FileService` interface and instead will get the standard `IADsService` interface.

Additional properties for `FileService` are:

- `Description`: A read/write string that describes the file service.

- `MaxUserCount`: A read/write integer value that identifies the maximum number of users allowed to run the service concurrently. A value of –1 indicates that no limit is set.

Additional methods for `FileService` are:

- `Resources()`: Gets an interface pointer on a collection object that represents current open resources for the file service.
- `Sessions()`: Gets an interface pointer on a collection object that represents current open sessions on the file service.

Listing 18-5 shows how you can display the standard and extended features of the `FileService` object. By iterating through each element in the `Resources` and `Sessions` collections, you can display a list of currently open files and active user sessions. You'll use this technique in the next section when you examine `Resource` and `Session` object properties.

LISTING 18-5

Viewing Resource and Sessions Usage

VBScript
fileservice.vbs

```
On Error Resume Next

Set s = GetObject("WinNT://seattle/zeta/lanmanserver,fileservice")

'Display service properties
WScript.Echo s.Class & " " & s.Name
WScript.Echo "==============================="
WScript.Echo "StartType: " & s.StartType
WScript.Echo "Description: " & s.Description
WScript.Echo "MaxUserCount: " & s.MaxUserCount
WScript.Echo "ServiceType: " & s.ServiceType
WScript.Echo "DisplayName: " & s.DisplayName
WScript.Echo "Path: " & s.Path
WScript.Echo "ErrorControl: " & s.ErrorControl
WScript.Echo "HostComputer: " & s.HostComputer
WScript.Echo "LoadOrderGroup: " & s.LoadOrderGroup
WScript.Echo "ServiceAccountName: " & s.ServiceAccountName
WScript.Echo "Dependencies: " & s.Dependencies
WScript.Echo "Status: " & s.Status

For Each resource In s.Resources
 WScript.Echo "Resource path: " & resource.Path
Next
For Each session In s.sessions
 WScript.Echo "Session name: " & session.Name
Next
```

continued

LISTING 18-5 *(continued)*

JScript
fileservice.js

```
var s = GetObject("WinNT://seattle/zeta/lanmanserver,fileservice")

//Display service properties
WScript.Echo(s.Class + " " + s.Name)
WScript.Echo("==============================")
WScript.Echo("StartType: " + s.StartType)
WScript.Echo("Description: " + s.Description)
WScript.Echo("MaxUserCount: " + s.MaxUserCount)
WScript.Echo("ServiceType: " + s.ServiceType)
WScript.Echo("DisplayName: " + s.DisplayName)
WScript.Echo("Path: " + s.Path)
WScript.Echo("ErrorControl: " + s.ErrorControl)
WScript.Echo("HostComputer: " + s.HostComputer)
WScript.Echo("LoadOrderGroup: " + s.LoadOrderGroup)
WScript.Echo("ServiceAccountName: " + s.ServiceAccountName)

try {
 WScript.Echo("Dependencies: " + s.Dependencies)
}
catch (e) {
  //property setting not available
}
try {
 WScript.Echo("Status: " + s.Get("Status"))
}
catch (e) {
  //property setting not available
}

 rList = new Enumerator(s.Resources());

 for (; !rList.atEnd(); rList.moveNext())
 {
  resource = rList.item()
  WScript.Echo("Resource path: " + resource.Path)
 }

 sList = new Enumerator(s.Sessions());

 for (; !sList.atEnd(); sList.moveNext())
 {
  session = sList.item()
  WScript.Echo("Session name: " + session.Name)
 }
```

Output

```
FileService lanmanserver
================================
StartType: 2
Description:
MaxUserCount: -1
ServiceType: 32
DisplayName: Server
Path: F:\WIN2000\System32\services.exe
ErrorControl: 1
HostComputer: WinNT://seattle/zeta
LoadOrderGroup:
ServiceAccountName: LocalSystem
Resource path: E:\myBooks\docs
Resource path: E:\myBooks\docs\chapter1.rtf
Session name: WRSTANEK\127.0.0.1
```

Working with Resource and Session objects

You use `Resource` objects to view open resources for a file service. The properties for `Resource` objects are:

- `LockCount`: The number of locks on a resource.

- `Path`: The file path of the resource.

- `User`: The name of the user who opened the resource.

- `UserPath`: An `AdsPath` string of the user object that is accessing the resource.

You use `Session` objects to view active user sessions for the file service. The properties for `Session` objects are:

- `Computer`: The name of the client workstation from which the session initiated.

- `ComputerPath`: The `AdsPath` of the related computer object.

- `ConnectTime`: The number of minutes since the session started.

- `IdleTime`: The number of minutes the session has been idle.

- `User`: The name of the user that initiated the session.

- `UserPath`: The `AdsPath` of the related user object.

All properties of `Resource` and `Session` objects are read-only. This means you can view them but cannot set them, which makes sense because these values are set automatically by the operating system.

Listing 18-6 shows a script that displays summary information for open files and user sessions on a specified computer. We've written the script in both VBScript and JScript so you can compare the implementation techniques. Note the format of property values in the output. With resources, entries can relate to folder paths and to file paths. Generally, if you have an entry for a file path, you'll also see an entry for the related folder path. With sessions, you'll see that the session name is a combination of the username and the IP address from which the session originates, such as WRSTANEK\127.0.0.1. You may also see entries that begin with a dollar sign ($), which indicates a computer account rather than a user account.

LISTING 18-6

Viewing Resource and Sessions Usage

VBScript
shareusage.vbs

```
' ***********************
' Script: Share Usage
' Version: 1.1.5
' Creation Date: 06/15/2008
' Last Modified: 07/21/2008
' Author: William R. Stanek
' Email: williamstanek@aol.com
' Copyright (c) 2008 William R. Stanek
' ***********************

On Error Resume Next
lf = Chr(13) & Chr(10)

WScript.Echo "=======================================" & lf
WScript.Echo "==     Share Usage Script     ==" & lf
WScript.Echo "=======================================" & lf

WScript.Echo "Enter local or remote host name: " & lf

host = WScript.StdIn.ReadLine()

On Error Resume Next

Set s = GetObject("WinNT://" & host & "/lanmanserver,fileservice")

'Display open files
WScript.Echo lf & s.Class & " " & s.Name
WScript.Echo "=============================="
WScript.Echo "Open Files: " & lf

For Each resource In s.Resources
  WScript.Echo "File or Folder Path: " & resource.Path
```

```
 WScript.Echo "Number of Locks: " & resource.LockCount
 WScript.Echo "User: " & resource.User & lf
Next

'Display user sessions
WScript.Echo "==============================="
WScript.Echo "User sessions: " & lf

For Each session In s.sessions
 WScript.Echo "Session name: " & session.Name
 WScript.Echo "User: " & session.User
 WScript.Echo "Computer: " & session.Computer
 WScript.Echo "Connect Time: " & session.ConnectTime
 WScript.Echo "Idle Time: " & session.IdleTime & lf
Next
```

JScript
shareusage.js

```
// ************************
// Script: Share Usage
// Version: 1.1.5
// Creation Date: 6/17/2008
// Last Modified: 7/21/2008
// Author: William R. Stanek
// Email: williamstanek@aol.com
// Copyright (c) 2008 William R. Stanek
// ************************

lf = "\r\n"

WScript.Echo("=========================================" + lf)
WScript.Echo("==    Share Usage Script    ==" + lf)
WScript.Echo("=========================================" + lf)

WScript.Echo("Enter local or remote host name: " + lf)

host = WScript.StdIn.ReadLine()

var s = GetObject("WinNT://" + host + "/lanmanserver,fileservice")

//Display open files
WScript.Echo(lf + s.Class + " " + s.Name)
WScript.Echo("==============================")
WScript.Echo("Open Files: " + lf)


 rList = new Enumerator(s.Resources());
```

continued

LISTING 18-6   *(continued)*

```
 for (; !rList.atEnd(); rList.moveNext())
 {
  resource = rList.item()
  WScript.Echo("File or Folder Path: " + resource.Path)
  WScript.Echo("Number of Locks: " + resource.LockCount)
  WScript.Echo("User: " + resource.User + lf)
 }

//Display user sessions
WScript.Echo("==============================")
WScript.Echo("User sessions: " + lf)

 sList = new Enumerator(s.Sessions());

 for (; !sList.atEnd(); sList.moveNext())
 {
  session = sList.item()
  WScript.Echo("Session name: " + session.Name)
  WScript.Echo("User: " + session.User)
  WScript.Echo("Computer: " + session.Computer)
  WScript.Echo("Connect Time: " + session.ConnectTime)
  WScript.Echo("Idle Time: " + session.IdleTime + lf)
 }
```

Output

```
=======================================

==   Share Usage Script   ==

=======================================

Enter local or remote host name:

zeta

FileService lanmanserver
==============================
Open Files:

File or Folder Path: E:\myBooks\docs
Number of Locks: 0
User: WRSTANEK

File or Folder Path: E:\myBooks\docs\chapter1.rtf
Number of Locks: 0
User: WRSTANEK
```

```
===============================
User sessions:

Session name: WRSTANEK\127.0.0.1
User: WRSTANEK
Computer: 127.0.0.1
Connect Time: 7259
Idle Time: 7236
```

In Windows scripts, you can close open files and end user sessions, using the Remove() method of the IADsCollection interface. However, you can only do this if the files or sessions are inactive or erroneously listed. The following example ends all inactive user sessions:

VBScript

```
Set s = GetObject("WinNT://zeta/lanmanserver,fileservice")
Set coll = fso.Sessions

For Each session In coll
 coll.Remove "Session", session.Name
Next
```

JScript

```
var s = GetObject("WinNT://" + host + "/lanmanserver,fileservice")

sList = new Enumerator(s.Sessions());

for (; !sList.atEnd(); sList.moveNext())
{
  session = sList.item()
  sList.Remove("Session", session.Name)
}
```

Summary

This chapter explored working with services, open resources, and user sessions. Services provide essential functions for Windows computers. You can use scripts to view service settings and to manage service configuration using the properties and methods of the IADsService interface. This interface is extended by IADsFileService and IADsFileServiceOperations, which provide additional features for FileService objects. These additional features enable you to work with open resources and user sessions. Groups of resources and sessions are represented by Resources and Sessions collections, which in turn, contain one or more Resource or Session objects.

Chapter 19

Maintaining Shared Directories, Printer Queues, and Print Jobs

In previous chapters, you learned how to manage network resources, in particular network drives and network printer connections. Now it's time to extend this knowledge so that you can create, control, and configure related resources; namely shared folders, print queues, and print jobs. A key concept on any network is resource sharing; both folders and printers can be shared.

When you share a folder, you make all of its files and subfolders available to network users. Authorized users can then access this shared folder by creating a network drive that points to the folder. Using ADSI, you can create shared folders and set shared folder properties.

When you share printers, you configure a printer for remote access over the network. If a user prints a document, the document is routed to a print queue where it is stored prior to printing. Documents in a print queue are referred to as print jobs. Print jobs can be handled in FIFO (first in, first out) fashion. They can also be printed according to their priority—for example, a print job with high priority is printed before a print job with low priority.

Working with Shared Folders

As you know, shared folders are used to make data available over the network. What you may not know is how shared folders generally are managed. Normally, you create and configure shared folders using Windows Explorer or Computer Management. Once you create a shared folder, you can also use Computer Management to view and manage both open resources and user sessions related to the shared folder.

You can also manage shared folders in Windows scripts. Chapter 10 showed you how to map network drives to access shares. Chapter 18 showed you how to view and manage open resources and user sessions for shares. Now let's look at scripting techniques that help you manage the shared folders.

Folder sharing essentials

As with open resources and user sessions, you access shared folders through the `FileService` object of the LanManServer service. After you obtain a pointer to the `FileService` object, you can then create file shares or work with existing file shares through the `FileShare` object. The following example looks at all file shares on a computer called Zeta:

```
Set fs = GetObject("WinNT://zeta/LanmanServer,FileService")
For Each sh In fs
    WScript.Echo sh.name
Next
```

The example returns a list of shares on Zeta, such as:

```
PRINT$
NETLOGON
SYSVOL
CorpDataShare
myBooks
```

The list does not show default shares (other than `PRINT$`). Default shares are shared folders created automatically by the operating system and are also referred to as administrative shares. If you use the `NET SHARE` command-line utility to list the shares on a computer, you'll see all shares (both default and standard). To see a list of all shares, type **net share** at the command line. The resulting output should look similar to the following:

```
Share name    Resource                                        Remark
------------------------------------------------------------------------------
I$            I:\                                             Default share
IPC$                                                          Remote IPC
D$            D:\                                             Default share
print$        F:\WIN2000\System32\spool\drivers
                                                              Printer Drivers
ADMIN$        F:\WIN2000                                      Remote Admin
C$            C:\                                             Default share
E$            E:\                                             Default share
F$            F:\                                             Default share
CorpDataShare
              F:\CorpData
myBooks       E:\myBooks
NETLOGON      F:\WIN2000\sysvol\sysvol\seattle.domain.com\SCRIPTS
                                                              Logon server share
SYSVOL        F:\WIN2000\sysvol\sysvol                        Logon server share
```

```
BrotherM       LPT1:                    Spooled   Brother MFC-5550
HPDeskJe       LPT1:                    Spooled   HP DeskJet 890C
The command completed successfully.
```

> **NOTE** Note that the last two entries in the code are for shared printers.

Table 19-1 provides an overview of how administrative shares are used.

TABLE 19-1

Using Administrative Shares

Share Name	Description
ADMIN$	Provides access to the operating system %SystemRoot% during remote administration
Driveletter$	Allows an administrator to connect to the root folder of a drive; shares are shown as C$, D$, E$, and so on.
FAX$	Supports network faxes
IPC$	Supports named pipes during remote access
Microsoft UAM Volume	User Access Manager volume; provides access control files for non-Windows users
NETLOGON	Supports the Net Logon service
PRINT$	Provides access to printer drivers, which are used with network printers
SYSVOL	Active Directory system volume; used by Active Directory

Examining shared folders and their properties

When you work with shared folders that already exist, you can obtain their objects directly through the WinNT provider. To do this, you use the following syntax for the ADsPath String:

```
WinNT://ComputerName/lanmanserver/ShareName,FileShare
```

where *ComputerName* is the name of the computer and *ShareName* is the actual name of the share, such as:

```
WinNT://Zeta/lanmanserver/netlogon,FileShare
```

Each shared folder has a set of properties that you can work with. These properties are summarized in Table 19-2.

TABLE 19-2

FileShare Object Properties

Property	Status	Value Type	Min. Range	Max. Range	Multiple Values
CurrentUserCount	RO	Integer	0	2147483647	False
Description	RW	String	0	257	False
HostComputer	RW	ADsPath String	0	256	False
MaxUserCount	RW	Integer	0	2147483647	False
Path	RW	Path String	0	340	False

Most of these properties are rather straightforward. CurrentUserCount returns the current number of users connected to this share. Description sets or gets a description of the file share. HostComputer sets or gets the ADsPath to the host computer on which the share resides. Path sets or gets the file path to shared directory. MaxUserCount sets or gets the maximum number of concurrent users for the share. If MaxUserCount is set to –1, there is no maximum set for the shared folder.

Listing 19-1 shows how you could display the properties of the Netlogon share and then change the maximum number of users.

LISTING 19-1

Examining Properties of Shared Folders

VBScript
foldershare.vbs

```
Set fs = GetObject("WinNT://zeta/LanmanServer/netlogon,fileshare")
WScript.Echo fs.Name
WScript.Echo "Current User Count: " & fs.CurrentUserCount
WScript.Echo "Description: " & fs.Description
WScript.Echo "Host Computer: " & fs.HostComputer
WScript.Echo "Maximum User Count: " & fs.MaxUserCount
WScript.Echo "File Path: " & fs.Path
```

JScript
foldershare.js

```
var fs = GetObject("WinNT://zeta/LanmanServer/netlogon,fileshare");
WScript.Echo(fs.Name);
WScript.Echo("Current User Count: " + fs.CurrentUserCount);
WScript.Echo("Description: " + fs.Description);
WScript.Echo("Host Computer: " + fs.HostComputer);
```

```
WScript.Echo("Maximum User Count: " + fs.MaxUserCount);
WScript.Echo("File Path: " + fs.Path);
```

Output

```
NETLOGON
Current User Count: 0
Description: Logon server share
Host Computer: WinNT://SEATTLE/zeta
Maximum User Count: -1
File Path: F:\WIN2000\sysvol\sysvol\seattle.domain.com\SCRIPTS
```

Creating and deleting shared folders

As with many other objects, you create and delete shared folders using the `Create()` and `Delete()` methods of the IADsContainer interface. Before you can call either of these methods, you must bind to the container for the LanManServer service, and then you can call `Create()` or `Delete()` as necessary.

The only mandatory properties for creating a shared folder are `Path` and `MaxUserCount`. However, you must also specify the name for the shared folder. Listing 19-2 creates a shared folder called CorpData.

LISTING 19-2

Creating Shared Folders

VBScript
createshare.vbs

```
Set cont = GetObject("WinNT://seattle/zeta/LanmanServer,FileService")
Set fs = cont.Create("FileShare", "CorpData")
fs.Path = "C:\Data\Users\Docs"
fs.MaxUserCount = -1
fs.SetInfo
```

JScript
createshare.js

```
var cont = GetObject("WinNT://seattle/zeta/LanmanServer,FileService");
var fs = cont.Create("FileShare", "CorpData");
fs.Path = "C:\\Data\\Users\\Docs";
fs.MaxUserCount = -1;
fs.SetInfo();
```

You delete shares using a similar technique. First you bind to the container for the `FileService` object. Then you delete the shared folder by name using the `Delete()` method, such as:

VBScript

```
Set cont = GetObject("WinNT://seattle/zeta/LanmanServer,FileService")
cont.Delete("FileShare", "CorpData")
```

JScript

```
var cont = GetObject("WinNT://seattle/zeta/LanmanServer,FileService");
cont.Delete("FileShare", "CorpData");
```

Managing Print Queues

Through print queues, administrators can view and manage printers and pending print jobs. In ADSI, print queues are controlled with the `PrintQueue` object, which is implemented through the `IADsPrintQueue` and `IADsPrintQueueOperations` interfaces.

Examining print queues

Each printer configured for use on the network can have one or more print queues associated with it. For example, you could configure one print queue to handle high-priority printing and another to handle low-priority printing. Both print queues could point to a network-attached printer, and through these print queues you could manage your printing.

In Windows scripts, you access print queues through the `Computer` object. Each print queue configured on the computer will have a unique object associated with it. The name of this object is the same as the shared printer name, which can be obtained by typing **net share** at the command prompt. If a printer is registered in Active Directory, you can also obtain shared printer names through the Find Printers dialog box. Follow these steps:

1. Click Start, point to Search, and then select For Printers. This displays the Find Printers dialog box.
2. Enter * in the Name field, and then click Find Now. The find dialog box will return a list of all printers that are on the network.
3. Right-click on the printer entry that you want to examine and then select Properties.
4. In the Properties dialog box, select the Sharing tab, and then note the shared name of the printer. This is the name you'll use to access the PrintQueue object for this printer.

In a script, you would obtain the name of print queues through the associated `Computer` object. For example, if a computer named Zeta is a print server and has several print queues attached to it, you could obtain the shared printer name by filtering the related container on the PrintQueue object, such as:

VBScript

```
Set c = GetObject("WinNT://Zeta,computer")
c.Filter = Array("PrintQueue")
n = 0

For Each p In c
 n = n + 1
 Set pq = GetObject(p.ADsPath)
 WScript.Echo "Print Queue " & CStr(n) & ": " & pq.Name
Next
```

Output

```
Print Queue 1: HPEngineering
Print Queue 2: HPMarketing
Print Queue 3: HPTechnology
```

Another way to examine PrintQueue objects is to use an Enumerator to examine all objects in the Computer object's container using a loop to search for the PrintQueue class, such as:

JScript

```
var comp = GetObject("WinNT://Zeta,Computer");
n = 0;

tlist = new Enumerator(comp);
for (; !tlist.atEnd(); tlist.moveNext())
 {
 s = tlist.item();
 if (s.Class == "PrintQueue") {
  n += 1;
  WScript.Echo("Print Queue " + n + ": " + s.Name);
 }
}
```

Output

```
Print Queue 1: HPEngineering
Print Queue 2: HPMarketing
Print Queue 3: HPTechnology
```

You could then manage the HPEngineering, HPMarketing, and HPTechnology print queues on Zeta. To manage the queues individually, you could use any of the following ADsPath strings:

```
WinNT://seattle/zeta/HPEngineering
WinNT://seattle/zeta/HPMarketing
WinNT://seattle/zeta/HPTechnology
```

You could also manipulate the print queues within the For loops, which would allow you to manage all of the print queues on a particular computer.

Using the PrintQueue object

The PrintQueue object has many properties associated with it. An overview of properties for the PrintQueue object is provided in Table 19-3. You use properties to examine and control configuration of the print queue.

TABLE 19-3

PrintQueue Object Properties

Property	Status	Value Type	Min. Range	Max. Range	Multiple Values
Action	RW	Integer	0	2147483647	False
Attributes	RW	Integer	0	2147483647	False
BannerPage	RW	Path String	0	340	False
Datatype	RW	String	0	256	False
DefaultJobPriority	RW	Integer	1	99	False
Description	RW	String	0	257	False
JobCount	RO	Integer	0	2147483647	False
Location	RW	String	0	256	False
Model	RW	String	0	256	False
NetAddresses	RW	String, Array	0	256	True
ObjectGUID	RO	String	0	256	False
PrintDevices	RW	String, Array	0	256	True
PrinterName	RW	String	0	256	False
PrintProcessor	RW	String	0	256	False
Priority	RW	Integer	1	99	False
StartTime	RW	Time String	n/a	n/a	False
Status	RO	Integer	0	16777216	False
UntilTime	RW	Time String	n/a	n/a	False

Listing 19-3 shows how you could display properties of print queues on a particular computer. Note the output values for each property. We discuss key properties and their uses in the next section.

LISTING 19-3

Working with Print Queues

VBScript
printqueue.vbs

```
On Error Resume Next

Set c = GetObject("WinNT://Zeta,computer")
c.Filter = Array("PrintQueue")

For Each p In c

 Set pq = GetObject(p.ADsPath)
 WScript.Echo "Shared Printer: " & pq.Name
 WScript.Echo "============================="
 WScript.Echo "Action " & pq.Action
 WScript.Echo "Attributes " & pq.Attributes
 WScript.Echo "Banner Page " & pq.BannerPage
 WScript.Echo "Data Type " & pq.Datatype
 WScript.Echo "Default Job Priority " & pq.DefaultJobPriority
 WScript.Echo "Description " & pq.Description
 WScript.Echo "Host Computer " & pq.HostComputer
 WScript.Echo "Job Count " & pq.JobCount
 WScript.Echo "Location " & pq.Location
 WScript.Echo "Model " & pq.Model
 WScript.Echo "Object GUID " & pq.ObjectGUID
 WScript.Echo "Print Devices " & pq.PrintDevices
 WScript.Echo "Print Processor " & pq.PrintProcessor
 WScript.Echo "Print Queue Name " & pq.PrinterName
 WScript.Echo "Queue Priority " & pq.Priority
 WScript.Echo "Start Time " & pq.StartTime
 WScript.Echo "Until Time " & pq.UntilTime

Next
```

Output

```
Shared Printer: HPEngineering
=============================
Action 1
Attributes 8776
Banner Page C:\WIN2000\system32\sysprint.sep
Data Type RAW
```

continued

421

LISTING 19-3   *(continued)*

```
Default Job Priority 0
Description Engineering Departmental Printer
Job Count 1
Location 16th Floor
Model HP LaserJet 8000
Object GUID {50DD3D14-25F3-4740-BB87-A1605BE46E95}
Print Devices LPT1:
Print Processor WinPrint
Print Queue Name HP8000Eng
Queue Priority 1
Start Time 4:00:00 PM
Until Time 4:00:00 PM
```

Using a banner page

The `PrintQueue` object properties are helpful in managing printers. One of the most useful properties is `BannerPage`, which lets you view or set the path to a banner-page file used to separate print
jobs. Banner pages can be used at the beginning of print jobs in order to clearly identify where one
print job starts and another ends. They also can be used to change the print device mode, such as
whether the print device uses PostScript or PCL (Printer Control Language).

Windows provides a default set of banner-page files. These files are saved in the `%SystemRoot%\`
`system32` folder with a .SEP file extension. Each file has a different use:

- `pcl.sep`: Switches the printer to PCL mode and prints a banner page before each
  document.

- `pscript.sep`: Sets the printer to PostScript mode but doesn't print a banner page.

- `sysprint.sep`: Sets the printer to PostScript mode and prints a banner page before each
  document.

If you don't like the banner pages provided, you can use the default banner page files as the basis for
new ones. You set the banner page for a printer as follows:

VBScript

```
Set pq = GetObject("WinNT://seattle/zeta/HPDeskJe,PrintQueue")

Set WshShell = WScript.CreateObject("WScript.Shell")
sysroot = WshShell.ExpandEnvironmentStrings("%SystemRoot%")

pq.BannerPage = sysroot & "\system32\sysprint.sep"
pq.SetInfo
```

JScript

```
var pq = GetObject("WinNT://seattle/zeta/HPDeskJe,PrintQueue");

var WshShell = WScript.CreateObject("WScript.Shell");
sysroot = WshShell.ExpandEnvironmentStrings("%SystemRoot%");

pq.BannerPage = sysroot + "\\system32\\sysprint.sep";
pq.SetInfo();
```

If you don't want a printer to use a banner page, set the `BannerPage` property to an empty string, such as:

VBScript

```
Set pq = GetObject("WinNT://seattle/zeta/HPDeskJe,PrintQueue")
pq.BannerPage = ""
pq.SetInfo
```

JScript

```
var pq = GetObject("WinNT://seattle/zeta/HPDeskJe,PrintQueue");
pq.BannerPage = "";
pq.SetInfo();
```

Working with general printer information

Many `PrintQueue` properties provide general information, such as the printer model or print device in use. Usually, you'll want to view this information, rather than set it. For example, you could create a script to obtain summary information on all printers on the network. The type of information you might collect could include the printer name, model, description, and location.

More technical information that you may want to gather for administrators includes:

- **Network Address:** Tells you the IP address of a network-attached printer. Printers can have multiple IP addresses.
- **Print Device:** Tells you how the printer is connected to the print server. Printers can be connected through one or more ports, such as LPT1 or LPT1 and LPT2.
- **Print processor:** Creates the raw print data necessary for printing. The format of the data is based on the data type set for the print processor. The primary print processor on Windows is WinPrint. This print processor supports several different data types.
- **Data type:** Identifies the data type. In most cases, the data type is controlled by the Print Spooler service. Because of this, the data type shown by the `DataType` property is rarely used.

If you move a printer from one location to another, you'll probably need to update the printer's location and description. You may also need to change the print device or network address. An example is shown as Listing 19-4.

LISTING 19-4

Setting Print Queue Information

VBScript
printinfo.vbs

```
Set pq = GetObject("WinNT://seattle/zeta/HPMarketing,PrintQueue")
pq.Location = "15th Floor SE"
pq.Description = "Color printer for marketing department"
pq.NetAddresses = "192.168.10.5"
pq.SetInfo
```

JScript
printinfo.vbs

```
var pq = GetObject("WinNT://seattle/zeta/HPMarketing,PrintQueue");
pq.Location = "15th Floor SE";
pq.Description = "Color printer for marketing department";
pq.NetAddresses = "192.168.10.5";
pq.SetInfo();
```

Prioritizing print queues and print jobs

Other `PrintQueue` properties control when and how documents are printed. When multiple print queues point to the same physical print device, you may want to control the priority of the print queue. In this way, you could have a high-priority print queue for documents that are needed immediately and a low-priority print queue for all other documents.

You control print queue priority with the `Priority` property. A priority of 1 is the lowest priority. A priority of 99 is the highest priority. If you create two print queues, one with a priority of 1 and the other with a priority of 99, documents in the second queue will always print before documents in the first queue.

Another way to control document printing is to set a default priority for print jobs. Print jobs always print in order of priority. Jobs with higher priority print before jobs with lower priority. Remember that the range of priorities is from 1 to 99.

The following example sets the queue priority to 10 and the default job priority to 1:

VBScript

```
Set pq = GetObject("WinNT://seattle/zeta/HPTechnology,PrintQueue")
pq.Priority = 10
pq.DefaultJobPriority = 1
pq.SetInfo
```

JScript

```
var pq = GetObject("WinNT://seattle/zeta/HPTechnology,PrintQueue");
pq.Priority = 10;
pq.DefaultJobPriority = 1;
pq.SetInfo();
```

Scheduling print queue availability

Print queues are either always available or available only during certain hours. You control print queue availability through the StartTime and UntilTime properties. If these properties are set to the same value, the print queue is always available. If these properties are set to different times, the print queue is only available during the specified time.

You could specify that a print queue is only available after normal business hours by setting StartTime to 5 p.m. and UntilTime to 9 a.m., such as:

VBScript

```
Set pq = GetObject("WinNT://seattle/zeta/HPTechnology2,PrintQueue")
pq.StartTime = "5:00:00 PM"
pq.UntilTime = "9:00:00 AM"
pq.SetInfo
```

JScript

```
var pq = GetObject("WinNT://seattle/zeta/HPTechnology2,PrintQueue");
pq.StartTime = "5:00:00 PM";
pq.UntilTime = "9:00:00 AM";
pq.SetInfo();
```

Checking print queue status

The print queue status tells you the status of the print queue and the physical print device. You can use the status to determine if the printer is jammed, out of paper, and much more.

Checking the status of a print queue is easy; you just obtain the value of the Status property, such as:

```
var pq = GetObject("WinNT://seattle/zeta/HPEngineering,PrintQueue")
WScript.Echo(pq.Status)
```

Understanding precisely what the status code means is more challenging than merely obtaining the status code because there is a fairly extensive list of status codes. Table 19-4 shows the list.

TABLE 19-4

Print Queue Status Codes

Constant	Code	Description
–	0	Print is running normally.
ADS_PRINTER_PAUSED	1	Print queue is paused.
ADS_PRINTER_PENDING_DELETION	2	Print queue is being deleted.
ADS_PRINTER_ERROR	3	Printer error
ADS_PRINTER_PAPER_JAM	4	Paper is jammed in the printer.
ADS_PRINTER_PAPER_OUT	5	Printer is out of paper.
ADS_PRINTER_MANUAL_FEED	6	Printer is set for manual feed.
ADS_PRINTER_PAPER_PROBLEM	7	Printer has a paper problem.
ADS_PRINTER_OFFLINE	8	Printer offline
ADS_PRINTER_IO_ACTIVE	256	Printer IO active
ADS_PRINTER_BUSY	512	Printer busy
ADS_PRINTER_PRINTING	1024	Printer is printing.
ADS_PRINTER_OUTPUT_BIN_FULL	2048	Printer output bin is full.
ADS_PRINTER_NOT_AVAILABLE	4096	Printer not available
ADS_PRINTER_WAITING	8192	Printer is waiting.
ADS_PRINTER_PROCESSING	16384	Printer is processing.
ADS_PRINTER_INITIALIZING	32768	Printer is initializing.
ADS_PRINTER_WARMING_UP	65536	Printer is warming up.
ADS_PRINTER_TONER_LOW	131072	Printer is low on toner.
ADS_PRINTER_NO_TONER	262144	Printer is out of toner.
ADS_PRINTER_PAGE_PUNT	524288	Printer page punt
ADS_PRINTER_USER_INTERVENTION	1048576	Printer user intervention
ADS_PRINTER_OUT_OF_MEMORY	2097152	Printer is out of memory.
ADS_PRINTER_DOOR_OPEN	4194304	Printer door is open.
ADS_PRINTER_SERVER_UNKNOWN	8388608	Printer server has unknown error.
ADS_PRINTER_POWER_SAVE	16777216	Printer is in power save mode.

Rather than trying to handle all possible printer problems in a script, you'll probably want to focus on handling the most common problems. For example, you could create a script that periodically polls all printers on the network, checking for problems and displaying a list of possible ways to resolve these problems.

Listing 19-5 shows a script that monitors printers on a specified print server. The script has two key subroutines: printMon and checkPrinter. The printMon subroutine controls how often the script checks printers. The basic technique is to use WScript.Sleep to set a wait interval. This interval is in milliseconds with 300,000 milliseconds equaling 5 minutes. The checkPrinter subroutine displays the status of printers. This is handled with a Select Case structure that checks the status code.

LISTING 19-5

Monitoring Printers

VBScript
printmonitor.vbs

```
lf = Chr(13) & Chr(10)

WScript.Echo "=======================================" & lf
WScript.Echo "==     Printer Monitor     ==" & lf
WScript.Echo "=======================================" & lf

WScript.Echo "Enter name of print server to monitor: " & lf
host = WScript.StdIn.ReadLine()
printMon()

'Check printers at 5 minute intervals
sub printMon()

 Set c = GetObject("WinNT://" & host & ",computer")

 c.Filter = Array("PrintQueue")

WScript.Echo lf & "======================================="
WScript.Echo "Checking Printers on " & host
WScript.Echo "======================================="

For Each pq In c
 If pq.Status > 0 Then CheckPrinter(pq)
Next

'Wait 5 minutes before calling printMon again
WScript.Sleep(300000)

printMon()
```

continued

LISTING 19-5   *(continued)*

```
End Sub

'Display printer status for non-normal conditions
sub checkPrinter(obj)

 WScript.Echo lf
 WScript.Echo "Print Queue Name: " & obj.Name
 WScript.Echo "Printer Model: " & obj.Model
 WScript.Echo "Printer Location: " & obj.Location
 WScript.Echo "======================================="

 Select Case obj.Status
  Case 1
   WScript.Echo "Print Queue is Paused."

  Case 3
   WScript.Echo "Printer Error!"

  Case 4
   WScript.Echo "Paper Jam!"

  Case 5
   WScript.Echo "Printer is out of paper!"

  Case 6
   WScript.Echo "Printer set to manual paper feed."

  Case 7
   WScript.Echo "Paper problem on printer!"

  Case 8
   WScript.Echo "Printer is offline."

  Case 131072
   WScript.Echo "Printer is low on toner."

  Case 262144
   WScript.Echo "Printer is out of toner!"

  Case Else
    WScript.Echo "Printer is changing states or has error."
    WScript.Echo "Status: " & CStr(pq.Status)

 End Select

 WScript.Echo "======================================="
 WScript.Echo "======================================="
```

```
End Sub
```

Output

```
=========================================
==    Printer Monitor    ==
=========================================


Enter name of print server to monitor:

Zeta


=========================================
Checking Printers on Zeta
=========================================


Print Queue Name: HPEngineering
Printer Model: HP LaserJet 8000
Printer Location: 16th Floor SW
=========================================
Print Queue is Paused.
=========================================
=========================================


Print Queue Name: HPMarketing
Printer Model: HP LaserJet 8000
Printer Location: 16th Floor NE
=========================================
Print Queue is Paused.
=========================================
=========================================
```

Managing print queues

In addition to properties, the `PrintQueue` object also has methods. These methods are used to pause, resume, and purge the print queue. You pause a print queue by invoking its `Pause` method, such as:

VBScript

```
Set pq = GetObject("WinNT://seattle/zeta/HPEngineering,PrintQueue")
pq.Pause
```

JScript

```
var pq = GetObject("WinNT://seattle/zeta/HPEngineering,PrintQueue");
pq.Pause();
```

To resume printing, the script can invoke the print queue's `Resume` method. If you want to delete all documents in a print queue, call its `Purge` method. Here's an example:

VBScript

```
Set pq = GetObject("WinNT://seattle/zeta/HPEngineering,PrintQueue")
pq.Purge
```

JScript

```
var pq = GetObject("WinNT://seattle/zeta/HPEngineering,PrintQueue");
pq.Purge();
```

 **Any document that has spooled to the printer and is in the printer's memory will continue to print.**

Another useful method of the `PrintQueue` object is `PrintJobs`. The `PrintJobs` method retrieves a pointer to a collection of print jobs managed by the print queue. You can then iterate through this collection of print jobs to manage individual documents that are waiting to be printed. Working with print jobs is discussed in the next section.

Controlling Print Jobs

Now that you know how to work with print queues, let's take a look at working with print jobs. A busy print queue can have dozens of documents waiting to be printed. All of these documents are represented as `PrintJob` objects in the `PrintJobs` collection.

Examining print job properties

Each `PrintJob` object has properties that you can view and set. These properties are summarized in Table 19-5.

TABLE 19-5

Properties of Print Jobs

Property	Status	Value Type	Min. Range	Max. Range	Multiple Values
Description	RW	String	0	256	False
HostPrintQueue	RO	ADsPath String	0	256	False
Notify	RW	String	0	256	False
PagesPrinted	RO	Integer	0	2147483647	False
Position	RW	Integer	0	2147483647	False

Property	Status	Value Type	Min. Range	Max. Range	Multiple Values
Priority	RW	Integer	1	99	False
Size	RO	Integer	0	2147483647	False
StartTime	RW	Time String	n/a	n/a	False
Status	RO	Integer	0	256	False
TimeElapsed	RO	Integer	0	2147483647	False
TimeSubmitted	RO	Time String	n/a	n/a	False
TotalPages	RO	Integer	0	2147483647	False
UntilTime	RW	Time String	n/a	n/a	False
User	RO	String	0	256	False

Listing 19-6 provides a detailed example of working with print job properties. As the listing shows, you access print jobs through the `PrintJobs` collection.

LISTING 19-6

Monitoring Printers

VBScript
printjobs.vbs

```
On Error Resume Next
Set pq = GetObject("WinNT://zeta/HPDeskJe,PrintQueue")

For Each pj in pq.PrintJobs

    WScript.Echo "Print Job: " & pj.Name
    WScript.Echo "============================="
    WScript.Echo "Description: " & pj.Description
    WScript.Echo "Host Print Queue: " & pj.HostPrintQueue
    WScript.Echo "Notify: " & pj.Notify
    WScript.Echo "Notify Path: " & pj.NotifyPath
    WScript.Echo "Pages Printed: " & pj.PagesPrinted
    WScript.Echo "Position: " & pj.Position
    WScript.Echo "Priority: " & pj.Priority
    WScript.Echo "Size: " & pj.Size
    WScript.Echo "Start Time: " & pj.StartTime
```

continued

LISTING 19-6 *(continued)*

```
    WScript.Echo "Status: " & pj.Status
    WScript.Echo "Time Elapsed: " & pj.TimeElapsed
    WScript.Echo "Time Submitted: " & pj.TimeSubmitted
    WScript.Echo "Total Pages: " & pj.TotalPages
    WScript.Echo "Until Time: " & pj.UntilTime
    WScript.Echo "User: " & pj.User
    WScript.Echo "User Path: " & pj.UserPath
    WScript.Echo "=============================="

Next
```

Output

```
Print Job 2
==============================
Description: Microsoft Word - addresses.doc
Host Print Queue: WinNT://SEATTLE/zeta/HPDeskJet
Notify: Administrator
Pages Printed: 0
Position: 1
Priority: 1
Size: 917328
Start Time: 4:00:00 PM
Status: 0
Time Elapsed: 0
Time Submitted: 5/15/2008 3:25:48 PM
Total Pages: 39
Until Time: 4:00:00 PM
User: Administrator
==============================
```

While most of the print job properties are self-explanatory, a few deserve more attention. These are:

- HostPrintQueue: The ADsPath string that names the print queue processing this print job.
- Notify: The user to be notified when the print job is completed.
- NotifyPath: The ADsPath string for the user to be notified when the job is completed.
- PagesPrinted: The total number of pages printed in the current job.
- Position: The numeric position of the print job in the print queue.
- Priority: The priority of the print job from 1 (lowest) to 99 (highest).
- User: The name of user who submitted the print job.
- UserPath: The ADsPath string of the user who submitted the print job.

Print jobs can also have a status. A status of zero (0) indicates a normal condition. Any other status indicates a possible problem. Status codes for print jobs are summarized in Table 19-6.

TABLE 19-6

Print Job Status Codes

Constant	Status Code	Description
–	0	Normal
ADS_JOB_PAUSED	1	Job is paused.
ADS_JOB_ERROR	2	Job error
ADS_JOB_DELETING	4	Job is being deleted.
ADS_JOB_PRINTING	8	Job is printing.
ADS_JOB_OFFLINE	16	Job is offline.
ADS_JOB_PAPEROUT	32	Paper is out.
ADS_JOB_PRINTED	64	Job printed.
ADS_JOB_DELETED	256	Job was deleted.

Monitoring print job status

You can check print job status conditions in much the same way as you can check print queue status conditions. In fact, with a few modifications, you can use the print monitor script to monitor print jobs, as well. To see how, examine Listing 19-7.

LISTING 19-7

Monitoring Printers and Print Jobs

VBScript
printmonitor2.vbs

```
lf = Chr(13) & Chr(10)

WScript.Echo "=======================================" & lf
WScript.Echo "==    Printer Monitor    ==" & lf
WScript.Echo "=======================================" & lf

WScript.Echo "Enter name of print server to monitor: " & lf
host = WScript.StdIn.ReadLine()
```

continued

LISTING 19-7   *(continued)*

```
printMon()

'Check printers at 5 minute intervals
sub printMon()

 Set c = GetObject("WinNT://" & host & ",computer")

 c.Filter = Array("PrintQueue")

 WScript.Echo lf & "========================================"
 WScript.Echo "Checking Printers on " & host
 WScript.Echo "========================================"

 For Each pq In c
  If pq.Status > 0 Then CheckPrinter(pq)

  For Each j in pq.PrintJobs
   checkPrintJobs(j)
  Next
Next

 'Wait 5 minutes before calling printMon again
 WScript.Sleep(300000)

 printMon()

End Sub

'Display printer status for non-normal conditions
sub checkPrinter(obj)

 WScript.Echo lf
 WScript.Echo "Print Queue Name: " & obj.Name
 WScript.Echo "Printer Model: " & obj.Model
 WScript.Echo "Printer Location: " & obj.Location
 WScript.Echo "========================================"

 Select Case obj.Status
  Case 1
   WScript.Echo "Print Queue is Paused."
  Case 3
   WScript.Echo "Printer Error!"
  Case 4
   WScript.Echo "Paper Jam!"
  Case 5
   WScript.Echo "Printer is out of paper!"
  Case 6
   WScript.Echo "Printer set to manual paper feed."
```

```
    Case 7
     WScript.Echo "Paper problem on printer!"
    Case 8
     WScript.Echo "Printer is offline."
    Case 131072
     WScript.Echo "Printer is low on toner."
    Case 262144
     WScript.Echo "Printer is out of toner!"
    Case Else
       WScript.Echo "Printer is changing states or has error."
       WScript.Echo "Status: " & CStr(pq.Status)
   End Select

   WScript.Echo "======================================"
   WScript.Echo "======================================"

End Sub

'Display printer job status for non-normal conditions
sub checkPrintJobs(pj)

  Select Case pj.Status
   Case 1

    WScript.Echo lf
    WScript.Echo "Print Job: " & pj.Description
    WScript.Echo "Position: " & pj.Position
    WScript.Echo "Pages Printed: " & pj.PagesPrinted
    WScript.Echo "Total Pages: " & pj.TotalPages
    WScript.Echo "Printed By: " & pj.User
    WScript.Echo "===================================="
    WScript.Echo "Print Job is Paused."
    WScript.Echo "===================================="

   Case 2

    WScript.Echo lf
    WScript.Echo "Print Job: " & pj.Description
    WScript.Echo "Position: " & pj.Position
    WScript.Echo "Pages Printed: " & pj.PagesPrinted
    WScript.Echo "Total Pages: " & pj.TotalPages
    WScript.Echo "Printed By: " & pj.User
    WScript.Echo "===================================="
    WScript.Echo "Print Job error."
    WScript.Echo "===================================="

  End Select

End Sub
```

continued

LISTING 19-7 *(continued)*

Output

```
=====================================

==   Printer Monitor   ==

=====================================

Enter name of print server to monitor:

Zeta

=====================================
Checking Printers on Zeta
=====================================

Print Queue Name: HPEngineering
Printer Model: HP LaserJet 8000
Printer Location: 16th Floor
=====================================
Print Queue is Paused.
=====================================
=====================================

Print Job: Microsoft Word - listings.doc
Position: 1
Pages Printed: 0
Total Pages: 39
Printed By: Administrator
=====================================
Print Job is Paused.
=====================================

Print Job: Test Page
Position: 2
Pages Printed: 0
Total Pages: 1
Printed By: Administrator
=====================================
Print Job is Paused.
=====================================
```

Pausing and resuming print jobs

As with print queues, print jobs can be paused and resumed. You use the Pause method to pause a print job and the Resume method to resume a print job. One reason to pause a print job would be to temporarily stop printing a large document to allow other documents to be printed first.

Listing 19-8 shows an example of how you could control print jobs through Pause and Resume. Anytime there are five or more documents in the print queue and the document being printed has more than 50 pages to print, the active document is paused and other documents are printed. Printing doesn't resume until several of the smaller documents have printed.

LISTING 19-8

Controlling Print Jobs with Pause and Resume

VBScript
controlprinting.vbs

```
lf = Chr(13) & Chr(10)

WScript.Echo "=======================================" & lf
WScript.Echo "==    Print Job Monitor    ==" & lf
WScript.Echo "=======================================" & lf

checkJobs()

sub checkJobs()
 Set c = GetObject("WinNT://Zeta,computer")
 c.Filter = Array("PrintQueue")

 'Initialize counter
 n = 0

 For Each pq In c

  For Each j in pq.PrintJobs
    n = n + 1
  Next

  If n > 5 Then
   For Each j in pq.PrintJobs
     If j.Status = 8 And j.TotalPages - j.PagesPrinted > 50 Then
       WScript.Echo "Pausing ... " & j.Description
       j.Pause
     End If
   Next
  End If
```

continued

LISTING 19-8   *(continued)*

```
  If n < 3 Then
   For Each j in pq.PrintJobs
     If j.Status = 1 Then
        WScript.Echo "Resuming ... " & j.Description
        j.Resume
     End If
   Next
  End If

 Next

 'Wait 5 minutes
 WScript.Sleep(300000)

 'Call self
 checkJobs()

end sub
```

Output

```
=======================================

==    Print Job Monitor    ==

=======================================


Pausing ... Microsoft Word - massiveprint.doc
Resuming ... Microsoft Word - massiveprint.doc
```

Summary

Resource sharing is an essential part of any network environment. With Windows scripts, you can manage and maintain many different types of network resources. This chapter focused on working with shared folders, print queues, and print jobs. As you learned, you can create, delete, and modify shared folders. With print queues and print jobs, you can move a few steps beyond normal maintenance by implementing monitoring scripts. These scripts help maintain the healthy status of print queues and print jobs with limited administrator intervention.

Chapter 20

Managing Active Directory Domain Extensions

A s you've seen in previous chapters, many features of Windows and Active Directory can be scripted with the WinNT ADSI provider. WinNT is useful for managing most core functions, including user, group, and computer accounts. However, when you want to perform more advanced manipulation of Windows or Active Directory, you'll need to use the LDAP (Lightweight Directory Access Protocol) ADSI provider. With LDAP, you can script the extended features of any Active Directory object.

Working with Naming Contexts and the RootDSE Object

Active Directory uses a multimaster approach for maintaining and replicating directory information. Because of this, you can use any domain controller to view and manage directory information and don't have to specify a specific server when working with Active Directory. In fact, with the LDAP provider you are encouraged not to specify a server in your AdsPaths. Instead, you should bind to the root of the directory tree and then select a naming context that you want to work with. In Active Directory, the RootDSE object represents the root of the directory tree.

Binding to a naming context

A naming context is a top-level container for the directory tree. Three naming contexts are available: domain container, schema container, and configuration container. Domain container contains users, groups, computers, organizational units, and other domain objects. Schema container provides access to schema objects. Configuration container contains sites, which in turn contain individual sites, subnets, intersite transports, and other configuration objects.

As you might expect, the domain container is the one you'll use the most. In most cases, you can bind to the domain container via the `defaultNamingContext` property of the `RootDSE` object, such as:

VBScript

```
Set rootDSE = GetObject("LDAP://rootDSE")
domainContainer = rootDSE.Get("defaultNamingContext")
```

JScript

```
var rootDSE = GetObject("LDAP://rootDSE");
domainContainer = rootDSE.Get("defaultNamingContext");
```

If the domain is `seattle.tvpress.com`, the following is the value of `domainContainer`:

```
DC=seattle,DC=tvpress,DC=com
```

You can then use the `domainContainer` variable when you work with objects in the domain. For example, instead of specifying the AdsPath:

```
LDAP://OU=Marketing,DC=seattle,DC=tvpress,DC=com
```

you would use the following:

```
LDAP://OU=Marketing," & domainContainer
```

or

```
LDAP://OU=Marketing," + domainContainer
```

> **TIP** A key reason for binding to `RootDSE` and then to the domain container is to ensure that your scripts work in any domain. For example, you could use the script in the `seattle.tvpress.com`, `newyork.tvpress.com` or `la.tvpress.com` domain. However, if you wanted to access objects in a domain other than the current domain, you must specify the AdsPath. You will also need to authenticate yourself in the domain as discussed in the section of Chapter 15 titled, "Introducing Active Directory Services Interfaces."

Using RootDSE properties

`defaultNamingContext` is only one of many properties for the `RootDSE` object. Other properties of this object are summarized in Table 20-1.

TABLE 20-1

Properties of the RootDSE Object

Property	Description	Value Type	Multi-valued
configurationNamingContext	The distinguished name for the configuration container	ADsPath String	False
currentTime	The time on the current directory server	Date Time	False
defaultNamingContext	The distinguished name for the domain of which the current directory server is a member; the value can be changed.	ADsPath String	False
DnsHostName	The DNS address for this directory server	String	False
dsServiceName	The distinguished name of the NTDS settings object for the current directory server	ADsPath String	False
HighestCommittedUSN	The Highest Update Sequence Number (USN) used on the current directory server; USNs are used in directory replication.	Integer	False
LdapServiceName	The Service Principal Name (SPN) for the current LDAP server; SPNs are used for mutual authentication.	String	False
namingContexts	The distinguished names for all naming contexts stored on the current directory server	Array	True
RootDomainNamingContext	The distinguished name for the root domain in the forest that contains the domain of which the current directory server is a member	ADsPath String	False
schemaNamingContext	The distinguished name of the schema container	ADsPath String	False
ServerName	The distinguished name of the server object for the current directory server	ADsPath String	False

continued

TABLE 20-1   *(continued)*

Property	Description	Value Type	Multi-valued
subschemaSubentry	The distinguished name of the subSchema object, which exposes supported attributes	ADsPath String	False
SupportedControl	Object identifiers (OIDs) for the extension controls supported by the current directory server	Array	True
SupportedLDAPVersion	The major LDAP versions supported by the current directory server	Array	True
SupportedSASLMechanisms	The supported security mechanisms for the current server	Array	True

Listing 20-1 provides a script that displays the values of RootDSE properties. Be sure to examine the output of the script. This output should give you a better understanding of how the RootDSE properties are used.

LISTING 20-1

Working with RootDSE

VBScript
rootdse.vbs

```
On Error Resume Next
Set obj = GetObject("LDAP://rootDSE")

WScript.Echo "Path: " & obj.AdsPath
WScript.Echo "Subschema: " & obj.subschemaSubentry
WScript.Echo "Service Name: " & obj.dsServiceName
WScript.Echo "Server Name: " & obj.ServerName
WScript.Echo "Default Naming Context: " & obj.defaultNamingContext
WScript.Echo "Schema Naming Context: " & obj.schemaNamingContext
WScript.Echo "Config Naming Context: " & obj.configurationNamingContext
WScript.Echo "Root Domain Naming Context: " & obj.RootDomainNamingContext
WScript.Echo "Highest USN: " & obj.HighestCommittedUSN
WScript.Echo "DNS Host Name: " & obj.DnsHostName
WScript.Echo "LDAP Service Name: " & obj.LdapServiceName
```

```
'Examine Multivalued properties
c = obj.namingContexts

For Each a In c
 WScript.Echo "Naming Context: " & a
Next

c = obj.SupportedControl
For Each a In c
 WScript.Echo "Supported Control: " & a
Next

c = obj.SupportedLDAPVersion
For Each a In c
 WScript.Echo "Supported LDAP Version: " & a
Next

c = obj.SupportedSASLMechanisms
For Each a In c
 WScript.Echo "Supported SASL: " & a
Next
```

Output

```
Path: LDAP://rootDSE

Subschema: CN=Aggregate,CN=Schema,CN=Configuration,
DC=seattle,DC=tvpress,DC=com

Service Name: CN=NTDS Settings,CN=ZETA,CN=Servers,CN=Default-First-Site,CN=Sit
es,CN=Configuration,DC=seattle,DC=tvpress,DC=com

Server Name CN=ZETA,CN=Servers,CN=Default-First-Site, CN=Sites,CN=Configuratio
n,DC=seattle,DC=tvpress,DC=com

Default Naming Context: DC=seattle,DC=tvpress,DC=com

Schema Naming Context: CN=Schema,CN=Configuration,DC=seattle, DC=tvpress,DC=com

Config Naming Context: CN=Configuration,DC=seattle,DC=tvpress,DC=com

Root Domain Naming Context: DC=seattle,DC=tvpress,DC=com

Highest USN: 2055

DNS Host Name: ZETA.seattle.domain.com

LDAP Service Name: seattle.domain.com:zeta$@SEATTLE.DOMAIN.COM
```

continued

LISTING 20-1 *(continued)*

```
Naming Context: CN=Schema,CN=Configuration,DC=seattle, DC=tvpress,DC=com
Naming Context: CN=Configuration,DC=seattle,DC=tvpress,DC=com
Naming Context: DC=seattle,DC=tvpress,DC=com

Supported Control: 1.2.840.113556.1.4.319
Supported Control: 1.2.840.113556.1.4.801
Supported Control: 1.2.840.113556.1.4.473

Supported LDAP Version: 3
Supported LDAP Version: 2

Supported SASL: GSSAPI
Supported SASL: GSS-SPNEGO
```

Accessing Active Directory Schema

One of the first things you'll notice when you set out to work with Active Directory is that there's an extremely rich feature set and as a result, even the most basic objects can have many properties. To help manage this complexity, Windows Support Tools includes a utility called ADSI Edit (adsiedit. exe). Using ADSI Edit, you can manage objects in the domain, configuration, and schema containers. The sections that follow provide an overview of installing and using ADSI Edit.

Installing and starting ADSI Edit

ADSI Edit is installed as part of the Windows Support Tools library. You install the support tools by completing the following steps:

1. Insert the Windows CD-ROM into the CD-ROM drive. Then when the Autorun screen appears, click Browse This CD. This starts Windows Explorer.

2. In Explorer, click Support, click Reskit, and then click Setup. This starts the Windows Support Tools Setup Wizard. Read the Welcome dialog box, and then click Next.

3. Enter your user information, and then continue by clicking Next.

4. Select the installation type Typical, and then click Next twice to start the installation.

5. Click Finish. The Support Tools will be installed on your computer.

You can now start ADSI Edit by clicking Start, pointing to Programs, pointing to Windows Support Tools, pointing to Tools, and then selecting ADSI Edit. As shown in Figure 20-1, ADSI Edit is used to access naming context and their objects. Each naming context has its own node. The node you'll use the most is Domain NC.

FIGURE 20-1

Use ADSI Edit to access naming contexts and their related objects.

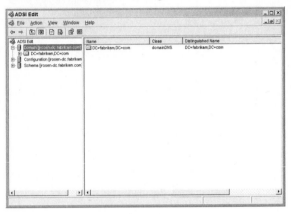

Examining the domain-naming context

In the Domain NC node, you can access the domain-naming context for each domain in the domain forest. As summarized in Table 20-2, each container stored in this node has an associated object class and distinguished name. Unlike Active Directory Users and Computers, both default and advanced containers are available, which is why you see the additional entries for LostAndFound, System, and Infrastructure.

TABLE 20-2

Domain NC Node Containers

Name	Object Class	Sample Distinguished Name
CN=Builtin	builtinDomain	CN=Builtin,DC=seattle,DC=tvpress,DC=com
CN=Computers	container	CN=Computers,DC=seattle,DC=tvpress,DC=com
OU=Domain Controllers	organizationalUnit	OU=Domain Controllers,DC=seattle,DC=tvpress, DC=com
CN=ForeignSecurity Principals	container	CN=ForeignSecurityPrincipals,DC=seattle,DC=tvpress, DC=com
CN=LostAndFound	lostAndFound	CN=LostAndFound,DC=seattle,DC=tvpress,DC=com
CN=System	container	CN=System,DC=seattle,DC=tvpress,DC=com
CN=Users	container	CN=Users,DC=seattle,DC=tvpress,DC=com
CN=Infrastructure	infrastructureUpdate	CN=Infrastructure,DC=seattle,DC=tvpress, DC=com

You create an instance of a container object when you bind to the distinguished name for the container. For example, you could bind to the System container using the ADsPath string:

```
CN=System,DC=seattle,DC=tvpress,DC=com
```

You could also access the System container through RootDSE, such as:

VBScript

```
Set rootDSE = GetObject("LDAP://rootDSE")
domainContainer = rootDSE.Get("defaultNamingContext")
Set sysObject = GetObject("LDAP://CN=System," & domainContainer)
```

JScript

```
var rootDSE = GetObject("LDAP://rootDSE");
domainContainer = rootDSE.Get("defaultNamingContext");
var sysObject = GetObject("LDAP://CN=System," + domainContainer);
```

Right-clicking an entry in the Domain NC node displays a menu that allows you to manage the selected container or object. Generally, only advanced administrators should move, rename, or create elements directly in ADSI Edit. More often, you'll use ADSI Edit to examine the properties of containers and objects. To do this, right-click on the element you want to examine, and then select Properties. This displays a dialog box similar to the one shown in Figure 20-2.

FIGURE 20-2

The Properties dialog box allows you to view attributes for the selected element.

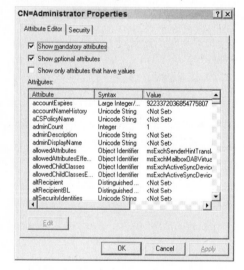

In the Attributes tab of the Properties dialog box, you can examine mandatory and optional properties of the selected element. The Attribute Values panel displays information for the currently selected property. Being able to view element attributes allows you to explore the properties of Active Directory objects. This is useful if the directory in your domain has been extended or reconfigured.

As you examine attributes, you'll note that the syntax types are a bit different than what you're used to because Active Directory supports different syntax types. The mapping between common attribute syntax types and property data types is as follows:

- `Boolean`: A Boolean value represented as True/False or 1/0
- `CaseExactString`: A case-sensitive `String`
- `CaseIgnoreString`: A string that isn't case-sensitive
- `DirectoryString`: A string that may contain directory or file path separators, such as `seattle.tvpress.com/Users`
- `DN`: An `AdsPath` string, such as CN=Users,DC=seattle, DC=tvpress, DC=com
- `GeneralizedTime`: A date/time value
- `INTEGER`: An integer value
- `INTEGER8`: An 8-bit integer value
- `OctetString`: A `String` containing hexadecimal values
- `OID`: An object identifier or class
- `ObjectSecurityDescriptor`: An integer value representing the security descriptor of the element
- `Time`: A date/time value
- `UTCTIME`: A UTC (Universal Time Coordinate) date/time value

Some object attributes are inherited and are not listed as normal object properties. For example, most objects support the mandatory attributes `instanceType`, `objectCategory`, and `objectClass`. These attributes are displayed in ADSI Edit but are not returned as either mandatory or optional attributes when you examine objects through scripts. Still, you usually can call these inherited attributes in scripts, as follows:

```
Set cont = GetObject("LDAP://OU=Engineering,DC=seattle,DC=tvpress,DC=com")
c = cont.objectClass
For Each a In c
 WScript.Echo "Object Class: " & a
Next
```

Common Active Directory objects

Active Directory distinguishes between various types of objects using object classes. The top-level object class for domain objects is `domainDNS`. This is the class for domains in the domain-naming context. Domain objects in turn contain other objects. The most commonly used object classes are as follows:

- `Computer`: Represents computer objects
- `Contact`: Represents contacts listed in Active Directory
- `Group`: Represents domain security and distribution groups
- `organizationalUnit`: Represents organizational units
- `user`: Represents user accounts

Each of these objects supports a different set of object properties. Because we've examined similar properties in previous chapters, we won't spend a lot of time covering these properties and will instead provide summary tables that you can use as quick references. Afterwards, we'll cover specific techniques for managing these objects.

Managing Computer Objects with LDAP

You can examine computer accounts and set properties that describe a particular computer with the WinNT ADSI provider. You can't, however, manage computer accounts, and this is where the LDAP provider comes in handy. Using the LDAP provider, you can create, rename, move, and delete computer accounts. To do this, you bind to the container or organizational unit that you want to work with and then invoke the appropriate method of the IADsContainer interface on the computer account, such as Create or Delete.

Active Directory computer object properties

Normally, computer objects are stored in the Computers container or the Domain Controllers organizational unit. However, you can store computer objects in any available container or organization unit. Table 20-3 provides a summary of computer object properties for Active Directory.

TABLE 20-3

Active Directory Computer Object Properties

Property	Status	Value Type	Min. Range	Max. Range	Multiple Values
accountDisabled	RW	Boolean	0	1	False
adminDescription	RW	DirectoryString	0	1024	False
adminDisplayName	RW	DirectoryString	1	256	False
CN	RO	DirectoryString	1	64	False

Property	Status	Value Type	Min. Range	Max. Range	Multiple Values
company	RW	DirectoryString	1	64	False
controlAccessRights	RO	OctetString	16	16	True
department	RW	DirectoryString	1	64	False
description	RW	DirectoryString	0	1024	True
destinationIndicator	RW	PrintableString	1	128	True
displayName	RW	DirectoryString	0	256	False
displayNamePrintable	RW	PrintableString	1	256	False
division	RW	DirectoryString	0	256	False
dNSHostName	RO	DirectoryString	0	2048	False
employeeID	RW	DirectoryString	0	16	False
extensionName	RW	DirectoryString	1	255	True
facsimileTelephone Number	RW	DirectoryString	1	64	False
givenName	RW	DirectoryString	1	64	False
homePhone	RW	DirectoryString	1	64	False
homePostalAddress	RW	DirectoryString	1	4096	False
info	RW	DirectoryString	1	1024	False
initials	RW	DirectoryString	1	6	False
international ISDNNumber	RW	NumericString	1	16	True
location	RW	DirectoryString	0	1024	False
mail	RW	DirectoryString	0	256	False
middleName	RW	DirectoryString	0	64	False
mobile	RW	DirectoryString	1	64	False
mSMQDigests	RW	OctetString	16	16	True
name	RW	DirectoryString	1	255	False
netbootGUID	RO	OctetString	16	16	False
networkAddress	RW	CaseIgnoreString	0	256	True

continued

TABLE 20-3 *(continued)*

Property	Status	Value Type	Min. Range	Max. Range	Multiple Values
nTSecurityDescriptor	RO	ObjectSecurity Descriptor	0	132096	False
objectGUID	RO	OctetString	16	16	False
objectSid	RO	OctetString	0	28	False
otherFacsimile TelephoneNumber	RW	DirectoryString	1	64	True
otherHomePhone	RW	DirectoryString	1	64	True
otherLogin Workstations	RW	DirectoryString	0	1024	True
otherMobile	RW	DirectoryString	1	64	True
otherPager	RW	DirectoryString	1	64	True
otherTelephone	RW	DirectoryString	1	64	True
ou	RW	DirectoryString	1	64	True
pager	RW	DirectoryString	1	64	False
personalTitle	RW	DirectoryString	1	64	False
physicalDelivery OfficeName	RW	DirectoryString	1	128	False
postalAddress	RW	DirectoryString	1	4096	True
postalCode	RW	DirectoryString	1	40	False
postOfficeBox	RW	DirectoryString	1	40	True
primaryInternational ISDNNumber	RW	DirectoryString	1	64	False
primaryTelexNumber	RW	DirectoryString	1	64	False
proxyAddresses	RW	DirectoryString	1	1123	True
registeredAddress	RW	OctetString	1	4096	True
sAMAccountName	RW	DirectoryString	0	256	False
siteGUID	RO	OctetString	16	16	False
street	RW	DirectoryString	1	1024	False

Property	Status	Value Type	Min. Range	Max. Range	Multiple Values
streetAddress	RW	DirectoryString	1	1024	False
telephoneNumber	RW	DirectoryString	1	64	False
telexNumber	RW	OctetString	1	32	True
textEncodedORAddress	RW	DirectoryString	1	1024	False
thumbnailLogo	RW	OctetString	1	32767	False
thumbnailPhoto	RW	OctetString	0	102400	False
title	RW	DirectoryString	1	64	False
userCert	RW	OctetString	0	32767	False
userParameters	RW	DirectoryString	0	32767	False
userPassword	RW	OctetString	1	128	True
userWorkstations	RW	DirectoryString	0	1024	False
wWWHomePage	RW	DirectoryString	1	2048	False
x121Address	RW	NumericString	1	15	True

Creating and deleting computer accounts with LDAP

To create a computer account, you must get the object for the container you want to work with and then invoke the container's Create method. The only properties that you must set when creating computer accounts are the common name and the Windows NT SAM account name. You could set these properties when creating an account for a computer called Omega, as shown in Listing 20-2.

LISTING 20-2

Creating a Computer Account

VBScript
createcomputer.vbs

```
Set cont = GetObject("LDAP://OU=Engineering,DC=seattle,DC=tvpress,DC=com")
Set comp = cont.Create("computer","CN=Omega")
comp.Put "samAccountName","Omega"
comp.SetInfo
```

continued

LISTING 20-2   *(continued)*

JScript
createcomputer.js

```
var cont = GetObject("LDAP://OU=Engineering, DC=seattle,DC=tvpress,DC=com");
var comp = cont.Create("computer","CN=Omega");
comp.Put("samAccountName","Omega");
comp.SetInfo()
```

You can delete a computer account stored in a container by invoking the container's `Delete` method. Here's how you would delete the computer account created in the previous listing:

VBScript

```
Set cont = GetObject("LDAP://OU=Engineering,DC=seattle,DC=tvpress,DC=com")
cont.Delete "computer","CN=Omega"
```

JScript

```
var cont = GetObject("LDAP://OU=Engineering, DC=seattle,DC=tvpress,DC=com");
cont.Delete("computer","CN=Omega");
```

Moving and renaming computer accounts with LDAP

Moving and renaming computer accounts are similar operations. When you move an account, you retrieve the destination container and then invoke the container's `MoveHere` method for the computer account you want to move. Listing 20-3 shows how you could move a computer object from the Computers container to the Engineering organizational unit.

LISTING 20-3

Moving a Computer Account

VBScript
movecomputer.vbs

```
'Get rootDSE
Set rootDSE = GetObject("LDAP://rootDSE")
domainCont = rootDSE.Get("defaultNamingContext")

'Get the destination container
set cont = GetObject("LDAP://OU=Engineering," & domainCont)

'Move object from original container to the destination
cont.MoveHere "LDAP://CN=Omega,CN=Computers," & domainCont, "CN=Omega"
```

JScript
movecomputer.js

```
//Get rootDSE
var rootDSE = GetObject("LDAP://rootDSE");
domainCont = rootDSE.Get("defaultNamingContext");

//Get the destination container
var cont = GetObject("LDAP://OU=Engineering," + domainCont);

//Move object from original container to the destination
cont.MoveHere("LDAP://CN=Omega,CN=Computers," + domainCont, "CN=Omega");
```

The first parameter for the MoveHere method is the current location of the computer object. The second parameter is the object name at the destination. Thus, as Listing 20-4 shows, you could rename a computer object that you are moving simply by specifying a different name as the second parameter.

LISTING 20-4

Moving and Renaming a Computer Account

VBScript
mrcomputer.vbs

```
'Get rootDSE
Set rootDSE = GetObject("LDAP://rootDSE")
domainCont = rootDSE.Get("defaultNamingContext")

'Get the destination container
set cont = GetObject("LDAP://OU=Marketing," & domainCont)

'Move object and specify new name
cont.MoveHere "LDAP://CN=Omega,CN=Computers," & domainCont, "CN=BobsComputer"
```

JScript
mrcomputer.js

```
//Get rootDSE
var rootDSE = GetObject("LDAP://rootDSE");
domainCont = rootDSE.Get("defaultNamingContext");

//Get the destination container
var cont = GetObject("LDAP://OU=Marketing," + domainCont);

//Move object and specify new name
cont.MoveHere("LDAP://CN=Omega,CN=Computers," + domainCont, "CN=BobsComputer");
```

If you want to rename an object without changing its container, set the destination container's ADsPath string to be the same as that of the original container. An example is shown as Listing 20-5.

LISTING 20-5

Renaming a Computer Account Without Moving It

VBScript
renamecomputer.vbs

```
'Get rootDSE
Set rootDSE = GetObject("LDAP://rootDSE")
domainCont = rootDSE.Get("defaultNamingContext")

'Get the destination container
set cont = GetObject("LDAP://CN=Computers," & domainCont)

'Move object and specify new name
cont.MoveHere "LDAP://CN=Omega,CN=Computers," & domainCont, "CN=Delta"
```

JScript
renamecomputer.js

```
//Get rootDSE
var rootDSE = GetObject("LDAP://rootDSE");
domainCont = rootDSE.Get("defaultNamingContext");

//Get the destination container
var cont = GetObject("LDAP://CN=Computers," + domainCont);

//Move object and specify new name
cont.MoveHere("LDAP://CN=Omega,CN=Computers," + domainCont, "CN=Delta");
```

Enabling and disabling computer accounts with LDAP

Computer accounts often need to be enabled or disabled. You enable a computer account to make it active and allow the computer to connect to the domain. To enable a computer account, you set the accountDisabled property to False, as in the following:

VBScript

```
Set comp = GetObject("LDAP://CN=Omega,OU=Sales,DC=seattle,DC=tvpress,DC=com")
comp.AccountDisabled = "False"
comp.SetInfo
```

JScript

```
var comp = GetObject("LDAP://CN=Omega,OU=Sales,DC=seattle,DC=tvpress,DC=com");
comp.AccountDisabled = "False";
comp.SetInfo();
```

You disable a computer account to deactivate it, which doesn't allow the computer to connect to the domain. However, disabling an account won't forcibly disconnect a computer from a domain. To disable a computer account, you set the accountDisabled property to True, as follows:

VBScript

```
Set comp = GetObject("LDAP://CN=Omega,OU=Sales,DC=seattle,DC=tvpress,DC=com")
comp.AccountDisabled = "True"
comp.SetInfo
```

JScript

```
var comp = GetObject("LDAP://CN=Omega,OU=Sales,DC=seattle,DC=tvpress,DC=com");
comp.AccountDisabled = "True";
comp.SetInfo();
```

Managing Contacts with LDAP

In Active Directory, a contact represents an address book entry. Generally, contacts provide names, addresses, and other information needed to contact a person or business. Table 20-4 provides a summary of properties for Active Directory contact objects.

TABLE 20-4

Active Directory Contact Object Properties

Property	Status	Value Type	Min. Range	Max. Range	Multiple Values
adminDescription	RW	DirectoryString	0	1024	False
adminDisplayName	RW	DirectoryString	1	256	False
cn	RO	DirectoryString	1	64	False
company	RW	DirectoryString	1	64	False
department	RW	DirectoryString	1	64	False
description	RW	DirectoryString	0	1024	True
destinationIndicator	RW	PrintableString	1	128	True

continued

TABLE 20-4   *(continued)*

Property	Status	Value Type	Min. Range	Max. Range	Multiple Values
displayName	RW	DirectoryString	0	256	False
displayNamePrintable	RW	PrintableString	1	256	False
division	RW	DirectoryString	0	256	False
employeeID	RW	DirectoryString	0	16	False
extensionName	RW	DirectoryString	1	255	True
facsimileTelephone Number	RW	DirectoryString	1	64	False
givenName	RW	DirectoryString	1	64	False
homePhone	RW	DirectoryString	1	64	False
homePostalAddress	RW	DirectoryString	1	4096	False
info	RW	DirectoryString	1	1024	False
initials	RW	DirectoryString	1	6	False
internationalISDNNumber	RW	NumericString	1	16	True
mail	RW	DirectoryString	0	256	False
middleName	RW	DirectoryString	0	64	False
mobile	RW	DirectoryString	1	64	False
name	RW	DirectoryString	1	255	False
nTSecurityDescriptor	RO	ObjectSecurity Descriptor	0	132096	False
objectGUID	RO	OctetString	16	16	False
otherFacsimile TelephoneNumber	RW	DirectoryString	1	64	True
otherHomePhone	RW	DirectoryString	1	64	True
otherMobile	RW	DirectoryString	1	64	True
otherPager	RW	DirectoryString	1	64	True
otherTelephone	RW	DirectoryString	1	64	True
ou	RW	DirectoryString	1	64	True
pager	RW	DirectoryString	1	64	False

Property	Status	Value Type	Min. Range	Max. Range	Multiple Values
personalTitle	RW	DirectoryString	1	64	False
physicalDelivery OfficeName	RW	DirectoryString	1	128	False
postalAddress	RW	DirectoryString	1	4096	True
postalCode	RW	DirectoryString	1	40	False
postOfficeBox	RW	DirectoryString	1	40	True
primaryInternational ISDNNumber	RW	DirectoryString	1	64	False
primaryTelexNumber	RW	DirectoryString	1	64	False
proxyAddresses	RW	DirectoryString	1	1123	True
registeredAddress	RW	OctetString	1	4096	True
sn	RW	DirectoryString	1	64	False
street	RW	DirectoryString	1	1024	False
streetAddress	RW	DirectoryString	1	1024	False
telephoneNumber	RW	DirectoryString	1	64	False
telexNumber	RW	OctetString	1	32	True
textEncodedORAddress	RW	DirectoryString	1	1024	False
thumbnailLogo	RW	OctetString	1	32767	False
thumbnailPhoto	RW	OctetString	0	102400	False
title	RW	DirectoryString	1	64	False
userCert	RW	OctetString	0	32767	False
userPassword	RW	OctetString	1	128	True
wWWHomePage	RW	DirectoryString	1	2048	False
x121Address	RW	NumericString	1	15	True

Using the LDAP provider, you can manage contacts in much the same way as you manage computer accounts. To do this, you bind to the container or organizational unit that you want to work with and then invoke the appropriate container method on the contact. Again, these methods are Create, Delete, and MoveHere.

The only property that you must set when creating a contact is the common name. You may also want to set the following properties:

- `company`: Company name
- `department`: Department name
- `title`: Job title
- `telephoneNumber`: Business telephone number
- `homePhone`: Home telephone number
- `givenName`: First name
- `initials`: Middle initial
- `sn`: Last name (surname)
- `displayName`: Display name in Active Directory
- `mail`: E-mail address

Listing 20-6 shows how you could create a contact in Active Directory.

LISTING 20-6

Creating a Contact

VBScript
createcontact.vbs

```
Set cont = GetObject("LDAP://OU=Marketing,DC=seattle,DC=tvpress,DC=com")
Set contact = cont.Create("contact","CN=Tony Green")
contact.company = "ABC Enterprises, Ltd."
contact.department = "Sales"
contact.title = "Sales Associate"
contact.telephoneNumber = "206-555-1212"
contact.homePhone = "253-555-1212"
contact.givenName = "Tony"
contact.initials = "R"
contact.sn = "Green"
contact.displayName = "Tony Green"
contact.mail = "tgreen@tvpress.com"
contact.SetInfo
```

JScript
createcontact.js

```
var cont = GetObject("LDAP://OU=Marketing,DC=seattle,DC=tvpress,DC=com");
var contact = cont.Create("contact","CN=Tony Green");
contact.company = "ABC Enterprises, Ltd.";
contact.department = "Sales";
contact.title = "Sales Associate";
```

```
contact.telephoneNumber = "206-555-1212";
contact.homePhone = "253-555-1212";
contact.givenName = "Tony";
contact.initials = "R";
contact.sn = "Green";
contact.displayName = "Tony Green";
contact.mail = "tgreen@tvpress.com";
contact.SetInfo();
```

Managing Groups with LDAP

In Chapter 17, you learned the basics for managing groups with the WinNT provider. Now let's look at how you manage groups with the LDAP provider. One of the first things you'll note is that on the surface the administration techniques are similar, but as you delve deeper, you'll find that the LDAP provider supports a richer feature set.

Active Directory group object properties

Table 20-5 provides a summary of properties for Active Directory group objects. Before you can work with a group object, you must bind to the container in which the group object resides, such as:

```
GetObject("LDAP://CN=Users,DC=seattle,DC=tvpress,DC=com")
```

Or you must access the group object directly, such as:

```
GetObject("LDAP://CN=Domain Users,CN=Users, DC=seattle,DC=tvpress,DC=com")
```

TABLE 20-5

Active Directory Group Object Properties

Property	Status	Value Type	Min. Range	Max. Range	Multiple Values
adminDescription	RW	DirectoryString	0	1024	False
adminDisplayName	RW	DirectoryString	1	256	False
cn	RO	DirectoryString	1	64	False
controlAccessRights	RO	OctetString	16	16	True
description	RW	DirectoryString	0	1024	True
displayName	RW	DirectoryString	0	256	False

continued

TABLE 20-5 *(continued)*

Property	Status	Value Type	Min. Range	Max. Range	Multiple Values
displayNamePrintable	RW	PrintableString	1	256	False
extensionName	RW	DirectoryString	1	255	True
groupType	RW	Integer	$-2\wedge31$	$2\wedge31$	False
info	RW	DirectoryString	1	1024	False
mail	RW	DirectoryString	0	256	False
name	RW	DirectoryString	1	255	False
nTSecurityDescriptor	RO	ObjectSecurity Descriptor	0	132096	False
objectGUID	RO	OctetString	16	16	False
objectSid	RO	OctetString	0	28	False
proxyAddresses	RW	DirectoryString	1	1123	True
sAMAccountName	RW	DirectoryString	0	256	False
telephoneNumber	RW	DirectoryString	1	64	False
textEncodedORAddress	RW	DirectoryString	1	1024	False
userCert	RW	OctetString	0	32767	False
wWWHomePage	RW	DirectoryString	1	2048	False

Creating groups with LDAP

Unlike WinNT, you can only use the LDAP provider to create global group accounts. You cannot use LDAP to create groups stored on local computers. Still, you create groups in much the same way. You access the container in which you want to place the group, and then invoke the container's Create method. Afterward, you can set properties for the group.

The only mandatory properties for groups are the common name and the Windows NT SAM account name. This means you could create a group account called Sales as follows:

VBScript

```
Set obj = GetObject("LDAP://CN=Users,DC=seattle,DC=tvpress,DC=com")
Set grp = obj.Create("group", "Sales")
grp.samAccountName = "sales"
grp.SetInfo
```

JScript

```
var obj = GetObject("LDAP://CN=Users,DC=seattle,DC=tvpress,DC=com");
var grp = obj.Create("group", "Sales");
grp.samAccountName = "sales";
grp.SetInfo();
```

You create a global security group by default. If you want to create a different type of group, you must set the `groupType` property when creating the group. This property is set to an integer value that represents the type of group to create. The following are valid values for `groupType`:

- 2 creates a global distribution group.
- 4 creates a domain-local distribution group.
- 8 creates a universal distribution group.
- -2147483646 creates a global security group.
- -2147483644 creates a domain-local security group.
- -2147483640 creates a universal security group.

NOTE Universal security groups cannot be created when using mixed-mode operations. You must be in native mode operations. In native mode, Active Directory only supports Windows domains and no longer supports Windows NT domains. So before you change modes, you should ensure that all Windows NT systems in the domain have been upgraded to Windows.

Listing 20-7 shows how you could create these group types in VBScript. You would use similar techniques for JScript.

LISTING 20-7

Creating Groups

VBScript
creategroups.vbs

```
'Create global distribution group
Set obj = GetObject("LDAP://CN=Users,DC=seattle,DC=tvpress,DC=com")
Set grp = obj.Create("group", "CN=MarketingGlobalDist")
grp.groupType = 2
grp.Put "samAccountName", "MarketingGD"
grp.SetInfo

'Create domain local distribution group
Set obj = GetObject("LDAP://CN=Users,DC=seattle,DC=tvpress,DC=com")
Set grp = obj.Create("group", "CN=MarketingDomainLocalDist")
grp.groupType = 4
grp.Put "samAccountName", "MarketingDD"
grp.SetInfo
```

continued

LISTING 20-7 *(continued)*

```
'Create universal distribution group
Set obj = GetObject("LDAP://CN=Users,DC=seattle,DC=tvpress,DC=com")
Set grp = obj.Create("group", "CN=MarketingUniversalDist")
grp.groupType = 8
grp.Put "samAccountName", "MarketingUD"
grp.SetInfo

'Create global security group
Set obj = GetObject("LDAP://CN=Users,DC=seattle,DC=tvpress,DC=com")
Set grp = obj.Create("group", "CN=MarketingGlobal")
grp.groupType = -2147483646
grp.Put "samAccountName", "MarketingG"
grp.SetInfo

'Create domain local security group
Set obj = GetObject("LDAP://CN=Users,DC=seattle,DC=tvpress,DC=com")
Set grp = obj.Create("group", "CN=MarketingDomainLocal")
grp.groupType = -2147483644
grp.Put "samAccountName", "MarketingD"
grp.SetInfo

'Create universal security group
Set obj = GetObject("LDAP://CN=Users,DC=seattle,DC=tvpress,DC=com")
Set grp = obj.Create("group", "CN=MarketingUniversal")
grp.groupType = -2147483640
grp.Put "samAccountName", "MarketingU"
grp.SetInfo
```

Deleting, moving, and renaming groups with LDAP

You can also delete, move, and rename groups. You can delete a group stored in a container by invoking the container's Delete method. Here's how you would delete a group called Marketing:

VBScript

```
Set cont = GetObject("LDAP://OU=Users,DC=seattle,DC=tvpress,DC=com")
cont.Delete "group","CN=Marketing"
```

JScript

```
var cont = GetObject("LDAP://OU=Users,DC=seattle,DC=tvpress,DC=com");
cont.Delete "group","CN=Marketing";
```

Moving and renaming groups is similar to moving and renaming computer accounts. You retrieve the destination container and then invoke the container's MoveHere method for the group you want to move. Listing 20-8 shows how you could move a group called SalesEng from the Users container to the Sales organizational unit.

LISTING 20-8

Moving a Group

VBScript
movegroup.vbs

```
'Get rootDSE
Set rootDSE = GetObject("LDAP://rootDSE")
domainCont = rootDSE.Get("defaultNamingContext")

'Get the destination container
set cont = GetObject("LDAP://OU=Sales," & domainCont)

'Move group from original container to the destination
cont.MoveHere "LDAP://CN=SalesEng,CN=Users," & domainCont, "CN=SalesEng"
```

JScript
movegroup.js

```
//Get rootDSE
var rootDSE = GetObject("LDAP://rootDSE");
domainCont = rootDSE.Get("defaultNamingContext");

//Get the destination container
var cont = GetObject("LDAP://OU=Sales," + domainCont);

//Move group from original container to the destination
cont.MoveHere("LDAP://CN=SalesEng,CN=Users," + domainCont, "CN=SalesEng");
```

To rename a group when you move it, you simply specify a different name as the second parameter for MoveHere. To rename a group and keep it in the same container, use the same value for the original and destination container, as shown in Listing 20-9.

LISTING 20-9

Renaming a Group

VBScript
renamegroup.vbs

```
'Get rootDSE
Set rootDSE = GetObject("LDAP://rootDSE")
domainCont = rootDSE.Get("defaultNamingContext")

'Get the destination container
set cont = GetObject("LDAP://OU=Engineering," & domainCont)
```

continued

LISTING 20-9 *(continued)*

```
'Move group from original container to the destination
cont.MoveHere "LDAP://CN=Coders,OU=Engineering," & domainCont, "CN=Developers"
```

JScript
renamegroup.js

```
//Get rootDSE
var rootDSE = GetObject("LDAP://rootDSE");
domainCont = rootDSE.Get("defaultNamingContext");

//Get the destination container
var cont = GetObject("LDAP://OU=Engineering," + domainCont);

//Move group from original container to the destination
cont.MoveHere("LDAP://CN=Coders,OU=Engineering," + domainCont, "CN=Developers");
```

Checking group membership with LDAP

One way to work with groups is to obtain a list of current members. You can do this by calling the group object's Members() method. The Members() method returns a collection of members using the IADsMembers interface. You can examine each member using a for loop, as shown in Listing 20-10.

LISTING 20-10

Checking Group Membership

VBScript
groupmembers.vbs

```
Set grp = GetObject("LDAP://CN=Marketing,CN=Users, DC=seattle,DC=domain,DC=com")

Set mList = grp.members
For Each member In mList
   WScript.Echo member.Name
Next
```

JScript
groupmembers.js

```
var grp = GetObject("LDAP://CN=Marketing,CN=Users, DC=seattle,DC=domain,DC=com");

mList = new Enumerator(grp.members());

for (; !mList.atEnd(); mList.moveNext())
{
```

```
s = mList.item();
WScript.Echo(s.Name);
}
```

To check for a specific member, you can use the IsMember () method. This method returns True
(1) if the user or group is a member of the group and False (0), otherwise. You could use IsMember
as follows:

VBScript

```
Set grp = GetObject("LDAP://CN=Marketing,CN=Users,
DC=seattle,DC=domain,DC=com")

mem = grp.IsMember("CN=William R. Stanek,CN=Users,
DC=seattle,DC=domain,DC=com")
WScript.Echo CStr(mem)
```

JScript

```
var grp = GetObject("LDAP://CN=Marketing,CN=Users,
DC=seattle,DC=domain,DC=com");

mem = grp.IsMember("CN=William R. Stanek,CN=Users,
DC=seattle,DC=domain,DC=com");
WScript.Echo(mem);
```

Adding and removing group members with LDAP

You can use the LDAP provider to add and remove members from a group, as well. First, obtain the
group object you want to work with, and then invoke Add or Remove as appropriate. After you add
or remove a member, you can use IsMember() to confirm the action, as follows:

VBScript

```
Set grp = GetObject("LDAP://CN=Marketing,CN=Users,
DC=seattle,DC=domain,DC=com")
grp.Add("CN=William R. Stanek,CN=Users,DC=seattle,DC=domain,DC=com")

WScript.Echo grp.IsMember("CN=William R. Stanek,CN=Users,
DC=seattle,DC=domain,DC=com")
```

JScript

```
var grp = GetObject("LDAP://CN=Marketing,CN=Users,
DC=seattle,DC=domain,DC=com");
grp.Add("CN=William R. Stanek,CN=Users,DC=seattle,DC=domain,DC=com");

WScript.Echo(grp.IsMember("CN=William R. Stanek,CN=Users,
DC=seattle,DC=domain,DC=com"));
```

Working with Organizational Units

Organizational units often are used to mirror business or functional structures. For example, if your organization has business groups called Technology, Marketing, and Operations, you may want to have organizational units with the same names. You could then add resources and accounts to these organizational units.

Examining organizational unit properties

Organizational units can be at different physical locations, as well. This is why contact information, such as addresses and telephone numbers, are associated with organizational units. Table 20-6 provides a summary of properties for organizational units.

TABLE 20-6

Properties for Organizational Units

Property	Status	Value Type	Min. Range	Max. Range	Multiple Values
adminDescription	RW	DirectoryString	0	1024	False
adminDisplayName	RW	DirectoryString	1	256	False
businessCategory	RW	DirectoryString	1	128	True
cn	RW	DirectoryString	1	64	False
description	RW	DirectoryString	0	1024	True
destinationIndicator	RW	PrintableString	1	128	True
displayName	RW	DirectoryString	0	256	False
displayNamePrintable	RW	PrintableString	1	256	False
extensionName	RW	DirectoryString	1	255	True
facsimileTelephoneNumber	RW	DirectoryString	1	64	False
internationalISDNNumber	RW	NumericString	1	16	True
name	RW	DirectoryString	1	255	False
nTSecurityDescriptor	RO	ObjectSecurityDescriptor	0	132096	False
objectGUID	RO	OctetString	16	16	False
ou	RW	DirectoryString	1	64	True
physicalDelivery OfficeName	RW	DirectoryString	1	128	False

Property	Status	Value Type	Min. Range	Max. Range	Multiple Values
postalAddress	RW	DirectoryString	1	4096	True
postalCode	RW	DirectoryString	1	40	False
postOfficeBox	RW	DirectoryString	1	40	True
proxyAddresses	RW	DirectoryString	1	1123	True
registeredAddress	RW	OctetString	1	4096	True
street	RW	DirectoryString	1	1024	False
telephoneNumber	RW	DirectoryString	1	64	False
telexNumber	RW	OctetString	1	32	True
thumbnailLogo	RW	OctetString	1	32767	False
userPassword	RW	OctetString	1	128	True
wWWHomePage	RW	DirectoryString	1	2048	False
x121Address	RW	NumericString	1	15	True

Creating organizational units

Organizational units can be created within the top-level domain container or within existing organizational units. When you create a unit in the top-level domain container, you bind to the domain-naming context and then invoke the Create method of this container. Otherwise, you bind to an existing organizational unit and then create a sub-unit by invoking the Create method.

The only property you must set is OU, which stores the name of the organizational unit. Listing 20-11 creates an organizational unit called Engineering.

LISTING 20-11

Creating an Organizational Unit

VBScript
createou.vbs

```
'Get domain naming context
Set obj = GetObject("LDAP://DC=seattle,DC=domain,DC=com")

'create ou object
Set ou = obj.Create("organizationalUnit","OU=Engineering")
```

continued

LISTING 20-11   *(continued)*

```
'Set the name of the ou
ou.ou = "Engineering"
ou.SetInfo
```

JScript
createou.js

```
//Get domain naming context
var obj = GetObject("LDAP://DC=seattle,DC=domain,DC=com");

//create ou object
var ou = obj.Create("organizationalUnit","OU=Engineering");

//set the name of the ou
ou.ou = "Engineering";
ou.SetInfo();
```

Modifying organizational units

You can work with existing organizational units in much the same way as you work with other objects. You bind to the `organizationalUnit` object:

```
GetObject("LDAP://OU=Marketing,DC=seattle,DC=tvpress,DC=com")
```

Then you set or get properties. You may also need to examine the objects within the organizational unit. One way to do this would be to obtain a list of all objects that it contains, as shown in Listing 20-12.

LISTING 20-12

Accessing Objects Within an Organizational Unit

VBScript
getobjs.vbs

```
Set ou = GetObject("LDAP://OU=Engineering,DC=seattle,DC=domain,DC=com")

For Each member In ou
    WScript.Echo member.Name
Next
```

JScript
getobjs.js

```
var ou = GetObject("LDAP://OU=Engineering,DC=seattle,DC=domain,DC=com");

mList = new Enumerator(ou);

for (; !mList.atEnd(); mList.moveNext())
{
 s = mList.item();
 WScript.Echo(s.Name);
}
```

Moving, renaming, and deleting organizational units

The LDAP provider supports the MoveHere method for moving and renaming organizational units. The following example moves Developers so that it is a sub-unit of Engineering:

VBScript

```
Set cont = GetObject("LDAP://OU=Engineering,DC=seattle,DC=domain,DC=com")
cont.MoveHere "LDAP://OU=Developers,DC=seattle,DC=domain,DC=com",
"OU=Developers"
```

JScript

```
var cont = GetObject("LDAP://OU=Engineering,DC=seattle,DC=domain,DC=com");
cont.MoveHere("LDAP://OU=Developers,DC=seattle,DC=domain,DC=com",
"OU=Developers");
```

You delete organizational units using the Delete method. An example follows:

VBScript

```
Set obj = GetObject("LDAP://DC=seattle,DC=domain,DC=com")
obj.Delete "organizationalUnit", "OU=Engineering"
```

JScript

```
var obj = GetObject("LDAP://DC=seattle,DC=domain,DC=com");
obj.Delete("organizationalUnit", "OU=Engineering");
```

Managing User Accounts with LDAP

Just about everything you learned about managing user accounts with WinNT can be applied to managing user accounts with LDAP. There are some important differences, however, and these differences are examined in this section.

Examining user object properties with LDAP

Table 20-7 provides a summary of properties for Active Directory user objects. Before you can work with user objects, you must bind to the container in which the objects reside, such as:

```
GetObject("LDAP://CN=Users,DC=seattle,DC=tvpress,DC=com")
```

Or you must access the user object directly, such as:

```
GetObject("LDAP://CN=William R. Stanek, OU=Technology,DC=seattle,
DC=tvpress,DC=com")
```

TABLE 20-7

Active Directory User Object Properties

Property	Status	Value Type	Min. Range	Max. Range	Multiple Values
adminDescription	RW	DirectoryString	0	1024	False
adminDisplayName	RW	DirectoryString	1	256	False
cn	RO	DirectoryString	1	64	False
company	RW	DirectoryString	1	64	False
controlAccessRights	RO	OctetString	16	16	True
department	RW	DirectoryString	1	64	False
description	RW	DirectoryString	0	1024	True
destinationIndicator	RW	PrintableString	1	128	True
displayName	RW	DirectoryString	0	256	False
displayNamePrintable	RW	PrintableString	1	256	False
division	RW	DirectoryString	0	256	False
employeeID	RW	DirectoryString	0	16	False
extensionName	RW	DirectoryString	1	255	True

Property	Status	Value Type	Min. Range	Max. Range	Multiple Values
facsimileTelephone Number	RW	DirectoryString	1	64	False
generationQualifier	RW	DirectoryString	1	64	False
givenName	RW	DirectoryString	1	64	False
homePhone	RW	DirectoryString	1	64	False
homePostalAddress	RW	DirectoryString	1	4096	False
info	RW	DirectoryString	1	1024	False
initials	RW	DirectoryString	1	6	False
internationalISDNNumber	RW	NumericString	1	16	True
mail	RW	DirectoryString	0	256	False
middleName	RW	DirectoryString	0	64	False
mobile	RW	DirectoryString	1	64	False
mSMQDigests	RW	OctetString	16	16	True
name	RW	DirectoryString	1	255	False
networkAddress	RW	CaseIgnoreString	0	256	True
nTSecurityDescriptor	RO	ObjectSecurity Descriptor	0	132096	False
objectGUID	RO	OctetString	16	16	False
objectSid	RO	OctetString	0	28	False
otherFacsimile TelephoneNumber	RW	DirectoryString	1	64	True
otherHomePhone	RW	DirectoryString	1	64	True
otherLoginWorkstations	RW	DirectoryString	0	1024	True
otherMobile	RW	DirectoryString	1	64	True
otherPager	RW	DirectoryString	1	64	True
otherTelephone	RW	DirectoryString	1	64	True
ou	RW	DirectoryString	1	64	True
pager	RW	DirectoryString	1	64	False

continued

TABLE 20-7 *(continued)*

Property	Status	Value Type	Min. Range	Max. Range	Multiple Values
personalTitle	RW	DirectoryString	1	64	False
physicalDelivery OfficeName	RW	DirectoryString	1	128	False
postalAddress	RW	DirectoryString	1	4096	True
postalCode	RW	DirectoryString	1	40	False
postOfficeBox	RW	DirectoryString	1	40	True
primaryInternational ISDNNumber	RW	DirectoryString	1	64	False
primaryTelexNumber	RW	DirectoryString	1	64	False
proxyAddresses	RW	DirectoryString	1	1123	True
registeredAddress	RW	OctetString	1	4096	True
sAMAccountName	RW	DirectoryString	0	256	False
sn	RW	DirectoryString	1	64	False
street	RW	DirectoryString	1	1024	False
streetAddress	RW	DirectoryString	1	1024	False
telephoneNumber	RW	DirectoryString	1	64	False
telexNumber	RW	OctetString	1	32	True
textEncodedORAddress	RW	DirectoryString	1	1024	False
thumbnailLogo	RW	OctetString	1	32767	False
thumbnailPhoto	RW	OctetString	0	102400	False
title	RW	DirectoryString	1	64	False
userCert	RW	OctetString	0	32767	False
userParameters	RW	DirectoryString	0	32767	False
userPassword	RW	OctetString	1	128	True
userWorkstations	RW	DirectoryString	0	1024	False
wWWHomePage	RW	DirectoryString	1	2048	False
x121Address	RW	NumericString	1	15	True

With user objects, the LDAP provider also supports a custom mapping between ADSI properties and Active Directory properties. These customizations only apply to specific properties and are designed to more closely resemble the fields that you'll find in Active Directory Users and Computers dialog boxes.

A partial list of custom mappings is shown in Table 20-8. Because of these custom mappings, your scripts can refer to the `givenName` property as FirstName, the `sn` property as LastName, and so on.

TABLE 20-8

Custom Mappings for User Object Properties

ADSI Properties	Active Directory Property
AccountDisabled	userAccountControl Mask
AccountExpirationDate	AccountExpires
BadLoginCount	BadPwdCount
Department	Department
Description	Description
Division	Division
EmailAddress	Mail
EmployeeID	EmployeeID
FaxNumber	FacsimileTelephoneNumber
FirstName	GivenName
FullName	DisplayName
HomeDirectory	HomeDirectory
HomePage	WWWHomePage
IsAccountLocked	UserAccountControl
Languages	Language
LastFailedLogin	BadPasswordTime
LastLogin	LastLogon
LastLogoff	LastLogoff
LastName	Sn
LoginHours	LogonHours
LoginScript	ScriptPath

continued

TABLE 20-8	(continued)
ADSI Properties	**Active Directory Property**
LoginWorkstations	UserWorkstations
Manager	Manager
MaxStorage	MaxStorage
NamePrefix	PersonalTitle
NameSuffix	GenerationQualifier
OfficeLocations	PhysicalDeliveryOfficeName
OtherName	MiddleName
PasswordLastChanged	PwdLastSet
PasswordRequired	UserAccountControl
Picture	ThumbnailPhoto
PostalAddresses	PostalAddress
PostalCodes	PostalCode
Profile	ProfilePath
SeeAlso	SeeAlso
TelephoneHome	HomePhone
TelephoneMobile	Mobile
TelephoneNumber	TelephoneNumber
TelephonePager	Pager
Title	Title

Creating user accounts with LDAP

While the WinNT provider allows you to create both local and domain user accounts, the LDAP provider can only create domain user accounts. Yet unlike WinNT, these domain accounts can be placed in any container or organizational unit, giving you additional flexibility.

To create a user account, you must specify the common name and the Windows NT SAM account name. All other properties are optional.

You could create a user account for William R. Stanek and place it in the Technology organizational unit as follows:

VBScript

```
Set obj = GetObject("LDAP://OU=Technology,DC=seattle,DC=domain,DC=com")
Set usr = obj.Create("user", "CN=William R. Stanek")
usr.samAccountName = "wrstanek"
usr.SetInfo
```

JScript

```
var obj = GetObject("LDAP://OU=Technology,DC=seattle,DC=domain,DC=com");
var usr = obj.Create("user", "CN=William R. Stanek");
usr.samAccountName = "wrstanek";
usr.SetInfo();
```

If no additional attributes are specified, the new user account is created with default property settings. These default property settings are as follows:

- Full Name (displayName) is blank.
- First Name (givenName) is blank.
- Last Name (sn) is blank.
- User Principal Name (UPN) is blank.
- Password is blank.
- Primary group is set to Domain Users.

User flags are also set on the account. These flags state that the user must change the password, the account is disabled, and the account never expires. User flags can be set using techniques similar to those discussed in Chapter 17. All of the flags discussed in Table 17-4 apply to LDAP user objects, as well. You set or view these flags through the userAccessControl property.

With LDAP, you must create a user account before you can set or change the password. The related methods are the same, however. You use SetPassword to set a password and ChangePassword to change a password, as follows:

VBScript

```
Set usr = GetObject("LDAP://CN=William R. Stanek,
  OU=Technology,DC=seattle,DC=domain,DC=com")
usr.SetPassword "NewPassword"

Set usr = GetObject("LDAP://CN=William R. Stanek,
  OU=Technology,DC=seattle,DC=domain,DC=com")
usr.ChangePassword "OldPassword","NewPassword"
```

JScript

```
var usr = GetObject("LDAP://CN=William R. Stanek,
  OU=Technology,DC=seattle,DC=domain,DC=com");
usr.SetPassword("NewPassword");

var usr = GetObject("LDAP://CN=William R. Stanek,
  OU=Technology,DC=seattle,DC=domain,DC=com");
usr.ChangePassword("OldPassword","NewPassword");
```

Setting user account flags

The LDAP implementation of the user object provides several advantages over the WinNT implementation, especially when it comes to setting account flags. Unlike WinNT, you can set any of the following properties directly and don't have to use the `userAccessControl` flags:

- User must change password
- Account disabled
- Account lockout
- Account expiration

You specify that the user must change his password with the `pwdLastSet` property. A value of zero (0) means the user must change his password at the next logon. A value of –1 clears this setting. In this example, you specify that William R. Stanek must change his password at the next logon:

VBScript

```
Set usr = GetObject("LDAP://CN=William R. Stanek, OU=Technology,DC=seattle,
DC=domain,DC=com")
usr.Put "pwdLastSet", CLng(0)
usr.SetInfo
```

JScript

```
var usr = GetObject("LDAP://CN=William R. Stanek, OU=Technology,DC=seattle,
DC=domain,DC=com");
usr.Put("pwdLastSet", 0);
usr.SetInfo();
```

You can disable a user account by setting the `AccountDisable` property to True (1). Then to enable the account, you would set `AccountDisable` to False (0), as follows:

VBScript

```
Set usr = GetObject("LDAP://CN=William R. Stanek,
  OU=Technology,DC=seattle,DC=domain,DC=com")
usr.AccountDisabled = False
usr.SetInfo
```

JScript

```
var usr = GetObject("LDAP://CN=William R. Stanek,
  OU=Technology,DC=seattle,DC=domain,DC=com");
usr.AccountDisabled = 0;
usr.SetInfo();
```

To unlock an account that has been locked out by the operating system, set the IsAccountLocked property to False (0), as follows:

VBScript

```
Set usr = GetObject("LDAP://CN=William R. Stanek,
  OU=Technology,DC=seattle,DC=domain,DC=com")
usr.IsAccountLocked = False
usr.SetInfo
```

JScript

```
var usr = GetObject("LDAP://CN=William R. Stanek,
  OU=Technology,DC=seattle,DC=domain,DC=com");
usr.IsAccountLocked = 0;
usr.SetInfo();
```

Only Windows can set IsAccountLocked to True (1). Typically, an account gets locked because a user (or intruder) repeatedly entered a bad password.

Other useful properties for managing user accounts are AccountExpirationDate and AccountExpires. If you want an account to expire on a specific date, set AccountExpirationDate to the desired date, as in the following:

VBScript

```
Set usr = GetObject("LDAP://CN=William R. Stanek,
  OU=Technology,DC=seattle,DC=domain,DC=com")
usr.AccountExpirationDate = "12/15/2001"
usr.SetInfo
```

JScript

```
var usr = GetObject("LDAP://CN=William R. Stanek,
  OU=Technology,DC=seattle,DC=domain,DC=com");
usr.AccountExpirationDate = "12/15/2001";
usr.SetInfo();
```

To specify that an account should never expire, set AccountExpires to –1, as follows:

VBScript

```
Set usr = GetObject("LDAP://CN=William R. Stanek,
  OU=Technology,DC=seattle,DC=domain,DC=com")
usr.AccountExpires = -1
usr.SetInfo
```

JScript

```
var usr = GetObject("LDAP://CN=William R. Stanek,
  OU=Technology,DC=seattle,DC=domain,DC=com");
usr.AccountExpires = -1;
usr.SetInfo();
```

Viewing group membership

As with WinNT, you can use the `Groups()` method to check group membership for users. The `Groups()` method returns a collection of group objects to which a user belongs. You could use this method to examine all of the groups William R. Stanek belongs to, as follows:

VBScript

```
Set usr = GetObject("LDAP://CN=William R. Stanek,
  OU=Technology,DC=seattle,DC=domain,DC=com")

For Each grp In usr.Groups
   WScript.Echo  grp.Name
Next
```

JScript

```
var usr = GetObject("LDAP://CN=William R. Stanek,
  OU=Technology,DC=seattle,DC=domain,DC=com");

mList = new Enumerator(usr.Groups());

for (; !mList.atEnd(); mList.moveNext())
{
 s = mList.item();
 WScript.Echo(s.Name);
}
```

Output

```
CN=Enterprise Admins
CN=Schema Admins
CN=Domain Admins
CN=Administrators
CN=Backup Operators
```

Moving, renaming, and deleting user accounts with LDAP

The LDAP provider supports the `MoveHere` method for moving and renaming user accounts, and the `Delete` method for deleting user accounts. You could move a user account to a different container, as Listing 20-13 demonstrates.

LISTING 20-13

Moving a User Account

VBScript
moveuser.vbs

```
'Get rootDSE
Set rootDSE = GetObject("LDAP://rootDSE")
domainCont = rootDSE.Get("defaultNamingContext")

'Get the destination container
Set cont = GetObject("LDAP://OU=Engineering," & domainCont)

'Move object from original container to the destination
cont.MoveHere "LDAP://CN=William R. Stanek,OU=Technology," & domainCont,
  "CN=William R. Stanek"
```

JScript
moveuser.js

```
//Get rootDSE
var rootDSE = GetObject("LDAP://rootDSE");
domainCont = rootDSE.Get("defaultNamingContext");

//Get the destination container
var cont = GetObject("LDAP://OU=Engineering," + domainCont);

//Move object from original container to the destination
cont.MoveHere("LDAP://CN=William R. Stanek,OU=Technology," + domainCont,
  "CN=William R. Stanek");
```

Summary

In this chapter, you used the LDAP ADSI provider to manage Active Directory objects. As you learned, many extensions are available for common objects, and you can use these extensions to manipulate objects in many different ways. Because this provider can access other LDAP-compliant technologies, you can apply everything you've learned in this chapter when scripting Exchange Server, as well as other LDAP-compliant servers. For example, you could create, move, and delete Exchange mailboxes using the techniques discussed in this chapter.

Part IV

Windows PowerShell

Part IV digs deep into Windows PowerShell, covering everything from input, output, and error handling to working with files to managing event logging and beyond. In Part IV, you'll learn exactly how you can use PowerShell to configure, manage, and troubleshoot Windows. You'll also learn how to use PowerShell with Active Directory Services Interfaces (ADSI) and Windows Management Instrumentation (WMI).

Chapter 21

Input, Output, and Error Handling in PowerShell

I t's important to learn early in your PowerShell career the range of options you have for output. Output can go into a variable, it can be sent to a file, it can be piped into another command, or it can be left to drop out to the console. One of the first lessons in this area to learn is that you don't have to do *anything* to get output. Writing in PowerShell gives you access to many facilities which control output and handle XML, HTML, and CSV formats with minimal effort. In fact, one of the reasons that people take up PowerShell in the first place is the small amount of work needed to produce well-formatted output.

This chapter is going to look at some of the inputs and outputs and some of the traps that might be there for people coming to PowerShell for other environments.

Output to the Console

Arguably the most famous piece of computer program is the one that appears at the start of Kernighan and Ritchie's *The C Programming Language*, which contains the line:

```
printf("Hello, world!\n\r");
```

Ever since that book appeared, people learning any new language have started with something to output some basic text on whatever *console device* they are using, be that a teletype printer, a terminal screen, or a text window in Windows. PowerShell refers to this window as its *host*. It is common to call this destination *standard output*.

In the batch language, which has been with us since the early days of DOS, you use the echo command when you want to output something to standard output. For example:

```
Echo Hello world
```

In PowerShell, if you enter the text string:

```
"Hello world"
```

PowerShell outputs "Hello World" back to you. What has happened here? You've got some output on the screen without ever giving a command to do that: CMD would have responded with the following:

```
'"hello world"' is not recognized as an internal or external command,
operable program or batch file.
```

PowerShell has parsed this line and decided you have given it a text string object: you've been clear by putting quotation marks around it that you wanted a string object. So what do you want to do with your string object? Do you want to put in a variable? No. Send it to a file? Didn't say so. Pipe it to a command? Haven't asked for that either. So PowerShell lets it fall out to the console.

Without the quotes around it, PowerShell assumes that text must be a command, but it can recognize numbers—in fact, you can check how it handles different kinds of input:

```
> ("hello").gettype().name
String
> (3).gettype().name
Int32
> (3.14159).gettype().name
Double
> ([wmiclass]"\\.\root\cimv2:win32_processor").gettype().name
ManagementClass
```

Without quotation marks, PowerShell looks for a command that matches the string. Of course commands with spaces in them need to be wrapped in quotes but entering 'C:\Program Files\ Internet Explorer\iexplore.exe' just returns the string. To execute what is in the string as a command you prefix the string with an ampersand (&):

```
& 'C:\Program Files\Internet Explorer\iexplore.exe'
```

A Little Diversion into Strings

In the last few paragraphs the single quote and double quotation mark have been used almost interchangeably.

PowerShell interprets this text:

```
& "C:\Program Files\Internet Explorer\iexplore.exe"
```

which uses double quotes in same way it would if the if single quotes were used as follows:

```
& 'C:\Program Files\Internet Explorer\iexplore.exe'
```

However, they are not quite the same; variables are wrapped in the double quoted version, so you could have entered:

```
> & "$Env:ProgramFiles\Internet Explorer\iexplore.exe"
```

But they are *not* expanded in the single quotation version—which causes an error in this case:

```
> & '$Env:ProgramFiles\Internet Explorer\iexplore.exe'
The term '$Env:ProgramFiles\Internet Explorer\iexplore.exe' is not
recognized as a cmdlet, function, operable program, or script file.
```

Strings can also be followed by a -f (format) operator, as in the following command:

```
'{0}\Internet Explorer\iexplore.exe' -f $env:programFiles
```

The {0} says to the –f operator "convert the parameter at position 0 to a string and insert it here."

Inside the braces, you can specify formatting for the string-conversion if need be. It is shorter to write:

```
"you specified a cylinder diameter of {1} and height {2}, giving
a volume of {0:0.00000} x ({1}/2)^2 x {2} = {3:0.000}" -f
$pi,$d,$h,($pi*$h*$d*$d/4)
```

than it is to write:

```
"you specified a cylinder diameter of " + $d + " and height " + $d + "
giving a volume of " + $pi.tostring("0.00000") + " x (" + $d + "/2)^2
x" +$h + " = " + ($pi*$h*$d*$d/4).toString("0.000")
```

It is even possible to use a hybrid—with both string expansion and the –f parameter in the same string:

```
"you specified a cylinder diameter of $d and height $h, giving a volume
of {0:0.00000} x ($d/2)^2 x $h = {1:0.000}" -f $pi ($pi*$h*$d*$d/4)
```

The settings you can use inside the braces or in a tostring( ) method are explained in more detail in Table 21-1. Most formats can include a digit, in the table 4 is used as an example, but other numbers could be used.

TABLE 21-1

Formatting codes and their results

Type	Code	Applied to 3.14159265358979	Applied to 31	Applied to 314159265358.979
Currency	c	$3.14	$31.00	$314,159,265,358.98
	C4	$3.1416	$31.0000	$314,159,265,358.9790
Decimal	D	Exception	31	Exception
	D4	Exception	0031	Exception
Exponential	E	3.141593E+000	3.100000e+001	3.141593e+011
	E4	3.1416e+000	3.1000e+001	3.1416e+011
Fixed point	F	3.14	31.00	314159265358.98
	f4	3.1416	31.0000	314159265358.9790
General	G	3.14159265358979	31	3.142e+11
	G4	3.142	31	314,159,265,358.9790
Number	N	3.14	31.00	314,159,265,358.98
	n4	3.1416	31.0000	314,159,265,358.9790
Percentage	p	314.16 %	3,100.00 %	31,415,926,535,897.90%
	p4	314.1593 %	3,100.0000 %	31,415,926,535,897.9000%
Round trip	r	3.1415926535897931	Exception	314159265358.979
	r4	3.1415926535897931	Exception	314159265358.979
Hex	x	Exception	1f	Exception
	x4	Exception	001f	Exception
Custom	00.00%	314.16%	3100.00%	31415926535897.90%
	##.##%	314.16%	3100%	31415926535897.90%
	#,###.##	3.14	31	314,159,265,358.98
	0,000.00	0,003.14	0,031.00	314,159,265,358.98

Custom formats can be built up for numbers as in the preceding examples. It is important to understand that different number formats will be treated differently in different cultures.

You can see what the settings are by querying a .NET object:

```
[System.Globalization.CultureInfo]::currentCulture.numberFormat
```

This object has properties, CurrencyGroupSlizes, NumberGroupSizes and PercentGroupSizes, which specify how many digits are grouped together: NumberDecimalSeparator allows Windows to cope with using the , and the . as the decimal point and CurrencySymbol lets Windows use $, £, €, or ¥ as needed.

You can examine the settings for each culture. For example, the following code:

```
[System.Globalization.CultureInfo]::GetCultureinfo("ja-jp").
numberFormat
```

will get the number format for Japanese. To discover the list of possible settings to pass in GetCultureInfo you can use the following:

```
[System.Globalization.CultureInfo]::GetCultures("installedWin32Culture
s")
```

There is a special culture named the invariant culture. Cynics might assume that this is English-US, but it is a mixture of US and international settings. The next table uses the date formats returned by:

```
[System.Globalization.CultureInfo]::InvariantCulture.datetimeformat
```

Dates can have more complex formatting, as shown in Table 21-2.

TABLE 21-2

Pre-defined date formatting codes

Code	Description	Format (invariant culture)
d	ShortDate pattern	`MM/dd/yyyy`
D	LongDate pattern	`dddd, dd MMMM yyyy`
f	Full date/time pattern (short time)	`dddd, dd MMMM yyyy HH:mm`
F	Full date/time pattern (long time)	`dddd, dd MMMM yyyy HH:mm:ss`
g	General date/time pattern (short time)	`MM/dd/yyyy HH:mm`
G	General date/time pattern (long time)	`MM/dd/yyyy HH:mm:ss`
M or m	Month day pattern	`MMMM dd`
o	Round-trip date/time pattern	`"yyyy'-'MM'-'dd'T'HH':'mm':'ss.` `fffffffK"`

continued

TABLE 21-2   *(continued)*

Code	Description	Format (invariant culture)
R or r	RFC1123 pattern	ddd, dd MMM yyyy HH':'mm':'ss 'GMT'
s	SortableDateTime pattern	yyyy'-'MM'-'dd'T'HH':'mm':'ss
t	ShortTime pattern "HH:mm"	HH:mm
T	LongTime pattern	HH:mm:ss
u	Universal SortableDate/Time pattern	yyyy'-'MM'-'dd HH':'mm':'ss'Z'
Y or y	YearMonth pattern	yyyy MMMM

Finally you can put custom date formats together using the terms in Table 21-3.

TABLE 21-3

Custom date formatting codes

Code	Meaning
h	h is the hour on the 12-hour clock without a leading 0.
	hh (plus any number of additional "h" specifiers) is the hour on the 12-hour clock: A single-digit hour is formatted with a leading 0.
	H is the hour on the 24-hour clock without a leading 0.
	HH (plus any number of additional "H" specifiers) is the hour on the 24-hour clock: A single-digit hour is formatted with a leading 0.
m	m is the minute formatted without a leading zero.
	mm (plus any number of additional "m" specifiers) is the minute; a single-digit minute is formatted with a leading zero.
s	s is the second, formatted as a number without a leading zero.
	ss (plus any number of additional "s" specifiers) is the second; a single-digit second is formatted with a leading zero.
f	Represents the seconds fraction. f is the most significant digit; ff is the two most significant . . .up to fffffff for the seven most significant, with trailing zeros included.
	F is the most significant digit; FF is the two most significant . . . up to FFFFFFF for the seven most significant, with trailing zeros omitted.

Code	Meaning
t	t represents the first character of the A.M./P.M. designator.
	tt (plus any number of additional "t" specifiers) represents the full A.M./P.M. designator.
d	d represents the day of the month as a number without a leading zero.
	dd represents the day of the month as a number; a single-digit day is formatted with a leading zero.
	ddd represents the abbreviated name of the day of the week.
	dddd (plus any number of additional "d" specifiers) represents the full name of the day of the week.
M	M represents the month as a number without a leading zero.
	MM represents the month as a number. A single-digit month is formatted with a leading zero.
	MMM represents the abbreviated name of the month.
	MMMM represents the full name of the month.
y	y represents the year as, at most, a two-digit number, without a leading zero.
	yy represents the year as, at most, a two-digit number. If the year is one of the first ten in a new century, it includes a leading zero.
	yyyy represents the year as a four-digit number. If the year has fewer than four digits, the number is padded with leading zeros to achieve four digits.
g	g (plus any number of additional "g" specifiers) represents the period or era (A.D. for example).
z	z represents the signed time zone offset in hours, without a leading zero.
	zz represents the signed time zone offset in hours; a single-digit offset is formatted with a leading zero.
	zzz (plus any number of additional "z" specifiers) is the time offset in hours and minutes.
	The offset is always displayed with a leading sign. A plus sign (+) indicates hours ahead of GMT, and a minus sign (-) indicates hours behind GMT. The offset ranges from –12 through +13. The offset is affected by daylight savings time.
	: is the time separator. It can be overridden by local settings.
	/ is the date separator. It can be overridden by local settings.
	" or ' can be used for quoted text. " should be preceded with the escape character (\).
	%x displays any one of the above on their own.
	Any other character is copied to the result.

Implicit and Explicit Output

You need to be aware of implicit and explicit outputs. As you've seen, you can just specify a string and PowerShell will send it to the host console. That means there is no need to tell a function that something should be returned. So the following function will work very nicely:

```
Function calc-cylinder
{"To calculate the volume of a cylinder using Pi(R^2)H"
"Enter the diameter of your cylinder"
$d=read-host
"Enter the height of your cylinder"
 $h=read-host
 $pi=[system.math]::pi
 "You specified a cylinder diameter of $d and height $h, giving
a volume of {0:0.00000} x ($d/2)^2 x $h = {1:0.000}" -f $pi,
($pi*$h*$d*$d/4)
 }
```

When you run it, it looks like this:

```
To calculate the volume of a cylinder using Pi(R^2)H
Enter the diameter of your cylinder
12
Enter the height of your cylinder
14
You specified a cylinder diameter of 12 and height 14, giving a volume
of 3.14159 x (12/2)^2 x 14 = 1319.469
```

You can improve the behavior of the function by allowing the user to pass it parameters, like this:

```
Function calc-cylinder
{Param ($d=(read-host -prompt "Enter the diameter") ,
        $h=(read-host -prompt "Enter the height"))
 "Calculating the volume of a cylinder using Pi (R^2) H"
 $pi=[system.math]::pi
 $result=($pi*$h*$d*$d/4)
 "You specified a cylinder diameter of $d and height $h, so the volume
is {0:0.00000} x ($d/2)^2 x $h " -f $pi
 $result
 }
```

So when you run the function, you get this:

```
> calc-cylinder -d 12 -h 14
Calculating the volume of a cylinder using Pi (R^2) H
You specified a cylinder diameter of 12 and height 14, so the volume is
3.14159 x (12/2)^2 x 14
1319.46891450771
```

You should be able to pass the function the bore and stroke of an engine (its cylinder diameter and height), and multiply the cylinder volume by the number of cylinders to get the total capacity of the engine, like this:

```
> (calc-cylinder -d 7.78 -h 10.5) * 4
Calculating the volume of a cylinder using Pi (R^2) H
You specified a cylinder diameter of 7.78 and height 10.5, so the
volume is 3.14159 x (7.78/2)^2 x 10.5
499.158389030554
Calculating the volume of a cylinder using Pi (R^2) H
You specified a cylinder diameter of 7.78 and height 10.5, so the
volume is 3.14159 x (7.78/2)^2 x 10.5
499.158389030554
Calculating the volume of a cylinder using Pi (R^2) H
You specified a cylinder diameter of 7.78 and height 10.5, so the
volume is 3.14159 x (7.78/2)^2 x 10.5
499.158389030554
Calculating the volume of a cylinder using Pi (R^2) H
You specified a cylinder diameter of 7.78 and height 10.5, so the
volume is 3.14159 x (7.78/2)^2 x 10.5
499.158389030554
```

Wait—that's not right and, no, it's not an error by the typesetter. PowerShell really has returned four copies of the calculation. Each one is an array containing two text strings and a double precision floating point number. How was PowerShell supposed to know what was the *true* result of the calculation and what was written to the screen to keep us informed?

The answer, of course, is that you need to stop *implying* to PowerShell that you want something printed on the screen and be explicit about it, using the Write-host Cmdlet.

```
Function calc-cylinder
{Param ($d=(read-host -prompt "Enter the diameter") ,$h=(read-host
-prompt "Enter the height"))
 Write-host "Calculating the volume of a cylinder using Pi (R^2) H"
 $pi=[system.math]::pi
 $result=($pi*$h*$d*$d/4)
 Write-host ("You specified a cylinder diameter of $d and height $h, so
the volume is {0:0.00000} x ($d/2)^2 x $h " -f $pi)
 $result
 }

> (calc-cylinder -d 7.78 -h 10.5) * 4
Calculating the volume of a cylinder using Pi (R^2) H
You specified a cylinder diameter of 7.78 and height 10.5, so the
volume is 3.14159 x (7.78/2)^2 x 10.5
1996.63355612222
```

Notice in the second Write-Host the string is wrapped in brackets; otherwise, PowerShell will assume that -f $pi is a parameter for Write-Host. Because -f is short for -foregroundColor this would mean you were trying to set a non-integer foreground color—which will cause an error.

Here, you can see two important guidelines at work:

- **Think about input parameters for the function.** Allow users to provide parameters; don't ask them to type in input by using the Read-Host Cmdlet unless it is necessary (for example, if a parameter is omitted.)

- **Try to divide function output into something you want to tell the user and something to be used by another operation.** If a function's sole job is only to display information, you are safe using implicit output; if its output is used by something else, then you aren't.

When you specify that something should be sent to the host console with Write-Host or by piping it to Out-Host, it is no longer an output of the function; this has a consequence for capturing what you do because, if you redirect calc-cylinder to a file, it does not affect what is written to the screen.

```
> (calc-cylinder -d 7.78 -h 10.5) > results.txt
Calculating the volume of a cylinder using Pi (R^2) H
You specified a cylinder diameter of 7.78 and height 10.5, so the
volume is 3.14159 x (7.78/2)^2 x 10.5
```

You can check what is in the file and you see it contains only the value:

```
> type results.txt
499.158389030554
```

Sometimes that is exactly what you want, and sometimes you want to have a record of what appeared on the screen. PowerShell provides two Cmdlets, Start-transcript and Stop-transcript, which do exactly that; PowerShell doesn't care what route something took to reach the console. If it got there it goes in the transcript. You'll see shortly why this is important.

Verbose and Debug Output

One of the problems any developer has to deal with when thinking about output is how much of it there should be.

In the preceding example, telling the user that the formula for a cylinder is $\pi r^2 h$ and what they passed into the function is probably going to be redundant most of the time in practice may annoy some users. Consider the case where someone is getting the wrong results. They know that a cylinder 30 units high and 10 units in diameter should have a volume a little less than 2500, but is turning out over 7,000. Wouldn't it be useful to show that calc-cylinder 30 10 treats the first parameter as the diameter not the height. What is the developer to do? Annoy one set of users with output that isn't needed? Or leave others floundering? What if those are the same users on different days?

Fortunately, PowerShell has an answer in `Write-Verbose`.

If you enter the command:

```
Write-Verbose "hello world"
```

at the command prompt on a default configuration of PowerShell, then *nothing happens*. And you'll be left wondering "How can that be called 'Verbose'?" PowerShell has a trick here: whereas CMD and UNIX shells have the concept of standard output and standard error, PowerShell has some other pipelines that you can write to. You can write to these pipelines with different `write-` commands, as shown in Table 21-4.

TABLE 21-4

PowerShell's write commands

`Cmdlet`	Description
Write-Output	Writes to the "success" pipeline, and is pretty much redundant because if PowerShell isn't told what else to do with something that's what it will do anyway.
Write-error	Writes to the error pipeline, which shows up in red on the screen
Write-Debug	Writes to warning pipeline, which shows up in yellow on the screen, prefixed with the word DEBUG
Write-verbose	Writes to warning pipeline, which shows up in yellow on the screen, prefixed with the word VERBOSE
Write-Warning	Writes to warning pipeline, which shows up in yellow on the screen, prefixed with the word WARNING

So there are probably two questions in your mind, one of which is "Why didn't `Write-Verbose` output anything?" The other is "Isn't it worse to have the text in yellow with the word VERBOSE in front of it?" The answer to these is the same: Debug, Error, Verbose, and Warning all have an associated preference variable, which can be set to `Silently Continue`, `Continue`, `Stop`, or `Inquire`.

By default, `$ErrorPreference` and `$WarningPreference` are set to `Continue`—that is, output the message but do not stop; and `$debugPrefence` and `$VerbosePreference` are set to `Silently Continue`—that is, ignore the message and proceed as if it hadn't even been written. `Stop` stops the script and `Inquire` asks the user if the script should continue.

So if you change the function you were using before to this:

```
Function calc-cylinder
{Param ($d=(read-host -prompt "Enter the diameter") ,$h=(read-host
-prompt "Enter the height"))
 Write-Verbose "Calculating the volume of a cylinder using Pi (R^2) H"
 $pi=[system.math]::pi
 $result=($pi*$h*$d*$d/4)
 Write-debug ("You specified a cylinder diameter of $d and height $h,
so the volume is {0:0.00000} x ($d/2)^2 x $h " -f $pi)
 $result
 }
```

When you run the function, you can change the preferences to give a better understanding of what the function is doing.

```
> $VerbosePreference="Continue"
> calc-cylinder 30 10
VERBOSE: Calculating the volume of a cylinder using Pi (R^2) H
7068.58347057703
> $DebugPreference="continue"
> calc-cylinder 30 10
VERBOSE: Calculating the volume of a cylinder using Pi (R^2) H
DEBUG: You specified a cylinder diameter of 30 and height 10, so the
volume is 3.14159 x (30/2)^2 x 10
7068.58347057703
```

Managing Different Outputs from Cmdlets

PowerShell has a standard set of parameters that most Cmdlets implement. These include -Confirm and -WhatIf, and -OutputBuffer, which controls the number of objects to be buffered between one command and the next one in the pipeline. In addition to these, there are five that control output: -Debug, -Verbose, -ErrorAction, -ErrorVariable, and -OutVariable.

- -Verbose will cause output to the verbose display regardless of the setting of $verbosePreference.

- -Debug will prompt the user if they wish to continue, regardless of the setting of $DebugPreference.

- -erroraction allows $errorActionPreference to be overridden for a single Cmdlet.

$ErrorActionPreference can be set with a scope for just a function or script like this:

```
$Local:ErrorActionPreference = "SilentlyContinue"
```

This will silence error reporting for every Cmdlet in the script or function.

To test access to an administrator-only registry key to see if the user is running with elevated privileges, you can use the following command and silence errors only for that Cmdlet and not for the whole script.

```
dir Microsoft.PowerShell.Core\Registry::HKEY_USERS\s-1-5-20 `
    -ErrorAction silentlycontinue | out-null
```

PowerShell has an automatic variable, $?, which queries the success of the last command so you could follow the previous line with:

```
if ($?) { write-host -ForegroundColor Green "This session is elevated"} `
else { write-host -ForegroundColor Red  "This session is not elevated."}
```

This is a pretty simple test; if the `dir` is successful, you must be an administrator and any error means you're not—but it would be better to try to check the error and confirm that it is access denied. PowerShell has another automatic variable, `Error[]`, an array that holds the history of errors. An error can be returned from the Cmdlet in a named variable. One important detail to note is that the variable name doesn't include a dollar ($) sign in this case. You can think of $ as meaning "the value of" in statements such as `$x=10 ; Write-host $x`. When you tell a Cmdlet to store the result in `x`, (without the $ sign) you're passing it a pointer to where something should go. So the preceding line can be extended like this:

```
dir Microsoft.PowerShell.Core\Registry::HKEY_USERS\s-1-5-20 `
    -ErrorAction silentlycontinue -errorVariable MyErr | out-null
```

Using `-ErrorVariable` (or `-OutVariable` for success output) does not redirect output but makes a copy of it, so simply writing the line as follows will *not* hide the line from the user,

```
dir Microsoft.PowerShell.Core\Registry::HKEY_USERS\s-1-5-20 `
    -errorVariable MyErr
```

In the same way, the following:

```
dir -Outvariable myFolder
```

is not the same as:

```
$myFolder = dir
```

The second line takes the output and stores it in a variable without returning any results, whereas the first returns the results of looking at the current directory *and* stores the results in a variable. This is similar to the `Tee-Object` Cmdlet, which can write an object to a file and output it as well or can store it in a variable and output it. For example:

```
dir | Tee-object -Variable myFolder
```

or

```
dir | Tee-object -FilePath MyFolder.Txt
```

In the case of the error example, the specified variable contains an array of error objects, which give rich information. They have an Exception property, which contains the text of the message. You can see what it is in this case:

```
> $myerr[0].Exception
Requested registry access is not allowed.
```

Error objects have a *target object* property, which is very useful in a loop that is processing multiple files because it will allow the one that caused the error to be identified. In this case, it will just contain the path to the registry key. They have an InvocationInfo property, which is an object containing the information about the command that caused the error. And they have a categoryinfo property, which is an object with information about the error itself. For this error you can discover more about it using the following code.

```
> $myerr[0].categoryInfo

Category    : PermissionDenied
Activity    : Get-ChildItem
Reason      : SecurityException
TargetName  : HKEY_USERS\s-1-5-20
TargetType  : String
```

So the dir command in the preceding code can be followed with a test like this:

```
if (-not $MyErr) { write-host -Foreground Green "This session is
elevated"} `
else { if ($myerr[0].categoryInfo.category -eq "PermissionDenied") `
            {write-host -Foreground Red   "This session is not
elevated."}
        Else  {write-host -Foreground Red   "Error testing elevation"} }
```

More on Error Output

Before we leave the question of the errors, let's examine a situation in which a script needs to generate an error on purpose. You have already seen that scripts can send output to the error display. In fact, write-error has parameters to allow it to set all the properties you looked at in the previous section. So write-error is not simply "output to the error channel," but "write an object into the error[] array" as well. This works very well for informational errors but there are some cases where you need a script or a function to terminate and display an error—perhaps the simplest case being when parameters are needed but not specified. PowerShell can put in a default expression for a parameter, so a Param statement at the start of a function might contain:

```
$Server="."
```

which will set the $server parameter to "." if no parameter is specified. But the expression can be something that is evaluated, so a parameter can be written as:

```
$path=$(Throw "you must specify a path")
```

Earlier in this chapter, we described a dollar sign ($) in front of a variable name as meaning *the value of*, and it is playing a similar role in the $() construction here—effectively saying to PowerShell *evaluate this*. Evaluating throw generates an error and breaks out of the script so, for example, a function to create a new Hyper-V hard disk is called without the required parameters. The result might be as follows:

```
> new-virtualHardDisk
You must specify a Path for the disk
At C:\Users\administrator\HYPERV.PS1:119 char:33
+ {Param ([String]$vhdPath=$(Throw( <<<< "You must specify a Path for
the disk")) , [int64]$size, $parentDisk, $server="."
,[Switch]$Fixed
,[Switch]$wait)
```

Throw can be placed anywhere in a script—in a function body, for example—and it will normally cause the function to exit. PowerShell also provides a Trap keyword to specify a code block to evaluate when an error is thrown. The error object becomes available in the script block specified by trap as $_, just like code piped into anything else. Trap is not the equivalent of on error goto found in languages such as Visual Basic, so something like the following will fail.

```
Trap {"You don't have administrator Access"}
dir Microsoft.PowerShell.Core\Registry::HKEY_USERS\s-1-5-20
```

If Trap can catch only exceptions that are explicitly thrown, then it does beg the question: Why not simply write the exception handler in the body of the script? There are two reasons for wanting to do this—first, the same handler or handlers might be needed in multiple places and Trap allows the script for them to be put in one place, making the script shorter and easier to maintain. Second, in a complex combination of conditions and loops, it may simply be easier to jump out using Throw. Trap allows the exit to be more graceful, closing connections for example, but it can also continue at the next command by including the Continue keyword.

Knowing which command Trap will consider to be *next* is something that requires a little understanding of PowerShell's command processing.

Consider this simple looking command:

```
1..5 | foreach {write-host $_ ; $_ * $_ ; write-host "after the
calculation"}
```

So we are going to take the numbers 1 to 5, echo the number to console, output its square as the result of the for loop, and then echo the words *after the calculation* to the console. Simple enough—so here's the output:

```
1
1
after the calculation
2
4
after the calculation
3
9
after the calculation
4
16
after the calculation
5
25
after the calculation
```

Nothing changes if you direct the output of the function using Out-Host. In other words, the output of the for loop gets processed before the next command inside the loop.

So let's introduce a throw and a trap into this:

```
trap
{$_.exception ; continue}
1..5 | foreach {write-host $_ ; $_ * $_ ; throw "An exception"
                write-host "after the calculation"} | out-host
write-host "All done"
```

So you have a trap, which will output the exception and continue—but where does it continue from? Immediately after the throw? At the next item in the loop? Somewhere else entirely? And does the output go through to the Out-Host? Here's the output:

```
1
1
An exception
All done
```

As before, what happens here is that as soon as there is some output it is sent to the next command in the pipeline. So the sequence begins, writes 1 to the console, passes 1*1 to Out-Host, throws an exception with the text "An exception", and then continues. You can see that PowerShell continues at the next command in the block—the whole of 1..5 | foreach |Out-Host is one command.

This is not always what you want. Suppose you are trying to catch problems opening one file in many and have a trap that records failures in more than one place in the script? Three important words may have passed you by in the previous paragraph. PowerShell continues at the next command in the block. The trick for this case is that the trap needs to be inside a foreach block, like this:

```
1..5 | foreach { trap{$_.exception ; continue}
              write-host $_
              $_ * $_
              throw "An exception"
              write-host "after the calculation"} | out-host
write-host "All done"
```

Now the output is:

```
1
1
An exception
after the calculation
2
4
An exception
after the calculation
3
9
An exception
after the calculation
4
16
An exception
after the calculation
5
25
An exception
after the calculation
All done
```

Of course the drawback of this is that if you are trying to trap things in more than one block, you have to put the trap command in each one—and if the block run by trap is large, it probably needs to be moved into its own function.

Session Transcripts

One of the shortcomings of redirection is that, by default, what it can do is limited. You can redirect the normal (success) pipeline to a file with the > sign—as you can in CMD.EXE—and >> will append to a file rather than overwrite it, but anything explicitly sent to the console does *not* get redirected.

You can also redirect things sent to the error pipeline with 2>, and PowerShell has a trick for merging errors into the success pipeline by using 2>&1. This allows errors and success output to be sent to the same file or into the same piped command. The debug, verbose, and warning pipelines can't be captured in the same way.

PowerShell provides a transcript facility with two Cmdlets, Start-Transcript and Stop-Transcript.

Where a series of commands in CMD would need to be sent to a file with > and >>, and the command itself is not recorded, everything that you can see by scrolling back up in the console window is captured in the transcript, the prompt, the commands entered and their parameters error, verbose and debug output as well as the normal session output. So let's see the transcript from the cylinder calculation example—just for completeness, there is an error at the end of it.

```
**********************
Windows PowerShell Transcript Start
Start time: 20080830202103
Username  : Contoso\james
Machine   : JAMES-2008 (Microsoft Windows NT 6.0.6001 Service Pack 1)
**********************
Transcript started, output file is C:\Users\james\Documents\PowerShell_
transcript.20080830202103.txt
PS C:\Users\james\Documents\windowsPowershell> calc-cylinder 30 10
7068.58347057703
PS C:\Users\james\Documents\windowsPowershell>
$DebugPreference="continue"
PS C:\Users\james\Documents\windowsPowershell> calc-cylinder 30 10
DEBUG: You specified a cylinder diameter of 30 and height 10, so the
volume is 3.14159 x (30/2)^2 x 10
7068.58347057703
PS C:\Users\james\Documents\windowsPowershell>
$VerbosePreference="Continue"
PS C:\Users\james\Documents\windowsPowershell> calc-cylinder 30 10
VERBOSE: Calculating the volume of a cylinder using Pi (R^2) H
DEBUG: You specified a cylinder diameter of 30 and height 10, so the
volume is 3.14159 x (30/2)^2 x 10
7068.58347057703
PS C:\Users\james\Documents\windowsPowershell> $debugPreference=silentl
yContinue
The term 'silentlyContinue' is not recognized as a cmdlet, function,
operable program, or script file. Verify the term and try again.
At line:1 char:33
+ $debugPreference=silentlyContinue <<<<
PS C:\Users\james\Documents\windowsPowershell> Stop-Transcript
**********************
Windows PowerShell Transcript End
End time: 20080830202205
**********************
```

Tracking Progress

In a lot of scripts, there is a delay while something happens, and giving progress updates—a progress bar or a percentage, for example—is difficult. In a Windows forms application, it is easy enough to update a number and there is a *gas gauge* control, there is no equivalent for a batch file.

PowerShell has a Write-Progress Cmdlet that allows activity to be tracked, without leaving anything permanently on the console. It has to be passed at least two parameters: -Activity is the overall description and -Status describes what is happening. In addition, -percentagecompete gives a visual progress indicator, -Secondsremaining shows how long the command can be expected to keep running. and -CurrentActivity shows more granular information about the task. The output displayed by Write-Progress looks like this:

```
activity
    Status
    [oooooooooooooooooo               ]
    00:01:10 remaining.
    Current Activity
```

Unlike the other write- Cmdlets, the output of Write-Progress is *not* captured by the transcript process.

It is possible for Write-Progress to display nested activities:

```
for($i = 1; $i -lt 101; $i++ )
  {write-progress -activity "Updating" -Status "customers->"
-percentComplete $i
    for($j = 1; $j -lt 101; $j++ )
{write-progress -activity "Updating" -status "customer-Orders " `
 -current "Customer ID $i" -seconds (10100-(100*$i)-$j) -id 1
}
  }
```

Here you can see two loops: The outer one contains a Write-Progress statement, which displays a progress bar, and the inner one contains another Write-Progress statement, which displays the seconds remaining and a current activity. The logic behind the Write-Progress Cmdlet is that the second has an -ID parameter and thus does not overwrite the information displayed by the first.

Information displayed by Write-Progress remains onscreen until the PowerShell prompt reappears. This means that if you want to test it, you cannot simply enter the Cmdlet on its own because no sooner has the text appeared, than it will disappear, so follow it with Sleep 5 to keep it on the screen for a few seconds. Conversely, a progress message can be removed early by calling Write-Progress with a -Completed switch; if more than one progress section is on display, the -ID is used to identify which has completed; -Activity and -Status switches are still required even though they are not displayed.

Taking More Control of Formatting

One of the things that puts the *Power* into PowerShell is its ability to work with objects, and objects have many properties, not all of which will be of interest to us. For example, if you get a list of processes with the `Get-Process` command, there are over 50 properties available. You might be happy with the default selection, but you may want to select your own. Similarly, there are situations where you don't want every item returned. It is quite common for people who are starting out with PowerShell to start by converting VB or VBScript code into PowerShell language but still retain all the paradigms of VB in the resulting code. Here is an example in PowerShell:

```
$procs=Get-Process
for($i = 0; $i -lt $procs.count; $i++ )
{if ($Procs[$i].product -match "Office")
    {write-host ($Procs[$i].name.padright(20) + " "+
    $Procs[$i].cpu.tostring("00000.00") + " " +
    $Procs[$i].VM.tostring().padleft(12))
    }
}
```

This is perfectly valid PowerShell. But a few things add complexity here.

The first of these is the technique of storing something as an array and then using its `Count` property in a loop that indexes into each item. You can simply pipe into `forEach-Object` (or one of its aliases, `forEach` or %) and refer to each object using $_, as follows:

```
Get-Process | forEach-object {if ($_.product -match "Office")
    {write-host ($_.name.padright(20) + " "+
    $_.cpu.tostring("00000.00") + " " +
    $_.VM.tostring().padleft(12))
    }
}
```

That's simpler, but a second improvement would be to filter the items *before* looping through them. `Get-Process` can be given the *names* of processes—but this requires passing a list of all the members of the product family, and querying for one which is not running will result in an error . So a better solution is to put a `Where-Object` Cmdlet between the `get` and the `for`, as follows:

```
Get-Process | where-object {$_.product -match "Office"}|
forEach-object {
    write-host ($_.name.padright(20) + " "+
    $_.cpu.tostring("00000.00") + " " +
    $_.VM.tostring().padleft(12))    }
```

Finally, you can use `Format-Table` to replace the whole *write in a loop* construction.

```
Get-Process| where-object {$_.product -match "Office"}|
 format-table -property ` Name,cpu,VM
```

Format-Table has an alias, ft, and if only one parameter is passed (in this case a single array) it is assumed to be -property. Where-Object can also be abbreviated to ? and Get-Process has a UNIX-style alias of PS, so at the command line the original half dozen lines of code could be pared down to this:

```
PS | ? {$_.product -match "Office"} | ft Name,cpu,VM
```

Before looking at some of the more sophisticated uses of Format-Table, it is worth mentioning its -autoSize and -wrap switches. If -autoSize is not specified, Format-Table simply divides the width of the screen by the number of properties to be displayed and displays each of the columns using that width—and it can output the information as it is returned by an earlier function in the pipeline. With -autoSize, it waits until all the data has been passed, and calculates the required widths. This is usually preferable. The -wrap switch allows data that is longer than its column width to be wrapped over multiple lines.

In addition, where there is too much data to display in table form, there is a Format-List Cmdlet that works in a similar way, but displays each item working down the screen rather than across. Format-List can be abbreviated to its alias, fl, and as with Format-Table, it is provided with one parameter that is assumed to be the list of properties. Sometimes it is useful when exploring objects to use | FL * rather than | GM to look at the properties with the get-member Cmdlet.

Format-table becomes particularly powerful when used with *calculated properties*. In their simplest form, calculated properties allow the label of a column in the table to be replaced with something easier to understand than the property name. For example, instead of CPU and VM, in the process example shown previously, you might want to display Total CPU Time and Virtual Memory.

A calculated property is written as an *associative array*—which some people know as a *hash table*—with an *expression* and (for Format-table) a *Label*. The syntax for declaring an *associative* array is:

```
@{<key1 = item1>; <key2 = item2>;…}
```

The sequence doesn't matter because an item is found using its key. The item for the Label key is a text string, and the item for the expression key is a script block enclosed in braces. So to rename fields in the earlier get-process command to give CPU and VM better labels, the command would look like this:

```
Get-Process| where-object {$_.product -match "Office"}|
  format-table -property `
Name, @{Label="Total CPU Time"; expression={$_.cpu}},
@{Label="Virtual memory"; expression={$_.VM} }
```

Of course the fields in this example aren't *calculating* anything; their expressions are just a property, which Format-Table retrieves and evaluates. Whatever is returned by expression appears in the table. You could put a more complex formula into the expression. For example, the following:

```
(Get-Date) - $_.StartTime
```

will return a TimeSpan object and you can use its Totalseconds property to give the total time a process has been running in seconds, using the following calculated property:

```
@{expression={ ((get-date) - $_.StartTime).totalSeconds};Label="Time
running" }
```

You can even calculate the percentage of CPU time that process has used over its life.

```
@{expression={ ($_.cpu/((get-date)-$_.StartTime).totalSeconds).
tostring("P3")}; Label="Lifetime CPU %" }
```

The toString("p3") at the end formats the result as a percentage to three places of decimals. Another use for calculated fields is to change the format of a property using the formatting laid out earlier in this chapter.

The important thing is that an expression is just a script block and whatever it returns appears in the table. Recall earlier how we pooh-poohed the idea of using a for loop to iterate through all the members of the array. Suppose you wanted to display a number next to them. That might seem like a reason for going back to the for loop, but PowerShell can evaluate any code in an expression—like something to increment a counter.

For example:

```
$Counter=-1
Get-Process| where-object {$_.product -match "Office"}|
 format-table -property `
@{Label="ID"; expression={ ($global:Counter++)} } , Name, cpu
```

This can be the basis for a simple menu. Instead of *piping* the processes into Format-Table, another of the Cmdlet's switches can specify an input object. Then a function asks the user to select one of the running processes.

```
Function choose-ProcessByProduct
{param ($product)
 $processes= Get-Process| where-object {$_.product -match
[string]$product}
 $Global:Counter=-1
 format-table -inputObject $processes -autosize  -property `
@{Label="ID"; expression={ ($global:Counter++)} } , Name, cpu
 $processes[(read-host "Which one ?")]
}
```

And this will produce something similar to the following, depending on what is running on the computer at the time.

```
>choose-ProcessByProduct office
ID Name                     CPU
-- ----                     ---
 0 communicator    2095.9046352
 1 EXCEL             86.5181546
 2 OUTLOOK         9681.9524634
 3 WINWORD        10828.2010111
Which one ?: 2

Handles NPM(K)  PM(K)  WS(K) VM(M)   CPU(s)   Id ProcessName
------- ------  -----  ----- -----   ------   -- -----------
   6442    190 324056 214940   951 9,682.03 5032 OUTLOOK
```

This looks fine until you realize one thing about the output of Format-Table. It has been relying on implicit output—which is great if you want to redirect your nicely formatted output to a file but not so nice if you want to store the chosen process in a variable, because this will happen:

```
> $P=choose-ProcessByProduct office
Which one ?:
```

What happened to all the information in the menu? The answer is that it was just output—PowerShell was told that the output of the choose function was to go into $P so it did what it was told!

Fortunately, this is easy to fix by piping the Format-Table into the Out-Host Cmdlet, like this:

```
format-table -inputObject $processes -autosize  -property `
@{Label="ID"; expression={ ($global:Counter++)} } , Name, cpu | out-Host
```

Sorting and Selecting Fields

So far, you've seen Implicit and Explicit output and how you can use Format-Table (or Format-List) to give nicely formatted output with relatively little work; before we leave calculated fields, let's look at two techniques that are useful for managing the properties of objects in output.

The first is the Select-Object Cmdlet. If you have a background in querying data from databases it is sometimes helpful to think of PowerShell building up a classic SQL query with a set of Cmdlets. So a query in SQL would typically be:

```
Select fields From source where condition Order By Field
```

or

```
Select fields From source where condition Group By Field
```

In PowerShell, you've seen that Get functions and Cmdlets (such as Get-Process, in the preceding examples) do the job of the From part. PowerShell has a Where-Object Cmdlet with an alias of where, which does the same job as the where clause.

PowerShell also has Cmdlets for sorting and grouping, for example:

```
Get-Process| where-object {$_.product -match "Office"}|
    sort-object -property name
```

As before, if the –property is not specified, PowerShell will assume that the first un-named parameter is the property field, so at a command line one could simplify this to:

```
PS | Sort Name,Vm
```

which will sort the processes by name and virtual memory (by writing name,VM the comma causes PowerShell's parser to treat Name and Vm as a single-array parameter rather than two separate string parameters). Like Format-Table, the Sort-Object Cmdlet will accept calculated fields, so the list of processes you obtained in the Format-Table example could be sorted with a calculated field.

```
Get-Process| where-object {$_.product -match "Office"}|
    sort @{expression={ ($_.cpu/((get-date)-$_.StartTime
    ).totalSeconds)}}
```

Note that the definition of the field doesn't have a name or label part, just an expression.

For grouping, PowerShell has a Group-Object Cmdlet. This returns group-info objects, each of which has a name property, a count property, and a Group property, which contains an array of the original objects. So the Get-Process command can return groups of objects based on the product they belong to using the following command:

```
get-process | Group-Object -Property product
```

From these groups, you might look at each of the groups returned and add up the CPU time of each of its members—like this:

```
get-process | Group-Object -Property product | foreach-object `
{$_.name ; $_.group | foreach-object -begin {$cpu=0} `
  -process {$cpu+=$_.CPU} -end {$cpu} }
```

Rather than using a loop to go through each group member and calculate a running total, you can use the PowerShell's Measure-Object Cmdlet. Measure-Object takes multiple objects—the groups in this case—and counts them and can be told to calculate the minimum, maximum, sum, and average for one or more properties, which would need quite a lot more script.

So a more efficient way to write the previous script is as follows:

```
get-process | Group-Object -Property product | foreach-object `
{$_.name ; ($_.group | Measure-Object -sum -property CPU).sum }
```

Grouping can use the same calculated properties that you use in both sorting and displaying the table. The only problem with this approach is that you may need to do the same calculation in more than one place—especially if you are sorting by a property and then showing it in a formatted table, which makes the process a bit unwieldy.

There are two ways around this. The first is to use the Select-Object Cmdlet; select does what you might expect—returning required fields, in SQL style. For example:

```
Select-object -property Name,VM,CPU, @{name="LifeTimeCPU"; expression=
{(($_.cpu/((get-date)-$_.StartTime ).totalSeconds.tostring("p"))}}
```

Although the sequence is not the same as SQL, you now have parts of a PowerShell command, which are equivalent to SQL's Select, Where, From, and Order by, although in PowerShell the order is Get | Where | Select | sort so the full command would be:

```
> Get-Process| where-object {$_.product -match "Office"}|
 Select-object -property Name,VM,CPU, @{name="LifeTimeCPU"; expression=
{((($_.cpu/((get-date)-$_.StartTime ).totalSeconds).tostring("p"))}} |
sort LifeTimeCPu |  Format-table -autosize -property Name,Vm,Cpu,
LifetimeCpu
```

This works nicely unless, for example, you want to be able to call the Kill()method for the process object because you'll find the method has gone. If you redirect the output of Select-Object into get-member, you get output like this:

```
    TypeName: System.Management.Automation.PSCustomObject

Name          MemberType    Definition
----          ----------    ----------
Equals        Method        System.Boolean Equals(Object obj)
GetHashCode   Method        System.Int32 GetHashCode()
GetType       Method        System.Type GetType()
ToString      Method        System.String ToString()
CPU           NoteProperty  System.Management.Automation.PSObject
                            CPU=2344.1334264
LifeTimeCPU   NoteProperty  System.Management.Automation.PSObject
                            LifeTimeCPU=0.28%
Name          NoteProperty  System.String Name=communicator
VM            NoteProperty  System.Int32 VM=403300352
```

The type has changed; Select-Object throws away the original Process object and creates a new PSCustomObject. It adds properties to it (you'll see what NoteProperties are about in a moment), but you've lost all the methods of the object, so you might want to look for another way.

If you were very sharp eyed in the choose- example, you might have noticed that when PowerShell outputs the details of a process object without any other instruction it uses a column titled

ProcessName, but all the subsequent examples simply used Name. PowerShell can add *members* to objects; in fact, under the surface, PowerShell does that for some existing .NET objects. For example, you can find out about the member with the name "Name" returned by get-Process, as follows:

```
> get-process | get-member -name "name"
    TypeName: System.Diagnostics.Process
Name MemberType    Definition
---- ----------    ----------
Name AliasProperty Name = ProcessName
```

The first thing this tells you is that you have a System.Diagnostics.Process .NET object. If you were to look up the properties of this object class on MSDN, you would find that it does not have a name property, only ProcessName. But the next thing that get-member says is that the member named "Name" has a member type of "Alias Property," which is defined as "Name=ProcessName." In other words, PowerShell has made the ProcessName property accessible using an alias of "name."

PowerShell's Add-Member Cmdlet adds AliasProperties, and about a dozen other member types. You saw NoteProperties in the previous section—they are properties that are set once— and ScriptProperties. For reasons known only to the people who designed it, when input is piped into Add-Member, it needs to be called with a -PassThrough switch. Otherwise, it adds the member and throws the result away.

To add a script property to the processes you have been looking at in the previous examples, the code is just slightly different. Instead of writing $_ for "the current one in the pipeline," you write $this, so the command would be:

```
> Get-Process| where-object {$_.product -match "Office"}|
add-member -PassThru -memberType scriptproperty -name LifeTimeCpu
-value { ($this.cpu/((get-date)-$this.StartTime ).totalSeconds)}
```

Just running this on its own will cause PowerShell to output the following:

```
Handles  NPM(K)    PM(K)   WS(K) VM(M)   CPU(s)     Id ProcessName
-------  ------    -----   ----- -----   ------     -- -----------
   2290      90    77676   79000   370 2,358.02   3572 communicator
    394      26    18128   28320   205     1.95   6696 EXCEL
   8146     222   373028  208884  1032  ...07.48   5032 OUTLOOK
   2384      83    57956   85804   386  ...36.40   4376 WINWORD
```

After adding a member, the the object is still a Process object: PowerShell knows which fields it should output for Process objects (you'll see how shortly) and the list of fields does not contain the new `LifeTimeCPU` property, so it doesn't appear in the table above but it's there—you can use it in `Sort-Object` and `Format-Table`.

```
> Get-Process| where-object {$_.product -match "Office"}|
 add-member -PassThru -memberType scriptproperty -name LifeTimeCpu
          -value {
              ($This.cpu/((get-date)-$This.StartTime ).totalSeconds)} |
 sort-object -Property lifetimeCpu |
 format-table -autosize -Property name,vm,cpu,@{Label="Lifetime CPU";
                               expression={$_.lifetimecpu.toString("P")}}


Name               VM          CPU Lifetime CPU
----               --          --- ------------
communicator  390860800  2364.7411585 0.27 %
WINWORD       407875584 11699.4041957 1.36 %
OUTLOOK      1108582400 12307.074891 1.43 %
```

We examine additional uses for `Add-Member` in later sections. But first there is a little aside about PowerShell understands how to format objects.

Changing How PowerShell Formats Objects

How is it, for example, that when you get information about files and let PowerShell output it, it always displays the folder the file is in, even if you do something like this?

```
> $d1 = dir *.ps1
> $d2 = dir pics\*.ps1
> $dlot=$d1+$d2
> $dlot
    Directory: Microsoft.PowerShell.Core\FileSystem::C:Stuff


Mode      LastWriteTime       Length Name
----      -------------       ------ ----
-a---    20/08/2007     15:16   2514 AD-e164.ps1

    Directory: Microsoft.PowerShell.Core\FileSystem::C:\Stuff\pics


Mode      LastWriteTime       Length Name
----      -------------       ------ ----
-a---    17/03/2008     13:47    224 reset.ps1
```

How does PowerShell *know*, not just to output `Mode`, `Last Write Time`, `Length` and `Name`, but also to put out a header for each change in the parent folder? How does it know which properties to output for a `process` object—and that `Non-Paged`, `Paged`, `Working Set`, and `Virtual Memory` should be converted to different units?

The answer to both of these questions lies in some XML files in the PowerShell home folder (under Windows\system32—the location is stored in $PsHome). These files are digitally signed and you must not change them: doing so would break the signatures and then PowerShell won't know how to format things. One of these files is named FileSystem.format.ps1xml, and if you look inside it you will find a section that goes like this:

```
<View>
  <Name>children</Name>
  <ViewSelectedBy>
    <SelectionSetName>FileSystemTypes</SelectionSetName>
  </ViewSelectedBy>
  <GroupBy>
    <PropertyName>PSParentPath</PropertyName>
    <CustomControlName>FileSystemTypes-GroupingFormat</
CustomControlName>
  </GroupBy>
  <TableControl>
    <TableHeaders>
      <TableColumnHeader>
       <Label>Mode</Label><Width>7</Width><Alignment>left</Alignment>
      </TableColumnHeader>
      <TableColumnHeader>
       <Label>LastWriteTime</Label><Width>25</Width><Alignment>right</
Alignment>
      </TableColumnHeader>
      <TableColumnHeader>
       <Label>Length</Label><Width>10</Width><Alignment>right</
Alignment>
      </TableColumnHeader>
      <TableColumnHeader/>
    </TableHeaders>
    <TableRowEntries><TableRowEntry>
      <Wrap/>
      <TableColumnItems>
        <TableColumnItem><PropertyName>Mode</PropertyName></
TableColumnItem>
        <TableColumnItem><ScriptBlock>
        [String]::Format("{0,10}  {1,8}", $_.LastWriteTime.
ToString("d"), $_.LastWriteTime.ToString("t"))
        </ScriptBlock></TableColumnItem>
        <TableColumnItem><PropertyName>Length</PropertyName></
TableColumnItem>
        <TableColumnItem><PropertyName>Name</PropertyName></
TableColumnItem>
      </TableColumnItems>
    </TableRowEntry></TableRowEntries>
  </TableControl>
</View>
```

You can see that the XML applies to file system types (which are defined elsewhere in the XML file) and it groups by the property `PSParentPath`. Then it defines a table control, with one section to define headers—with familiar looking labels—and another section to define the data part which contains a mixture of properties from the object and script.

In the same way, `DotNetTypes.format.ps1xml` describes how a number of types should be displayed. You can create a new version of this file with a pared down entry for `System.Diagnostics.process`, with some of the fields removed.

```
<Configuration><ViewDefinitions><View>
  <Name>process</Name>
  <ViewSelectedBy>
    <TypeName>System.Diagnostics.Process</TypeName>
    <TypeName>Deserialized.System.Diagnostics.Process</TypeName>
  </ViewSelectedBy>
  <TableControl>
    <TableHeaders>
      <TableColumnHeader>
        <Label>VM(M)  </Label><Width> 5</Width><Alignment>right</
Alignment>
      </TableColumnHeader>
      <TableColumnHeader>
        <Label>CPU(s) </Label><Width> 8</Width><Alignment>right</
Alignment>
      </TableColumnHeader>
      <TableColumnHeader />
    </TableHeaders>
    <TableRowEntries><TableRowEntry><TableColumnItems>
      <TableColumnItem>
        <ScriptBlock>[int]($_.VM / 1048576)</ScriptBlock>
      </TableColumnItem>
       <TableColumnItem>
        <ScriptBlock>if ($_.CPU -ne $()) { $_.CPU.ToString("N")}</
ScriptBlock>
      </TableColumnItem>
      <TableColumnItem>
        <PropertyName>ProcessName</PropertyName>
      </TableColumnItem>
    </TableColumnItems></TableRowEntry></TableRowEntries>
  </TableControl>
</View></ViewDefinitions></Configuration>
```

This can be loaded with the `Update-FormatData` Cmdlet. To add a file to the collection used for formatting, it is called with a -PrePend or -Append switch. PowerShell applies a rule of *first definition wins* so the file needs to be loaded with a -prepend switch. The file that defines the format for a process can be updated and tested using the same example as shown previously, like this:

```
> Update-FormatData -PrependPath My.Format.PS1XML
> Get-Process| where-object {$_.product -match "Office"}

VM(M)  CPU(s)  ProcessName
-----  ------  -----------
  262   20.14  communicator
  187    2.04  EXCEL
  535  110.51  OUTLOOK
  326  367.32  WINWORD
```

Because you have seen the structure of the file and removed columns you don't want, adding columns to the view is not difficult.

You can add a heading, as follows:

```
<TableColumnHeader>
  <Label>Life CPU</Label>
  <Width>8</Width>
  <Alignment>right</Alignment>
</TableColumnHeader>
```

And the same code block you used before:

```
<TableColumnItem>
  <ScriptBlock>
    {((($_.cpu/((get-date)-$_.StartTime ).totalSeconds).tostring("p"))}
  </ScriptBlock>
</TableColumnItem>
```

The `Update-FormatData` Cmdlet doesn't need to be told to add the file a second time, so if the file is saved, you can run the update again and get the new format with our custom field.

```
> Update-FormatData
> Get-Process| where-object {$_.product -match "Office"}
VM(M)  CPU(s)  Life CPU ProcessName
-----  ------  -------- -----------
  263   20.23  0.09 %  communicator
  187    2.07  0.01 %  EXCEL
  523  111.10  0.52 %  OUTLOOK
  309  381.80  1.79 %  WINWORD
```

The *format* data defines the default formatting that PowerShell uses when outputting the object. As we mentioned before, PowerShell adds some properties to types, and these are defined in `types.ps1XML`. As with the format, you must not change the original files but you can create your XML file and, using the `Update-TypeData` Cmdlet, you can *spot weld* extra properties onto any type.

Creating Custom Objects on Demand

You've seen in the previous section that new properties can be added to a type for the duration of a session by using the Update-TypeData Cmdlet, and earlier you saw how properties could be added to an object as it is processed using the Add-member Cmdlet. But there are other circumstances in which you don't have an object to start with, but it would be more useful to be able to deal with an object than, for example, a block of XML.

The following example comes from the same Hyper-V management library used as an example in Chapter 25 on WMI. Hyper-V provides a system called Key-Value Pair exchange, which allows the host computer to tell its virtual machines information such as its own name, and the name by which it refers to them. In return, the guest machines report back which operating system they are running, and their fully qualified domain name. The WMI object that returns the Key value pairs has a property that contains an array of blocks of XML. Each block looks something like the following:

```xml
<INSTANCE CLASSNAME="Msvm_KvpExchangeDataItem">
  <PROPERTY NAME="Caption" PROPAGATED="true" TYPE="string">
  </PROPERTY>
  <PROPERTY NAME="Data" TYPE="string">
    <VALUE>UK-DC.Contoso.com</VALUE>
  </PROPERTY>
  <PROPERTY NAME="Description" PROPAGATED="true" TYPE="string">
  </PROPERTY>
  <PROPERTY NAME="ElementName" PROPAGATED="true"TYPE="string">
  </PROPERTY>
  <PROPERTY NAME="Name" TYPE="string">
    <VALUE>FullyQualifiedDomainName</VALUE>
  </PROPERTY>
  <PROPERTY NAME="Source" TYPE="uint16">
    <VALUE>2</VALUE>
</PROPERTY>
</INSTANCE>
```

The ideal would be to have a single object with properties for FullyQualifiedDomainName, OSName, OSVersion, and so on, and this piece of script will produce just such an object:

```powershell
$KVPComponent.GuestIntrinsicExchangeItems |
  forEach -begin { $KVPObj = New-Object -TypeName System.Object } `
        -process {([xml]$_).SelectNodes("/INSTANCE/PROPERTY") |
                  forEach -process {if ($_.name -eq "Name") {$propName=$_.value}
                                    if ($_.name -eq "Data") {$Propdata=$_.value}}
                      -end {Add-Member -inputObject $KvpObj -MemberType `
                            NoteProperty -Name $PropName -Value $PropData}}
              -end {$KvpObj}
```

The script contains two loops, one inside the other. The outer loop uses one of the features that PowerShell provides in the Foreach-Object Cmdlet, which was covered in Chapter 4. This offers you the capability to have three script blocks, named `begin`, `process`, and `end`. In this case, `begin` creates a new object with a type of `system.object`, and `end` returns that object. In between, the `process` script block adds properties to the object.

The inner loop doesn't need a `Begin` block but has a `process` block, which looks for `/Instance/Property` nodes within the XML and picks out the name and data ones, and stores them. When the inner loop has looked at each of the property nodes it adds a property to the `System.object`. The name of the property is the "name" `/instance/property` node and the value of the property is its "data" `/instance/property` node. So when processing the preceding XML, the code in the inner loop will pick out `FullyQualifiedDomainName` and `UK-DC.Contoso.com`. When all the XML blocks have been processed, the output looks like this:

```
FullyQualifiedDomainName : UK-DC-WDS.Roadshow.com
OSName                   : Windows Server (R) 2008 Enterprise
OSVersion                : 6.0.6001
CSDVersion               : Service Pack 1
OSMajorVersion           : 6
OSMinorVersion           : 0
OSBuildNumber            : 6001
OSPlatformId             : 2
ServicePackMajor         : 1
ServicePackMinor         : 0
SuiteMask                : 18
ProductType              : 2
ProcessorArchitecture    : 9
```

Techniques for Switching in Output

One of the common things needed in the output of a PowerShell command is to return different text as a result of different codes returned by other commands—for example, ProductType or SuiteMask in the previous example. PowerShell's associative arrays—or hash tables—provide a useful way of doing this.

It would be possible to expand the product type as follows:

```
If ($kvpobj.ProductType -eq 1) {"WorkStation"}
If ($kvpobj.ProductType-eq 2) {"Domain controller"}
If ($kvpobk.ProductType-eq 3) {"Server"}
```

This can be improved a little by using a `switch` statement:

```
switch ($kvpobj.ProductType {
  1 {"WorkStation"}
  2{"Domain controller"}

  3 {"Server}
}
```

This can be reduced to a single line by using a hash table:

```
@{1="WorkStation";2="Domain controller";3="Server"}.[int]$kvpobj
.ProductType
```

The hash table is enclosed in the @{ } construction and defines each possible ProductType code as a *key*, with the descriptions as the associated *value*. Using a .Key qualifier with a hash table returns the value associated with that key, and in this case the key is held in the ProductType field.

An extension to this technique is to use a hash table to expand a bitmap mask construction. In these cases, a number is built up using 1 to mean one thing, 2 to mean another, 4 another, 8, 16, and 32 further flags. This is the case with the suitemask property in the Hyper-V key/value pair example shown previously. Each of these columns can be checked using the -band (binary AND) in multiple if statements like this:

```
If ($kvpobj.SuiteMask -band 1){" Small Business"}
If ($kvpobj.SuiteMask -band 2){" Enterprise"}
If ($kvpobj.SuiteMask -band 4 ){"BackOffice"}
If ($kvpobj.SuiteMask -band 8 ){"Communications"}
```

But with many values to test, it becomes quite a long process.

Here is the same thing in one line using a hash table. One long line defines the hash table itself and the second looks up the keys (1,2,4,8, and so on). If -band shows a match with a key, then the value associated with that key is output:

```
$suites=@{1="Small Business"; 2="Enterprise"; 4="BackOffice";
8="Communications"; 16="Terminal"; 32="Small Business Restricted";
64="Embedded NT";128="Data Center"; 256="Single User";
512="Personal";1024="Blade"}
Foreach ($Key in $suites.keys){if ($KvpObj.suiteMask -band $key)
{$suites.$key}}
```

Additional Output Cmdlets

You have seen already that you can control *what* PowerShell outputs and you saw that PowerShell has both implicit output—where output just goes to the console for want of being sent anywhere else—and explicit output where you explicitly send output to a particular destination. You saw the different *pipes* for success, error, debug, and warning, and that you could use Write-Host or pipe information into Out-Host to explicitly display it on the console.

PowerShell has six built-in out- Cmdlets to output information received via the pipe, two useful export- Cmdlets to save information in CSV or XML format, and a ConvertTo-HTML Cmdlet.

You have seen some of the Out- commands already, particularly Out-Host, which sends output from a function or Cmdlet to the console rather than relying on implicit output. For short pieces of text in a function it is usually easier to use `Write-Host`, but when dealing with the output of a function or another Cmdlet—such as `Format-Table`—it is easier to pipe input into `Out-Host` which has a `-paging` switch that allows output to be displayed a page at a time.

PowerShell doesn't have a `More` Cmdlet; by default, it creates a function for a `More`, which is a wrapper for `Out-Host -paging`. Because there is a tiny risk that `More` won't exist on a machine, if you don't know where a script is going to be run, it is safest to use `Out-Host` in your own scripts.

You have also seen `Out-Null`, which serves the same purpose as `> Nul` in CMD—it throws away output. PowerShell understands that `Nul` is a three-letter device name (such as Con, Prn, and the LPT and COM names) and will only allow commands to be redirected to files, not devices. It uses the four-letter `Null` for the name of its variable and in the in the `out-` command.

PowerShell also has `Out-Default`, which takes input and outputs it to wherever it was going to go anyway. It doesn't really serve any purpose at all. The following:

    AnyCommand | out-Default

gives the same results as:

    Anycommand

`Out-File` is functionally equivalent using the redirection operator `>`, except that it takes switches. `-NoClobber` is common to Cmdlets, which write to files and says "Don't over-write an existing file." `-whatif` and `-Confirm` report what the command would have done and confirm the action respectively. And `-Width` truncates lines after a given number of characters. `Out-File` also takes a parameter to specify different kinds of text encoding (ANSI, Unicode, and so on).

One of the limitations of the `Format-Table` Cmdlet is that it is scaled to the width of the screen; one of the uses for the `Out-String` Cmdlet is to specify an alternate width so you could use the following command to get a detailed directory that could be viewed in another program.

    dir | format-table -property * -auto | Out-String -Width 800 >
    bigtable.txt

The last of the built-in `Out-` Cmdlets is `Out-Printer`. The ability to use `> LPT1` to get a quick output has long gone from windows scripting, and `Out-Printer` puts it back. `Out-Printer` will print to the default printer or it can be given a `-name` parameter to switch to a different one. You can discover and change printer settings using WMI. (See Chapter 25 for more details.) There are many extensions to the range of `Out-` commands. Some are provided in snap-ins for PowerShell but they can be as simple as using aliases. PowerShell can pipe text into normal Windows programs such as `clip.exe`. Some people like to define an alias to map `clip` to `Out-Clipboard`.

Outputting in Specific File Formats

The ConvertTo-HTML Cmdlet can save an enormous amount of script because you can take a set of objects and output them as an HTML table with one simple Cmdlet rather than using dozens of lines of script to write each of the HTML tags around the data you need.

Typically the output of ConvertTo-HTML is sent to a file, either by using the > operator or by using the Out-File Cmdlet. Like other commands you have seen, ConvertTo-HTML takes a -properties switch. Without it, the Cmdlet will build an HMTL table with a column for every property in the objects passed to it. So for example, you can take the processes you looked at before and send them to ConvertTo-HTML and open the result.

```
get-process | where {$_.product -match "office"} | convertto-Html >
Process.htm
invoke-item process.htm
```

But this will give a very wide table because every property of the processes is included. You could go back to the earlier example and pass the ConvertTo-HTML Cmdlet the same -Property parameter that was used for format table.

```
Get-Process| where-object {$_.product -match "Office"}| convertTO-
Html -property Name, @{Label="Total CPU Time"; expression={$_.cpu}},@
{Label="Virtual memory"; expression={$_.VM} } , @{expression={
($_.cpu/((get-date)-$_.StartTime).totalSeconds).tostring("P3")};
Label="Lifetime CPU %" }
```

The output of ConvertTo-HTML is an array of strings containing an HTML table. The Cmdlet takes -Title, -head, and —Body switches to allow the page to be given a title and additional content to be added as the head section or at the start of the body section. The strings in the array can be manipulated like any others; for example, everything in the table can be right aligned with the following code:

```
ConvertTo-Html | foreach-object ($_.replace("<td>",
"<td  alight=right>")
```

In addition to producing formatted output, the Export- Cmdlets allow PowerShell to produce text output that is designed to be read by another program. Export-CSV creates a CSV file.

First, it outputs the type of the first object (prefixed with a # sign). This allows PowerShell to import from the file and create the correct kind of object, but it can confuse other importers so it can be disabled with a -NoTypeInformation switch.

Next, PowerShell examines the properties of the first item, and adds a header row to the data, just as it would if formatting a table or converting to HTML. Next it outputs those properties for each of the objects it was passed. If the information passed to the command contains more than one type of data—for example, `DIR | export-csv "My-Directory.csv"` will export both File objects and directory objects—only one type and one header row are written and these are based on the first object. For each subsequent object, PowerShell attempts to output properties matching those found on the first one. With the output of `DIR` this is not a major problem as a lot of properties are common to both `FileInfo` and `DirectoryInfo` objects. In other cases, it may cause blank or nonsense output.

As is normal with CSV, special techniques are needed for text items. As the online help explains:

> "Property values that contain commas, double quotes, leading or trailing spaces, or line breaks are put in double quotes before being written to the CSV file. Any double quotes contained in a property are redoubled to indicate that they are literal."

Neither of the `Export-` Cmdlets take the `-property` switch because they are designed to take information and output it in a way that can be imported at a later stage, so any formatting or custom field creation needs to be done earlier in the pipeline.

The second `Export-` Cmdlet is `Export-CliXML` and this exports to an XML representation, which can be re-imported later. Unlike a CSV file, which is a flat table, an XML document can contain levels of hierarchy, so `Export-CliXML` has a `-Depth` switch, which will control the expansion of child objects when they are exported. If this isn't specified, `Export-CliXML` will look at the settings in `types.psxml` to decide the depth for each object.

For example, without specifying a depth switch, `DIR | Export-CliXML` will export an XML file that simply details the files and subdirectories. With a depth switch these are each of the properties might be expanded, so the XML file contains the properties for each item's parent, and drive that it is stored on and so on.

Every Export Has a Corresponding Import

Everything in this chapter so far has concentrated on output, which shouldn't be a surprise as a lot of work in PowerShell is getting information from somewhere and displaying it. The other side of the coin—input—tends to be a smaller part of the story.

First of all, the `Export-` Cmdlets you have just seen have companion `Import-` Cmdlets, so information exported with `Export-CliXML` can be imported directly with `import-CliXML`, and the result will be a facsimile of the original objects. For example, the following:

```
$myDir = Dir $env:userProfile -recurse
```

will take a snapshot of the state of the files and directories in the users home folder, and these can be compared with the state of the same folders as they stand at a later time. However, if PowerShell is closed, the variable will be lost. By using:

```
Dir $env:userProfile -recurse | export-CliXML -Path MyDir.xml
```

the information is saved and when it is reloaded PowerShell rebuilds the same `FileInfo` and `DirectoryInfo` objects—not some text representation of them. The depth specified for the export will determine if some of the associated objects are present or not.

The two `-CliXML` Cmdlets use a specific schema designed to allow objects to be exported in this way, but it is not designed for handling generic XML.

Handling XML in PowerShell is reasonably simple, thanks to an `[XML]` type accelerator. This allows an XML file to be read and processed into an `XMLDocument` object like this:

```
$x=[xml](get-content C:\Windows\System32\WindowsPowerShell\v1.0\types.
ps1xml)
```

The result is a .NET `system.xml.XmlDocument` object with all the associated properties and methods.

Processing XML is a subject for a book in its own right, so here we will just make two quick observations. First, an `XMLDocument` object has a normal object hierarchy, so you can refer to `$x.Types` `.Type` to get an object for each of the *type* nodes in the file. Second, you can also use XPath notation to select nodes, using one of the methods built into the `XMLDocument` object. So you can write:

```
$x.selectNodes("/Types/Type [Name='System.Array']")
```

and this will select *type* nodes inside the root *Types* node which contain a name set to `System.Array`.

Just as `Export-CliXML` has a companion, so does `Export-CSV`. Because a wide range of tools can save or export in CSV format there are many applications for CSV data from provisioning services for users based on an export from an HR system through to Geo-tagging photographs using the log from a GPS device. And, of course, using a spreadsheet package such as Microsoft Excel makes it easy to prepare data for a script.

As we mentioned before, by default the first row of a CSV file created with the `Export-CSV` Cmdlet is the type of the object being exported. On import, if there is no type found in the first line, then PowerShell creates custom management objects for each row of data. `Import CSV` is dependent on having a header row at the start of the CSV file, which sets the property names for the custom object. You'll see shortly how to deal with a file that does not have a header row.

Any text file can be read using the `Get-Content` Cmdlet, and this returns an array of text strings. In fact, `Get-Content` can also be used with an `-encoding` switch, and this allows different kinds of text to be selected or for the file to be flagged as a binary file. The `Type` and `cat` commands are aliases for `Get-Content`, although many people find it is somehow more natural to use `Type` *Filename* as a command to see the contents of a file at the command prompt and `Get-Content` to read it in to a variable. The `cat` command in UNIX is short for concatenate and `Get-Content` can be told to read multiple files—and concatenate their output—in three different ways:

```
Dir *.txt -recurse | get-Content
Get-Content *.txt
Get-Content gps.csv,Sdm.csv
```

Usually, PowerShell will be asked to do some other processing with the file so the result of `Get-Content` will either be assigned to a variable or piped into another command. For example, if the file comes from a GPS logger it might be piped into the `Where-Object` Cmdlet to select only the lines that are tagged as the "Recommend minimum Data"—which begin `$GPRMC` and drop all the other lines of diagnostic information.

```
dir *.gps | get-content | where {$_ -like '$GPRM*'}
```

`Get-Content` returns an array of strings and this has a useful side effect. This example uses GPS data deliberately because although the rows of data are comma-separated, the file does not have a header row. But it is possible to add one by concatenating two string arrays together, so the following code will add a header row to the data:

```
@("Type,Time,status,latitude,NS,longitude,EW,Speed,bearing,Date,blank,ch
ecksum") + (dir *.gps | get-content | where {$_ -like '$GPRM*'} > Temp.CSV
```

Now that the data has been written to a file, you can import it with `Import-CSV`—which will only read from files, and won't take input from the pipe (at least in PowerShell V1). Feeding the results into `Get-Member` shows the names that were used in the header are now properties of a custom object.

```
PS C:\Users\jamesone\Documents\windowsPowershell> import-csv temp.csv | GM
    TypeName: System.Management.Automation.PSCustomObject

Name          MemberType   Definition
----          ----------   ----------
Equals        Method       System.Boolean Equals(Object obj)
GetHashCode   Method       System.Int32 GetHashCode()
GetType       Method       System.Type GetType()
.ToString     Method       System.String ToString()
bearing       NoteProperty System.String bearing=73.06
blank         NoteProperty System.String blank=
checksum      NoteProperty System.String checksum=*2F
Date          NoteProperty System.String Date=030708
EW            NoteProperty System.String EW=W
latitude      NoteProperty System.String latitude=5325.5023
longitude     NoteProperty System.String longitude=00255.0864
NS            NoteProperty System.String NS=N
Speed         NoteProperty System.String Speed=4.869933
status        NoteProperty System.String status=A
Time          NoteProperty System.String Time=070445.647
Type          NoteProperty System.String Type=$GPRMC
```

More on Selecting Text

It is often convenient to use `Get-Content | where` either at the command prompt (perhaps shortening `Get-Content` to one of its aliases ,GC, Type or Cat) or in a script. But there is another Cmdlet that is useful for getting just the matching strings: `Select-String`. This is a mixture of the DOS `find` command and the UNIX `grep` command: unlike these two it doesn't return simple strings, but PowerShell objects that contain the line number, file name, and the line of text. The drawback to using `Select-String` is that its output is not the matching text, and the text itself needs to be referenced using the `.line` property. But it has a number of benefits—not least that its default output shows file names and line numbers when looking for text.

Used at the command line, `Select-String` gives a quick way to answer questions such as "Which of these files contain this text," and even "Which ones have lots of occurrences of the text I'm seeking."

```
select-string *.ps1 -Pattern "Get-WmiObject" -SimpleMatch  | group
filename
```

Notice the use of `-SimpleMatch`—normally the pattern is a regular expression that allows much more sophisticated searching, but at the price of needing to learn a new language for expressing search terms. Chapter 30 has a brief guide to using regular expressions.

Sometimes it is useful to output the first few lines of a file, so the previous example could be modified to show the first few lines at the start of a script by calling `Get-Content` and specifying the number of lines it should read with the `-TotalCount` parameter.

```
select-string *.ps1 -Pattern "Get-WmiObject" -SimpleMatch  | group
filename | foreach-object {$_.name; get-content $_.name -totalcount 5}
```

Using `-TotalCount` allows you to specify the first *n* lines. You can also use the `Select-Object` Cmdlet to select the first or last *n* lines. It is more efficient to read only the first five lines than to use `Select-Object` to throw the others away, but `Select-Object` is useful if the notes that explain a file are placed at the end.

```
select-string *.ps1 -Pattern "Get-WmiObject" -SimpleMatch  | group
filename | foreach-object {$_.name; get-content $_.name | select-object
-last 5}
```

And these two can be combined. If you know you want lines 95 to 99, you can tell `Get-Content` to read the first 99 lines with `-TotalCount 99` and then select the last five of those.

Because PowerShell text strings are .NET string objects, they have all the methods that .NET provides for strings, which makes it very easy to select text within a string, or replace parts of a string, or split strings. For example, if a file just contains a list of file paths, you can output the extensions by splitting each line at any `.` characters and outputting the last one.

```
Get-content fileList.txt | foreach-object {$_.split(".")[-1]}
```

Or you can output the drive letter by splitting at any colon (:) characters and outputting the first one.

```
Get-content fileList.txt | foreach-object {$_.split(":")[0]}
```

User Input

The last kind of input to consider is that which comes from the user. As was pointed out earlier, it is better to allow the user to pass a parameter as a string but sometimes you need or want the user to input something—for example, the user may run a command that presents a set of choices based on the state of the system and then pipes their selection into another command.

For this, PowerShell provides the Read-Host Cmdlet. Just as Write-Host writes to the console in its role as "standard output" so Read-Host reads from the console in the role of "standard input" .

Read-Host takes only two possible parameters: the "prompt" text and a switch, -asSecureString, to say "This is a password; display stars and store the result as a secure string." Secure strings can be passed in places where credentials are expected.

The result that comes back from Read-Host is a string, and if multiple inputs are required the string can be split using the Split() method you saw previously.

Summary

In this chapter, you have had a tour of a lot of different parts of PowerShell covering everything from how you can take an input object and convert it to a well-formatted table through how to take input from the user. On the way, you have seen how simple it is for PowerShell to read from and process files and how it can sort, group, and calculate properties. You should be able to see the flexibility PowerShell offers—indeed sometimes it seems to give you multiple ways to accomplish a task without a clear-cut way of picking the best one. What should have become clear is how PowerShell gives you simple building blocks that can be piped together to great effect with minimal amounts of programming required.

Chapter 22

Working with Files and the Registry in PowerShell

W orking with files is one of the most basic roles that a shell must fill. In this chapter you'll see how PowerShell does that, but also how it uses providers to make the same commands valid file-systems, the registry and more.

Using PSDrives, Accessing the File System, Mapping Drives

First, a little history …

Back in the 1970s, the CP/M operating system used a convention of A: for the first floppy disk drive and B: for the second, and this was duplicated in the first version of MS-DOS. When support for hard disks was needed, DOS 2.0 named the first hard disk volume C:, and added hierarchical directories in a similar style to UNIX ones—the two most obvious differences being, first, that UNIX uses the forward slash (/) to separate directories on the path whereas Microsoft operating systems use the backward slash (\ ), and second, that UNIX mounts additional disks into a hierarchy with a single root, where traditionally each volume in a Microsoft operating system has a separate root. In fact, from the early days of DOS, Microsoft operating systems have featured the command SUBST, which allows a long path to be presented as its own drive letter.

Current Microsoft operating systems don't *require* a drive letter per disk. Like UNIX, they can mount a volume into a directory on an existing file system, but in most cases users expect each disk volume to have its own drive letter.

Microsoft's early networking products introduced "Universal Naming Convention" (UNC) names and a set of NET commands, such as NET USE and NET SHARE, which are still valid 20 years later. Connections to shared files on a network server are typically presented using drive letters.

Anyone who has worked with a Microsoft command processor will expect to have access to drives in exactly the same way in PowerShell. PowerShell takes the idea of drives a little further with *providers*.

Providers allow things that would not normally look like a drive to be presented as one. The built-in snap-ins have the following providers (see Table 22-1), As well as a provider for the file systems, which provides the traditional A: , C: and so on.

TABLE 22-1

PowerShell Providers

Provider Name	Snap-In	Provides Access To
Alias	Microsoft.PowerShell.Core	PowerShell Aliases
Function	Microsoft.PowerShell.Core	PowerShell Functions
Variable	Microsoft.PowerShell.Core	PowerShell Variables
Environment	Microsoft.PowerShell.Core	System Environment Variables
Registry	Microsoft.PowerShell.Core	System Registry
Certificate	Microsoft.PowerShell.Core	The System Certificate Store

Additional snap-ins can add providers. For example, the PowerShell Community Extensions (www.codeplex.com/pscx) has providers for Internet Explorer's Common RSS Feed store, the .NET Global Assembly Cache, and Directory Services.

So you can use commands such as the following:

```
DIR Microsoft.PowerShell.Core\Registry::HKEY_CURRENT_USER
DIR Microsoft.PowerShell.Core\FileSystem::c:\
```

Or, if you have the Community Extensions installed, you can use the following:

```
DIR PSCX\FeedStore::
```

This syntax is painfully longwinded—although as you will see in a moment, you may want to use it occasionally.

PowerShell defines drives and you can see what has been defined with the `Get-PSDrive` command. Typically, it might show something like this:

```
Name          Provider        Root
----          --------        ----
Alias         Alias
C             FileSystem      C:\
cert          Certificate     \
D             FileSystem      D:\
E             FileSystem      E:\
Env           Environment
Function      Function
HKCU          Registry        HKEY_CURRENT_USER
HKLM          Registry        HKEY_LOCAL_MACHINE
HKUSERS       Registry        HKEY_USERS
Variable      Variable
```

`Get-PSDrive` has companion Cmdlets, `Remove-PSDrive` and `New-PSDrive`.

You can remove all the non–file system drives, which PowerShell defines for you. For example:

```
Remove-PSDrive -PSProvider Registry -name *
```

will remove all the drives created by the registry provider and

```
Remove-PSDrive FUNCTION
```

will remove the Function drive. You can put it back with

```
New-PSdrive -PSProvider Function -name Function -Root \
```

If you want to create a drive for your home directory, you can, like this:

```
New-PSdrive -PSProvider FileSystem -name Home `
-Root C:\users\administrator
```

The flat providers (`ENV`, `ALIAS`, and `FUNCTION`) can be treated like variable scopes. For example, `$Env:UserProfile` will return the `UserProfile` variable (equivalent to `%UserProfile%` in CMD.EXE, or a batch file). So the previous command could have been written as:

```
New-PSdrive -PSProvider FileSystem -name Home `
-Root $env:UserProfile
```

Note that the trailing colon is *not* included when specifying the name of the drive to be created, although it is used when the drive is referenced after creation.

As mentioned, it is not necessary to add a drive to access something. For example, to determine whether PowerShell is running with *elevated* privileges on Windows Vista or Windows Server 2008, you can test to see if accessing part of the Registry that is only available to administrators generates an error.

Rather than creating a drive for the HKEYUSERS branch and then deleting it, you can use the following:

```
Dir Microsoft.PowerShell.Core\Registry::HKEY_USERS\S-1-5-20
```

You'll see later how to test for errors and to suppress error messages.

Changing (setting) locations

Anyone who has used CMD.EXE or COMMAND.COM knows that entering D: changes the current drive to D:, and CD D: will not change the current location to drive D:, but will tell you which directory on D: is the current one; CD D:\STUFF changes the active directory on D: but doesn't make D: the active drive.

PowerShell has a more generic Set-Location Cmdlet, which combines both of these tasks. It is also aliased to CD, ChDir, and SL. Set-Location is used to change drives as well. However, rather than forcing those who have grown up with the other shells to change their ways, PowerShell has *functions* A:, B:, C:, and so on all the way up to Z:. You can see the content of one of these with the command:

```
$Function:D:
```

This tells you that the body of the function is:

```
Set-Location D:
```

If you have a look at the functions: drive, you'll see there are no functions for changing to the other predefined drives, although there is nothing to stop you from adding commands for ENV:, Variable:, and the others listed and any drives you create.

In addition to Set-Location, PowerShell has a Get-Location Cmdlet, which is aliased to PWD (print working directory), the UNIX version of the same thing.

Getting child items (a.k.a. getting a directory) and testing paths

Although PowerShell supports the DIR and PS commands known by users of earlier Microsoft and UNIX shells, these are actually aliases for the Get-ChildItem Cmdlet.

Get-ChildItem returns the contents of a directory or, with the -recurse switch, a directory and all its subdirectories. Using the DIR alias you can enter the following commands:

```
DIR
DIR *.JPG
DIR Photos
```

All three commands work as they would in CMD.EXE or COMMAND.COM. The first returns the contents of the current directory. The second returns files with a .jpg extension, and the third returns files in a Photos subdirectory. Where the older shells have a /S switch for subdirectories, PowerShell uses `-recurse` because it needs only enough to tell it apart from the other switches; you can use this command:

```
Dir -r
```

as the equivalent of the command `dir /s` in CMD.EXE.

However, from this point the behavior of `Get-ChildItem`, and its aliases `DIR` and `LS`, is different from what you would experience in CMD.EXE. For example, in PowerShell, you can type:

```
Dir 'May photos' , 'June photos'
```

and get the contents of two directories, or you can type:

```
Dir '*.ps1', '*.txt'
```

to get PowerShell script files and text files in the current directory. If the first Parameter in the command line is not named, PowerShell treats it as the `-Path` parameter, if multiple items are supplied separated by commas they are treated as one parameter.

When the `-recurse` switch is used, the Cmdlet treats it as "recurse through these directories" so the following two commands work differently from what you might have been used to. The following code:

```
Dir *Photos -recurse
```

will take the directories `Jan Photos`, `Feb Photos`, `Mar Photos`, `Apr Photos`, and so on and recurse through their contents and subdirectories. This command:

```
Dir *.jpg -recurse
```

won't return anything—unlike `dir *.jpg /s` in CMD.EXE. If you want to include .jpg files only, the command is:

```
Dir -recurse -include *.jpg
```

And you can combine a collection of paths to be recursed and then filter the results.

```
Dir *Photos -recurse -include *.jpg,*.Jpeg
```

`-include` allows a list of values, and so does its companion, the `-exclude` switch. So you can build up a command like this:

```
Dir *Photos -recurse -include *.jpg,*.Jpeg -exclude _IMG*
```

One important thing to note is that `include` and `exclude` work only if `DIR` is told to fetch something first, so:

```
Dir -include *.jpg
```

won't return anything.

You can use the `Where-Object` Cmdlet to filter the items returned. However all the objects will be returned, and `Where-Object` will discarded some, which is less efficient than using `-Include` and `-Exclude` switches; so you should try to use these where possible. But using `Where-Object` gives greater flexibility because it can work with complex conditions on any the properties of the object. The command:

```
Dir | Get-Member
```

will show the properties of `FileInfo` and `DirectoryInfo` objects to see what properties you can use in `Where-Object`. For example, the `length` property holds the file *size* so you can filter to files smaller than 1MB in size with the following command.

```
Dir | Where-Object {$_.length -lt 1mb}
```

The test in `Where-Object` is a PowerShell code block that can do pretty much anything provided it returns `true` or `false`. For example:

```
Dir | Where-Object {test-path ("Photos\" + $_.name)}
```

will return those files in the current directory, which are also in the Photos subfolder.

`Test-Path` takes the `-include` and `-exclude` switches in the same way as `dir`, and it tests to see if there is something that matches the specified path. An easy way to think of it is that if `Dir <something>` would return anything, `Test-Path <something>` will return `true`.

`Test-path` can also test to see if an item is a container or a leaf node, and it can test to see if the path is valid, even if the item does not exist.

Other path Cmdlets worth noting:

- `Resolve-Path` converts a partial path to a fully qualified one.
- `Split-Path` cuts the path at the last \ character and returns the directory part by default; with the other switches it can return the file part or the drive part.
- `Join-Path` links the directory and file part, and unlike simply joining the two strings it handles the common problem of deciding if a \ character is present at the end of the path.

Like other Cmdlets, they can be used with multiple files, but the following example is designed for processing a single file. It is from a function that saves an image of a running virtual machine as a

JPEG file. It takes a parameter for the JPEG path; the .NET assemblies for handling bitmaps require a fully qualified path to be specified but the function needs to cope with several possibilities:

- No path is specified at all.

- Multiple virtual machines are piped into the function, so the function needs to give each JPEG a name based on the name of the VM (its element name property).

- A file name is specified without a path.

- A relative path is specified—for example IMAGES instead of C:\users\administrator\images.

- Folder names might be written with a trailing \ or without it.

So the code in the function ends up as follows:

```
if ($JpegPath -eq $null) {$JpegPath = $pwd}
if (test-path $JpegPath -pathtype container) {$JpegPath =`
     join-Path $JpegPath ($VMSettings.elementName + ".JPG") }
$Folder = split-path $JpegPath
if ($folder -eq "" ) {$JpegPath  = join-Path $pwd $JpegPath }
else  {$jpegpath=$jpegpath.Replace($Folder , (resolve-path `
          $folder)) }
```

The first line of the preceding code says that if no path is specified, make the path the current directory.

The second says that if the path is a directory, add the Virtual Machine's element name and .JPG to the path. The Join-Path Cmdlet handles the directory being written with or without the trailing \.

If just a file was specified, then neither of the previous lines will have done anything. The next line splits the directory part of the path from the file name, and if there is no directory part, the current directory is added. If there is a directory part, then it is resolved and the unresolved name replaced with a fully qualified one. Resolve-Path won't expand a path to a file that doesn't exist yet—hence the trick of replacing the unresolved directory with the resolved one.

Copying, deleting and renaming files

As you may have come to expect by now, PowerShell has its own Cmdlets for copying, deleting, and renaming files or other objects made visible through providers.

The Copy-Item Cmdlet has aliases cp (like UNIX) and Copy (like the Microsoft shells).

Remove-Item deletes both files and directories and has aliases rm, rmdir, del, erase, and rd.

Move-Item combines Copy and Remove and has the alias move.

And finally, `Rename-Item` has an alias, `ren`.

Through their aliases, these Cmdlets can be used in a very similar way to their counterparts in CMD.

So you can use the following:

```
Copy *.jpg  photos
Ren IMG_1234.JPG  DIVE1234.JPG
Del  IMG_1234.JPG
Rd OldData
```

Because PowerShell tries to be consistent, the `-recurse`, `-include`, and `-exclude` switches work with `Copy-Item` and `Remove-Item` in the same way as they do with `Get-ChildItem`, and all three support `-force` to allow them to handle read-only files. They also support `-whatif` and `-confirm` switches, which are implemented by many Cmdlets. `-whatif` shows what the command would do and `-confirm` asks for confirmation before carrying it out.

One area where these Cmdlets differ from their CMD.EXE equivalents is in the use of the pipe. Users of CMD.EXE may well have sent the output of `DIR` to `MORE` or to `SORT` or `FIND`. The idea of piping it to `delete`, `rename`, or `copy` might seem a bit alien. The previous section showed a command:

```
DIR | Where-Object {test-path ("Photos\" + $_.name)}
```

which will return the files in the current directory that are also in the Photos subdirectory. Because those files are duplicates, you can delete them with the following:

```
DIR | Where-Object {test-path ("Photos\" + $_.name)} | DEL
```

Remember that `Get-ChildItem` (or its alias `Dir`) returns file objects; if you don't tell PowerShell to process them, it outputs them to the screen. Piping it into `Remove-Item` (or its aliases) will delete the files. In this case, `Where-Object` just filters out some of the objects you don't want to process.

One place where usage differs between CMD.EXE and PowerShell is with the `rename` command. In CMD, you can issue the command `Ren *.JPEG *.JPG`, and this will rename all the files with a .JPEG extension to .JPG. This doesn't work in PowerShell: `Rename-Item` takes items individually and renames them. It is possible to perform complex rename operations by piping files into `Rename-Item` and setting the name to something based on the name of the file object. For example:

```
dir _igp* |  rename-item  -newname {$_.name.replace("_IGP","Party") }
```

Creating and deleting directories

As you have just seen, PowerShell does not differentiate between deleting a file and removing a directory: `Del` and `RD` are both aliased to `Remove-Item`. If you use `Remove-Item`, or one of its aliases and specify a non-empty directory, without using the `-recurse` switch, then PowerShell will prompt to ask if you want to delete the directory and all its contents.

PowerShell's `New-Item` Cmdlet needs to be told explicitly to create a directory, so there is an `MD` function rather than an alias.

File properties and attributes

As you saw in the section on getting child items, file objects in PowerShell have properties; and there are several ways to access them—one is to get the file with `Get-Item` or `Get-ChildItem`. This is usually the easiest if you need to examine the properties of several items. To get the properties of a single item, PowerShell provides the `Get-ItemProperty` Cmdlet.

Viewing and setting ACL permissions

PowerShell has `Get-Acl` and `Set-Acl` Cmdlets for manipulating access control lists.

`Get-Acl` returns a .NET, `System.Security.AccessControl.FileSecurity` or `System.Security.AccessControl.DirectorySecurity` object when used against the files system. (There is a `System.Security.AccessControl.RegistrySecurity` object, which is returned if it is run against the registry). `Set-Acl` takes one of these objects and applies it. Because PowerShell can manipulate .NET objects, it is possible to build the security object from scratch; however, the most common use of `Set-Acl` is to copy an ACL from one place to another.

One unusual thing about `Set-Acl` is that it accepts either the file(s) to be ACL'd or the security object from the pipe. PowerShell's online help gives the following examples (the first pipes the ACL into `Set-Acl`, and the second pipes in the objects to be permissioned):

```
get-acl c:\dog.txt | set-acl -path C:\cat.txt
```

and

```
$newACL = get-acl file0.txt
get-childitem c:\temp -recurse -include *.txt -force | set-acl
-aclobject $newacl
```

In many cases, it will be easier to use the `CACLS` or The New `iCACLS` command-line utility to set ACLs as one would from CMD.

The name `GET-Acl` is slightly misleading as it returns all the security information for an object, not just the Access Control List, as you can see:

```
> Get-Acl . | Format-List
Path   : Microsoft.PowerShell.Core\FileSystem::C:\Users\james\
         Documents\windowsPowershell
Owner  : LONDON\james
Group  : LONDON\Domain Users
Access : LONDON\james Allow  FullControl
         LONDON\james Allow  268435456
         NT AUTHORITY\SYSTEM Allow  FullControl
```

```
                    NT AUTHORITY\SYSTEM Allow  268435456
                    BUILTIN\Administrators Allow  FullControl
                    BUILTIN\Administrators Allow  268435456
        Audit  :
        Sddl   : O:S-1-5-21-1721254763-462695806-1538882281-
                    46340G:DUD:(A;ID;FA;;;S-1-5-21-1721254763-462695806-
                    1538882281-46340)(A;OICIIOID;GA;;;S-1-5-21-1721254763-
                    462695806-1538882281-46340)(A;ID;FA;;;SY)(A;OICIIOID;GA;;;SY)
                    (A;ID;FA;;;BA)(A;OICIIOID;GA;;;BA)
```

The access entry is itself made up of File System Access rule objects (or Registry Access rule objects), and you can explore the rules by sending them to Format-list,

```
> (get-acl .)
      .access[0] | format-list

FileSystemRights  : FullControl
AccessControlType : Allow
IdentityReference : EUROPE\jamesone
IsInherited       : True
InheritanceFlags  : None
PropagationFlags  : None
```

You can see that PowerShell expands the flags to meaningful text—for example, displaying Allow or Deny instead of 0 or 1. It has a textual representation of the more common rights, such as Full Control. In the preceding example, non-standard combinations are parsed as follows:

TABLE 22-2

Rights, Codes and their Meanings

Value	Meaning
1	ReadData/ListDirectory
2	WriteData/CreateFiles
4	AppendData/CreateDirectories
8	ReadExtendedAttributes
16	WriteExtendedAttributes
32	ExecuteFile/TraverseDirectory
64	DeleteSubdirectoriesAndFiles
128	ReadAttributes
256	WriteAttributes
131072	ReadPermissions

Value	Meaning
262144	ChangePermissions
524288	TakeOwnership
1048576	Synchronize

Working with file items: reading their content, creating and adding to them

In CMD there is a TYPE command that types the contents of a file to the screen. In UNIX, the cat command can be used to do the same. PowerShell has a Cmdlet, Get-Content, which has aliases of Type and Cat.

Get-Content is closer to the UNIX cat, in that it can concatenate the content of multiple files. For example, the following:

```
Get-Content blog-utils.ps1, GPS.ps1
```

returns the contents of two PowerShell scripts concatenated.

Get-Content returns an array of text strings that can be piped into something else, so the following command finds lines in PowerShell scripts that contain the term webclient

```
Get-Content *.ps1 | Where-Object { $_ -like "*webclient*" }
```

Because the content returned is an array of strings, you can use normal array notation to return subsets of the file; for example:

```
(get-content myFile.Txt)[0]
(get-content myFile.Txt)[1,2,7]
(get-content myFile.Txt)[0..19]
```

Get-Content has companions: Add-Content and Set-Content.

Add-Content appends content to the end of an existing file; for example:

```
Add-content week.log (get-content Monday.log,Tuesday.log,
    Wednesday.log,Thursday.log,Friday.log)

Add-content *.PS1 "# Note: this is a sample use at your own risk"
```

The first appears no different from using the >> "append results to a file" redirection operator, which is used in other shells and supported in PowerShell. The second shows that Add-Content is more flexible and can add to multiple files. The same is true of Set-Content; used with a single file, it is no different from the > "create a file with results" redirection operator but it, too, can work with multiple files. For example:

```
Set-Content *day.log ("Log Reset " + (get-date))
```

One other thing worth noting is that PowerShell has a shorthand syntax for getting the content of a single file—${path}—which treats the file pointed to by path as if it were a variable. This can be useful—but the path is fixed as with a variable name—so it is less useful when the name of the file isn't known in advance.

Selecting strings and working with text data

It is often necessary to process a text file in some way and there are two basic common patterns— either to filter the lines in the text or to run a command against each line—which might return a modified version of the line.

In addition to selecting the lines in a file by knowing their position, PowerShell allows lines to be filtered using the Where-Object Cmdlet, which you saw earlier for filtering child items in a folder. One of the most important things to remember is that the expressions used in Where-Object use operators that begin with a minus sign and are written as text rather than symbols, so you use:

-eq	For "Is equal to," not	=
-ge	For "Is greater than or equal to," not	>=
-gt	For "Is greater than," not	>
-lt	For "Is less than," not	<
-le	For "Is less than or equal to," not	<=
-ne	For "Is not equal to," not	<>
-and	Not	and
-or	Not	or

It is a fairly common mistake to test for something in a where or if statement with the equal (=) sign, which *assigns* a value rather than *testing* for it. PowerShell will process this as a valid command—it just won't give the desired results.

The following command returns all the non-blank lines in a file:

```
Get-Content MyScript.ps1 | where-object {$_ -ne ""}
```

PowerShell has -like and –Contains operators. Contains is sometimes incorrectly used; it is *not* like the contains predicate in the free text searches of some SQL dialects. Contains returns True if one member of an array matches the argument. For example:

```
> "boo" -contains "o"
False
> "b","o","o" -contains "o"
True
```

-Like works in a similar way to the Like predicate in SQL: the asterisk (*) is used for "anything" and the question mark (?) is used for a single character. For example:

```
> "boo"  -like "b*"
True
> "boo"  -like "b"
False
> "boo" -like "b??"
True
> "boo" -like "b?"
False
> "b","o","o" -like "b*"
b
```

Notice in the last example, the -like operator returns the matching members of the array.

PowerShell is able to process regular expressions with the -match operator. Regular expressions are both powerful and complex and we will not discuss them in detail here. But testing for lines which either begin or end with a given substring are operations which are so commonly needed that it is worth looking at them. We might use the form:

```
$_.substring(0,9) -eq "# example"
```

However, it can be a chore to count the characters and if you know that ^ means "starting" and $ means "ending" in a regular expression you can write:

```
$_ -match "^# example"
```

-Like, -Contains, and -Match all have negative versions (-NotLike, -NotContains, and -NotMatch) so the preceding example could also be used to filter out lines that begin with # (comments), like this:

```
Get-Content MyScript.ps1 | Where-Object {($_ -notmatch "^#")
   -and ($_ -ne "")}
```

This could be piped into the Measure-object Cmdlet to find the number of lines of "real" script in the file, as follows:

```
Get-Content MyScript.ps1 | Where-Object {($_ -notmatch "^#")
   -and ($_ -ne "")} | measure-object -count
```

Finally, when handling strings it is useful to know if the comparisons are case-sensitive or not. PowerShell normally treats strings in a case-*insensitive* way, but all the operators listed in this section can be prefixed with a *C* for case-sensitive, or an *I* to make them explicitly case-Insensitive.

Typically, when processing a file, it's necessary to do something with each line of it and you can do this with the Foreach-Object command. A simple example would be to look at each line and replace one piece of text with another; because strings in PowerShell are .NET string objects, they have all the properties and methods you'd find in a .NET language, including `replace()` (which *is* case-sensitive); for example, this command will replace all instances of a variable $file with $fileName:

```
Get-Content MyScript.ps1 |ForEach-Object {$_.replace("$file",
"$FileName")
```

Parsing text

As was just mentioned, PowerShell strings are .NET strings and they have a split function. For example, if a string is separated by commas, it can be converted into an array of strings;

```
Get-Content GPS-Data.CSV | ForEach-Object {$_.split(",")}
```

This will turn the content from an array of text strings to an array of arrays of text strings.

However, for comma-separated files with a header row, it is easier to use the `Import-CSV` Cmdlet. If the file doesn't have a header file, then it is quite easy to add one: the result of `Get-Content` is an array of strings. A new array can be defined with the syntax `@(Element0,Element1,Element2)`, so a single element array can be defined containing the first row line of the file and joined to the rest of the file; the header row can be added to a GPS log file like this:

```
@("Type,Time,status,latitude,NS,longitude,EW,Speed,bearing,Date,
blank,checksum")+ (Get-Content GPS.LOG) > Gps-Data.CSV
```

The critical thing when importing a CSV file, instead of parsing the raw text, is that its fields become properties of an array of objects.

```
> Import-Csv Gps-Data.CSV | Get-Member
    TypeName: System.Management.Automation.PSCustomObject
```

Name	MemberType	Definition
Equals	Method	System.Boolean Equals(Object obj)
GetHashCode	Method	System.Int32 GetHashCode()
GetType	Method	System.Type GetType()
ToString	Method	System.String ToString()
bearing	NoteProperty	System.String bearing=73.06
blank	NoteProperty	System.String blank=
checksum	NoteProperty	System.String checksum=*2F
Date	NoteProperty	System.String Date=030708
EW	NoteProperty	System.String EW=W
latitude	NoteProperty	System.String latitude=5325.5023
longitude	NoteProperty	System.String longitude=00255.0864
NS	NoteProperty	System.String NS=N
Speed	NoteProperty	System.String Speed=4.869933
status	NoteProperty	System.String status=A
Time	NoteProperty	System.String Time=070445.647
Type	NoteProperty	System.String Type=$GPRMC

Notice that the type is a "PSCustomObject"—building these objects with your own custom scripts is covered in Chapters 21 and 30; the process may use items from an array created by calling `Split()`, or any of the other string methods.

In addition to using `Where-Object` to filter out rows—for example, filtering this GPS data to only the Navigation data rows (the ones where the type field is `$GPRMC`)—PowerShell has another useful tool for filtering (and calculating) columns: `Select-Object`. For example:

```
Import-CSV temp.CSV | Where-Object {$_.type -eq '$GPRMC'} |
Select-Object Date,time, Latitude, NS, Longitude, EW
```

Converting a text file into an XML document is very straight forward; for example:

```
[xml](get-content "..\Remote Assistance Logs\20080523132838.xml")
```

The syntax of `– [type] Something` is used in many contexts; for example:

```
[Char]65
```

The preceding code takes the number 65 and converts it to an ASCII character (A in this case). This *type accelerator* syntax is used in many places in PowerShell—you saw the XML version used in Chapter 21, and it will be used to convert a path into an AD object or a WMI object in Chapters 24 and 25.

Working with the Registry

So far, everything you have seen has used the File System Provider. However, at the start of the chapter, you saw there were other providers, including one for the Registry; this provider creates two drives by default—HKCU, for the HKEY_CURRENT_USER hive, and HKLM, for the HKEY_LOCAL_MACHINE hive. Other drives can be set up for any part of the Registry and it can be referenced with the full provider path as well.

Navigation in the Registry is the same as navigation in the file system—`Set-Location` (or its alias CD), `Push-Location`, `Pop-Location` (and their aliases `PushD` and `PopD`), `Get-ChildItem` (its aliases `DIR` and `ls`), and `Get-Item` all work in the same way.

The major difference between working with the File System and working with the Registry is that the Registry *keys* (the items in the left pane in `REGEDIT`) can be both containers and leaf nodes in the tree, and treated as *items*. They can be created in the same way as directories in the file system with `New-Item`. (The registry provider ignores the `-type` parameter for `New-Item` so it is possible to use the `MD` function and treat registry keys as directories.)

Registry values (the items in the right pane in REGEDIT) are treated as item-properties. They are *not* leaf nodes in the Registry tree. You can see this in the different way that a dir command works in the Registry, compared with the file system.

```
PS HKCU:\software\microsoft> dir

    Hive: Microsoft.PowerShell.Core\Registry::HKEY_CURRENT_USER\
        software\microsoft

SKC  VC Name                           Property
---  -- ----                           --------
  1   0 .NETFramework                   {}
  1   0 Active Setup                    {}

  0   1 Calc                            {layout}

  2   0 Works Suite                     {}
```

The SKC and VC columns are the *Sub-Key Count* and *Value Count* respectively. The following command returns all the values inside the key.

```
PS HKCU:\software\microsoft> Get-ItemProperty calc

PSPath       : Microsoft.PowerShell.Core\Registry::HKEY_CURRENT_USER\
               software\microsoft\calc
PSParentPath : Microsoft.PowerShell.Core\Registry::HKEY_CURRENT_USER\
               software\microsoft
PSChildName  : calc
PSDrive      : HKCU
PSProvider   : Microsoft.PowerShell.Core\Registry
layout       : 0
```

There are two ways to get an individual property:

```
PS HKCU:\Software\Microsoft> $properties=( Get-ItemProperty
                                            -Path Calc )
PS HKCU:\Software\Microsoft> $properties.layout
0

PS HKCU:\software\microsoft> (Get-ItemProperty -Path Calc
-Name "Layout").layout
0
```

The first is more useful if more than one value needs to be examined, and the second is more useful when only one value is needed.

Values can be changed with the Set-ItemProperty Cmdlet. For example:

```
set-ItemProperty -Path Calc -Name "Layout" 1
```

Values can be added to a key with `New-ItemProperty`, and like creating new items in the file system, it is necessary to use the `-PropertyType` switch. The property type can be:

- `String`
- `ExpandString`
- `Binary`
- `DWord`
- `MultiString`
- `QWord`
- `Unknown`

For example:

```
New-ItemProperty -Path HKCU:\Software\Microsoft\Calc `
-Name "test" -Value "This is a test" -PropertyType string
```

Finally, a value can be removed from a key using the following syntax:

```
Remove-ItemProperty -Path calc -Name "test"
```

Summary

In this chapter, you have seen the main commands for working with files, which can be used at the prompt in PowerShell in a very similar way to their equivalents in CMD.EXE. By using aliases, PowerShell allows the same command names to be used—albeit with different switches than their CMD.EXE equivalents.

You have also seen that by using *providers,* PowerShell allows you to use the same commands to access the registry as you would to work with files. This consistency—for example using `new-item` or `get-childItem` to do the same job with different kinds of objects—means you do not have to spend time learning new commands to work with different kinds of objects. Deleting a function uses the same command as deleting a file, which uses the same command as deleting a certificate.

Chapter 23

Event Logging, Services, and Process Monitoring with PowerShell

I
t is important for any shell to allow a system administrator to manage the programs running a system. These may be normal user mode processes or they may be services which run in the background. This chapter looks at the tools PowerShell provides for managing both of these events as well as examining the information the programs record in the event log.

Working with Services

Microsoft environments have had command-line tools for managing network services since the days of DOS and MS-NET, and the NET.EXE command still provides much of the same functionality as it did back then: Net Start, Net Stop, Net Share, and Net Use commands from 20 years ago have remained constant through the change to OS/2 LAN Manager, Windows NT, and Server 2000, 2003, and 2008 and as the client has changed from DOS/Windows to Windows NT–based, including Windows XP and Windows Vista. The command has evolved to take on the ability to manage accounts and groups and to pause and resume services as well as simply starting and stopping them.

The Net Start command returns a list of running services; as a traditional text-based command, it can be run in PowerShell and have its output piped into something. For example, the following command checks which services containing "Windows" in their name are running on a Windows Vista Ultimate computer:

```
> net start | where {$_ -like "*Windows*" }
These Windows services are started:
    Windows Audio
    Windows Audio Endpoint Builder
    Windows Backup
```

```
Windows Defender
Windows Driver Foundation - User-mode Driver Framework
Windows Error Reporting Service
Windows Event Log
Windows Firewall
Windows Image Acquisition (WIA)
Windows Management Instrumentation
Windows Media Center Extender Service
Windows Media Center Receiver Service
Windows Media Center Scheduler Service
Windows Mobile-2003-based device connectivity
Windows Mobile-based device connectivity
Windows Search
Windows Time
Windows Update
```

If you look at the top of the list, you can see this command line returned the title from NET.EXE. In cases like this, the old world worked purely with text, but when you want to do anything with the returned services the information returned by NET.EXE is too limited—even if you made the effort to parse it. You can't get a list of services that are not running, or identify which services start automatically. In short: you can see why PowerShell needs to implement something better.

Before looking at PowerShell's commands, however, it is worth taking a moment to consider access to services through WMI because it provides a different but overlapping set of features.

There is a WMI object class in the Root/CIMV2 namespace named Win32_Service that provides access to the services, and like any other WMI class, it can be accessed on remote machines. It can offer greater flexibility, although it can be more complicated because you need to deal with the objects that are in a less processed state than if you use the Cmdlets that PowerShell provides.

You can see the kind of flexibility in the WMI objects just by getting the first few, like this:

```
> Get-WmiObject win32_service  | select-object -First 5


ExitCode   : 0
Name       : AeLookupSvc
ProcessId  : 460
StartMode  : Auto
State      : Running
Status     : OK

ExitCode   : 1077
Name       : ALG
ProcessId  : 0
StartMode  : Manual
State      : Stopped
Status     : OK
```

```
ExitCode   : 0
Name       : Appinfo
ProcessId  : 460
StartMode  : Manual
State      : Running
Status     : OK

ExitCode   : 1077
Name       : AppMgmt
ProcessId  : 0
StartMode  : Manual
State      : Stopped
Status     : OK

ExitCode   : 0
Name       : AudioEndpointBuilder
ProcessId  : 396
StartMode  : Auto
State      : Running
Status     : OK
```

So you can see that some of the services—such as "ALG"—are in an OK state even though they are stopped. WMI gives access to more properties than the PowerShell commands, including the ProcessID, Description, and the AccountName used to start it and the ExitCode you can see in the preceding examples.

One facility of NET.EXE that is useful even when using something else to manage the services is the HELPMSG sub-command, which expands return codes to a text message. For example, you might be curious what 1077 means in the exit codes of several of the services in the previous example. You can find out like this:

```
> net helpmsg 1077
No attempts to start the service have been made since the last boot.
```

In addition to the six default properties that are defined as the default output in types.ps1xml, there are other useful properties and methods you can access on the WMI object; you can discover these by piping the output of the Get-WMIObject command into Get-Member. For example, you would usually want to see the display name field rather than the shorthand *name*.

PowerShell has its own Get-Service command, which returns .NET service objects that have slightly different properties and methods from those provided by WMI. You can get a tabulated list of the services as follows:

```
> get-Service | sort-object -property displayname | select -first 5 |
Format-Table -autosize -Property DisplayName, ServiceName, Status, ServiceType

DisplayName                         ServiceName  Status   ServiceType
-----------                         -----------  ------   -----------
Application Experience              AeLookupSvc  Running  Win32ShareProcess
```

```
Application Information                 Appinfo    Running Win32ShareProcess
Application Layer Gateway Service       ALG        Stopped  Win32OwnProcess
Application Management                  AppMgmt    Stopped  Win32ShareProcess
Background Intelligent Transfer Service BITS       Running  Win32ShareProcess
```

The Name of a service is a short name that is used internally by Windows. This is different from what is normally shown to users: therefore Get-Service is flexible about the passing of names. It supports a -Name parameter, which is considered to be best practice in PowerShell because when something has a name, it should be possible to ask for it by name, as in this example:

```
> get-service -Name *network*
Status    Name              DisplayName
------    ----              -----------
Stopped   WMPNetworkSvc     Windows Media Player Network Sharin...
```

As with many other commands you have seen already, Get-Service has an alias, in this case GSV, and if the first parameter is not labeled, it is assumed to be the -Name parameter, so the previous command can be entered at the prompt using a little less typing by putting it in the form:

```
Gsv *network*
```

However, most people will want to refer to this service by its *display* name so in addition to the -Name parameter, Get-Service can take a -DisplayName parameter. Changing the preceding example from -Name to -DisplayName finds more services:

```
> Get-Service -DisplayName *network*

Status    Name              DisplayName
------    ----              -----------
Running   napagent          Network Access Protection Agent
Running   Netman            Network Connections
Running   netprofm          Network List Service
Running   NlaSvc            Network Location Awareness
Running   nsi               Network Store Interface Service
Stopped   p2pimsvc          Peer Networking Identity Manager
Stopped   p2psvc            Peer Networking Grouping
Stopped   WMPNetworkSvc     Windows Media Player Network Sharin...
```

As before, the command can be abbreviated for entry at the prompt. However, the Cmdlet takes both -Debug and -DisplayName parameters so -DisplayName can't be shortened to -d At least -di must be given.

Like the Get-ChildItem Cmdlet (or its alias Dir), Get-Service (or Gsv) supports an -Include parameter, which acts on the name field, and can be modified with an -Exclude parameter. But it doesn't have a switch for just running, just stopped, just auto-started, or just manually-started services. Although it is less efficient to get all the services and then filter them using Where-Object, the number of services on any machine is small enough for this not to be considered a problem, so it is perfectly acceptable to construct a command like the following:

```
Get-Service | where-object {($_.name -like "lanman*") -and
                           ($_.Status -eq "running")}

Status    Name              DisplayName
------    ----              -----------
Running   LanmanServer      Server
Running   LanmanWorkstation Workstation
```

Starting, Stopping, Suspending, Resuming, and Restarting Services

PowerShell has five Cmdlets: Start-Service, Stop-Service, Restart-Service (which is stop followed by start), Suspend-Service, and Resume-Service.

These do pretty much what you would expect them to—with the capability to act on more than one service at once being one of the more obvious improvements over their NET.EXE equivalents.

Stopping a service

Although most things about the Stop-Service Cmdlet are obvious, remember that stopping services is a privileged operation and if you start PowerShell on Windows Vista or Server 2008 as an administrative user, but without saying you want to run PowerShell *as administrator*, you'll get an error when you try to start or stop the service.

Windows services can register dependency relationships with each other, and these can be quite complex. For example, a dozen services depend on the Plug and Play service, and the Workstation service depends on four others. So what happens when you try to stop a service that has other services depending on it? The following example puts that to the test.

```
> Stop-Service AudioEndpointBuilder
Stop-Service : Cannot stop service 'Windows Audio Endpoint Builder
(AudioEndpointBuilder)' because it has dependent services. It can only
be stopped if the Force flag is set.
```

When the Stop-Service Cmdlet is given a single unnamed parameter, it assumes it to be the -Name parameter, which can be a wildcard. audioE* would have worked just as well here. Like Get-Service, you can filter out services you don't want to stop with the -Exclude switch. And just as you can retrieve a service by its display name with Get-Service, you can specify -DisplayName, which can be truncated at the command prompt to -di. Stop-Service has an alias of SpSv for command-line use if you want to minimize your typing.

PowerShell requires the -force flag, even if the dependent services are not running. If you specify it, they are stopped, but unlike the Net command, you won't be told what the dependent services are, or what *their* dependents are. They're just stopped.

In a script, this is probably what you want anyway. You can check before putting the script into production what services (if any) depend on the one you want to stop and specify the -Force switch. Your script(s) can then take responsibility for restarting the services. How?

A service, running or not, has two properties: DependentServices and ServicesDependedOn. These are arrays that contain not just the name of the services but the .NET ServiceController objects. So before you stop a service, you can discover which of its dependent services are running. If you store this information, you can restart the dependents after you have completed the action for which they needed to be stopped. For example:

```
$dep=(get-Service audioEndPointBuilder).DependentServices |
where-object {$_.status -eq "running"}
Stop-service -name audioEndPointBuilder -force
Take some action
Start-Service audioEndPointBuilder
$dep | Start-Service
```

The last line of this example shows something else that is useful about Stop-Service and the others: they can take input from the pipe.

Starting a service

The Start-Service Cmdlet is no more complicated to understand than Stop-Service, and takes the same parameters. Services can be identified by DisplayName or internal name, can be filtered using -Exclude, and can be passed via the pipe. If what is piped into these Cmdlets is a string or array of strings, the Cmdlets assume they are being passed the name(s) of the service(s).

If a service depends on others that are not running, those services will be silently started without the need for any switch, and attempting to start a service that is already running will not cause any error.

Restarting a service

The Restart-Service Cmdlet delivers the same behavior as calling Stop-Service and then calling Start-Service with identical parameters. Quite commonly, if a service's settings are changed, the quickest way to get them to take effect is to restart the service.

The same rules apply to restarting as stopping. It requires administrator privileges, and if the service has dependents, the Cmdlet needs the -Force switch. Restarting a service does *not* restart its dependents, so some method is needed for restarting them. Here is another method, which is more general than the preceding one, in that it will restart any service that has been stopped—either because multiple services were restarted or because a service's dependents had their own dependents.

It is possible to capture all the running services before one or more other services are restarted and then restart any of the services that have become stopped. If services need to be started in a given order, their dependencies should ensure that those that are needed earlier are auto-started if called out of sequence. This could be done as follows:

```
$srv=Get-Service | where {$_.status -eq "running"}
$serviceList | Restart-service
$srv | get-service | where-object {$_.status -ne "running"} | Start-Service
```

There is an alternate way to write the last line, as you will see in a moment.

Suspending and resuming services

Not all services accept the command to pause (or suspend operations), and those that do, behave in different ways. Some will stop processing requests entirely. Others will continue to process requests but won't allow new users to connect. Some even use the pause request as a method to tell the service to take some action without ever going into a paused state. As with starting and stopping services, pause and resume are privileged operations and attempting to run them in a non-elevated session will cause an error.

PowerShell provides a `Suspend-Service` Cmdlet; with a companion `Resume-Service`. You can check which of the services accept the suspend request by checking the property `CanPauseAndContinue`, like this:

```
Get-service | where-object{$_.canPauseAndContinue}
Status    Name                 DisplayName
------    ----                 -----------
Running   LanmanServer         Server
Running   LanmanWorkstation    Workstation
Running   Netlogon             Netlogon
Running   seclogon             Secondary Logon
Running   stisvc               Windows Image Acquisition (WIA)
Running   TapiSrv              Telephony
Running   WerSvc               Windows Error Reporting Service
Running   Winmgmt              Windows Management Instrumentation
```

Rather confusingly, the Cmdlets use the verbs `Suspend` and `Resume`, but the objects returned by `Get-Service` have methods named `Pause()` and `Continue()`—in addition to `start()` and `Stop()`. The Cmdlets provide a shortcut, so the following:

```
(Get-service -Name lanmanServer).pause()
```

is equivalent to:

```
Suspend-Service LanManServer
```

So the alternate version of the example in the restart section would be to use the `start()` method on the `ServiceController` object rather than using the `Start-Service` Cmdlet, like this:

```
$srv | get-service | foreach-Object {if ($_.status -ne "running")
                                     {$_.Start()}}
```

Configuring services

PowerShell has a `Set-Service` Cmdlet, which allows:

- The startup type of a service to be toggled between Automatic, Manual, and Disabled
- The Long description to be changed
- The Display name to be changed

The first two can be seen in the Services Management console, but can only be viewed in PowerShell by using WMI.

The description of the Windows Vista Bluetooth Service is blank by default and it can be set by getting the object and piping it into `Set-Service`, as follows:

```
Get-Service -DisplayName "Bluetooth*" |
set-service -Description "Supports Bluetooth Devices"
```

The short name for the service is `BthServ`, but it is easier to find the service with a display name that starts `Bluetooth` and pipe it into `Set-Service`. If you know the name you could enter the command as:

```
set-service -name BthServ -Description "Supports Bluetooth Devices"
```

`Set-Service` lets you change the display name by specifying a `-DisplayName` parameter and change the startup type to `Automatic`, `Manual`, or `Disabled` by specifying a `-StartUpType` switch. For example:

```
set-service -name BthServ -StartupType manual
```

Setting service properties, like the other tasks you have already seen with services, requires an elevated PowerShell session.

It is possible to discover more about services by looking at the `Win32_Service` WMI object. For example, the following will give a list of running services and their associated process IDs and the account used to start them:

```
> Gwmi win32_service | where {$_.started} | select name, displayname,
StartName, ProcessID | sort ProcessID | ft * -a
```

Working with Processes

Services are a special class of processes that run in the background to enable some system feature. Once running—and especially if you have discovered the service's process ID—you can work with its process object. In addition, any user tasks—including PowerShell itself—will have an associated process.

Starting, finding, and stopping processes

It is more-or-less axiomatic that a shell should make it easy to start a process: In PowerShell, if you enter a command, it first checks to see if it is defined as an alias. If not, the command checks to see if it is defined as a function, and if neither is found, then PowerShell checks the path to see if it can find a script or executable program with that name. For example, the following:

```
notepad  MyScript.ps1
```

will edit a file in Notepad. However, if you enter:

```
New-Alias notepad calc
function notepad {write-host "Oh no"}
```

the alias *wins*.

One important consideration is how to be clear that a file name contain spaces is a single entity. In the old CMD shell, all that was needed was to wrap the command in quotation marks. However, that tells PowerShell *This is a string* so PowerShell uses the ampersand (&) to say *execute this*. You can see this if you type \p [tab]. When the path expands to program files, PowerShell converts the line to & 'Program Files'.

PowerShell has a Get-Process Cmdlet that returns System.Diagnostics.Process .NET objects. You saw in the section "Changing How PowerShell Formats Objects" in Chapter 21 that types can have extra properties added to them using definitions in Types.PS1XML. The process object has 51 properties of its own plus another six alias properties and seven script properties added by the types file. That's obviously a rich source of information when trying to find out what is going on with processes. However, there are additional properties that can be found through WMI. For example, in task manager you can view the command line used to start a process, but it's not available from the .NET object. You can get the information from the Win32_Process WMI object. But Get-Process is convenient. It gives a table of information, and processes can be easily found by name or process ID, and it can be invoked from the command line using an alias: either GP or PS. For example, Ps calc will get a process object without your having to use the Get-WMIObject command, specify the Win32_process class, and filter it to the item with the process name of Calc.

Get-Process gives access to a useful subset of properties needed when checking on the operation of processes: their start time, CPU time (privileged and UserMode), priority, threads, handles, and memory (Working Set, Paged Memory, NonPaged Memory, Virtual Memory, and Private Memory, with the peaks in Paged, Virtual, and Working Set), plus the window title, path to the executable, and file version, product, and company name. Any of these can be used in the condition of Where-Object. For example:

```
Get-Process | where-object {$_.mainWindowTitle -like "*calc*" }

Handles  NPM(K)    PM(K)      WS(K) VM(M)   CPU(s)     Id ProcessName
-------  ------    -----      ----- -----   ------     -- -----------
     53       6     2248       8876    80     0.16   7888 calc
```

The process object has a threads property, which allows you to see whether threads are executing or waiting and, if so, what for.

Access to the file versions is useful when trying to detect differences in behavior between two systems that should be identical. The process object allows you to drill into the modules loaded by the application, and see beyond the program which was started and look at the information for each of the modules that it calls. So if you have two applications that should be the same but are acting differently you can check the versions of the modules they load, as follows:

```
(Gp calc).modules |sort fileVersion | ft -a -w moduleName, fileversion

ModuleName     FileVersion
----------     -----------
USP10.dll      1.0626.6001.18000 (longhorn_rtm.080118-1840)
CLBCatQ.DLL    2001.12.6931.18000 (longhorn_rtm.080118-1840)
ole32.dll      6.0.6000.16386 (vista_rtm.061101-2205)
SHLWAPI.dll    6.0.6000.16386 (vista_rtm.061101-2205)
MSCTF.dll      6.0.6000.16386 (vista_rtm.061101-2205)
uxtheme.dll    6.0.6000.16386 (vista_rtm.061101-2205)
calc.exe       6.0.6000.16386 (vista_rtm.061101-2205)
OLEAUT32.dll   6.0.6001.18000
LPK.DLL        6.0.6001.18000 (longhorn_rtm.080118-1840)
SHELL32.dll    6.0.6001.18000 (longhorn_rtm.080118-1840)
ntdll.dll      6.0.6001.18000 (longhorn_rtm.080118-1840)
kernel32.dll   6.0.6001.18000 (longhorn_rtm.080118-1840)
IMM32.DLL      6.0.6001.18000 (longhorn_rtm.080118-1840)
ADVAPI32.dll   6.0.6001.18000 (longhorn_rtm.080118-1840)
RPCRT4.dll     6.0.6001.18000 (longhorn_rtm.080118-1840)
USER32.dll     6.0.6001.18000 (longhorn_rtm.080118-1840)
GDI32.dll      6.0.6001.18023 (vistasp1_gdr.080221-1537)
comctl32.dll   6.10 (longhorn_rtm.080118-1840)
msvcrt.dll     7.0.6001.18000 (longhorn_rtm.080118-1840)
```

The modules listed above are for Calculator running on Windows Vista. As you can see, some of the DLLs loaded follow the normal operating system versioning (6.0.xxxx.xxxxx) and others don't. You can look at the file description to see what these DLLs are (for example, USP10.DLL is the Uniscribe Unicode Script Processor). You can also see that most of the DLLs are from the RTM version of Windows Vista, but some are from Service Pack 1, which synched with the release of Server 2008 (aka, Longhorn). The numbers at the end are the build date and time, so the Vista RTM build is November 1, 2006, and the Longhorn RTM ones are January 18, 2008. You might notice one of the files (GDI32) has a later build number (18023 instead of 18000) and was built on February 21, 2008, so you could reasonably assume that this file has been patched from Windows Update. It is this sort of information that can help you to identify differences in patches between machines.

There are three ways to bring a process to an end. Both the .NET object returned by the Get-Process and the WMI Win32_Process object have Kill() methods; there is also a Stop-Process Cmdlet. All three of the following will end a running instance of Calculator.

```
(get-process -Name calc).kill()
get-process -name calc | Stop-Process
stop-process -name Calc
```

Of these, the first will work only if the there is a single instance of Calculator running and the second form is usually combined with a Where-Object{}to identify a specific instance.

One final thing to investigate before leaving processes is the question of which user owns a process—or which processes belong to a given user session.

As you will learn in Chapter 25, WMI objects can be linked together using an Associators Of WMI query. Win32_Process objects are linked to Win32_logonSession objects.

```
>$p=gwmi -q "select * from win32_process where name='calc.exe'"
> gwmi -q "associators of {$p} where classdefsonly"
Win32_ComputerSystem                        Win32_LogonSession
CIM_DataFile
```

Investigating this a little further shows that a win32_LogonSession object doesn't contain the name of the user but is linked to a Win32_Account object via a Win32_LoggedOnUser object:

```
> $l=gwmi -q "associators of {$p} where resultclass=win32_logonSession"
> gwmi -q "associators of {$l} where classdefsonly"
Win32_Process                               Win32_Account

> gwmi -q "references of {$l} where classdefsonly"
Win32_SessionProcess                        Win32_LoggedOnUser
```

So you can obtain the user details from the `Win32_Account` object. One caveat is that if the user has logged on with cached credentials, it won't be possible to get their associated `Win32_Account` object. Instead, their name can be found by parsing the `Antecedent` property of the logged on user account.

It is possible to work the other way, and get all the logged on user accounts and display the user and associated processes, as in the following example.

```
Function Get-UserProcess{
Param ($Server=".")
Get-wmiobject -computerName $server -class Win32_LoggedOnUser |
Foreach-object {
    $d=[wmi]$_.dependent ;
     $Processes=get-wmiobject -query "associators of {$d} where
                                    resultclass=Win32_process"
    If ($Processes -ne $null)
        {$_.antecedent ;
          Format-table -autosize -wrap -inputobject $processes `
                        -property name, commandline, Processid}
    }
}
```

Working with Event Logs

Many different kinds of troubleshooting and process or service management lead to the Windows event logs.

PowerShell has a single Cmdlet for working with event logs, `Get-EventLog`, which takes the common PowerShell parameters and four parameters of its own.

- `-Logname`: Identifies the log from which events are to be fetched.
- `-newest`: Returns the most recent *n* events.
- `-asString`: Returns the events as strings and not objects.
- `-List`: Changes the behavior of the Cmdlet so that it returns the logs themselves and not the events they contain. `-List` and `-logname` can't be combined.

Clearing an event log

When used with the -list switch, Get-EventLog returns System.Diagnostics.EventLog .NET objects. By default, these are presented like this:

```
> Get-EventLog  -list

Max(K) Retain OverflowAction       Entries Name
------ ------ ---------------      ------- ----
15,168      0 OverwriteAsNeeded     28,251 Application
15,168      0 OverwriteAsNeeded          0 DFS Replication
20,480      0 OverwriteAsNeeded          0 Hardware Events
   512      7 OverwriteOlder             0 Internet Explorer
20,480      0 OverwriteAsNeeded          0 Key Management Service
 8,192      0 OverwriteAsNeeded      3,467 Media Center
16,384      0 OverwriteAsNeeded         28 Microsoft Office Diagnostics
16,384      0 OverwriteAsNeeded        621 Microsoft Office Sessions
30,016      0 OverwriteAsNeeded     54,937 Security
15,168      0 OverwriteAsNeeded     32,666 System
15,360      0 OverwriteAsNeeded     18,648 Windows PowerShell
```

In fact, the type formatting XML files (in this case DotNetTypes.format.ps1xml) have worked some magic here because the column names are not "Max(k)", "Retain", and "Name". Piping the output into Get-Member shows the names are actually MaximumKilobytes, MinimumRetention Days, and Log. Get-Member also shows a Clear() method, which clears the log.

The way to get a single log file is to request the list of event logs and filter down to the one you are interested in; you can then call the clear() method () on that log, like this:

```
((Get-EventLog  -list) | where {$_.log -match "Windows PowerShell"} ).clear()
```

This syntax doesn't seem intuitive; you would expect to use something like Get-EventLog "Windows Powershell" but this will return the entries in the PowerShell log, not the log itself.

Exporting event logs

Before clearing a log, it is a good idea to export it. PowerShell can export a log simply by getting the EventLog entries and piping the results into Export-Csv or Export-Clixml

Windows' event viewer tool has its own .EVTx binary format—but also exports CSV files. It can only import EVTx files back so if you want to read events in Event viewer, you need to use it to export them. However, in many cases what is desired is to have a log that can be processed in Excel or imported into a database, and CSV format is good enough for this. For example, this will create a CSV file and load it into Excel (assuming Excel is present, and the default program for CSV files):

```
get-eventlog "windows powershell" | export-csv powershell-events.csv
Invoke-Item powershell-events.csv
```

Figure 23-1 shows examining an Event log using filtering in Excel.

FIGURE 23-1

Examining an Event log using filtering in Excel

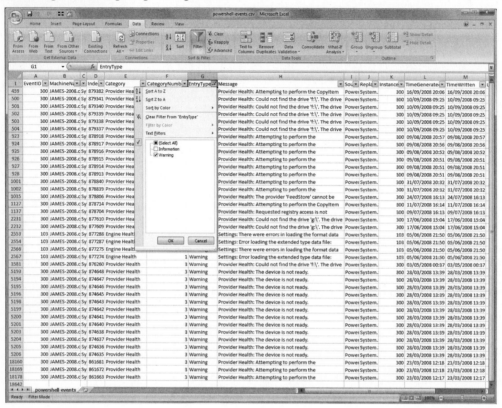

Finding entries in the event log

Get-eventlog will return entries that have an ID, a category, an entry type (Warning, Error, or Information), a message, and a time stamp. These properties can be used in a Where-Object or a group-object command. For example:

```
Get-EventLog "WindowsPowerShell" | Group-Object -Property entryType |

  ft -a name, count

Name        Count
----        -----
Information 18609
Warning        39
```

```
>Get-EventLog "Windows PowerShell" | where {$_.entryType -eq "Warning"} |
 group category  | ft name,count -a

Name             Count
----             -----
Provider Health    35
Engine Health       4

> Get-EventLog "Windows PowerShell" | where {($_.entryType -eq "Warning")
-and ($_.category -eq "Engine Health")} | ft -a timegenerated, message

TimeGenerated        Message
-------------        -------
05/06/2008 21:50:46  Settings: There were errors in loading the format
                               data file:
05/06/2008 21:50:46  Settings: Error loading the extended type data file:...
05/06/2008 21:50:42  Settings: There were errors in loading the format
                               data file:
05/06/2008 21:50:41  Settings: Error loading the extended type data file:...
```

To save processing time, it is often easiest to specify the -newest switch so that instead of processing many thousands of entries, you can limit it to the first few hundred. For example:

```
> Get-EventLog "Windows PowerShell" -newest 1000 |
    where {($_.entryType -eq "Warning")}  | ft -a timegenerated,message
```

By getting the Log object—as you would to clear it—you can also reference an entries object as one of its properties. 0 is the oldest entry, so you can get the oldest events like this:

```
((Get-EventLog  -list) |
   where {$_.log -match "Windows PowerShell"} ).entries[0..20]
```

In fact, you can add a Script property to each log to show the oldest entry:

```
> Get-EventLog  -list | Add-Member -PassThru -Name "Oldest" `
-MemberType ScriptProperty -Value {$this.entries[0].TimeGenerated} |
 ft -a log,oldest

Log                  Oldest
---                  ------
Application          09/02/2008 16:26:14
DFS Replication
HardwareEvents
Internet Explorer
Key Management Service
Security             07/07/2008 12:12:56
System               01/07/2008 09:47:05
Windows PowerShell   23/03/2008 11:16:00
```

(Some of the logs are empty so they have no "oldest" entry.)

Summary

In this chapter you've seen how PowerShell works with events, processes, and services. Through its built-in Cmdlets, it provides a functionality that extends what was previously available from the command prompt in Windows environments. In cases where these don't go far enough, the capability to access WMI and .NET objects easily means that PowerShell is a very useful aid in system management and troubleshooting. This is a slightly different use case for PowerShell because often it is positioned as a tool for automating tasks, which could be done with GUI tools, but which are repeated and so are scripted for reasons of efficiency. In the case of investigating process behavior, PowerShell is giving access to options that aren't accessible through the GUI tools provided with Windows.

Chapter 24

Working with Active Directory Using ADSI and PowerShell

ADSI—the Active Directory Services Interface—allows you to query directory services. Three different kinds of directories are commonly used in the Microsoft world:

- WinNT allows access to the local computer, and Windows NT (pre–Windows 2000) domains.

- LDAP accesses an Active Directory Domain Controller using the LDAP protocol.

- GC accesses an Active Directory Global Catalog server.

A Quick Introduction to Active Directory

Active Directory is a replicated database that holds information about objects that are to be centrally managed—for example, Users, Groups and Computers. The set of object *classes* that can be stored is extensible, so anything that needs to be managed centrally can have an object definition added to AD. Exchange 2000 was the first major application to use Active Directory to store its information. It uses AD as its mail directory and defines extra classes for mail stores, gateways, and so on.

In addition to classes, AD defines a set of *attributes* (properties) for those classes. The set of attributes is also extensible. Any attribute can be added to any existing class. So, for example, Exchange does not define a new class for a mail-enabled user. Instead, the attributes that it needs—the users' mail addresses, where their mailboxes are stored, and so on—are defined as new attributes that are added to the existing user object class. The definitions of attributes and objects are referred to as the Active Directory *Schema*.

AD groups computers into *Domains*, each of which has a DNS style name—for example, Contoso.com. Domains with contiguous names (for example, Contoso.com, Americas.Contoso.com, and Europe. Contoso.com), can be grouped into *trees*, and multiple trees (or other non-contiguous domains) can be grouped into *forests*. In each domain one or more *Domain Controllers* (DCs) holds the database; but each Domain Controller only holds a subset of the information for the whole forest.

A DC stores the complete database information for objects in its own domain; in other words it holds all their attributes. A Domain controller that is designated as a *Global Catalog* server also stores all objects outside its domain, but it holds only *a partial replica* of them—a read-only subset of their attributes. Each attribute in the AD Schema has a flag to indicate whether it is a member of this Partial Replica Set, and whether it is indexed for fast retrieval.

The AD database is divided into *partitions* known as *Contexts*. Each Domain has its own context, and this context is replicated to all the Domain Controllers in the domain. The Schema has a context, and another context holds configuration information: these are replicated to every Domain Controller in the forest.

To make management of objects in the domain easier, domains support *containers*, like folders in the file system. The directory entry for an object can be moved between containers in its domain, and it has a path that includes the domain and container hierarchy, which can be used to identify it (because the path can change AD objects also have a globally unique ID, which remains constant).

Directory activities

Any activity with Active Directory can be broken down into one of three tasks:

- Creating new objects (of a class which is defined in the Schema)
- Finding objects in the directory
- Modifying objects that have been found or created

In the real world, activities are often combinations of these tasks—for example, "Find all the user entries that match certain criteria and set an attribute on them." Or "Produce a report showing which users are enabled for service X." Or it might be to provide diagnostic information about a service, or to find some information that is used as a parameter in undertaking some other task.

Caution

At the risk of stating the obvious: *Erroneous changes to AD can also have serious consequences*, so you should always develop and test scripts that make changes to the directory in a separate environment before using them in production.

The second caution is less obvious. When making changes to the directory entries for services objects or attributes those services use on other classes, you should check that that the service supports making an update simply by changing the attribute(s) in Active Directory, or whether you need to go through some other interface. In some cases, direct manipulation of AD appears to work but is unsupported and may cause issues later. For example, in Office Communications Server there is a WMI object for managing OCS-enabled users. It is also possible to enable a user by setting the correct AD attributes; only the WMI method is supported.

PowerShell and ADSI

When version 1 of PowerShell was released it attracted some criticism for the weakness of its AD support. Microsoft has said that this will be improved in future versions.

This has given rise to a number of third-party tools to ease the management of AD (for example, Quest has made the PowerShell part of its management tools available free of charge—see `www.quest.com/powershell/activeroles-server.aspx`). If you have full control of the environment, then it is worth investigating these tools because they reduce the amount of script that is needed to accomplish a given task. However, if you are writing scripts that will be used on machines that you don't control then you won't be able to rely on these tools being present, and you will need to write several lines of PowerShell using the built-in ADSI type accelerator and generic .NET classes. Active Directory objects are not as easy to explore as COM, .NET, and WMI ones so more expertise—or more reference material—is required to work them.

Getting Entries from AD with [ADSI]

Explicitly or implicitly, queries for an object use an *Active Directory Service Path* (ADSpath). ADSI will attempt to discover a Domain Controller for an `LDAP` query and a Global Catalog server for a `GC` query; but some understanding is needed of whether an object will be found on the default Domain Controller, and if a Global Catalog server is queried, whether the attributes of interest are found on GCs. In some cases an object will be a different domain and the desired attribute will not be on the GC, so it will be necessary to specify the directory server.

An ADSpath is written in the style of a URI:

```
AccessMethod://Server:Port/resource
```

For example:

```
LDAP://localhost:389/RootDSE
LDAP://localhost/RootDSE
LDAP://RootDSE
```

The access method is *case sensitive*—you must write LDAP and GC in uppercase—using lowercase results in an error.

```
> [adsi]"ldap://rootdse"
out-lineoutput : Exception retrieving member
"ClassId2e4f51ef21dd47e99d3c952918aff9cd": "Unknown error (0x80005000)"
```

RootDSE is a special object—we examine it shortly.

> **NOTE**   All the examples in this chapter will use LDAP, and we will assume that it will work cor-
> rectly against the default server and port. In your own scripts, you may need to use GC
> or WinNT providers, or specify the server or port explicitly.

The path for an AD entry is known as a distinguished name and looks something like this:

```
"cn=UK-DC-WDS,ou=Domain Controllers,dc=contoso,dc=com"
```

This notation reads from least significant to most significant: you could read the path above aloud like this:

> The object with the Common Name UK-DC-WDS,
> which is a member of the Organizational Unit Domain controllers,
> which is a member of the Domain Component Contoso,
> which is a member of the Domain Component com.

Many people would read this by splitting the path into groups and reading the Domain Components forwards and the rest working backwards "contoso.com / Domain Controllers ou / UK-DC-WDS object".

When it comes to getting Directory entries in PowerShell, you will see there is more than one way to do it (you may grow to feel that any task in PowerShell can be accomplished in more than one way). The first way is the [ADSI] Type Accelerator.

Like other Type Accelerators [ADSI] takes one kind of object and flips it another. In this case, it takes an ADSpath as a string and returns a System.DirectoryServices.DirectoryEntry object like this:

```
> [adsi]"LDAP://rootdse"
currentTime                    : {20081010110949.0Z}
subschemaSubentry              : {CN=Aggregate,CN=Schema,CN=
                                 Configuration,DC=Contoso,DC=com}
dsServiceName                  : {CN=NTDS Settings,CN=UK-DC-
                                 WDS,CN=Servers,CN=Default-First-Site-
                                 Name,CN=Sites,CN=Configuration
                                 ,DC=Contoso,DC=com}
namingContexts                 : {DC=Contoso,DC=com,
                                 CN=Configuration,DC=Contoso
                                 ,DC=com, CN=Schema,CN=Configuration,
                                 DC=Contoso, DC=com, DC=DomainDnsZones,
                                 DC=Contoso,DC=com...}
```

```
defaultNamingContext           : {DC=Contoso,DC=com}
schemaNamingContext            : {CN=Schema,CN=Configuration,DC=Contoso
                                 ,DC=com}
configurationNamingContext     : {CN=Configuration,DC=Contoso,DC=com}
rootDomainNamingContext        : {DC=Contoso,DC=com}
supportedControl               : {1.2.840.113556.1.4.319,
                                 1.2.840.113556.1.4.801
                                 , 1.2.840.113556.1.4.473,
                                 1.2.840.113556.1.4.52
                                 8...}
supportedLDAPVersion           : {3, 2}
supportedLDAPPolicies          : {MaxPoolThreads, MaxDatagramRecv,
                                 MaxReceiveBuffer, InitRecvTimeout...}
highestCommittedUSN            : {205014}
supportedSASLMechanisms        : {GSSAPI, GSS-SPNEGO, EXTERNAL,
                                 DIGEST-MD5}
dnsHostName                    : {UK-DC-WDS.Contoso.com}
ldapServiceName                : {Contoso.com:uk-dc-wds$@CONTOSO.COM}
serverName                     : {CN=UK-DC-WDS,CN=Servers,CN=Default-
                                 First-Site-Name,CN=Sites,CN=
                                 Configuration,DC=Contoso,DC=com}
supportedCapabilities          : {1.2.840.113556.1.4.800,
                                 1.2.840.113556.1.4.167
                                 0, 1.2.840.113556.1.4.1791,
                                 1.2.840.113556.1.4.
                                 1935}
isSynchronized                 : {TRUE}
isGlobalCatalogReady           : {TRUE}
domainFunctionality            : {3}
forestFunctionality            : {3}
domainControllerFunctionality  : {3}
```

Here, you can see the RootDSE giving information about the LDAP service—from the current time, through different names used for the service (its DNS name, LDAP-Service, or Service-Principal name and the location in AD where its configuration is stored). Querying RootDSE also shows you a list of the different contexts the LDAP server can service, in this case the list is:

- DC=Contoso,DC=com

- CN=Configuration,DC=Contoso,DC=com

- CN=Schema,CN=Configuration,DC=Contoso,DC=com

- DC=DomainDnsZones,DC=Contoso,DC=com

RootDSE also shows the ADSpath for the Schema, configuration, root domain, and current domain (default) contexts (which might not be stored on this server).

You can also see that the service reports its forest, domain, and domain-controller levels (all Server 2008) and that it is synchronized within the domain and between domains as a Global Catalog server, so this is the first case of being able to use information from ADSI for diagnostic purposes.

The next thing you can try is to get the *default domain naming context*: If you know the domain where you are working, you can enter it in the form LDAP://dc=Contoso,dc=com or you can get it by reference to the DefaultNamingContext property of RootDSE—which is more useful if you don't know where the script is going to be run.

```
> [adsi]("LDAP://" + ([adsi]"LDAP://rootdse").defaultNamingContext)
distinguishedName
-----------------
{DC=Contoso,DC=com}
```

In fact, there is a shortcut: [ADSI]"" will return the default naming context.

At first glance it seems that you can use all the properties of the objects returned by [ADSI] using the conventional dotted notation—such as .defaultNamingContext; however, with ADSI, frustration lurks round every corner. If you pipe the previous command into format-list (or FL *), you find a line like this:

```
creationTime                    : {System.__ComObject}
```

Unfortunately, there isn't any easy way to convert this to something you can work with—although we present a solution shortly.

The next annoyance you may notice is that if you pipe this object into Get-Member (or GM), it lists the *properties* you saw on the previous page but it doesn't list any *methods*. This means you have to look outside PowerShell to find what you can do with the object. This isn't a bad thing for authors of books on scripting, but compared with other objects you work with in PowerShell, it is certainly a drag.

The final annoyance (for now) is that this object is the root of the domain; it has some container and OU objects underneath but none of the properties appear to be *children*. In Chapter 25, you will see that objects that PowerShell has "tweaked" can also have a PSBASE property, which contains the base object. So you can get to the children (and some methods) using this object. Here's an example that uses an empty string to return the current domain, and then gets the objects at the top level of the domain:

```
> ([adsi]"").psbase.children | ft -a objectClass, distinguishedName

objectClass                 distinguishedName
-----------                 -----------------
{top, builtinDomain}        {CN=Builtin,DC=Contoso,DC=com}
{top, container}            {CN=Computers,DC=Contoso,DC=com}
{top, organizationalUnit}   {OU=Domain Controllers,DC=Contoso,DC=com}
{top, container}            {CN=ForeignSecurityPrincipals,DC=Contoso,
                            DC=com}
{top, infrastructureUpdate} {CN=Infrastructure,DC=Contoso,DC=com}
{top, lostAndFound}         {CN=LostAndFound,DC=Contoso,DC=com}
```

```
{top, msDS-QuotaContainer}   {CN=NTDS Quotas,DC=Contoso,DC=com}
{top, container}             {CN=Program Data,DC=Contoso,DC=com}
{top, container}             {CN=System,DC=Contoso,DC=com}
{top, container}             {CN=Users,DC=Contoso,DC=com}
```

You can see that some of the containers at the top of the domain are special-purpose ones with their own special classes. Some of the default containers are of a type `container` and some belong to the `OrganizationalUnit` class.

Creating Objects

One of the hidden methods for a directory entry is named `create()`; you might expect the following command to create a new OU in the root of the domain with the name My OU:

```
>  ([adsi]"").Create("organizationalUnit", "ou=My OU")
distinguishedName
-----------------
{}
```

If you check for the presence of the OU, it isn't there; you need to commit the changes.

```
$o=([adsi]"").Create("organizationalUnit", "ou=My OU")
$o.setinfo()
```

You need to be aware of some potentially frustrating behavior with the conventional dotted notation.

```
> $o=([adsi]"").Create("organizationalUnit", "ou=Management")
> $o.Description="I'm an OU"
> $o.setinfo()
Exception calling "setinfo" with "0" argument(s): "A constraint
violation occurred. (Exception from HRESULT: 0x8007202F)"
```

Instead of using this syntax, the property needs to be assigned with a `Put()` method:

```
> $o.put("Description","I'm an OU")
> $o.setinfo()
>
```

It's good practice to always use the `put` method, but not using it doesn't always cause an error. For example, the following:

```
> $o=([adsi]"").Create("organizationalUnit", "ou=Third OU")
> $o.setinfo()
> $o.Description="Another OU"
> $o.setinfo()
>
```

produces no error.

Getting Directory Entries with the Searcher

If you pipe the objects you have created or fetched with the [ADSI] type accelerator into Get-Member, it reports that they belong to the System.DirectoryServices.DirectoryEntry .NET class, but there is another way to get objects of that class, which is to use the DirectorySearcher object. The following is an example of the searcher in use, to find all users in the domain, regardless of the container they are in:

```
>  (new-Object directoryServices.DirectorySearcher("(objectclass=user)")
).findall()


Path                                    Properties
----                                    ----------
LDAP://CN=Administrator,CN=Users,DC=... {primarygroupid; iscriticalsystemobj...
LDAP://CN=Guest,CN=Users,DC=Contoso...  {iscriticalsystemobject, samaccountn...
LDAP://CN=UK-DC-WDS,OU=Domain Contro... {primarygroupid, iscriticalsystemobj...
LDAP://CN=WIN-PQS6KIOLM1W,CN=Compute... {primarygroupid, iscriticalsystemobj...
LDAP://CN=GROMMIT,CN=Computers,DC=Ro... {primarygroupid, iscriticalsystemobj...
LDAP://CN=WALLACE,CN=Computers,DC=Ro... {primarygroupid, iscriticalsystemobj...
LDAP://CN=James,CN=Users,DC=Contoso...  {lastlogontimestamp, countrycode, sa...
LDAP://CN=user1,CN=Users,DC=Contoso...  {samaccountname, useraccountcontrol,...
LDAP://CN=lisa,CN=Users,DC=Contoso,...  {samaccountname, useraccountcontrol,...
```

When requesting a new system.directoryServices.DirectorySearcher object, PowerShell will look for the object under the system part of the .NET object hierarchy, so the New-Object Cmdlet can be given a -typeName parameter, which is allowed to omit the word *system*. In the preceding example, the -typeName has been omitted as well; New-Object will assume that an unnamed parameter is the type name. Although this is fine when entering commands at the PowerShell prompt, in scripts you should try to use the full names and be clear about parameter naming.

There are different parameter combinations when requesting a new directorySearcher, as shown in Table 24-1.

TABLE 24-1

Directory searcher creation Parameters

Parameters passed in to a new searcher	Meaning
( )	No parameters, returns all the properties of all the objects in the default naming context without any kind of filtering.
(String)	Specifies a filter, in LDAP syntax: only objects matching this filter are returned.
(String, String[])	Specifies a filter, and an array containing the names of properties to load; other properties are discarded.

Parameters passed in to a new searcher	Meaning
`(String, String[], SearchScope)`	Specifies a filter, properties to load, and a search scope, which is either "Base" (which returns only the object), "OneLevel" (which returns all the objects children), or "Subtree," which is the default and searches recursively through all the containers and sub-containers below the start point.
`(DirectoryEntry)`	Specifies the search root — where the search should start — and returns all the properties of every object below the start point.
`(DirectoryEntry, string)`	Specifies the search root and a filter. Returns only those objects matching the filter below the start point.
`(DirectoryEntry, String, String[])`	Specifies the search root, a filter, and an array of properties to load.
`(DirectoryEntry, String, String[], SearchScope)`	Specifies the search root, a filter, properties to load, and the search scope (base, Onelevel, or Subtree)

Notice that if you specify the search root, you pass a directory entry object, and the easiest way to get the object is with the [ADSI] type accelerator.

The values passed in creating the searcher can be set on the object after it is created, using its `SearchRoot, Filter, PropertiesToLoad,` and `SearchScope` properties.

There are additional properties, which can be set on the searcher object, as shown in Table 24-2.

TABLE 24-2

Directory Searcher properties

Property Name	Use
`PageSize`	Sets the number of items to be returned in at a time. By default it is 0, meaning return all the results together.
`Sort`	A `System.DirectoryServices.SortOption` object. This has two properties: one named `Direction` — which is either `Ascending` or `Descending` and the other named `propertyName`,
`PropertyNamesOnly`	Retrieves the property names for each object but not the values they contain.
`SizeLimit`	Sets a maximum number of items to return. This is especially useful in test scenarios, where an incorrectly formulated search could return tens of thousands of items.
`TombStone`	Specifies if deleted objects are to be returned.

The searcher object class provides two main methods: FindAll(), which returns all the matching objects, and FindOne(), which returns only the first one.

Using the scopes with the searcher, it is possible to get the immediate children of an object: Previously you saw that the DirectoryEntry could be obtained with the [ADSI] type accelerator and then its PSbase.Children property could be examined. With the searcher, it is possible to get the top-level containers in the domain by writing the following:

```
>$searcher= New-Object directoryServices.DirectorySearcher([ADSI]"")
>$searcher.SearchScope="oneLevel"
>$searcher.FindAll() | format-Table
Path                                Properties
----                                ----------
LDAP://CN=Builtin,DC=Contoso,DC=com    {uascompat, objectguid, nextrid, obj...
LDAP://CN=Computers,DC=Contoso,DC=com  {iscriticalsystemobject, systemflags...
LDAP://OU=Domain Controllers,DC=Road... {iscriticalsystemobject, systemflags...
LDAP://CN=ForeignSecurityPrincipals,... {iscriticalsystemobject, systemflags...
LDAP://CN=Infrastructure,DC=Contoso... {iscriticalsystemobject, systemflags...
LDAP://CN=LostAndFound,DC=Contoso,D... {iscriticalsystemobject, systemflags...
LDAP://OU=Management,DC=Contoso,DC=com {objectclass, usncreated, name, obje...
LDAP://OU=My OU,DC=Contoso,DC=com      {objectclass, usncreated, name, obje...
LDAP://CN=NTDS Quotas,DC=Contoso,DC... {iscriticalsystemobject, systemflags...
LDAP://CN=Program Data,DC=Contoso,D... {objectclass, usncreated, name, obje...
LDAP://CN=System,DC=Contoso,DC=com     {iscriticalsystemobject, systemflags...
LDAP://CN=Users,DC=Contoso,DC=com      {iscriticalsystemobject, systemflags...
```

The searcher doesn't return directoryentry objects, as the [ADSI] type accelerator does, but SearchResult objects. These have only two properties (Path and Properties) and the single method, getdirectoryEntry().

The properties collection has some case sensitivity, which may cause you some frustration until you get used to it. If you use the type accelerator, you might see something like the following:

```
> ([adsi]"LDAP://CN=Administrator,CN=Users,DC=Contoso,DC=com")  | fl *

objectClass              : {top, person, organizationalPerson, user}
cn                       : {Administrator}
description              : {Built-in account for administering the
                           computer/domain}
distinguishedName        : {CN=Administrator,CN=Users,DC=Contoso,DC=com}
instanceType             : {4}
whenCreated              : {4/22/2008 5:31:54 AM}
whenChanged              : {10/5/2008 8:21:17 AM}
uSNCreated               : {System.__ComObject}
lastLogon                : {System.__ComObject}
```

As you can see, the property names are in *mixed case*.

Try the same with the searcher, like this:

```
>$searcher.SearchRoot=[adsi]"LDAP://CN=Administrator,CN=Users,DC=Contoso,
DC=com"
>$searcher.SearchScope="base"
>$searcher.Findone().properties

Name                           Value
----                           -----
objectclass                    {top, person, organizationalPerson, user}
cn                             {Administrator}
description                    {Built-in account for administering the compu...
distinguishedname              {CN=Administrator,CN=Users,DC=Contoso,DC=com}
whencreated                    {4/22/2008 5:31:54 AM}
whenchanged                    {10/5/2008 8:21:17 AM}
usncreated                     {8194}
lastlogon                      {128681052251349570}
```

The property names are *all lowercase*—but notice that usnCreated has become a readable Update Sequence Number instead of an unreadable object. WhenCreated has become a date and so has lastlogon.

The properties property of a SearchResult object is a collection with the usual count and item members. There are two ways to get a property from the collection: dotted notation and the item parameterized property:

```
> $searcher.Findone().properties.distinguishedName
> $searcher.Findone().properties.item("distinguishedName")
CN=Administrator,CN=Users,DC=Contoso,DC=com
> $searcher.Findone().properties.distinguishedname
CN=Administrator,CN=Users,DC=Contoso,DC=com
```

The attempt to get the distinguishedName with an uppercase *N* fails when using the dotted form but succeeds when using the item() form. The dotted form works only if the name is all lowercase, even if it is normally returned in mixed case. When writing scripts, you might choose to use the more verbose Item() syntax. When you are in a hurry and trying to discover something at the command prompt, and you want to use the shorter dotted notation, you will find that this is exactly the time you are likely to forget about this case behavior.

It's a date Jim, but not as we know it

In the previous section, you saw that the COM objects had changed into dates, and there was a comment that lastLogon had become a date, but if you look at what was returned in the example, 128681052251349570 doesn't look like a date. It is what is referred to as FileTime format. According to MSDN:

A Windows file time is a 64-bit value that represents the number of 100-nanosecond intervals that have elapsed since 12:00 midnight, January 1, 1601 A.D. (C.E.) Coordinated Universal Time (UTC).

Of the many ways of writing a time, that's one of the more obtuse. Fortunately, the .NET `System.DateTime` class provides a `fromFileTime()` method for converting these numbers to a conventional date. Unfortunately, AD doesn't return a 64 bit integer but a string, which must be converted first, and PowerShell's normal casting syntax—`[int64]$lastlogon`—doesn't work. Instead, you need to use the `Parse()` method provided by the `int64` class; this can parse numbers in decimal or hex. By default, `parse()` assumes the string is a decimal number, but it can take a bitwise array of flags to tell it the number is something else. `515` is the combination of flags used for hex numbers. (The `Win32_QuickFixEngineeering` WMI class returns install dates as FileTimes, in hex, which must entitle its authors to consideration for a "Most obfuscated time format devised" award.).

The following is a utility function to do the conversion:

```
Function Convertto-DateTime
{Param ($FileTime , [Switch]$Hex )
 If ($hex)
     {$Number = [int64]::parse($filetime , 515) }
else
     {$Number = [int64]::parse($filetime) }
 [system.datetime]::FromFileTime($number)
 }
```

LDAP filters

All this talk of the difficulties with properties might leave you wondering if the `DirectorySearcher` object is actually better avoided. However, because it is able to return an object, the children of an object, or an arbitrary set of objects found by searching the directory, and is accessible from anything that can access .NET objects, it is still very useful.

Its search ability is based on LDAP filters, and LDAP syntax is the last new thing to learn. At times, it may be tempting to get all the Active Directory objects and then filter them down to the set that you want to work with using PowerShell's `Where-Object` Cmdlet. But doing so would mean asking AD to send many more objects over the network—potentially tens of thousands—only for PowerShell to discard them. So this approach should be avoided, which requires at least a basic understanding of filters. It is possible to query AD using an ActiveX Data Objects (ADO) provider, but this introduces its own problems and won't be discussed here.

Note also that AD maintains indexes on properties, which are commonly used for searching and sorting, so it is able to do these things more efficiently than PowerShell Cmdlets, which don't have the benefit of being able to use the indexes.

The expressions that are used in LDAP filters usually take one of the following forms:

- (attribute = value)
- (attribute >= value)
- (attribute <= value)

The asterisk (*) symbol is used as a Wildcard, so you can search for *Operators, Domain*, *Admin*, or simply *.

The ! prefix operator negates an expression.

A filter is made up of either a single expression or a compound expression using either the "&" prefix operator for "and" or the "|" prefix operator for "or" to group expressions together. The grouped expression is wrapped in brackets.

So whereas in SQL you would write:

```
where (expression1) and (expression2) and (expression3)
```

or in a PowerShell Where-Object Cmdlet you would write:

```
where-object {(expression1) -and (expression2) -and (expression3)
```

in LDAP you write:

```
(&(expression1)(expression2)(expression3))
```

The directory doesn't return properties that are part of the definition for a class but which are not set for given entry. One common task is to find all the objects where a property *has* been set, which is where testing for a wildcard is most useful. A typical task is to search for all mail-enabled users—or in AD terms, all entries with an object class of user and an e-mail property set to anything. The filter for that would look like this:

```
(&(objectClass=user)(email=*))
```

To find users who are *not* mail enabled, there are two ways to write the filter:

```
(&(objectClass=user)(!(email=*)))
```

or

```
(&(objectClass=user)(!email=*))
```

You can combine and conditions with or conditions. For example, the following filter:

```
(&(objectClass=user) (|(givenName=Lisa)(givenName=James))  )
```

selects all directory entries for the user object class where the given name is either Lisa or James.

Building a library of AD functions

It can be useful to have functions to wrap the Searcher object. For example, here is a function to return properties in a more PowerShell-focused way:

```
Function Get-ADEntryProperties
{ param($Root="", [String]$Scope="Subtree", [String]$Filter)
 $Searcher = New-Object system.directoryServices.DirectorySearcher([adsi]$Root)
 $Searcher.SearchScope = $Scope
 If ($filter) {$Searcher.Filter = $Filter}
 $Searcher.findAll() |
    foreach-object {$p=$_.Properties
       $p.propertyNames |
          foreach-object -begin {$ADObj = New-Object -TypeName System.Object}`
             -process {if ($P.item($_).count -eq 1)
                         {Add-Member -inputObject $ADObj -MemberType NoteProperty`
                                     -Name $_ -Value $P.item($_)[0]}
                      else {Add-Member -inputObject $ADObj -MemberType NoteProperty`
                                       -Name $_ -Value $P.item($_)}
                       }`
             -end {$ADObj} }
}
```

Let's examine how this function works, line by line.

The function takes root and Scope parameters. Note that by naming these root and scope instead of using the searchRoot and SearchScope names used by the Searcher object, they can be identified with -r and -s for easy entry at the command prompt. $root is set to an empty string if no value is passed for it, and if $scope isn't passed it is set to Subtree, the final parameter is the filter.

The searcher object is created with a Search Root, the scope is set, and if the filter was passed as a parameter then the filter property is set on the object Then the findall method is called and the results piped into a for loop.

For each directory entry retrieved, the function creates a new object and works through the entry's property names, adding each one with its associated value to the new object. Because a lot of the properties are arrays with a single item, there is logic in the loop to strip these items out of the array. Once all the properties have been processed, one object is returned for each directory entry found.

Here are a couple of examples of using the function—first a formatted list of the top-level containers in the domain:

```
>  Get-ADEntryProperties -root "LDAP://DC=contoso,DC=com" -scope "onelevel" |
       ft name,distinguishedName -a
```

```
name                          distinguishedname
----                          -----------------
Builtin                       CN=Builtin,DC=Contoso,DC=com
Computers                     CN=Computers,DC=Contoso,DC=com
Domain Controllers            OU=Domain Controllers,DC=Contoso,DC=com
ForeignSecurityPrincipals     CN=ForeignSecurityPrincipals,DC=Contoso,DC=com
Infrastructure                CN=Infrastructure,DC=Contoso,DC=com
LostAndFound                  CN=LostAndFound,DC=Contoso,DC=com
My OU                         OU=My OU,DC=Contoso,DC=com
NTDS Quotas                   CN=NTDS Quotas,DC=Contoso,DC=com
Program Data                  CN=Program Data,DC=Contoso,DC=com
System                        CN=System,DC=Contoso,DC=com
Users                         CN=Users,DC=Contoso,DC=com
```

Another use would be to export all the objects that matched particular criteria—for example all computer objects in the domain:

```
Get-ADEntryproperties  -filter "(objectclass=computer)" |
    export-csv computer.csv
```

The second function returns selected directory entries from AD—either a single item, given its path (which is doing the same job as the type accelerator), or its children, or all the objects in a branch of the directory, filtered with an LDAP filter.

```
Function Get-ADEntry
{ param($Root="", [String]$Scope="Subtree", [String]$Filter)
  $Searcher = New-Object system.directoryServices.
DirectorySearcher([adsi]$Root)
  $Searcher.SearchScope = $Scope
  If ($filter) {$Searcher.Filter = $Filter}
  $Searcher.findAll() | foreach-object {$_.GetDirectoryEntry()}
}
```

This is a basic form of the function. It hasn't been written to accept piped input, and doesn't check that the search root is a valid string. Even in this short form, it can be put to good use in a variety of ways—first getting all the objects within a container, and the objects *they* contain. Notice that computer entries can be containers, holding *Service Connection Point* entries.

```
> Get-ADEntry -root "LDAP://CN=Computers,DC=Contoso,DC=com"
distinguishedName
-----------------
{CN=Computers,DC=Contoso,DC=com}
{CN=WIN-PQS6KIOLM1W,CN=Computers,DC=Contoso,DC=com}
{CN=Windows Virtual Machine,CN=WIN-PQS6KIOLM1W,CN=Computers,
DC=Contoso,DC=com}
{CN=MSVMM,CN=WIN-PQS6KIOLM1W,CN=Computers,DC=Contoso,DC=com}
{CN=GROMMIT,CN=Computers,DC=Contoso,DC=com}
{CN=Microsoft Hyper-V,CN=GROMMIT,CN=Computers,DC=Contoso,DC=com}
{CN=WALLACE,CN=Computers,DC=Contoso,DC=com}
{CN=Microsoft Hyper-V,CN=WALLACE,CN=Computers,DC=Contoso,DC=com}
```

The next example just gets the directory entries in the container, without looking at any contents they might have. (Note that this is not the best way to search for computer objects.)

```
> Get-ADEntry -root "LDAP://CN=Computers,DC=Contoso,DC=com" `
-scope "OneLevel"
distinguishedName
-----------------
{CN=GROMMIT,CN=Computers,DC=Contoso,DC=com}
{CN=WALLACE,CN=Computers,DC=Contoso,DC=com}
{CN=WIN-PQS6KIOLM1W,CN=Computers,DC=Contoso,DC=com}
```

This search filters out the container itself and any grandchildren—it simply returns children. So if the container has child OUs, it will return them but not the computers they contain. To search just for computers in this container, you can use the following command:

```
> Get-ADEntry -root "LDAP://CN=Computers,DC=Contoso,DC=com" `
-filter "(ObjectClass="Computer")"
distinguishedName
-----------------
{CN=GROMMIT,CN=Computers,DC=Contoso,DC=com}
{CN=WALLACE,CN=Computers,DC=Contoso,DC=com}
{CN=WIN-PQS6KIOLM1W,CN=Computers,DC=Contoso,DC=com}
```

And you could get a single entry from a container:

```
> Get-ADEntry -root "LDAP://CN=Computers,DC=Contoso,DC=com" `
-filter "(name=grommit)"
distinguishedName
-----------------
{CN=GROMMIT,CN=Computers,DC=Contoso,DC=com}
```

In reality, you probably wouldn't request the entry named `Grommit` in the `Computers` container. Instead you'd ask for the entry named `Grommit` anywhere in the domain and, perhaps, qualify it by filtering down to entries for computer objects, as in the following example:

```
>(Get-ADEntry  -filter "(&(objectclass=computer)(name=grommit))"
).psbase.moveto( [ADSI]"LDAP://OU=My OU,DC=Contoso,DC=com" )
```

This last example uses the `moveTo()` method of the Directory entry object to move items to a different container. Move and some of the other methods are discussed shortly.

Finding related entries in AD

One further kind of query is available through the searcher object, and that is the `Attribute scoped query`. The most obvious use for this is checking on group memberships. It works by finding the `Search-Root` directory entry and examining one of its attributes. The selected attribute must contain the distinguished names of other entries: the searcher then returns *those* entries. For example, you can find the entries that are members of the Built-in Administrators group by using its `member` property:

```
> $searcher.SearchRoot=
           [adsi]"LDAP://CN=Administrators,CN=Builtin,DC=Contoso,DC=com"
> $searcher.SearchScope="base"
> $searcher.Filter=$null
> $searcher.AttributeScopeQuery="Member"
> $searcher.FindAll()

Path                                Properties
----                                ----------
LDAP://CN=Administrator,CN=Users,DC=... {primarygroupid, iscriticalsystemobj...
LDAP://CN=Enterprise Admins,CN=Users... {admincount, iscriticalsystemobject,...
LDAP://CN=Domain Admins,CN=Users,DC=... {admincount, iscriticalsystemobject,...
```

Alternatively, you can discover groups that a user belongs to by using the `MemberOf` property, as follows:

```
> $searcher.SearchRoot=[adsi]"LDAP://CN=Administrator,CN=USers,DC=Contoso,
                              DC=com"
> $searcher.AttributeScopeQuery="MemberOf"
> $searcher.FindAll()

Path                                Properties
----                                ----------
LDAP://CN=Administrators,CN=Builtin,... {admincount, iscriticalsystemobject,...
LDAP://CN=Schema Admins,CN=Users,DC=... {admincount, iscriticalsystemobject,...
LDAP://CN=Enterprise Admins,CN=Users... {admincount, iscriticalsystemobject,...
LDAP://CN=Domain Admins,CN=Users,DC=... {admincount, iscriticalsystemobject,...
LDAP://CN=Group Policy Creator Owner... {iscriticalsystemobject, samaccountn...
```

Attribute scoped queries can be used anywhere that one entry has a property that points to other objects: manager/direct reports relationships, for example. It might be useful to create a function for this:

```
Function Get-ADReleation
{param($Root, [String]$Property, [String]$Filter)
 $Searcher = New-Object system.directoryServices
                        .DirectorySearcher([adsi]$Root)
 $Searcher.SearchScope = "Base"
 $Searcher.AttributeScopeQuery=$property
 If ($filter) {$Searcher.Filter = $Filter}
 $Searcher.findAll() | foreach-object {$_.GetDirectoryEntry()}}
```

This function can be improved to take input from the pipe, and perform some validation of the parameters, but as it stands now it can find out memberships and direct reports. For example:

```
> Get-ADReleation -root "LDAP://CN=James,CN=Users,DC=Contoso,DC=Com" `
    -property "DirectReports"
distinguishedName
-----------------
{CN=lisa,CN=Users,DC=Contoso,DC=com}
```

This function can be used as the basis for other functions, for example:

```
Function Get-ADGroupMemberEntry
{Param ($groupName)
 $root=Get-ADEntry -Filter "(&(name=$groupName)(objectclass=group))"
 Get-ADReleation -root $root -property "Member"}
```

The function can be used as follows:

```
> Get-ADGroupMemberEntry "administrators"

distinguishedName
-----------------
{CN=Administrator,CN=Users,DC=Contoso,DC=com}
{CN=Enterprise Admins,CN=Users,DC=Contoso,DC=com}
{CN=Domain Admins,CN=Users,DC=Contoso,DC=com}
```

Operations on Directory Entries

Examples you have already seen in this chapter have used the Create and Move methods of the Directory entry object being used. It doesn't matter whether the object is obtained using the [ADSI] Type accelerator or the DirectorySearcher object; the process is the same.

Creating objects

As you saw earlier in this chapter, entries have a `Create()` method, which takes `ObjectClass` and `Name` parameters:

```
>  ([adsi]"").Create("organizationalUnit", "ou=My OU")
```

Common objects you might want to create include organizational units, users, and groups.

The syntax is `$DirectoryEntry.Create("ObjectClass", "name" )`

If you are not sure about the Object class to use, you can either look at the class of an existing object of the same type, or you can examine the AD Schema using the ADSIedit utility.

The name is written as the local name within the container. This is normally in the form `cn=`, the exception being for Organizational Units. In the distinguished name, they form an `ou=` element and this is used in the name, as in the preceding example.

You can get the container, which will hold the new object either using the `[ADSI]` type accelerator, as you saw before, or using the DirectorySearcher object—the functions that were defined for in the previous section to get an entry do exactly that, they could be used in the following code to create a new user.

```
$usersContainer= get-adentry -filter  "(&(name=users)
(objectclass=container))"
$newUser=$usersContainer.create("user","cn=paul")
$newUser.put("SamAccountName","Paul")
$newUser.put("Description", "New Starter")
$newUser.setinfo()
```

Every item in the directory is an ActiveDirectoryEntry object, even though the entries represent different kinds of objects. In other words, although `Users` are one class of object and `Groups` are a different class, they are both represented by directory entries, which are handled in exactly the same way. The only difference between creating a user and a group is the class name in the `create` statement.

```
$GroupsContainer= get-adentry -filter "(&(name=users)
(objectclass=container))"
$newGroup=$groupsContainer.create("group","cn=Sales")
$newGroup.put("SamAccountName","Sales")
$newGroup.put("Description", "Sales")
$newGroup.setinfo()
```

In both of these examples, you can see that the SAMAccountName property is set; this is the name used in the form Domain\Name. If it is not set, AD will assign a quasi-random one.

You'll also notice that if you create a user account in this way it begins life in a disabled state.

Setting single-valued properties

Active Directory allows the set of attributes to be extended and so to discover some properties it may be necessary to see what they are set to on an existing entry, or examine the AD Schema using the ADSIedit utility. In many cases, you can discover information about a property by searching for its name in the MSDN library (http://msdn.microsoft.com/en-us/library/default.aspx).

There are some properties you will want to set on objects when you create them—for example, changing the flags on a user account so that the user is able to log on, and setting the user's password, SAM Account Name, and User Principal Name. In the case of groups, the AD ObjectClass is the same whether the group is a Distribution Group or a Security Group and whether its scope is Domain-Local, Global, or Universal. You set a flag on the group to change its type and scope. Finally, there are different ways of setting an attribute, depending on whether you are adding a member to a list or overwriting what is already there.

User Account Control flags

If you examine a newly created directory entry for a user account, you will see it has a property named UserAccountControl, and by default on a Windows Server 2008 AD domain, this is set to 546 (0x00000222).

The value is made up from the ADS User Flags, which are set as shown in Table 24-3.

TABLE 24-3

ADS user flags

Value	Name	Meaning
1	SCRIPT	Doesn't apply to AD
2	ACCOUNTDISABLE	Account disabled
8	HOMEDIR_REQUIRED	Home Directory is required.
16	LOCKOUT	The Account is locked out.
32	PASSWD_NOTREQD	No Password is required.
64	PASSWD_CANT_CHANGE	Read only—ACLs mean user can't change the password.
128	ENCRYPTED_TEXT_PASSWORD_ALLOWED	This user can send their password as encrypted text.
256	TEMP_DUPLICATE_ACCOUNT	A local account for users from another domain, not visible to other domains
512	NORMAL_ACCOUNT	This is a normal user account.

Value	Name	Meaning
2048	INTERDOMAIN_TRUST_ACCOUNT	This is an account for a domain trust relationship.
4096	WORKSTATION_TRUST_ACCOUNT	This is an account for a Member server or Workstation.
8192	SERVER_TRUST_ACCOUNT	This is an account for a Domain Controller.
65536	DONT_EXPIRE_PASSWD	This User's password never expires.
131072	MNS_LOGON_ACCOUNT	This is a Majority node Set account for fail-over clustering.
262144	SMARTCARD_REQUIRED	The user must use a smart card to log on.
524288	TRUSTED_FOR_DELEGATION	This is a service account, which can impersonate other users.
1048576	NOT_DELEGATED	This account may not be impersonated by a service account.
2097152	USE_DES_KEY_ONLY	This account must use DES encryption for keys.
4194304	DONT_REQUIRE_PREAUTH	Kerberos authentication is not required.
8388608	PASSWORD_EXPIRED	Read only—user's password has expired.
16777216	TRUSTED_TO_AUTHENTICATE_FOR_DELEGATION	This service account can log on as an impersonated user.

So the default value, 546, is 512 + 32 + 2—ordinary account, no password required, and account disabled. You can set the value to 512 or 544, when creating the user to enable the account.

Setting passwords

Although it is stored in Active Directory, a user's password is not accessible as a property. Instead, there is a setpassword() method, so that you can set a user's initial password. Having set the password, you can force the user to change it by setting the pwdLastSet field to 0, for example.

```
$newuser.SetPassword("TopSecret!")
$newUser.put("UserAccountControl", 544)
$newUser.put("pwdlastSet", 0)
$newUser.setinfo()
```

Setting group types

There is a similar issue with flags when creating groups; by default, groups are created as Global security groups. Some changes of scope are allowed after creation but it is better to set the type of group you want when it is created.

The flags for the different types of group are:

2	Global Group
4	Local Group
8	Universal Group
2147483648 (0x80000000)	Security enabled

To create a group as a security-enabled local group, use the following:

```
$newGroup=$groupsContainer.create("group","cn=Marketing")
$newGroup.put("SamAccountName","Marketing")
$newGroup.put("Description", "Marketing Local Group")
$newGroup.put("GroupType", 0x80000004 )
$newGroup.setinfo()
```

Adding to (and deleting from) multivalued properties

Calling the Put() method will overwrite an existing property, and when a property can hold only a single value, that is exactly what you want to happen. But when a property can be multivalued, you usually want to append rather than overwrite. There is a "Put-Extended" method, PutEx(). In fact, there are four operations that you may want to perform, which are chosen by passing a flag to PutEx.

1	Clear	Remove the property from the object
2	Update	Replace the existing values
3	Append	Add extra values to a multi-valued field
4	Delete	Remove values from a multi valued field

Note that the properties must be an array, so the following syntax will cause an error:

```
$newGroup.putex(3, "member", $newuser.distinguishedName)
```

The correct syntax is:

```
$newGroup.putex(3, "member",@( $newuser.distinguishedName))
```

The same PutEx() syntax can be used with the MemberOf attribute of users and manager and reports, or even the multivalued phone number fields.

In the example, it is safe to assume that a newly created user is not a member of a newly created group. However, you should be aware that adding a user to a group they already belong to will cause an error when the SetInfo() method is called to save the changes. So the following would be safer in a script:

```
If (-not($Group.member -contains $user.distinguishedName))
{ $Group.putex(3, "member",@( $user.distinguishedName)) }
```

Moving and deleting objects

You saw earlier that the psbase property of the directory entry object has a MoveTo() method for moving objects from one place to another. For example:

```
$usersContainer=get-adentry -f "(&(name=my*)(objectclass=organizational
                                                        Unit))"
$user=get-adentry -f "(&(name=lisa)(objectclass=user))"
$user.psbase.moveto($usersContainer)
```

There are two ways to delete objects in Active Directory. The simpler, safer way works in a similar way to create() a first get a container, and then call its delete() method, specifying object class and name.

```
$usersContainer=get-adentry -f "(&(name=users)(objectclass=container))"
$newUser=$usersContainer.delete("user","cn=paul")
```

The second way is rather more severe because it deletes all the objects below a given point in the directory, and that is the deleteTree() method of the psbase property. Following on from the previous example, this will delete both the OU and the user entry that was moved into it.

```
$usersContainer.psbase.deleteTree()
```

Testing for the presence of an entry

One final use for the directory entry object is to test to see if a given entry exists. For example, the following code:

```
[System.DirectoryServices.DirectoryEntry]::exists( "LDAP://CN=Administr
ator,CN=Users,DC=Contoso,DC=com")
```

returns True if the administrator account can be found at its default location and False otherwise.

Summary

This chapter has deliberately set out to be a "warts and all" examination of working with AD in PowerShell. Some people have said that it is simply too difficult, but you have seen how PowerShell can be used to carry out most Active Directory tasks, and although there are certainly areas that can be improved—especially by adding some of the third-party tools that are available—PowerShell is still a very useful tool for carrying out many AD tasks, especially with the aid of a few lines of script to automate the parts of the process. It is worth building your own library of functions for specific tasks you need to carry out; and the ones provided in this chapter can be used as a starting point.

Chapter 25

Working with WMI in PowerShell

PowerShell has the capability to work with all three of the major kinds of objects in Windows: .NET, COM, and WMI. Windows Management Instrumentation is a general method for managing Windows components and applications, both on the local machine and on other machines over the network.

The number of WMI objects available in current versions of Windows can seem bewildering at first. We won't try to list every available WMI object; rather, we'll look at how to discover what is available and make use of it in your own scripts.

First of all, WMI objects are arranged into *namespaces*. A namespace is a collection of related WMI objects. The objects belong to *classes*. And several *instances* may exist of each class.

Here's a simple case of getting the drives on the local computer:

```
> Get-WmiObject -namespace root\cimv2 -class win32_
logicalDisk

DeviceID     : C:
DriveType    : 3
ProviderName :
FreeSpace    : 5735075840
Size         : 99929288704
VolumeName   :
```

```
DeviceID      : D:
DriveType     : 5
ProviderName :
FreeSpace     :
Size          :
VolumeName    :

DeviceID      : E:
DriveType     : 2
ProviderName :
FreeSpace     : 106528768
Size          : 1018822656
VolumeName    :
```

As you can see, each Logical disk object has a `DeviceID`—the drive letter, a `Drivetype`—that indicates whether it is a hard disk, CD/DVD, and so on.

It is often necessary to look up information about the WMI object returned, and the best place is Microsoft's MSDN website. If you go to `http://msdn.microsoft.com/library` and search for "Win32_LogicalDisk class" you will get a complete list of the properties and methods available, and an explanation of what each does, including a table of the drive types.

The command line in the preceding code is deliberately verbose. In most situations, it could simply be written as:

```
Gwmi win32_logicalDisk
```

`Get-WMIObject` has an alias, `GWMI`. If only one parameter is passed to it without naming it, then it is assumed to be `Class`. In this shortened version, the `-Namespace` has been omitted. Windows has a default namespace and this starts as one named `root\CIMv2`, but it can be changed from the computer management MMC console.

Figure 25-1 shows how to configure the default WMI namespace.

If most of your WMI work is with a different namespace, you can make that one the default to save you from having to enter it at the command line again and again. Of course, this carries the risk that any script that *assumes* that the default namespace hasn't been changed will break. So when writing a script, it is always best to explicitly specify the namespace. If you are working at the command line, you can dispense with it and with the `-Class` parameter label.

Configuring the default WMI namespace.

Displaying WMI Information

One of the common things you want with WMI is to get some information and report it (or a subset of it) in a nicely formatted way. This is where PowerShell's format-table Cmdlet can be a great help, and it is worth taking a moment to look at some techniques we use with format-table before you move on to look at more sophisticated ways of querying WMI.

The simplest way to use format-table is just to pipe the objects output from one command into it. Often, output is more readable if the columns are sized automatically, with the -autosize switch. For example:

```
>Get-WmiObject -class win32_logicalDisk | format-table -autosize

DeviceID DriveType ProviderName FreeSpace        Size VolumeName
-------- --------- ------------ ---------        ---- ----------
C:           3                   5708292096 99929288704
D:           5
E:                               106528768   1018822656
```

As with most PowerShell Cmdlets, `Format-Table` has an alias to reduce the amount of typing needed when working interactively. FT can be used as an alias for `Format-Table` and the `-Autosize` can be shortened to simply `-a`.

It's quite rare that the default properties are the ones that are actually wanted. So `Format-Table` will usually be called with the `-property` switch, as follows:

```
> Get-WmiObject win32_logicalDisk  | format-table `
  -property deviceID,drivetype,filesystem,freespace -autosize

deviceID drivetype filesystem  freespace
-------- --------- ----------  ---------
C:               3 NTFS        6190678016
D:               5
E:               2 FAT          106528768
Z:               4
```

This is all fine—except that `DeviceID` isn't great as a column name, `driveType` isn't very easy to understand, and `FreeSpace` isn't very easy to read—so not that fine at all really. `Format-Table` (and other PowerShell Cmdlets that accept lists of properties, such as `Select-Object`) can create custom fields. These are defined using PowerShell's hash table syntax with a *label* part and an *expression* part. The simplest kind of custom field changes the column heading, like this:

```
@{label= "drive"; expression={$_.DeviceID} }
```

The next simplest custom field is one that reformats text. Because PowerShell text strings are .NET text strings, PowerShell can access all the formatting available in .NET. Other types—such as the Unsigned 64 bit integer used for FreeSpace, have a `ToString()` method, which can take a formatting string, as follows:

```
@{Label="Free-Space"; Expression={$_.freeSpace.tostring("#,###")}}
```

However, because the expression is a PowerShell code block, it can contain long and intricate pieces of code. Examples of tricks you can use with custom fields appear in Chapters 21 and 30.

People who are moving over to PowerShell from scripting in Visual Basic, for example, might write something like this to output the list of drives:

```
$MyDrives= Get-WmiObject win32_logicalDisk
Write-host "deviceID drivetype filesystem  freespace"
Foreach ($Drive in $mydrives) {
    $DriveLetter=$Drive.DeviceID.padRight(5)
    switch ($Drive.DriveType) {0 {$Dt="Unknown          "}
                               1 {$Dt="No Root Directory "}
                               2 {$Dt="Removable disk    "}
                               3 {$Dt="Local disk        "}
                               4 {$Dt="Network drive     "}
                               5 {$Dt="Compact Disk      "}
                               6 {$Dt="RAM Disk          "}}
```

```
If ($Drive.FileSystem -ne $null) {
        $filesystem = $Drive.FileSystem.PadRight(10)}
Write-host $DriveLetter,$dt,$filesystem,$drive.freespace }
```

Most of what you see here is doing work that could be done by `Format-Table`—indeed, a `For` loop to generate output is a sure sign of someone new to PowerShell. But what about the `Switch`? That can go in the expression code block for a custom property in `Format-List` or `Format-Table`, but there is a more compact way of doing the same thing, using one of PowerShell's built-in features— the hash table or associative array, which can be declared and accessed like this:

```
>$days=@{"January"=31;"February"=28;"March"=31;"April"=30;"June"=30}
>$days["January"]
31
```

The preceding two lines can be joined to form a single line—although in this case you are looking for the name of a drive type based on the value in the drive type property:

```
@{ 0= "Unknown"; 1="No Root Directory";  2="Removable Disk";
3="Local Disk" ; 4= "Network Drive";  5="Compact Disc";
6=" RAM Disk"}[[int]$drive.DriveType]
```

And this can be put into an expression in a `Format-Table`—so now you have a more complex `Format-Table` line. Although this wraps down multiple lines in print (and you can split lines for readability), this function is one line:

```
Function Get-DiskInfo
{Get-WmiObject -nameSpace "root\cimv2" -class win32_logicalDisk |
 format-table -autosize -property
     @{label="Drive"; expression={$_.DeviceID}}, Filesystem,
     @{label="DriveType"; Expression={@{0="Unknown";
       1="No Root Directory";  2="Removable Disk"; 3="Local Disk";
       4="Network Drive";  5="Compact Disc";
       6="RAM Disk"}[[int]$_.DriveType]  }},
     @{Label="Free-Space";Expression={$_.freeSpace.tostring("#,###")}}
 }
```

If you are working with the same class of object that you want to display in a specific format, you can define an XML file for it, as shown in Chapter 21 in the section "Changing How PowerShell Formats Objects."

In that section, the `Win32_logical disk` object is one that has a predefined XML entry, but you can define your own XML file to override defaults. To get the same result as the function in the example, the XML would look like this:

```
<Configuration><ViewDefinitions><View>
  <Name>process</Name>
  <ViewSelectedBy>
```

```
        <TypeName>System.Management.ManagementObject#root\cimv2\win32_logicalDisk
        </TypeName>
    </ViewSelectedBy>
    <TableControl>
      <TableHeaders>
        <TableColumnHeader>
          <Label>Drive</Label><Width>5</Width><Alignment>right</Alignment>
        </TableColumnHeader>
        <TableColumnHeader>
          <Label>DriveType</Label><Width>20</Width><Alignment>right</Alignment>
        </TableColumnHeader>
        <TableColumnHeader>
          <Label>Free Space</Label><Width>20</Width><Alignment>right</Alignment>
        </TableColumnHeader>
      </TableHeaders>
      <TableRowEntries><TableRowEntry><TableColumnItems>
        <TableColumnItem>
          <PropertyName>DeviceID</PropertyName>
        </TableColumnItem>
        <TableColumnItem>
          <ScriptBlock>@{0="Unknown"; 1="No Root Directory"; 2="Removable Disk";
                       3="Local Disk"; 4="Network Drive";  5="Compact Disc";
                       6="RAM Disk"}[[int]$_.DriveType] </ScriptBlock>
        </TableColumnItem>
         <TableColumnItem>
          <ScriptBlock>$_.freeSpace.tostring("#,###") </ScriptBlock>
        </TableColumnItem>
      </TableColumnItems></TableRowEntry></TableRowEntries>
    </TableControl>
  </View></ViewDefinitions></Configuration>
```

This approach is useful when you are writing functions that query WMI to produce something which is then piped into another function. Otherwise you need one function to get objects and a second function to output them nicely.

Querying WMI

In the previous section, you saw that Get-WMIObject could retrieve all the instances of a particular class of object. In fact, beneath the surface Get-WMIObject is using a SQL-like syntax—the WMI Query Language (WQL). There are two ways of writing the queries.

Choosing to how to write the query

One method to get WMI objects is to write select statements in WQL. For example:

```
Get-WMIObject -Query "Select * From WIN32_LogicalDrive"
```

The other is one you have seen already: the `-Class` parameter.

```
Get-WMIObject -Class WIN32_LogicalDrive
```

These two commands are equivalent and make the same query of WMI. WQL uses the same `Where` clause structure as conventional SQL, allowing queries like this:

```
Get-WMIObject -Query "Select * From WIN32_LogicalDrive where DeviceID='C:'"
```

What about the same thing in the `-Class` syntax? One way to do this would be to use PowerShell's `where-object` Cmdlet:

```
Get-WMIObject -Class WIN32_LogicalDrive | where-object {$_.DeviceID -eq "C:")
```

Note that PowerShell's `where-object` Cmdlet uses the `-eq` operator for "is equal to" where WQL uses the equal (=) sign, even when it is invoked from PowerShell.

There are cases where it is necessary to use `Where-Object`—for example, when searching for a regular expression with the `-match` operator, which has no equivalent in WQL. But as a rule it is best to avoid using `Where-Object` if criteria can be specified at the `get` stage. To understand why, imagine that instead of retrieving one drive from a list of five, you are querying `Win32_UserAccount` objects on a domain controller to find one user among 5,000 or even 50,000. Obviously, a form that retrieves many objects and passes every one into `where-object` only to throw most of them away is much less efficient than one that returns only the required objects in the first place, which is what the `where` WQL clause does.

Just as the `—Class` switch is, in effect, a way of specifying a `FROM` clause, `Get-WMIobject` has a `-Filter` switch to specify a `WHERE` clause, and a `-Property` switch to handle selecting fields. For example, the following:

```
Get-WmiObject -Property freeSpace, Filesystem `
 -class win32_logicalDisk -filter "deviceID='C:'"
```

is identical to:

```
Get-WmiObject -query "Select freeSpace, Filesystem from win32_logicalDisk
 where deviceID='C:'"
```

Sometimes when PowerShell offers two ways of carrying out the same task, it is easy to see which circumstances favor one method and which favor the other. For example, one might mean less typing when entering commands interactively at the prompt, and the other might make a script easier to understand. In this case, any query that has a `Select...From...Where` structure, can be written using the `-class`, `-filter`, `-property` form of `Get-WMIObject`. Only a few special queries that don't use `Select` must be written in WQL form; for the majority it is a matter of personal choice: any script that builds a `where` clause can also build a `-filter` parameter and so on.

Finding WMI objects by association

So what are the WQL queries that don't use `SELECT`? WMI allows objects to define *associations*—relationships with each other—and these can be queried with WQL using the `Associators of` and `References of` statements. The most common use is to get one object and then get those associated with it, like this:

```
> $CDrive=(Get-WmiObject -query "Select * from win32_logicalDisk where
deviceID='C:'")
>Get-WmiObject -query "ASSOCIATORS OF {$CDrive}"


Hidden                  :
Archive                 :
EightDotThreeFileName   :
FileSize                :
Name                    : c:\
Compressed              :
Encrypted               :
Readable                : True

NumberOfBlocks    : 195174400
BootPartition     : True
Name              : Disk #0, Partition #1
PrimaryPartition  : True
Size              : 99929292800
Index             : 1

Domain               : Contoso.com
Manufacturer         : Dell Inc.
Model                : Latitude D820
Name                 : JAMES-2008
PrimaryOwnerName     : James
TotalPhysicalMemory  : 3486859264
```

The `associators of` statement uses the WMI path to the object, but when the string is wrapped in double quotes, PowerShell expands the variable `$CDrive` to its path. In other words:

```
"ASSOCIATORS OF {$CDrive}"
```

is the same as:

```
'ASSOCIATORS OF {\\JAMES-2008\root\cimv2:Win32_LogicalDisk.DeviceID="C:"}'
```

Connected items can be retrieved based on the *nature* of the connection, and the references of statement is helpful in discovering information about the relationships. Because the links between objects form many-to-many relationships, objects only rarely have properties to point to other, connected objects. Instead, WMI uses an intermediate object type—for example, a Win_32LogicalDiskRootDirectory object joins a Win32_logicaldisk object to the Win32_directory object, which represents its root directory. These *association classes* define roles for objects, which they connect—the most common one being to say that one is a part that is contained by the other—which is a container.

The following diagram shows the relationships for the three objects connected to the Logical disk in the preceding example.

Win32_logicaldisk	Links through	Win32_ LogicaldiskRootDirectory (AssocClass)	To	Win32_directory (ResultClass)
Win32_logicaldisk	Links through	Win32_ LogicalDiskToPartition (AssocClass)	To	Win32_DiskPartition (ResultClass)
Win32_logicaldisk	Links through	Win32_SystemServices (AssocClass)	To	Win32_computerSystem (ResultClass)
Win32_LogicalDisk	Is a part of	Win32_computerSystem		
Win32_LogicalDisk	Is a group containing	Win32_Directory		
Win32_LogicalDisk	Is a dependent of	Win32_DiskPartition		

You can discover the association classes in the middle by using the references of statement; for example:

```
>Get-wmiobject -Query "references of {$cdrive}"

__CLASS        : Win32_LogicalDiskRootDirectory
GroupComponent : \\JAMES-2008\root\CIMV2:Win32_LogicalDisk
                 .DeviceID="C:"
PartComponent  : \\JAMES-2008\root\cimv2:Win32_Directory.Name="C:\\"

__CLASS        : Win32_SystemDevices
GroupComponent : \\JAMES-2008\root\cimv2:Win32_ComputerSystem
                 .Name="JAMES-2008"
PartComponent  : \\JAMES-2008\root\cimv2:Win32_LogicalDisk
                 .DeviceID="C:"

__CLASS        : Win32_LogicalDiskToPartition
Antecedent     : \\JAMES-2008\root\cimv2:Win32_DiskPartition
                 .DeviceID="Disk #0, Partition #1"
Dependent      : \\JAMES-2008\root\cimv2:Win32_LogicalDisk
                 .DeviceID="C:"
EndingAddress  : 100028907519
StartingAddress : 99614720
```

With an understanding of these relationships, it is easier to understand the special WHERE terms used by the associators of statement. Although it uses the same where keyword, the clause is different from the Where clause in a Select statement in the following ways:

- Properties of the WMI object can't be used; fields have to be part of the association reference. They include AssocClass and ResultClass, ResultRole and Role, and ClassDefsOnly.

- The only operator that can be used in a where clause is =. (There is no "like," and no <>.)

- Terms being sought are not enclosed in quotes (that is: where ResultClass= Win32_Directory, not where ResultClass= 'Win32_Directory').

- Where multiple parts are specified, there is an implied AND, the AND is not written, and there is no option to specify OR or NOT.

The first example of an associators of query you saw was:

```
Get-WmiObject -query "ASSOCIATORS OF {$CDrive}"
```

It would be unusual to ask "What objects are connected with this object *in any way*?" This command returns three different types of objects. The classes of the result objects can be discovered using an Associators of query with a where classDefsOnly clause. The classes of the intermediate association objects can be discovered with a references of query with the same where ClassDefs only clause.

```
> get-wmiobject -query "ASSOCIATORS OF {$cdrive} where classdefsonly"

Win32_Directory                           Win32_ComputerSystem
Win32_DiskPartition

> get-wmiobject -query "references OF {$cdrive} where classdefsonly"

Win32_LogicalDiskRootDirectory            Win32_SystemDevices
Win32_LogicalDiskToPartition
```

When a script needs to find an object by association, generally we know the class of that object. For example, we know we want the disk partition for drive C: , so Associators of is called with a where clause, which specifies the ResultClass—the Win32_diskPartition class.

```
get-wmiobject -query "ASSOCIATORS OF {$cdrive} where ResultClass=
Win32_DiskPartition"
```

Some types of connections can link to more than one type of object, and because these queries do not support the use of OR, the objects cannot be retrieved by specifying multiple result classes in a Where clause. In this case, the objects can be found using AssocClass in the Where clause and specifying the intermediate object discovered with a references of query.

Here's how the same query would be written based on the type of association that links the objects, rather than the type of the result object:

```
get-wmiobject -query "associators OF {$cdrive} where AssocClass=
Win32_LogicalDiskToPartition"
```

Each reference object contains two properties, which define the nature of relationship. In the preceding example, `Win32_LogicalDiskRootDirectory` and `Win32_SystemDevices` define a link between a `PartComponent` and a `GroupComponent` that contains it, and the `Win32_LogicalDiskToPartition` object defines a link between an `Antecedent` (parent) and a `Dependent` (child).

So it is also possible to find an object by specifying the `role` of the starting object, or the `resultRole` result object, so testing for `role=groupComponent` is the same as testing for `resultRole=PartComponent`, and vice versa.

For example, one can find the objects contained within the `WIN32_computer`:

```
> $pc= get-wmiobject win32_computerSystem
>get-wmiobject -query "associators OF {$pc} where role=groupcomponent
classdefsonly"
```

```
Win32_BIOS                     Win32_LoadOrderGroup
Win32_UserAccount              Win32_SystemDriver
Win32_Process                  Win32_Service
Win32_OperatingSystem          Win32_Environment
Win32_DMAChannel               Win32_IRQResource
Win32_DeviceMemoryAddress      Win32_PortResource
Win32_MotherboardDevice        Win32_Bus
Win32_SoundDevice              Win32_PnPEntity
Win32_1394Controller           Win32_Battery
Win32_IDEController            Win32_PortableBattery
Win32_POTSModem               Win32_Printer
Win32_Processor               Win32_CDROMDrive
Win32_DiskDrive               Win32_DiskPartition
Win32_Fan                     Win32_Keyboard
Win32_LogicalDisk             Win32_MappedLogicalDisk
Win32_MemoryArray             Win32_MemoryDevice
Win32_PCMCIAController         Win32_PointingDevice
Win32_SCSIController          Win32_NetworkAdapter
Win32_USBController           Win32_USBHub
Win32_Volume                  Win32_CacheMemory
Win32_DesktopMonitor          Win32_TemperatureProbe
Win32_VideoController         Win32_SerialPort
Win32_NetworkConnection
```

The WMI Type Accelerators

In addition to the different forms of querying for an object, PowerShell implements a *type accelerator* for WMI.

You may have seen Type Accelerators within PowerShell without even realizing it. For example:

- [String]123 converts the number 123 to a text string: "123"
- [char[]][String]123 converts that to an array of characters, "1", "2", "3"
- Byte[]] [char[]][String]123 coverts it to a byte array with ASCII representations of "1", "2" and "3", the numbers 49, 50, and 51.

Putting [WMI] in front of something returns a WMI object—but what can it convert? The answer is that every WMI object has a unique path that identifies it, which is in the form:

```
\\Server\namespace:Class.identifier
```

The identifier might be some kind of DeviceID, or process handle, or any other property of the object that is unique, the most common one being Name. For example:

```
([wmi]'\\JAMES-2008\root\cimv2:Win32_ComputerSystem.Name="JAMES-2008"')
```

The preceding code returns the same object as:

```
Get-WmiObject -computerName James-2008 -namespace root\cimv2 -query
"Select * from Win32_computersystem where name='James-2008' "
```

The second syntax is generally easier to read and supports filters and passing of multiple objects; -computerName can be an array of computers. But there are cases where it is necessary to use the path—for example, when one WMI object gives a path as a reference to another object.

An example of this is in Windows Server 2008 Hyper-V. Hyper-V is Microsoft's new virtualization technology, which allows a single computer to be divided into multiple *Virtual Machines*, each of which runs its own operating system. Hyper-V doesn't include any PowerShell Cmdlets, but it does provide a lot of WMI objects. A Virtual Machine object has an associated hard disk object, objects that represent memory, network cards, and so on.

Some of the WMI objects for Hyper-V include methods that start a job running in the background—for example, saving the state of a Virtual Machine, or compacting a Virtual Hard Disk file. There is a WMI object to represent the job, and the path to this object is returned by the method that sets the job in motion.

Scripts to check the State property of the WMIJob object have been posted in several places. Here is a PowerShell function to do it.

```
Function Test-WMIJob
{param ([String]$JobID, [Switch]$Wait )
    $Job = [WMI]$JobID
    if ($job -ne $null) {
        while (($job.jobstate -eq 4) -and $wait) {
        Start-Sleep -seconds 1
         $Job.PSBase.Get() }
        @{2="New"; 3="Starting"; 4="Running $($job.PercentComplete)%";
5="Suspended"; 6="Shutting Down"; 7="Completed"; 8="Terminated";
9="Killed"; 10="Exception"; 11="Service"}[[int]$Job.JobState]
}}
```

Reviewing this line by line:

- The function takes a -Wait switch, and a -JobID parameter, which is expected to be a string, and is immediately converted to a WMI object.

- Assuming an object was found, the function checks its JobState property.

- If this is 4, "Running," and the wait switch was specified, it goes into a loop of sleeping for 1 second, and checking the job again.

- Finally it uses a hash table to translate the JobState property to text—the technique that was introduced in Chapter 4.

PowerShell version 1 does not make all the methods available from the WMI object accessible directly as properties of the PowerShell object, so PSBASE is used to get to the methods of the underlying object—as in the Get(), which is used to check for the updated state of the job.

There is a second WMI type accelerator, [WMICLASS], which returns an object that describes the class, including a list of the classes properties and methods. For example, you can see all the properties defined on an account object:

```
> ([wmiclass]"\\.\root\cimv2:Win32_account").psbase.properties |
    Format-Table -Property name,type -autosize
```

```
Name            Type
----            ----
Caption         String
Description     String
Domain          String
InstallDate     DateTime
LocalAccount    Boolean
Name            String
SID             String
SIDType         UInt8
Status          String
```

The path used includes the computer name (".." indentifies the local computer in the example) so it is possible to see classes that are defined on remote computers.

The object returned by [WMIClass] always includes a method named createInstance, but whether this can be used to create an object in the underlying OS depends on the object. For example, the following code:

```
$CPU=([wmiclass]"\\.\root\cimv2:Win32_processor").createInstance()
```

creates an object that describes a processor. Obviously, it can't add a CPU to the system, and trying to save the newly created object back to the OS will fail. For logical objects—such as user accounts—whether a new objected can be saved (with the Put() method described later) depends on how the WMI provider is implemented. In the case of accounts, WMI does not let us circumvent the normal account creation methods. Here, and in several situations when working with WMI objects, you need a knowledge of the object itself. For objects that are part of the operating system, the information is found on Microsoft's MSDN website. Links do change on the site so the easiest way to find information is to search at http://msdn.microsoft.com/library.

Querying Across Computers

So far all the queries in this chapter have run on the local computer. In the previous section, you saw that the paths used by the PowerShell type accelerators contain the name of the target computer. The Get-WmiObject Cmdlet supports a -computerName parameter that allows it to run across multiple computers—assuming that the firewall rules on the destination computer allow it. By default, rules in the *Remote Administration* firewall group are disabled and need to be enabled—either through the management console or with a NetSh command. The following is the version for Server 2008 (including Server core); other operating systems may vary:

```
netsh advfirewall firewall set rule group="Remote Administration" new
enable=yes
```

In the Get-WmiObject command, the -computerName switch routes the WMI command to another server. PowerShell has a principle that if multiple items can be gracefully supported, then they should be, so the computer name can actually be an array of names.

```
Get-WmiObject -computerName LocalHost,James-2008 -namespace root\cimv2 `
              -class win32_logicalDisk
```

The name Localhost or a dot (.) character can be used to represent the local machine. When writing PowerShell functions and filters that use WMI, it is a good practice to accept the computer name as a parameter and default it to "." as in the following example, which retrieves virtual machines running under Hyper-V on server 2008.

```
Function Get-VM
{Param ($Name="%", $Server="." )
 $Name=$Name.replace("*","%")
 $WQL="Select * From MsVM_ComputerSystem Where ElementName Like 'Name'
AND Caption Like 'Virtual%' "
Get-WmiObject -computername $Server -NameSpace "root\virtualization"
-Query $WQL
}
```

You can see that the function doesn't use the name `ComputerName` for any of its parameters—this function is part of a wider library, and in different places `ComputerName` might mean the virtual machine or the server hosting the virtual machine. In addition, there is a piece of general advice:

> GET Cmdlets should support -NAME. A VERY large percentage of the time people do a
> GET, they want a specific item or a set of NAMED items so you should hotrod this
> experience by directly supporting it. NAME should take multiple inputs and support
> wildcards, e.g., "get-process -name *ss,a*"
>
> —Jeffrey Snover, writing on the PowerShell blog

In the function as shown, there is no support for multiple names for the virtual machines (although other functions in the same library do support arrays of names, but do so by calling `Get-VM` for each one). However, it does support wildcards. The function anticipates that people will want to write `Core*` for machines beginning "core" rather than following the WQL and SQL convention of `Core%` for a wildcard. So it replaces * with %. If the server parameter holds multiple names, then `Get-WmiObject` will be invoked with those names, and no special coding needs to be done to support multiple servers. To ensure that function works when no server is specified it defaults the parameter to "."

You can see it also creates a variable, WQL, to hold the query. The full version of the function has additional switches—`-Running`, `-Stopped`, and `-Supsended`—which extend the query so it only returns virtual machines in one of those states.

There is one final point to make about this function: it returns the objects in their natural state, which makes it easy to pipe its output into another command. For example, to put running VMs into a suspended (saved) state, the full version of the function supports this command line:

```
Get-vm -running | suspend-VM
```

Unless some formatting XML is loaded (see the section "Changing How PowerShell Formats Objects" in Chapter 21) the raw WMI object will be displayed. This makes `Get-VM`'s output when used on its own a little ugly. The alternatives are:

- Write a format XML file and load it when needed.
- Give `Get-VM` a `-Formatted` switch, so sometimes it outputs objects and sometimes not.
- Write a "List-VM" function, which produces formatted output.

Logging on to the remote computer

WMI will pass the logged-on user's credentials through to another computer but if these are not the required ones, a `-credential` switch can be used, either with a string containing a user name (which will cause the user to be prompted for a password), or a variable that holds credentials securely. A script can use:

```
$MyCred = Get-Credential
```

And PowerShell will prompt the user for logon details. Thereafter, all the `Get-WmiObject` commands can use `-Credential $myCred`. However, there is a limitation that credentials can't be passed to the local computer. If a script needs to pass credentials to remote servers and retrieve information from the local server, two different forms of the command need to be specified, one without the `-credential` switch for the local machine and one with the switch for remote ones. Because the local machine can be specified using "LocalHost" or any other alias, its short name, fully qualified domain name, or IP address, or simply ".", trapping this can be awkward.

Discovering WMI Objects

So far, this chapter has assumed that you know which objects you want to get using the `Get-WMIObject` Cmdlet. WMI objects are documented on Microsoft's MSDN website but sometimes it is necessary to browse and discover the objects that might be used to accomplish a task. Sometimes a known object will lead to a desired one using `associators of`, as seen earlier in this chapter, but at other times it may be necessary to explore a namespace, and examine objects to discover whether something you want to use in script is available as an object.

One of the first questions to answer is, "What namespaces are available on this computer?"

The `root` namespace has a `__namespace` class, so to get a list of the available namespaces, you can get those objects, like this:

```
Get-WmiObject -Namespace root -class __namespace | Select-Object name
```

When you know the available namespaces, it is then possible to list the classes they contain. For example, this will give a list of all the object types in the `root\cimV2` namespace:

```
Get-WmiObject -Namespace root\cimV2 -list | Sort-Object -Property name
```

It is sometimes useful to filter out the names that begin with two underscore characters. For example, the following will dump out an entire namespace to a file that can then be studied to find a property, a name, or a known value—but only with the "real" properties, not the "housekeeping" ones.

```
> $ns="root\securityCenter"
> Get-WmiObject -Namespace $ns -list | where-object {$_.name -notmatch
"__"} | foreach-object {GetWmiObject -Namespace $ns -class $_.name} >
temp.txt
```

WMI Object Properties

All WMI objects have some common properties that are used for the internal housekeeping—these properties begin with two underscore characters and include the object's class, `__NAMESPACE`, `__PATH` (which was used with the [`WMI`] type accelerator earlier in this chapter), and `__SERVER` (the computer which generated it). The `__Server` property is useful when a PowerShell function is passed a WMI object and can't be sure which server that object came from and needs to get a related object. For example, when managing Server-2008 Hyper-V remotely, `$VM` might point to a virtual machine running on a remote server; an `associators of` query can be used to get the `Settings` object for that virtual machine, but only if it is run against the correct server, so the command to run the query uses the __Server property of $VM to direct it to the right server:

```
Get-WmiObject -ComputerName $vm.__Server -NameSpace "root\
virtualization" -Query "Associators Of {$VM} Where ResultClass =
MsVM_VirtualSystemSettingData"
```

The __class property can be useful for checking that the right kind of WMI object has been passed to or returned from a function; PowerShell can test the type of a parameter or variable but only to the level of knowing it is a WMI object—not the WMI class the object represents—using code similar to this:

```
if ($VM -is [System.Management.ManagementObject]) {do something}
else {write-host "A WMI object was needed"}
```

Updating WMI Objects

The properties of WMI objects seen in PowerShell are static—that is, if the underlying object changes, WMI doesn't have a method to automatically propagate that change through to a variable in PowerShell. (In fact, in version 1, PowerShell can't respond to any kind of event from WMI.) To work around this, the objects have an underlying GET() method, which you saw in the test-wmiJob function. If the GET() were omitted then this function would loop forever.

Properties can be flagged read-only or read-write—but PowerShell treats all properties as read-write. When the PUT() method is called to write back updated properties, then only the writeable properties are committed. This can be confusing because superficially PowerShell lets you do impossible things with WMI properties. Earlier, you retrieved a logical disk object so you could try setting its free space through WMI. Clearly that makes no sense. You can't make more space on the disk just by saying "Make it so" and yet it appears that you can.

```
> $cdrive

DeviceID     : C:
DriveType    : 3
ProviderName :
FreeSpace    : 8255655936
Size         : 99929288704
VolumeName   :

> $cdrive.FreeSpace=100GB
> $cdrive

DeviceID     : C:
DriveType    : 3
ProviderName :
FreeSpace    : 107374182400
Size         : 99929288704
VolumeName   :
```

So it appears this disk—which is only 93GB in size—now has 100GB of free space, which is, of course, impossible. You can even save this information back. (Note that this will only work if the PowerShell session is running with administrative privileges.)

```
> $cdrive.put()

Path            : \\localhost\root\cimv2:Win32_LogicalDisk.DeviceID="C:"
RelativePath    : Win32_LogicalDisk.DeviceID="C:"
Server          : localhost
NamespacePath   : root\cimv2
ClassName       : Win32_LogicalDisk
IsClass         : False
IsInstance      : True
IsSingleton     : False

> $cdrive

DeviceID     : C:
DriveType    : 3
ProviderName :
FreeSpace    : 107374182400
Size         : 99929288704
VolumeName   :
```

Only by using the GET() method can you see that the property was never saved back.

```
> $cdrive.psbase.get()
> $cdrive

DeviceID     : C:
DriveType    : 3
ProviderName :
FreeSpace    : 8255655936
Size         : 99929288704
VolumeName   :
```

Other properties *can* be changed simply by setting them to something else and calling the Put() method, which writes them back. Some can only be changed by calling special purpose methods. For example, in the preceding examples, you can see that the volume name is blank. You can set the volume name, save it using Put(), and verify it has been saved with Get().

```
> $cdrive.VolumeName="Windows_Boot"
> $cdrive.Put()

Path            : \\localhost\root\cimv2:Win32_LogicalDisk.DeviceID="C:"
RelativePath    : Win32_LogicalDisk.DeviceID="C:"
Server          : localhost
NamespacePath   : root\cimv2
ClassName       : Win32_LogicalDisk
```

```
IsClass       : False
IsInstance    : True
IsSingleton   : False

> $cdrive.get
> $cdrive

DeviceID      : C:
DriveType     : 3
ProviderName  :
FreeSpace     : 8257511424
Size          : 99929288704
VolumeName    : Windows_Boot
```

Other properties can be changed only by calling methods specially provided. For example, the win32_computerSystem object has Name and Domain properties. You can change the domain of a computer or its name, but not by simply setting them to their new values and calling Put(). Instead there are methods named JoinDomainOrWorkgroup(), UnjoinDomainOrWorkgroup(), and Rename() and these handle the complexities of, for example, specifying an account, which can be used to join the domain.

WMI Object Methods

Many WMI objects don't implement any methods aside from Get() and Put(). For those objects that are part of Windows, the objects are documented on MSDN, with an entry for each method explaining what parameters it takes and what it returns; it is usually easiest to find the details by searching at http://msdn.microsoft.com/library.

There are two ways to invoke a method: the most common is to call it with the "dotted" notation, as follows:

```
$cdRes=$cdrive.chkdsk($false,$false,$false,$false,$false,$false)
```

$cdRes has a .returnValue property, and may have additional properties depending on the method; for example, some of the methods used to manage Hyper-V return a value to say they have started a process and then have a Job property, which allows the process to be tracked.

There is an alternative syntax, which some people find easier to use, and that is to call the underlying InvokeMethod method of the WMI object. This uses a single array of arguments for passed and returned parameters. For example:

```
$arguments=@($false,$false,$false,$false,$false,$false)
$chkres=$cdrive.psbase.invokemethod("chkdsk",$arguments)
```

$chkres holds the value that was in $cdres.returnValue in the previous example. With this syntax, a value returned—such as the job in the Hyper-V case—will be found in the arguments array.

A Case Study for WMI: Server 2008 Hyper-V

Hyper-V, the virtualization stack for Windows Server 2008, does not provide a command-line interface, but it does provide a large number of WMI objects, which can be used from PowerShell. In writing a library, to manage Hyper-V from PowerShell, the same WMI techniques were used again and again.

Hyper-V defines many object classes to handle different aspects of a virtual machine, and it defines three important *management* classes. The *Image Management Service* deals with virtual hard disks, the *Virtual System Management Service* deals with the virtual machines, and the *Virtual Switch Management Service* handles networking. Generally, to find information about a Virtual Machine you need to call Get-WMIObject with the right query. The put() method is not used to saving changes; instead, to create, change, or delete something, the management services are used.

To get a piece of information about a Virtual Machine, or to change it, an MSVM_ComputerSystem object is usually required. Often the difficult part of writing functions is trying to anticipate how the user wants to invoke them, and what he or she expects to be returned. Typically, the user might want to pass a name of a virtual machine, rather than the WMI object that represents it. Consider the simple case of starting VMs. The user might want to call the following:

```
Start-VM London-DC
Start-VM -server HVtest1 -VM London-DC
Start-VM London-DC,Paris-DC,NewYork-DC,Munich-DC
$myDCList= "London-DC","Paris-DC"; Start-VM $MyDCList
Start-VM *DC -Server HvTest1,HvTest2
Get-vm *DC -Server HvTest1,HvTest2 | Start-VM
```

The last one—a requirement to accept piped input, made it easier to make the command a *filter*, rather than a *function*. Each item is piped into a filter individually and is accessible via the $_ variable.

So, many of the commands follow a template like this:

```
Filter Set-VMState
{Param ($VM , $state, $Server=".")
 if ($VM -eq $null) {$VM=$_}
 if ($VM -is [String]) {$VM=(Get-VM -Name $VM -Server $Server) }
 if ($VM -is [Array]) {$VM | ForEach-Object {Set-VMState -VM $_ -State
$state -Server $Server} }
 if ($VM -is [System.Management.ManagementObject]) {
        $result = $VM.RequestStateChange($State)
        $Result.Job }
 $VM=$null
}
```

The first step is to see if a $VM parameter has been passed at all. If not, the function looks to the pipe for input. Any variables set in the filter will be preserved for subsequent objects piped in so $VM is set to null at the end. Otherwise, piping ten objects into the filter will result in the same command being run against the first one ten times.

If $VM is a single text string—either because it was passed as a parameter, or because a string was piped in—then it is replaced with matching MSVM_ComputerSystem object(s) obtained by calling the Get-VM function from earlier in this chapter Get-VM will handle wildcards in $VM and multiple servers in $Server. If an array is passed to the filter or returned by Get-VM, the function is called recursively for each of its items. This has the side effect of being able to process an array that contains MSVM_ComputerSystem objects, unique machine names as strings, or wildcarded names or a mixture.

The function then makes sure it has a WMI object, and calls its RequestStateChange() method.

What should the output of the filter be? Should it return the text State of VM <name> was changed? Should it return the resultCode for calling the RequestStateChange method—which might indicate "Job started"? Should it return the JobID? If the filter is simply invoked like this:

```
Set-VMState -VM "London-DC" -State $vmstate.running
```

then what does the user want to see? And if set-vmState is called from another function, what does that function need? The two may not be the same.

It is sometimes useful to return some text as the result of the function—that is not to formally prefix it with write-host or pipe it to out-host—but doing that will make things harder for another function. This problem is discussed in more detail in Chapter 21. Put simply when writing a function, you must decide if any returned text should be,

- Returned as a result, which is passed into a variable or another command in the pipleline
- Explicitly sent to the console for the user to see
- Sent to the Verbose channel using the Write-Verbose Cmdlet to give output for the user only if the variable $verbosepreference has be set to request it.

This function might use something like the following:

```
Write-Verbose "Changing state of $($vm.elementName)"
```

Returning the only JobID as the result of the function allows another function (or the user) to find out what happened to the request to start the VM.

To avoid writing the same function four times to request different state changes for Start, Stop, Suspend, Pause these tasks have been given functions which are just wrappers around the set-VMState filter. Each tests to see if it needs to pass a named parameter or one from the pipe, and if the -wait switch is specified it calls the test-WMIjob function shown earlier in this chapter:

```
Filter Start-VM
{Param ($VM , $server, [Switch]$wait)
 if ($VM -eq $null) {
      $JobID=(Set-VMState -VM $_ -Server $server -State $vmState.running)
 }
  else {
      $jobID=(Set-VMState -VM $VM -Server $server -State $vmState.running)
 }
  if ($wait) {test-wmijob $jobID -wait}
  else       {$jobid}
 }
```

Finally, the script that defines these functions also defines a hash table containing each of the possible states for a VM, so instead of requesting that state be set to 2 (which would send the reader of the script to the reference materials to find out what 2 represents), the call to Set-VMstate uses $VMState.running. The hash table—or *associative array* as PowerShell calls it—is declared like this:

```
$VMState=@{"Running"=2 ; "Stopped"=3; "Paused"=32768;
"Suspended"=32769; "Starting"=32770; "Snapshotting"=32771;
"Saving"=32773; "Stopping"=32774 }
```

Summary

In this chapter you have seen:

- How you can discover WMI objects—either by association from a known object or by finding first namespaces and then classes within a namespace

- How to query for objects using the [WMI] type accelerator and different forms of the Get-WMIObject command—with both Select and Associators of forms of WQL

- The properties of WMI objects and how they can be presented in a way that is easier to read than the raw output of the object

- How properties can be changed, including the need to use GET to find or verify changes and PUT to send changes back

- Some practical points around building PowerShell scripts that use WMI

Often, working with any kind of object—whether it is WMI, COM, or .NET, and in whatever language, whether it is PowerShell, VB, or C#—the language that manipulates the object is usually the easy part to learn, and the reusable part. It is exactly the same process to get a WMI object that represents a logical disk on Windows XP as it is to get one that represents a Hyper-V virtual machine on Windows Server 2008. And you pass a command to the logical disk to say "run a chkDsk" in the same way that you pass a command to the VM to say "change state to 'running.'" The technique for finding a partition object from a logical disk is the same technique used to find the machine settings object from a virtual machine. A trick that is useful to format one object for display can be useful for any object, and so on. In the `cimV2` namespace alone, there are over 1,000 object classes. Adding applications or operating system options adds to the number of available objects, so the question to ask is not "What can PowerShell do for these objects?" but "What objects are available for PowerShell to leverage?"

Part V

Windows Scripting Libraries

Now that you've worked through parts I, II, III and IV, you should be ready to tackle any job using Windows scripting. But rather than start from scratch, it would be good to begin with a set of tools. Part V provides you those tools. The five chapters in this Part develop a set of script libraries that you can incorporate into your own projects: file system and administration utilities, network and system administration utilities, account management utilities and general PowerShell utilities. With these tools, you're well on your way to creating your own Windows scripting projects. Good luck!

Chapter 26

Library: File-System Utilities

The file-system utility library provides functions for working with files and folders. Through batch script (.WS) files, you can access these utility functions in any of your scripts. The sections that follow show you the source of the library, as well as how the library can be used.

IN THIS CHAPTER

Creating the file-system utility library

Using the file-system utility library

Working with library methods

Examining the File-System Utility Library

Listing 26-1 shows the file-system utility library script. When calling this script from JScript, be sure to pass path information in JScript format with double slashes as folder separators. You do not need to do this from VBScript. Windows Script Host automatically transforms VBScript paths into JScript paths when you call JScript functions from VBScript.

LISTING 26-1

File-System Utility Library

filesystemlib.js

```
// ***********************
// Script: File System Utility Library
// Version: 1.1.5
// Creation Date: 06/15/2008
// Last Modified: 07/05/2008
// Author: William R. Stanek
// E-mail: williamstanek@aol.com
```

continued

LISTING 26-1   *(continued)*

```
// ************************
// Description: Provides a utility library for working
//              with files and folders.
// ************************
// Copyright (c) 2008 William R. Stanek
// You have a royalty-free right to use these applications, provided
// that you give credit to the author AND agree that the author has
// no warranty, obligations or liability for any of these library
// functions.
// ************************

function GetFolderContents(folderPath, separator)
{
  var contents, fpath, sep;
  fpath = folderPath
  sep = separator

  contents = "";
  contents += "Folders:" + sep
  contents += "============================" + sep
  contents += GetSubFolders(fpath, sep).
  contents += sep + "Files:" + sep
  contents += "============================" + sep
  contents += GetFiles(fpath, sep)

  return(contents);
}

function GetSubFolders(folderPath, separator)
{
  var fs, f, fc, s;

  s = "";

  fs = new ActiveXObject("Scripting.FileSystemObject");
  f = fs.GetFolder(folderPath);
  fc = new Enumerator(f.SubFolders);

  for (; !fc.atEnd(); fc.moveNext())
  {
   s += fc.item();
   s += separator
  }

  return(s);
}
```

```
function GetFiles(folderPath, separator)
{
  var fs, f, fc, s;

  s = "";

  fs = new ActiveXObject ("Scripting.FileSystemObject");
  f = fs.GetFolder(folderPath);
  fc = new Enumerator(f.Files);

  for (; !fc.atEnd(); fc.moveNext())
  {
   s += fc.item();
   s += separator
  }

  return(s);
}

function CheckExists(filePath)
{
  var fs, s;

  s = "False";

  fs = new ActiveXObject("Scripting.FileSystemObject");

  if (fs.FolderExists(filePath))
    s = "True";
  else if (fs.FileExists(filePath))
    s = "True";

  return(s);
}

function GetInfo(filePath)
{
  var fs, f, s;

  fs = new ActiveXObject("Scripting.FileSystemObject");

  if (fs.FolderExists(filePath))
    f = fs.GetFolder(filePath);
  else if (fs.FileExists(filePath))
    f = fs.GetFile(filePath);

  s = "Name: " + f.Name + "\r\n";
  s += "Path: " + f.Path + "\r\n";
  s += "Date Created: " + f.DateCreated + "\r\n";
```

continued

609

LISTING 26-1   *(continued)*

```
  s += "Date Last Accessed: " + f.DateLastAccessed + "\r\n";
  s += "Date Last Modified: " + f.DateLastModified;

  return(s);
}

function GetSize(filePath)
{
  var fs, f, s;

  fs = new ActiveXObject("Scripting.FileSystemObject");
  f = fs.GetFolder(filePath);

  if (fs.FolderExists(filePath))
    f = fs.GetFolder(filePath);
  else if (fs.FileExists(filePath))
    f = fs.GetFile(filePath);

  s = f.size;

  return(s);
}

function GetType(filePath)
{
  var fs, f, s;

  fs = new ActiveXObject("Scripting.FileSystemObject");
  f = fs.GetFolder(filePath);

  if (fs.FolderExists(filePath))
    f = fs.GetFolder(filePath);
  else if (fs.FileExists(filePath))
    f = fs.GetFile(filePath);

  s = f.type;

  return(s);
}

function CheckParentFolder(filePath)
{
  var fs, s = "";

  fs = new ActiveXObject("Scripting.FileSystemObject");
  s += fs.GetParentFolderName(filePath);
```

```
  return(s);
}

function SetArchiveAttribute(folderName)
{
  var fs, f, fc, s;

  fs = new ActiveXObject("Scripting.FileSystemObject");
  f = fs.GetFolder(folderName);
  fc = new Enumerator(f.Files);
  s = "";

  for (; !fc.atEnd(); fc.moveNext())
  {
    theFile = fs.GetFile(fc.item());

    if (!(theFile.attributes && 32))
    {
     theFile.attributes = theFile.attributes + 32;
    }


  }
  return("Finished!");
}

function ClearArchiveAttribute(folderName)
{
  var fs, f, fc, s;

  fs = new ActiveXObject("Scripting.FileSystemObject");
  f = fs.GetFolder(folderName);
  fc = new Enumerator(f.Files);
  s = "";

  for (; !fc.atEnd(); fc.moveNext())
  {
    theFile = fs.GetFile(fc.item());

    if (theFile.attributes && 32)
    {
     theFile.attributes = theFile.attributes - 32;
    }


  }
  return("Finished!");
}
```

continued

LISTING 26-1 *(continued)*

```javascript
function SetReadOnly(folderName)
{
  var fs, f, fc, s;

  fs = new ActiveXObject("Scripting.FileSystemObject");
  f = fs.GetFolder(folderName);
  fc = new Enumerator(f.Files);
  s = "";

  for (; !fc.atEnd(); fc.moveNext())
  {
    theFile = fs.GetFile(fc.item());

    theFile.attributes = 1;
  }
  return("Finished!");
}


function ClearReadOnly(folderName)
{
  var fs, f, fc, s;

  fs = new ActiveXObject("Scripting.FileSystemObject");
  f = fs.GetFolder(folderName);
  fc = new Enumerator(f.Files);
  s = "";

  for (; !fc.atEnd(); fc.moveNext())
  {
    theFile = fs.GetFile(fc.item());

    theFile.attributes = 0;
  }
  return("Finished!");
}

function SetHiddenSystem(folderName)
{
  var fs, f, fc, s;

  fs = new ActiveXObject("Scripting.FileSystemObject");
  f = fs.GetFolder(folderName);
  fc = new Enumerator(f.Files);
  s = "";

  for (; !fc.atEnd(); fc.moveNext())
```

```
  {
    theFile = fs.GetFile(fc.item());

    theFile.attributes = 6;

  }
  return("Finished!");
}


function SetNormal(folderName)
{
  var fs, f, fc, s;

  fs = new ActiveXObject("Scripting.FileSystemObject");
  f = fs.GetFolder(folderName);
  fc = new Enumerator(f.Files);
  s = "";

  for (; !fc.atEnd(); fc.moveNext())
  {
    theFile = fs.GetFile(fc.item());

    theFile.attributes = 0;
  }
  return("Finished!");
}

function ListSpecialFolders(sep)
{
  var s;

  s = "";
  s += "=============================================================" + sep;
  s += "Special Folders List" + sep;
  s += "                    Scripting Bible" + sep;
  s += "                    by William R. Stanek" + sep;
  s += "=============================================================" + sep;
  s += "AllUsersDesktop:    Desktop shortcuts for all users." + sep;
  s += "AllUsersPrograms:   Programs menu options for all users." + sep;
  s += "AllUsersStartMenu:  Start menu options for all users." + sep;
  s += "AllUsersStartup:    Startup applications for all users." + sep;
  s += "Desktop:            Desktop shortcuts for the current user." + sep;
  s += "Favorites:          Favorites menu shortcuts for the current user." + sep;
  s += "Fonts:              Fonts folder shortcuts for the current user." + sep;
  s += "MyDocuments:        My Documents menu shortcuts for the current user." + sep;
  s += "NetHood:            Network Neighborhood shortcuts for the current user." + sep;
  s += "Printers:           Printers folder shortcuts for the current user." + sep;
```

continued

LISTING 26-1   *(continued)*

```javascript
    s += "Programs:         Programs menu options for the current user." + sep;
    s += "Recent:           Recently used document shortcuts for the current user." + sep;
    s += "SendTo:           SendTo menu shortcuts for the current user." + sep;
    s += "StartMenu:        Start menu shortcuts for the current user." + sep;
    s += "Startup:          Startup applications for the current user." + sep;
    s += "Templates:        Templates folder shortcuts for the current user." + sep;
    s += "=========================================================" + sep;

    return(s);
}

function NewShortcut(sfolder, sname, stype, starget)
{
    var ws = WScript.CreateObject("WScript.Shell");

    pmenu = ws.SpecialFolders(sfolder);

    var scut = ws.CreateShortcut(pmenu + "\\" + sname + "." + stype);
    scut.TargetPath = starget;

    scut.Save();
}

function CheckMenu(mname)
{
    var fs, f, fc, s;
    fs = new ActiveXObject("Scripting.FileSystemObject");
    var ws = WScript.CreateObject ("WScript.Shell")
    smenu = ws.SpecialFolders(mname)

    f = fs.GetFolder(smenu);
    fc = new Enumerator(f.Files);
    s = "";
    for (; !fc.atEnd(); fc.moveNext())
    {
        theFile = fs.GetFile(fc.item());
        s += theFile + "\r\n"
    }
    return (s)
}

function CheckMenu2(mname)
{
    var fs, f, fc, s;

    var ws = WScript.CreateObject("WScript.Shell");
    smenu = ws.SpecialFolders(mname);
```

```
  fs = new ActiveXObject("Scripting.FileSystemObject");
  f = fs.GetFolder(smenu);
  fc = new Enumerator(f.Files);
  s = "";

  for (; !fc.atEnd(); fc.moveNext())
  {
   f1 = fs.GetFile(fc.item());
   s += f1.name + "\r\n"
  }
  return (s)
}

function NewMenu(sfolder, mname)
{
  var s;
  s = "False"

  var ws = WScript.CreateObject("WScript.Shell");
  pmenu = ws.SpecialFolders(sfolder);

  if (sfolder == "AllUsersPrograms" || sfolder == "AllUsersStart" || sfolder ==
"Programs" || sfolder == "StartMenu") {

    fs = new ActiveXObject("Scripting.FileSystemObject");
    var foldr = fs.CreateFolder(pmenu + "\\" + mname)
    s = "True"

  }
  return(s)
}

function AddMenuOption(sfolder, mname, sname, stype, starget)
{
  var ws = WScript.CreateObject("WScript.Shell");
  pmenu = ws.SpecialFolders(sfolder);

  var scut = ws.CreateShortcut(pmenu + "\\" + mname + "\\" + sname + "." + stype);
  scut.TargetPath = starget;

  scut.Save()
}

function CopyFile2Desktop(filePath)
{
  var fs, test;

  var ws = WScript.CreateObject("WScript.Shell");
  pmenu = ws.SpecialFolders("Desktop");
```

continued

615

LISTING 26-1   *(continued)*

```
  fs = new ActiveXObject("Scripting.FileSystemObject");
  fs.CopyFile(filePath, pmenu + "\\");
}

function MoveFile2Desktop(filePath)
{
  var ws = WScript.CreateObject("WScript.Shell");
  pmenu = ws.SpecialFolders("Desktop");

  fs = new ActiveXObject("Scripting.FileSystemObject");
  fs.MoveFile(filePath, pmenu + "\\");
}

function CopyFolder2Desktop(filePath)
{
  var fs, test;

  var ws = WScript.CreateObject("WScript.Shell");
  pmenu = ws.SpecialFolders("Desktop");

  fs = new ActiveXObject("Scripting.FileSystemObject");
  fs.CopyFolder(filePath, pmenu + "\\");
}

function MoveFolder2Desktop(filePath)
{
  var ws = WScript.CreateObject("WScript.Shell");
  pmenu = ws.SpecialFolders("Desktop");

  fs = new ActiveXObject("Scripting.FileSystemObject");
  fs.MoveFolder(filePath, pmenu + "\\");
}


function NewFile(filePath)
{
  var fs, s = filePath;
  fs = new ActiveXObject("Scripting.FileSystemObject");

  if (!fs.FileExists(filePath)) {
    var theFile = fs.CreateTextFile(filePath);
    s += " created."
  } else
    s += " already exists.";

  return(s);
}
```

```
function NewFolder(folderPath)
{
  var fs, s = folderPath;
  fs = new ActiveXObject("Scripting.FileSystemObject");

  if (!fs.FolderExists(folderPath)) {
    var foldr = fs.CreateFolder(folderPath);
    s += " created."
  } else
    s += " already exists.";

  return(s);
}

function AddDesktop(sname,trgt)
{

var ws = WScript.CreateObject ("WScript.Shell")
dsktop = ws.SpecialFolders("Desktop")

var scut = ws.CreateShortcut (dsktop + "\\" + sname + ".LNK")
scut.TargetPath = trgt
scut.Save()

}

function AddDesktopURL(sname,trgt)
{

var ws = WScript.CreateObject ("WScript.Shell")
dsktop = ws.SpecialFolders("Desktop")

var scut = ws.CreateShortcut (dsktop + "\\" + sname + ".URL")
scut.TargetPath = trgt
scut.Save()

}

function AddStartMenu(sname,trgt)
{

var ws = WScript.CreateObject ("WScript.Shell")
smenu = ws.SpecialFolders("StartMenu")
var scut = ws.CreateShortcut (smenu + "\\" + sname + ".LNK")
scut.TargetPath = trgt
scut.Save()

}
```

continued

617

LISTING 26-1   *(continued)*

```
function AddStartMenuURL(sname,trgt)
{

var ws = WScript.CreateObject ("WScript.Shell")
smenu = ws.SpecialFolders("StartMenu")
var scut = ws.CreateShortcut (smenu + "\\" + sname + ".URL")
scut.TargetPath = trgt
scut.Save()

}

function DeleteShortcut(sfolder, sname)
{
  var ws = WScript.CreateObject("WScript.Shell");
  smenu = ws.SpecialFolders(sfolder);

  fs = new ActiveXObject("Scripting.FileSystemObject");
  f = fs.GetFile(smenu + "\\" + sname);

  f.Delete();
}

function DeleteFile(filePath)
{
  var fs;
  fs = new ActiveXObject("Scripting.FileSystemObject");

  fs.DeleteFile(filePath);
}

function DeleteFolder(folderPath)
{
  var fs;
  fs = new ActiveXObject("Scripting.FileSystemObject");

  fs.DeleteFolder(folderPath);
}
```

Using the File-System Utility Library

The file-system utility library has many functions that you can call from other scripts. Most of the functions expect to be passed a folder path, such as:

```
D:\\Working
```

or a file path, such as:

```
D:\\working\\data.txt
```

There are a few exceptions, such as `GetFolderContents`, `GetSubFolders`, and `GetFiles`, that expect additional parameters.

Using GetSubFolders, GetFiles, and GetFolderContents

The `GetSubFolders` and `GetFiles` functions return a list of subfolders or files in the referenced folder. These functions expect to be passed a folder path and a character to display as a separator. This separator can be a space, a comma, or a special formatting character, such as \r\n for carriage return and line feed. Here's an example of how you can call `GetFiles`:

```
theList = GetFiles("C:\\WinnT", "\r\n")
```

If you use a .WS file, you don't have to place the `GetFiles` function in your script. Instead, you can handle the function like a library call. With a .WS file, you can use `GetFiles` as follows:

```
<Job ID="CreateFolders">
  <Script LANGUAGE="JScript" SRC="filesystemlib.js" />
  <Script LANGUAGE="JScript">
          theList = GetFiles("C:\\WinnT", "\r\n")
          WScript.Echo(theList)
  </Script>
</Job>
```

The `GetFolderContents` function returns a list of all subfolders and files in the referenced folder. The function does this by obtaining the output of both `GetSubFolders` and `GetFiles`, and then formatting the output using the separator you've specified, such as:

```
Folders:
==========================
E:\working\data1
E:\working\data2
E:\working\data3
E:\working\samples
E:\working\data_back

Files:
==========================
E:\working\document1.txt
E:\working\document2.txt
E:\working\document3.txt
E:\working\document4.txt
E:\working\document5.txt
E:\working\document6.txt
```

Using CheckExists

You can use the CheckExists function to determine if a resource that you want to work with exists. The function expects to be passed a file or folder path, and returns True if the resource exists and False otherwise. An interesting feature of this function is the If ... Else If construct that tests whether the path you've supplied references a folder of a file:

```
if (fs.FolderExists(filePath))
    s = "True";
else if (fs.FileExists(filePath))
    s = "True";
```

Here, you test for the existence of the file path as a folder and as a file. The If ... Else If construct allows a single function to work with files and folders, and it is used by many other functions in the system utility library, including GetInfo, GetSize, and GetType.

Using GetInfo, GetSize, and GetType

The GetInfo function expects to be passed a file or folder path, and returns summary information for the file or folder. This information is placed on separate lines using \r\n and includes:

- File or folder name
- File or folder path
- Date created
- Date last accessed
- Date last modified

The GetSize and GetType functions also return file or folder information. GetSize returns the byte size of the file or folder. GetType returns the file or folder type. A similar function is CheckParentFolder. This function returns the name of the parent folder for the specified resource.

Setting and clearing file attributes

The utility library also has functions for working with file attributes. These functions are:

- SetReadOnly: Sets the read-only attribute
- ClearReadOnly: Clears the read-only attribute
- SetArchiveAttribute: Sets the archive attribute
- ClearArchiveAttribute: Clears the archive attribute
- SetHiddenSystem: Sets the hidden and system attributes
- SetNormalAttribute: Clears all other attributes and sets the normal attribute

These functions set the attributes on all files in a referenced folder, but they do not go through sub-folders. Keep in mind that you can't change the archive attribute on read-only files. Because of this, you may want to call `ClearReadOnly` before calling `SetArchiveAttribute` or `ClearArchive Attribute`.

You can set the read-only attribute on all files in the `D:\working` folder as follows:

```
SetReadOnly("D:\\Working")
```

If you use a .WS file, you don't have to place the `SetReadOnly` function in your script. Instead, you can handle the function like a library call, such as:

```
<Job ID="CreateFolders">
  <Script LANGUAGE="JScript" SRC="adminlib.js" />
  <Script LANGUAGE="JScript">
          ret = SetReadOnly("D:\\Working")
          WScript.Echo(ret)
  </Script>
</Job>
```

The set and clear functions use an `Enumerator` object to move through each file in the referenced folder. To obtain a file object, the function calls `GetFile` with the name of the current item in the enumerator list. The `file` object is then used to set or clear the appropriate attribute, such as:

```
theFile = fs.GetFile(fc.item());
if (theFile.attributes && 32)
{
    theFile.attributes = theFile.attributes - 32;
}
```

Working with special folders, shortcuts, and menus

You can use the `ListSpecialFolders` function to display a formatted list of all the special folders available. This is useful so script users can obtain a list of special folders that they may want to work with. For example, if you prompt users to enter the name of a special folder to manage and they don't know the folder name, they can leave it blank or type "?" to obtain a list of special folders.

The function expects to be passed a line separator, which could be `\r\n` for output to the command line, a dialog box, or HTML tags, such as `<BR>`, for display in a browser window. With `\r\n`, the output of the function looks like this:

```
==========================================================
Special Folders List
                   Scripting Bible
                   by William R. Stanek
==========================================================
AllUsersDesktop:     Desktop shortcuts for all users.
AllUsersPrograms:    Programs menu options for all users.
```

```
AllUsersStartMenu:    Start menu options for all users.
AllUsersStartup:      Startup applications for all users.
Desktop:              Desktop shortcuts for the current user.
Favorites:            Favorites menu shortcuts for the current user.
Fonts:                Fonts folder shortcuts for the current user.
MyDocuments:          My Documents menu shortcuts for the current user.
NetHood:              Network Neighborhood shortcuts for the current user.
Printers:             Printers folder shortcuts for the current user.
Programs:             Programs menu options for the current user.
Recent:               Recently used document shortcuts for the current user.
SendTo:               SendTo menu shortcuts for the current user.
StartMenu:            Start menu shortcuts for the current user.
Startup:              Startup applications for the current user.
Templates:            Templates folder shortcuts for the current user.
=========================================================
```

Once you know which special folder you want to work with, you can add items to the special folder using NewShortcut. The NewShortcut function can be used to create link and URL shortcuts. It can also be used to add start items, menu options, and desktop links. When you use this function, you must pass in the following parameters:

- sfolder: The name of the special folder to use, such as Programs
- sname: The name of the shortcut, such as My Home Page
- stype: The type of the shortcut, either LNK or URL
- starget: The target of the shortcut, such as http://www.tvpress.com

The following example creates a URL shortcut on the Programs menu:

```
NewShortcut("Programs", "My Home Page", "URL", "http://www.tvpress.com/")
```

Other useful functions for working with menus and menu options are NewMenu and AddMenuOption. You use NewMenu to create a new menu and AddMenuOption to add options to the menu.

The NewMenu function expects to be passed the name of a special folder that represents one of the following menus:

- AllUsersPrograms
- AllUsersStart
- Programs
- StartMenu

It also expects to be passed the name of the menu to create. With this in mind, you could call NewMenu as follows:

```
NewMenu ("Programs", "Quick Access")
```

You can then use the AddMenuOption function to add options to this menu. You could also use this function to add options to any existing menus, provided they are submenus of Programs or Start. The AddMenuOption function expects to be passed the following arguments:

- sfolder: The name of the special folder to use, such as Programs
- mname: The name of the submenu to work with, such as Quick Access
- sname: The name of the shortcut, such as My Home Page
- stype: The type of the shortcut; either LNK or URL
- starget: The target of the shortcut, such as http://www.tvpress.com

The following is an example of calling this function:

```
AddMenuOption ("Programs", "Quick Access", "My Home Page", "URL",
"http://www.tvpress.com")
```

Managing menu options

The CheckMenu and CheckMenu2 functions are designed to help you track and manage menu options. You can pass the function the name of a special menu and the function returns a list of all options assigned through this menu. The CheckMenu function returns the full file path to the menu options, such as:

```
F:\Documents and Settings\Administrator.ZETA\Start Menu\Programs\
Internet Explorer.LNK

F:\Documents and Settings\Administrator.ZETA\Start Menu\Programs\My
Home Page.URL

F:\Documents and Settings\Administrator.ZETA\Start Menu\Programs\
Outlook Express.LNK
```

The CheckMenu2 function returns the option name only, such as:

```
Internet Explorer.LNK
My Home Page.URL
Outlook Express.LNK
```

You can use these functions in several ways. If you are trying to determine whether a particular option is assigned to the current user or all users, you can call `CheckMenu` or `CheckMenu2` once with a current user menu and a second time with an all users menu, such as:

```
WScript.Echo(CheckMenu(StartMenu))
WScript.Echo("=================")
WScript.Echo(CheckMenu(AllUsersStartMenu))
```

Because the `CheckMenu` function returns the complete file path to the options, you can use the function to delete menu options, as well. To see how, let's work through an example. Listing 26-2 obtains a list of options on the Programs menu for the current user and all users on the system. These options are written to a text file (`menuoptions.txt`). The script uses `WriteChar` from `iolib.js` and `CheckMenu` from `filesystemlib.js`.

LISTING 26-2

Getting All Menu Options

getoptions.WS

```
<Job ID="GetMenuOptions">
  <Script LANGUAGE="JScript" SRC="iolib.js" />
  <Script LANGUAGE="JScript" SRC="filesystemlib.js" />

  <Script LANGUAGE="VBScript">
    theOptions = CheckMenu("Programs")
    ret = WriteChar("d:\\menuoptions.txt", theOptions)
    theOptions = CheckMenu("AllUsersPrograms")
    ret = WriteChar("d:\\menuoptions.txt", theOptions)
</Script>
</Job>
```

menuoptions.txt

```
D:\WINNT\Profiles\All Users\Start Menu\Programs\Access.LNK
D:\WINNT\Profiles\All Users\Start Menu\Programs\Excel.LNK
D:\WINNT\Profiles\All Users\Start Menu\Programs\FrontPage.LNK
D:\WINNT\Profiles\All Users\Start Menu\Programs\PowerPoint.LNK
D:\WINNT\Profiles\All Users\Start Menu\Programs\Word.LNK
D:\WINNT\Profiles\All Users\Start Menu\Programs\PhotoDraw.LNK
D:\WINNT\Profiles\All Users\Start Menu\Programs\Web Script.LNK
D:\WINNT\Profiles\All Users\Start Menu\Programs\Web Script2.LNK
D:\WINNT\Profiles\All Users\Start Menu\Programs\Web Script3.LNK
```

You then edit the `menuoptions.txt` file and remove menu options that you don't want to keep. Afterward, you run Listing 26-3 to remove the options from the menu. The script uses `ReadLineN` from `iolib.js` and `DeleteFile` from `filesystemlib.js`.

LISTING 26-3

Deleting Multiple Menu Options

deleteoptions.WS

```
<Job ID="DeleteOptions">
  <Script LANGUAGE="JScript" SRC="adminlib.js" />
  <Script LANGUAGE="JScript" SRC="filelib.js" />
  <Script LANGUAGE="VBScript">
  Dim numLines, theFile
  numLines = 4

  theFile = "d:\menuoptions.txt"

  For i = 1 to numLines Step 1

    theShortcut = ReadLineN(theFile, i)
    ret = DeleteFile(theShortcut)

  Next
  </Script>
</Job>
```

 If you use this script, be sure to update the `numLines` variable so that it reflects the actual number of lines in the `menuoptions.txt` file.

Adding to the desktop and Start menu

To quickly add shortcuts to the desktop or Start menu for the current user, use the `AddDesktop`, `AddDesktopURL`, `AddStartMenu`, and `AddStartMenuURL` functions. While `AddDesktop` and `AddStartMenu` create link shortcuts, `AddDesktopURL` and `AddStartMenuURL` create URL shortcuts. These functions accept the same parameters: the name of the shortcut (without the LNK or URL extension) and the target path of the shortcut.

Listing 26-4 shows how you can use these functions in order to add multiple desktop and menu shortcuts. The listing uses the file utility library, as well as the network resource library. The file `options.txt` contains the shortcuts being added to the desktop. The file `adesktop.WS` contains a batch script, with the main script written in VBScript.

LISTING 26-4

Adding Multiple Shortcuts

options.txt

```
WinScripting Home
http://www.tvpress.com/winscripting/
WinScripting Microsoft
http://msdn.microsoft.com/scripting/
WinScripting for IIS 7.0
http://msdn.microsoft.com/library/sdkdoc/iisref/aore2xpu.htm
```

adesktop.WS

```
<Job ID="AddShortcuts">
  <Script LANGUAGE="JScript" SRC="iolib.js" />
  <Script LANGUAGE="JScript" SRC="filesystemlib.js" />

  <Script LANGUAGE="VBScript">
  Dim numLines, theFile
  numLines = 6

  theFile = "D:\datatest.txt"

  For i = 1 to numLines Step 2

   theShortcut = ReadLineN(theFile, i)
   theTarget = ReadLineN(theFile, i+1)
   ret = AddDesktopURL(theShortcut, theTarget)

  Next
  </Script>
</Job>
```

Because this is the first time we've called JScript from VBScript via the utility libraries, let's take a quick look at some key concepts. As the script shows, when you call a JScript function that uses file paths, you don't need to use the JScript syntax. File paths are automatically converted for you, which is why you can set the file path as:

```
D:\datatest.txt
```

However, you do have to use a slightly different syntax when calling functions that don't return values. The script uses:

```
ret = AddDesktopURL(theShortcut, theTarget)
```

rather than:

```
AddDesktopURL(theShortcut, theTarget)
```

Even though the AddDesktopURL function doesn't return a value, you can call the function as though it does return a value. If you don't do this, VBScript thinks the function is a subroutine, and you cannot use parentheses when calling a subroutine.

An interesting feature of the script is the use of a For Next loop to read from the file two lines at a time. In the first iteration of the For loop, lines 1 and 2 are read from the options.txt file. The value of line 1 is assigned as the shortcut name. The value of line 2 is assigned as the target path. Then the AddDesktopURL function is called with these values. In the second iteration of the For loop, lines 3 and 4 are read from the options.txt file, and so on.

Other useful desktop functions are CopyFile2Desktop and MoveFile2Desktop. These functions expect to be passed a file path and then for the file to be either copied or moved to the Windows desktop. You can move a file to the desktop as follows:

```
MoveFile2Desktop("D:\\Working\\document1.txt")
```

Two functions with similar usage are CopyFolder2Desktop and MoveFolder2Desktop. These functions expect to be passed a folder path and then for the folder to be either copied or moved to the Windows desktop. You can copy a folder to the desktop as follows:

```
MoveFile2Desktop("D:\\Working\\Data")
```

Using NewFolder and NewFile

You can use the NewFolder function to create a new folder, provided the folder doesn't already exist. If you wanted to create a folder at D:\Working\Data, you could use the following call:

```
WScript.Echo(NewFolder("D:\\working\\data"))
```

The value returned from NewFolder would either be:

```
D:\working\data created.
```

or

```
D:\working\data already exists.
```

The NewFile function can be used in much the same way. The key difference is that you pass NewFile the file path you want to create, instead of a folder path, such as:

```
WScript.Echo(NewFile("D:\\working\\data\\document1.txt"))
```

Using DeleteFile, DeleteFolder, and DeleteShortcut

The `DeleteFile` and `DeleteFolder` functions are used to delete files and folders, respectively. You can use wildcards when calling these functions, such as:

```
DeleteFile("D:\\working\\*.txt")
```

 Be careful when using the delete functions. Never pass a reference to a root folder, such as `C:\`.

You use `DeleteShortcut` to delete shortcuts. The function expects to be passed the name of a special folder containing the shortcut and the full name of the shortcut. For example, you could delete a shortcut called My Home Page from the Programs menu as follows:

```
DeleteShortcut("Programs", "\My Home Page.URL")
```

If the shortcut is on a submenu, be sure to enter the submenu path as part of the shortcut name, such as:

```
DeleteShortcut("Programs", "Quick Access\\My Home Page.URL")
```

Summary

This chapter developed a utility library for working with file systems. You can call the functions of this library from your own scripts at any time. The next chapter provides a utility library for handling input and output.

Chapter 27

Library: I/O Utilities

IN THIS CHAPTER

Creating the I/O utility library

Using the I/O utility library

Working with library methods

The I/O utility library provides functions for handling input and output. With these functions, you'll be able to read files, write files, obtain input, and display output. Through batch script (.WS) files, you can access these utility functions in any of your scripts. The sections that follow show the source for the library, as well as how the library can be used.

Examining the I/O Utility Library

The code for the I/O utility library is shown in Listing 27-1. When using this script from JScript, be sure to pass path information in JScript format with double slashes as folder separators. With other scripting languages, you normally don't have to use double slashes.

LISTING 27-1

I/O utility library

iolib.js

```
// ***********************
// Script: I/O Utility Library
// Version: 1.1.5
// Creation Date: 05/20/2008
// Last Modified: 06/15/2008
// Author: William R. Stanek
// Email: williamstanek@aol.com
// ***********************
// Description: Provides a utility library for reading
//              and writing files.
```

continued

LISTING 27-1   *(continued)*

```
// ************************
// Copyright (c) 2008 William R. Stanek
// You have a royalty-free right to use these applications,
// provided that you give credit to the author AND agree that
// the author has no warranty, obligations or liability for
// any of these library functions.
// ************************

function DisplayConsolePrompt(promptText)
{

    lf = "\r\n"
    WScript.Echo(promptText + lf)

    r = WScript.StdIn.ReadLine()

    return(r)
}

function ReadFromKeyboard(scriptname, promptText)
{

    lf = "\r\n"
    WScript.Echo("=========================================" + lf)
    WScript.Echo(scriptname + lf)
    WScript.Echo("=========================================" + lf)

    WScript.Echo(promptText + lf)

    r = WScript.StdIn.ReadLine()

    return(r)
}

function ReadFile(theFile)
{
  var fs, f, r;
  var ForReading = 1;

  fs = new ActiveXObject("Scripting.FileSystemObject");
  f = fs.OpenTextFile(theFile, ForReading);
  r = f.ReadAll();

  return(r);
}

function ReadLineN(theFile,n)
```

```
{
  var fs, f, r;
  var ForReading = 1;

  n—

  fs = new ActiveXObject("Scripting.FileSystemObject");
  f = fs.OpenTextFile(theFile, ForReading);

  for (a = 0; a < n; a++) {
   if (!f.AtEndOfStream) {
    f.SkipLine()
   }
  }
  r =  f.ReadLine();

  return(r);
}

function ReadCharN(theFile,s,n)
{
  var fs, f, r;
  var ForReading = 1;

  fs = new ActiveXObject("Scripting.FileSystemObject");
  f = fs.OpenTextFile(theFile, ForReading);

  f.Skip(s);
  r =  f.Read(n);

  return(r);
}

function WriteLine(theFile,theLine)
{
  var fs, f;
  var ForWriting = 2, ForAppending = 8;

  fs = new ActiveXObject("Scripting.FileSystemObject")

  if (fs.FileExists(theFile))
   var f = fs.OpenTextFile (theFile, ForAppending)
  else
   var f = fs.OpenTextFile (theFile, ForWriting, "True")

  f.WriteLine(theLine);
  f.Close();
}
```

continued

LISTING 27-1   *(continued)*

```
function WriteChar(theFile,theString)
{
  var fs, f;
  var ForWriting = 2, ForAppending = 8;

  fs = new ActiveXObject("Scripting.FileSystemObject")

  if (fs.FileExists(theFile))
   var f = fs.OpenTextFile (theFile, ForAppending)
  else
   var f = fs.OpenTextFile (theFile, ForWriting, "True")

  f.Write(theString);
  f.Close();
}

function DisplayDialog(text, timeout, title, buttonType)
{
   var answ;

  if (timeout == null)
    timeout = 10
  if (title == null)
    title = "Input Required"
  if (buttonType == null)
    buttonType = 3

  var w = WScript.CreateObject("WScript.Shell");
  answ = w.Popup(text, timeout, title, buttonType)
  return(answ)
}

function GetResponse(text, timeout, title, buttonType)
{
   var s, answer;

  answer = DisplayDialog(text, timeout, title, buttonType)

  s = "";

  switch (answer) {
   case 1 :
     s = "ok";
     break;

   case 2 :
     s = "cancel";
```

```
      break;

   case 3 :
     s = "abort";
     break;

   case 4 :
     s = "retry";
     break;

   case 5 :
     s = "ignore";
     break;

   case 6 :
     s = "yes";
     break;

   case 7 :
     s = "no";
     break;

   default :
    s = "none"
    break
    }

   return(s)
}

function GetErrorInfo(e, sep)
{

   var s;
   s = "";

   s += "Error Type:   " + e + sep
   s += "Description: " + e.description + sep;
   s += "Error Code:   "
   s += e.number & 0xFFFF;
   s += sep;

   return(s)
}

function WriteEvent(status)
{
   var s;
   s = ""
```

continued

LISTING 27-1 *(continued)*

```
var ws = WScript.CreateObject("WScript.Shell")

if (status == 0) {
//successful execution
s = WScript.ScriptName + " completed successfully."
ws.LogEvent(0, s)
}
else {
//failed execution
s = WScript.ScriptName + " did not execute properly."
s += "\r\n " + WScript.ScriptFullName
s += "\r\n " + WScript.FullName
ws.LogEvent(1, s)
}

}
```

Using the I/O Utility Library

As you examined the source code, you probably noted two general types of functions: those for handling file I/O and those for handling other types of I/O tasks. Let's look at the file I/O functions first and then look at the other I/O functions.

Handling file I/O with the utility library

File I/O tasks make several assumptions. First of all, text files are assumed to be in the default format for the system, which is normally ASCII text. Most of the file I/O functions also expect to be passed a file path, such as:

```
D:\\working\\document1.txt
```

One of the most basic utility functions is ReadFile. This function reads an entire file and returns the contents for you to work with. You could use ReadFile to display the contents of a file in a pop-up dialog as follows:

```
var w = WScript.CreateObject("WScript.Shell");
w.Popup (ReadFile("D:\\document1.txt"))
```

If you use a .WS file, you don't have to place the ReadFile function in your script. Instead, you can handle the function like a library call. With a .WS file, you could use ReadFile as follows:

```
<Job ID="ReadFile">
  <Script LANGUAGE="JScript" SRC="filelib.js" />
```

```
<Script LANGUAGE="JScript">
        theFile = ReadFile("D:\\data.txt")
        WScript.Echo(theFile)
</Script>
</Job>
```

Other functions in the library can be used in similar ways as well. Use the ReadLineN function to read a specific line in a file, such as the fifth line. If you want to read the fifth line in the file, pass in the file name and then the integer value 5, such as:

```
theLine = ReadLineN("D:\\document.txt",5)
```

The ReadLineN function skips four lines in the file and then reads the fifth line. The contents of this line are then returned. To read the first line in the file, you could pass in 1 as the line parameter, such as:

```
theLine = ReadLineN("D:\\document1.txt",1)
```

NOTE Keep in mind that you cannot try to read a line that doesn't exist. For example, if the file contains 12 lines, you can't try to read the 14th line. If you do, no value is returned.

The ReadCharN function is used to read a specific group of characters in a file. For example, if you know that the file contains fixed-length records with each record having 50 characters, you could read in the third record by telling ReadCharN to skip 100 characters and then read 50 characters, such as:

```
theRecord = ReadLineN("D:\\data.txt",100,50)
```

The utility library also provides functions for writing to files. The WriteLine function writes a line to a file. The WriteChar function writes a block of characters to a file. You can use these functions to write onto new files or to append onto existing files. To ensure that existing files are appended, rather than overwritten, the functions make use of the following If Else construct:

```
if (fs.FileExists(theFile))
    var f = fs.OpenTextFile (theFile, ForAppending)
else
    var f = fs.OpenTextFile (theFile, ForWriting, "True")
```

Again, this conditional test checks for a file's existence. If the file exists, it is opened in ForAppending mode. Otherwise, the file is opened in ForWriting mode. You could use the WriteLine function as follows:

```
theFile = "D:\\mydata.txt"
theLine = "William Stanek, wrstane, wrs@tvpress.com, x7789"
WriteLine(theFile,theLine)
```

In a .wsc file you could use WriteLine in much the same way:

```
<Job ID="WriteFile">
  <Script LANGUAGE="JScript" SRC="filelib.js" />
```

```
<Script LANGUAGE="JScript">
  theFile = "D:\\mydata.txt"
  theLine = "William Stanek, wrstane, wrs@tvpress.com, x7789"
  WriteLine(theFile,theLine)
</Script>
</Job>
```

Handling other I/O tasks with the utility library

The I/O utility library also provides functions for handling essential I/O tasks. Two key functions are DisplayConsolePrompt and ReadFromKeyboard. When called from a script using the CScript host, the DisplayConsolePrompt function displays a message at the command prompt and waits for the user to enter a line of information. The function then returns the user's response to the caller. You could use this function anytime you need to obtain input from a user. If you wanted the user to enter the name of a remote system to work with, you could call DisplayConsolePrompt like this:

```
response = DisplayConsolePrompt("Please Enter Remote System Name:")
```

The ReadFromKeyboard function takes this idea a bit further. Not only can you supply a prompt to display, but you can also enter banner text to display to the user. For example, if you called ReadFromKeyboard as follows:

```
response = ReadFromKeyboard("File Administration Script", "Please Enter
Remote System Name:")
```

the user would see the following output at the command prompt:

```
========================================

File Administration Script

========================================

Please Enter Remote System Name:
```

If you would rather display a pop-up dialog, you can use the DisplayDialog function, instead. This function provides a quick and easy way to get input from users through pop-up dialogs. To see how this works, you'll need to give the function a test run. Try calling DisplayDialog as follows:

```
answ = DisplayDialog("Shall We Continue?")
```

You should see a pop-up dialog with the following default settings:

- Title set to "Input Required"
- Timeout set to ten seconds
- Button type set to Yes/No/Cancel

If necessary, you can override the default settings. Simply enter the parameters you'd like to set, such as:

```
answ = DisplayDialog("Shall We Continue?", 20, "Continue Y/N?")
```

Although the `DisplayDialog` function doesn't analyze the user response, the `GetResponse` function does. Using `GetResponse`, you can determine which button a user pressed and then handle the response appropriately. The text values returned by `GetResponse` are:

- ok
- cancel
- abort
- retry
- ignore
- yes
- no
- none

You can call `GetResponse` just as you call `DisplayDialog`, but you can do a bit more with the response—and you don't need to worry about which numeric values equate to which answer types. Here's an example:

```
answ = GetResponse("Shall We Continue?")

if (answ = "yes") {
 //answered yes; handle response
} else
 //answered no or didn't respond; handle response
}
```

When you want to handle or track problems with scripts, you'll find that the `GetErrorInfo` and `WriteEvent` functions are very useful. The `GetErrorInfo` function can be used to examine errors that occur during execution, and it normally is used with try catch statements, such as:

```
try {
  x = data
}
catch(e) {
  WScript.Echo(GetErrorInfo(e, "\r\n"))
}
```

If the `data` variable isn't defined, `GetErrorInfo` returns the following results:

```
Error Type:  [object Error]
Description: 'data' is undefined
```

```
Error Code:  5009
```

These results could then be displayed to the current user.

The `WriteEvent` function writes events to the Application Log on the local system. The type of event written depends on how a status flag is set when the function is called. If the status is set to 0, the function writes an informational event with the description:

```
ScriptName completed successfully.
```

such as:

```
myscript.ws completed successfully.
```

If the status is set to 1, the function writes an error event with the following description:

```
ScriptName completed successfully.
 ScriptPath
 WSHPath
```

such as:

```
myscript.ws did not execute properly.
 E:\scripts\myscript.ws
 F:\WIN2000\system32\cscript.exe
```

You could use `WriteEvent` in a script as follows:

```
//script body here using a status flag
//to track success or failure

WriteEvent(status)
```

Summary

This chapter developed a utility library for handling input and output. You can call the functions of this library from your own scripts at any time. The next chapter discusses a network resource library.

Chapter 28

Library: Network Resource Utilities

The network resource library provides functions for working with drives, network shares, services, open resources, and user sessions. The sections that follow show the source for the script, as well as how the script can be used.

IN THIS CHAPTER

Creating the network resource library

Using the network resource library

Working with library methods

Examining the Network Resource Utility Library

Listing 28-1 shows the source code for the network resource library. Key features implemented in this library are discussed in Chapters 10, 18, and 19.

LISTING 28-1

Managing Network Resources

netreslib.js

```
// ************************
// Script: Network Resource Library
// Version: 1.1.8
// Creation Date: 04/30/2008
// Last Modified: 05/15/2008
// Author: William R. Stanek
// Email: williamstanek@aol.com
// ************************
// Description: Provides a utility library for
//              managing network resources.
// ************************
```

continued

LISTING 28-1   *(continued)*

```javascript
// Copyright (c) 2008 William R. Stanek
// You have a royalty-free right to use these applications, provided
// that you give credit to the author AND agree that the author has
// no warranty, obligations or liability for any of these library
// functions.
// ************************

function GetDriveInfo()
{
  var fs, d, e, s, t, wnet, cname;

  wNet = WScript.CreateObject("WScript.Network");
  cname = wNet.ComputerName;

  fs = new ActiveXObject ("Scripting.FileSystemObject");
  e = new Enumerator(fs.Drives);
  s = "";
  s += "=========================" + "\r\n";
  s += cname + "\r\n";
  s += "=========================" + "\r\n";

  for (; !e.atEnd(); e.moveNext())
  {

    d = e.item();
    switch (d.DriveType)
    {
    case 0: t = "Unknown"; break;
    case 1: t = "Removable"; break;
    case 2: t = "Fixed"; break;
    case 3: t = "Network"; break;
    case 4: t = "CD-ROM"; break;
    case 5: t = "RAM Disk"; break;
    }
    s += "Drive " + d.DriveLetter + ": - " + t + "\r\n";
    if (d.ShareName)
     s += " Share: " + d.ShareName + "\r\n";
    s += "Total space " + Math.round(d.TotalSize/1048576);
    s += " Mbytes" + "\r\n";
    s += "Free Space: " + Math.round(d.FreeSpace/1048576);
    s += " Mbytes" + "\r\n";
    s += "=========================" + "\r\n";
  }
  return(s);
}

function GetDriveInfo2()
```

```
{
  var fs, d, e, s, t, wnet, cname;

  wNet = WScript.CreateObject("WScript.Network");
  cname = wNet.ComputerName;

  fs = new ActiveXObject ("Scripting.FileSystemObject");
  e = new Enumerator(fs.Drives);
  s = "";
  s += "==========================" + "\r\n";
  s += cname + "\r\n";
  s += "==========================" + "\r\n";

  for (; !e.atEnd(); e.moveNext())
  {

    d = e.item();
  if ((d.DriveType < 2) || (d.DriveType > 3))
      continue;

    switch (d.DriveType)
    {
    case 0: t = "Unknown"; break;
    case 1: t = "Removable"; break;
    case 2: t = "Fixed"; break;
    case 3: t = "Network"; break;
    case 4: t = "CD-ROM"; break;
    case 5: t = "RAM Disk"; break;
    }
    s += "Drive " + d.DriveLetter + ": - " + t + "\r\n";
    if (d.ShareName)
     s += " Share: " + d.ShareName + "\r\n";
    s += "Total space " + Math.round(d.TotalSize/1048576) ;
    s += " Mbytes" + "\r\n";
    s += "Free Space: " + Math.round(d.FreeSpace/1048576);
    s += " Mbytes" + "\r\n";
    s += "==========================" + "\r\n";
  }
    return(s);
}

function CheckFreeSpace()
{
  var fs, d, e, s, tspace, fspace, wnet, cname;

  wnet = WScript.CreateObject("WScript.Network");
  cname = wnet.ComputerName;

  fs = new ActiveXObject ("Scripting.FileSystemObject");
```

continued

LISTING 28-1   *(continued)*

```
    e = new Enumerator(fs.Drives);
    s = "";
    s += "=========================" + "\r\n";
    s += cname + "\r\n";
    s += "=========================" + "\r\n";

    for (; !e.atEnd(); e.moveNext())
    {

      d = e.item();
      if ((d.DriveType < 2) || (d.DriveType > 3))
        continue
      tspace = Math.round(d.TotalSize/1048576);
      fspace = Math.round(d.FreeSpace/1048576);
      if (fspace < (tspace*.1))
       {
        s += "Drive " + d.DriveLetter;
        if (d.VolumName)
         s += "Volume: " + d.VolumName;
        if (d.ShareName)
         s += " Share: " + d.ShareName;
        s += "\r\n!!!" + "\r\n";
        s += "Free Space: " + fspace;
        s += " Mbytes" + "\r\n";
        s += "!!!" + "\r\n";
       }

    }
    return(s);
}

function MapDrive(drv, nshare)
{

    fs = new ActiveXObject("Scripting.FileSystemObject");
    if (fs.DriveExists(drv))
     {
      var wn = WScript.CreateObject ("WScript.Network");
      wn.RemoveNetworkDrive(drv);
     }
    else
     {
      var wn = WScript.CreateObject ("WScript.Network");
      wn.MapNetworkDrive(drv, nshare);
     }
}
```

```javascript
function defPrinter(dp)
{
 var wn = WScript.CreateObject("WScript.Network");
 wn.SetDefaultPrinter (dp);
}

function AddPrinter(prntr, pshare)
{
 var wn = WScript.CreateObject("WScript.Network");
 wn.AddPrinterConnection(prntr, pshare);
}

function RemPrinter(prntr)
{
 var wn = WScript.CreateObject("WScript.Network");
 wn.RemovePrinterConnection (prntr);
}

function getServiceInfo(domain,system)
{
  var lf, ret, tlist;
  lf = "\r\n";
  ret = "";

  var comp = GetObject("WinNT://" + domain + "/" + system);
  tlist = new Enumerator(comp);

  for (; !tlist.atEnd(); tlist.moveNext())
  {

   s = tlist.item();

   if (s.Class == "Service") {

       //Display service properties
       ret += s.Class + " " + s.Name + lf;
       ret += "==============================" + lf;
       ret += "StartType: " + s.StartType + lf;
       ret += "ServiceType: " + s.ServiceType + lf;
       ret += "DisplayName: " + s.DisplayName + lf;
       ret += "Path: " + s.Path + lf;
       ret += "ErrorControl: " + s.ErrorControl + lf;
       ret += "HostComputer: " + s.HostComputer + lf;
       ret += "LoadOrderGroup: " + s.LoadOrderGroup + lf;
       ret += "ServiceAccountName: " + s.ServiceAccountName + lf;

       try {
        ret += "Dependencies: " + s.Dependencies + lf;
       }
```

continued

643

LISTING 28-1   *(continued)*

```javascript
      catch (e) {
       //property setting not available or is array
       }
      try {
      //services can have multiple dependencies
       e = s.Dependencies.toArray();
        for (opt in e)
        {
          ret += "Dependencies: " + e[opt] + lf;
        }
      }
      catch (e) {
        //property setting not available
      }
      try {
        ret += "Status: " + s.Get("Status") + lf;
      }
      catch (e) {
        //property setting not available
      }

    }

    ret += lf;

  }

  return (ret);
}

function checkService(domain, system, service)
{

  var lf, ret, tlist;
  lf = "\r\n";
  ret = "";

  var comp = GetObject("WinNT://" + domain + "/" + system);
  tlist = new Enumerator(comp);

  for (; !tlist.atEnd(); tlist.moveNext())
  {

   s = tlist.item();

   if (s.Class == "Service") {
```

```
if (s.DisplayName == service || s.Name == service) {

    ret += "=========================================" + lf;
    ret += "Checking status of " + s.Name + lf;

    switch (s.Status) {
    case 1 :
        ret += "=========================================" + lf;
        ret += "Service not running." + lf;
        ret += "=========================================" + lf;
        break;
    case 2 :
        ret += "=========================================" + lf;
        ret += "Service is starting..." + lf;
        ret += "=========================================" + lf;
        break;
    case 3 :
        ret += "=========================================" + lf;
        ret += "Service is stopping..." + lf;
        ret += "=========================================" + lf;
        break;
    case 4 :
        ret += "=========================================" + lf;
        ret += "Service is running normally." + lf;
        ret += "=========================================" + lf;
        break;
    case 5 :
        ret += "=========================================" + lf;
        ret += "Service is resuming..." + lf;
        ret += "=========================================" + lf;
        break;
    case 6 :
        ret += "=========================================" + lf;
        ret += "Service is pausing." + lf;
        ret += "=========================================" + lf;
        break;
    case 7 :
        ret += "=========================================" + lf;
        ret += "Service is paused." + lf;
        ret += "=========================================" + lf;
        break;
    case 8 :
        ret += "=========================================" + lf;
        ret += "Service error!" + lf;
        ret += "=========================================" + lf;
        break;
    }
  }
}
```

continued

LISTING 28-1   *(continued)*

```
    }

    return (ret);

}

function startService(domain, system, service)
{

  var lf, ret;
  lf = "\r\n";
  ret = "";

  var s = GetObject("WinNT://" + domain + "/" + system + "/" + service +
  ",service");

  if (s.Status == 1) {
     s.Start();
     ret += "=======================================" + lf;
     ret += "Starting Service..." + s.Name + lf;
     ret += "=======================================" + lf;

  } else {
     ret += "=======================================" + lf;
     ret += s.Name + " may already be started." +lf;
     ret += "=======================================" + lf;
     ret += checkService(domain, system, service)
  }

  return (ret);

}

function stopService(domain, system, service)
{

  var lf, ret;
  lf = "\r\n";
  ret = "";

  var s = GetObject("WinNT://" + domain + "/" + system + "/" + service +
  ",service");

  if (s.Status == 4) {
     s.Stop();
     ret += "=======================================" + lf;
     ret += "Stopping Service..." + s.Name + lf;
```

```
      ret += "=======================================" + lf;

   } else {
      ret += "=======================================" + lf;
      ret += s.Name + " may already be stopped." +lf;
      ret += "=======================================" + lf;
      ret += checkService(domain, system, service)
   }

   return (ret);

}

function pauseService(domain, system, service)
{

   var lf, ret;
   lf = "\r\n";
   ret = "";

   var s = GetObject("WinNT://" + domain + "/" + system + "/" + service +
   ",service");

   if (s.Status == 4) {
      s.Pause();
      ret += "=======================================" + lf;
      ret += "Pausing Service..." + s.Name + lf;
      ret += "=======================================" + lf;

   } else {
      ret += "=======================================" + lf;
      ret += s.Name + " may already be paused." +lf;
      ret += "=======================================" + lf;
      ret += checkService(domain, system, service)
   }

   return (ret);

}

function resumeService(domain, system, service)
{

   var lf, ret;
   lf = "\r\n";
   ret = "";

   var s = GetObject("WinNT://" + domain + "/" + system + "/" + service +
   ",service");
```

continued

LISTING 28-1   *(continued)*

```
  if (s.Status == 7) {
     s.Continue();
     ret += "=======================================" + lf;
     ret += "Resuming Service..." + s.Name + lf;
     ret += "=======================================" + lf;

  } else {
     ret += "=======================================" + lf;
     ret += s.Name + " may already be running." +lf;
     ret += "=======================================" + lf;
     ret += checkService(domain, system, service)
  }

  return (ret);

}

function checkRS(domain, system)
{
  var lf, rList, sList, resource, ret, session;

  lf = "\r\n";
  var s = GetObject("WinNT://" + domain + "/" + system +
  "/lanmanserver,fileservice");

  ret = "";
  ret += "===============================" + lf;
  ret += "Checking Resources and Sessions" + lf;
  ret += lf;
  ret += s.HostComputer + lf;
  ret += "===============================" + lf;

  rList = new Enumerator(s.Resources());

   for (; !rList.atEnd(); rList.moveNext())
   {
    resource = rList.item();
    ret += "Resource path: " + resource.Path + lf;
   }

  sList = new Enumerator(s.Sessions());

   for (; !sList.atEnd(); sList.moveNext())
   {
    session = sList.item();
    ret += "Session name: " + session.Name + lf;
   }
```

```
    return (ret);
}

function viewDetailedRS(domain, system)
{

  var lf, rList, sList, resource, ret, session;

  lf = "\r\n";
  var s = GetObject("WinNT://" + domain + "/" + system +
  "/lanmanserver,fileservice");

  ret = "";
  ret += "==============================" + lf;
  ret += "Getting Detailed Information" + lf;
  ret += "for Resources and Sessions" + lf + lf;
  ret += s.HostComputer + lf;
  ret += "==============================" + lf;

  ret += "==============================" +lf;
  ret += "Open Files: " + lf +lf;

  rList = new Enumerator(s.Resources());

  for (; !rList.atEnd(); rList.moveNext())
  {
   resource = rList.item()
   ret += "File or Folder Path: " + resource.Path +lf;
   ret += "Number of Locks: " + resource.LockCount +lf;
   ret += "User: " + resource.User + lf
  }


  ret += "==============================" +lf;
  ret += "User Sessions: " + lf + lf;

  sList = new Enumerator(s.Sessions());

  for (; !sList.atEnd(); sList.moveNext())
  {
   session = sList.item()
   ret += "Session name: " + session.Name +lf;
   ret += "User: " + session.User +lf;
   ret += "Computer: " + session.Computer +lf;
   ret += "Connect Time: " + session.ConnectTime +lf;
   ret += "Idle Time: " + session.IdleTime +lf;

  }
```

continued

LISTING 28-1 *(continued)*

```
    ret += "===============================" +lf;
    return (ret);
}

function viewShareInfo(domain, system, share)
{
  var lf, ret;

  lf = "\r\n";
  ret = "";

  var fs = GetObject("WinNT://" + domain + "/" + system + "/LanmanServer/" +
  share + ",fileshare");

  ret += "===============================" +lf;
  ret += fs.Name + " Information " + lf;
  ret += "===============================" +lf;
  ret += "Current User Count: " + fs.CurrentUserCount + lf;
  ret += "Description: " + fs.Description + lf;
  ret += "Host Computer: " + fs.HostComputer + lf;
  ret += "Maximum User Count: " + fs.MaxUserCount + lf;
  ret += "File Path: " + fs.Path + lf;
  ret += "===============================" +lf;

  return (ret);
}

function createShare(domain, system, sharename, path)
{

  var lf;

  lf = "\r\n";
  var s = GetObject("WinNT://" + domain + "/" + system +
  "/LanmanServer,fileservice");

  val = "";

  var fs = s.Create("FileShare", sharename);
  fs.Path = path;
  fs.MaxUserCount = -1;
  fs.SetInfo();

}

function deleteShare(domain, system, sharename)
{
```

```
var lf;

lf = "\r\n";
var s = GetObject("WinNT://" + domain + "/" + system +
"/LanmanServer,fileservice");

val = "";

var fs = s.Delete("FileShare", sharename);

}
```

Using the Network Resource Utility Library

As you've seen from Listing 28-1, the network resource utility library provides many custom functions. Calling these ready-to-use functions from within your own scripts can save you time and effort.

Using GetDriveInfo

The GetDriveInfo function returns a summary of all drives on a system. If you want to run the script as a nightly AT job, you can log the information to a file using the .wsf file shown in Listing 28-2. This script uses the I/O utility library (iolib.js) and the network resource library (netreslib.js).

The results of the script are stored in a file called logfile.txt. Sample output for this file is shown in the listing. Because the WriteChar function appends to existing files, information is added to the log file each time you run the script.

LISTING 28-2

Getting and Logging Drive Information

logdriveinfo.wsf

```
<Job ID="LogDriveInfo">
  <Script LANGUAGE="JScript" SRC="iolib.js" />
  <Script LANGUAGE="JScript" SRC="netreslib.js" />
  <Script LANGUAGE="JScript">
   checkDrive = GetDriveInfo()
   WriteChar("logfile.txt",checkdrive)
  </Script>
</Job>
```

continued

LISTING 28-2   *(continued)*

Output into logfile.txt

```
========================
ZETA
========================
Drive C: - Fixed
Total space 2047 Mbytes
Free Space: 564 Mbytes
========================
Drive G: - Removable
Total space 96 Mbytes
Free Space: 39 Mbytes
========================
Drive H: - CD-ROM
Total space 584 Mbytes
Free Space: 0 Mbytes
========================
```

The GetDriveInfo function, as currently written, checks all drives on the system, including removable drives. These drives must have media. If they don't, you may see a prompt asking you to check the drive. To get a report of fixed and network drives only, use the GetDriveInfo2 function. These statements within the For loop cause the function to skip checks for removable and CD-ROM drives:

```
if ((d.DriveType < 2) || (d.DriveType > 3))
     continue
```

Using CheckFreeSpace

Another useful function for tracking drive info is CheckFreeSpace. CheckFreeSpace returns a warning if a fixed or network drive has less than 10 percent free space available. The code that checks for free space is:

```
tspace = Math.round(d.TotalSize/1048576)
fspace = Math.round(d.FreeSpace/1048576)
if (fspace < (tspace*.1))
```

Here, you take the total free space and multiply by .1 to come up with a value to compare to the amount of free space. The code that checks the free space percentage is easily updated. For example, if you want to report errors when there is 25 percent free space, you can update the function as follows:

```
tspace = Math.round(d.TotalSize/1048576)
fspace = Math.round(d.FreeSpace/1048576)
if (fspace < (tspace*.25))
```

The CheckFreeSpace function can also be run as a nightly AT job. Listing 28-3 shows a sample .wsf file that maps a network share and then updates a central log file. Sample output for this log file is shown.

LISTING 28-3

Examining Free Space on a System

checkdriveinfo.wsf

```
<Job ID="DriveInfo">
  <Script LANGUAGE="JScript" SRC="iolib.js" />
  <Script LANGUAGE="JScript" SRC="netreslib.js" />
  <Script LANGUAGE="JScript">
  checkDrive = CheckFreeSpace()
  MapDrive("X:", "\\\\Omega\\data")
  WriteChar("X:\\dspace.log",checkdrive)
  MapDrive("X:")
  </Script>
</Job>
```

Output into dspace.log

```
========================
ZETA
========================
Drive C
!!!
Free Space: 8 Mbytes
!!!
========================
OMEGA
========================
Drive C
!!!
Free Space: 12 Mbytes
!!!
```

Using MapDrive

MapDrive provides a single function for connecting and disconnecting drives. If the drive referenced in the first parameter exists, the drive is disconnected. Otherwise, the drive is connected to the network share passed in the second parameter. You can use MapDrive to connect a drive as follows:

```
MapDrive("Z:", "\\\\Zeta\\logs")
```

Later, you can disconnect the drive by calling:

```
MapDrive("Z:")
```

Working with printers

The network resource library also has functions for working with printers. These functions are defPrinter for setting a default printer, AddPrinter for adding a printer connection, and RemPrinter for removing a printer connection. The first parameter for all of these functions is the local name of the printer you are working with. AddPrinter expects a second parameter, which is the name of the network printer share you are connecting. You can call AddPrinter in a script as follows:

```
AddPrinter("MarketingPrinter", "\\\\Omega\\Prtrs\\Marketing")
```

Viewing, checking, and managing services

You'll find two key functions for viewing and checking Windows services: getServiceInfo and checkService. The getServiceInfo function provides a detailed summary of all services on a specified computer. For example, you could examine all the services on a computer called Jupiter in the Marketing domain as follows:

```
WScript.Echo(getServiceInfo("Marketing","Jupiter"))
```

The results would look similar to the following:

```
Service Alerter
===============================
StartType: 2
ServiceType: 32
DisplayName: Alerter
Path: F:\WINNT\System32\services.exe
ErrorControl: 1
HostComputer: WinNT://marketing/jupiter
LoadOrderGroup:
ServiceAccountName: LocalSystem
Dependencies: LanmanWorkstation

Service AppMgmt
===============================
StartType: 3
ServiceType: 32
DisplayName: Application Management
Path: F:\WINNT\system32\services.exe
ErrorControl: 1
HostComputer: WinNT://marketing/jupiter
```

```
LoadOrderGroup:
ServiceAccountName: LocalSystem
...
...
Service Wmi
===============================
StartType: 3
ServiceType: 32
DisplayName: Windows Management Instrumentation Driver Extensions
Path: F:\WINNT\system32\Services.exe
ErrorControl: 1
HostComputer: WinNT://marketing/jupiter
LoadOrderGroup:
ServiceAccountName: LocalSystem
```

The checkService function displays the status of a service on a specified system. The service can be referenced by display name or by the actual service name. For example, you could reference the WinMgmt service:

```
WScript.Echo(checkService("seattle", "Zeta", "WinMgmt"))
```

or the Windows Management Instrumentation service:

```
WScript.Echo(checkService("seattle", "Zeta",
"Windows Management Instrumentation"))
```

If the service is running normally, the output you see is:

```
==========================================
Checking status of WinMgmt
==========================================
Service is running normally.
==========================================
```

If you need to manage services on a remote system, you'll find that the startService, stopService, pauseService, and resumeService functions are very handy. As the names imply, these functions start, stop, pause, or resume services, respectively. Be sure to specify the domain, system, and service name when calling these functions, such as:

```
WScript.Echo(startService("seattle", "Zeta", "WinMgmt"))
```

The return value from the function tells you one of two things. If the service was stopped, you'll get the following message:

```
==========================================
Starting Service...WinMgmt
==========================================
```

This message tells you that the service is being started. If the service wasn't stopped, however, you'll get this message:

```
==========================================
WinMgmt may already be started.
==========================================
==========================================
Checking status of WinMgmt
==========================================
Service is running normally.
==========================================
```

The function displays a message that tells you the service may already be started and then calls the `checkService` function in order to obtain a more precise status.

Using checkRS and viewDetailedRS

The `checkRS` and `viewDetailedRS` functions display information about open resources and user sessions. `checkRS` returns summary information. `viewDetailedRS` returns detailed information. Both functions expect to be passed a domain and system name to work with, such as:

```
WScript.Echo(checkRS("seattle", "zeta"))
```

The return values from `checkRS` are formatted as follows:

```
==============================
Checking Resources and Sessions

WinNT://seattle/zeta
==============================
Resource path: E:\myBooks
Resource path: E:\myBooks\Apartments.doc
Session name: ADMINISTRATOR\127.0.0.1
```

The return values from `viewDetailedRS` are formatted like this:

```
==============================
Getting Detailed Information
for Resources and Sessions

WinNT://seattle/zeta
==============================
==============================
Open Files:

File or Folder Path: E:\myBooks
Number of Locks: 0
User: ADMINISTRATOR
File or Folder Path: E:\myBooks\Apartments.doc
```

```
Number of Locks: 3
User: ADMINISTRATOR
==============================
User Sessions:

Session name: ADMINISTRATOR\127.0.0.1
User: ADMINISTRATOR
Computer: 127.0.0.1
Connect Time: 819
Idle Time: 803
==============================
```

Using viewShareInfo, createShare, and deleteShare

The final set of utility functions is designed to work with network shares. You use `viewShareInfo` to obtain summary information for a named share. Here's how you could examine the netlogon share on a computer called Goldbug in the Gemini domain:

```
WScript.Echo(viewShareInfo("Gemini", "Goldbug", "netlogon"))
```

The return value would look similar to the following:

```
==============================
NETLOGON Information
==============================
Current User Count: 0
Description: Logon server share
Host Computer: WinNT://gemini/goldbug
Maximum User Count: -1
File Path: F:\WINNT\sysvol\sysvol\gemini.com\SCRIPTS
==============================
```

The `createShare` function provides a quick and easy way to create shared folders on remote computers. Just call the function with the domain name, remote system name, share name, and folder path, such as:

```
createShare("gemini", "goldbug", "UserData", "e:\\Users\\Data")
```

Don't worry if you make a mistake; you can use the `deleteShare` function to delete the share:

```
deleteShare("gemini", "goldbug", "UserData")
```

Summary

This chapter developed a utility library for managing network resources. Through batch script (.wsf) files, you can access these utility functions in any of your scripts. The next chapter provides a utility library for managing accounts.

Chapter 29

Library: Account Management Utilities

IN THIS CHAPTER

Creating the account
management library

Using the account management
library

Working with library methods

As you set out to manage accounts, you may want to keep the account management library in mind. This library provides functions for managing user, group, and computer accounts, as well as domain account policies. Through batch scripts (.wsf) files, you can access these utility functions in any of your scripts.

Building the Account Management Library

Listing 29-1 provides the source code for the account management library. As you examine the listing, note the function names and how the functions are implemented. If you have specific questions on the techniques used in the listing, you'll find related discussions in Chapters 17 and 20.

LISTING 29-1

Account Management Utility Library

accountlib.js

```
// ************************
// Script: Account Management Library
// Version: 1.1.5
// Creation Date: 04/22/2008
// Last Modified: 05/05/2008
// Author: William R. Stanek
// E-mail: williamstanek@aol.com
```

continued

LISTING 29-1   (continued)

```
// ************************
// Description: Provides a utility library for
//              managing Windows accounts.
// ************************
// Copyright (c) 2008 William R. Stanek
// You have a royalty-free right to use these applications,.
// provided that you give credit to the author AND agree that
// the author has no warranty, obligations or liability for any
// of these library functions.
// ************************


//Domain management functions

function setMinPasswordLength(domain, passLength)
{
  var dom = GetObject("WinNT://" + domain);
  dom.Put("MinPasswordLength", passLength);
  dom.SetInfo();

  return ("Minimum Password Length: " + dom.Get("MinPasswordLength"));

}

function setPasswordAge(domain, minAge, maxAge)
{
  var lf, ret, passMinAge, passMaxAge;
  lf = "\r\n";
  ret = "";

  var dom = GetObject("WinNT://" + domain);
  dom.Put("MinPasswordAge", 86400 * minAge);
  dom.Put("MaxPasswordAge", 86400 * maxAge);
  dom.SetInfo();

  passMinAge = dom.Get("MinPasswordAge") / 86400;
  passMaxAge = dom.Get("MaxPasswordAge") / 86400;

  ret += "Minimum Password Age: " + passMinAge + " days" + lf;
  ret += "Maximum Password Age: " + passMaxAge + " days";

  return (ret);
}

function setPasswordHistory(domain, histLength)
{
  var ret;
  ret = "";
```

```
  var dom = GetObject("WinNT://" + domain);
  dom.Put("PasswordHistoryLength", histLength);
  dom.SetInfo();

  return("Password History Length: " + dom.Get("PasswordHistoryLength"));
}

function setAccountLockoutInfo(domain, maxBad, unlockInt, lockoutObs)
{

  var lf, ret, maxBad, autoU, lockO;
  lf = "\r\n";
  ret = "";

  var dom = GetObject("WinNT://" + domain);
  dom.Put("MaxBadPasswordsAllowed", maxBad);
  dom.Put("AutoUnlockInterval", 60 * unlockInt);
  dom.Put("LockoutObservationInterval", 60 * lockoutObs);
  dom.SetInfo();

  maxBad = dom.Get("MaxBadPasswordsAllowed");
  autoU = dom.Get("AutoUnlockInterval") / 60;
  lockO = dom.Get("LockoutObservationInterval") / 60;

  ret += "Maximum Bad Passwords Allowed: " + maxBad + lf;
  ret += "AutoLock Interval: " + autoU + " minutes" + lf;
  ret += "Lockout Observation Interval: " + lockO + " minutes";

  return (ret);
}

//Computer management functions

function getAllComputers() {

  var lf, ret;
  lf = "\r\n";
  ret = "";


  var prov = GetObject("WinNT:");
  tlist = new Enumerator(prov);

  for (; !tlist.atEnd(); tlist.moveNext())
   {

   s = new Enumerator(tlist.item());

   for (; !s.atEnd(); s.moveNext())
```

continued

LISTING 29-1   *(continued)*

```javascript
    {

      o = s.item();
      if (o.Class == "Computer") {

        try {
          ret += o.Class + " " + o.Name + lf;
          ret += " Owner: " + o.Owner + lf;
          ret += " Division: " + o.Division + lf;
          ret += " OperatingSystem: " + o.OperatingSystem + lf;
          ret += " OS Version: " + o.OperatingSystemVersion + lf;
          ret += " Processor: " + o.Processor + lf;
          ret += " ProcessorCount: " + o.ProcessorCount + lf;
        }
        catch(e) {

          ret += " Not online at this time" + lf;
        }
      }
    }
  }

  return (ret);
}

function getDomainComputers(domain) {

  var lf, ret;
  lf = "\r\n";
  ret = "";

  var dom = GetObject("WinNT://" + domain);

  s = new Enumerator(dom);

  for (; !s.atEnd(); s.moveNext())
  {

    o = s.item();
    if (o.Class == "Computer") {

      try {
        ret += o.Class + " " + o.Name + lf;
        ret += " Owner: " + o.Owner + lf;
        ret += " Division: " + o.Division + lf;
        ret += " OperatingSystem: " + o.OperatingSystem + lf;
        ret += " OS Version: " + o.OperatingSystemVersion + lf;
```

```
        ret += " Processor: " + o.Processor + lf;
        ret += " ProcessorCount: " + o.ProcessorCount + lf;
        }
      catch(e) {

        ret += " Not online at this time" + lf;
        }
      }
    }

  return (ret);
}

function createComputerAccount(container, computer) {

  var rootDSE = GetObject("LDAP://rootDSE");
  domainCont = rootDSE.Get("defaultNamingContext");

  try {
    var cont = GetObject("LDAP://OU=" + container + "," + domainCont);
  }
  catch(e) {
    var cont = GetObject("LDAP://CN=" + container + "," + domainCont);
  }

  var comp = cont.Create("computer","CN=" + computer);

  comp.Put("samAccountName",computer);
  comp.SetInfo();

}

function createEnabledComputerAccount(container, computer) {

  var rootDSE = GetObject("LDAP://rootDSE");
  domainCont = rootDSE.Get("defaultNamingContext");

  try {
    var cont = GetObject("LDAP://OU=" + container + "," + domainCont);
  }
  catch(e) {
    var cont = GetObject("LDAP://CN=" + container + "," + domainCont);
  }

  var comp = cont.Create("computer","CN=" + computer);

  comp.Put("samAccountName",computer);
  comp.SetInfo();
```

continued

LISTING 29-1   *(continued)*

```
  comp.AccountDisabled = "False";
  comp.SetInfo();
}

function deleteComputerAccount(container, computer) {

  var rootDSE = GetObject("LDAP://rootDSE");
  domainCont = rootDSE.Get("defaultNamingContext");

  try {
    var cont = GetObject("LDAP://OU=" + container + "," + domainCont);
  }
  catch(e) {
    var cont = GetObject("LDAP://CN=" + container + "," + domainCont);
  }

  cont.Delete("computer","CN=" + computer);

}

function enableComputerAccount(container, computer) {

  var rootDSE = GetObject("LDAP://rootDSE");
  domainCont = rootDSE.Get("defaultNamingContext");

  try {
    var cont = GetObject("LDAP://OU=" + container + "," + domainCont);
  }
  catch(e) {
    var cont = GetObject("LDAP://CN=" + container + "," + domainCont);
  }

  var comp = cont.GetObject("computer","CN=" + computer);

  comp.AccountDisabled = "False";
  comp.SetInfo();
}

function disableComputerAccount(container, computer) {

  var rootDSE = GetObject("LDAP://rootDSE");
  domainCont = rootDSE.Get("defaultNamingContext");

  try {
    var cont = GetObject("LDAP://OU=" + container + "," + domainCont);
  }
  catch(e) {
    var cont = GetObject("LDAP://CN=" + container + "," + domainCont);
```

```
  }

  var comp = cont.GetObject("computer","CN=" + computer);

  comp.AccountDisabled = "True";
  comp.SetInfo();
}

//User management functions

function createLocalUser(computer, user, password) {

  var obj = GetObject("WinNT://" + computer)
  var usr = obj.Create("user", user)
  usr.SetPassword(password)
  usr.SetInfo()

}

function deleteLocalUser(computer, user) {

  var obj = GetObject("WinNT://" + computer)
  obj.Delete("user", user)

}


function createUser(container, fullName, first, last, samName, password) {

  var rootDSE = GetObject("LDAP://rootDSE");
  domainCont = rootDSE.Get("defaultNamingContext");

  try {
    var cont = GetObject("LDAP://OU=" + container + "," + domainCont);
  }
  catch(e) {
    var cont = GetObject("LDAP://CN=" + container + "," + domainCont);
  }

  var usr = cont.Create("user", "CN=" + fullName);
  usr.samAccountName = samName;
  usr.displayName = fullName;
  usr.givenName = first;
  usr.sn = last;
  usr.userPrincipalName = samName

  usr.SetInfo();

  usr.AccountDisabled = 0;
```

continued

LISTING 29-1   (continued)

```
  usr.SetPassword(password);
  usr.SetInfo();

}

function deleteUser(container, displayName) {

  var rootDSE = GetObject("LDAP://rootDSE");
  domainCont = rootDSE.Get("defaultNamingContext");

  try {
    var cont = GetObject("LDAP://OU=" + container + "," + domainCont);
  }
  catch(e) {
    var cont = GetObject("LDAP://CN=" + container + "," + domainCont);
  }

  cont.Delete("User", "CN=" + displayName);

}

function userMustChangePassword(container, displayName) {

  var rootDSE = GetObject("LDAP://rootDSE");
  domainCont = rootDSE.Get("defaultNamingContext");

  try {
    var cont = GetObject("LDAP://OU=" + container + "," + domainCont);
  }
  catch(e) {
    var cont = GetObject("LDAP://CN=" + container + "," + domainCont);
  }

  var usr = cont.GetObject("User", "CN=" + displayName);

  usr.Put("pwdLastSet", 0)
  usr.SetInfo()

}

function enableUserAccount(displayName) {

  var rootDSE = GetObject("LDAP://rootDSE");
  domainCont = rootDSE.Get("defaultNamingContext");

  try {
    var cont = GetObject("LDAP://" + domainCont);
```

```
  }
  catch(e) {
    var cont = GetObject("LDAP://" + domainCont);
  }

  var usr = cont.GetObject("User", "CN=" + displayName);

  usr.AccountDisabled = 0
  usr.SetInfo()

}

function enableUserAccount(container, displayName) {

  var rootDSE = GetObject("LDAP://rootDSE");
  domainCont = rootDSE.Get("defaultNamingContext");

  try {
    var cont = GetObject("LDAP://OU=" + container + "," + domainCont);
  }
  catch(e) {
    var cont = GetObject("LDAP://CN=" + container + "," + domainCont);
  }

  var usr = cont.GetObject("User", "CN=" + displayName);

  usr.AccountDisabled = 0
  usr.SetInfo()

}

function disableUserAccount(container, displayName) {

  var rootDSE = GetObject("LDAP://rootDSE");
  domainCont = rootDSE.Get("defaultNamingContext");

  try {
    var cont = GetObject("LDAP://OU=" + container + "," + domainCont);
  }
  catch(e) {
    var cont = GetObject("LDAP://CN=" + container + "," + domainCont);
  }

  var usr = cont.GetObject("User", "CN=" + displayName);

  usr.AccountDisabled = 1
  usr.SetInfo()

}
```

continued

LISTING 29-1   *(continued)*

```
function unlockUserAccount(container, displayName) {

  var rootDSE = GetObject("LDAP://rootDSE");
  domainCont = rootDSE.Get("defaultNamingContext");

  try {
    var cont = GetObject("LDAP://OU=" + container + "," + domainCont);
  }
  catch(e) {
    var cont = GetObject("LDAP://CN=" + container + "," + domainCont);
  }

  var usr = cont.GetObject("User", "CN=" + displayName);

  usr.IsAccountLocked = 0
  usr.SetInfo()

}

function changePassword(container, displayName, password) {

  var rootDSE = GetObject("LDAP://rootDSE");
  domainCont = rootDSE.Get("defaultNamingContext");

  try {
    var cont = GetObject("LDAP://OU=" + container + "," + domainCont);
  }
  catch(e) {
    var cont = GetObject("LDAP://CN=" + container + "," + domainCont);
  }

  var usr = cont.GetObject("User", "CN=" + displayName);

  usr.SetPassword(password)
  usr.SetInfo()

}

function accountExpiration(container, displayName, dateString) {

  var rootDSE = GetObject("LDAP://rootDSE");
  domainCont = rootDSE.Get("defaultNamingContext");

  try {
    var cont = GetObject("LDAP://OU=" + container + "," + domainCont);
  }
  catch(e) {
```

```
    var cont = GetObject("LDAP://CN=" + container + "," + domainCont);
  }

  var usr = cont.GetObject("User", "CN=" + displayName);

  usr.AccountExpirationDate = dateString
  usr.SetInfo()

}

//Group management functions

function createGDistGroup (container, groupName, groupSAMName)
{

  var rootDSE = GetObject("LDAP://rootDSE");
  domainCont = rootDSE.Get("defaultNamingContext");

  try {
    var cont = GetObject("LDAP://OU=" + container + "," + domainCont);
  }
  catch(e) {
    var cont = GetObject("LDAP://CN=" + container + "," + domainCont);
  }

  var grp = cont.Create("group", "CN=" + groupName)

  grp.groupType = 2

  if (groupSAMName == null)
    grp.Put("samAccountName", groupName)
  else
    grp.Put("samAccountName", groupSAMName)

  grp.SetInfo()

}

function createDLDistGroup (container, groupName, groupSAMName)
{

  var rootDSE = GetObject("LDAP://rootDSE");
  domainCont = rootDSE.Get("defaultNamingContext");

  try {
    var cont = GetObject("LDAP://OU=" + container + "," + domainCont);
  }
  catch(e) {
    var cont = GetObject("LDAP://CN=" + container + "," + domainCont);
```

continued

LISTING 29-1   *(continued)*

```
  }

  var grp = cont.Create("group", "CN=" + groupName)

  grp.groupType = 4

  if (groupSAMName == null)
    grp.Put("samAccountName", groupName)
  else
    grp.Put("samAccountName", groupSAMName)

  grp.SetInfo()

}

function createUDistGroup (container, groupName, groupSAMName)
{

  var rootDSE = GetObject("LDAP://rootDSE");
  domainCont = rootDSE.Get("defaultNamingContext");

  try {
    var cont = GetObject("LDAP://OU=" + container + "," + domainCont);
  }
  catch(e) {
    var cont = GetObject("LDAP://CN=" + container + "," + domainCont);
  }

  var grp = cont.Create("group", "CN=" + groupName)

  grp.groupType = 8

  if (groupSAMName == null)
    grp.Put("samAccountName", groupName)
  else
    grp.Put("samAccountName", groupSAMName)

  grp.SetInfo()

}

function createGSecGroup (container, groupName, groupSAMName)
{

  var rootDSE = GetObject("LDAP://rootDSE");
  domainCont = rootDSE.Get("defaultNamingContext");
```

```
  try {
    var cont = GetObject("LDAP://OU=" + container + "," + domainCont);
  }
  catch(e) {
    var cont = GetObject("LDAP://CN=" + container + "," + domainCont);
  }

  var grp = cont.Create("group", "CN=" + groupName)

  grp.groupType = -2147483646

  if (groupSAMName == null)
    grp.Put("samAccountName", groupName)
  else
    grp.Put("samAccountName", groupSAMName)

  grp.SetInfo()

}

function createDLSecGroup (container, groupName, groupSAMName)
{

  var rootDSE = GetObject("LDAP://rootDSE");
  domainCont = rootDSE.Get("defaultNamingContext");

  try {
    var cont = GetObject("LDAP://OU=" + container + "," + domainCont);
  }
  catch(e) {
    var cont = GetObject("LDAP://CN=" + container + "," + domainCont);
  }

  var grp = cont.Create("group", "CN=" + groupName)

  grp.groupType = -2147483644

  if (groupSAMName == null)
    grp.Put("samAccountName", groupName)
  else
    grp.Put("samAccountName", groupSAMName)

  grp.SetInfo()

}

function createUSecGroup (container, groupName, groupSAMName)
{
```

continued

LISTING 29-1   *(continued)*

```
  var rootDSE = GetObject("LDAP://rootDSE");
  domainCont = rootDSE.Get("defaultNamingContext");

  try {
    var cont = GetObject("LDAP://OU=" + container + "," + domainCont);
  }
  catch(e) {
    var cont = GetObject("LDAP://CN=" + container + "," + domainCont);
  }

  var grp = cont.Create("group", "CN=" + groupName)

  grp.groupType = -2147483640

  if (groupSAMName == null)
    grp.Put("samAccountName", groupName)
  else
    grp.Put("samAccountName", groupSAMName)

  grp.SetInfo()

}

function deleteGroup (container, groupName)
{

  var rootDSE = GetObject("LDAP://rootDSE");
  domainCont = rootDSE.Get("defaultNamingContext");

  try {
    var cont = GetObject("LDAP://OU=" + container + "," + domainCont);
  }
  catch(e) {
    var cont = GetObject("LDAP://CN=" + container + "," + domainCont);
  }

  cont.Delete("group", "CN=" + groupName)

}

function createLocalGroup(computer, groupName) {

  var obj = GetObject("WinNT://" + computer)
  var grp = obj.Create("group", groupName)
  grp.SetInfo()

}
```

```
function deleteLocalGroup(computer, groupName) {

  var obj = GetObject("WinNT://" + computer)
  obj.Delete("group", groupName)

}

//General computer, group and user functions

function moveAccount(orig, dest, comp) {

  var rootDSE = GetObject("LDAP://rootDSE");
  domainCont = rootDSE.Get("defaultNamingContext");

  try {
    var cont = GetObject("LDAP://OU=" + dest + "," + domainCont);
  }
  catch(e) {
    var cont = GetObject("LDAP://CN=" + dest + "," + domainCont);
  }

  try {
    cont.MoveHere("LDAP://CN=" + comp + ",OU=" + orig + "," + domainCont, "CN=" +
comp);
  }
  catch(e) {
    cont.MoveHere("LDAP://CN=" + comp + ",CN=" + orig + "," + domainCont, "CN=" +
comp);
  }

}

function mrAccount(orig, dest, comp, newcomp) {

  var rootDSE = GetObject("LDAP://rootDSE");
  domainCont = rootDSE.Get("defaultNamingContext");

  try {
    var cont = GetObject("LDAP://OU=" + dest + "," + domainCont);
  }
  catch(e) {
    var cont = GetObject("LDAP://CN=" + dest + "," + domainCont);
  }

  try {
    cont.MoveHere("LDAP://CN=" + comp + ",OU=" + orig + "," + domainCont, "CN=" +
newcomp);
  }
  catch(e) {
```

continued

LISTING 29-1   *(continued)*

```
      cont.MoveHere("LDAP://CN=" + comp + ",CN=" + orig + "," + domainCont, "CN=" +
newcomp);
  }

}

function renameAccount(orig, comp, newcomp) {

  var rootDSE = GetObject("LDAP://rootDSE");
  domainCont = rootDSE.Get("defaultNamingContext");

  try {
    var cont = GetObject("LDAP://OU=" + orig + "," + domainCont);
  }
  catch(e) {
    var cont = GetObject("LDAP://CN=" + orig + "," + domainCont);
  }

  try {
    cont.MoveHere("LDAP://CN=" + comp + ",OU=" + orig + "," + domainCont, "CN=" +
newcomp);
  }
  catch(e) {
    cont.MoveHere("LDAP://CN=" + comp + ",CN=" + orig + "," + domainCont, "CN=" +
newcomp);
  }

}

//check functions

function checkUserGroups(domain, userSAMName) {

  var lf, ret;
  lf = "\r\n";
  ret = "";

  var ntusr = GetObject("WinNT://" + domain + "/" + userSAMName)
  ntList = new Enumerator(ntusr.Groups());

  ret += "=================================" + lf;
  ret += userSAMName + " is a member of: " + lf + lf;

  for (; !ntList.atEnd(); ntList.moveNext())
  {
   s = ntList.item();
   ret += s.Name + lf;
  }
```

```
  return (ret);
}

function checkGroupMembership()
{

  var lf, ret;
  lf = "\r\n";
  ret = "";

  var prov = GetObject("WinNT:")
  tlist = new Enumerator(prov)

  for (; !tlist.atEnd(); tlist.moveNext())
   {

   s = new Enumerator(tlist.item())

   for (; !s.atEnd(); s.moveNext())
    {

    o = s.item();
    if (o.Class == "User") {


      ret += "=====================================" + lf;
      if (o.FullName == "")
       ret += "Account: " + o.Name + lf;
      else
       ret += "Account: " + o.FullName + lf;

      mList = new Enumerator(o.Groups());

      for (; !mList.atEnd(); mList.moveNext())
      {
       usr = mList.item();
       ret += usr.Name + lf;
      }

    }
   }
  }

 return (ret);
}


function checkComputerAccounts() {
```

continued

LISTING 29-1 *(continued)*

```javascript
//This function only checks the Computers and Domain Controllers containers
var lf, ret;
lf = "\r\n";
ret = "";

var prov = GetObject("WinNT:")

tlist = new Enumerator(prov)

for (; !tlist.atEnd(); tlist.moveNext())
 {

 s = new Enumerator(tlist.item());

 for (; !s.atEnd(); s.moveNext())
  {

  o = s.item();
   if (o.Class == "Computer") {

    if (o.AccountDisabled == "True") {

      ret += o.Name + " is disabled" + lf;

    }

   }

  }
 }

 return (ret);
}

function checkUserAccounts() {

 //This function checks all containers for users
 var lf, ret;
 lf = "\r\n";
 ret = "";

 var prov = GetObject("WinNT:");
 tlist = new Enumerator(prov);

 for (; !tlist.atEnd(); tlist.moveNext())
  {
```

```
s = new Enumerator(tlist.item());

for (; !s.atEnd(); s.moveNext())
 {

 o = s.item();
  if (o.Class == "User") {

    if (o.AccountDisabled == 1) {

      ret += o.Name + " is disabled" + lf;

    }


    if (o.IsAccountLocked == 1) {

      ret += o.Name + " is locked" + lf;

    }
  }
 }
}

return (ret);

}
```

Using the Account Management Utilities

The account management library has more than 36 utility functions. After reviewing the source code for the utility library, you are probably ready to put these functions to work on your network. Still, you may need to take a brief look at how the functions are used, and the usage details are exactly what you'll find in the sections that follow.

Configuring domain account policies with the library utilities

The account management library includes four functions for configuring account policies. Each function sets one or more account policy in the designated domain and is used as follows:

- setMinPasswordLength: Sets the minimum password length.
- setPasswordAge: Sets the minimum and maximum password age in days.

- `setAccountLockoutInfo`: Sets the maximum number of bad passwords allowed, the auto unlock interval, and the lockout observation interval. Both intervals are specified in minutes.

- `setPasswordHistory`: Sets the password history length.

Listing 29-2 shows how you could use these functions in a batch script (.wsf) file.

LISTING 29-2

Setting Domain Account Policies with the Utility Library

logdriveinfo.wsf

```
<Job ID="SetDomainAccountPolicy">
  <Script LANGUAGE="JScript" SRC="accountlib.js" />

  <Script LANGUAGE="JScript">
      WScript.Echo(setMinPasswordLength("seattle", 8))
      WScript.Echo(setPasswordAge("seattle", 5, 60))
      WScript.Echo(setAccountLockoutInfo("seattle", 5, 60, 5))
      WScript.Echo(setPasswordHistory("seattle", 5))
  </Script>
</Job>
```

Output

```
Minimum Password Length: 8
Minimum Password Age: 5 days
Maximum Password Age: 60 days
Maximum Bad Passwords Allowed: 5
AutoLock Interval: 60 minutes
Lockout Observation Interval: 5 minutes
Password History Length: 5
```

Managing groups with the library utilities

In the account management library, you'll find a large section of functions for working with groups. As you know from previous discussions, there are several different types of groups, and each type of group has different characteristics. To manage local groups, you can use the `createLocalGroup` and `deleteLocalGroup` functions. When using these functions, be sure to reference the name of the local computer and local group to work with. The following example shows how you could create a local group called `LocalMarketing` on a computer called Harpo:

```
createLocalGroup("Harpo", "LocalMarketing")
```

If you later wanted to delete the group, you could call deleteLocalGroup with the same parameters:

```
deleteLocalGroup("Harpo", "LocalMarketing")
```

You'll also find functions for creating domain security and distribution groups. These functions are:

- createDLDistGroup: Creates a domain-local distribution group
- createGDistGroup: Creates a global distribution group
- createUDistGroup: Creates a universal distribution group
- createDLSecGroup: Creates a domain-local security group
- createGSecGroup: Creates a global security group
- createUSecGroup: Creates a universal security group

You call these functions with the name of the container or organizational unit in which the group should be created and the name of the group, such as:

```
createDLDistGroup ("Engineering", "EngLocalMail")
```

You don't need to specify the CN= or OU= designator. This information is added automatically using the following try catch statement:

```
try {
  var cont = GetObject("LDAP://OU=" + container + "," +
  domainCont);
}
catch(e) {
  var cont = GetObject("LDAP://CN=" + container + "," +
  domainCont);
}
```

NOTE You'll see similar try catch statements used throughout this library. The primary reason to use these statements is to make it easier to manage domain resources—you don't need to worry whether you are referencing a container or an organizational unit.

To delete domain groups, use the deleteGroup function. Because this function has the same syntax, it can be used as follows:

```
deleteGroup("Engineering", "EngLocalMail")
```

Another useful function for working with groups is checkGroupMembership. You can use this function to display or log the group membership of all users in the domain. An example of logging group membership is shown in Listing 29-3.

LISTING 29-3

Getting and Logging Group Membership Information

logmeminfo.wsf

```
<Job ID="LogMemInfo">
  <Script LANGUAGE="JScript" SRC="accountlib.js" />
  <Script LANGUAGE="JScript" SRC="iolib.js" />

  <Script LANGUAGE="JScript">
          WriteChar("logfile.txt",checkGroupMembership())
  </Script>
</Job>
```

Output into logfile.txt

```
====================================
Account: Administrator
Enterprise Admins
Schema Admins
Group Policy Creator Owners
Domain Admins
Domain Users
Administrators
====================================
Account: Guest
Domain Guests
Domain Users
Guests
====================================
Account: Henry Brown
Domain Users
====================================

...

...
====================================
Account: William R. Stanek
Domain Admins
Domain Users
Administrators
====================================
```

Managing users with the library utilities

Like groups, user accounts can be managed locally and in the domain. To manage local user accounts, you can use the createLocalUser and deleteLocalUser functions. When creating a local account, pass in the name of the computer on which to create the account, the name of the account, and the account password. The following example creates an account for tjbrown on a computer called Groucho:

```
createLocalUser("Groucho", "tjbrown", "changeMe")
```

Later, you could delete the account using deleteLocalUser:

```
deleteLocalUser("Groucho", "tjbrown")
```

Creating and deleting domain user accounts is a bit different. When you create a domain account with the utility library, you must pass in the following parameters in this order:

- Container or organizational unit in which the new account should be created
- Full name for the account
- First name
- Last name
- Login name (This parameter also sets the SAM account name.)
- Password

An example follows:

```
createUser("Engineering", "Henry Brown", "Henry", "Brown",
"hbrown", "radicalmamma")
```

The deleteUser function has only two parameters—the container name and the user display name. Following this, you could delete the previous account with this function call:

```
deleteUser("Engineering", "Henry Brown")
```

Functions are also provided to unlock, enable, disable, and force the user to change passwords on the next login. These functions are unlockUserAccount, enableUserAccount, disableUser Account, and userMustChangePassword. The syntax for these functions is as follows:

```
unlockUserAccount("Engineering", "Henry Brown")
enableUserAccount("Engineering", "Henry Brown")
disableUserAccount("Engineering", "Henry Brown")
userMustChangePassword("Engineering", "Henry Brown")
```

Additional utility functions are provided, as well. changePassword is used to set a new password for a user. In this example, you set Harold's password to brownBears:

```
changePassword("Engineering", "Harold Brown", "brownBears")
```

accountExpiration sets the expiration date on the named account. Use a date string to set a specific expiration date:

```
accountExpiration("Engineering", "Harold Brown", "12/31/99")
```

Or use -1 to specify that the account has no expiration date:

```
accountExpiration("Engineering", "Harold Brown", -1)
```

checkUserAccounts returns a list of all accounts that are locked or disabled. You don't need to pass in any parameters when calling this function. Thus, you could call checkUserAccounts as follows:

```
WScript.Echo(checkUserAccounts())
```

And you'd then get a list of locked or disabled accounts:

```
Guest is disabled
krbtgt is disabled
```

The final utility function for working with user accounts is checkUserGroups. This function displays the group membership of a named user. Because the WinNT provider is used to obtain this list, you should be sure to pass in the SAM account name rather than the display name, as well as the NT domain name. In this example, you check the seattle domain for the group membership of wrstanek:

```
checkUserGroups("seattle", "wrstanek")
```

The result is as follows:

```
==================================
wrstanek is a member of:

Enterprise Admins
Domain Admins
Domain Users
Administrators
```

Managing computers with the library utilities

Computer accounts can also be managed with this library. The key functions are the following:

- createComputerAccount: Used to create new computer accounts but not enable them
- createEnabledComputerAccount: Used to create and enable new computer accounts
- deleteComputerAccount: Used to delete computer accounts
- disableComputerAccount: Used to disable computer accounts
- enableComputerAccount: Used to enable computer accounts

These functions all have the same syntax. You pass in the name of container or organization units for the computer account, as well as the account name, such as:

```
createComputerAccount("Computers", "Zippo")
createEnabledComputerAccount("Computers", "Zippo")
deleteComputerAccount("Computers", "Zippo")
disableComputerAccount("Engineering", "Jupiter")
enableComputerAccount("Engineering", "Jupiter")
```

You'll find other utility functions for working with computer accounts, as well. Use getDomain Computers to obtain information on all active computers in the named domain. You could log information for computers in the seattle domain as shown in Listing 29-4.

LISTING 29-4

Obtaining Computer Account Information

logmeminfo.wsf

```
<Job ID="LogMemInfo">
  <Script LANGUAGE="JScript" SRC="accountlib.js" />
  <Script LANGUAGE="JScript" SRC="iolib.js" />

  <Script LANGUAGE="JScript">
          WriteChar("logfile.txt", getDomainComputers("seattle"))
  </Script>
</Job>
```

Output into logfile.txt

```
Computer HARPO
 Not online at this time
Computer OMEGA
 Not online at this time
Computer ZETA
 Owner: William Stanek
 Division: Web@Work
 OperatingSystem: Windows NT
 OS Version: 5.0
 Processor: x86 Family 6 Model 3 Stepping 3
 ProcessorCount: Uniprocessor Free
```

---

getAllComputers returns a similar list for all domains in the domain forest. With check ComputerAccounts, you can check the status of computer accounts in the domain forest. Simply call the function:

```
WScript.Echo(checkComputerAccounts())
```

You'll obtain a list of all disabled computers, such as:

```
Harpo is disabled
Omega is disabled
```

Functions for renaming and moving accounts

We've taken a look at nearly all of the functions in the utility library. The only remaining functions to discuss are the multipurpose functions:

- moveAccount: Used to move computer, user, and group accounts
- renameAccount: Used to rename computer, user, and group accounts
- mrAccount: Used to move and rename computer, user, and group accounts

These functions are easy to use. You pass moveAccount the original container name, the destination container name, and the name of the object to move, such as:

```
moveAccount("Engineering", "Marketing", "Henry Brown")
```

You pass renameAccount the current container, the current name, and the new name for the account, such as:

```
renameAccount("Engineering", "Henry Brown", "Harold Brown")
```

You pass mrAccount the original container name, the destination container name, the name of the object to move, and the new name, such as:

```
mrAccount("Marketing", "Engineering", "Henry Brown", "Harold Brown")
```

That's all there is to it. The functions handle the behind-the-scenes work for you.

Summary

The account management utilities provide a great starting point for managing user, group, and computer accounts. If you want to use these functions in your own scripts, be sure to use batch script (.wsf) files. Remember that you can combine multiple libraries, as well as multiple scripts.

Chapter 30

Library: Building a PowerShell Library

IN THIS CHAPTER

Customizing the PowerShell environment

Building network utilities, with COM, WMI, and .NET

Regular expressions and advanced text processing

I n this chapter, you will see some useful techniques to draw on when building your own functions, filters, and scripts. The idea is not so much to give you "101 useful PowerShell scripts," but rather to build some scripts so you can see techniques that can be applied in many different contexts. First, let's look at how to get PowerShell the way you want it.

Customizing Your PowerShell Environment

There are several ways that you might want to customize the environment for PowerShell. You can use the *profile* if you would like every session to have:

- Additional PowerShell snap-ins loaded
- User-defined functions pre-loaded from a script
- Additional .NET libraries available
- Additional or redefined aliases
- Additional variables predefined
- Customized prompt behavior or window title
- Customized colors

The profile is just a PowerShell script and, as described in Chapter 4, the execution policy of the machine needs to be set to allow scripts to run and may require the profile script to be signed. A Group Policy template file is available from Microsoft's website (go to www.microsoft.com/ downloads and search for PowerShell ADM). This allows the permissions to be set centrally for particular computers or users. For example, a Group Policy object could apply to an Active Directory OU containing servers to require scripts to be signed.

Before looking at things you can add to a profile script, it would be useful to consider what can be done without resorting to scripts at all.

Snap-ins present a problem: If security dictates that the default policy of PowerShell is not to run any scripts at all, how is a product that uses PowerShell supposed to provide the user with a shell with its snap-ins preloaded? If you look at such products, you find they tend to have an icon labeled "PowerShell – product name." Examining the command for these icons, you find that they start PowerShell with the PsConsoleFile parameter. The PS console file is an XML file with a .psc1 extension that lists additional snap-ins. These files aren't signed and can't run scripts—or stop the default profile running. To avoid writing your own XML file, you can use a Cmdlet, Export-Console, which exports an XML file which will then load all the currently loaded snap-ins. For example:

```
export-console -path CustomConsole.psc1
```

A PowerShell shortcut can be created with the following command line:

```
powershell.exe -PsConsoleFile CustomConsole.psc1
```

While on the subject of shortcuts, it is the shortcut that sets the default window title for PowerShell and PowerShell's default background color. If you just run PowerShell.exe without using the short-cut, it will come up in traditional CMD-style black. If you want to specify custom colors—either to make it clear you have loaded a special-purpose configuration of the shell, or just because you might like retro-looking green on black, then this is the easiest place to do it.

One useful technique on Windows Vista and Server 2008 is to configure a second PowerShell shortcut for administrative tasks. By default, both of these operating systems start programs with reduced privileges for users other than the built-in Administrator. Any other user who is a member of the Administrators group will get a reduced privilege shell unless they request otherwise. In the shortcut, you can set the option to "Run as Administrator." In the shortcut's properties, simply go to Shortcut tab and click the Advanced button to set it. You can then change the window title to Windows PowerShell [Administrator] on the General properties page. Because you tend not to look at the window title much when actually using the shell, here is a good case for setting a custom color scheme. Another reason for doing this is that a script may change the window title while PowerShell is running.

If you are creating custom shortcuts to start PowerShell, you can run a script that defines functions, variables, and aliases. If you launch PowerShell with a command line, it will normally exit on com-pletion. The script needs to be specified as a -noExit parameter to avoid PowerShell closing. To ensure that whatever is defined in the script remains after the script has finished, it needs to be dot sourced. So the command becomes:

```
powershell.exe -NoExit ". CustomScript.ps1"
```

Exploring the PowerShell host

If you look at the PowerShell variables (for example, by entering the command `Dir Variable;`), you will see there is one named `Host`. PowerShell is modular and does not need to be run in the command-line mode. Indeed, there are various Microsoft and third-party tools that run PowerShell inside other programs. If you check what is in `$host`, you'll discover some information about the environment where PowerShell is hosted. The command window will look something like this:

```
> $host
Name                : ConsoleHost
Version             : 1.0.0.0
InstanceId          : cf160ee7-d19e-48ea-8f0a-f8a092b44755
UI                  : System.Management.Automation.Internal.Host
                      InternalHostUserInterface
CurrentCulture      : en-GB
CurrentUICulture    : en-US
PrivateData         : Microsoft.PowerShell.ConsoleHost+ConsoleColorProxy
```

Notice that although this was returned by a machine running in British English, the PowerShell UI remains in U.S. English.

There are two properties of interest here, `PrivateData` and `UI`.

The `UI` property contains a single object, `RAW UI`, which you can examine like this:

```
> $host.ui.rawui
ForegroundColor       : DarkYellow
BackgroundColor       : DarkMagenta
CursorPosition        : 0,79
WindowPosition        : 0,23
CursorSize            : 25
BufferSize            : 140,80
WindowSize            : 140,57
MaxWindowSize         : 140,57
MaxPhysicalWindowSize : 160,57
KeyAvailable          : False
WindowTitle           : Windows PowerShell
```

Most of these properties can be ignored, but you can see the foreground and background colors and the window title.

Chapter 21 had a small piece of code to test to see if the user was able to exercise administrative privileges; as described earlier, it's good to have a separate shortcut to start PowerShell as Administrator with different colors and window title. But what if the user just right-clicks the normal PowerShell shortcut and chooses Run as Administrator? Then the window title won't be changed and the screen colors won't be set; so this would be the kind of thing that could be run from a profile.

```
dir Microsoft.PowerShell.Core\Registry::HKEY_USERS\s-1-5-20 `
    -ErrorAction silentlycontinue -errorVariable MyErr | out-null
$global:Admin=(-not $myerr)
If ($global:admin) {$host.ui.rawui.ForegroundColor="yellow"
                    $host.ui.rawui.windowtitle += "[Administrator]"}
```

This piece of script sets a variable for other scripts to check to see if the user is an administrator, rather than just setting the title and foreground color. That way, any script which runs later in the session can check to see if the variable is set and then change its behavior according to its value.

You can also see and customize colors in `$Host.PrivateData`.

```
> $host.PrivateData

ErrorForegroundColor      : Red
ErrorBackgroundColor      : Black
WarningForegroundColor    : Yellow
WarningBackgroundColor    : Black
DebugForegroundColor      : Yellow
DebugBackgroundColor      : Black
VerboseForegroundColor    : Yellow
VerboseBackgroundColor    : Black
ProgressForegroundColor   : Yellow
ProgressBackgroundColor   : DarkCyan
```

You may already have noticed that the background when PowerShell returns an error or writes to the `Debug`, `Error`, `Verbose`, or `Warning` pipes is always black. There is nothing to set these colors when the Windows shortcut tells PowerShell what the background should be. (Normally it is set to `Dark Magenta`, a label that actually corresponds to "PowerShell blue.") You can set the colors for both the text and the background; for example:

```
$host.PrivateData.errorbackgroundColor="DarkMagenta"
```

Of course, this assumes that the background color *is* PowerShell blue, so it is safer to set it to `$host.ui.rawui.backgroundColor`.

PowerShell has a shorthand way of assigning multiple variables to the same value; all the backgrounds can be set with one long line, as follows:

```
$host.PrivateData.errorBackgroundColor =
$host.PrivateData.warningBackgroundColor =
$host.PrivateData.DebugBackgroundColor =
$host.PrivateData.VerboseBackgroundColor = $host.ui.rawui.backgroundColor
```

If you change the background color, you may think the error text has changed to a different foreground color. This is actually an illusion, although you may need to take a screenshot of a window with errors before and after the change and check the pixel color values in a paint program to prove it to yourself!

If you want to have different foreground colors, you can. For example, you might add color to differentiate between Warning, Verbose, and Debug text.

The PowerShell prompt

Veterans of MS-DOS may remember that in the Autoexec.bat file—DOS's equivalent of a profile— you would usually have a PROMPT command. This set an environment variable, also named PROMPT. If it was not set, DOS would have a prompt of C>. To get it to show the path, the prompt would be set to pg ($p being the path and $g being a greater-than sign). The default was changed so that CMD.EXE defaults to pg if nothing else is set, but you can still use prompt [$D] pg to display the date in square brackets before the path, just as you could in the 1980s.

PowerShell has a different approach to the prompt. It manages its own prompt, independent of any prompt you might have in CMD. In fact, if you start PowerShell from inside CMD, it doesn't open a new window, but if you look for a variable named prompt it doesn't have one. There's a prompt function instead. You can see what its code block is by using the following:

```
PS C:\> type function:prompt
'PS ' + $(Get-Location) + $(if ($nestedpromptlevel -ge 1) { '>>' }) + '> '
```

Get-Location is the equivalent of the UNIX "Print Working Directory" command pwd. In fact, it has an alias of pwd. So this function just returns PS, the location, and a greater-than sign: the familiar PowerShell prompt. The prompt is a function—whatever it returns becomes the prompt for the next line. So you could replicate that 80s-style prompt like this:

```
Function prompt {"[" + (get-Date).toString("d") +"]" + (Get-Location) + ">"}
```

But it is a function—so it could do anything. For example, in preparing this book, the publisher works with an 80-column page width for text so the examples have a shortened prompt, but it is still necessary to know the current location. To do this, the prompt function can be changed to show the current location on the window title, and just set the prompt to a minimal >.

```
Function prompt {$host.ui.rawui.windowtitle = Get-Location ; ">"}
```

Adding more to the environment

The prompt is an example of a function that sits naturally in the profile, but you may well have others. Often you will want to load functions, which are contained in a script. Remember that these need to be *dot sourced*. Normally when a script runs, any functions that it defines are only "in scope" for the lifetime of the script. As soon as the script completes, the functions effectively vanish. Prefixing a function or script with a dot tells PowerShell: *"Run this in the current scope, not in its own."* The profile runs at the global level in PowerShell itself, so variables, functions, and aliases it affects are global and accessible for the life of the PowerShell session. But any scripts that it calls need to be dot sourced if they are to leave anything behind.

Snap-ins can be loaded by starting PowerShell with a console file, but this technique is best used for loading different combinations of snap-ins in different sessions. If you always use the same snap-in(s), an `Add-PsSnapIn` command can be added to the profile. For example, Windows Server Backup in Server 2008 has a PowerShell snap-in to manage the backup configuration. This can be made available in every session by adding a line to your profile.

```
Add-PsSnapIn Windows.ServerBackup
```

This way, the backup Cmdlets are always available so you don't have to run the `Add-PsSnapIn` command in every session. However, one word of caution. If you become too used to a snap-in being loaded, it is very easy to forget that you need to explicitly load it when taking a script you have developed to another machine.

The same warning applies to loading .NET assemblies. For example, if you do a lot of work processing photos and want to have the .NET library that gives access to them, then you need to load the library, and the following line can be added to your profile.

```
[reflection.assembly]::loadfile(
"C:\Windows\Microsoft.NET\Framework\v2.0.50727\System.Drawing.dll")
```

Having done so, it is easy to forget that `System.drawing.bitMap` is not a class that PowerShell understands by default. In the same way customizations to object properties that are loaded from XML using the `Update-TypeData` or `Update-FormatData` Cmdlets can be added through the profile, you must remember to explicitly load them on other computers.

As the profile can run any code you could enter at the prompt, you can set variables for use later in the session and define your own aliases. Again, the same warning applies. Aliases of your own will work in scripts on your machine, but taken to another machine without the same aliases they will fail. Some people avoid using any aliases in scripts. Some will allow `CD`, `DIR`, `TYPE`, and others, which are used in the same way that they have been for more than 20 years. Others think it is fine to use PowerShell-defined aliases such as `%` or `GCI`, even away from the prompt. Most people, however, will draw the line at user-defined aliases in a script.

It is still helpful to define new aliases to ease navigation at the command prompt. For example, PowerShell has `Push-Location` and `Pop-Location` Cmdlets to stack previous folder locations. (A stack is a last-in first-out data structure. Items are said to be *pushed* onto the top of the stack and *popped* off again.) Some of the old add-ons for DOS maintained a directory history so it might be nice to do the same in PowerShell: You use `CD` to move to a new directory, and `CD-` to retrace your steps.

To do this, you need to delete the initial alias, which maps CD onto Set-location, and re-alias it to Push-location. Then a new alias CD- can be created for Pop-Location, like this:

```
del Alias:\cd
set-alias -Name cd -Value push-location
set-alias -Name "cd-" -value Pop-Location
```

Now that you know how to configure your environment to work with PowerShell in the way that you want to, it's time to look at some of the functions that you build inside it.

A Generic "choose" Function

Frequently you need to ask users to choose from a set of objects. Sometimes you do this because the user didn't bother to supply the object as a parameter. Sometimes when the command is entered, the user can't know what choices are available, and sometimes it is quicker to choose from a list than it is to enter the selection as a parameter. For example, consider the two command lines for starting virtual machines:

```
Start-vm -VM "London 2008 DC","Paris 2003 SQL"
```

and

```
Choose-vm | start-vm
```

So how to write a Choose- function?

In Chapter 21, you saw the following choose function created as a demonstration of the power of calculated fields in get-table:

```
Function choose-ProcessByProduct
{param ($product)
 $processes= Get-Process| where-object {$_.product -match
[string]$product}
 $Global:Counter=-1
 format-table -inputObject $processes -autosize -property `
@{Label="ID"; expression={ ($global:Counter++)} } , Name, cpu
 $processes[(read-host "Which one ?")]
 }
```

You can rewrite this function as required for each object type you need. So if virtual machines have a Get-VM command, you could insert that, change a few names, and make yourself a choose-VM function.

You have also seen the split() method for text strings; the user's input can be split into an array of items. PowerShell arrays can take an array of indices, so the read-host command can accept comma-separated inputs that can then be split to an array of integers like this:

```
[int[]](Read-Host "Which one(s) ?").Split(",")
```

You can see that this function is gradually getting harder to maintain. The usual way of creating a new Choose- function is to copy an existing one and modify it to suit a new purpose, but as more variations are introduced, the scope for introducing errors increases.

What would be better would be a function that could be handed an array of any object, told which properties to display, get the user to make a single or multiple selection, and return the select object(s). And here it is:

```
Function Choose-List {Param ($InputObject, $Property, [Switch]$multiple)
If ($inputObject -is [Array]) {
   $Global:counter=-1
   $Property=@(@{Label="ID"; Expression={ ($global:Counter++) }}) + $Property
   $InputObject | format-table -autosize -property $Property | out-host
   if ($multiple){$InputObject[[int[]](Read-Host "Which one(s)?").Split(",")]}
   else           { $InputObject[      (Read-Host "Which one ?")        ]}
   }
else {$inputObject}
}
```

Let's break this down line by line:

- The function is passed an array of input objects, a list of properties, and a switch to indicate whether it can return multiple objects.

- If $InputObject is not an array— that is, if it is a single object or empty, then it is returned; otherwise the rest of the code executes.

- $counter starts at –1. This isn't intuitive; the first item in the array has an index of 0 . $counter will be incremented and displayed as a single operation. So counter has to start at 1 less than the first number. The first time it is displayed it will be incremented to 0, and each object will be displayed with a number which matches its array index and The counter needs to be global; otherwise it will be reset between one object being passed to format-table and the next.

- $Property is an array that contains the properties to be displayed. The calculated field to increment and display, $counter, is defined as the only element in a new array, and that array is joined onto $property.

- $input is piped into format-table, which uses $property to choose the columns. The result is explicitly sent to the console; otherwise it would be treated as a result of the function.

- If the -multiple switch was specified, the user is prompted for multiple inputs, which are split and used as the array indices. If it was not, then the user is asked for a single input, which is used as the array index. The select item(s) from the array are returned.

So the `Choose-VM` function, which was mooted previously, is just a way to call `Choose-List`.

```
Function Choose-VM
{param ($Server=".")
 choose-list -multiple -InputObject (Get-VM -Server $Server) `
        -Property @(@{Label="VM Name"; Expression={$_.ElementName}})}
```

In this case, `Get-VM` is another PowerShell function that uses WMI to return objects representing virtual machines. A calculated field is used to display the `ElementName` property with a column heading of `VM Name`, and this is wrapped in `@( )` to make it an array with one item instead of single string.

There will be more uses for this `choose-` function in the next section.

Network Utilities

There can scarcely be an IT professional who hasn't used `Ping` to test network connectivity and `IPConfig` to return information about TCP/IP configuration or manage DHCP settings. Because they are command-line programs, it is perfectly valid to run either of these programs in a PowerShell session but `IPconfig` returns text output. You can't pipe that output into `ping`, and it is hard work to extract just the default gateway or DNS server. The best you can do is copy and paste from the results of `IPconfig` into the command line for `Ping`.

In this section, we will have a look at PowerShell implementations of `Ping` and `IPconfig`.

Finding network adapters

A good place to start would be to get a list of network adapters, and WMI has a ready-made class to provide just that. The following code:

```
Get-WmiObject -nameSpace Root\cimv2 -class Win32_Networkadapter
```

will return the nework adapters on the local computer, so that they can be used in a function. You might want to get only certain adapters so it's better to use a query in the function, like this:

```
Function Get-NetworkAdapter
{Param ($Name="%")
 Get-WmiObject -nameSpace Root\cimv2 '
        -Query "Select * from  Win32_Networkadapter where name like '$name' "}
```

When `Get-NetworkAdapter "%wireless%"` is run, it might return something like this:

```
__GENUS                        : 2
__CLASS                        : Win32_NetworkAdapter
__SUPERCLASS                   : CIM_NetworkAdapter
__DYNASTY                      : CIM_ManagedSystemElement
__RELPATH                      : Win32_NetworkAdapter.DeviceID="9"
```

```
__PROPERTY_COUNT               : 40
__DERIVATION                   : {CIM_NetworkAdapter, CIM_LogicalDevice,
                                  CIM_LogicalElement, CIM_ManagedSystemElement}
__SERVER                       : JAMES-2008
__NAMESPACE                    : Root\cimv2
__PATH                         : \\JAMES-2008\Root\cimv2:Win32_NetworkAdapter
                                  .DeviceID="9"
AdapterType                    : Ethernet 802.3
AdapterTypeId                  : 0
AutoSense                      :
Availability                   : 3
Caption                        : [00000009] Intel(R) Wireless WiFi Link 4965AGN
ConfigManagerErrorCode         : 0
ConfigManagerUserConfig        : False
CreationClassName              : Win32_NetworkAdapter
Description                    : Intel(R) Wireless WiFi Link 4965AGN
DeviceID                       : 9
ErrorCleared                   :
ErrorDescription               :
GUID                           : {B5186613-6363-4AC7-BE32-6B0F04C6D28E}
Index                          : 9
InstallDate                    :
Installed                      : True
InterfaceIndex                 : 11
LastErrorCode                  :
MACAddress                     : 00:21:5C:03:1B:BD
Manufacturer                   : Intel Corporation
MaxNumberControlled            : 0
MaxSpeed                       :
Name                           : Intel(R) Wireless WiFi Link 4965AGN
NetConnectionID                : Wireless Network
NetConnectionStatus            : 2
NetEnabled                     : True
NetworkAddresses               :
PermanentAddress               :
PhysicalAdapter                : True
PNPDeviceID                    : PCI\VEN_8086&DEV_4230&SUBSYS_11118086&REV_61\
                                  FF031BBD00
PowerManagementCapabilities    :
PowerManagementSupported       : False
ProductName                    : Intel(R) Wireless WiFi Link 4965AGN
ServiceName                    : NETw4v64
Speed                          : 54000000
Status                         :
StatusInfo                     :
SystemCreationClassName        : Win32_ComputerSystem
SystemName                     : JAMES-2008
TimeOfLastReset                : 20080921111111.375199+060
```

This is a good start but it is probably not the way you want to see the information, so the next step is to try piping it into Format-Table.

```
Get-NetworkAdapter | format-table -property Name, MACAddress, speed -autosize

Name                                            MACAddress          speed
----                                            ----------          -----
WAN Miniport (SSTP)
WAN Miniport (L2TP)
WAN Miniport (PPTP)                             50:50:54:50:30:30
WAN Miniport (PPPOE)                            33:50:6F:45:30:30
WAN Miniport (IPv6)
WAN Miniport (Network Monitor)
Intel(R) 82566MM Gigabit Network Connection    00:1C:25:BC:C2:76
Wired Virtual Network                          00:1C:25:BC:C2:76 10000000000
WAN Miniport (IP)
Intel(R) Wireless WiFi Link 4965AGN            00:21:5C:03:1B:BD 54000000
isatap.{B5186613-6363-4AC7-BE32-6B0F04C6D28E}                     100000
RAS Async Adapter
Teredo Tunneling Pseudo-Interface              02:00:54:55:4E:01 1073741824
Microsoft Virtual Network Switch Adapter
Internal Virtual Network                       00:15:5D:01:68:01 10000000000
isatap.{D1F84CFF-7092-4720-AEEA-A2D583381787D}                    100000
6TO4 Adapter                                                      100000
Microsoft Windows Mobile Remote Adapter
isatap.{FF66572F-8568-49F2-92A0-2D4A722E719E}                     100000
```

That's better—so the function can be adapted to use Format-Table.

```
Function Get-NetworkAdapter
{Param ($Name="%" , [switch]$Formatted)
$nic=Get-WmiObject -nameSpace Root\cimv2 `
        -Query "Select * from  Win32_Networkadapter where name like '$name' "
if ($formatted) {format-table -autosize -inputObject $nic -property Name, ,
MACAddress   , speed }
else  {$nic}
}

> Get-NetworkAdapter "intel%" -f
Name                                            MACAddress          speed
----                                            ----------          -----
Intel(R) 82566MM Gigabit Network Connection    00:1C:25:BC:C2:76
Intel(R) Wireless WiFi Link 4965AGN            00:21:5C:03:1B:BD 54000000
```

It is worth noting that you could leave Get-NetworkAdapter outputting the raw WMI object and define a formatting XML file instead of using Format-Table. You have multiple options to choose from and which one is "right" will vary with the circumstances.

The list of network adapters isn't in order so it would be good to sort it by name. Also, notice that the speed column is blank for the first one because in this case the cable was disconnected. The parameters passed to Format-Table can be adapted to show disconnected if the speed is null. With a sort added and a calculated speed column, the function looks like this:

```
Function Get-NetworkAdapter {Param ($Name="%" , [switch]$Formatted)
  $nic=Get-WmiObject -nameSpace Root\cimv2 `
           -Query "Select * from Win32_Networkadapter where name like '$name' " |
           sort-object -property name
  if ($formatted) {
       format-table -autosize -inputObject $nic -property Name, MACAddress,
           @{Label="Speed"; Expression={if ($_.Speed -eq $null) {"Disconnected"}
                                        else {$_.Speed}} } }
  else {$nic}
}


> Get-NetworkAdapter  -f

Name                                              MACAddress        Speed
----                                              ----------        -----
6T04 Adapter                                                        100000
Intel(R) 82566MM Gigabit Network Connection       00:1C:25:BC:C2:76 Disconnected
Intel(R) Wireless WiFi Link 4965AGN               00:21:5C:03:1B:BD     54000000
Internal Virtual Network                          00:15:5D:01:68:01  10000000000
isatap.{B5186613-6363-4AC7-BE32-6B0F04C6D28E}                        100000
isatap.{D1F84CFF-7092-4720-AEEA-A2D58381787D}                        100000
isatap.{FF66572F-8568-49F2-92A0-2D4A722E719E}                        100000
Microsoft Virtual Network Switch Adapter                            Disconnected
Microsoft Windows Mobile Remote Adapter                             Disconnected
RAS Async Adapter                                                   Disconnected
Teredo Tunneling Pseudo-Interface                 02:00:54:55:4E:01   1073741824
WAN Miniport (IP)                                                  Disconnected
WAN Miniport (IPv6)                                                Disconnected
WAN Miniport (L2TP)                                                Disconnected
WAN Miniport (Network Monitor)                                    Disconnected
WAN Miniport (PPPOE)                              33:50:6F:45:30:30 Disconnected
WAN Miniport (PPTP)                               50:50:54:50:30:30 Disconnected
WAN Miniport (SSTP)                                                Disconnected
Wired Virtual Network                             00:1C:25:BC:C2:76  10000000000
```

Two final modifications complete the function.

First, it is looking at the local computer only, so it might be useful to add a parameter for the target server. WMI properties use the name __Server, but the Get-WMIObject Cmdlet uses a -computerName parameter. Which you use is up to you, but it is a good idea to be consistent.

Second, most users expect to be able to use * for a wildcard rather than the SQL style % so the final version of the function can replace * with % so they don't need to adapt.

```
Function Get-NetworkAdapter {Param ($Name="%", $Server=".", [switch]$Formatted)
 $name=$name.replace("*","%")
 $nic=Get-WmiObject -nameSpace Root\cimv2 -computername $Server `
         -Query "Select * from Win32_Networkadapter where name like '$name' " |
         sort-object -property name
 if ($formatted) {
     format-table -autosize -inputObject $nic -property Name, MACAddress,
         @{Label="Speed"; Expression={if ($_.Speed -eq $null) {"Disconnected"}
                                       else {$_.Speed}} } }
 else  {$nic}
 }
```

This would also be a good place to create a `Choose-NetworkAdapter` function.

```
Function Choose-NetworkAdapter {param ($Server=".")
 choose-list -InputObject (Get-networkAdapter -Server $Server) `
            -multiple -Property name,MacAddress}
```

Now you can get one or more network adapter(s) by choosing with this function or by specifying the name to the `Get-NetworkAdapter`. It's time to put the object to use.

Get-Ipconfig

`IPconfig` is an example of a command-line program that just looks *wrong* from a PowerShell perspective. For example, where other TCP/IP utilities use a minus sign (-) for their switches, `IPconfig` uses a forward slash (/). Its functionality seems to have grown without being planned.

On modern versions of Windows, `IPconfig` does three main things. It tells you the IP configuration, manages automatic configuration (`/release` and `/renew`) and manages DNS behavior (`/FlushDNS` and `/RegisterDNS` and `/DisplayDNS`). This last one is interesting: Windows has a DNS cache that holds mappings of names to IP addresses. It also has an ARP cache that holds the mappings of IP addresses to MAC addresses. A separate program (`ARP.EXE`) gives access to the ARP cache, but DNS cache support has been lashed onto `IPconfig`. If things were consistent, either ARP would be part of `IPconfig` or DNS would have its own tool.

How would PowerShell approach this with the benefit of starting a design from scratch? First, it would use a `Verb-Noun` name. The psychology of this shouldn't be underestimated; if you have a command named `Get-IpConfiguration` you would start other functions with names like `Release-IpConfiguration`, `Renew-Ipconfiguration` and so on. The change is subtle but important; the meaning of the command is in the name, not the switches.

Second, if there is a tool for selecting network adapters, then it should be possible to pass one or more network adapters as a parameter to any of these commands. But it should also be possible to pass a name to the command as well.

In Chapter 25, you saw that you could go from an object to its associated objects and that it was possible to discover the classes with `classdefsonly`. In this case, you could do the following:

```
> $nic=choose-networkAdapter
> gwmi -q "associators of {$nic} where classDefsOnly"

Win32_ComputerSystem                        Win32_PnPEntity
Win32_NetworkAdapterConfiguration           Win32_IRQResource
Win32_DeviceMemoryAddress                   Win32_NetworkProtocol
Win32_SystemDriver
```

If you were exploring the WMI objects, you would probably look at the `Win32_NetworkProtocol` class first, but this contains entries for different members of the IP family (TCP/IPv4, UDP/IPv4, TCP/IPv6, and UDP/IPv6) so that's not it. Next you would look at the properties of `Win32_NetworkAdapterConfiguration`:

```
gwmi -q "associators of {$nic} where resultClass=
Win32_NetworkAdapterConfiguration" | gm
```

This returns about 70 properties, which look useful.

These include:

- `Description, MACAddress, ServiceName`
- `IPEnabled, IPAddress, DefaultIPGateway, IPSubnet`
- `DHCPEnabled, DHCPServer, DHCPLeaseObtained and DHCPLeaseExpires`
- `DNSHostName, DNSDomain, DNSServerSearchOrder,`
  `DNSDomainSuffixSearchOrder, DNSEnabledForWINSResolution`
- `WINSPrimaryServer, WINSSecondaryServer, WINSEnableLMHostsLookup,`
  `WINSScopeID`

There isn't a good way to show these as a table so for the full list it's necessary to use `Format-List`. However, a function could easily have switches for two formats—in the following example that's what the `-Short` and `-all` switches are used for.

```
Function get-IpConfig {Param ($nic , [Switch]$Short,  [Switch]$All)
$config=Get-wmiObject -query "associators of {$nic} where resultClass=
Win32_NetworkAdapterConfiguration"
If ($short) {$config | format-table -autosize -property IPAddress,
                     DefaultIPGateway  , IPSubnet }
Else {if ($all) {$config | format-list -property Description, ServiceName,
                  MACAddress, IPAddress, DefaultIPGateway , IPSubnet ,
                  DHCPEnabled , DHCPServer , DHCPLeaseObtained ,
                  DHCPLeaseExpires , DNSHostName , DNSDomain ,
                  DNSServerSearchOrder, DNSDomainSuffixSearchOrder ,
                  DNSEnabledForWINSResolution, WINSPrimaryServer ,
```

```
                        WINSSecondaryServer , WINSEnableLMHostsLookup,
                        WINSScopeID}
           Else {$Config} }
       }
```

This can be used in multiple ways—first, to return the object that will display a default set of properties:

```
> get-ipconfig $nic
DHCPEnabled        : True
IPAddress          : {192.168.1.101, fe80::a9bc:5965:f841:3862}
DefaultIPGateway   : {192.168.1.1}
DNSDomain          :
ServiceName        : BCM43XV
Description        : Broadcom 802.11g Network Adapter
Index              : 5
```

This set of properties is defined in Types.psXML (see Chapter 21 for how you can redefine it). Used this way, the function returns the WMI object, which gives rise to a second way to use it—to get one property:

```
> (get-ipconfig $nic).DNSServerSearchOrder
194.168.4.100
194.168.8.100
```

Notice that DNSSearchServerOrder is a single array property so it has more than one value.

The other way to use the Function is to take advantage of the the formatted outputs which it defines—first the short form as a single line per network card:

```
> get-ipconfig $nic -short

IPAddress                                   DefaultIPGateway IPSubnet
---------                                   ---------------- --------
{192.168.1.101, fe80::a9bc:5965:f841:3862} {192.168.1.1}    {255.255.255.0, 64}
```

And then the long form as a list:

```
> get-ipconfig $nic -all

Description        : Broadcom 802.11g Network Adapter
ServiceName        : BCM43XV
MACAddress         : 00:19:7D:3A:1F:AB
IPAddress          : {192.168.1.101, fe80::a9bc:5965:f841:3862}
DefaultIPGateway   : {192.168.1.1}
IPSubnet           : {255.255.255.0, 64}
DHCPEnabled        : True
DHCPServer         : 192.168.1.1
DHCPLeaseObtained  : 20080922182725.000000+060
```

```
DHCPLeaseExpires              : 20080923182725.000000+060
DNSHostName                   : JAMESONE09
DNSDomain                     :
DNSServerSearchOrder          : {194.168.4.100, 194.168.8.100}
DNSDomainSuffixSearchOrder    :
DNSEnabledForWINSResolution   : False
WINSPrimaryServer             :
WINSSecondaryServer           :
WINSEnableLMHostsLookup       : True
WINSScopeID                   :
```

Another feature is worth noting here—the time format. And this is a good news/bad news story. First the bad news: WMI uses a time format defined by the DTMF, and it is a format that isn't used anywhere in .NET. You can use the [System.DateTime]::parseExact method for many date formats, formats. That doesn't work here because the DTMF specifies that a time offset, in minutes, must be written at the end of the time. In the the example above the offset is +060 meaning one hour ahead of UTC. The good news is that there is a method specific to this time format but it doesn't stop there. If you pipe a WMI object into get-member you'll find this:

```
ConvertFromDateTime    ScriptMethod System.Object ConvertFromDateTime();
ConvertToDateTime      ScriptMethod System.Object ConvertToDateTime();
```

The ScriptMethods are specified in Types.PS1XML but they are defined once for all WMI objects; each WMI type can also have its own section. You investigate the script method by referring to it without putting brackets and parameters after it. PowerShell will show you all its members—it is, after all, just another object. One of these members is named script, so as a shortcut, you can enter the following:

```
> (get-ipconfig $nic).ConvertToDateTime.script
[System.Management.ManagementDateTimeConverter]::ToDateTime($args[0])
```

The examples to date have used named parameters, although strictly speaking anything that takes only a single parameter doesn't need to give it a name. The ConvertToDateTime script uses this approach and so uses $args[0] to refer to the first (and only) parameter it is passed. It calls the ToDateTime() method of the System.Management.ManagementDateTimeConverter class, which was created specifically to solve this problem. If you are thinking about creating your own PS1XML file for a WMI class, which contains dates, it is worth defining a script property that outputs the reformatted date. As it is, you can call this method when formatting the list.

But before adding the formatting, there are some other things that need to be fixed:

- After the trouble of creating a function to choose Network Adapters, there is no way to pipe its output into the function.

- The function can't take a name—only a WMI object.

- The function will fail if passed multiple WMI objects.

So here is a template to overcome these problems:

```
Filter Verb-Noun
{ Param($Noun)
 If ($Noun -eq $null   )  {$Noun=$_ }
 If ($Noun -is [String])  {$Noun=(Get-noun $noun) }
 If ($Noun -is [Array] )  {$Noun | forEach-object {verb-noun $_} }
 If ($Noun -is [NounClass){do the work }
 $noun=$null
}
```

Let's review this line by line:

- The first line has changed from a *function* declaration to a *filter*. Functions and filters are interchangeable in most circumstances but they handle piped input differently. A filter receives each item and treats it as *the current one*, $_.

- If the *noun* parameter is empty, it is set to whatever is in the pipe (which might be nothing). At this stage $noun might be a string, a single WMI object, an array, or nothing.

- At this point different functions based on the template may vary their behavior if nothing is passed via the parameter or via the pipe. As presented the function will do nothing if it isn't given a -noun parameter, and to get all the possible options, it needs to be invoked with -noun *. This wouldn't be the expected behavior for the Get-Ipconfig function so the first line can be modified:

  ```
  If ($Noun -eq $null)  {if ($_) {$Noun=$_} else {$noun="*" }
  ```

- If $noun is a single string, then the filter calls another function (Get-Noun) to get the object(s) represented by that string: typically the string will be a name and the function will return the object with that name. However, the name might be a wildcard, in which case Get-Noun will return an array.

- If the filter was given an array of objects, or an array of strings, or if it was given a single string that matched multiple objects, then the function is called recursively for each one. This allows it to cope with being given parameters that are mixed or nested arrays.

- At this stage, $noun might be a WMI object. It might be empty, it might be an array—because execution will continue after the recursive calls for each object. It might be some other type that was passed in error. So the work of the function is only done if it is the right type.

- The variables in a filter remain in scope for the lifetime of the pipeline where it is used; they are not cleared each time a new item is passed. So, $noun is set to null at the end: failure to do this will mean the filter runs once for each object passed but each time it processes the first one again.

All the work of the function is done in the section marked "do the work," but there is another change to insert here—that is, the WMI object being worked on might come from a different server so any calls to Get-WMIObject in this section need to explicitly specify the -computerName parameter as $noun.__server.

One other change to apply to the function is to include only the response if the IPEnabled property is true. Otherwise, various unused NICs and pseudo NICs are listed. So when you apply these changes and the date formatting to the existing function it becomes:

```
Filter get-IpConfig
  {Param ($nic , $server="." , [Switch]$Short, [Switch]$All)
If ($nic -eq $null)     {if ($_) {$Nic=$_} else {$nic= "*" }}
If ($Nic -is [String])  {$Nic=(Get-NetworkAdapter $nic)}
If ($nic -is [Array] ){$nic| forEach-Object {
                  if ($all) {get-ipconfig -nic $_ -Server $server -all}
                  else {if ($short) {get-ipconfig -nic $_ -server $Server -short}
                        else { get-ipconfig -nic $_ -server $Server }}}}
If ($nic -is [System.Management.ManagementObject]){
   $config=Get-wmiObject -computerName $nic.__server -query "associators of
                  {$nic} where resultClass=Win32_NetworkAdapterConfiguration" |
                  Where {$_.IPEnabled}
  If ($short) {$config | format-table -autosize -property IPAddress,
                      DefaultIPGateway  , IPSubnet }
  Else {if ($all){$config |
                  format-list -property Description, ServiceName,
                  MACAddress, IPAddress, DefaultIPGateway , IPSubnet ,
                  DHCPEnabled , DHCPServer ,
                  @{Label="LeaseObtained";
                    expression={$_.convertToDateTime( $_.DHCPLeaseObtained)}},
                  @{Label="LeaseExpires";
                    expression={$_.convertToDateTime( $_.DHCPLeaseExpires)}},
                  DNSHostName , DNSDomain , DNSServerSearchOrder,
                  DNSDomainSuffixSearchOrder , DNSEnabledForWINSResolution,
                  WINSPrimaryServer ,WINSSecondaryServer ,
                  WINSEnableLMHostsLookup, WINSScopeID}
        Else {$Config} }}
$nic=$null
}
```

Now any of the following commands will work:

```
get-ipconfig
get-ipconfig "Broadcom 802.11g Network Adapter"
get-ipconfig broad*
get-ipconfig broad*,blue*
get-ipconfig broad* -sh
get-ipconfig broad* -all
get-ipconfig -nic broad* -all
$myNic=choose-networkAdapter  ; get-ipconfig -nic $mynic
```

```
choose-networkAdapter | Get-ipconfig
choose-networkAdapter | Get-ipconfig -all
choose-networkAdapter | Get-ipconfig | foreach {$_.dnsServerSearchOrder}
```

Ping

Ping is one of the standard tools that IT professionals have grown used to over the years to test to see if a computer is *alive*. Ping is the name of the program that sends an ICMP Echo request: it's not an infallible indicator (the firewall in Windows Server 2008 blocks ICMP Echo by default), and just because IP packets can reach a server doesn't mean that all the required services you need are running. Ping leaves you in a bit of a quandary when it comes to PowerShell: is ping a verb (*Ping the server*) or a noun (*Send a ping to the server*). The examples will treat it as a verb so the function will be `Ping-Host`.

Writing your own code to send ICMP packets out and check for responses is just too hard. Fortunately, WMI provides a `PingStatus` object and querying this object generates a ping.

```
Get-WmiObject -query "Select * from  Win32_PingStatus where
Address='192.168.1.1' and ResolveAddressNames = True and recordRoute=1"
```

To get this nicely formatted it can be piped into `Format-Table`; for example:

```
Get-WmiObject -query "Select * from  Win32_PingStatus where
Address='192.168.1.1' and ResolveAddressNames = True and recordRoute=1" |
Format-table -autosize -property ProtocolAddressResolved , ResponseTime ,
ResponseTimeToLive , StatusCode
```

All that is needed is to wrap this in a function, or rather a filter, because it will need to be called in more than one way; for example:

```
Ping-host 192.168.1.1,"www.microsoft.com"
Get-ipconfig | foreach { $_.DNSServerSearchOrder | Ping-host }
```

The same template that was used before can be used again—except that in this case there is less work to do resolving types. So the filter looks like this:

```
Filter Ping-host {Param ($target, $server="." , [switch]$formatted )
If ($target -eq $null) ($target=$_}
If ($target -is [Array] ){$target| forEach-Object {
                    if ($formatted) {ping-host -target $target -formatted}
                    else {ping-host -target $target } }}
If ($target -is [string] ){
    $pingResult= Get-WmiObject -query "Select * from  Win32_PingStatus where
            Address='$target' and ResolveAddressNames = True and recordRoute=1"
    If ($formatted) {$pingResult | Format-table -autosize `
                            -property Address, ProtocolAddressResolved ,
                            ResponseTime , ResponseTimeToLive , StatusCode}
    Else {$pingResult}}
}
```

Incidentally, you saw at the start of this chapter that PowerShell uses $host to mean the console, so don't try to define a variable or parameter using the name "Host." This function can be called with another parameter or it can take its input from Get-IPconfig, as follows:

```
> Get-ipconfig | foreach { $_.DNSServerSearchOrder | Ping-host -f}
Address         ProtocolAddressResolved ResponseTime ResponseTimeToLive StatusCode
-------         ----------------------- ------------ ------------------ ----------
194.168.4.100 194.168.4.100                      10                251          0


Address         ProtocolAddressResolved ResponseTime ResponseTimeToLive StatusCode
-------         ----------------------- ------------ ------------------ ----------
194.168.4.100 194.168.4.100                      19                251          0
```

Because the filter outputs a table for each object, it generates duplicate headers—to remove these it is better to pass the output of all the pings as objects into format-table like this:

```
> Get-ipconfig | foreach { $_.DNSServerSearchOrder | Ping-host | format-
table -autosize -Property Address, ProtocolAddressResolved , ResponseTime ,
ResponseTimeToLive , StatusCode }

Address         ProtocolAddressResolved ResponseTime ResponseTimeToLive StatusCode
-------         ----------------------- ------------ ------------------ ----------
194.168.4.100 194.168.4.100                      11                251          0
194.168.4.100 194.168.4.100                      11                251          0
```

Clever Uses for Hash Tables

Back in Chapter 4 you saw that PowerShell can store information in an Associative Array or hash table. This is useful for avoiding the switch statement and many lines of code to decode a response. In the example, ping returns a status code. 0 means OK but there are 22 other status codes. Quite often, a script will contain something like this every time the user should see the meaning instead of the code:

```
switch ($a) {
    0 {"OK"}
    11001 {" Buffer Too Small "}
    11002 {" Destination Net Unreachable" }
    11003 {" Destination Host Unreachable "}
<etc for 22 lines>
    }
```

You can define the codes centrally and look them up as needed. Here's the definition:

```
$PingStatusCode=@{0="Success" ; 11001="Buffer Too Small" ; 11002="Destination
Net Unreachable" ; 11003="Destination Host Unreachable" ; 11004="Destination
Protocol Unreachable"; 11005="Destination Port Unreachable";11006="No
Resources";11007="Bad Option";11008="Hardware Error";11009="Packet Too
```

```
Big"; 11010="Request Timed Out"; 11011="Bad Request"; 11012="Bad Route";
11013="TimeToLive Expired Transit"; 11014="TimeToLive Expired Reassembly";
11015="Parameter Problem"; 11016="Source Quench"; 11017="Option Too Big";
11018="Bad Destination"; 11032="Negotiating IPSEC"; 11050="General Failure" }
```

So now $PingStatusCode[11032] returns Negotiating IPSEC. As you saw in Chapter 20, extra note properties can be added to an object using the add-member command.

```
Add-member -inputObject $PingResult -name "statusText" -memberType NoteProperty
-value $PingStatusCode[[int]PingResult_.statusCode]
```

This is a lot more efficient than writing the add-member 22 times in a switch statement. It can be inserted into the Ping-Host filter immediately after the line where $PingResult is assigned. From then on, the .statusText property can be used in other commands.

You can use a similar trick when each bit in a byte or integer value means something. For example, some WMI functions return a *suite mask*, which identifies which parts of Windows are installed. For example, a 1 in the "2s" bit says "This is Enterprise Edition;" a 1 in the "16s" column says "This supports Terminal Services connection," and so on. There are ten of these flags and it is common to see something like this:

```
[string[]]$Descriptions=@()
If (KvpObj.suiteMask -band 1) {descriptions+= "Small business"}
If (KvpObj.suiteMask -band 2) {descriptions+= "Enterprise"}
If (KvpObj.suiteMask -band 4) {descriptions+= "BackOffice"}
```

The if statement uses the bitwise AND operator (sometimes also called a binary AND). This compares each of the bits in the 2 operands and returns a 1 if both are true and a 0 if either or both is false. There is a companion bitwise OR, which returns a 1 if either or both bits is true and 0 only if both bits are false.

For example:

```
        9 1001          9 1001
-bAND   4 0100   -bOR 4 0100
        0 0000         13 1101

        9 1001          9 1001
-bAND   8 1000   -bOR 8 1000
        8 1000          9 1001
```

All the different meanings can be stored in a hash table:

```
$suites=@{1="Small Business"; 2="Enterprise"; 4="BackOffice";
8="Communications"; 16="Terminal"; 32="Small Business Restricted"; 64="Embedded
NT"; 128="Data Center";256="Single User"; 512="Personal"; 1024="Blade"}
```

A hash table has a Keys property that contains all its keys (1, 2, 4, 8, 16, 32, 64, 128, 256, 512, 1024 in this case), so it is easy to loop through the keys and perform a bitwise AND between the key and the value of the flags. If it returns anything other than zero, the value part of the hash table element can be added to an array:

```
$suites.keys  | foreach -begin {[String[]]$descriptions= @()} -process
{if ($KvpObj.suiteMask -bAND $_) {$descriptions += $suites[$_]} } -end
{$descriptions}
```

So a dozen lines have been reduced to two.

COM Objects: A Firewall Tool

So far, this chapter has looked extensively at WMI objects, which can be retrieved with the `get-WMIobject` Cmdlet. PowerShell can work with COM and .NET objects as well. To return to the theme of Networking utilities, this section will look at the COM object used to manage the firewall on a Vista or Server 2008 machine.

Apart from using a different Cmdlet to obtain the object the process for working with this object is the same as the ones you have seen before. PowerShell uses the `New-Object` Cmdlet to obtain COM and .NET objects—it assumes that the object is a .NET object (which will be covered a little later in this chapter) unless the `-COMObject` switch is specified.

For the firewall, the object that's required is the `HNetCfg.FwPolicy2` object.

So to get the object, the command is:

```
$fw=New-object -comObject HNetCfg.FwPolicy2
```

The first thing you can test with this object is the type(s) of network the computer is connected to. There are four values that can appear in profile types:

- Domain = 1
- Private = 2
- Public = 4
- All = 2147483647

You can see which is/are in use with the following:

```
$fw.CurrentProfileTypes
```

You can use a hash table in the same way as the ping example in the previous section. To test the bit mask for the different types, use the following:

```
$FWprofileTypes= @{1GB="All";1="Domain"; 2="Private" ; 4="Public"}
Function Convert-FWProfileType
{Param ($ProfileCode)
```

```
$FWprofileTypes.keys | foreach -begin {[String[]]$descriptions= @()} `
 -process {if ($profileCode -bAND $_) {$descriptions +=
$FWProfileTypes[$_]} } -end {$descriptions}}

> $fw=New-object -comObject HNetCfg.FwPolicy2
> Convert-fwprofileType  $fw.CurrentProfileTypes
Private
```

Each class of network allows the firewall to be turned on or off, and the default inbound or outbound action can be set to block or allow. So the following line will show the state of the firewall for each:

```
> 1,2,4 | foreach-object {" {0,8} Networks enabled:
  {1,5} defaults:  inbound {2}, outbound {3}" -f $FWProfileTypes[$_],
$fw.Firewallenabled($_), $fw.DefaultInboundAction($_),
$fw.DefaultOutboundAction($_) }

  Domain Networks enabled:  True defaults:  inbound 0, outbound 1
 Private Networks enabled:  True defaults:  inbound 0, outbound 1
  Public Networks enabled:  True defaults:  inbound 0, outbound 1
```

You might know what 0 and 1 mean in this context, but it would be better to define a hash table to decode it to "block" and "allow."

```
$FwAction=@{1="Allow"; 0="Block"}
```

As you can see in the preceding example, FireWallEnabled, DefaultInboundAction, and DefaultOutBoundAction are parameterized properties—that is to say, they take a value using the same syntax as a method (rather than using the square brackets of an array) but return a fixed value, not a calculated one. So here is a function to test the state of the firewall. It looks at each of the networks and outputs an object with the network's name, the state of those properties, and a fourth one, BlockAllInboundTraffic:

```
Function Test-Firewall {
  $fw=New-object -comObject HNetCfg.FwPolicy2
  "Active Profiles(s) :" + (Convert-fwprofileType  $fw.CurrentProfileTypes)
  @(1,2,4) | select @{name="Network Type";expression={$fwProfileTypes[$_]}},
    @{Name="Firewall Enabled";expression={$fw.FireWallEnabled($_)}},
    @{Name="Block all inbound";expression={$fw.BlockAllInboundTraffic($_)}},
    @{name="Default In";expression={$FwAction[$fw.DefaultInboundAction($_)]}},
    @{Name="Default Out";expression={$FwAction[$fw.DefaultOutboundAction($_)]}}|
    Format-Table -auto
}
```

This is the same information that appears in the management console for the firewall, with the important difference that you can base scripted actions on the results of the functions. Figure 30-1 shows the MMC console.

FIGURE 30-1

The MMC console

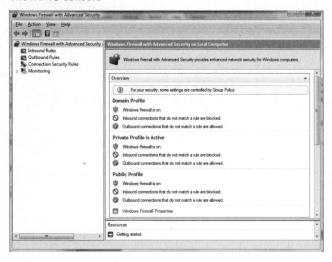

The MMC console also shows rules that define how the firewall behaves for each type of traffic.

A rule can specify to allow blocking behavior of inbound or outbound connections for:

- Any combination of profiles
- A program or a service
- A protocol TCP, UDP, ICMP, GRE, and so on
- A connection to or from specific ports (80 for HTTP, 25 for Mail, and so on)
- A connection to or from specific addresses

Figure 30-2 shows the rules in the MMC.

The `rules` property of the `FWPolicy` object contains a collection of `rule` objects with these properties.

A function can get the rules, and it makes sense to allow them to be filtered by criteria:

```
Function Get-FireWallRule
{Param ($Name, $Direction, $Enabled, $Protocol, $profile, $action)
 $Rules=(New-object -comObject HNetCfg.FwPolicy2).rules
 If ($name)      {$rules= $rules | where-object {$_.name -like $name}}
 If ($direction) {$rules= $rules | where-object {$_.direction -eq $direction}}
 If ($Enabled)   {$rules= $rules | where-object {$_.Enabled -eq $Enabled}}
```

```
If ($protocol)  {$rules= $rules | where-object {$_.protocol -eq $protocol}}
If ($profile)   {$rules= $rules | where-object {$_.Profiles -bAND $profile}}
If ($Action)    {$rules= $rules | where-object {$_.Action -eq $Action}}
$rules}
```

FIGURE 30-2

The rules in the MMC

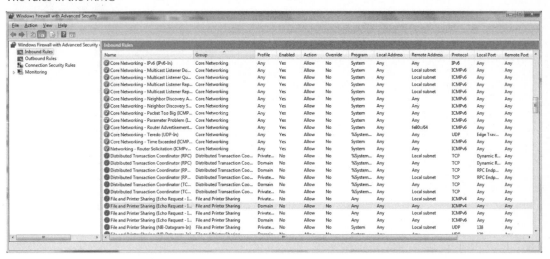

The function can be invoked as:

```
> Get-FireWallRule -protocol 1 -direction 1 -profile 1 -name *echo* -enabled
$false
```

But it would be useful to define hash tables that work both ways for the profile type, the Protocol, and the direction. For example the direction would define 1="inbound" and "inbound"=1.

```
$FWprofileTypes= @{1GB="All";1="Domain"; 2="Private" ; 4="Public";
                   "all"= 2147483647; "Domain"=1; "Private"=2; "Public"=4}
$FwAction=@{1="Allow"; 0="Block"; "Allow"=1;"block"=0}
$FwProtocols=@{1="ICMPv4";2="IGMP";6="TCP";17="UDP";41="IPv6";43="IPv6Route";
44="IPv6Frag";47="GRE";58="ICMPv6";59="IPv6NoNxt";60="IPv6Opts";112="VRRP";
113="PGM";115="L2TP";
"ICMPv4"=1;"IGMP"=2;"TCP"=6;"UDP"=17;"IPv6"=41;"IPv6Route"=43;
"IPv6Frag"=44;"GRE"=47;"ICMPv6"=48;"IPv6NoNxt"=59;"IPv6Opts"=60;"VRRP"=112;
"PGM"=113;"L2TP"=115}
$FWDirection=@{1="Inbound"; 2="outbound"; "Inbound"=1;"outbound"=2}
```

With these in place, it is possible to call the function with meaningful names rather than codes for the different parameters. For example:

```
> Get-FireWallRule -protocol $fwprotocols.icmpv4 `
-profile $FWprofileTypes.domain `
 -name *echo* -direction $fwDirection.inbound

Name              : File and Printer Sharing (Echo Request - ICMPv4-In)
Description       : Echo Request messages are sent as ping requests to
                    other nodes.
ApplicationName   :
serviceName       :
Protocol          : 1
LocalPorts        :
RemotePorts       :
LocalAddresses    : *
RemoteAddresses   : *
IcmpTypesAndCodes : 8:*
Direction         : 1
Interfaces        :
InterfaceTypes    : All
Enabled           : False
Grouping          : @FirewallAPI.dll,-28502
Profiles          : 1
EdgeTraversal     : False
Action            : 1
```

You can see one unfortunate way that the object is implemented here and that is the text string used for the grouping field is abstracted out into a DLL. You can look at the Grouping column in the UI to match up the value Grouping field (in this case @FirewallAPI.dll,-28502) with the text File and Printer Sharing. The group name can be used in either the DLL form or as the full text with the methods EnableRuleGroup() and IsRuleGroupEnabled(). The former enables or disables a group, and the latter checks to see its status. For example:

```
> $fw.IsRuleGroupEnabled($fwProfileTypes.all,"@FirewallAPI.dll,-28502")
False
> $fw.EnableRuleGroup($fwProfileTypes.all,"File and Printer Sharing")
> $fw.IsRuleGroupEnabled($fwProfileTypes.all,"@FirewallAPI.dll,-28502")
True
```

These functions give you an easier-to-use alternative for the NetSh utility if you need a script to configure multiple machines to have the same set of firewall rules. In addition to enabling or disabling rules by group, you can enable them individually by retrieving the rule with the Get-FireWall rule function and setting their `Enabled` property to `$True`. There is no separate action to commit the change so a command like the one that follows will take effect immediately:

```
(Get-FireWallRule -protocol $fwprotocols.icmpv4 `
-profile $FWprofileTypes.domain  -name *echo* -direction $fwDirection.inbound
).enabled=$true
```

Note that it requires elevated privileges to change firewall rules (although not to view them), so on a default installation of Windows Vista or Server 2008, a user—other than the built-in Administrator who runs PowerShell without specifying "Run as Administrator"—will get an "Access Denied" error.

The ability of the script to return the settings of the firewall without elevating to run the management console is obviously a useful one, as a non-administrative user can use it to gather diagnostic information. The `Get-FireRule` function can be piped into Export-CSV, or even modified to create a CSV and mail it to a support person trying to troubleshoot a problem.

The other obvious thing to do with the output of a `Get-FirewallRule` is to format it with `Format-List` and/or `FormatTable`:

```
> get-firewallRule -direction $fwdirection["inbound"] | select -last 5 |
format-table -wrap -property Name,@{Label="Action"; expression={$Fwaction[$_
.action]}}, @{Label="Protocol"; expression={$FwProtocols[$_.protocol]}},
localPorts
```

Name	Action	Protocol	LocalPorts
Core Networking - Internet Group Management Protocol (IGMP-In)	Allow	IGMP	
Core Networking - Dynamic Host Configuration Protocol (DHCP-In)	Allow	UDP	68
Core Networking - Teredo	Allow	UDP	Teredo
Core Networking - IPv6 (IPv6-In)	Allow	IPv6	
Secure Socket Tunneling Protocol (SSTP-In)	Allow	TCP	443

You can decide which of the columns to allow. With the limited column width here, the example uses only four columns, but with a wider display you can use any combination of the following:

```
Enabled
@{Label="In/Out";expression={$FwDirection[$_.direction]}}
localPorts
remoteports
Servicename
ApplicationName
```

Using .NET Objects to Access Mail and Web Services

In the previous section on getting information about the firewall, I mentioned that the information can be exported to a CSV file and then mailed to a support person. Up to this point, I haven't explained how to send a mail message so this would be a good place to explore how you can do that.

Sending mail

As with many other things you have seen with PowerShell, there is more than one way to send a mail message, but the two methods can be summarized as either: interact with an e-mail client on the computer where PowerShell is running, and use it to assemble and send a message as the currently signed-in user. Or, connect to a mail server (typically an SMTP server) and pass it a message that has been composed inside PowerShell, which it can then deliver. The second option is covered later. In the first example, we will consider how to send mail with Microsoft Outlook, which, like the firewall, uses a COM object model.

To get access to Outlook, it is first necessary to request the `Outlook.application` COM object. If you want to explore Outlook, you can use its `GetNamespace` method and request the "MAPI" namespace—then all the folders within Outlook are available to you. In current versions of Outlook, it is possible to create an item from the application object without having to go to the folder where it will exist when created, which cuts the process for creating a new message down to two lines of code:

```
$OL=new-object -comobject "Outlook.Application"
$Msg=$ol.CreateItem(0)
```

The 0 tells `createitem()` that you are requesting a "mail note" item (you might be requesting an appointment, contact, or task). The mail note has a `Send()` method; all that a script needs to do is to specify to whom the message is addressed (by setting a `To` property), its subject line (a `Subject` property), and body (an `HTMLBody` or `Body` Property), and call the `Send` method.

```
$msg.to="james@contoso.com"
$msg.subject="Message sent from PowerShell"
$msg.body="This message was sent from PowerShell"
$msg.send
```

The message also has an `attachments` property—which refers to an attachments collection. Adding an attachment is as simple as calling the `add` method of this collection with the path of the file that you want to attach. All of this can be packaged as a PowerShell function, as follows:

```
Function Send-OutlookMail
{Param ($To,
       $Subject = "Auto-Mail",
       $Body    = "Automated mail from PowerShell",
       $Attach , [Switch]$HTMLBody)
  $ol= New-Object -comobject "Outlook.application"
```

```
    $msg= $ol.CreateItem(0)
    $msg.to=$to
    $msg.subject=$Subject
    if ($HmtlBody) {$msg.Hmtlbody=$body} else {$msg.body=$body}
    foreach ($f in $attach){$msg.attachments.add((resolve-path $f).path)}
    $msg.send()
    }
```

With the function in place, it can be called to send details of how the firewall is configured:

```
    Get-Firewall | Export-CSV -path firewall.csv
    send-outlookmail "james@contoso.com" -attach firewall.csv
```

This works well, although Outlook is likely to put up one or two warnings in the process—the new versions know that they are vectors for viruses and spam mailings so they warn the user if some other program tries to get information out or send messages.

Figure 30-3 shows Outlook warning messages.

FIGURE 30-3

Outlook warning messages

There is a more important issue: servers tend not to have a mail client configured so using Outlook to send mail is ruled out. The alternative uses .NET objects instead of COM ones and sends the mail via an SMTP server. Removing the dependency on any particular mail client can simplify the process of sending mail. However, the problems with spam, phishing mails, and viruses have meant that many organizations restrict what can be done with their SMTP connections—even the internal ones. Connections may be limited to specific IP addresses, they may require IPSec to prove a machine is a valid member of a corporate network, or user authentication (and the .NET object has an option to log on with the current user's credentials to make this easier). If the SMTP server is based on Microsoft Exchange, then it may require the From address on the mail message to be that of a mailbox linked to the login used. So just going directly to an SMTP server may not be as simple as it appears here.

The principle is much the same; instead of the client software creating a message object that has a send method, the .NET objects have a message created as a free standing object and passed to the client object's send method. The properties to be set on the message are similar, between SMTP and Outlook. The one difference is that whereas Outlook has separate `Body` and `HTMLBody` proper-ties, the .NET SMTP message has a single `body` property, and a separate property of the message `IsBodyHTML` identifies the format. The final difference is that Outlook "knows" its server and user-name, but the .NET objects need to be told the name or IP address of the server and address of the sender that the mail should appear to come from.

```
Function Send-SMTPMail {
 Param($From    = "NoReply@contoso.com",
       $To
       $Subject = "Auto-Mail",
       $Body    = "Automated mail from PowerShell",
       $SMTPhost="smtp.contoso.com",
       $Attach, [Switch]$HTMLBody, [Switch]$UseCredentials)

 $SMTPclient = new-object System.Net.Mail.SmtpClient $SMTPhost
 if ($UseCredentials) {$SMTPCLient.UseDefaultCredentials = $true}
 $Msg = new-object System.Net.Mail.MailMessage $from, $to, $subject, $body
 if ($HTMLBody) {$msg.IsBodyHtml = $true}
 if ($attach) { Foreach ($f in $Attach)
                       {$data=new-object System.Net.Mail.Attachment $f
                        $msg.Attachments.Add($data)
 $client.Send($msg)}
```

So to send the same firewall configuration information, the two commands needed would be:

```
Get-Firewall | Export-CSV -path firewall.csv
send-Smtpmail -smtpHost Smtp.contoso.com -to "james@contoso.com" `
-from "$env:userName@contoso.com" -attach firewall.csv
```

Using the Web client object and XML

In addition to the SMTP client, the .NET classes include a `WebClient` class, which can upload files or post information to a web site, and get information from a web site. We take the Web for granted, but it is often useful to be able to process information obtained from the Internet in PowerShell. So this section will look at a range of tasks you can take on with a little knowledge of the relevant objects.

Getting a Web client object is as simple as any other object:

```
$web=New-Object system.net.webclient
```

If you look at this object with `get-member`, you will find it has eight upload and six download methods. Each of these are doubled-up because they have a normal, *synchronous* version, which waits for completion before returning control to whatever called it, and an *asynchronous* version, which returns control immediately and then triggers an event to say that the task has been com-pleted. PowerShell V1 doesn't provide the tools for handling events (although Microsoft has said future versions will). However, in most scripts there is very little the script can be doing while wait-ing for a process to complete—so this isn't much of a loss.

The upload and download methods can send or receive a string, an array of bytes, or a file, and for uploading there is an additional method to upload name/value pairs. The following examples concentrate on downloads.

To begin with, you can get the contents of the Microsoft home page, as follows:

```
$MsHome   = $web.downloadString("http://www.microsoft.com")
```

$MSHome is now very large string containing the Microsoft home page, and you can process this as required. The Webclient object has a ResponseHeaders property, which contains the headers that describe the transaction that returned the page. So you can investigate what type of file was returned, and the version of the software running on the Web server as follows:

```
> $web.responseheaders
Pragma
Content-Length
Cache-Control
Content-Type
Date
Expires
P3P
Server
X-AspNet-Version
X-Powered-By
> $web.responseheaders["Content-Type"]
text/html; charset=utf-8
> $web.responseheaders["Server"]
Microsoft-IIS/7.0
> $web.responseheaders["X-AspNet-Version"]
2.0.50727
```

So you can see it would be easy to write a short function to discover what version of software a particular site or server was running.

```
function Test-WebServer
{Param ($Site=$(Throw "you must specify a site to test"))
 if (-not ($site).tolower().startswith("http")) {$site= "http://$site"}
 $null =  $web.downloadString($site)
 "$Site is running " + $web.responseheaders["Server"]
 }

> test-webserver www.microsoft.com
http://www.microsoft.com is running Microsoft-IIS/7.0
```

Downloading a page to get the headers might be useful for cataloguing servers internally or if you are curious to know what software is being used by a site. It is far more likely you will want to do some processing of the text in the page that was downloaded; so the next example will get an RSS feed and parse its XML.

I have touched on XML only briefly up to this point, so let me take this opportunity to look at how XML is handled in PowerShell.

The first step is to get the page, which is easy enough; this example is going to process the feed for the PowerShell library for Hyper-V on Microsoft's *codeplex* open source repository (www.codeplex.com/psHyperV), which has already been mentioned. You can download the RSS feed and convert it from a string to an XML document using the [XML]type accelerator, as follows:

```
$web=New-Object system.net.webclient
$rssPage=$web.downloadString(
            "http://www.codeplex.com/PSHyperv/Project/ProjectRss.aspx")
$feed=[Xml]$rssPage
```

$Feed now contains a .NET system.xml.xmlDocument object and this can be processed in PowerShell in the same way that it can in other languages. You can see the top-level element and start to explore like this:

```
> $feed
xml                xml-stylesheet                                      rss
---                --------------                                      ---
version="1.0"    type="text/xsl" ref="http://www.codeplex.com/rss.xsl"   rss
```

"RSS" in the column named RSS is an indication that RSS is a sub-object that can be explored itself, but xml and xml-stylesheet are top-level properties of the document.

```
> $feed.rss

version                              channel
-------                              -------
2.0                                  channel
```

"Channel" in the column named Channel is an indication that Channel is a sub-object that can be explored itself, and version is a property of the RSS tag.

```
> $feed.rss.channel
format-default : The member "Item" is already present.
```

Wait . . . that's not good. Unfortunately, the .NET object has a member with the name item and each piece of information in the RSS feed is tagged <item>...</item> in the XML. PowerShell is trying to call two things item, and that won't work. To carry on with this exploration, a little cheating is required. Because the whole page is in a string, and strings have a .replace() method, you can change all the instances of <item> and </item> to use a safe name such as RSSitem, and *then* convert that to XML and carry on as before.

```
>$feed2=[xml]($rssPage.replace("item>","RSSitem>"))
>$feed2
xml                xml-stylesheet                                          rss
---                --------------                                          ---
version="1.0"      type="text/xsl" ref="http://www.codeplex.com/rss.xsl"   rss

>$feed2.rss
version                             channel
-------                             -------
2.0                                 channel

$feed2.rss.channel
title              link              description        RSSitem
-----              ----              -----------        -------
PowerShell manag…  http://www.codep...  A project to pro...  {RSSitem, RSSite...

> $feed2.rss.channel.rssitem[-1]
title       : Commented Issue: Add support for capturing a thumbnail JPG of a r
              unning VM
link        : http://www.codeplex.com/PSHyperv/WorkItem/View.aspx?WorkItemId=28
              45
description : Title says it all. <br />This has been added for builds after 0.9
              <br />Comments: ** Comment from web user: jamesone ** <p></p><p>&
              #42;&#42; Closed by jamesone 8&#47;10&#47;2008 3&#58;56 PM</p>
author      : jamesone
pubDate     : Sun, 10 Aug 2008 22:56:59 GMT
guid        : guid
```

When you understand the hierarchy within the XML document, you can use its SelectNodes() method to select each of the channels in the feed. Usually, a feed will have only one channel, but if it has more than one the following will return an array:

```
$channels=$feed2.SelectNodes("/rss/channel")
```

So at the command prompt, you could use a line like the following to work through each of the channels, output its title, and then output a table of its items. In a script, you wouldn't use % for foreach-object or ft for format-table, but it's fine at the prompt.

```
> $channels | % {$_.Title ; $_.SelectNodes("RSSitem")| ft title, pubdate }
PowerShell management Library for Hyper-V
title                              pubDate
-----                              -------
Created Issue: Difficult to determin...  Tue, 23 Sep 2008 00:09:36 GMT
Created Issue: Delete multiple (all)...  Tue, 23 Sep 2008 00:07:28 GMT
New Post: commands are doing nothing     Mon, 15 Sep 2008 20:09:30 GMT
```

```
New Post: commands are doing nothing      Mon, 15 Sep 2008 14:31:17 GMT
New Post: Totally confused                Fri, 12 Sep 2008 18:46:05 GMT
New Post: command are doing nothing       Fri, 12 Sep 2008 10:27:22 GMT
New Post: Totally confused                Fri, 12 Sep 2008 10:20:50 GMT
New Post: Totally confused                Thu, 11 Sep 2008 04:04:31 GMT
Commented Feature: Add Get-VMSummary...    Wed, 27 Aug 2008 21:42:02 GMT
Commented Issue: Add Get-VMSummaryIn...    Tue, 26 Aug 2008 23:50:37 GMT
Updated Release: 0.95a Beta (Aug 19,...    Tue, 26 Aug 2008 19:32:05 GMT
Created Issue: Add Get-VMSummaryInfo...     Sat, 23 Aug 2008 00:06:57 GMT
Released: 0.95 Beta (Aug 19, 2008)        Tue, 19 Aug 2008 09:47:01 GMT
Updated Release: 0.95 Beta (Aug 19, ...    Tue, 19 Aug 2008 09:47:01 GMT
Closed Issue: Add -force and -start ...    Mon, 18 Aug 2008 23:25:54 GMT
Closed Issue: VHD Items still outsta...    Mon, 18 Aug 2008 23:25:23 GMT
Commented Issue: VHD Items still out...     Mon, 18 Aug 2008 23:25:05 GMT
Updated Wiki: Home                        Mon, 18 Aug 2008 23:12:21 GMT
Reopened Issue: Add support for capt...     Sun, 10 Aug 2008 22:57:00 GMT
Commented Issue: Add support for cap...     Sun, 10 Aug 2008 22:56:59 GMT
```

Notice that inside the loop there is no leading / on the path to the RSS item in the `SelectNodes` because it is not starting at the root element of the document. If you knew the feed was a single channel, you could write it more simply as: `$feed2.SelectNodes("/rss/channel/RSSitem")`. And if the clash of names isn't going to impact you, then you could avoid changing the tags in the document. In fact, you dispense with the variables completely and write:

```
([xml]($web.downloadString(
"http://www.codeplex.com/PSHyperv/Project/ProjectRss.aspx"))).SelectNodes(
"/rss/channel/item") | ft Title,pubdate
```

Regular Expressions

When looking at text—whether from a disk file or a page downloaded from the Internet or in the property of a management object—it is often necessary to find items that match a particular pattern. PowerShell provides a simple operator, `-like`, which can check for basic wildcards. In many places, this is all that is needed—for example, looking through a log file for lines that contain the word "Error" or looking through a script for lines that don't begin with a # (these are comments in PowerShell). On other occasions, a simple wildcard doesn't work. The following paragraphs explain an example.

There is a format for writing phone numbers known as E.164, which says phone numbers are written in the form

```
+ national code (area code) Local Number.
```

For example, a U.S. number might be written +1 (212) 555 1234, or a British number might be written +44 (123) 456789.

However, when dialing a national number in Britain, the area code is written as (0123) 456789. This has given rise to a British habit of writing numbers as +44 (0) 123 456789. This confuses computers when they try to dial numbers and people from outside the country don't know if the 0 should be dialed or not (it shouldn't—calls will not connect). The problem is, how do you recognize a number that is written incorrectly when there are so many options for how to write it?

- 440123456789
- +440123456789
- +44 0123456789
- +44 0 123456789
- +44 (0) 123456789
- +44(0)123456789

There isn't a way to write this with a wildcard syntax, so the text would need some kind of pre-processing before testing to see if the number was valid. But that would strip out spaces and brackets, which make the number easier to read. The task of a regular expression is to identify any of the preceding forms with a single template for incorrectly written numbers.

A regular expression describes text as combinations of:

- Specific characters (such as A or 9)
- Ranges of characters (such as A–F)
- Classes of characters (such as letters, white-space, or digits)

An expression can specify how many times a character can appear. It can appear:

- Any number of times, including zero
- At least once
- A specified number of times

So the bad UK phone numbers:

- Begin with a plus sign (sometimes)
- Then 44 (always)
- Then a space (sometimes)
- Then an open bracket (sometimes)
- Then a zero
- Then a close bracket (sometimes)
- Then a space (sometimes)

This can be written as a single regular expression.

Expressed as set of instructions in English, we want to tell PowerShell "Find a match if the expression starts with zero or one plus signs, 44, zero or more spaces, zero or one open bracket, 0, zero or one close bracket and zero or more spaces."

It's time to dive into regular expression syntax:

- **The start or end of the expression:** Regular expressions use the ^ sign to mean "Start" and the $ sign to mean "End." In the example, the expression being sought is at the beginning.

- **Symbols:** Regular expressions use \ as an escape character, so if you want to find the $ sign in the text, you write it as \$ to distinguish it from using $ to mean "end." In the example, the + sign is written \+ and brackets \(and \).

- **Specific characters:** Provided it doesn't need to be escaped you can write the character you are looking for so 0 matches "0" and a matches "a". In the example, the pattern the characters looked for are 44 and 0.

- **Ranges and groups of characters are written wrapped in square brackets:** [aeiou] means "any of a, e, i , o, or u" and [a-e] means "anything in the range a to e inclusive."

- **Alternates are separated with the pipe symbol:** dog|Cat means "either dog or cat"; a|e|i|o|u is equivalent to [aeiou].

- **Classes of characters:** \s means "any space," \w means "any word character—letter or digit" and \d means "any digit." The writing of classes is *case-sensitive*. \S means "any non-space," \W means any non-word, and \D means "any non-digit." The example is going to look for space characters.

- **Repetition:** * means "any number of occurrences of the previous term, including 0"; + means "at least one occurrence"; and ? means "0 or 1 occurrences." {n} means exactly n occurrences, and {n,m} means between n and m occurrences. The example needs to look for 0 or 1 plus signs and brackets and any number of spaces.

So the expression builds up like this:

^	begin
\+?	+ sign zero or once
44	The text "44"
\s*	Any number of spaces (including none)
\(?	(sign zero or once

0	The text 0
\)?	) sign zero or once
\s*	Any number of spaces (including none)

When the whole expression is put together, you can see why people sometimes describe regular expressions as "write only"; the expression to recognize all those bad phone numbers is:

```
^\+?44\s*\(?0\)?\s*
```

PowerShell has two basic comparison operators for regular expressions, `-Match` and `-NotMatch`, and as with other comparison operators these are implicitly case-insensitive. They have explicitly case-insensitive versions (`-iMatch` and `-iNotMatch`) and case-sensitive versions (`-cMatch` and `-cNotMatch`).

This regular expression can be used with `-Match` to test if a phone number is one of the badly formatted ones. For example, both of the following lines return `true`:

```
"440123456789" -match "^\+?44\s*\(?0\)?\s*"
"+44 (0) 123456789" -match "^\+?44\s*\(?0\)?\s*"
```

So far so good. Bad numbers can be identified, but in a case like this you would want to substitute the correct text (+44) in place of the text that gave the match. For that, PowerShell provides a `-Replace` operator, which will make the change but return the string unmodified if no match is found.

```
> "+44 (0) 123456789" -replace "^\+?44\s*\(?0\)?\s*","+44 "
+44 123456789

> "+44 (208) 123456" -replace "^\+?44\s*\(?0\)?\s*","+44 "
+44 (208) 123456
```

The PowerShell regular expression operators are based on another .NET class, `System.Text.RegularExpressions.Regex`.

Using this class directly allows you to do some more sophisticated things using multiple matches. PowerShell's `-match` operator is concerned only with the question "Does this text give a match with this expression?", not "There are many matches in this text: where can they all be found?" Suppose that instead of wanting to know whether someone has entered a phone number correctly, you wanted to pull out all the hyperlinks from a Web page. That's a harder proposition, isn't it?

In HTML, a link is written as:

```
<a href="http://www.microsoft.com/powershell">Some text </a>
```

The `<a>` tag can have other text in it, but the `href=` part is unique. So a match would be `href=` followed by the double-quote (`"`) sign followed by any number of non-space characters (word characters exclude the punctuation, which is valid in a URL) and then another `"` sign so the expression is:

```
'href=\"\S*\'
```

To get a `regex` object based on this expression, you can use the `[regex]` type accelerator, and this has a `.Matches()` method, which returns each of the matches found. So if a page has been downloaded and stored in `$Webpage` already (the RSS feed page from a blog would be a good one to use for this), the following will return all the matches:

```
([regex]'href=\"\S*\" ').matches($WebPage)
```

You can examine the properties of the matches by piping the results of this command into `get-member`. There is an `Index` property, which gives the offset in the string and a `length` property, which gives the length of the matching text. But most useful is the `Value` property, which gives the matching text. By using `replace()` to strip off `"` signs and the leading `href=` the following will give all the URLs on a given page:

```
([regex]'href=\"\S*\" ').matches($WebPage) | % {$_.value.replace('href=',""
).replace('"','')} | sort -unique
```

You can follow the links to other pages by building this into a function and calling it recursively, and if writing for a script it would be better to replace the `%` and `Sort` aliases in the preceding code with their full forms (`Foreach-Object` and `Sort-Object`).

```
Function crawl-Url {Param ($Site=$(Throw "you must specify a site to Crawl") ,
                          $level=0, $maxLevels=3 )
  if ($global:web -eq $null) {$global:web = New-Object system.net.webclient}
  if (-not ($site).tolower().startswith("http")) {$site= "http://$site"}
  ([regex]'href=\"\S*\" ').matches($web.downloadString($site) ) |
          Foreach-object {$_.value.replace('href=',"").replace('"','')} |
          sort-object -unique |
          foreach {"$site links to $_"
                  $level ++
                  if($level -lt $maxLevels){crawl-url -site $_ -level $level}
                  }
  }
```

Normally, variables would be declared in the scope of the function, but here, a variable that holds the `web` object is declared as a global variable. That way, each time the function is called, the same object can be reused, instead of creating one afresh for each recursive pass through the function. There could be thousands of such passes.

More Advanced Text Processing—Discovering Script Dependencies

This section draws two techniques together—using regular expressions from the previous section and another technique for linking an item to the closest match—and it will end with some ways that you can develop this "fuzzy join" idea.

There is a PowerShell Cmdlet that hasn't been introduced yet, which makes use of regular expressions, and is a powerful tool for complex textual searches. The Cmdlet is Select-String.

If you see Select-String mentioned in online discussions, it seems to be in the form:

Q. Is there any easy way to find which of my scripts use the WebClient WMI object?

A. Sure. Use this:

```
> select-string -path *.ps1 "webclient"
```

If you try this for yourself, you will get output similar to the following:

```
blog-utils.ps1:73:  $results=[xml](new-object System.Net.WebClient).UploadStrin
g($postUrl, $postTemplate)
get-usersblog.ps1:246: $result=(new-object System.Net.WebClient).UploadString($
postURL , $postTemplate)
```

Each item of output shows the file name, line number in the file, and the matching line itself, but it wouldn't be PowerShell if this just returned text and not an object. Sending the last of the items returned in the preceding example to Format-List shows the members of the MatchInfo object:

```
IgnoreCase : True
LineNumber : 246
Line       : $result=(new-object System.Net.WebClient).UploadString($postURL ,
             $postTemplate)
Filename   : get-usersblog.ps1
Path       : C:\Users\james\Documents\windowsPowershell\get-usersblog.ps1
Pattern    : webclient
```

This is starting to look useful: it can identify which files contain matches, and tell you where in the file a match was found, and what matched—*pattern* sounds like a regular expression.

The parameters for Select-String include standard -path, -include, and -exclude parameters just like Get-ChildItem to tell it *where* to look (although it can take input from the pipe as well).

To tell it *what* to look for, it has a `-pattern` parameter, which specifies a regular expression, and there is a `-SimpleMatch` switch to say the pattern isn't a regular expression. As usual, PowerShell is implicitly case-insensitive and `Select-String` has a `-caseSensitive` switch to say if matches should be case-sensitive.

Finally, for people who just want to know which files contain something without getting the details for each occurrence, there is a `-List` switch, which stops examining a file after the first occurrence is found.

So the next example is going to use a couple of lines of PowerShell to find all the `function` and `filter` declarations in a script. Before using `Select-String`, however, it would be a good idea to remove comments from the files because they may give bogus references to a function.

A comment line begins with a # but it may have any number of spaces in front of it so this is a good case for a regular expression. The following reads the script—minus comments—into `-$script`:

```
$script=(Get-Content .\hyperv.ps1 | where {$_ -notMatch "^\s*#"})
```

Next, `Select-string` can use *multiple* regular expressions to return a list of functions and filters. The regular expressions are simple—lines that begin with "Function" or "Filter." You can see the behavior of `Select-String`:

```
$script | Select-String  -pattern "^Function","^filter"  |
  ft -auto lineNumber,line,  pattern
```

```
LineNumber Line                              Pattern
---------- ----                              -------
        12 Function Choose-List              ^Function
        24 Function Out-Tree                 ^Function
        33 Function Choose-Tree              ^Function
        55 Filter Convert-DiskIDtoDrives     ^filter
        62 Filter Test-WMIJob                ^filter
        74 Function test-Admin               ^Function
        85 Function Get-VhdDefaultPath       ^Function
        91 Function New-VHD                  ^Function
       109 Filter Mount-VHD                  ^filter
       137 Filter UnMount-VHD                ^filter
       151 Function Compact-VHD              ^Function
       163 Filter Get-VHDInfo                ^filter
       182 Function Expand-VHD               ^Function
```

This can be passed into `Add-Member` to add a script property, which is the name of the function or filter. To get this, the "filter " or "function" can be replaced with an empty string using the `-Replace` regular expression operator, which you saw in the previous section. To allow for functions that are written as a single line or for authors whose personal style is to write the opening brace on the same line as the function declaration, rather than on the next line, the result can be split at { and only the first part kept. Finally, any superfluous spaces can be trimmed off, and the result stored to be used a little later in the process:

```
$functions=$script | Select-String  -pattern "^Function","^filter" |
Add-Member -PassThru -MemberType scriptProperty -Name FunctionName `
-Value {($this.line -replace "Function|Filter","").split("{")[0].trim()}
```

So $functions now contains a collection of function and filter names.

With the ability of Select-String to take multiple items as its Pattern parameter, the entire list of function names can be passed to it. To do this, first a single line isolates the function names from the $functions array. Then a second line can use Select-String to return all the lines that contain any of those function names. To reduce the false matches, it is better to search for the name followed by a space. Even so, there will be some false matches because Select-String will return the lines where functions are declared, but a where-object will filter these out. Rather than using two terms in the where part, a single regular expression can match Function or Filter.

```
$bareFunctions = $functions | foreach {$_.functionName +" "}
$script | Select-String -simplematch $bareFunctions |
    Where {($_.line -notmatch "^Function|^filter")}
```

The objects returned by this command have a pattern property, which contains whichever of the patterns in the array (function names) generated a match on that line—in other words, the function being called, and the line number where the match occurred. The following shows just a few of the matches:

```
> $script | Select-String -simplematch $bareFunctions |
 Where {($_.line -notmatch "^Function|^filter")} |
select -last 5 | ft -auto lineNumber,  pattern

LineNumber Pattern
---------- -------
      1039 New-VM
      1069 Get-VM
      1070 Get-VMJPEG
      1071 Get-VMSettingData
      1114 test-Admin
```

So far, the two fragments of script have obtained a list of where all the functions begin, and a list of where all function calls occur. What's needed in order to be able say "function X calls function Y" is to find the last declaration with a line number before the call (that's the declaration of the function that is making the call). In some senses this is like doing a join between database tables, and isolating the required item. This can be done by piping the command which has been built up in the preceding paragraphs into Add-Member.

```
Add-Member {($functions | where {$_.lineNumber -lt $this.lineNumber} |
select -last 1).functionName } -Name "IsCalledBy" -PassThru `
-MemberType scriptProperty
```

This adds an IsCalledBy property to each item. Its value is calculated by a script block that filters down the list of function declarations to the ones before this line (the where) and pares it down to the last one (the select) and just returns its functionname property.

This will give all the matches—including duplicates and functions that recursively call themselves. A where will remove the recursive calls, and the duplicates can be removed and the data sorted by piping that into Sort-Object:

```
sort Pattern,calls -unique | where {$_.pattern -ne $_.Calls}
```

And finally this might be formatted or otherwise processed by piping into format-table. The final command is seven Cmdlets piped together:

```
$Script | Select-String | where | add-member | sort | where | format

$script | Select-String -simplematch $bareFunctions |
Where-object{($_.line -notmatch "^Function|^filter")} |
 Add-Member -Name "IsCalledBy" -PassThru -MemberType scriptProperty -value `
     {($functions | where-object {$_.lineNumber -lt $this.lineNumber} |
         select -last 1).functionName } |sort-object Pattern,isCalledBy -unique|
where {$_.pattern -ne $_.IsCalledBy+" "} | ft pattern,isCalledBy
```

All this can be put into a function:

```
Function Get-FunctionLinks
{param ($fileName)
$script=(Get-Content $fileName | where {$_ -notMatch "^\s*#"})
$functions=$script | Select-String  -pattern "^Function","^filter" |
   Add-Member -PassThru  -MemberType scriptProperty -Name FunctionName `
       -Value {($this.line -replace "Function|Filter","").split("{")[0].trim()}
$bareFunctions = $functions | foreach-object {$_.functionname +" "}
$script | Select-String -simplematch $bareFunctions |
  Where-object{-not(($_.line -match "^Function|filter"))}|
  Add-Member -Name "IsCalledBy" -PassThru -MemberType scriptProperty -value `
      {($functions | where-object {$_.lineNumber -lt $this.lineNumber} |
         Select-object -last 1).functionName } |
  sort-object Pattern,isCalledBy -unique|
  where-object {$_.pattern -ne $_.IsCalledBy+" "}
}
```

The preceding code was used to produce a diagram that illustrates the complex relationships between the functions in the library for HyperV at `www.codeplex.com/psHyperv`.

You can access a version of this diagram via our downloads page at `www.wiley.com/go/powershellbible`.

Scripts or Fuctions: Checking How a Script Was Invoked

Often you will find that the PowerShell needed to carry out a task is provided as a .PS1 file. In practice, a function is just block of code that is stored in memory, and the same block of code can be stored in a .PS1 file. Unless you count copying and pasting, the only way to load stored functions into a PowerShell session is by dot sourcing a .PS1 file containing the functions. So you might wonder if there is a definitive way of deciding on filter, function, or script? Generally, if input is going to be piped into it, then it is best implemented as a filter. Which is better? To write a single .PS1file with many functions in which you dot source, or many .PS1 files each containing a task-specific script? In a lot of cases, it will be a matter of personal preference. A collection of interrelated tasks are generally better as functions. Anything you expect to use more than once in a session is more efficient as a function.

But this presents a problem because PowerShell is two different things—it is a programming language and it is a shell, a successor to COMMAND.COM and CMD.EXE. In those shells, if you had a batch file that set an *environment* variable, the variable would still be set when you left the batch file. Most programming languages, on the other hand, have a concept of *scope*—what happens in a function stays in the function. So when PowerShell runs a script, it leaves nothing behind—unless you expressly specify a dot in front of it to say "run this in the current scope, not a scope for the script." The syntax came from the UNIX world, and regularly causes problems for those who are new to PowerShell and are trying to load a useful script. It doesn't help that, in PowerShell, the current folder is not on the path so scripts frequently have to be invoked as `.\script.ps1` and to stay resident as `. .\script.ps1`. It is very easy to miss the leading dot.

There is a solution to this, which is to check how the script was run, and that can be discovered using an automatic variable—`$myInvocation`.

`$MyInvocation` will tell you which line of a calling script was the one that launched the current one, and what the command line was, and so on. It has a line property that returns the command line used to call the script. This can be tested and the user running the script told that the functions, filters, and variables defined in the script have not been loaded. For example:

```
if ($myinvocation.line -notmatch "^\.\s") {write-host -ForegroundColor red
"No Functions were loaded - you need to invoke with . scriptname "}
```

$MyInvocation also has a scriptName property, but it needs to be used inside a function. It will give the name of the script that called the function. Used on its own, like the line property in the previous example, it will normally be blank. You can test the behavior by creating a function and a script like this:

```
> set-content Invoke.ps1 "where_am_I -fake parameter"
> function where_am_i {$myInvocation}
1> .\invoke
MyCommand         : where_am_i
ScriptLineNumber  : 1
OffsetInLine      : -2147483648
ScriptName        : C:\Users\jamesone\Documents\windowsPowershell\Invoke.ps1
Line              : where_am_I -fake parameter
```

The function can be in the script or outside, but it can discover which line from which script called it. You can use Split-Path to divide the folder from the file name, so scripts can load format files and the like, which are found in the same folder.

Summary

This chapter has given you a tour of PowerShell techniques that you can use in your own scripts; you have seen how to use the major classes of objects and how to get information from web sites. You had a brief introduction to regular expressions and saw how PowerShell Cmdlets can build into very powerful commands. Quite large projects can be undertaken with knowledge of only ten or so PowerShell topics:

- Parameter passing
- Array handling
- String methods
- Get-WmiObject and NewObject
- If...else (and the associated conditions)
- Looping (especially foreach-object)
- Where-Object
- Select-Object
- Measure-Object
- Format-Table and Format-List

Of course, even a book many times the size of this one would not be able to cover every possible use of every object and every Cmdlet. Fortunately, PowerShell has developed a strong Internet community, with many people blogging about it. `http://Microsoft.com/powershell` has links to many of the interesting third-party sites where extensions are available, and there are many blogs. Jeffrey Snover, the father of PowerShell, writes at `http://blogs.msdn.com/powershell` and frequently links to other bloggers. There are also user groups in Europe and North America. So if it isn't covered here, there is usually somewhere you can turn for help.

One important thing to remember is that to do useful scripting work you will only need to use a subset of the available Cmdlets I examined two large projects of my own that total near 2,500 lines. They used 26 Cmdlets between them, and 7 out of 8 calls to a Cmdlet used the ten most popular.

```
Read-host, Write-host, Out-Host, Out-Null, Write-Error, WriteProgress
and WriteOutput.
Join-Path, Split-Path, Resolve-Path and Test-Path
Format-table, Format-List, export-CSV, Import-CSV
For-eachObject, Where-object, Sort-Object, Select-Object, Add-Member ,
Measure-Object
New-Object, Get-WmiObject, Get-EventLog
Start-Sleep and Set-Alias.
```

You don't need to know a lot of PowerShell to get started...what are you waiting for?

Part VI

Appendixes

Appendix A

Windows Scripting API

U se the Windows Script Host Quick Reference to help you quickly find and determine usage for elements you want to work with. The reference is organized by element and by object.

XML Elements

<?XML ?>

```
<?XML
  version="version"
  [standalone="yes"] ?>
```

<runtime>

```
<runtime>
  Self-documentation code. Contains <description>, <example>, <usage>,
<named>, and <unnamed> elements.
</runtime>
```

<description>

```
<description>
  Script description in one or more lines.
</description>
```

<example>

```
<example>
  Usage example for the job.
</example>
```

\<usage\>

```
<usage>
  Usage text that overrides other example and descriptive text.
</usage>
```

\<named\>

```
<named>
  name="ArgName"
  helpstring="HelpText"
  [type="string|boolean|simple"]
  [required="true|false"] />
```

\<unnamed\>

```
<unnamed>
  name="PlaceHolderName"
  helpstring="HelpText"
  [many="true|false"]
  [required="true|false"] />
```

\<package\>

```
<package>
    Code for one or more jobs. Contains <job> elements.
</package>
```

\<job\>

```
<job [id="JobID"]>
 Job code. Contains <?job?>, <object>, <reference>, <resource>, and
<script> elements.
</job>
```

\<?job ?\>

```
<?job
  [error="flag"]
  [debug="flag"] ?>
```

\<object\>

```
<object
  id="objectID"
  [classid="clsid:GUID" | progid="programID"]
  [events="true|false" />
```

\<reference\>

```
<reference
  [object="progID" | guid="typelibGUID"]
  [version="version"] />
```

\<resource\>

```
<resource id="resourceID">
    Isolated string or number
</resource>
```

\<script\>

```
<script
 language="language"
[src="path"]>
      script code
</script>
```

getResource Static Method

Returns the contents of a \<resource\> element as a string.

Usage: VBScript

```
<resource id="ResourceIdentifier"> Resource Text </resource>

<script language="VBScript">
 WScript.Echo getResource("ResourceIdentifier")
</script>
```

Usage: JScript

```
<resource id=" ResourceIdentifier "> Resource Text </resource>

<script language="JScript">
 WScript.Echo(getResource("ResourceIdentifier"));
</script>
```

Drives Collection

Creating: VBScript

```
Set WshNetwork = WScript.CreateObject("WScript.Network")
Set drives = WshNetwork.EnumNetworkDrives
```

Creating: JScript

```
var WshNetwork = WScript.CreateObject("WScript.Network")
var drives = WshNetwork.EnumNetworkDrives
```

Properties

```
object.Count          (Returns: integer)
object.length
object.Item(integer)
```

Printers Collection

Creating: VBScript

```
Set WshNetwork = WScript.CreateObject("WScript.Network")
Set printers = WshNetwork.EnumPrinterConnections
```

Creating: JScript

```
var WshNetwork = WScript.CreateObject("WScript.Network")
var printers = WshNetwork.EnumPrinterConnections
```

Properties

```
object.Count          (Returns: integer)
object.length
object.Item(integer)
```

StdIn Stream*

Creating

```
Set StdIn = WScript.StdIn
var StdIn = WScript.StdIn
```

*Accessible only in CScript.exe.

Methods

```
WScript.StdIn.Close()
WScript.StdIn.Read(characters)
```

```
WScript.StdIn.ReadAll()
WScript.StdIn.ReadLine()
WScript.StdIn.Skip(characters)
WScript.StdIn.SkipLine()
```

Properties

```
WScript.StdIn.AtEndOfLine        (Returns: boolean flag)
WScript.StdIn.AtEndOfStream        (Returns: boolean flag)
WScript.StdIn.Column        (Returns: integer)
WScript.StdIn.Line        (Returns: integer)
```

StdErr Stream*

Creating

```
Set StdErr = WScript.StdErr
var StdErr = WScript.StdErr
```

*Accessible only in CScript.exe.

Methods

```
WScript.StdErr.Close()
WScript.StdErr.Write("text")
WScript.StdErr.WriteBlankLines(numberOfLines)
WScript.StdErr.WriteLine(["text"])
```

StdOut Stream*

Creating

```
Set StdOut = WScript.StdOut
var StdOut = WScript.StdOut
```

*Accessible only in CScript.exe.

Methods

```
WScript.StdOut.Close()
WScript.StdOut.Write("text")
WScript.StdOut.WriteBlankLines(numberOfLines)
WScript.StdOut.WriteLine(["text"])
```

WshArguments Collection

Creating

```
Set args = WScript.Arguments
var args = WScript.Arguments
```

Methods

```
object.Count()          (Returns: integer)
object.ShowUsage()        (Returns: string)
```

Properties

```
object.length
object.Item(integer)
object.Named          (Returns: WshNamed collection)
object.Unnamed          (Returns: WshUnnamed collection)
```

WshNamed Collection

Creating

```
Set argsNamed = WScript.Arguments.Named
var argsNamed = WScript.Arguments.Named
```

Method

```
object.Count()          (Returns: integer)
```

Properties

```
object.length
object.Item(integer)
```

WshUnnamed Collection

Creating

```
Set argsUnnamed = WScript.Arguments.Unnamed
var argsUnnamed = WScript.Arguments.Unnamed
```

Method

```
object.Count()          (Returns: integer)
```

Properties

```
object.length
object.Item(integer)
```

Script.Signer Object

Creating

```
Set Signer = CreateObject("Scripting.Signer")
var Signer = new ActiveXObject("Scripting.Signer")
```

Method

```
object.Sign(FileExtension, ScriptToSign, Certificate[, CertStore])
object.SignFile(ScriptToSign, Certificate[, CertStore])
object.Verify(FileExtension, ScriptToVerify, PromptUser])
object.VerifyFile(ScriptToVerify, PromptUser])
```

WScript Object

Creating

Top-level object; forming the root of the object hierarchy.

Methods

```
WScript.ConnectObject(objectName,
                      eventPrefix)
WScript.CreateObject(objectName
                     [,eventPrefix])
WScript.DisconnectObject(objectName)
WScript.Echo([Arg1]
            [,Arg2]
            [,ArgN])
WScript.GetObject(pathToFileContainingAutomationObject
                  [,programID]
                  [,eventPrefix])
WScript.Quit([errorCode])
WScript.Sleep(numberOfMilliseconds)
```

Properties

```
WScript.Arguments            (Returns: WshArguments collection)
WScript.BuildVersion           (Returns: integer)
WScript.FullName     (Returns: string; full path to host executable)
WScript.Interactive  (Returns: Boolean)
WScript.Name          (Returns: string; name of WScript object)
WScript.Path (Returns: string; directory where script host resides)
WScript.ScriptFullName(Returns: string; full path to current script)
WScript.ScriptName       (Returns: string; name of current script)
WScript.StdErr           (Returns: StdErr stream)
WScript.StdIn          (Returns: StdIn stream)
WScript.StdOut          (Returns: StdOut stream)
WScript.Version          (Returns: script; script host version)
```

WshController Object

Creating

```
Set Controller = WScript.CreateObject("WSHController")
var Controller = WScript.CreateObject("WSHController")
```

Method

```
object.CreateScript("scriptPathAndArgs"[, RemoteComputer])
```

WshEnvironment Object

Creating: VBScript

```
Set WshShell = WScript.CreateObject("WScript.Shell")
Set WshEnv = WshShell.Environment("EnvironmentVariableType")
```

Creating: JScript

```
var WshShell = WScript.CreateObject("WScript.Shell")
var WshEnv = WshShell.Environment("EnvironmentVariableType")
```

Methods

```
object.Count()         (Returns: integer)
object.remove("environmentVariableToDelete")
```

Properties

```
object.length
object.Item("folderName")
```

WshNetwork Object

Creating

```
Set wn = WScript.CreateObject("WScript.Network")
var wn = WScript.CreateObject("WScript.Network")
```

Methods

```
object.AddPrinterConnection("localPort",
                            "networkPrinterPath"
                            [,"storeProfileFlag"]
                            [,"userName"]
                            [,"password"])
object.AddWindowsPrinterConnection("networkPrinterPath")
object.EnumNetworkDrives()
object.EnumPrinterConnections()
object.MapNetworkDrive("driveLetter",
                       "networkShare",
                       [,"storeProfileFlag"]
                       [,"userName"]
                       [,"password"])
object.RemoveNetworkDrive("driveLetterOrNetworkPath"
                          [,"forceFlag"]
                          [,"updateProfileFlag"])
object.RemovePrinterConnection("printerPortOrNetworkPath"
                               [,"forceFlag"]
                               [,"updateProfileFlag"])
object.SetDefaultPrinter("remotePrinterName")
```

Properties

```
object.ComputerName     (Returns: string; current computer name)
object.UserDomain       (Returns: string; current user domain)
object.UserName         (Returns: string; current user name)
```

WshRemote Object

Creating: VBScript

```
Set Controller = WScript.CreateObject("WSHController")
Set RemoteScript = Controller.CreateScript("ScriptToRun","RemoteComp")
```

Creating: JScript

```
var Controller = WScript.CreateObject("WSHController");
var RemoteScript = Controller.CreateScript("ScriptToRun","RemoteComp");
```

Methods

```
object.Execute()
object.Terminate()
```

Properties

```
object.Error (Returns: WshRemoteError object)
object.Status (Returns: status value)
```

Events

```
object_End()
object_Error()
object_Start()
```

WshRemoteError Object

Returned by the Error property of the WshRemote object.

Properties

```
object.Character (Returns: signed long integer; position of error)
object.Description (Returns: string; description of error)
object.Line (Returns: unsigned long integer; line number of error)
object.Number (Returns: unsigned long integer; number of error)
object.Source (Returns: string; source object that caused error)
object.String (Returns: string; source code that caused error)
```

WshScriptExec Object

Creating: VBScript

```
Set WshShell = CreateObject("WScript.Shell")
Set progExec = WshShell.Exec("ProgramToRun")
```

Creating: JScript

```
var WshShell = new ActiveXObject("WScript.Shell");
var progExec = WshShell.Exec("ProgramToRun");
```

Methods

```
object.Terminate()
```

Properties

```
object.ExitCode      (Returns:exit code)
object.ProcessID     (Returns: program's process id for activation)
object.Status        (Returns:status code)
object.StdErr        (Returns:stderr stream)
object.StdIn         (Returns:stdin stream)
object.StdOut        (Returns:stdout stream)
```

WshShell Object

Creating

```
Set ws = WScript.CreateObject("WScript.Shell")
var ws = WScript.CreateObject("WScript.Shell")
```

Methods

```
object.AppActivate("appTitle")
object.CreateShortcut(shortcutNamePath)
object.Exec("programToRun")
object.ExpandEnvironmentStrings(environmentVariableToExpand)
object.LogEvent(eventType,
                "eventDescription"
                [,"targetSystem"])
object.Popup("popupText",
```

```
                          [secondsToWait]
                          [,"popupTitle"]
                          [,buttonType])
            object.RegDelete("pathToRegistryKeyOrValue")
            object.RegRead("pathToRegistryKeyOrValue")
            object.RegWrite("pathToRegistryKeyOrValue"
                          valueToWrite
                          [,dataType])
            object.Run("command"
                    [,windowStyle]
                    ["waitOnReturnFlag"])
            object.SendKeys("keysToSend")
```

Properties

```
            object.CurrentDirectory [= "PathToUseAsCurrent"]
            object.Environment(["environmentVariableType"])
            object.SpecialFolders("specialFolderName")
```

WshShortcut Object

Creating: VBScript

```
            Set WshShell = WScript.CreateObject("WScript.Shell")
            Set linkShortcut = WshShell.CreateShortcut("Name.LNK")
```

Creating: JScript

```
            var WshShell = WScript.CreateObject("WScript.Shell")
            var linkShortcut = WshShell.CreateShortcut("Name.LNK")
```

Methods

```
            object.Save()
```

Properties

```
            object.Arguments = "argString"
            object.Description = "shortcutDescription"
            object.FullName          (Returns: string; full file path to shortcut)
            object.Hotkey = "hotKey"
            object.IconLocation = "iconPath, iconIndex"
            object.RelativePath = "relativePath"
            object.TargetPath = "filePath"
            object.WindowStyle = "windowStyle"
            object.WorkingDirectory = "workingDirectory"
```

WshSpecialFolders Object

Creating: VBScript

```
Set WshShell = WScript.CreateObject("WScript.Shell")
folder = WshShell.SpecialFolders("SpecialFolderName")
```

Creating: JScript

```
var WshShell = WScript.CreateObject("WScript.Shell")
folder = WshShell.SpecialFolders("SpecialFolderName")
```

Method

```
object.Count()                    (Returns: integer)
```

Properties

```
object.length
object.Item("folderName")
```

WshUrlShortcut Object

Creating: VBScript

```
Set WshShell = WScript.CreateObject("WScript.Shell")
Set urlShortcut = WshShell.CreateShortcut("Name.URL")
```

Creating: JScript

```
var WshShell = WScript.CreateObject("WScript.Shell")
var urlShortcut = WshShell.CreateShortcut("Name.URL")
```

Methods

```
object.Save()
```

Properties

```
object.FullName          (Returns: string; full file path to shortcut)
object.TargetPath = "urlPath"
```

Appendix B

Core ADSI Reference

ctive Directory Service Interfaces provide the core objects used to script directory services, computer resources, and networks. This appendix provides a quick reference for key interfaces, and their related properties and methods. The reference is not meant to be exhaustive; rather, the focus is on the most commonly used features in Windows scripts.

Using This Reference

ADSI providers implement the interfaces examined in this appendix. In Chapter 21, you learned about system providers, specifically WinNT, LDAP, NDS, and NWCOMPAT. These providers implement different subsets of these interfaces. Because each object implements multiple interfaces and there is almost always overlap between objects, it isn't practical to map out each object separately.

Instead, you'll use Tables 21-2 through 21-5 in Chapter 21 and this appendix to map out the core features of an object. For example, if you wanted to determine the complete set of methods and properties that are available for the WinNT `Computer` object, you would look at Table 21-3 and see that the object implements `IADs`, `IADsComputer`, `IADsComputerOperations`, `IADsContainer`, and `IADsPropertyList`. You would then examine each of these interfaces in order to determine available properties and methods that may be available to the WinNT `Computer` object.

With the LDAP and NDS providers, keep in mind that `GenObject` provides basic services for most objects. For example, with the LDAP `Group` object, Table 21-2 shows that `Group` implements

- `IADsGroup`
- `IADsExtension`

and GenObject implements

- IADs
- IADsContainer
- IADsDeleteOps
- IADsObjectOptions
- IADsPropertyList
- IDirectoryObject
- IDirectorySearch

Thus, the combination of features for these interfaces represents the total set of methods and properties that may be available to the Group object.

ADSI Interfaces

The sections that follow provide a quick reference for ADSI interfaces. ADSI providers and ADSI are completely extensible. This means that new versions of providers and ADSI may add or change key features. *Providers don't have to implement all the features of an interface, either.*

IADs

The IADs interface provides the core features for all ADSI objects. You obtain a pointer to this interface when you bind to an object, as follows:

```
Set user = GetObject("LDAP://CN=William Stanek,CN=Users
,DC=TVPRESS, DC=Com")
user.Put "givenName", "William"
user.Put "sn", "Stanek"
user.SetInfo
```

Properties

AdsPath

Value: String   **Gettable:** Yes   **Settable:** No

Description: The object's ADsPath that uniquely identifies this object from all others.

Class

Value: String   **Gettable:** Yes   **Settable:** No

Description: The name of the object's class.

GUID

Value: String   **Gettable:** Yes   **Settable:** No

Description: The GUID of the object from the directory store.

Name

Value: String   **Gettable:** Yes   **Settable:** No

Description: The object's relative name.

Parent

Value: String   **Gettable:** Yes   **Settable:** No

Description: The ADsPath string for the parent of the object.

Schema

Value: String   **Gettable:** Yes   **Settable:** No

Description: The ADsPath string to the schema class object for this object.

Methods

Get("propertyName")

Returns: String or array

Description: Gets a property Value from the property cache.

GetEx("propertyName")

Returns: Array

Description: Gets an array of cached property Values.

GetInfo()

Returns: Error status

Description: Gets property Values for an object from the directory store and loads them into the property cache. Called implicitly the first time you get an object's property. Overwrites any previously cached values for the object.

GetInfoEx("propertyName")

Returns: Error status

Description: Gets the Values for the select property from the directory store and loads them into the property cache.

Put("propertyName", valueString)

Returns: Error status

Description: Sets a new Value in the property cache.

PutEx(Flag, "propertyName", valueArray)

Returns: Error status

Description: Sets an array of cached Values.

SetInfo()

Returns: Error status

Description: Saves the object's cached Values to the data store.

IADsAcl

The IADsAcl interface is used to work with ACL attribute Values in Novell NetWare Directory Services (NDS).

Properties

Privileges

Value: Number   **Gettable:** Yes   **Settable:** Yes

Description: The privilege setting.

ProtectedAttrName

Value: String   **Gettable:** Yes   **Settable:** Yes

Description: The name of the protected attribute.

SubjectName

Value: String   **Gettable:** Yes   **Settable:** Yes

Description: The name of the subject.

Method

CopyAcl()

Returns: Error status

Description: Makes a copy of an existing ACL.

IADsADSystemInfo

The `IADsADSystemInfo` interface provides information about Windows computers in Windows domains. You obtain a pointer to this interface when you bind to an object, as follows:

```
Dim wincomputer
Set wincomputer = CreateObject("ADwincomputertemInfo")
Response.Write "User: " & wincomputer.UserName
Response.Write "Computer: " & wincomputer.ComputerName
Response.Write "Domain: " & wincomputer.DomainDNSName
Response.Write "PDC Role Owner: " & wincomputer.PDCRoleOwner
```

Properties

ComputerName

Value: String   **Gettable**: Yes   **Settable**: No

Description: The distinguished name of the local computer.

DomainDNSName

Value: String   **Gettable**: Yes   **Settable**: No

Description: The DNS name of the local computer domain.

DomainShortName

Value: String   **Gettable**: Yes   **Settable**: No

Description: The domain component of the local domain name.

ForestDNSName

Value: String   **Gettable**: Yes   **Settable**: No

Description: The DNS name of the local computer forest.

IsNativeMode

Value: Boolean   **Gettable**: Yes   **Settable**: No

Description: Boolean Value that indicates whether the local computer's domain is running in Windows 2000 native or higher mode, or Windows 2000 mixed mode.

PDCRoleOwner

Value: String   **Gettable**: Yes   **Settable**: No

Description: The distinguished name of the domain controller that owns the PDC emulate role in the local computer domain.

SchemaRoleOwner

Value: String   **Gettable:** Yes   **Settable:** No

Description: The distinguished name of the domain controller that owns the Schema Master role in the local computer domain.

SiteName

Value: String   **Gettable:** Yes   **Settable:** No

Description: The name of the local computer site.

UserName

Value: String   **Gettable:** Yes   **Settable:** No

Description: The distinguished name of the currently logged on user or the user context under which the thread is running.

Method

GetAnyDCName()

Returns: String.

Description: Method obtains the DNS name of an available domain controller in the local computer's domain.

GetDCSiteName()

Returns: String.

Description: Method obtains the name of the Active Directory site that contains the local computer.

RefreshSchemaCache()

Returns: Error code.

Description: Method performs an immediate update to the schema so that you can view the schema with all current changes.

GetTrees()

Returns: Array of strings.

Description: Method obtains the DNS names of all directory trees in the local computer's forest.

IADsBackLink

The `IADsBackLink` interface is used to access the Back Link attribute in Novell NetWare Directory Services (NDS).

Properties

ObjectName

Value: String   **Gettable:** Yes   **Settable:** Yes

Description: The name of an object to which the Back Link is attached.

RemoteID

Value: Number   **Gettable:** Yes   **Settable:** Yes

Description: The numeric identifier of a remote server.

IADsCaseIgnoreList

The `IADsCaseIgnoreList` interface is used to access the Case Ignore List attribute in Novell NetWare Directory Services (NDS).

Property

CaseIgnoreList

Value: Array   **Gettable:** Yes   **Settable:** Yes

Description: A sequence of case-insensitive strings.

IADsClass

The `IADsClass` interface is designed for managing schema class objects. You access an object's schema class through its `Schema` property, as follows:

```
Set obj = GetObject("WinNT://zeta,computer")
Set cls = GetObject(obj.Schema)

For Each p in cls.MandatoryProperties
    WScript.Echo "Mandatory: " & p
Next
For Each p in cls.OptionalProperties
    WScript.Echo "Optional: " & p
Next
```

Properties

Abstract

Value: Boolean   **Gettable:** Yes   **Settable:** Yes

Description: Boolean Value that indicates whether the schema class is abstract.

AuxDerivedFrom

Value: Array   **Gettable:** Yes   **Settable:** Yes

Description: Array of AdsPath strings that specify the super Auxiliary classes of this schema class.

Auxiliary

Value: Boolean   **Gettable:** Yes   **Settable:** Yes

Description: Boolean Value that determines whether this schema class is an Auxiliary class.

CLSID

Value: String   **Gettable:** Yes   **Settable:** Yes

Description: A provider-specific string that identifies the COM object that implements this schema class.

Container

Value: Boolean   **Gettable:** Yes   **Settable:** Yes

Description: Boolean Value that indicates whether this is a Container object.

Containment

Value: Array   **Gettable:** Yes   **Settable:** Yes

Description: Array of strings that identify object types that can be contained within this container.

DerivedFrom

Value: Array   **Gettable:** Yes   **Settable:** Yes

Description: Array of AdsPath strings that indicate which classes this class is derived from.

HelpFileContext

Value: String   **Gettable:** Yes   **Settable:** Yes

Description: The context identifier for an optional help file.

HelpFileName

Value: String   **Gettable:** Yes   **Settable:** Yes

Description: The name of an optional help file.

MandatoryProperties

Value: Array   **Gettable:** Yes   **Settable:** Yes

Description: An array of strings that lists the mandatory properties for an ADSI object.

NamingProperties

Value: Array   **Gettable:** Yes   **Settable:** Yes

Description: An array of strings that list the properties that are used for naming attributes.

OID

Value: String   **Gettable:** Yes   **Settable:** Yes

Description: The directory-specific object identifier.

OptionalProperties

Value: Array   **Gettable:** Yes   **Settable:** Yes

Description: An array of strings that list the optional properties for an ADSI object.

PossibleSuperiors

Value: Array   **Gettable:** Yes   **Settable:** Yes

Description: An array of `AdsPath` strings that lists classes that can contain instances of this class.

PrimaryInterface

Value: String   **Gettable:** Yes   **Settable:** No

Description: The globally unique identifier of the interface defining this schema class.

Method

Qualifiers()

Returns: Collection of ADSI objects

Description: Method obtains a collection with additional provider-specific limits on the object class. (Not currently implemented)

IADsCollection

The `IADsCollection` interface is used to manage collections. Two special types of collections are `IADsContainer` and `IADsMembers`. You can obtain a collection of session objects as follows:

```
Set fso = GetObject("WinNT://zeta/LanmanServer")
Set coll = fso.Sessions

For Each session In coll
  WScript.Echo "Session name: " & session.Name
Next
```

Methods

Add(Object)

Returns: Error status

Description: Adds an object to the collection. Some collections don't support adding objects.

Remove(Object)

Returns: Error status

Description: Removes an object from the collection. Some collections don't support removing objects.

GetObject(Object)

Returns: Error status

Description: Gets the specified object. Some collections don't support this method.

IADsComputer

The IADsComputer interface is used to manage computers on a network. You can use this interface when you bind to a computer object, as follows:

```
Set comp = GetObject("WinNT://zeta,computer")
If (comp.Class = "Computer") Then
 'Do the following
End If
```

Properties

ComputerID

Value: String   **Gettable:** Yes   **Settable:** No

Description: The globally unique identifier for this machine.

Department

Value: String   **Gettable:** Yes   **Settable:** Yes

Description: The department to which this computer belongs.

Description

Value: String   **Gettable:** Yes   **Settable:** Yes

Description: The description of this computer.

Division

Value: String   **Gettable:** Yes   **Settable:** Yes

Description: The division to which this computer belongs.

Location

Value: String   **Gettable:** Yes   **Settable:** Yes

Description: The physical location of this computer.

MemorySize

Value: Number   **Gettable:** Yes   **Settable:** Yes

Description: The amount of RAM in MB.

Model

Value: String   **Gettable:** Yes   **Settable:** Yes

Description: The model of this computer.

NetAddresses

Value: Array   **Gettable:** Yes   **Settable:** Yes

Description: The network addresses of the computer.

OperatingSystem

Value: String   **Gettable:** Yes   **Settable:** Yes

Description: The installed operating system in use.

OperatingSystemVersion

Value: String   **Gettable:** Yes   **Settable:** Yes

Description: The version of installed operating system in use.

Owner

Value: String   **Gettable:** Yes   **Settable:** Yes

Description: The owner of this computer.

PrimaryUser

Value: String   **Gettable:** Yes   **Settable:** Yes

Description: The contact person for this computer.

Processor

Value: String   **Gettable:** Yes   **Settable:** Yes

Description: The type of CPU.

ProcessorCount

Value: Number   **Gettable:** Yes   **Settable:** Yes

Description: The number of processors installed in this computer.

Role

Value: String   **Gettable:** Yes   **Settable:** Yes

Description: The role of this computer, such as server or workstation.

Site

Value: String   **Gettable:** Yes   **Settable:** No

Description: The globally unique identifier for the site to which the computer belongs.

StorageCapacity

Value: Number   **Gettable:** Yes   **Settable:** Yes

Description: The size of disk space in MB.

IADsComputerOperations

The `IADsComputerOperations` interface provides extended functions for computers. You can bind to a `Computer` object and use this interface as follows:

```
Set user = GetObject("WinNT://domainName/computerName,computer")
```

Methods

Shutdown("rebootFlag")

Returns: Error status

Description: Executes a remote shutdown of a computer. Set rebootFlag to true for reboot after shutdown.

Status()

Returns: Status code

Description: Returns the current operations status of the computer.

IADsContainer

The `IADsContainer` interface enables container objects to create, delete, and manage contained ADSI objects. You obtain a pointer to this interface when you bind to a container object, as follows:

```
Set obj = GetObject("WinNT://zeta,computer")
Set cls = GetObject(obj.Schema)
If (cls.Container = TRUE) then
    WScript.Echo "The object is a container."
Else
    WScript.Echo "The object is not a container."
End If
```

Properties

Count

Value: Number   **Gettable:** Yes   **Settable:** No

Description: The number of directory objects in the container or the number of filtered items.

Filter

Value: Array   **Gettable:** Yes   **Settable:** Yes

Description: Items in the array represent object classes.

Hints

Value: Array   **Gettable:** Yes   **Settable:** Yes

Description: Items in the array represent properties found in the schema definition.

Methods

CopyHere("AdsPath","newName")

Returns: Error status

Description: Creates a copy of an object within a directory.

Create("objectClass","relativeName")

Returns: Error status

Description: Creates a new object within a container.

Delete("objectClass","relativeName")

Returns: Error status

Description: Deletes a specified object from a container.

GetObject("objectClass","relativeName")

Returns: Error status

Description: Gets interface for a named object.

MoveHere("AdsPathToObject","relativeName")

Returns: Error status

Description: Moves or renames an object within a directory.

IADsDeleteOps

The `IADsDeleteOps` interface provides a method that an object can use to delete itself from the directory store. With container objects, the method also deletes all objects within the container. If the object doesn't implement this interface, you can delete the object via the parent object. You can use `IADsDeleteOps` to delete an object as follows:

```
Set cont = GetObject("LDAP://OU=marketing,DC=tvpress,DC=com")
cont.DeleteObject(0)
```

Method

DeleteObject(Flag)

Returns: Error status

Description: Deletes the object from the directory. Set the deletion flag to zero.

IADsDomain

The `IADsDomain` interface is designed for managing resources in domains. You can use this interface when you bind to a domain object, as in the following:

```
Set comp = GetObject("WinNT://zeta ")
If (comp.Class = "Domain") Then
 'Do the following
End If
```

Properties

AutoUnlockInterval

Value: Number   **Gettable:** Yes   **Settable:** Yes

Description: The minimum time that can elapse before a locked account is automatically re-enabled.

IsWorkgroup

Value: Boolean   **Gettable:** Yes   **Settable:** No

Description: A Boolean that determines whether the computer is a member of a workgroup, rather than a domain.

LockoutObservationInterval

Value: Number   **Gettable:** Yes   **Settable:** Yes

Description: The time interval during which the bad password counter is increased.

MaxBadPasswordsAllowed

Value: Number   **Gettable:** Yes   **Settable:** Yes

Description: The maximum bad password logins before the account is locked out.

MaxPasswordAge

Value: Number   **Gettable:** Yes   **Settable:** Yes

Description: The maximum time that can elapse before a password must be changed.

MinPasswordAge

Value: Number   **Gettable:** Yes   **Settable:** Yes

Description: The minimum time that can elapse before a password can be changed.

MinPasswordLength

Value: Number   **Gettable:** Yes   **Settable:** Yes

Description: The minimum number of characters required in a password.

PasswordAttributes

Value: Number   **Gettable:** Yes   **Settable:** Yes

Description: The restrictions on passwords. Restrictions are set with the following:

- `PASSWORD_ATTR_NONE` or 0x00000000
- `PASSWORD_ATTR_MIXED_CASE` or 0x00000001
- `PASSWORD_ATTR_COMPLEX` or 0x00000002

With `PASSWORD_ATTR_COMPLEX`, the password must include at least one punctuation mark or non-printable character.

PasswordHistoryLength

Value: Number   **Gettable:** Yes   **Settable:** Yes

Description: The number of passwords saved in the password history. Users cannot reuse a password in the history list.

IADsEmail

The `IADsEmail` interface is used to access the Email Address attribute in Novell NetWare Directory Services (NDS).

Properties

Address

Value: String   **Gettable:** Yes   **Settable:** Yes

Description: The e-mail address of the user.

Type

Value: Number   **Gettable:** Yes   **Settable:** Yes

Description: The type of the e-mail message.

IADsExtension

The `IADsExtension` interface provides features for extending ADSI. Used with interfaces that extend core ADSI. You won't normally access this interface directly in scripts.

IADsFaxNumber

The `IADsFaxNumber` interface is used to access the Facsimile Telephone Number attribute in Novell NetWare Directory Services (NDS).

Properties

Parameters

Value: Array   **Gettable:** Yes   **Settable:** Yes

Description: Parameters for the fax machine.

TelephoneNumber

Value: String   **Gettable:** Yes   **Settable:** Yes

Description: The telephone number of the fax machine.

IADsFileService

The IADsFileService interface is used to manage file services. This interface inherits from IADsService, and only additional properties are detailed in this section. You can use this interface when you bind to a file service, as follows:

```
Set fs = GetObject("WinNT://zeta/LanmanServer")

fs.Description = "WinNT file service."
n = fs.MaxUserCount
If n = -1 Then
    WScript.Echo "No limit on LanmanServer."
Else
    WScript.Echo n & " users are allowed."
End If
```

To access active sessions or open resources used by the file service, you have to go through the IADsFileServiceOperations interface.

Properties

Description

Value: String   **Gettable:** Yes   **Settable:** Yes

Description: The description of the file service.

MaxUserCount

Value: Number   **Gettable:** Yes   **Settable:** Yes

Description: The maximum number of users allowed to run the service concurrently. A Value of –1 indicates no limit is set.

IADsFileServiceOperations

The IADsFileServiceOperations interface provides extended functions for file services. You can bind to a FileService object and use this interface as follows:

```
Set user = GetObject("WinNT://domainName/computerName/LanmanServer")
```

The IADsFileServiceOperations interface allows you to work with open resources and active sessions of the file service through IADsSession and IADsResource, respectively. You can use these collections as follows:

```
Set fso = GetObject("WinNT://zeta/LanmanServer")
For Each resource In fso.Resources
    WScript.Echo "Resource path: " & resource.Path
```

```
Next
For Each session In fso.sessions
    WScript.Echo "Session name: " & session.Name
Next
```

Methods

Resources()

Returns: Resource collection

Description: Gets an interface pointer on a collection object that represents current open resources for this file service.

Sessions()

Returns: Sessions Collection

Description: Gets an interface pointer on a collection object that represents current open sessions on this file service.

IADsFileShare

The IADsFileShare interface is used to manage shared folders. You can use this interface when you bind to the LanmanServer service on the host computer, as in the following:

```
Set fso = GetObject("WinNT://seattle/zeta/LanmanServer")
Set fs = fso.Create("FileShare", "Test")
WScript.Echo fs.Class
fs.Path = "F:\test"
fs.SetInfo
```

Properties

CurrentUserCount

Value: Number   **Gettable:** Yes   **Settable:** No

Description: The current number of users connected to this share.

Description

Value: String   **Gettable:** Yes   **Settable:** Yes

Description: The description of the file share.

HostComputer

Value: String   **Gettable:** Yes   **Settable:** Yes

Description: The AdsPath reference to the host computer.

Path

Value: String   **Gettable:** Yes   **Settable:** Yes

Description: The file system path to a shared directory.

MaxUserCount

Value: Number   **Gettable:** Yes   **Settable:** Yes

Description: The maximum number of concurrent users for the share.

IADsGroup

The `IADsGroup` interface is used to manage group membership. You can use this interface when you bind to a Group object, as follows:

```
Set grp = GetObject("LDAP://CN=Backup Operators,CN=Builtin,DC=seattle,D
C=domain,DC=com")

grp.Add("LDAP://CN=William R. Stanek,CN=Users,DC=seattle,DC=domain,DC=c
om")

WScript.Echo grp.IsMember("LDAP://CN=William R. Stanek,CN=Users,DC=seat
tle,DC=domain,DC=com")
```

Property

Description

Value: String   **Gettable:** Yes   **Settable:** Yes

Description: The description of the group.

Methods

Add("AdsPathString")

Returns: Error status

Description: Adds an object to a group.

IsMember("AdsPathString")

Returns: Membership flag

Description: Determines whether the user or group is a member. A nonzero Value indicates that the user is a member of the group.

Members("AdsPathString")

Returns: Members object collection

Description: Gets the Members object collection that you can use to iterate through group membership.

Remove("AdsPathString")

Returns: Error status

Description: Removes an object from a group.

IADsHold

The IADsHold interface is used to access the Hold attribute in Novell NetWare Directory Services (NDS).

Properties

Amount

Value: Number   **Gettable:** Yes   **Settable:** Yes

Description: The amount charged against the user for the period on hold.

ObjectName

Value: String   **Gettable:** Yes   **Settable:** Yes

Description: The name of the object on hold.

IADsLargeInteger

The IADsLargeInteger interface is used to manipulate 64-bit integers of the LargeInteger type. Use the formula:

```
largeInt = HighPart * 2³² + LowPart
```

Properties

HighPart

Value: Number   **Gettable:** Yes   **Settable:** Yes

Description: The high part of the integer.

LowPart

Value: Number   **Gettable:** Yes   **Settable:** Yes

Description: The low part of the integer.

IADsLocality

The IADsLocality interface represents the geographical location of a directory element and is used to manage locality. The interface supports organizing accounts by location, organization, and organizational unit. IADsLocality implements IADsContainer. You can access this interface as follows:

```
Set dom = getObject("LDAP://zeta/DC=tvpress, DC=com")
Set loc = dom.GetObject("locality","L=myLocality")
```

Properties

Description

Value: String   **Gettable:** Yes   **Settable:** Yes

Description: The description of the locality.

LocalityName

Value: String   **Gettable:** Yes   **Settable:** Yes

Description: The name of the locality.

PostalAddress

Value: String   **Gettable:** Yes   **Settable:** Yes

Description: The main post office address of the locality.

SeeAlso

Value: String   **Gettable:** Yes   **Settable:** Yes

Description: Other information relevant to the locality.

IADsMembers

The IADsMembers interface is used to manage a collection of objects that belong to a group. You can use this interface when you get the Members object collection, as follows:

```
Set grp = GetObject("LDAP://CN=Administrators,CN=Builtin,
DC=seattle,DC=domain,DC=com")

grp.members.filter = Array("user")
For each usr in grp.members
    WScript.Echo usr.Name & "," & usr.Class & "," & usr.AdsPath
Next
```

Properties

Count

Value: String   **Gettable:** Yes   **Settable:** No

Description: The number of members.

Filter

Value: String   **Gettable:** Yes   **Settable:** Yes

Description: The filter for selection.

IADsNamespaces

The `IADsNamespaces` interface is used to manage namespace objects. You obtain a pointer to this interface when you bind to the object using the "ADs:" string, as in the following:

```
Set ns = GetObject("ADs:")
```

Property

DefaultContainer

Value: Array   **Gettable:** Yes   **Settable:** Yes

Description: The default container name for the current user. You can set this property by assigning an AdsPath. You do not need to call `SetInfo()`.

IADsNetAddress

The `IADsNetAddress` interface is used to access the Net Address attribute in Novell NetWare Directory Services (NDS).

Properties

Address

Value: Array   **Gettable:** Yes   **Settable:** Yes

Description: The network addresses supported.

AddressType

Value: Number   **Gettable:** Yes   **Settable:** Yes

Description: The communication protocol supported.

IADsO

The `IADsO` interface is used to manage the organization to which an account belongs. `IADsO` implements `IADsContainer`. You can use this interface when you obtain a pointer to the domain object, as follows:

```
Set prov = GetObject("LDAP:")
Set org = prov.OpenDSObject("LDAP://DC=SEATTLE,DC=DOMAIN,DC=COM",
"wrstanek@seattle.domain.com","stanek", ADS_SECURE_AUTHENTICATION)

org.Filter = Array("organization")
For each o in org
    WScript.Echo "Fax number of " & o.Name & " : " & o.Description
Next
```

Properties

Description

Value: String   **Gettable:** Yes   **Settable:** Yes

Description: The description of the organization.

FaxNumber

Value: String   **Gettable:** Yes   **Settable:** Yes

Description: The fax number of the organization.

LocalityName

Value: String   **Gettable:** Yes   **Settable:** Yes

Description: The name of the organization.

PostalAddress

Value: String   **Gettable:** Yes   **Settable:** Yes

Description: The postal address of the organization.

SeeAlso

Value: String   **Gettable:** Yes   **Settable:** Yes

Description: The other information relevant to this organization.

TelephoneNumber

Value: String   **Gettable:** Yes   **Settable:** Yes

Description: The telephone number of the organization.

IADsObjectOptions

The `IADsObjectOptions` interface for accessing provider-specific options of an ADSI object. These options are primarily used when searching the directory, as in the following:

```
Set cont = GetObject("LDAP://DC=seattle,DC=domain,DC=com")
srvName = cont.GetOption(ADS_OPTION_SERVERNAME)
WScript.Echo "Server Name for connection: " & srvName
PageSize = cont.GetOption(ADS_OPTION_PAGE_SIZE)
```

Methods

GetOption(optionConstantOrValue)

Returns: Error status

Description: Gets an option. Options are:

- `ADS_OPTION_SERVERNAME` or 0,
- `ADS_OPTION_REFERRALS` or 1,
- `ADS_OPTION_PAGE_SIZE` or 2,
- `ADS_OPTION_SECURITY_MASK` or 3,
- `ADS_OPTION_MUTUAL_AUTH_STATUS` or 4,
- `ADS_OPTION_QUOTA` or 5,
- `ADS_OPTION_PASSWORD_PORTNUMBER` or 6,
- `ADS_OPTION_PASSWORD_METHOD` or 7,
- `ADS_OPTION_ACCUMULATIVE_MODIFICATION` or 8,
- `ADS_OPTION_SKIP_SID_LOOKUP` or 9

SetOption(optionConstantOrValue, integerValue)

Returns: Error status

Description: Sets an option.

IADsOctetList

The `IADsOctetList` interface is used to access the `OctetList` attribute in Novell NetWare Directory Services (NDS).

Property

OctetList

Value: Array   **Gettable:** Yes   **Settable:** Yes

Description: An ordered sequence of byte arrays.

IADsOpenDSObject

The IADsOpenDSObject interface is designed to obtain an object reference securely. You obtain a pointer to this interface when you bind to the ADSI provider that you want to work with, as follows:

```
Set prov = GetObject("WinNT:")
Set user = prov.OpenDSObject("WinNT://" & NTDomain & "/" &
NTUser,"wrstane","jiggyPop", ADS_SECURE_AUTHENTICATION)
```

Method

OpenDSObject(ADSPath, UserID, Password, Flags)

Returns: Pointer to the object

Description: Binds to an ADSI object using the specified credentials.

IADsOU

The IADsOU interface is used to manage the organizational unit to which an account belongs. IADsOU implements IADsContainer. You can use this interface when you obtain a pointer to the domain object, as in the following:

```
Set prov = GetObject("LDAP:")
Set org = prov.OpenDSObject("LDAP://DC=SEATTLE,DC=DOMAIN,DC=COM",
"wrstanek@seattle.domain.com","stanek", ADS_SECURE_AUTHENTICATION)

org.Filter = Array("OrganizationalUnit")
For each o in org
    WScript.Echo "Category " & o.BusinessCategory & " : " &
        o.Description
Next
```

Properties

BusinessCategory

Value: String   **Gettable:** Yes   **Settable:** Yes

Description: The business function of the organizational unit.

Description

Value: String   **Gettable:** Yes   **Settable:** Yes

Description: The description of the organizational unit.

FaxNumber

Value: String   **Gettable:** Yes   **Settable:** Yes

Description: The fax number of the unit.

LocalityName

Value: String   **Gettable:** Yes   **Settable:** Yes

Description: The physical location of the unit.

PostalAddress

Value: String   **Gettable:** Yes   **Settable:** Yes

Description: The post office address of the unit.

SeeAlso

Value: String   **Gettable:** Yes   **Settable:** Yes

Description: Other information relevant to the unit.

TelephoneNumber

Value: String   **Gettable:** Yes   **Settable:** Yes

Description: The telephone number of the unit.

IADsPath

The IAdsPath interface is used to access the Path attribute in Novell NetWare Directory Services (NDS).

Properties

Path

Value: String   **Gettable:** Yes   **Settable:** Yes

Description: The file path for a directory.

Type

Value: Number   **Gettable:** Yes   **Settable:** Yes

Description: The type of file system.

VolumeName

Value: String   **Gettable:** Yes   **Settable:** Yes

Description: The name of the volume.

IADsPathname

The IAdsPathname interface is used to examine, extract, and construct paths. You can use this interface with any AdsPath.

Property

EscapedMode

Value: Number   **Gettable:** Yes   **Settable:** Yes

Description: The mode for escaping a path. Valid modes are:

```
ADS_ESCAPEDMODE_DEFAULT or 1
ADS_ESCAPEDMODE_ON or 2
ADS_ESCAPEDMODE_OFF or 3
```

Methods

AddLeafElement("leafElement")

Returns: Error status

Description: Adds an element to the end of the object path.

CopyPath()

Returns: Error status

Description: Instantiates an object with the same path as the current AdsPath.

GetElement(index)

Returns: Error status

Description: Gets the leaf element stored at the index.

GetEscapedElement(number,stringToEscape)

Returns: Escaped string

Description: Takes a path string with special characters and returns the string with escaped Values. The *number* parameter is reserved for future use, so just enter 0.

GetNumElements()

Returns: Number

Description: Gets the number of elements in the path.

RemoveLeafElement()

Returns: Error status

Description: Removes the last element from the path.

Retrieve(formatType)

Returns: AdsPath string

Description: Retrieves a path with a specific format. Formats are:

- ADS_FORMAT_WINDOWS or 1
- ADS_FORMAT_WINDOWS_NO_SERVER or 2
- ADS_FORMAT_WINDOWS_DN or 3
- ADS_FORMAT_WINDOWS_PARENT or 4
- ADS_FORMAT_X500 or 5
- ADS_FORMAT_X500_NO_SERVER or 6
- ADS_FORMAT_X500_DN or 7
- ADS_FORMAT_X500_PARENT or 8
- ADS_FORMAT_SERVER or 9
- ADS_FORMAT_PROVIDER or 10
- ADS_FORMAT_NAMESPACE or 10
- ADS_FORMAT_LEAF or 11

Set("AdsPath",optionType)

Returns: Error status

Description: Sets an AdsPath string with specific type. Option types are:

- ADS_SETTYPE_FULL or 1
- ADS_SETTYPE_PROVIDER or 2
- ADS_SETTYPE_NAMESPACE or 2
- ADS_SETTYPE_SERVER or 3
- ADS_SETTYPE_DN or 4

SetDisplayType(displayType)

Returns: Error status

Description: Determines how a path is to be displayed. Display types are:

- ADS_DISPLAY_FULL or 1
- ADS_DISPLAY_VALUE_ONLY or 2

IADsPostalAddress

The IADsPostalAddress interface is used to access the Postal Address attribute in Novell NetWare Directory Services (NDS).

Properties

PostalAddress

Value: Array   **Gettable:** Yes   **Settable:** Yes

Description: The postal address of the user.

IADsPrintJob

The IADsPrintJob interface represents print jobs. Use the IADsPrintJobOperations interface to manage print jobs. You can access this interface through a PrintQueue object, as follows:

```
Set pq = GetObject("WinNT://zeta/HPDeskJe")
Set pqo = pq
For Each pj in pqo.PrintJobs
    WScript.Echo pj.class
    WScript.Echo pj.description
    WScript.Echo pj.HostPrintQueue
    Set pjo = pj
    If Hex(pjo.status) = 10 Then
       ' if document is printing; pause it
       pjo.Pause
    Else
       pjo.Resume
    End If
Next
```

Properties

Description

Value: String   **Gettable:** Yes   **Settable:** Yes

Description: The description of the print job.

HostPrintQueue

Value: String   **Gettable:** Yes   **Settable:** No

Description: An ADsPath string that names the print queue processing this print job.

Notify

Value: String   **Gettable:** Yes   **Settable:** Yes

Description: The user to be notified when the job is completed.

NotifyPath

Value: String   **Gettable:** Yes   **Settable:** Yes

Description: An `AdsPath` string for the user to be notified when the job is completed.

Priority

Value: Number   **Gettable:** Yes   **Settable:** Yes

Description: The priority of the print job.

Size

Value: Number   **Gettable:** Yes   **Settable:** No

Description: The size of the print job in bytes.

StartTime

Value: Date   **Gettable:** Yes   **Settable:** Yes

Description: The earliest time when the print job should be started.

TimeSubmitted

Value: Date   **Gettable:** Yes   **Settable:** No

Description: The time when the job was submitted to the print queue.

TotalPages

Value: Number   **Gettable:** Yes   **Settable:** No

Description: The total number of pages in the print job.

UntilTime

Value: Date   **Gettable:** Yes   **Settable:** Yes

Description: The time when the print job should be stopped.

User

Value: String   **Gettable:** Yes   **Settable:** No

Description: The name of user who submitted the print job.

UserPath

Value: String   **Gettable:** Yes   **Settable:** No

Description: The `AdsPath` string for the user who submitted the print job.

IADsPrintJobOperations

The IADsPrintJobOperations interface provides extended functions for print jobs. You can use this interface when you obtain a PrintJob object, as follows:

```
Set pqo = GetObject("WinNT://zeta/HPDeskJe")
For each pj in pqo.PrintJobs
 set pjo = pj
 WScript.Echo "Print job status: " & Hex(pjo.status)
Next
```

Properties

PagesPrinted

Value: Number   **Gettable:** Yes   **Settable:** No

Description: The total number of pages printed for the current job.

Position

Value: Number   **Gettable:** Yes   **Settable:** Yes

Description: The numeric position of print job in the print queue.

Status

Value: Number   **Gettable:** Yes   **Settable:** Yes

Description: The status of print job as a hexadecimal Value. The values are:

- ADS_JOB_PAUSED or 0x00000001
- ADS_JOB_ERROR or 0x00000002
- ADS_JOB_DELETING or 0x00000004
- ADS_JOB_PRINTING or 0x00000010
- ADS_JOB_OFFLINE or 0x00000020
- ADS_JOB_PAPEROUT or 0x00000040
- ADS_JOB_PRINTED or 0x00000080
- ADS_JOB_DELETED or 0x00000100

TimeElapsed

Value: Number   **Gettable:** Yes   **Settable:** No

Description: The elapsed time in seconds since the job started printing.

Methods

Pause()

Returns: Error status

Description: Pauses the print job.

Resume()

Returns: Error status

Description: Resumes the print job.

IADsPrintQueue

The IADsPrintQueue interface represents a printer on a network. You can use the IADsPrintQueueOperations interface to control printer queues. You can use the interface when you obtain a PrintQueue object, as follows:

```
Set pq = GetObject("WinNT://zeta/HPDeskJe")
```

You could examine all print queues as follows:

```
Set comp = GetObject("WinNT://zeta,computer")
comp.Filter = Array("PrintQueue")
For Each p In comp
 Set pq = GetObject(p.ADsPath)
 WScript.Echo pq.Name & " is a " & pq.Model
Next
```

Properties

BannerPage

Value: String   **Gettable:** Yes   **Settable:** Yes

Description: The file path to a banner-page file used to separate print jobs.

Datatype

Value: String   **Gettable:** Yes   **Settable:** Yes

Description: The data type that can be processed by the print queue.

DefaultJobPriority

Value: Number   **Gettable:** Yes   **Settable:** Yes
      or String

Description: The default priority assigned to each print job.

Description

Value: String   **Gettable:** Yes   **Settable:** Yes

Description: The description of the print queue.

Location

Value: String   **Gettable:** Yes   **Settable:** Yes

Description: A description of the print queue location.

Model

Value: String   **Gettable:** Yes   **Settable:** Yes

Description: The name of the driver used by the print queue.

NetAddresses

Value: Array   **Gettable:** Yes   **Settable:** Yes

Description: The network IP addresses for the printer (if applicable).

PrintDevices

Value: Array   **Gettable:** Yes   **Settable:** Yes

Description: The names of print devices that the print queue uses as spooling devices.

PrinterPath

Value: String   **Gettable:** Yes   **Settable:** Yes

Description: The network path (for a shared printer).

PrintProcessor

Value: String   **Gettable:** Yes   **Settable:** Yes

Description: The print processor associated with the print queue.

Priority

Value: Number   **Gettable:** Yes   **Settable:** Yes

Description: The priority of this printer object's job queue.

StartTime

Value: Date   **Gettable:** Yes   **Settable:** Yes

Description: The time when the print queue starts processing jobs.

UntilTime

Value: Date   **Gettable:** Yes   **Settable:** Yes

Description: The time at which the print queue stops processing jobs.

IADsPrintQueueOperations

The `IADsPrintQueueOperations` interface provides extended features for print queues. You can work with this interface by getting a pointer to a `PrintQueue` object, as follows:

```
Set pqo = GetObject("WinNT://zeta/HPDeskJe")
If pqo.Status = ADS_PRINTER_TONER_LOW Then
  WScript.Echo "The printer is low on toner."
End If
```

Property

Status

Value: Number   **Gettable:** Yes   **Settable:** No

Description: The current status of the print queue. Valid status codes are:

- ADS_PRINTER_PAUSED or 0x00000001
- ADS_PRINTER_PENDING_DELETION or 0x00000002
- ADS_PRINTER_ERROR or 0x00000003
- ADS_PRINTER_PAPER_JAM or 0x00000004
- ADS_PRINTER_PAPER_OUT or 0x00000005
- ADS_PRINTER_MANUAL_FEED or 0x00000006
- ADS_PRINTER_PAPER_PROBLEM or 0x00000007
- ADS_PRINTER_OFFLINE or 0x00000008
- ADS_PRINTER_IO_ACTIVE or 0x00000100
- ADS_PRINTER_BUSY or 0x00000200
- ADS_PRINTER_PRINTING or 0x00000400
- ADS_PRINTER_OUTPUT_BIN_FULL or 0x00000800
- ADS_PRINTER_NOT_AVAILABLE or 0x00001000
- ADS_PRINTER_WAITING or 0x00002000
- ADS_PRINTER_PROCESSING or 0x00004000
- ADS_PRINTER_INITIALIZING or 0x00008000
- ADS_PRINTER_WARMING_UP or 0x00010000
- ADS_PRINTER_TONER_LOW or 0x00020000

- ADS_PRINTER_NO_TONER or 0x00040000
- ADS_PRINTER_PAGE_PUNT or 0x00080000
- ADS_PRINTER_USER_INTERVENTION or 0x00100000
- ADS_PRINTER_OUT_OF_MEMORY or 0x00200000
- ADS_PRINTER_DOOR_OPEN or 0x00400000
- ADS_PRINTER_SERVER_UNKNOWN or 0x00800000
- ADS_PRINTER_POWER_SAVE or 0x01000000

Methods

Pause()

Returns: Error status

Description: Pauses the print queue.

PrintJobs()

Returns: Print Job Collection

Description: Retrieves a pointer to a collection of print jobs that are managed by the print queue.

Purge()

Returns: Error status

Description: Deletes all jobs from the print queue.

Resume()

Returns: Error status

Description: Resumes the print queue.

IADsProperty

The IADsProperty interface is designed for managing attributes for schema objects. You gain access to an object's properties by binding to the parent schema object, as follows:

```
Set obj = GetObject("WinNT://zeta,computer")
Set cl = GetObject(obj.Schema)
Set sc = GetObject(cl.Parent)
Set prop = sc.GetObject("Property","Owner")
WScript.Echo "Attribute: " & prop.Name
WScript.Echo "Syntax: " & prop.Syntax
WScript.Echo "MaxRange: " & prop.MaxRange
WScript.Echo "MinRange: " & prop.MinRange
WScript.Echo "Multivalued:" & prop.Multivalued
```

Properties

MaxRange

Value: Number   **Gettable:** Yes   **Settable:** Yes

Description: The upper limit of Values for the property.

MinRange

Value: Number   **Gettable:** Yes   **Settable:** Yes

Description: The lower limit of Values for the property.

MultiValued

Value: Boolean   **Gettable:** Yes   **Settable:** Yes

Description: The Boolean Value indicates whether this property supports multiple values.

OID

Value: String   **Gettable:** Yes   **Settable:** Yes

Description: The directory-specific object identifier.

Syntax

Value: String   **Gettable:** Yes   **Settable:** Yes

Description: The property type, such as `String`.

Method

Qualifiers()

Returns: Collection of ADSI objects

Description: Method obtains a collection with additional provider-specific limits on the property.

IADsPropertyEntry

The `IADsPropertyEntry` interface allows a user to specify how a property's Values can be manipulated. To access a property entry, use the `Item` property or call the `GetPropertyItem` method on the `IADsPropertyList` interface, as in the following:

```
Set plist = GetObject("LDAP://zeta/DC=TVPRESS,DC=com")
plist.GetInfo
Set pentry = plist.GetPropertyItem("dc", ADSTYPE_CASE_IGNORE_STRING)
```

Properties

ADS_Type

Value: String   **Gettable:** Yes   **Settable:** Yes

Description: The data type of the property.

ControlCode

Value: String   **Gettable:** Yes   **Settable:** Yes

Description: A constant that specifies the operation to be performed on the property. These constants are ADS_PROPERTY_CLEAR, ADS_PROPERTY_UPDATE, ADS_PROPERTY_APPEND, and ADS_PROPERTY_DELETE.

Name

Value: String   **Gettable:** Yes   **Settable:** Yes

Description: The name of the property entry.

Values

Value: Array   **Gettable:** Yes   **Settable:** Yes

Description: Array representing the Values of the property.

IADsPropertyList

The IADsPropertyList interface is used to manage property entries in the property cache. You gain access to this interface when you load an object's properties into the property cache, as follows:

```
Set plist = GetObject("LDAP://zeta/DC=TVPRESS,DC=com")
plist.GetInfo
```

Property

PropertyCount

Value: String   **Gettable:** Yes   **Settable:** No

Description: The number of properties in the property list.

Methods

GetPropertyItem("propertyName",propertyTypeConstant)

Returns: Property entry

Description: Use this method to obtain a property entry. The normal constant is ADSTYPE_CASE_IGNORE_STRING.

Item(propertyNameOrIndex)

Returns: Property entry

Description: Obtains a property entry by name or index.

Next()

Returns: Property entry

Description: Obtains the next item in the cached property list.

PurgePropertyList()

Returns: Error status

Description: Deletes the cached property list for the object.

PutPropertyItem(propertyEntry)

Returns: Error status

Description: Updates a Value in the cached property list.

Reset()

Returns: Error status

Description: Moves back to the start of the cached property list.

ResetPropertyItem(propertyNameOrIndex)

Returns: Error status

Description: Removes a property from the cached property list by name or by index.

Skip(numberToSkip)

Returns: Error status

Description: Skips a specified number of items in the cached property list.

IADsPropertyValue

The IADsPropertyValue interface represents a property value in a property entry. You can obtain this interface through the Values property of IADsPropertyEntry, as follows:

```
Set plist = GetObject("WinNT://tvpress/zeta/administrator,user")
plist.GetInfo

Set pentry = plist.GetPropertyItem("description", ADSTYPE_CASE_IGNORE_
STRING)
```

```
For Each v In pentry.Values
    Set pval = v
    WScript.Echo pval.CaseIgnoreString
    pval.Clear
Next
```

Properties

ADsType

Value: Number   **Gettable:** Yes   **Settable:** Yes

Description: A constant representing a property's data type.

Boolean

Value: Boolean   **Gettable:** Yes   **Settable:** Yes

Description: A Boolean Value.

CaseExactString

Value: String   **Gettable:** Yes   **Settable:** Yes

Description: A case-sensitive string.

CaseIgnoreString

Value: String   **Gettable:** Yes   **Settable:** Yes

Description: A case-insensitive string.

DNString

Value: String   **Gettable:** Yes   **Settable:** Yes

Description: An object's distinguished name.

Integer

Value: Number   **Gettable:** Yes   **Settable:** Yes

Description: An integer Value.

LargeInteger

Value: Number   **Gettable:** Yes   **Settable:** Yes

Description: A large integer Value.

NumericString

Value: String   **Gettable:** Yes   **Settable:** Yes

Description: A string to be treated as a number.

OctetString

Value: String   **Gettable:** Yes   **Settable:** Yes

Description: A string of eight-bit characters.

PrintableString

Value: String   **Gettable:** Yes   **Settable:** Yes

Description: A printable string.

SecurityDescriptor

Value: Interface   **Gettable:** Yes   **Settable:** Yes
Pointer

Description: A security descriptor of type `IADsSecurityDescriptor`.

UTCTime

Value: String   **Gettable:** Yes   **Settable:** Yes

Description: A date in Coordinated Universal Time format.

Method

Clear()

Returns: Error status

Description: Clears the current Values of the `PropertyValue` object.

IADsPropertyValue2

The `IADsPropertyValue2` interface represents a property value in a property entry, including new and custom-defined data types. You can obtain this interface through the `Values` property of `IADsPropertyEntry`, as follows:

```
Set plist = GetObject("LDAP://server18/DC=cpandl,DC=com")
plist.GetInfo

Set pentry = plist.GetPropertyItem("description", ADSTYPE_CASE_IGNORE_
STRING)

For Each v In pentry.Values
    Set pval = v
    WScript.Echo pval.GetObjectProperty
    pval.Clear
Next
```

Properties

GetObjectProperty

Value: Variant   **Gettable:** Yes   **Settable:** No

Description: A pointer to a Variant that receives the requested attribute Value.

PutObjectProperty

Value: Variant   **Gettable:** No   **Settable:** Yes

Description: A pointer to a Variant that contains the new attribute Value.

IADsReplicaPointer

The IADsReplicaPointer interface is used to access the Replica Pointer attribute in Novell NetWare Directory Services (NDS).

Properties

Count

Value: Number   **Gettable:** Yes   **Settable:** Yes

Description: The number of existing replicas.

ReplicaAddressHints

Value: Array   **Gettable:** Yes   **Settable:** Yes

Description: A network address suggested as a node where a name server might be located.

ReplicaNumber

Value: Number   **Gettable:** Yes   **Settable:** Yes

Description: The ID number of the replica.

ReplicaType

Value: Number   **Gettable:** Yes   **Settable:** Yes

Description: A Value indicating the type of replica as master, secondary, or read-only.

ServerName

Value: String   **Gettable:** Yes   **Settable:** Yes

Description: The name of the server holding the replica.

IADsResource

The IADsResource interface is used to manage open resources for a file service. You can obtain a collection of resources through the FileService object, as follows:

```
Set fso = GetObject("WinNT://zeta/LanmanServer")
If (IsEmpty(fso) = False) Then
    For Each resource In fso.resources
        WScript.Echo "Resource name: " & resource.name
        WScript.Echo "Resource path: " & resource.path
    Next
End If
```

Properties

LockCount

Value: Number   **Gettable:** Yes   **Settable:** No

Description: The number of locks on a resource.

Path

Value: String   **Gettable:** Yes   **Settable:** No

Description: The file path of the resource.

User

Value: String   **Gettable:** Yes   **Settable:** No

Description: The name of the user who opened the resource.

UserPath

Value: String   **Gettable:** Yes   **Settable:** No

Description: The AdsPath string of the user object that is accessing the resource.

IADsSession

The IADsSession interface is used to manage active user sessions for the file service. You can access this interface through the FileService object, as follows:

```
Set fso = GetObject("WinNT://zeta/LanmanServer")
Set s = fso.Sessions
```

Properties

Computer

Value: String   **Gettable:** Yes   **Settable:** No

Description: The name of the client workstation from which the session initiated.

ComputerPath

Value: String   **Gettable:** Yes   **Settable:** No

Description: The ADsPath of the related computer object.

ConnectTime

Value: Number   **Gettable:** Yes   **Settable:** No

Description: The number of minutes since the session began.

IdleTime

Value: Number   **Gettable:** Yes   **Settable:** No

Description: The number of minutes that the session has been idle.

User

Value: String   **Gettable:** Yes   **Settable:** No

Description: The name of user who initiated the session.

UserPath

Value: String   **Gettable:** Yes   **Settable:** No

Description: The ADsPath of the related user object.

IADsService

The IADsService interface is used to manage services on a computer. Services are accessed through the IADsComputer interface, as follows:

```
Set comp = GetObject("WinNT://seattle/zeta/alerter,service")
```

The IADsFileService and IADsFileServiceOperations interfaces provide additional features for file services.

Properties

Dependencies

Value: Array   **Gettable:** Yes   **Settable:** Yes

Description: An array of services that must be running before this service can run.

DisplayName

Value: String   **Gettable:** Yes   **Settable:** Yes

Description: The display name of this service.

ErrorControl

Value: Number   **Gettable:** Yes   **Settable:** Yes

Description: The actions taken in case of service failure. Permissible actions are:

- `ADS_SERVICE_ERROR_IGNORE` or `0x00000000`
- `ADS_SERVICE_ERROR_NORMAL` or `0x00000001`
- `ADS_SERVICE_ERROR_SEVERE` or `0x00000002`
- `ADS_SERVICE_ERROR_CRITICAL` or `0x00000003`

HostComputer

Value: String   **Gettable:** Yes   **Settable:** Yes

Description: The `AdsPath` string of the host computer running the service.

LoadOrderGroup

Value: String   **Gettable:** Yes   **Settable:** Yes

Description: The load order group of which the service is a member.

Path

Value: String   **Gettable:** Yes   **Settable:** Yes

Description: The path and filename of the executable for the service.

ServiceAccountName

Value: String   **Gettable:** Yes   **Settable:** Yes

Description: The name of the account used by the service at startup.

ServiceAccountPath

Value: String   **Gettable:** Yes   **Settable:** Yes

Description: The AdsPath string of the startup account.

ServiceType

Value: Number   **Gettable:** Yes   **Settable:** Yes

Description: The process type in which the service runs. Valid types are:

- ADS_SERVICE_KERNEL_DRIVER or 0x00000001
- ADS_SERVICE_FILE_SYSTEM_DRIVER or 0x00000002
- ADS_SERVICE_OWN_PROCESS or 0x00000010
- ADS_SERVICE_SHARE_PROCESS or 0x00000020

StartType

Value: Number   **Gettable:** Yes   **Settable:** Yes

Description: The start type for the service. Valid types are:

- **ADSI Service Start Type**

  ```
  ADS_SERVICE_BOOT_START
  ADS_SERVICE_SYSTEM_START
  ADS_SERVICE_AUTO_START
  ADS_SERVICE_DEMAND_START
  ADS_SERVICE_DISABLED
  ```

- **Win32 Service Start Type**

  ```
  ADS_SERVICE_BOOT_START
  ADS_SERVICE_SYSTEM_START
  ADS_SERVICE_AUTO_START
  ADS_SERVICE_DEMAND_START
  ADS_SERVICE_DISABLED
  ```

StartupParameters

Value: String   **Gettable:** Yes   **Settable:** Yes

Description: Parameters passed to the service at startup.

Version

Value: String   **Gettable:** Yes   **Settable:** Yes

Description: The version of the service.

IADsServiceOperations

The IADsServiceOperations interface provides extended features for services. File service and file-service operations are managed through IADsFileService and IADsFileService Operations. You can access this interface through the Services object, as follows:

```
Set comp = GetObject("WinNT://zeta,computer")
Set serv = comp.GetObject("Service", "alerter")
```

Property

Status

Value: Number   **Gettable:** Yes   **Settable:** No

Description: The current status of the service. Valid status codes are:

- ADS_SERVICE_STOPPED or 0x00000001
- ADS_SERVICE_START_PENDING or 0x00000002
- ADS_SERVICE_STOP_PENDING or 0x00000003
- ADS_SERVICE_RUNNING or 0x00000004
- ADS_SERVICE_CONTINUE_PENDING or 0x00000005
- ADS_SERVICE_PAUSE_PENDING or 0x00000006
- ADS_SERVICE_PAUSED or 0x00000007
- ADS_SERVICE_ERROR or 0x00000008

Methods

Start()

Returns: Error status

Description: Starts the service.

Stop()

Returns: Error status

Description: Stops the service.

Pause()

Returns: Error status

Description: Pauses the service.

Continue()

Returns: Error status

Description: Resumes a paused service.

SetPassword("newPassword")

Returns: Error status

Description: Sets a new password to be used with the service startup account.

IADsSyntax

The IADsSyntax interface is designed for managing syntax in the schema. You obtain a pointer to this interface when you bind to a property of a schema object, as follows:

```
Set obj = GetObject("WinNT://zeta,computer")
Set cl = GetObject(obj.Schema)
Set sc = GetObject(cl.Parent)
Set prop = sc.GetObject("Property","Owner")
Set synt = GetObject(sc.ADsPath & "/" & prop.Syntax)
WScript.Echo "Automation data type: " & synt.OleAutoDataType
```

Property

OleAutoDataType

Value: Number   **Gettable:** Yes   **Settable:** Yes

Description: Indicates the virtual type constant for the property.

IADsTimestamp

The IADsTimestamp interface is used to access the Timestamp attribute in Novell NetWare Directory Services (NDS).

EventID

Value: Number   **Gettable:** Yes   **Settable:** Yes

Description: An event identifier.

WholeSeconds

Value: Number   **Gettable:** Yes   **Settable:** Yes

Description: The number of whole seconds relative to 12:00 a.m., 1 January, 1970, Universal Time Coordinate (UTC).

IADsTypedName

The `IADsTypedName` interface is used to access the Typed Name attribute in Novell NetWare Directory Services (NDS).

Properties

Interval

Value: Number   **Gettable:** Yes   **Settable:** Yes

Description: The frequency of object references.

Level

Value: Number   **Gettable:** Yes   **Settable:** Yes

Description: The priority level of the object.

ObjectName

Value: String   **Gettable:** Yes   **Settable:** Yes

Description: The name of the object.

IADsUser

The `IADsUser` interface is used to manage user accounts. You can bind to local and domain accounts. To bind to local accounts, use the following syntax:

```
Set user = GetObject("WinNT://computerName/userName,user")
```

To bind to domain accounts, use:

```
Set user = GetObject("WinNT://domainName/userName,user")
```

or use:

```
Set user = GetObject("LDAP://CN=userName,CN=Users, DC=ChildDomain,DC=Domain,DC=RootDomain")
```

Properties

AccountDisabled

Value: Boolean   **Gettable:** Yes   **Settable:** Yes

Description: Boolean that indicates whether the account is disabled.

AccountExpirationDate

Value: Date   **Gettable:** Yes   **Settable:** Yes

Description: The expiration date and time of the user account.

BadLoginAddress

Value: String   **Gettable:** Yes   **Settable:** No

Description: The address that last caused a bad login for the account.

BadLoginCount

Value: Number   **Gettable:** Yes   **Settable:** No

Description: The number of the bad login attempts since login count was last reset.

Department

Value: String   **Gettable:** Yes   **Settable:** Yes

Description: The organizational unit associated with the account.

Description

Value: String   **Gettable:** Yes   **Settable:** Yes

Description: The description of the account.

Division

Value: String   **Gettable:** Yes   **Settable:** Yes

Description: The division associated with the account.

EmailAddress

Value: String   **Gettable:** Yes   **Settable:** Yes

Description: The e-mail address of the account.

EmployeeID

Value: String   **Gettable:** Yes   **Settable:** Yes

Description: The employee ID number associated with the account.

FaxNumber

Value: String or Array   **Gettable:** Yes   **Settable:** Yes

Description: The list of fax numbers associated with the account.

FirstName

Value: String   **Gettable:** Yes   **Settable:** Yes

Description: The first name of the user.

FullName

Value: String   **Gettable:** Yes   **Settable:** Yes

Description: The full name of the user.

GraceLoginsAllowed

Value: Number   **Gettable:** Yes   **Settable:** Yes

Description: The number of times the user can log on after the password has expired.

GraceLoginsRemaining

Value: Number   **Gettable:** Yes   **Settable:** Yes

Description: The number of grace logins remaining.

HomeDirectory

Value: String   **Gettable:** Yes   **Settable:** Yes

Description: The home directory of the user.

HomePage

Value: String   **Gettable:** Yes   **Settable:** Yes

Description: The URL of the user's home page.

IsAccountLocked

Value: Boolean   **Gettable:** Yes   **Settable:** Yes

Description: A Boolean that indicates whether the account is locked.

Languages

Value: Array   **Gettable:** Yes   **Settable:** Yes

Description: An array of acceptable natural languages.

LastFailedLogin

Value: Date   **Gettable:** Yes   **Settable:** No

Description: The date and time of the last failed login.

LastLogin

Value: Date   **Gettable:** Yes   **Settable:** No

Description: The date and time of the last login.

LastLogoff

Value: Date   **Gettable:** Yes   **Settable:** No

Description: The date and time of the last logoff.

LastName

Value: String   **Gettable:** Yes   **Settable:** Yes

Description: The last name of the user.

LoginHours

Value: Array   **Gettable:** Yes   **Settable:** Yes

Description: An array of Values that indicate the time periods during each day of the week that the user can log on.

LoginScript

Value: String   **Gettable:** Yes   **Settable:** Yes

Description: The login script path for the account.

LoginWorkstations

Value: Array   **Gettable:** Yes   **Settable:** Yes

Description: An array of computer names or IP addresses from which the user can log on.

Manager

Value: String   **Gettable:** Yes   **Settable:** Yes

Description: The manager of the user.

MaxLogins

Value: Number   **Gettable:** Yes   **Settable:** Yes

Description: The maximum number of simultaneous login sessions allowed for the account.

MaxStorage

Value: Number   **Gettable:** Yes   **Settable:** Yes

Description: The maximum amount of disk space allowed for the user.

NamePrefix

Value: String   **Gettable:** Yes   **Settable:** Yes

Description: The name prefix of the user, such as Mr. or Mrs.

NameSuffix

Value: String   **Gettable:** Yes   **Settable:** Yes

Description: The name suffix of the user, such as Jr.

OfficeLocations

Value: Array or String   **Gettable:** Yes   **Settable:** Yes

Description: Office locations for the user.

OtherName

Value: String   **Gettable:** Yes   **Settable:** Yes

Description: An additional name of the user, such as a middle name.

PasswordExpirationDate

Value: Date   **Gettable:** Yes   **Settable:** Yes

Description: The date and time when the account password expires.

PasswordLastChanged

Value: Date   **Gettable:** Yes   **Settable:** No

Description: The date and time when the password was last changed.

PasswordMinimumLength

Value: Number   **Gettable:** Yes   **Settable:** Yes

Description: The minimum number of characters allowed in a password.

PasswordRequired

Value: Boolean   **Gettable:** Yes   **Settable:** Yes

Description: Boolean Value that indicates whether a password is required.

Picture

Value: Array   **Gettable:** Yes   **Settable:** Yes

Description: An octet string array of bytes that hold a picture of the user.

PostalAddresses

Value: Array   **Gettable:** Yes   **Settable:** Yes

Description: An array that holds addresses associated with the account.

PostalCodes

Value: Array   **Gettable:** Yes   **Settable:** Yes

Description: An array of zip codes for the postal addresses.

Profile

Value: String   **Gettable:** Yes   **Settable:** Yes

Description: The path to the user's profile.

RequireUniquePassword

Value: Boolean   **Gettable:** Yes   **Settable:** Yes

Description: Boolean Value that indicates whether a new password must be different from ones in the password history.

SeeAlso

Value: Array   **Gettable:** Yes   **Settable:** Yes

Description: Array of `AdsPath` strings for other objects related to this user.

TelephoneHome

Value: Array or String   **Gettable:** Yes   **Settable:** Yes

Description: An array of home phone numbers for the user.

TelephoneMobile

Value: Array or String   **Gettable:** Yes   **Settable:** Yes

Description: An array of mobile phone numbers for the user.

TelephoneNumber

Value: Array or String   **Gettable:** Yes   **Settable:** Yes

Description: An array of work-related phone numbers for the user.

TelephonePager

Value: Array   **Gettable:** Yes   **Settable:** Yes

Description: An array of pager numbers for the user.

Title

Value: String   **Gettable:** Yes   **Settable:** Yes

Description: The user's job title.

Methods

ChangePassword("oldPassword","newPassword")

Returns: Error status

Description: Changes the password for the account.

Groups()

Returns: Error status

Description: Obtains a collection of groups (IADsMembers) to which the user account belongs.

SetPassword("password")

Returns: Error status

Description: Sets the password for a new account.

IDirectoryObject

The IDirectoryObject interface provides non-Automation clients with direct access to directory service objects. Only non-Automation clients can call the methods of IDirectoryObject. Automation clients cannot use IDirectoryObject and instead use the IADs interface.

IDirectorySearch

The IDirectorySearch interface allows non-Automation clients to query the directory. Only non-Automation clients can call the methods of IDirectorySearch. Automation clients cannot use IDirectorySearch and instead use the IADs interface.

ADSI Error Codes

As you've seen in this reference, many methods return an error code. The type of error code you see depends on the ADSI provider that you are using. With WinNT, NDS, and NWCOMPAT, you normally see error codes in the form:

- 0x80005xxx E_ADS_* for standard errors
- 0x00005xxx S_ADS_* for severe errors

The LDAP provider, on the other hand, maps all errors to Win32 errors. Because of this, you'll normally see error codes in the form:

- 0x8007xxxx LDAP_* for LDAP errors
- 0x8007xxxx ERROR_* for Win32 errors

Table B-1 summarizes standard error codes.

TABLE B-1

Standard ADSI Error Codes

Error Code	Error Message	Description
0x00005011	S_ADS_ERRORSOCCURRED	One or more errors occurred.
0x00005012	S_ADS_NOMORE_ROWS	Search operation reached the last row.
0x00005013	S_ADS_NOMORE_COLUMNS	Search operation reached the last column for the current row.
0x80005000	E_ADS_BAD_PATHNAME	An invalid ADSI pathname was passed.
0x80005001	E_ADS_INVALID_DOMAIN_OBJECT	An unknown ADSI domain object was requested.
0x80005002	E_ADS_INVALID_USER_OBJECT	An unknown ADSI user object was requested.
0x80005003	E_ADS_INVALID_COMPUTER_OBJECT	An unknown ADSI computer object was requested.
0x80005004	E_ADS_UNKNOWN_OBJECT	An unknown ADSI object was requested.
0x80005005	E_ADS_PROPERTY_NOT_SET	The specified ADSI property was not set.
0x80005006	E_ADS_PROPERTY_NOT_SUPPORTED	The specified ADSI property is not supported.
0x80005007	E_ADS_PROPERTY_INVALID	The specified ADSI property is invalid
0x80005008	E_ADS_BAD_PARAMETER	One or more input parameters are invalid.
0x80005009	E_ADS_OBJECT_UNBOUND	The specified ADSI object is not bound to the remote resource.
0x8000500A	E_ADS_PROPERTY_NOT_MODIFIED	The specified ADSI object has not been modified.
0x8000500B	E_ADS_PROPERTY_MODIFIED	The specified ADSI object has been modified.

continued

TABLE B-1	(continued)	
Error Code	**Error Message**	**Description**
0x8000500C	E_ADS_CANT_CONVERT_DATATYPE	The data type cannot be converted.
0x8000500D	E_ADS_PROPERTY_NOT_FOUND	The property cannot be found in the cache.
0x8000500E	E_ADS_OBJECT_EXISTS	The ADSI object exists.
0x8000500F	E_ADS_SCHEMA_VIOLATION	The action violates the directory service schema rules.
0x80005010	E_ADS_COLUMN_NOT_SET	The specified column in the ADSI was not set.
0x80005014	E_ADS_INVALID_FILTER	The specified search filter is invalid.

Table B-2 summarizes LDAP error codes and provides the corresponding Win32 error codes.

TABLE B-2

LDAP Error Codes with Win32

ADSI Error Code	LDAP Error Message	Win32 Error Message	Description
0	LDAP_SUCCESS	NO_ERROR	Operation succeeded.
0x80070005	LDAP_INSUFFICIENT_RIGHTS	ERROR_ACCESS_DENIED	User doesn't have sufficient access rights.
0x80070008	LDAP_NO_MEMORY	ERROR_NOT_ENOUGH_MEMORY	System is out of memory.
0x8007001f	LDAP_OTHER	ERROR_GEN_FAILURE	Unknown error occurred.
0x800700ea	LDAP_PARTIAL_RESULTS	ERROR_MORE_DATA	Partial results received.
0x800700ea	LDAP_MORE_RESULTS_TO_RETURN	ERROR_MORE_DATA	More results are to be returned.
0x800704c7	LDAP_USER_CANCELLED	ERROR_CANCELLED	User cancelled the operation.
0x800704c9	LDAP_CONNECT_ERROR	ERROR_CONNECTION_REFUSED	Cannot establish the connection.
0x8007052e	LDAP_INVALID_CREDENTIALS	ERROR_LOGON_FAILURE	Logon failure
0x800705b4	LDAP_TIMEOUT	ERROR_TIMEOUT	The search timed out.

ADSI Error Code	LDAP Error Message	Win32 Error Message	Description
0x80071392	LDAP_ALREADY_EXISTS	ERROR_OBJECT_ALREADY_EXISTS	The object already exists.
0x8007200a	LDAP_NO_SUCH_ATTRIBUTE	ERROR_DS_NO_ATTRIBUTE_OR_VALUE	Requested attribute does not exist.
0x8007200b	LDAP_INVALID_SYNTAX	ERROR_DS_INVALID_ATTRIBUTE_SYNTAX	The syntax is invalid.
0x8007200c	LDAP_UNDEFINED_TYPE	ERROR_DS_ATTRIBUTE_TYPE_UNDEFINED	Type is not defined.
0x8007200d	LDAP_ATTRIBUTE_OR_VALUE_EXISTS	ERROR_DS_ATTRIBUTE_OR_VALUE_EXISTS	The attribute exists or value has been assigned.
0x8007200e	LDAP_BUSY	ERROR_DS_BUSY	The server is busy.
0x8007200f	LDAP_UNAVAILABLE	ERROR_DS_UNAVAILABLE	The server is not available.
0x80072014	LDAP_OBJECT_CLASS_VIOLATION	ERROR_DS_OBJ_CLASS_VIOLATION	Object class violation
0x80072015	LDAP_NOT_ALLOWED_ON_NONLEAF	ERROR_DS_CANT_ON_NON_LEAF	Operation is not allowed on a non-leaf object.
0x80072016	LDAP_NOT_ALLOWED_ON_RDN	ERROR_DS_CANT_ON_RDN	Operation is not allowed on relative name.
0x80072017	LDAP_NO_OBJECT_CLASS_MODS	ERROR_DS_CANT_MOD_OBJ_CLASS	Cannot modify object class
0x80072020	LDAP_OPERATIONS_ERROR	ERROR_DS_OPERATIONS_ERROR	Operations error occurred.
0x80072021	LDAP_PROTOCOL_ERROR	ERROR_DS_PROTOCOL_ERROR	Protocol error occurred.
0x80072022	LDAP_TIMELIMIT_EXCEEDED	ERROR_DS_TIMELIMIT_EXCEEDED	Time limit exceeded.
0x80072023	LDAP_SIZELIMIT_EXCEEDED	ERROR_DS_SIZELIMIT_EXCEEDED	Size limit exceeded
0x80072024	LDAP_ADMIN_LIMIT_EXCEEDED	ERROR_DS_ADMIN_LIMIT_EXCEEDED	Administration limit on the server exceeded.
0x80072025	LDAP_COMPARE_FALSE	ERROR_DS_COMPARE_FALSE	Compare yielded FALSE.
0x80072026	LDAP_COMPARE_TRUE	ERROR_DS_COMPARE_TRUE	Compare yielded TRUE.
0x80072027	LDAP_AUTH_METHOD_NOT_SUPPORTED	ERROR_DS_AUTH_METHOD_NOT_SUPPORTED	Authentication method is not supported.

continued

TABLE B-2	*(continued)*		
ADSI Error Code	**LDAP Error Message**	**Win32 Error Message**	**Description**
0x80072028	LDAP_STRONG_AUTH_ REQUIRED	ERROR_DS_STRONG_AUTH_ REQUIRED	Strong authentication is required.
0x80072029	LDAP_INAPPROPRIATE_ AUTH	ERROR_DS_ INAPPROPRIATE_AUTH	Authentication is inappropriate.
0x8007202a	LDAP_AUTH_UNKNOWN	ERROR_DS_AUTH_UNKNOWN	Unknown authentication error occurred.
0x8007202b	LDAP_REFERRAL	ERROR_DS_REFERRAL	Referral error
0x8007202c	LDAP_UNAVAILABLE_ CRIT_EXTENSION	ERROR_DS_UNAVAILABLE_ CRIT_EXTENSION	Critical extension is unavailable.
0x8007202d	LDAP_CONFIDENTIALITY_ REQUIRED	ERROR_DS_ CONFIDENTIALITY_ REQUIRED	Confidentiality is required.
0x8007202e	LDAP_INAPPROPRIATE_ MATCHING	ERROR_DS_ INAPPROPRIATE_MATCHING	Inappropriate matching error
0x8007202f	LDAP_CONSTRAINT_ VIOLATION	ERROR_DS_CONSTRAINT_ VIOLATION	Constraint violation
0x80072030	LDAP_NO_SUCH_OBJECT	ERROR_DS_NO_SUCH_ OBJECT	Object does not exist.
0x80072031	LDAP_ALIAS_PROBLEM	ERROR_DS_ALIAS_PROBLEM	Alias is invalid.
0x80072032	LDAP_INVALID_DN_ SYNTAX	ERROR_DS_INVALID_DN_ SYNTAX	Distinguished name has an invalid syntax.
0x80072033	LDAP_IS_LEAF	ERROR_DS_IS_LEAF	Object is a leaf.
0x80072034	LDAP_ALIAS_DEREF_ PROBLEM	ERROR_DS_ALIAS_DEREF_ PROBLEM	Cannot remove reference for the alias.
0x80072035	LDAP_UNWILLING_TO_ PERFORM	ERROR_DS_UNWILLING_TO_ PERFORM	Invalid operation
0x80072036	LDAP_LOOP_DETECT	ERROR_DS_LOOP_DETECT	Loop was detected.
0x80072037	LDAP_NAMING_VIOLATION	ERROR_DS_NAMING_ VIOLATION	Naming violation
0x80072038	LDAP_RESULTS_TOO_ LARGE	ERROR_DS_OBJECT_ RESULTS_TOO_LARGE	Results returned are too large.
0x80072039	LDAP_AFFECTS_ MULTIPLE_DSAS	ERROR_DS_AFFECTS_ MULTIPLE_DSAS	Multiple directory service agents are affected.

ADSI Error Code	LDAP Error Message	Win32 Error Message	Description
0x8007203a	LDAP_SERVER_DOWN	ERROR_DS_SERVER_DOWN	Cannot contact the LDAP server.
0x8007203b	LDAP_LOCAL_ERROR	ERROR_DS_LOCAL_ERROR	Local error occurred.
0x8007203c	LDAP_ENCODING_ERROR	ERROR_DS_ENCODING_ ERROR	Encoding error occurred.
0x8007203d	LDAP_DECODING_ERROR	ERROR_DS_DECODING_ ERROR	Decoding error occurred.
0x8007203e	LDAP_FILTER_ERROR	ERROR_DS_FILTER_ UNKNOWN	Search filter is bad.
0x8007203f	LDAP_PARAM_ERROR	ERROR_DS_PARAM_ERROR	A bad parameter was passed.
0x80072040	LDAP_NOT_SUPPORTED	ERROR_DS_NOT_SUPPORTED	Feature is not supported.
0x80072041	LDAP_NO_RESULTS_ RETURNED	ERROR_DS_NO_RESULTS_ RETURNED	Results are not returned.
0x80072042	LDAP_CONTROL_NOT_ FOUND	ERROR_DS_CONTROL_NOT_ FOUND	Control was not found.
0x80072043	LDAP_CLIENT_LOOP	ERROR_DS_CLIENT_LOOP	Client loop was detected.
0x80072044	LDAP_REFERRAL_LIMIT_ EXCEEDED	ERROR_DS_REFERRAL_ LIMIT_EXCEEDED	Referral limit has been exceeded.

Table B-3 summarizes LDAP error codes and provides the corresponding Win32 error codes for ADSI 2.0.

TABLE B-3

LDAP Error Codes with Win32 for ADSI 2.0

ADSI Error Code	LDAP Error Message	Win32 Error Message	Description
0	LDAP_SUCCESS	NO_ERROR	Operation succeeded.
0x80070002	LDAP_NO_SUCH_OBJECT	ERROR_FILE_NOT_FOUND	Object does not exist.
0x80070005	LDAP_AUTH_METHOD_NOT_ SUPPORTED	ERROR_ACCESS_DENIED	Authentication method not supported.
0x80070005	LDAP_STRONG_AUTH_ REQUIRED	ERROR_ACCESS_DENIED	Requires strong authentication

continued

TABLE B-3	*(continued)*		
ADSI Error Code	**LDAP Error Message**	**Win32 Error Message**	**Description**
0x80070005	LDAP_INAPPROPRIATE_ AUTH	ERROR_ACCESS_DENIED	Inappropriate authentication
0x80070005	LDAP_INSUFFICIENT_ RIGHTS	ERROR_ACCESS_DENIED	User has insufficient access rights.
0x80070005	LDAP_AUTH_UNKNOWN	ERROR_ACCESS_DENIED	Unknown authentication error occurred.
0x80070008	LDAP_NO_MEMORY	ERROR_NOT_ENOUGH_ MEMORY	System is out of memory.
0x8007001F	LDAP_OTHER	ERROR_GEN_FAILURE	Unknown error occurred.
0x8007001F	LDAP_LOCAL_ERROR	ERROR_GEN_FAILURE	Local error occurred.
0x80070037	LDAP_UNAVAILABLE	ERROR_DEV_NOT_EXIST	Server is not available.
0x8007003A	LDAP_SERVER_DOWN	ERROR_BAD_NET_RESP	Cannot contact the LDAP server.
0x8007003B	LDAP_ENCODING_ERROR	ERROR_UNEXP_NET_ERR	Encoding error occurred.
0x8007003B	LDAP_DECODING_ERROR	ERROR_UNEXP_NET_ERR	Decoding error occurred.
0x80070044	LDAP_ADMIN_LIMIT_ EXCEEDED	ERROR_TOO_MANY_NAMES	Exceeded administration limit on the server.
0x80070056	LDAP_INVALID_ CREDENTIALS	ERROR_INVALID_PASSWORD	Invalid credential
0x80070057	LDAP_INVALID_DN_ SYNTAX	ERROR_INVALID_ PARAMETER	Distinguished name has an invalid syntax.
0x80070057	LDAP_NAMING_VIOLATION	ERROR_INVALID_ PARAMETER	Naming violation
0x80070057	LDAP_OBJECT_CLASS_ VIOLATION	ERROR_INVALID_ PARAMETER	Object class violation
0x80070057	LDAP_FILTER_ERROR	ERROR_INVALID_ PARAMETER	Search filter is bad.
0x80070057	LDAP_PARAM_ERROR	ERROR_INVALID_ PARAMETER	Bad parameter was passed to a routine.
0X8007006E	LDAP_OPERATIONS_ERROR	ERROR_OPEN_FAILED	Operation error occurred.
0x8007007A	LDAP_RESULTS_TOO_ LARGE	ERROR_INSUFFICIENT_ BUFFER	Results set is too large.

ADSI Error Code	LDAP Error Message	Win32 Error Message	Description
0x8007007B	LDAP_INVALID_SYNTAX	ERROR_INVALID_NAME	Invalid syntax
0x8007007C	LDAP_PROTOCOL_ERROR	ERROR_INVALID_LEVEL	Protocol error
0x800700B7	LDAP_ALREADY_EXISTS	ERROR_ALREADY_EXISTS	Object already exists.
0x800700EA	LDAP_PARTIAL_RESULTS	ERROR_MORE_DATA	Partial results and referrals received.
0x800700EA	LDAP_BUSY	ERROR_BUSY	Server is busy.
0x800703EB	LDAP_UNWILLING_TO_ PERFORM	ERROR_CAN_NOT_COMPLETE	Server cannot perform operation.
0x8007041D	LDAP_TIMEOUT	ERROR_SERVICE_REQUEST_ TIMEOUT	Search timed out.
0x800704B8	LDAP_COMPARE_FALSE	ERROR_EXTENDED_ERROR	Compare yielded FALSE.
0x800704B8	LDAP_COMPARE_TRUE	ERROR_EXTENDED_ERROR	Compare yielded TRUE.
0x800704B8	LDAP_REFERRAL	ERROR_EXTENDED_ERROR	Cannot resolve referral.
0x800704B8	LDAP_UNAVAILABLE_ CRIT_EXTENSION	ERROR_EXTENDED_ERROR	Critical extension is unavailable.
0x800704B8	LDAP_NO_SUCH_ ATTRIBUTE	ERROR_EXTENDED_ERROR	Requested attribute does not exist.
0x800704B8	LDAP_UNDEFINED_TYPE	ERROR_EXTENDED_ERROR	Type is not defined.
0x800704B8	LDAP_INAPPROPRIATE_ MATCHING	ERROR_EXTENDED_ERROR	There was an inappropriate matching.
0x800704B8	LDAP_CONSTRAINT_ VIOLATION	ERROR_EXTENDED_ERROR	There was a constrain violation.
0x800704B8	LDAP_ATTRIBUTE_OR_ VALUE_EXISTS	ERROR_EXTENDED_ERROR	The attribute exists or the value has been assigned.
0x800704B8	LDAP_ALIAS_PROBLEM	ERROR_EXTENDED_ERROR	Alias is invalid.
0x800704B8	LDAP_IS_LEAF	ERROR_EXTENDED_ERROR	Object is a leaf.
0x800704B8	LDAP_ALIAS_DEREF_ PROBLEM	ERROR_EXTENDED_ERROR	Cannot dereference the alias.
0x800704B8	LDAP_LOOP_DETECT	ERROR_EXTENDED_ERROR	Loop was detected.
0x800704B8	LDAP_NOT_ALLOWED_ON_ NONLEAF	ERROR_EXTENDED_ERROR	Operation is not allowed on a non-leaf object.

continued

TABLE B-3	*(continued)*		
ADSI Error Code	**LDAP Error Message**	**Win32 Error Message**	**Description**
0x800704B8	LDAP_NOT_ALLOWED_ON_RDN	ERROR_EXTENDED_ERROR	Operation is not allowed on RDN.
0x800704B8	LDAP_NO_OBJECT_CLASS_MODS	ERROR_EXTENDED_ERROR	Cannot modify object class.
0x800704B8	LDAP_AFFECTS_MULTIPLE_DSAS	ERROR_EXTENDED_ERROR	Multiple directory service agents are affected.
0x800704C7	LDAP_USER_CANCELLED	ERROR_CANCELLED	User has canceled the operation.
0x80070718	LDAP_TIMELIMIT_EXCEEDED	ERROR_NOT_ENOUGH_QUOTA	Exceeded time limit.
0x80070718	LDAP_SIZELIMIT_EXCEEDED	ERROR_NOT_ENOUGH_QUOTA	Exceeded size limit.

Appendix C

Essential Command-Line Utilities for Use with WSH

Command-line utilities provide some of the most powerful and useful features you'll find anywhere. Using command-line utilities, you often can replace dozens of lines of code with a few simple statements. As you explore Windows you'll find that hundreds of utilities are available and all of them can be run within your Windows scripts.

In this appendix, we've selected the top utilities that you may want to use. You'll find a quick reference for commands as well as detailed entries on command usage and syntax. All examples show command-line and Windows script syntax.

ARP

```
ARP -a [inet_addr] [-N if_addr]
ARP -d inet_addr [if_addr]
ARP -s inet_addr eth_addr [if_addr]
```

eth_addr	Sets the physical MAC address in hexadecimal format, such as HH-HH-HH-HH-HH-HH where H is a hexadecimal value from 0 to F. Each network adapter card has a built-in MAC address.
if_addr	Sets the IP address of the interface whose address translation table should be modified. If you don't specify an address, the first available interface is used.
inet_addr	Sets an Internet address.
-a	Displays current ARP entries.
-d	Deletes the specified entry.
-g	Same as -a.
-N if_addr	Displays the ARP entries for the network interface specified by if_addr.
-s	Adds the host and associates the Internet address inet_addr with the physical address eth_addr. The physical address is given as six hexadecimal bytes separated by hyphens. The entry is permanent.

Details:

ARP displays and modifies the IP-to-physical address translation tables used by the address resolution protocol (ARP). Address Resolution Protocol (ARP) cache is maintained by Windows 2000 workstations and servers. Use the ARP command to view and manage this cache.

Use IPCONFIG to get a list of MAC addresses for a system's network adapter cards. If you PING an IP address on the LAN, the address is automatically added to the ARP cache.

Command Shell

```
arp -d 192.168.15.25
```

VBScript

```
Set ws = WScript.CreateObject("WScript.Shell")
ret = ws.Run("arp -d 192.168.15.25",0,"True")
```

JScript

```
var ws = WScript.CreateObject("WScript.Shell");
ws.Run("arp -d 192.168.15.25",0,"True")
```

ASSOC

```
ASSOC [.ext[=[fileType]]]
```

.ext   Specifies the file extension to associate the file type with.

fileType   Specifies the file type to associate with the file extension.

Details:

ASSOC displays and modifies file associations. If you enter **ASSOC** by itself, it displays all file associations. If you enter **ASSOC** followed by a file extension, it displays the file association for that extension.

Command Shell

```
assoc .xml=xmfile
```

VBScript

```
Set ws = WScript.CreateObject("WScript.Shell")
ret = ws.Run("assoc .xml=xmfile",0,"True")
```

JScript

```
var ws = WScript.CreateObject("WScript.Shell");
ws.Run("assoc .xml=xmfile",0,"True")
```

AT

```
AT [\\computername] [ [id] [/DELETE] | /DELETE [/YES]]
AT [\\computername] time [/INTERACTIVE]
AT [ /EVERY:date[,...] | /NEXT:date[,...]] "command"
```

`"command"`	Sets the command or script to run at the designated time.
`/delete`	Cancels a scheduled task. If `id` is omitted, all scheduled commands on the system are canceled.
`/every:date[,...]`	Runs the command on a recurring basis on each weekday or day of the month specified. Valid values are M, T, W, Th, F, S, Su, or 1 through 31. Separate consecutive days with dashes. Separate non-consecutive days with commas.
`/interactive`	Allows the job to interact with the desktop.
`/next:date[,...]`	Runs the task on a specific weekday or day of month. This is a non-recurring task.
`/yes`	Forces a confirmation prompt before deleting scheduled tasks.
`\\computername`	Sets a remote computer on which the task should run. If omitted, tasks are scheduled on the local computer.
`id`	The identification number assigned to a scheduled task.
`time`	Sets the time when command is to run in the format HH:MM. Time is set on a 24-hour clock (00:00 – 23:59).

Details:

AT schedules commands and programs to execute at a specific date and time. Tasks can be scheduled to run on a one-time or recurring basis. To list currently scheduled tasks, enter the **AT** command on a line by itself. See also Schtasks.

Command Shell

```
at 00:15 /every:M "backup.vbs"
at 01:00 /next:Su "rm c:\temp\*.tmp"
at 1 /delete
```

VBScript

```
Set ws = WScript.CreateObject("WScript.Shell")
ret = ws.Run("at 00:15 /every:M 'backup.vbs'",0,"True")
```

JScript

```
var ws = WScript.CreateObject("WScript.Shell");
ws.Run("at 00:15 /every:M 'backup.vbs'",0,"True")
```

ATTRIB

```
ATTRIB [+R | -R] [+A | -A ] [+S | -S] [+H | -H] [+I | -I]
       [drive:][path][filename] [/S [/D] [/L]]
```

[drive:]	Sets the drive to work with.
[path]filename	Sets the file path to work with.
+	Sets an attribute.
-	Clears an attribute.
R	Specifies that you want to set or clear the Read-only file attribute.
A	Specifies that you want to set or clear the Archive file attribute.
S	Specifies that you want to set or clear the System file attribute.
H	Specifies that you want to set or clear the Hidden file attribute.
I	Specifies that you want to set or clear the Indexed file attribute.
/D	Processes folders as well as files.
/L	Works on the attributes of the Symbolic Link versus the target of the Symbolic Link.
/S	Processes matching files in the current folder and subfolders.

Details:

ATTRIB displays and modifies file attributes. If you enter **ATTRIB** with a file path and no other parameters, you can examine file attributes of files. You can use ATTRIB to specify whether files and folders should be marked as read-only, hidden, and system. You can also specify whether files and folders should be indexed.

Command Shell

```
attrib +R /S /D c:\data\archive
```

VBScript

```
Set ws = WScript.CreateObject("WScript.Shell")
ret = ws.Run("attrib +R /S /D c:\data\archive",0,"True")
```

JScript

```
var ws = WScript.CreateObject("WScript.Shell");
ws.Run("attrib +R /S /D c:\\data\\archive",0,"True")
```

CACLS

```
CACLS filepath [/T] [/M] [/L] [/S[:SDDL]] [/E] [/C] [/G user:perm]
              [/R user [...]] [/P user:perm [...]] [/D user [...]]
```

`filepath`	Sets the name of the file or filepath to work with.
`user`	Specifies the name of a user or group to work with, such as BUILTIN\Users, BUILTIN\Administrators, NT AUTHORITY\System, or NT AUTHORITY\ Terminal Server User. For domains, you can specify a domain user account using the format DOMAIN\Username, such as CPANDL\WilliamS for the WilliamS account in the Cpandl.com domain.
`perm`	Sets the permission to assign as R for Read, W for Write, C for Change, or F for Full Control.
`/C`	Continues processing even when you receive access denied errors.
`/D user`	Denies specified user access.
`/E`	Edits the ACL instead of replacing it.
`/G user:perm`	Grant specified user access rights.
`/L`	Works on the Symbolic Link itself instead of the link target.
`/M`	Changes ACLs of volumes mounted to a directory.
`/P user:perm`	Replaces specified user's access rights.
`/R user`	Revokes specified user's access rights (only valid with /E).
`/S`	Displays the SDDL string.
`/S:SDDL`	Replaces the ACLs with those specified in the SDDL string. Not valid with /E, /G, /R, /P, or /D.
`/T`	Changes access control lists (ACLs) of specified files in the current directory and all subdirectories.

Details:

CACLS displays and modifies the access control lists (ACLs) of files or folders. If you use CACLS without parameters, you can view the ACL on the specified file or directory. When you display ACLs, CACLS uses the following abbreviations:

- CI for Container Inherit, which means the ACE will be inherited by directories.
- ID for Inherited, which means the ACE was inherited from the parent directory's ACL.
- IO for Inherit Only, which means the ACE does not apply to the current file/directory.
- OI for Object Inherit, which means the ACE will be inherited by files.

Command Shell

```
cacls '%CommonProgramFiles%\Microsoft Shared\VGX\vgx.dll' /P BUILTIN\
Users:R BUILTIN\Administrators:F 'NT AUTHORITY\SYSTEM:F' 'NT AUTHORITY\
TERMINAL SERVER USER:C'
```

VBScript

```
Set ws = WScript.CreateObject("WScript.Shell")
ret = ws.Run("cacls '%CommonProgramFiles%\Microsoft Shared\VGX\vgx.dll'
/P BUILTIN\Users:R BUILTIN\Administrators:F 'NT AUTHORITY\SYSTEM:F' 'NT
AUTHORITY\TERMINAL SERVER USER:C'",0,"True")
```

JScript

```
var ws = WScript.CreateObject("WScript.Shell");
ws.Run("cacls '%CommonProgramFiles%\\Microsoft Shared\\VGX\\vgx.dll' /P
BUILTIN\\Users:R BUILTIN\\Administrators:F 'NT AUTHORITY\\SYSTEM:F' 'NT
AUTHORITY\\TERMINAL SERVER USER:C'",0,"True")
```

CHKDSK

Checks a disk for errors and displays a report.

```
CHKDSK [drive:][[path]filename][/F][/V][/R][/X][/I][/C][/L[:size]]
```

[drive:]	Sets the drive to check.
[path]filename	Sets the files and directories to check for fragmentation (FAT only).
/C	Skips checking cycles in folder structure.
/F	Fixes errors on the disk.
/I	On NTFS, performs basic index checks instead of extended checks.
/L:size	On NTFS, changes size of the check disk log (in KB). If size is not specified, the current size is displayed.
/R	Finds bad sectors and recovers readable information.
/V	Lists each file as it is checked.
/X	Forces the drive to dismount if necessary before performing CHKDSK. This option also fixes errors.

Details:

CHKDSK checks a disk for errors and displays a report.

Command Shell

```
chkdsk /F /R c:
chkdsk c: d:
```

VBScript

```
Set ws = WScript.CreateObject("WScript.Shell")
ret = ws.Run("chkdsk /F /R c:",0,"True")
```

JScript

```
var ws = WScript.CreateObject("WScript.Shell");
ws.Run("chkdsk /F /R c:",0,"True")
```

COMPACT

```
COMPACT [/C | /U] [/S[:dir]] [/A] [/I] [/F] [/Q] [filename [...]]
```

filename	Sets the files or directories to compress.
/A	Displays or compresses files with the hidden or system attributes. These files are omitted by default.
/C	Compresses the specified files, directories, and/or drives. Directories will be marked so that files added afterward will be compressed.
/F	Forces compression or decompression on all specified files and directories, even those which are already flagged as compressed. Otherwise, flagged files and directories are skipped by default.
/I	Ignores errors. By default, COMPACT stops when an error is encountered.
/Q	Sets quiet mode so only essential information is reported.
/S	Includes subdirectories.
/U	Decompresses the specified files, directories, and/or drives. Directories will be marked so that files added afterward will not be compressed.

Details:

COMPACT displays or alters the compression of files on NTFS partitions. If you use COMPACT without parameters, you can view the compression state of the current directory and any files it contains. You can use multiple filenames and wildcards.

Command Shell

```
compact /I /C c:\working\scripts
compact /F /U d:\
```

VBScript

```
Set ws = WScript.CreateObject("WScript.Shell")
ret = ws.Run("compact /I /C c:\working\scripts",0,"True")
```

JScript

```
var ws = WScript.CreateObject("WScript.Shell");
ws.Run("compact /I /C c:\\working\\scripts",0,"True")
```

CONVERT

```
CONVERT drive: /FS:NTFS [/V] [/X]
[/CVTAREA:filename] [/NOSECURITY]
```

`drive:`	Sets the drive to convert to NTFS.
`/FS:NTFS`	Switch needed to convert the volume to NTFS.
`/V`	Run-in verbose mode.
`/X`	Forces the volume to dismount if necessary.
`/CVTAREA:filename`	Sets the name of a file in the root directory to use as a placeholder for NTFS system files.
`/NOSECURITY`	Removes security settings from converted files.

Details:

CONVERT converts FAT volumes to NTFS. If you try to convert the current drive or any drive being used by the operating system, the command prompts you to convert the drive on reboot. If you accept, a flag is set and the drive is converted the next time you reboot the system. If you decline, the operation is canceled.

Command Shell

```
convert d: /FS:NTFS
convert d: /FS:NTFS /V
```

VBScript

```
Set ws = WScript.CreateObject("WScript.Shell")
ret = ws.Run("convert d: /FS:NTFS",0,"True")
```

JScript

```
var ws = WScript.CreateObject("WScript.Shell");
ws.Run("convert d: /FS:NTFS",0,"True")
```

DATE

```
DATE [/T | mm-dd-yy]
```

`mm-dd-yy`	Sets the date in MM-DD-YYYY format. mm can be 1–12. dd can be 1–31. yy can be 80–99 or 1980–2079.
`/T`	Displays current date.

Details:

DATE displays or sets the date. Type in date and press Enter to set the date interactively.

Command Shell

```
date
date 04-11-2002
```

VBScript

```
Set ws = WScript.CreateObject("WScript.Shell")
ret = ws.Run("date 04-11-2002",0,"True")
```

JScript

```
var ws = WScript.CreateObject("WScript.Shell");
ws.Run("date 04-11-2002",0,"True")
```

DRIVERQUERY

```
DRIVERQUERY [/S system [/U username [/P [password]]]]
            [/FO format] [/NH] [/SI] [/V]
```

/S system	Sets the remote system to connect to (if any).
/U [domain\]user	Sets the alternate user context under which the command should execute. With domain accounts, you can specify the domain user account to use in Domain\User format, such as CPANDL\WilliamS for the WilliamS account in the Cpandl.com domain.
/P [password]	Sets the password for the alternate user context. If you don't provide a password when you specify a user context, you are prompted for a password.
/FO format	Specifies the type of output to display. Valid formats are TABLE, LIST, and CSV.
/NH	Turns off display of the column header row used with TABLE and CSV formats.
/SI	Displays information about signed drivers.
/V	Displays verbose output. Not valid with /SI.

Details:

By default, DRIVERQUERY displays a list of installed device drivers by module name, display name, driver type, and date linked. When you are working with signed drivers, DRIVERQUERY displays a list of devices with installed drivers by device name, inf name, signing status, and manufacturer. The standard output format is TABLE, but you can also use LIST for a formatted list of CSV for a list with comma-separated values.

Command Shell

```
driverquery
driverquery /s server87 /u cpandl\williams /si
```

VBScript

```
Set ws = WScript.CreateObject("WScript.Shell")
ret = ws.Run("driverquery /s server87 /u cpandl\williams /si",0,"True")
```

JScript

```
var ws = WScript.CreateObject("WScript.Shell");
ws.Run("driverquery /s server87 /u cpandl\williams /si",0,"True")
```

EXPAND

```
EXPAND [-r] source destination
EXPAND -r source [destination]
EXPAND -D source.cab [-f:files]
EXPAND source.cab -F:files destination
```

`-D`	Displays list of source files.
`-F:files`	List of files to expand from a .cab file.
`-r`	Rename expanded files.
`source`	Source files to be expanded.
`destination`	Destination filepath.

Details:

EXPAND decompresses files compressed with the Microsoft distribution format or files stored in .CAB files. You can use wildcards when specifying the source files. Also, if you don't specify a destination path, the current directory is used.

Command Shell

```
expand -r setup.ex_
expand *.ex_ d:\working\distro\
```

VBScript

```
Set ws = WScript.CreateObject("WScript.Shell")
ret = ws.Run("expand -r setup.ex_",0,"True")
```

JScript

```
var ws = WScript.CreateObject("WScript.Shell");
ws.Run("expand -r setup.ex_",0,"True")
```

FC

```
FC [/A] [/C] [/L] [/LBn] [/N] [/OFFLINE] [/T] [/U] [/W] [/nnnn]
    [drive1:][path1]filename1 [drive2:][path2]filename2
FC /B [drive1:][path1]filename1 [drive2:][path2]filename2
```

`[drive1:][path1]` `filename1`	Source file for comparison.
`[drive2:][path2]` `filename2`	Target file to use in comparison.
`/nnnn`	When attempting to resync ASCII text files, this specifies the number of lines that must match before the command considers an area to be identical. By default, two lines must match before the command considers an area to be identical.
`/A`	Displays only the first and last lines for each set of differences.
`/B`	Performs a binary comparison.
`/C`	Disregards whether letters in the comparison are upper- or lowercase.
`/L`	Compares files as ASCII text.
`/LBn`	Sets the maximum consecutive mismatches before FC cancels the operation.
`/N`	Displays the line numbers on an ASCII comparison.
`/OFFLINE`	Does not skip files with the offline attribute set.
`/T`	FC can compare tabs within files to spacing to detect differences. By default, FC converts tabs to spaces for comparisons. To turn this feature off, use this switch.
`/U`	Compare files as Unicode rather than ASCII.
`/W`	Ignores white space (tabs and spaces) for comparison. Multiple spaces and tabs are converted to a single space for the comparison.

Details:

FC compares two files and displays the differences between them. In binary mode, FC displays all differences. In ASCII/Unicode mode, FC looks for differences area by area. The size of these areas are set with /nnnn, /0050 for example.

Command Shell

```
fc /A /LB50 /0004 attitude.txt changes.txt
fc /B cr.bin cr2.bin
```

Windows Script

compare.bat

```
fc /A /LB50 /0004 attitude.txt changes.txt >> log.txt
fc /B cr.bin cr2.bin >> log.txt
```

compare.vbs

```
Set ws = WScript.CreateObject("WScript.Shell")
ret = ws.Run("compare.bat",0,"True")
```

compare.js

```
var ws = WScript.CreateObject("WScript.Shell");
ws.Run("compare.bat",0,"True")
```

FORMAT

```
FORMAT drive: [/FS:file-system] [/V:label] [/Q | /P:passes]
              [/A:size] [/C] [/X]
FORMAT drive: [/V:label] [/Q | /P:passes] [/F:size]
FORMAT drive: [/V:label] [/Q | /P:passes] [/T:tracks /N:sectors]
FORMAT drive: [/V:label] [/Q | /P:passes]
FORMAT drive: [/Q]
```

drive:	Sets the letter of the drive to format.
/A:size	Overrides the default allocation unit size. NTFS supports 512, 1024, 2048, 4096, 8192, 16K, 32K, and 64K. FAT supports 8192, 16K, 32K, 64K, 128K, and 256K. NTFS compression is not supported for allocation unit sizes above 4096K.
/C	Turn on file compression.
/F:size	Sets the size of the floppy disk to format. Common sizes are 360 or 1.2 for 5.25-inch disks, and 1.44 or 2.88 for 3.5-inch disks.
/FS:file-system	Sets the type of the file system as FAT or NTFS.
/N:sectors	Sets the number of sectors per track. Used with /T and cannot be used with /F.
/P:passes	Sets the number of passes for zeroing out sectors.
/Q	Performs a quick format.
/T:tracks	Sets the number of tracks per disk side.
/V:label	Sets the volume label.
/X	Forces the drive to dismount before formatting if necessary.

Details:

FORMAT formats a floppy disk or hard drive for use with Windows 2000.

Command Shell

```
format e: /FS:NTFS /C /V:Secondary
format a: /Q
```

VBScript

```
Set ws = WScript.CreateObject("WScript.Shell")
ret = ws.Run("format e: /FS:NTFS /C /V:Secondary",0,"True")
```

JScript

```
var ws = WScript.CreateObject("WScript.Shell");
ws.Run("format e: /FS:NTFS /C /V:Secondary",0,"True")
```

FTP

```
FTP [-v] [-d] [-i] [-n] [-g] [-s:filename] [-a] [-A] [-x:sendbuffer]
    [-r:recvbuffer] [-b:asynccount] [-w:windowsize] [host]
```

host	Sets the hostname or IP address of the remote host to which you want to connect.
-a	Uses any available local interface to bind data connection. Can sometimes resolve connectivity problems.
-A	Specifies that you want to log on anonymously.
-b:asynccount	Sets the async count, overriding the default count of 3.
-d	Sets debug mode, which displays all messages sent between the client and the server.
-g	Allows you to use wildcards when setting file and path names.
-i	Turns off interactive mode when you are transferring multiple files. Used to perform unattended transfers.
-n	Turns off auto-login during the initial connection.
-r:recvbuffer	Sets the receive buffer size, overriding the default buffer size of 8192 bytes.
-s:filename	Designates a text file containing FTP commands; the commands will automatically run after FTP starts.
-v	Turns off display of remote server responses.
-w:buffersize	Sets a new transfer buffer size, overriding the default buffer size of 4096 bytes.
-x:sendbuffer	Sets the send buffer size, overriding the default buffer size of 8192 bytes.

Details:

FTP transfers files using FTP (File Transfer Protocol). When you transfer files in scripts using FTP, be sure to use a transfer file which can contain any available FTP commands and to turn off interactive prompts for transferring multiple files. The following FTP commands are available once you start the utility:

!	Exits to the command shell.
?	Gets command help.
append	Starts a download in the current directory and appends to an existing file (if available) rather than overwriting the file.
ascii	Sets transfers mode to ASCII text. Use this with text file transfers to preserve end-of-line designators.
bell	Turns beep on/off for confirmation of command completion. Default setting is off.
binary	Sets transfer mode to binary. Use with executables and other binary file types.
bye	Exits to the command shell.
cd	Changes the remote working directory.
close	Closes FTP session, but doesn't exit the FTP utility.
debug	Turns debug mode on/off. Default setting is off.
delete	Deletes a file.
dir	Lists contents of directory on the system you are connected to for transfers.
disconnect	Closes the connection to the remote system.
get	Downloads a file from the remote system.
glob	Allows you to use wildcards when naming files and directories.
hash	Turns hash mark printing on/off. If this property is set, the # character prints each time the buffer is transferred, providing a visual cue for progress.
lcd	Changes the working directory on the local system, such as lcd c:\winnt\ system32.
literal	Sends arbitrary FTP command.
ls	Lists contents of remote directory. Because the command is designed after the UNIX ls, all normal ls flags are available, such as ls -l or ls -lsa.
mdelete	Deletes multiple files on the remote system.
mdir	Lists contents of multiple remote directories.
mget	Downloads multiple files from the remote system.
mkdir	Creates a directory on the remote system.
mls	Lists contents of multiple remote directories.
mput	Sends multiple files to the remote system.

open	Opens a connection to a remote system specified following the command, such as open idg.com.
prompt	Turns prompt mode on/off for mget, mput, and mdelete. Default mode is off.
put	Sends a file to the remote system.
pwd	Prints working directory on remote machine.
quit	Quits FTP sessions and exits to the command shell.
quote	Sends arbitrary FTP command.
recv	Downloads a file from the remote system.
remotehelp	Gets help from remote server.
rename	Renames a file on the remote system.
rmdir	Removes a directory on the remote system.
send	Sends a file to the remote system.
status	Gets the current status.
trace	Traces the IP route of the file transfer.
type	Sets the transfer type and toggles between ASCII and binary.
user	Starts logon procedure to change users while connected to a remote host.
verbose	Turns verbose mode on/off. Default is off.

Command Shell

```
ftp -i -g -s:tranf.txt idg.com
ftp -i idg.com
```

VBScript

```
Set ws = WScript.CreateObject("WScript.Shell")
ret = ws.Run("ftp -i -g -s:tranf.txt idg.com",0,"True")
```

JScript

```
var ws = WScript.CreateObject("WScript.Shell");
ws.Run("ftp -i -g -s:tranf.txt idg.com",0,"True")
```

FTYPE

```
FTYPE [fileType[=[command]]]
```

fileType	Sets the file type to examine or change.
command	Sets the launch command to use when opening files of this type.

Details:

FTYPE displays or modifies file types used in file extension associations. To display the current file types, enter **FTYPE** without any parameters. To delete an existing file type, set its launch command to an empty string, such as:

```
ftype perl=
```

If passing arguments, %0 or %1 is substituted with the filename being launched through the association. %* gets all the parameters and %2 gets the first parameter, %3 the second, and so on. %~*n* gets all the remaining parameters starting with the *n*th parameter, where *n* may be between 2 and 9.

Command Shell

```
ASSOC .pl=Perl
FTYPE Perl=c:\winnt\system32\perl.exe %1 %*
```

VBScript

```
Set ws = WScript.CreateObject("WScript.Shell")
ret = ws.Run("ASSOC .pl=Perl",0,"True")
ret = ws.Run("FTYPE Perl=c:\winnt\system32\perl.exe %1 %*",0,"True")
```

JScript

```
var ws = WScript.CreateObject("WScript.Shell");
ws.Run("ASSOC .pl=Perl",0,"True")
ws.Run("FTYPE Perl=c:\\winnt\\system32\\perl.exe %1 %*",0,"True")
```

IPCONFIG

```
ipconfig [/allcomparments]
ipconfig [/all | /release [adapter] | /renew [adapter]
         | /release6 [adapter] | /renew6 [adapter]
         | /flushdns | /registerdns | /displaydns
         | /showclassid adapter
         | /setclassid adapter [classidtoset]
]
```

adapter	Name of the adapter or pattern with * to match any character and ? to match one character.
classidtoset	Sets the DHCP class ID.
/all	Displays full configuration information.
/allcompartments	Displays information for all DNS compartments.
/displaydns	Displays the contents of the DNS resolve cache.
/flushdns	Flushes the DNS resolve cache.

/registerdns	Refreshes all DHCP leases and re-registers DNS names.
/release	Releases the IPv4 address for the specified adapter.
/release6	Releases the IPv6 address for the specified adapter.
/renew	Renews the IPv4 address for the specified adapter.
/renew6	Renews the IPv6 address for the specified adapter.
/setclassid	Modifies the DHCP class ID.
/showclassid	Shows all the DHCP class IDs for the adapter.

Details:

IPCONFIG displays TCP/IP configuration values. The /release and /renew switches are useful when your network uses DHCP. /renew forces the computer to request new address information from the DHCP server. /release forces the computer to release the dynamic IP address assigned by the DHCP server.

Command Shell

```
ipconfig /renew
ipconfig /release
```

VBScript

```
Set ws = WScript.CreateObject("WScript.Shell")
ret = ws.Run("ipconfig /renew",0,"True")
```

JScript

```
var ws = WScript.CreateObject("WScript.Shell");
ws.Run("ipconfig /renew",0,"True")
```

NBTSTAT

```
NBTSTAT [-a remotename] [-A IP_address] [-c] [-n]
        [-r] [-R] [-RR] [-s] [-S] [interval] ]
```

interval	Redisplays selected statistics, pausing interval seconds between each display. Press Ctrl+C to stop redisplaying statistics.
-A IP_address	Displays a remote computer's statistics by IP address.
-a remotename	Displays a remote computer's statistics by NetBIOS name.
-c	Displays the local computer's name cache including IP addresses.
-n	Displays local NetBIOS names.
-RR	Sends release to WINS and then starts WINS refresh.

-R	Reloads LMHOSTS after deleting the names from the NetBIOS name cache.
-r	Displays statistics for names resolved by broadcast and via WINS.
-S	Displays all client and server sessions by IP addresses.
-s	Displays all client and server sessions, converting destination IP addresses to hostnames via the local HOSTS file.

Details:

NBTSTAT displays status of NetBIOS over TCP/IP. NBTSTAT is useful for obtaining local and remote system NetBIOS information.

Command Shell

```
nbtstat -a mars1
nbtstat -A 192.152.16.8
nbtstat -c
```

VBScript

```
Set ws = WScript.CreateObject("WScript.Shell")
ret = ws.Run("nbtstat -A 192.152.16.8",0,"True")
```

JScript

```
var ws = WScript.CreateObject("WScript.Shell");
ws.Run("nbtstat -A 192.152.16.8",0,"True")
```

NET ACCOUNTS

```
NET ACCOUNTS [/FORCELOGOFF:{minutes | NO}] [/MINPWLEN:length]
             [/MAXPWAGE:{days | UNLIMITED}] [/MINPWAGE:days]
             [/UNIQUEPW:number] [/DOMAIN]
```

/DOMAIN	Specifies that the operation should be performed on the primary domain controller of the current domain. Otherwise, the operation is performed on the local computer. (Applies only to Windows 2000 workstations that are members of an NT domain. By default, Windows 2000 servers perform operations on the primary domain controller.)
/FORCELOGOFF: {minutes | NO}	Sets the time, in minutes, before a user is forced to log off when the account expires or valid logon hours expire. Users receive a warning prior to being logged off. By default, the option is set to NO, which prevents forced log off.
/MAXPWAGE: {days | UNLIMITED}	Sets the number of days that a password is valid. The default is 90 days and the range is 1–49,710 days.

/MINPWAGE:days	Sets the minimum number of days before a user can change a password. The default is 0, which sets no minimum time. The range is 0–49710.
/MINPWLEN:length	Sets the minimum number of characters for a password. The default is 6 characters and the range is 0–14.
/UNIQUEPW:number	Specifies the number of unique passwords a user must use before being able to reuse a password. The default is 5 and the range is 0–24.

Details:

NET ACCOUNTS manages user account and password policies. Use NET ACCOUNTS to manage user and password policies. To manage the accounts themselves, use NET USER, NET GROUP, or NET LOCALGROUP.

Command Shell

```
net accounts /domain /minpwlen:8 /maxpwage:45 /minpwage:10
```

VBScript

```
Set ws = WScript.CreateObject("WScript.Shell")
ret = ws.Run("net accounts /domain /minpwlen:8 /maxpwage:45 /
minpwage:10",0,"True")
```

JScript

```
var ws = WScript.CreateObject("WScript.Shell");
ws.Run("net accounts /domain /minpwlen:8 /maxpwage:45 /
minpwage:10",0,"True")
```

NET COMPUTER

```
NET COMPUTER \\computername {/ADD | /DEL}
```

\\computername	Sets the computer to add or delete from the domain.
/ADD	Adds the specified computer to the domain.
/DEL	Removes the specified computer from the domain.

Details:

NET COMPUTER adds or removes computers from a domain. The command is available only on Windows 2000 servers and is only applicable to the default domain.

Command Shell

```
net computer \\pluto8 /del
net computer \\saturn /add
```

VBScript

```
Set ws = WScript.CreateObject("WScript.Shell")
ret = ws.Run("net computer \\saturn /add",0,"True")
```

JScript

```
var ws = WScript.CreateObject("WScript.Shell");
ws.Run("net computer \\\\saturn /add",0,"True")
```

NET CONFIG SERVER

```
NET CONFIG SERVER [/AUTODISCONNECT:time] [/SRVCOMMENT:"text"]
                  [/HIDDEN:{YES | NO}]
```

/AUTODISCONNECT:time   Sets the number of minutes a user's session can be inactive before it is disconnected. The default is 15 minutes. The range is –1 to 65535 minutes. Use –1 to have the service never disconnect user sessions.

/SRVCOMMENT:"text"   Adds a comment for the server that is displayed in browse lists such as in Server Manager or NET VIEW. Enclose the comments in quotation marks and use up to 48 characters.

/HIDDEN:{YES | NO}   Allows you to prevent the server from being displayed in browser lists. The default is NO. Although a server is hidden from view, it is still accessible.

Details:

NET CONFIG SERVER displays or modifies configuration information for the server service. Enter **NET CONFIG SERVER** on a line by itself to see the current configuration of the server service.

Command Shell

```
net config server
net config server /autodisconnect:10 /hidden:yes
```

VBScript

```
Set ws = WScript.CreateObject("WScript.Shell")
ret = ws.Run("net config server /autodisconnect:10 /
hidden:yes",0,"True")
```

JScript

```
var ws = WScript.CreateObject("WScript.Shell");
ws.Run("net config server /autodisconnect:10 /hidden:yes",0,"True")
```

NET CONFIG WORKSTATION

```
NET CONFIG WORKSTATION [/CHARCOUNT:bytes]
                       [/CHARTIME:msec]
                       [/CHARWAIT:sec]
```

/CHARCOUNT:bytes   Sets the number of bytes Windows 2000 collects before sending the data to a communication device. The default is 16 bytes and the range is 0–65535 bytes. If /CHARTIME:msec is also set, Windows 2000 acts on whichever condition is satisfied first.

/CHARTIME:msec   Sets the amount of time in milliseconds that Windows 2000 collects data before sending the data to a communication device. The default is 250 milliseconds and the range is 0–65535000 milliseconds. If /CHARCOUNT:bytes is also set, Windows 2000 acts on whichever condition is satisfied first.

/CHARWAIT:sec   Sets the number of seconds that Windows 2000 waits for a communication device to become available. The default is 3600 seconds and the range is 0–65535 seconds.

Details:

NET CONFIG WORKSTATION displays or modifies configuration information for the workstation service. Enter **NET CONFIG WORKSTATION** on a line by itself to see the current configuration of the workstation service.

Command Shell

```
net config workstation
net config workstation /charcount:32
```

VBScript

```
Set ws = WScript.CreateObject("WScript.Shell")
ret = ws.Run("net config workstation /charcount:32",0,"True")
```

JScript

```
var ws = WScript.CreateObject("WScript.Shell");
ws.Run("net config workstation /charcount:32",0,"True")
```

NET CONTINUE

```
NET CONTINUE service
```

service   The service to resume.

Details:

Use NET CONTINUE to resume a paused service. Services that can be paused and resumed include: File Server For Macintosh, Lpdsvc, Net Logon, Network DDE, Network DDE DSDM, NT LM Security Support Provider, Remote Access Server, Server, Simple TCP/IP Services, Task Scheduler, and Workstation.

Command Shell

```
net continue "file server for macintosh"
```

VBScript

```
Set ws = WScript.CreateObject("WScript.Shell")
ret = ws.Run("net continue 'file server for macintosh'",0,"True")
```

JScript

```
var ws = WScript.CreateObject("WScript.Shell");
ws.Run("net continue 'file server for macintosh'",0,"True")
```

NET FILE

```
NET FILE [id [/CLOSE]]
```

id   The open file's identification number.

/CLOSE   Closes an open file and releases locked records.

Details:

NET FILE manages open files on a server. Enter **NET FILE** by itself to display a complete listing of open files, which includes the name of the user who has the file open and the number of file locks (if applicable).

Command Shell

```
net file
net file 0001 /CLOSE
```

VBScript

```
Set ws = WScript.CreateObject("WScript.Shell")
ret = ws.Run("net file 0001 /CLOSE",0,"True")
```

JScript

```
var ws = WScript.CreateObject("WScript.Shell");
ws.Run("net file 0001 /CLOSE",0,"True")
```

NET GROUP

```
NET GROUP [groupname [/COMMENT:"text"]] [/DOMAIN]
NET GROUP groupname {/ADD [/COMMENT:"text"] | /DELETE}
          [/DOMAIN]
NET GROUP groupname username [...] {/ADD | /DELETE} [/DOMAIN]
```

groupname	Sets the name of the global group to work with. To view a list of users in the global group, specify only the group name.
username[...]	Lists one or more usernames to add to or remove from a global group. Use spaces to separate multiple usernames.
/ADD	Creates a global group, or adds a username to an existing global group.
/COMMENT:"text"	Adds an optional description for the global group. The comment can have up to 48 characters and must be enclosed in quotation marks.
/DELETE	Removes a global group, or removes a username from a global group.
/DOMAIN	Specifies that the operation should be performed on the primary domain controller of the current domain. Otherwise, the operation is performed on the local computer. (Applies only to Windows 2000 workstations that are members of an NT domain. By default, Windows 2000 servers perform operations on the primary domain controller.)

Details:

NET GROUP manages global groups. Enter **NET GROUP** by itself to see a list of all global groups. Be sure to use quotation marks in group or usernames that have spaces.

Command Shell

```
net group "domain admins"
net group "domain admins" wrstanek /add
```

VBScript

```
Set ws = WScript.CreateObject("WScript.Shell")
ret = ws.Run("net group 'domain admins' wrstanek /add",0,"True")
```

JScript

```
var ws = WScript.CreateObject("WScript.Shell");
ws.Run("net group 'domain admins' wrstanek /add",0,"True")
```

NET LOCALGROUP

```
NET LOCALGROUP [groupname [/COMMENT:"text"]] [/DOMAIN]
NET LOCALGROUP groupname {/ADD [/COMMENT:"text"] | /DELETE}
```

```
                              [/DOMAIN]
         NET LOCALGROUP groupname name [...] {/ADD | /DELETE} [/DOMAIN]
```

groupname	Sets the name of the local group to work with. To view a list of users in the local group, specify only the group name.
username[...]	Lists one or more usernames to add to or remove from a local group. Use spaces to separate multiple usernames.
/ADD	Creates a local group, or adds a username to an existing local group.
/COMMENT:"text"	Adds an optional description for the local group. The comment can have up to 48 characters and must be enclosed in quotation marks.
/DELETE	Removes a local group, or removes a username from a local group.
/DOMAIN	Specifies that the operation should be performed on the primary domain controller of the current domain. Otherwise, the operation is performed on the local computer. (Applies only to Windows 2000 workstations that are members of an NT domain. By default, Windows 2000 servers perform operations on the primary domain controller.)

Details:

NET LOCALGROUP manages local groups. Enter **NET LOCALGROUP** by itself to see a list of all local groups. Be sure to use quotation marks in group or usernames that have spaces.

Command Shell

```
net localgroup "account operators"
net localgroup "account operators" wrstanek /add
```

VBScript

```
Set ws = WScript.CreateObject("WScript.Shell")
ret = ws.Run("net localgroup 'account operators' wrstanek /
add",0,"True")
```

JScript

```
var ws = WScript.CreateObject("WScript.Shell");
ws.Run("net localgroup 'account operators' wrstanek /add",0,"True")
```

NET PAUSE

```
NET PAUSE service
```

service   The service to put on hold.

Details:

NET PAUSE suspends a service and puts it on hold. When you use NET PAUSE to pause a service, you can use NET CONTINUE to resume it. Services that can be paused and resumed include File Server For Macintosh, Lpdsvc, Net Logon, Network DDE, Network DDE DSDM, NT LM Security Support Provider, Remoteboot, Remote Access Server, Server, Simple TCP/IP Services, Task Scheduler, and Workstation.

Command Shell

```
net pause "task scheduler"
```

VBScript

```
Set ws = WScript.CreateObject("WScript.Shell")
ret = ws.Run("net pause 'task scheduler'",0,"True")
```

JScript

```
var ws = WScript.CreateObject("WScript.Shell");
ws.Run("net pause 'task scheduler'",0,"True")
```

NET PRINT

```
NET PRINT \\computername\sharename
NET PRINT [\computername] job# [/HOLD | /RELEASE | /DELETE]
```

\\computername	The name of the computer sharing the printer queue.
sharename	The name of the shared printer queue.
job#	The number assigned to the print job in the print queue.
/DELETE	Removes a job from a queue.
/HOLD	Pauses the print job.
/RELEASE	Releases a print job that is held.

Details:

NET PRINT displays print jobs and shared queues. Use NET PRINT to manage shared printer queues and display queue status. To manage the shared printers themselves, use NET SHARE.

Command Shell

```
net print \\zeta\eng1
net print 0043 /delete
```

VBScript

```
Set ws = WScript.CreateObject("WScript.Shell")
ret = ws.Run("net print 0043 /delete",0,"True")
```

JScript

```
var ws = WScript.CreateObject("WScript.Shell");
ws.Run("net print 0043 /delete",0,"True")
```

NET SESSION

```
NET SESSION [\\computername] [/DELETE]
```

\\computername　　The name of the Windows 2000 server you want to examine.

/DELETE　　Disconnects the local computer and the designated workstation or server, closing all open files for the session. If you don't specify a computer name, all sessions are ended.

Details:

NET SESSION lists or disconnects sessions between the local computer and other computers on the network. Enter **NET SESSION** to examine the local computer's sessions. Enter **NET SESSION computername** to examine sessions on another computer. This command works only on servers.

Command Shell

```
net session \\pluto
net session \\jupiter /delete
```

VBScript

```
Set ws = WScript.CreateObject("WScript.Shell")
ret = ws.Run("net session \\jupiter /delete",0,"True")
```

JScript

```
var ws = WScript.CreateObject("WScript.Shell");
ws.Run("net session \\\\jupiter /delete",0,"True")
```

NET SHARE

```
NET SHARE sharename
NET SHARE sharename=drive:path [/USERS:number | /UNLIMITED]
                              [/REMARK:"text"]
                              [/CACHE:Manual | Automatic | No]
NET SHARE sharename [/USERS:number | /UNLIMITED]
```

```
                        [/REMARK:"text"]
                        [/CACHE:Manual | Automatic | No]
       NET SHARE {sharename | devicename | drive:path} /DELETE
```

`devicename`	Sets one or more printers shared by *sharename*. You can use LPT1: through LPT9:.
`drive:path`	Sets the complete path of the directory to be shared.
`sharename`	Sets the network name of the shared resource.
`/CACHE:Automatic`	Enables offline client caching with automatic updates.
`/CACHE:Manual`	Enables offline client caching with manual updates.
`/CACHE:No`	Disables offline client caching.
`/DELETE`	Stops sharing the specified resource.
`/REMARK:"text"`	Adds an optional comment about the shared resource. Quotation marks are mandatory.
`/UNLIMITED`	Specifies that an unlimited number of users can simultaneously access the shared resource.
`/USERS:number`	Sets the maximum number of users who can simultaneously access the shared resource.

Details:

`NET SHARE` manages shared printers and directories. Enter **NET SHARE** with a share name only to display information about the specified share.

Command Shell

```
net share netdata="r:\network\data\" /unlimited
net share netdata /delete
```

VBScript

```
Set ws = WScript.CreateObject("WScript.Shell")
ret = ws.Run("net share netdata /delete",0,"True")
```

JScript

```
var ws = WScript.CreateObject("WScript.Shell");
ws.Run("net share netdata /delete",0,"True")
```

NET START

```
       NET START [service]
```

`service`   The service to start. Enclose service names that have spaces in quotation marks.

Details:

NET START starts network services or lists network services that are running. Enter **NET START** by itself to list running services. Services you can start on workstations and servers include Alerter, Client Service For Netware, Clipbook Server, Computer Browser, DHCP Client, Directory Replicator, Eventlog, LPDSVC, Messenger, Net Logon, Network DDE, Network DDE DSDM, Network Monitoring Agent, NT LM Security Support Provider, Plug and Play, Remote Access Connection Manager, Remote Access ISNSAP Service, Remote Access Server, Remote Procedure Call (RPC) Locator, Remote Procedure Call (RPC) Service, Server, Simple TCP/IP Services, SNMP, Spooler, Task Scheduler, TCPIP NetBIOS Helper, Ups, and Workstation.

These additional services are available only on Windows 2000 servers: File Server For Macintosh, Gateway Service For Netware, Microsoft DHCP Server, Print Server For Macintosh, and Windows Internet Name Service.

NET START can also start network services not provided with the Windows 2000 operating system.

Command Shell

```
net start "Microsoft DHCP Server"
net start "Windows Internet Name Service"
```

VBScript

```
Set ws = WScript.CreateObject("WScript.Shell")
ret = ws.Run("net start 'Windows Internet Name Service'",0,"True")
```

JScript

```
var ws = WScript.CreateObject("WScript.Shell");
ws.Run("net start 'Windows Internet Name Service'",0,"True")
```

NET STATISTICS

```
NET STATISTICS [WORKSTATION | SERVER]
```

SERVER   Displays Server service statistics.

WORKSTATION   Displays Workstation service statistics.

Details:

NET STATISTICS displays workstation and server statistics. Enter **NET STATISTICS** by itself to list the services for which statistics are currently available.

Command Shell

```
net statistics workstation
net statistics server
```

Windows Script
stats.bat

```
net statistics workstation >> log.txt
net statistics server >> log.txt
```

compare.vbs

```
Set ws = WScript.CreateObject("WScript.Shell")
ret = ws.Run("stats.bat",0,"True")
```

compare.js

```
var ws = WScript.CreateObject("WScript.Shell");
ws.Run("stats.bat",0,"True")
```

NET STOP

```
NET STOP service
```

service   The service to stop. Enclose service names with spaces in quotation marks.

Details:

NET STOP stops network services. Stopping a service cancels any network connections that the service is running. You must have administrator privileges to stop services. The EventLog service cannot be stopped.

Services you can stop on workstations and servers include: Alerter, Client Service For Netware, Clipbook Server, Computer Browser, DHCP Client, Directory Replicator, LPDSVC, Messenger, Net Logon, Network DDE, Network DDE DSDM, Network Monitoring Agent, NT LM Security Support Provider, Plug and Play, Remote Access Connection Manager, Remote Access ISNSAP Service, Remote Access Server, Remote Procedure Call (RPC) Locator, Remote Procedure Call (RPC) Service, Server, Simple TCP/IP Services, SNMP, Spooler, Task Scheduler, TCPIP NetBIOS Helper, Ups, and Workstation.

These additional services are available only on Windows 2000 servers: File Server For Macintosh, Gateway Service For NetWare, Microsoft DHCP Server, Print Server For Macintosh, and Windows Internet Name Service.

NET STOP can also start network services not provided with Windows 2000.

Command Shell

```
net stop "Microsoft DHCP Server"
net stop "Windows Internet Name Service"
```

VBScript

```
Set ws = WScript.CreateObject("WScript.Shell")
ret = ws.Run("net stop 'Windows Internet Name Service'",0,"True")
```

JScript

```
var ws = WScript.CreateObject("WScript.Shell");
ws.Run("net stop 'Windows Internet Name Service'",0,"True")
```

NET TIME

```
NET TIME [\\computername | /DOMAIN[:domainname] |
         /RTSDOMAIN[:domainname]] [/SET]
         [\\computername] /QUERYSNTP
         [\\computername] /SETSNTP[:server_list]
```

\\computername	The name of a server with which you want to check or synchronize.
/DOMAIN[:domainname]	Specifies that the computer should synchronize with the Primary Domain Controller for the designated domain.
/RTSDOMAIN[:domainname]	Specifies that the computer should synchronize with a Reliable Time Server for the designated domain.
/SET	Synchronizes the computer's time with the time on the specified server or domain.
/QUERYSNTP	Displays the currently configured NTP server for the computer.
/SETSNTP: server_list	Sets the NTP time servers that the computer should use. Enter DNS names or IP addresses separated by spaces.

Details:

NET TIME displays time and synchronizes time with remote computers. Enter **NET TIME** by itself to display the current date and time on the network's timeserver (which is normally the primary domain controller).

Command Shell

```
net time /SETSNTP:pluto.tvpress.com
```

VBScript

```
Set ws = WScript.CreateObject("WScript.Shell")
ret = ws.Run("net time /SETSNTP:pluto.tvpress.com",0,"True")
```

JScript

```
var ws = WScript.CreateObject("WScript.Shell");
ws.Run("net time /SETSNTP:pluto.tvpress.com",0,"True")
```

NET USE

```
NET USE [devicename | *] [\\computername\sharename[\volume]
        [password | *]] [/USER:[domainname\]username]
        [/USER:[username@domainname]
        [[/DELETE] | [/PERSISTENT:{YES | NO}]]
NET USE [devicename | *] [password | *]] [/HOME]
NET USE [/PERSISTENT:{YES | NO}]
```

Prompts for a required password are as follows:

\\computername	The UNC name of the server to connect to. If the computer name contains blank characters, enclose the double backslash (\\) and the computer name and enclose the share in quotation marks, such as "\\PLUTO\NETDATA".
devicename	Assigns a device to connect to or disconnect from. A device name is either a disk drive (lettered D: through Z:) or a printer (LPT1: through LPT9:). Type an asterisk instead of a specific device name to assign the next available device name.
domainname	Sets a domain. Otherwise, the current domain is used.
password	The password needed to access the shared resource.
username	The username with which to log on.
/DELETE	Disconnects the specified connection.
/HOME	Connects a user to their home directory.
/PERSISTENT	Determines whether the connection is persistent. The default is the last setting used.
\sharename	The network name of the shared resource.
/USER	Used to set the username for the connection (if it is different than the currently logged in user's name).
\volume	Sets a NetWare volume on the server. Client Services for Netware or Gateway Service for Netware must be running.
YES	Makes connections persistent, which saves connections as they are made and restores them at next logon.
NO	Makes a temporary connection, which is disconnected when the user logs off.

Details:

NET USE manages remote connections. Enter **NET USE** by itself to display a list of network connections.

Command Shell

```
net use \\pluto\netdata * /persistent
net use \\pluto\netdata /delete
```

VBScript

```
Set ws = WScript.CreateObject("WScript.Shell")
ret = ws.Run("net use \\pluto\netdata /delete",0,"True")
```

JScript

```
var ws = WScript.CreateObject("WScript.Shell");
ws.Run("net use \\\\pluto\\netdata /delete",0,"True")
```

NET USER

```
NET USER [username [password | *] [options]] [/DOMAIN]
NET USER username {password | *} /ADD [options] [/DOMAIN]
NET USER username [/DELETE] [/DOMAIN]
```

The following are prompts for the password:

password	Assigns or changes a password for a user account.
username	Sets the name of the user account to create, view, or modify.
/ADD	Adds a user account.
/DELETE	Removes a user account.
/DOMAIN	Specifies that the operation should be performed on the primary domain controller of the current domain. Otherwise, the operation is performed on the local computer. (Applies only to Windows 2000 workstations that are members of an NT domain. By default, Windows 2000 servers perform operations on the primary domain controller.)

Options:

/ACTIVE:{YES | NO}	Enables or disables a user account. If the account is not active, the user cannot log on. The default is YES.
/COMMENT:"text"	Sets a description of up to 48 characters for the account. Enclose the text in quotation marks.
/COUNTRYCODE:nnn	Sets the operating system country code for the user's help and error messages. A value of 0 is the default.
/EXPIRES:{date | NEVER}	Determines whether the user's account expires. The default is NEVER. Expiration dates can be in mm/dd/yy or dd/mm/yy, depending on the country code.
/FULLNAME:"name"	Sets the user's full name. Enclose the name in quotation marks.
/HOMEDIR:pathname	Sets the path of the user's home directory. The path must exist before you can use it.
/PASSWORDCHG:{YES | NO}	Determines whether users can change their own password. The default is YES.

`/PASSWORDREQ:{YES	NO}`	Determines whether a user account must have a password. The default is `YES`.
`/PROFILEPATH[:path]`	Sets a path for the user's logon profile.
`/SCRIPTPATH:pathname`	Sets the location of the user's logon script.
`/TIMES:{times	ALL}`	Specifies the times and days a user is allowed to log on. Times are expressed as day[-day][,day[-day]],time[-time][,time [-time]] and limited to one-hour increments. Days can be spelled out or abbreviated (M, T, W, Th, F, Sa, Su). Hours can be 12- or 24-hour notation. For 12-hour notation, use AM or PM. The value `ALL` means a user can always log on. A null value (blank) means a user can never log on. Separate day and time entries with commas, and units of time with semicolons.
`/USERCOMMENT:"text"`	Allows a user comment to be added or changed.
`/WORKSTATIONS:{computer name[,...]	*}`	Lists as many as eight workstations from which a user can log on to the network. If `/WORKSTATIONS` has no list, or if the list is `*`, the user can log on from any computer.

Details:

`NET USER` manages user accounts. Enter `NET USER` by itself to list the user accounts for the server. The command works only on servers.

When you want to create or modify domain accounts, be sure to enter `/DOMAIN`.

Command Shell

```
net user wrstanek happydayz /ADD
net user wrstanek /DELETE
```

VBScript

```
Set ws = WScript.CreateObject("WScript.Shell")
ret = ws.Run("net user wrstanek /DELETE",0,"True")
```

JScript

```
var ws = WScript.CreateObject("WScript.Shell");
ws.Run("net user wrstanek /DELETE",0,"True")
```

NET VIEW

```
NET VIEW [\\computername | /DOMAIN[:domainname]]
NET VIEW /NETWORK:NW [\\computername]
```

\\computername	Specifies the computer whose shared resources you want to view.
/DOMAIN:domainname	Sets the domain for which you want to view computers that have resources available. If the domain name is omitted, all domains on the network are listed.
/NETWORK:NW	Displays all the servers on a NetWare network. If a computer name is specified, only the resources available on that computer are displayed.

Details:

NET VIEW displays available network resources. Enter **NET VIEW** without options to display a list of computers in the current domain or network.

Command Shell

```
net view \\delta
net view /domain:engineering
```

Windows Script

view.bat

```
net view \\delta >> log.txt
net view /domain:engineering >> log.txt
```

compare.vbs

```
Set ws = WScript.CreateObject("WScript.Shell")
ret = ws.Run("view.bat",0,"True")
```

compare.js

```
var ws = WScript.CreateObject("WScript.Shell");
ws.Run("view.bat",0,"True")
```

NETSTAT

```
NETSTAT [-a] [-b] [-e] [-f] [-n] [-o] [-p protocol] [-r] [-s] [-t]
[interval]
```

interval	Redisplays selected statistics, pausing between each display. Press CTRL+C to stop redisplaying statistics. If this option is omitted, information is only displayed once.
-a	Displays connections and listening ports.
-b	Displays the executable that created each connection or listening port.
-e	Displays Ethernet statistics. This may be combined with -s to obtain additional details.
-f	Displays the fully qualified domain name for foreign addresses.
-n	Displays IP addresses and port numbers rather than computer names.

-o	Displays the ID of the owning process for each connection.
-p protocol	Shows connections for the specified protocol (TCP or UDP). If the -s option is used with -p, you can view protocol information for TCP, UDP, ICMP, or IP.
-r	Displays the contents of the routing table.
-s	Displays per-protocol statistics. By default, statistics are shown for TCP, UDP, ICMP, and IP. Use with -p to examine a specific protocol.
-t	Displays the current offload state of each connection.

Details:

NETSTAT displays status of network connections as well as protocol statistics. Unlike most other commands, most options provide completely different types of information. TCP/IP networking must be installed.

Command Shell

```
netstat -a
netstat -s -p TCP
```

Windows Script

nstats.bat

```
netstat -a >> log.txt
netstat -s -p TCP >> log.txt
```

compare.vbs

```
Set ws = WScript.CreateObject("WScript.Shell")
ret = ws.Run("nstats.bat",0,"True")
```

compare.js

```
var ws = WScript.CreateObject("WScript.Shell");
ws.Run("nstats.bat",0,"True")
```

NSLOOKUP

```
NSLOOKUP [-option] [computer | server]
```

-option	An option to perform a query with; in the form -command=value or -command. The most commonly used command is querytype, which sets the type of record you want to examine. Record types include A, CNAME, MX, NS, PTR, and SOA.
computer	The hostname or IP address you want to look up in DNS.
server	The DNS server to use for the lookup. If you don't specify a server, the default name server is used.

Details:

NSLOOKUP shows the status of Domain Name System (DNS) for servers and workstations with DNS resolution. To use this command, TCP/IP networking must be configured. DNS lookup can be performed interactively or non-interactively. DNS lookups are most useful if you need to look up the IP address of a known host or examine DNS entries. If you want to see if a particular Internet host is available, PING is a better command to use.

Command Shell

```
nslookup www.tvpress.com
nslookup -querytype=mx tvpress.com
```

Windows Script

ns.bat

```
nslookup www.tvpress.com >> log.txt
nslookup -querytype=mx tvpress.com >> log.txt
```

compare.vbs

```
Set ws = WScript.CreateObject("WScript.Shell")
ret = ws.Run("ns.bat",0,"True")
```

compare.js

```
var ws = WScript.CreateObject("WScript.Shell");
ws.Run("ns.bat",0,"True")
```

PATH

```
PATH [[drive:]path[;...][;%PATH%]
PATH ;
```

[drive:]   Sets the drive to check.

path   Sets the directory path.

Details:

PATH displays or sets a search path for executable files. The command path is set during logon using system and user environment variables, namely the %PATH% variable. To view current path setting, type PATH on a line by itself and press Enter. The directory order in the command path indicates the search order used by the command shell when looking for executables and scripts.

Update existing path information by appending a new path to the %PATH% environment variable, for example:

```
path %PATH%;c:\scripts\networking
```

Clear the path by entering the following:

```
path ;
```

Command Shell

```
path
path c:\scripts\networking;%PATH%
```

VBScript

```
Set ws = WScript.CreateObject("WScript.Shell")
ret = ws.Run("path c:\scripts\networking;%PATH%",0,"True")
```

JScript

```
var ws = WScript.CreateObject("WScript.Shell");
ws.Run("path c:\\scripts\\networking;%PATH%",0,"True")
```

PING

```
PING [-t] [-a] [-n count] [-l size] [-f] [-i TTL] [-v TOS]
     [-r count] [-s count] [[-j host-list] | [-k host-list]]
     [-w timeout] [-R] [-S srcaddr] [-4] [-6] destination-list
```

`destination-list`	A list of computers to ping; specified by hostname or IP address. If NetBIOS resolution is enabled for the computer/domain, you can also use NetBIOS names (the computer name is an NT domain).
`-a`	Resolve IP addresses to hostnames when pinging.
`-f`	Specifies that the ping packet shouldn't be fragmented when it goes through gateways.
`-i TTL`	Sets a Time To Live value.
`-j host-list`	Sets the packet route using the host list. The route doesn't have to include all potential gateways. Use spaces to separate hostnames.
`-k host-list`	Sets a strict packet route using the host list. The route must be inclusive of all gateways. Use spaces to separate hostnames.
`-l size`	The number of bytes to send in the ping. The default is 64 and the maximum is 8192.
`-n count`	Number of times to ping the specified computer. The default is 4.
`-r count`	Displays the route taken by the ping packets. `Count` determines the number of hops to count from 1 to 9.
`-R`	With IPv6, uses the routing header to test the reverse route.
`-s count`	The timestamp for the number of hops set by `count`.

`-S srcaddr`	With IPv6, sets the source address to use.
`-t`	Ping repeatedly until interrupted.
`-v TOS`	Sets the type of service.
`-w timeout`	A timeout set in milliseconds.
`-4`	Forces using IPv4.
`-6`	Forces using IPv6.

Details:

`PING` sends data to a computer to determine if a network connection can be established. TCP/IP networking must be configured. `PING` is a good command to use before trying to work with an Internet resource. If the ping returns a bad IP address or host unreachable, it means the computer you want to work with isn't available.

Command Shell

```
ping -t www.idg.com
ping -n 50 www.idg.com
```

VBScript

```
Set ws = WScript.CreateObject("WScript.Shell")
ret = ws.Run("ping www.idg.com",0,"True")
if ret <> 0 Then
  WScript.Echo "Error!"
Else
  WScript.Echo "Success"
End If
```

JScript

```
var ws = WScript.CreateObject("WScript.Shell")
ret = ws.Run("ping www.idg.com",0,"True")
if (ret != 0)
  WScript.Echo("Error!")
else
  WScript.Echo("Success")
```

RECOVER

```
RECOVER [drive:][path]filename
```

`[drive:][path]filename`   Sets the drive, directory, or file to recover.

Details:

`RECOVER` recovers readable information from a bad or defective disk.

Command Shell

```
recover a:
```

VBScript

```
Set ws = WScript.CreateObject("WScript.Shell")
ret = ws.Run("recover a:",0,"True")
```

JScript

```
var ws = WScript.CreateObject("WScript.Shell");
ws.Run("recover a:",0,"True")
```

ROUTE

```
ROUTE [-f] [-p] [-4|-6] [command [destination] [MASK netmask] [gateway]
     [METRIC metric]]
```

-f	Clears the routing tables of gateway entries. This option is executed before running any of the available route commands.
-p	When used with the ADD command, makes the route persistent so it continues to exist when the system is restarted. When used with the PRINT command, prints a list of persistent routes.
-4	Forces using IPv4.
-6	Forces using IPv6.
command	Allows you to specify one of these route commands:
PRINT:	Prints a route.
ADD:	Adds a route.
DELETE:	Deletes a route.
CHANGE:	Modifies a route.
destination	Sets the route destination host.
MASK netmask	A subnet mask to associate with the route entry. The default network mask is 255.255.255.255.
gateway	The gateway for the route.
METRIC costmetric	Sets a numeric cost metric for the route. Valid values are from 1 to 9999.

Details:

ROUTE manages network routing tables. If you use a hostname for the destination rather than an IP address, ROUTE looks in the NETWORKS file to resolve the destination to an IP address. If you use a hostname for a gateway, ROUTE looks in the HOSTS file to resolve the host to an IP address. If the command is PRINT or DELETE, you can use wildcards for the destination and gateway.

The cost metric is useful in determining which route the local computer attempts to use first. Routes with a metric of 1 are always attempted before routes with higher-cost metrics.

Command Shell

```
route -p add mail.idg.com 255.255.255.0 214.15.8.2 1
route delete mail.idg.com 214.*
```

VBScript

```
Set ws = WScript.CreateObject("WScript.Shell")
ret = ws.Run("route delete mail.idg.com 214.*",0,"True")
```

JScript

```
var ws = WScript.CreateObject("WScript.Shell");
ws.Run("route delete mail.idg.com 214.*",0,"True")
```

SCHTASKS

```
SCHTASKS /parameter [arguments]
```

`Parameter:` Allows you to specify one of these route commands:

`/Create:` Creates a new schedule task.

`/Delete:` Deletes the scheduled task(s).

`/Query:` Displays all scheduled tasks.

`/Change:` Changes the properties of scheduled task.

`/Run:` Runs the scheduled task immediately.

`/End:` Stops the currently running scheduled task.

`/?:` Displays the help message.

Details:

SCHTASKS enables an administrator to create delete, query, change, run and end scheduled tasks on a local or remote system. To get detailed help on each parameter, use the /?.

Command Shell

```
schtasks /query
time /run /?
```

VBScript

```
Set ws = WScript.CreateObject("WScript.Shell")
ret = ws.Run("schtasks /query",1,"True")
```

JScript

```
var ws = WScript.CreateObject("WScript.Shell");
ws.Run("schtasks /query",1,"True")
```

TIME

```
TIME [time | /T]
```

time   Sets the time in [HH:[MM:[SS.[hh]]]][A|P] format.

/T   Displays the current time without a prompt.

Details:

TIME displays or sets the system time. TIME is normally set on a 24-hour clock. You can also set an AM or PM value if you use the A or P modifiers. Valid values are:

- Hours: 0 to 23
- Minutes: 0 to 59
- Seconds: 0 to 59
- Hundredths: 0 to 99

Command Shell

```
time /t
time 22:50
```

VBScript

```
Set ws = WScript.CreateObject("WScript.Shell")
ret = ws.Run("time 22:50",0,"True")
```

JScript

```
var ws = WScript.CreateObject("WScript.Shell");
ws.Run("time 22:50",0,"True")
```

TRACERT

```
TRACERT [-d] [-h maximum_hops] [-j host-list]
        [-w timeout] [-R] [-S srcaddr] [-4] [-6] target_name
```

target_name   The remote computer to locate.

-d	Does not convert IP addresses for hops.
-h maximum_hops	The maximum number of hops between the local computer and the target.
-j host-list	Sets the trace route using the host list. The route doesn't have to include all potential gateways. Use spaces to separate hostnames.
-R	With IPv6, uses the routing header to test the reverse route.
-S srcaddr	With IPv6, sets the source address to use.
-w timeout	Waits the specified number of milliseconds before timing out.
-4	Forces using IPv4.
-6	Forces using IPv6.

Details:

TRACERT displays the path between the local computer and a remote computer. Tracing the route between two computers is extremely helpful in troubleshooting network routing problems.

Command Shell

```
tracert tvpress.com
tracert -d tvpress.com
```

Windows Script

trace.bat

```
tracert tvpress.com >> log.txt
tracert -d tvpress.com >> log.txt
```

compare.vbs

```
Set ws = WScript.CreateObject("WScript.Shell")
ret = ws.Run("trace.bat",0,"True")
```

compare.js

```
var ws = WScript.CreateObject("WScript.Shell");
ws.Run("trace.bat",0,"True")
```

Index

E

X

The books you
read to succeed.

Get the most out of the latest software and leading-edge technologies
with a Wiley Bible—your one-stop reference.

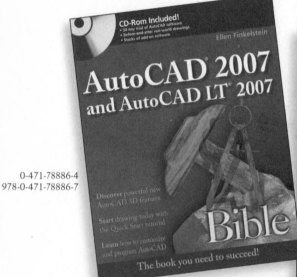

CD-Rom Included!
• 30-day trial of AutoCAD software
• Before-and-after real-world drawings
• Stacks of add-on software

Ellen Finkelstein

AutoCAD 2007
and AutoCAD LT 2007

Discover powerful new
AutoCAD 3D features

Start drawing today with
the Quick Start tutorial

Learn how to customize
and program AutoCAD

Bible

The book you need to succeed!

0-471-78886-4
978-0-471-78886-7

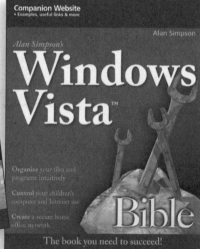

Companion Website
• Examples, useful links & more

Alan Simpson

Alan Simpson's

**Windows
Vista**™

Organize your files and
programs intuitively

Control your children's
computer and Internet use

Create a secure home
office network

Bible

The book you need to succeed!

0-470-04030-0
978-0-470-04030-0

"Paul is a data architect, database developer, and trainer. All three of his areas of expertise
are embodied in the book with great examples. If you want to learn SQL Server 2005, this
book is for you."
Wayne Snyder, Managing Consultant, Mariner

Paul Nielsen

SQL Server™
2005

Discover expanded features
for DBAs and programmers

Write stored procedures
and increase productivity

Integrate XML and
Web servers

Bible

The book you need to succeed!

0-7645-4256-7
978-0-7645-4256-5

DVD Included!   Full-color Insert
• Examples and content from the book   • 16-page full-color insert with
• Models and textures you can customize   cutting-edge examples
• Searchable PDF of book

Kelly L. Murdock

3ds Max 9

Model and animate from
day one with Quick Start

Create red-hot
gaming animations

Discover 3ds Max 9's
new features

Bible

The book you need to succeed!

0-470-10089-3
978-0-470-10089-9

Here's an example:

```
ProvObj.OpenDSObject("WinNT://TVPRESS/Administrator", "wrstane",
"jiggyPop", ADS_SECURE_CREDENTIALS)
```

When you use this method with other providers, be sure to use the correct syntax. For example, with the LDAP provider and Active Directory, you must specify the user ID in the format:

```
Username@domain
```

Here is an example:

```
wrstanek@seattle.tvpress.com
```

You should also be sure to use the correct flags. Most of the time you'll want to use the ADS_SECURE_CREDENTIALS flag, which tells the provider to request secure authentication. Still, there are times when you may want to use a different flag. You may also want to use multiple flags, and you can do this as well.

Table 15-6 provides a summary of the available flags. Because the flags represent constant values, you use multiple flags by adding together the flag values or by adding the constants themselves. While the constants are available in VBScript, they aren't available in JScript. Thus in JScript, you'll have to assign the constant a value, or simply use the expected value. The constant values are specified in octal format and use the 0x prefix.

TABLE 15-6

Flags for Use with OpenDSObject

Flag	Constant Value	Description
ADS_SECURE_ AUTHENTICATION	0x1	Requests secure authentication
ADS_USE_ ENCRYPTION	0x2	Tells ADSI to use SSL (Secure Socket Layer) encryption whenever exchanging data over the network; you must have a Certificate Server installed to use this option.
ADS_USE_SSL	0x2	Tells ADSI to use SSL (Secure Socket Layer) encryption. You must have a Certificate Server installed to use this option.
ADS_READONLY_ SERVER	0x4	Allows the provider to use a read-only connection
ADS_PROMPT_ CREDENTIALS	0x8	Tells ADSI to prompt for user credentials when the authentication is initiated. An interface must be available to display the prompt.

continued

TABLE 15-6   *(continued)*

Flag	Constant Value	Description
ADS_NO_AUTHENTICATION	0x10	Requests no authentication; the WinNT provider does not support this flag. With Active Directory, the security context is set as "Everyone."
ADS_FAST_BIND	0x20	Requests quick bind with minimum interfaces only (rather than full-interface support)
ADS_USE_SIGNING	0x40	Checks data integrity to ensure the data received is the same as the data sent; to use this flag, you must also set the ADS_SECURE_AUTHENTICATION flag.
ADS_USE_SEALING	0x80	Tells ADSI to use Kerberos encryption. To use this flag, you must also set the ADS_SECURE_AUTHENTICATION flag.

Listing 15-2 shows a more complete example of working with OpenDSObject. Technically, when you obtain a reference to the provider object, you are obtaining a reference to the root of the provider's namespace. You can then work your way through this namespace in a variety of ways. As you examine the listing, compare the VBScript and the JScript code carefully and note the differences. You should also note the output, which demonstrates that the local Administrator account accessed by the WinNT provider is different from the domain Administrator account accessed by the LDAP provider. The accounts have different GUIDs and thus, they are different.

LISTING 15-2

Authenticating Your Access to the Directory

VBScript
auth.vbs

```
NTDomain = "seattle"
NTUser = "Administrator"

Set prov = GetObject("WinNT:")
Set user = prov.OpenDSObject("WinNT://" & NTDomain & "/" & NTUser,
"wrstane","jiggyPop", ADS_SECURE_AUTHENTICATION)

'Work with the object
WScript.Echo user.Name
WScript.Echo user.Class
WScript.Echo user.GUID
WScript.Echo ""

Container = "CN=Administrator,CN=Users,DC=SEATTLE,DC=DOMAIN,DC=COM"
```

```
Set prov2 = GetObject("LDAP:")
Set user2 = prov2.OpenDSObject("LDAP://" & Container, "wrstanek@seattle.domain
.com","snoreLoud", ADS_SECURE_AUTHENTICATION)

'Work with the object
WScript.Echo user2.Name
WScript.Echo user2.Class
WScript.Echo user2.GUID
WScript.Echo ""
```

JScript
auth.js

```
ADS_SECURE_AUTHENTICATION  = 0x1

NTDomain = "seattle"
NTUser = "Administrator"

var prov = GetObject("WinNT:")
var user = prov.OpenDSObject("WinNT://" + NTDomain + "/" +
  NTUser,"wrstane","jiggyPop", ADS_SECURE_AUTHENTICATION)

//Work with the object
WScript.Echo(user.Name)
WScript.Echo(user.Class)
WScript.Echo(user.GUID)
WScript.Echo("")

Container = "CN=Administrator,CN=Users,DC=SEATTLE,DC=DOMAIN,DC=COM"

var prov2 = GetObject("LDAP:")
var user2 = prov2.OpenDSObject("LDAP://" + Container,
  "wrstanek@seattle.domain.com","snoreLoud", ADS_SECURE_AUTHENTICATION)

//Work with the object
WScript.Echo(user2.Name)
WScript.Echo(user2.Class)
WScript.Echo(user2.GUID)
WScript.Echo("")
```

Output

```
Administrator
User
{D83F1060-1E71-11CF-B1F3-02608C9E7553}

CN=Administrator
user
21fa96966f2b5341ba91257c73996825
```

> **NOTE** The script returns the local and domain administrators accounts. These accounts are differ-
> ent and the *Globally Unique Identifier (GUID)* associated with the accounts shows this. As
> you set out to work with the providers, don't forget that local objects are different than domain objects.

Accessing properties and updating objects

Providers access objects through various interfaces. The core interface is IADs. This interface defines
a set of properties and methods for working with objects. These properties and methods are examined in the sections that follow.

Working with IADs Properties

IADs properties you'll want to use in Windows scripts are summarized in Table 15-7. These properties allow you to examine (but not set) object properties.

TABLE 15-7

IADs Properties for Windows Scripts

Properties	Description	Sample Return Value
AdsPath	Retrieves the object's AdsPath	LDAP://CN=Administrator, CN=Users,DC=SEATTLE, DC=DOMAIN,DC=COM
Class	Retrieves the name of the object's class	User
GUID	Retrieves the GUID of the object	21fa96966f2b5341ba91257c73996825
Name	Retrieves the object's relative name	CN=Administrator
Parent	Retrieves the AdsPath string for the parent object	LDAP://CN=Users,DC=SEATTLE,DC=DOMAIN,DC=COM
Schema	Retrieves the AdsPath string for the related schema class object	LDAP://schema/user

The AdsPath strings for the parent and schema are very useful in your Windows scripts. You can
use these strings to retrieve the related parent and schema objects. Another useful property is GUID.
GUID returns the globally unique identifier that was assigned when the object instance was created.
Globally unique identifiers are 128-bit numbers that are guaranteed to be unique in the namespace.
Once an object is created, the GUID never changes—even if the object is moved or renamed. Thus,
while the AdsPath string to the object may change, the GUID won't. Because of this, you may want
to use GUIDs to examine and manage objects in scripts.

Listing 15-3 provides a detailed example of how you read property values and display them. You'll
also see an example of using the parent and schema properties to retrieve the related objects.